[Top]_The Linn Cove Viaduct around Grandfather Mtn._ N.C. DIVISION OF TOURISM FILM & SPORTS DEVELOPMENT
[Bottom] _Rainbow Falls in Transylvania County is beautiful from the walkway._ CONSTANCE E. RICHARDS

[Top] *Blue Ridge Mountains.* N.C. DIVISION OF TOURISM FILM & SPORTS DEVELOPMENT
[Bottom] *The Appalachian Trail.* N.C. DIVISION OF TOURISM FILM & SPORTS DEVELOPMENT

Asheville's skyline is aglow against the backdrop of the Blue Ridge Mountains.

Soaring art deco buildings identify Asheville's distinctive skyline.

Musicians perform at the Mountain Dance and Folk Festival in Asheville.
ASHEVILLE CONVENTION & VISITORS BUREAU

Having grassroots fun is easy at Shindig-on-the-Green. ASHEVILLE CONVENTION & VISITORS BUREAU

[Top] *This old mill is in Buncombe County in the Southern Mountains.* CONSTANCE E. RICHARDS
[Bottom] *Pisgah National Forest.* N.C. DIVISION OF TOURISM FILM & SPORTS DEVELOPMENT

The western North Carolina mountains are home to hundreds of waterfalls, like this one near Asheville.

Wall Street shops in downtown Asheville are popular with both people and their pets.
ASHEVILLE CONVENTION & VISITORS BUREAU

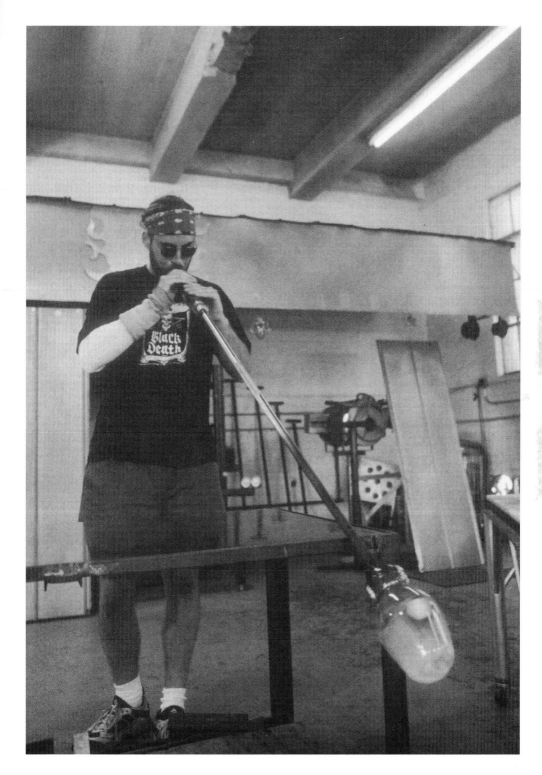

Great Southern Glassworks is a working glassblowing studio in Asheville. CONTANCE E. RICHARDS

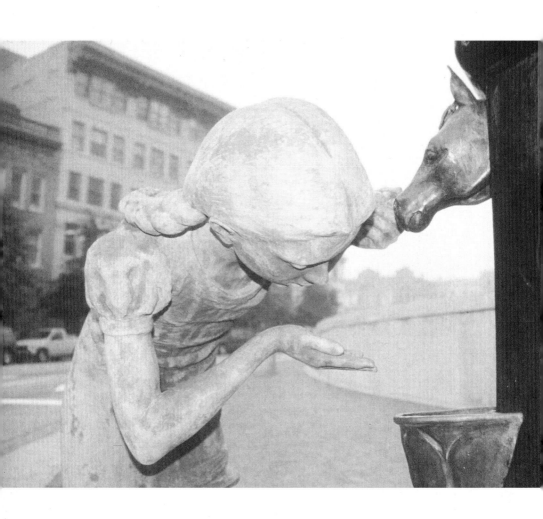

Asheville's Urban Trail features public art like this bronze sculpture of a girl getting a drink of water from a horse-head fountain. ASHEVILLE CONVENTION & VISITORS BUREAU

The Grove Arcade in downtown Asheville houses an open market, shops, and restaurants.

Peaceful mountain vistas greet visitors in western North Carolina.
ASHEVILLE CONVENTION & VISITORS BUREAU

CONTENTS

CONTENTS

Directory of Maps

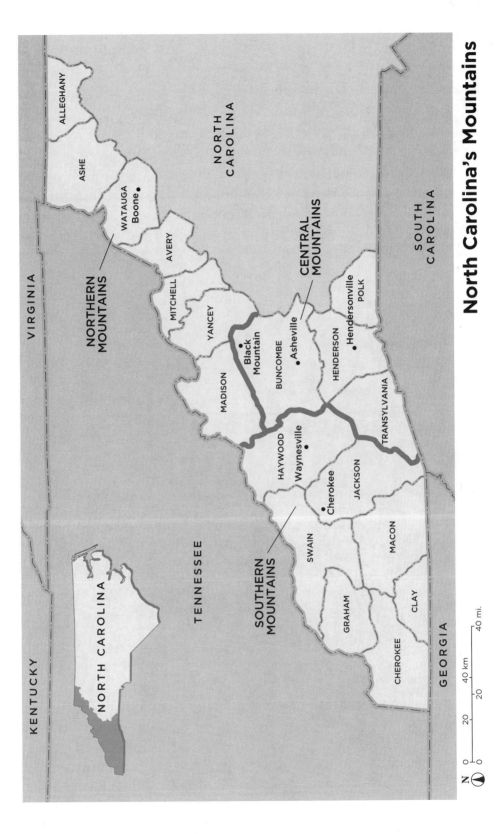

North Carolina's Mountains

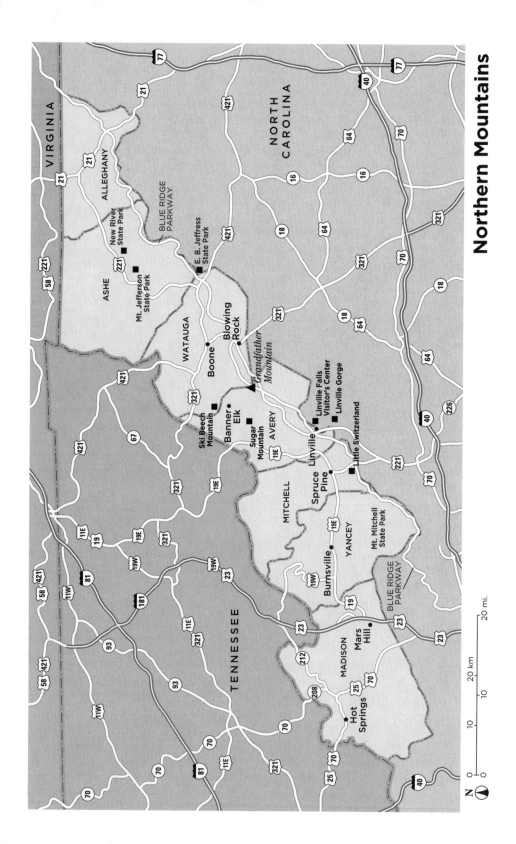

Northern Mountains

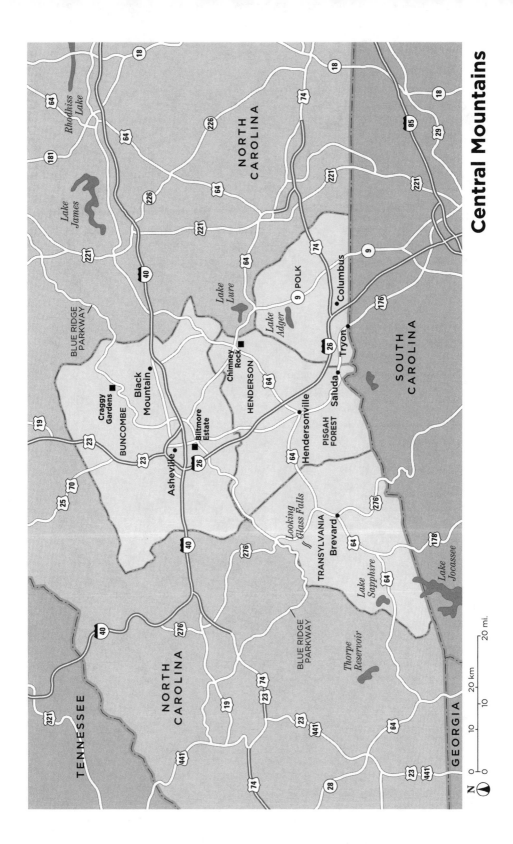

Central Mountains

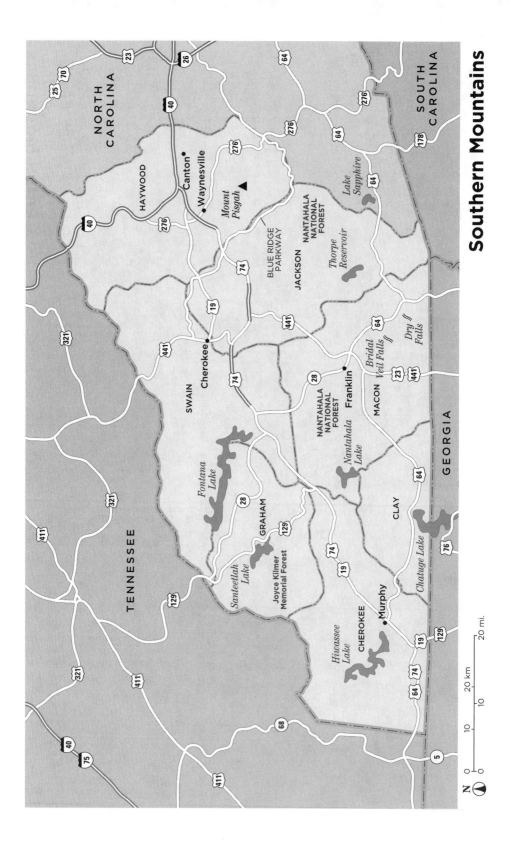

Southern Mountains

PREFACE

Welcome to North Carolina's mountains, a hospitable place, steeped in ancestral tradition, but awash in the influx of new ideas, industry, and people.

Those of us who were lucky enough to be born here, or whose ancestors stem from these mountains, grew up hiking the trails hooded by flowering rhododendron, splashing around chilly mountain-stream-fed swimming holes, and catching lightning bugs in dewy green fields at twilight. The mountains always beckon to us as our childhood home. Others of us, who have serendipitously found our way here, speak of a magnetism of the Blue Ridge Mountains of North Carolina. Together we make a fascinating blend of old and new, city and country.

The influx of new residents in these mountains has been phenomenal over the past decade. Newcomers live side by side with neighbors whose families have been here for generations.

Asheville, the largest city in Western North Carolina, has evolved into a lively city of professionals, artists, writers, New Agers, hippies, students, retirees, young adults, and everything in between. Walking the spirited streets day or night, you'll observe skateboarders, bicyclists, people enjoying a drink or meal under colorful awnings at sidewalk cafes, and shoppers scouring the antique shops and art galleries. On any given evening the music clubs and auditoriums host concerts—classical, bluegrass, reggae, ska, funk, rock, folk, modern dance, guest ballet performances—and any number of other cultural events. Yet even with so much to do, the pace is still slower and more personal than in large American urban centers—just a few visits to a downtown eatery and the owner will know you by name. Many well-known writers, artists, sculptors, artisans, producers, and play-wrights have chosen this area as their home or second home, enjoying the benefits of the town's intellectual offerings close to the bounty of the wilderness. Thomas Wolfe, O. Henry, and George Vanderbilt are but a few of the historical names who preceded them. (See our Area Overview and Arts and Culture chapters as well as our chapter on Biltmore Estate and Winery.)

The outdoors are, of course, another drawing point of this region. Pisgah Forest to the west formed the nucleus of what was to become America's first national forest; Mount Mitchell, the highest mountain on the eastern seaboard, is to the east of Pisgah. Numerous state parks thread through these mountains. Just a short drive from the city will take you to waterfalls, streams, rivers, gorges, and any other number of outdoor wonders. Every season is a good one here: Mild winters mean sweater weather with a bit of rain, perhaps occasional snow, and skiing in the higher elevations; spring is a glorious mix of sunshine and blooming azaleas and rhododendron; summers aren't too hot for hiking, but hot enough for dipping into a frigid mountain stream on the way; and autumn, well, that's when the mountains radiate their ancient magic. Stepping out into the late-October sunshine with a crisp, clear sky stretched overhead, you can lose yourself in wave after wave of colored splendor—reds, oranges, yellows, and golds, set off against occasional splashes of evergreens. (Read more about this in our Recreation and Blue Ridge Parkway chapters.)

This is also the home of the Cherokee Indians. We are invited to observe the traditions of these Native Americans in Cherokee, North Carolina, to the south. The Ocanoluftee Indian Village, for example, tastefully re-creates an 18th-century community with traditional ornamentation, living quarters, and working conditions. (You will read more about the Cherokees in our chapter on the Cherokee Indian Reservation.)

Crafts are well served in these mountains. Traditional mountain craft making abounds, as do crafts and art with a contemporary twist. You might find a studio next to fields of flowering tobacco plants, still a mainstay in North Carolina farming. Visit the farmers' markets in our towns and go home with baskets of juicy tomatoes, sweet corn, yams, baby squash, strawberries, cherries, apples, not to mention jars of homemade jams, jellies, relishes, apple butter, and honey. (Read more in our Mountain Crafts chapter.)

Whether you are just visiting, considering the mountains as a new home, or have just moved here, you'll be pleased with the balance that this area maintains. As for dining, an important part of travel-ing and enjoying a community, our Restaurants chapter discusses the best down-home cookin' to be found, as well as the plethora of fine gourmet and ethnic eating establishments that have opened their doors to accommodate every palate. Traditional bed-and-breakfasts and inns are scattered throughout the mountains, and modern resorts, many with superb golfing opportunities and other outdoor activities, as well as simpler hotels and motels mean you can choose your dream accommodation while you are here. Perhaps you would prefer to stay in a log cabin deep in a cove...It won't be a problem. (You can find your heart's desire in our Bed-and-Breakfasts and Country Inns and Other Accommodations chapters.)

The mixture of outdoor activities and cultural attractions, town and country, tradition and influx of progressive ideas is what keeps us here—and others coming.

ACKNOWLEDGMENTS

Thank you to the chambers of commerce and visitor center of Alleghany County, Ashe County, Avery County, Banner Elk, Beech Mountain, Blowing Rock, Madison County, Mitchell County, Yancey County, Watauga County, and Haywood County; the Boone Area Chamber of Commerce; High Country Host; Asheville Chamber of Commerce; and to all of the kind participants in this book who have kindly provided information and great experiences.

A very special thank you and much love to my parents Irene Dillingham Richards and Ken Richards for instilling in me a love of travel at a very young age, as well as an understanding that all places can be delightful and interesting if you just look.

Thank you to many friends scattered throughout the world now for their encouragement in trying out this American adventure and for remaining close even though you are thousands of miles away. I still miss you! Thank you to Vadim for encouragement in many endeavors.

Last, but not least, a big thank you to my North Carolina–based friends. You've made me feel right at home.

—Constance E. Richards

Without the support of the staff and volunteers of chambers of commerce and visitor centers in the cities and counties of Clay, Cherokee, Graham, Haywood, Henderson, Jackson, Macon, Polk, Swain, and Transylvania, as well as the Cherokee Indian Reservation, this seventh edition would not be as complete as it is. A special tip of the hat to all the folks of the mountains who have shared their experiences in such a generous manner. A special thanks to all those who have toured these mountains with me, adding important comments noted in this book.

An eternal word of thanks to our daughter, Constance, who has given me a "Father's Day" for life in inviting me to again coauthor this seventh edition with her. And to my wife Irene, in addition to all you are, you opened the world and the people of these mountains to me. In proofing my writing, you lived up to your legacy of... being my "refiner." I love you both.

To our readers, we wish you a good journey.

—Kenneth L. Richards

HOW TO USE THIS BOOK ⑦

Even after preparing six editions of this book, we continue to roam western North Carolina's beautiful peaks and valleys, its towns and forests, seeking out the new and revisiting the old to bring you the best of all that's wonderful here. A glimpse of the area includes 18 dynamic counties, plus the mountainous sections of Polk and Rutherford Counties. Covering so much ground—or simply thumbing through our guide—can be overwhelming. Here then is our road map through this seventh edition, allowing you to become a true "Insider" to North Carolina's mountains.

We've divided Western North Carolina into the following three sections: the Northern Mountains, Central Mountains, and Southern Mountains. Within each section we've listed the counties alphabetically, not geographically. Under those county headings, we've again put most listings in alphabetical order. County lines are somewhat arbitrary. For example, Highlands is in Macon County, and Cashiers, 10 miles away, is in Jackson County. However, the local people refer to the Highlands-Cashiers area as if it were a single unit.

In some cases we move away from this region/county format, such as when listing backcountry outfitters or other recreational specialists who serve the whole region. In such cases we list the towns as part of the address where their main headquarters are located.

In the Shopping Destinations chapter, we have listed them under their northern, central, and southern mountain headings. The shops are then listed in alphabetical order within those headings. Part of the fun of shopping is to discover great finds. You might discover yours in any little town

or roadside stand or establishment. With that in mind, we've listed the "discoveries" that are worth a special trip because they're filled with great stores or fantastic little shops.

A good place to begin this book is with the Area Overview chapter. From there you can go to regions or subjects that specifically interest you.

We've included maps so you can orient yourself to each region. Be alert to the fact that name places can be confusing based on multiple spellings and multiple locations. One example is that of the town of Cherokee on the Cherokee Indian Reservation (the Qualla Boundary) in the northwestern part of the state in Jackson and Swain Counties, while the county of Cherokee is some miles away in the far reaches of southwest North Carolina. (Its county seat is Murphy.) They are two entirely separate entities and areas.

Likewise, you will see the same name applied to wholly different locations or geographical formations. For example, down around Clay County the name Tusquitee is given to a bald, a creek, a community, and a chain of mountains. There are also two Hiwassees. The one we write about is the name of a large lake in Cherokee County, but there is also the nearby Georgia town of Hiwassee on Lake Chatuge, a body of water that covers part of Clay County in North Carolina and Towns County just over the border in Georgia.

Native American names can also present a problem: On some maps you'll find a river in Jackson County spelled Tuckasegee. On other maps it is spelled Tuckaseigee. We've chosen the former version. Likewise, some maps list a Jackson County lake as Lake Glenville; others call it Lake Thorpe.

The Cherokee, descendants of those native inhabitants who developed a culture in these mountains over time, provide a rich heritage of legends and lore. We have included some of these materials throughout this book. Volumes have been written about the Cherokee. Our designated chapter leads you to the Qualla Reservation in Cherokee, North Carolina. You can discover and live the lore firsthand.

Listed in "Close-Ups" boxes throughout this Insiders' Guide are some of the classic scenic views. Have your camera ready and find your own. "Close-ups" also allow us to feature a place, an event, or a person in greater depth.

Scattered throughout the book are Insiders' tips (indicated by 🅸), which offer quick insights and handy information.

With population movements, new roads and highways, relocating industries, and other factors of our modern world, change is evident everywhere. Nothing but the great and rugged peaks of this oldest mountain range in the world stays the same. We hope that we've enhanced your experience of Western North Carolina by making this an easy and enjoyable guide to use.

AREA OVERVIEW

Welcome to the North Carolina Mountains. They are as rich in history, folklore, indigenous culture, and natural wonder as you have been led to believe. Come join us on a journey through mossy coves and hollows, over wildflower-studded pasture lands and dewy forest trails, past gurgling mountain streams and mellifluous water-falls, into the green valleys and onto the misty blue ridges that comprise this glorious mountain range. Let your clock stand still for a moment and revel in the rejuvenating air, water, and earth of North Carolina's mountains.

Each county in Western North Carolina bears its own individual geographical features, history, and lifestyle. Each major town deserves a chapter, from cultural, educational, and medical centers like Asheville and Boone to the smaller pastoral settlements of Blowing Rock and Lake Lure. Many of these smaller mountain settlements and villages are made distinct by becoming "incorporated," indicating that they are legal townships unto themselves with their own tax bases and may not be swallowed up by the next larger town that might be growing beyond its boundaries.

In this chapter we offer "thumbnail sketches" of the area's counties. After reading even more about each of the counties under their headings in the more specialized chapters that follow, we trust you will be sufficiently inspired to come out here to explore and discover these mountain enclaves for yourself.

NORTHERN MOUNTAINS

Alleghany County

Tucked up against the border of Virginia is rural Alleghany County, the northernmost of North Carolina's mountain counties. Only 230 square miles, Alleghany is one of the smallest counties in the state. It was once known as "the lost province," and for good reason, because it can only be reached by winding two-lane roads. Alleghany County has a moderate climate, with distinct seasonal changes. Snow is not uncommon here, but the elevation, which ranges from 2,500 to 4,000 feet, does not sustain the winter sports more common in neighboring counties.

Indian hunters roamed this land thousands of years ago, but it was the ruggedly independent Scotch-Irish, English, and German pioneers who settled these hills and valleys in the late 1700s. The county was officially established in 1859 from parts of the surrounding counties of Ashe, Surry, and Wilkes. The name Alleghany is derived from the Indian word for "fine stream," which is fitting for an area nourished by the New River, one of the oldest rivers in the world. According to historians, this ancient river was named by surveyor Peter Jefferson, Thomas's father, who was surprised to find another "new" river behind the mountains.

The geographic remoteness of this county is more a blessing than a hindrance, for Alleghany County's natural isolation has preserved the rural America of 30 years

The northern mountain counties are Christmas tree country. Families have been farming Christmas trees here for generations. The Fraser Fir is a dark green color and one of the most desirable trees on the market. Even heavy ornaments can be hung from its strong boughs. The silvery undersides of the soft needles are pleasant to the touch, and the tree retains them throughout the holiday season. The White Pine is also an excellent Christmas tree.

ago. The pace is gentler in this small county of just 11,550 people. It's a friendly place where everyone knows everyone, where children can grow up never knowing a stranger, and where trust is an unspoken certainty. Many in Alleghany County still live on family land that has been handed down for generations. And in tiny Sparta, the county seat with a population of only 2,000, Main Street is not just a location but an atmosphere.

Seven percent of the county's labor force of 5,000 works in agriculture-related businesses, such as tobacco, beef cattle, corn, and hay. Christmas tree production is the fastest growing farm industry in the county, and outside manufacturing like Martin Marietta Manufacturing is being established as well as Sparta Industries, makers of Dr. Grabow's presmoked pipes; New River Artisans, manufacturers of custom-designed rugs; and NAPCO, makers of "Trivial Pursuit" game boards. Economic development is expected to continue in Alleghany County, especially with the improvement of the county's roads.

But it is still a joy to ride the winding two-laners of Alleghany County, up and down its spectacular rolling hills and along its far-reaching pastures. In an era of shrinking rural farmland, the expanse of unspoiled beauty is striking. Just a few minutes to the east is the Blue Ridge Parkway, which had its historical beginning in 1935 at nearby Cumberland Knob and forms some 30 miles of the eastern boundary of the county. Then drive a little farther south on the parkway to Doughton

Park, with its network of hiking trails and camping facilities. The easily accessible New River, well known among canoeing enthusiasts, provides easy and inexpensive opportunities for outdoor recreation.

For more information contact the Alleghany County Chamber of Commerce, P.O. Box 1237, Sparta, NC 28675; (336) 372-5473, (800) 372-5473; www. sparta-nc.com.

Ashe County

Ashe County, the extreme northwestern mountain county bordered by Tennessee and Virginia, is marked by the curling length of the New River, one of this country's few north-flowing rivers. The New River's pervasive presence in Ashe is responsible for much of the unique character of this remote North Carolina county. Like its eastern neighbor Alleghany, Ashe County has enjoyed its isolation, allowing it to retain the more relaxed flavor of yesteryear.

Shawnee, Creek, and Cherokee Indian hunters preceded European settlers, who arrived here in the 1750s, erecting their first permanent settlement in 1771 along Helton Creek. Ashe County's early settlers were part of the famous contingent of "overmountain men" who fought the decisive battle of King's Mountain during the Revolutionary War. By 1799 these lands were formally organized as a county and named for the Revolutionary patriot and North Carolina governor, Samuel Ashe. It was not until the mid-1800s that sizable Ashe County lost part of its original 977 square miles to the formation of Watauga and Alleghany Counties, leaving it at its present 427 square miles.

The county seat was established at Jeffersonton in 1803. The town, named for Thomas Jefferson, is known today as Jefferson and lies 1 mile east of West Jefferson. The separately incorporated town of West Jefferson began as a lumber industry

You can see three states from Mount Jefferson in Ashe County. This vantage point is especially breathtaking at sunset. Take US 221 from Jefferson, turning onto SR 1152, and drive all the way to the top to the parking area. The Summit Trail is just a fraction of a mile from the highest point on Mount Jefferson.

village when the railroad made its way here in 1914. Other villages sprang up along the path of the growing rail service. But the decline of the railroad in the decades after World War I had a detrimental effect on rural counties such as Ashe, and the ultimate termination of the county's rail service in 1927 served to isolate the area economically as well as physically.

The 1990s, however, proved to be a time of growth. A combination of Christmas tree farms, golf, and tourism began the revitalization. Ashe's pristine landscape and less-complicated lifestyle also attract new blood, particularly retirees. The county is actively seeking industrial growth, beckoning business with vastly improved and widened county roads.

The prominence of the New River in Ashe County and New River State Park make canoeing and camping popular activities in the area. Mount Jefferson, at an altitude of 4,683 feet, rises majestically out of a 474-acre state park, filled with easy-to-moderate hiking trails abundant with wildflowers. A cave near the top of the mountain is said to have sheltered runaway slaves during the Civil War. The Churches of the Frescoes in West Jefferson and Glendale Springs (see our Arts and Culture chapter) have gained national attention and brought surprising numbers of visitors to the remote hilltops of Ashe County.

With only 10 percent of the county population of 23,000 living in the towns of Jefferson and West Jefferson, Ashe County is still largely rural. Villages cluster at crossroads, and individual farms crown the hillsides. There is no roadside clutter here—the scenic hillsides are dotted with grazing cows and the ubiquitous fragrant stands of Christmas trees. Its proximity to bustling Boone, just 30 minutes away, makes Ashe County an appealing destination for the city person with a country heart.

For more information contact the Ashe County Chamber of Commerce, P.O. Box 31, West Jefferson, NC 28694; (336) 246–9550; www.ashechamber.com.

Avery County

Avery County, with a population of roughly 15,000 today, is a curious mix of peaceful rural life and sophisticated tourism. Settlement came slowly to this rugged place. Indians and mountain men alike hunted the land, yet few pioneers chose to make these peaks their home. One who did was the locally well-known settler William Linville, who came with his sons in 1766 only to be slain by hostile Indians near the spectacular waterfall and gorge that now bear his name.

This high mountain land is harsh in winter, but its clear air and cool summer temperatures attracted tourists as early as the 1870s. Boarding houses opened in Banner Elk to serve the seasonal visitors, and in 1891 the town of Linville was founded as a summer community for the wealthy. Roads continued to develop around the advancing railroad spurs that pushed through the area, opening remote ridges and valleys. Even so, the twists and turns of the topography left pockets of rural settlement untouched. It was not until 1911 that Avery County, named for Revolutionary patriot Waightstill Avery, was officially formed, making it the newest and one of the smallest counties in North Carolina (only 247 square miles). Newland is the county seat.

Waightstill Avery was a lawyer in peacetime. In one heated debate with Andrew Jackson, these two combatants elected to settle their differences with a duel. A quirk of the law in North Carolina read that one could make a challenge, but the duel could not be fought within the boundaries of the state. So at sunrise on the selected morning, the men met on the field of valor in Jonesborough, Tennessee, just over the state line. Even stranger, neither wished to harm the other. Thus they fired their dueling pistols into the air, shook hands, and had a beaker of whiskey to celebrate their newborn friendship. Jackson even offered a gift to Avery. The whole problem had arisen from the

5

CLOSE-UP

"Tar Heels"

The "Old North State" is self-descriptive. "Tar Heels" is another matter. Some versions have it birthed during the Revolutionary War at the battle of King's Mountain. Others claim that it derives from the tar pits found in the eastern part of the state.

Those in Western North Carolina give credit to Zeb Vance, who claimed that his North Carolina troops had "stick-to-itiveness" during the War Between the States. He once chided Virginians of the Grand Army, saying that if they had had "Tar on your heels, you would have stuck yesterday in the fight, instead of running."

so-called Bacon Law. Wrapped like a book, the package contained a slab of bacon.

Many visitors, now lowland residents, have returned for generations and maintain beautiful second homes in the exclusive areas of Grandfather Mountain, Elk River, and Linville Ridge. Banner Elk, home of Lees-McRae College and the famous Woolly Worm Festival, is also a popular skiing and golf resort community. Beech Mountain, the mile-high winter sport community, straddles Avery and neighboring Watauga Counties. These two communities are the more populated, tourism-driven parts of Avery County, while outlying areas of rural farmland continue much as they were early in the century.

Tiny Crossnore, in southern Avery County, was settled in 1833 and incorporated in 1925. Known for the Crossnore School established in 1911 to educate mountain children, this community is a pleasant reminder of early Western North Carolina town life. The county has a strong tradition in crafts, ranging from pottery and quilts to jewelry and furniture. Today Avery County also boasts the South's highest ski slopes, nine major golf

resorts (public and private), and a number of natural landmarks.

The only notable changes in the rural landscape of Avery County are the geometric patterns of green that cover the hills around Linville, a sign of Avery County's successful Christmas tree industry, in which over 900 families are active.

For more information contact the Avery County Chamber of Commerce, P.O. Box 700, Newland, NC 28657. Or contact the Banner Elk COC at (800) 972-2183, www.banner-elk.com, or the Beech Mountain COC at (800) 468-5506, www.beechmtn.com.

Madison County

The rugged terrain of this western county, bisected by the powerful French Broad River, reflects the self-reliant spirit of the local folk and their industrious predecessors.

Madison County lies northwest of Buncombe County, bordered by Haywood and Yancey Counties and the state of Tennessee. Formed in 1851 from parts of Buncombe and Yancey Counties, Madison County is named for America's fourth president, James Madison. The county is largely rural and has a population of only 17,500, with 48 percent of that population living on farms (the highest percentage in the state). The remainder live in family homes with acreage or in the towns of Mars Hill, Hot Springs, or Marshall, the county seat.

Agriculture—wheat, cattle, corn, and tobacco farming—is still the primary source of income here, but some small manufacturing has also moved into the county. In the last 20 years, an increasing number of artisans and craftspeople have made Madison County home, finding the solitude of the county's heavily wooded mountains conducive to their work. After 11 years of planning and construction, Interstate 26 opened a corridor through Madison County in 2003, connecting South Carolina to the Ohio Valley.

Mars Hill, the county's largest town, lies 20 minutes northwest of Asheville. As the home of Baptist-affiliated Mars Hill College, it is defined both by its scholastic roots and by the rugged individualism of Madison County's heritage. Attractive old brick storefronts face Main Street, a two-lane artery so narrow you could almost jump over it. Although the town remains pretty much as it was 50 years ago, the infusion of newcomers is increasing. Main Street, for example, now has two stoplights, and growth is creeping up the hill from the interstate. Being a college town, the ubiquitous coffeehouse has also made an appearance. Mars Hill is home to the Rural Life Museum and the Southern Appalachian Repertory Theater, and there is skiing nearby at Wolf Laurel. Still, this remains a charming old-fashioned hamlet that is kept dynamic by the presence of Mars Hill College.

Marshall, about 15 minutes west of Mars Hill, straddles the narrow hillsides cut by the French Broad River. Established around 1851, this town is much as it was at the turn of the century. The river has seen to that. Its ebb and flow, and frequent overflows, seem to have suspended the

city in time—this is Marshall's charm. Homes hug the hillsides surrounding the town. The cupola-topped courthouse, designed by Richard Sharp Smith of Biltmore Estate fame, commands a position at a crossroads within walking distance of the river. The town's self-appointed philosophers still convene on the courthouse benches along Main Street. Another prominent town landmark is the elementary school on the island in the middle of the river. Needless to say, students here have long looked forward to flood holidays as much as snow days.

As early as the 1830s, Hot Springs was host to wealthy visitors in search of the healing powers of its springs. A number of hotels, taverns, and boardinghouses sprang up, only to fade away in later years. Today the town is experiencing a revival as travelers, day-trippers, retirees, and summer residents converge on the hills and settle into old hotels that are now quaint bed-and-breakfast inns. The Hot Springs Spa has also been reborn (see our Attractions chapter). Easy access to the French Broad River makes white-water rafting an important part of the town's tourist economy. And with the Appalachian Trail winding through town, Hot Springs is a popular respite for weary hikers.

For more information contact the Madison County Chamber of Commerce, (828) 689-9351, P.O. Box 1527, Mars Hill, NC 28754; (877) 262-3476; www.madison county-nc.com.

Mitchell County

Mitchell County was formed in 1861 from portions of five counties: Yancey, Burke, Caldwell, McDowell, and Watauga. With a population of 14,500 today, this county of only 220 square miles was named in honor of Dr. Elisha Mitchell, explorer of famed Mount Mitchell, the highest peak east of the Mississippi. The county is bordered by Tennessee and Avery, Yancey and McDowell Counties. Mining of quartz, feldspar, and mica are major industries here. In fact the Spruce Pine Mining District is recognized the world over for its ultrapure quartz, which is vital to the computer industry. Agricultural products such as tobacco, corn, apples, and more recently Christmas trees are also important in the county.

Spruce Pine is the largest town in the county with a population close to 3,000. Bakersville, the county seat, is surrounded by the long-established communities of Rock Creek, Cane Creek, Mine Creek, and Toe Cane. These tiny towns, nestled in the twisting mountain coves of Mitchell County, are home to generations of families. The origins of other delightfully named hamlets such as Loafer's Glory, Relief, Ledger, Bandana, and Altapass are worthy of note. Loafer's Glory, about 3 miles north of Bakersville on N.C. Highway 226, was christened by the wives of the community after they observed the unabashed loitering of their men on the front porch of the community store. Relief is named for a once-popular cure-all tonic, Dr. Hart's Relief, which was sold in the community at Squire Peterson's Store around 1870. No doubt the popularity of the tonic came from the large volume of alcohol it contained. The community of Ledger was named for the ledger book sent to Washington, D.C., by community residents who were trying to establish the amount of mail passing through the area and their need for a local post office. The railroad played a part in naming two Mitchell County hamlets: Bandana got its name from the bandana a railroad brakeman used to locate a proper site for a railroad station. The Clinchfield Railroad, passing over these mountains from Tennessee, reached its highest point at the aptly named community of Altapass before heading down the mountain.

The proliferation of gem mines in Mitchell County has long made this county popular with rock hounds. The North Carolina Museum of Minerals is just off the Blue Ridge Parkway (see our chapter on Rockhounding). Mitchell County is also home to the Penland School of Crafts. Sitting atop a mountain ridge, this internationally acclaimed school of the arts draws talented craftspeople and artists from all over the world (see our Mountain Crafts chapter).

For more information contact the Mitchell County Chamber of Commerce, Route 1, P.O. Box 796, Spruce Pine, NC 28777; (828) 765-9483, (800) 227-3912; www.mitchell-county.com.

Watauga County

This county of 39,500 lies at the heart of North Carolina's high country. Formed in 1849, Watauga's 320 square miles are bordered by Tennessee and Avery, Ashe, Wilkes, and Caldwell Counties. It was named for the Watauga River, which rises near Grandfather Mountain and flows north into Tennessee, where it converges with the Holston River. *Watauga* is an Indian word for "beautiful water."

An early emphasis on education led to the development of Watauga County as a center of higher education. The county was largely rural until 1899, when the Dougherty brothers founded the Watauga Academy in Boone, the forerunner of Appalachian State University. Part of the University of North Carolina system, ASU plays an important role in the growth of the area, with thriving Boone, the county seat, at its heart. Boone's permanent resident population of 14,000 doubles with the addition of the students and swells even more with the arrival of tourists throughout the year. The cultural base of the university and the town's tourist-geared entertainment offer something for everyone.

Boone has become a magnet for tourism and related industries. Its many restaurants, for example, have turned the city into a dining destination. The climate is suited for both winter and summer sport, with golf and skiing the prime diversions in the county. Resorts such as Hound Ears, Hawksnest, Seven Devils, and Beech Mountain (partially in Avery

County) offer a multitude of recreation options. And potters, weavers, painters, storytellers, traditional mountain musicians, actors, and artisans fill the area with creative energy.

Blowing Rock, 15 minutes south of Boone, is a picturesque mountain town perched on a ridge overlooking the John's River Gorge. The town takes it name from the rock formation over the gorge that creates an unusual current of air spiraling up from the valley below. The view from the Blowing Rock is breathtaking, as is the scenery from nearly every vantage point in town. Charming specialty stores and fine restaurants line Main Street, and excellent bed-and-breakfast inns are scattered along Blowing Rock's side streets, just a few steps from downtown. You can walk to almost everything here, including the town square, which is the scene of concerts and art shows in summer. Tourism is important to Blowing Rock, so the town leadership is working to retain its villagelike character.

Foscoe, on N.C. Highway 105 leading into Boone, has become known for its selection of craft and antique shops. The community is blessed with a glorious view of Grandfather Mountain in nearby Avery County.

Valle Crucis, in central Watauga County, is also off N.C. 105 at the junction of Dutch Creek and the Watauga River. Established as an Episcopal mission in 1842, it retains a largely rural character and has become a popular site for summer homes, unique restaurants, renowned inns, and unusual shopping.

Despite the busy pace of the tourist meccas, Watauga County offers plenty of quiet countryside. Heading toward Tennessee you can see some of the most scenic farmland in Western North Carolina. U.S. Highway 321 winds up, down, and around hillsides studded with craggy rocks and threaded with lazy, meandering creeks.

For more information contact the Boone Area Chamber of Commerce and Convention & Visitors Bureau, 208 Howard Street, Boone, NC 28607; (828) 264-2225, (800) 852-9506; www.visitboonenc.com; High Country Host, 1700 Blowing Rock Road, Boone, NC 28607; (828) 264-1299, (800) 438-7500; Blowing Rock Chamber of Commerce, P.O. Box 406, Blowing Rock, NC 28605; (828) 295-7851; www.highcountryhost.com.

Yancey County

Indians and mountaineers played vital parts in the development of Yancey County. The area was a thoroughfare for Cherokee Indians who roamed these rich hunting grounds. But the path of the Scotch-Irish settlers seeking a new country also led to these mountains and the fertile valleys, which are fed by Yancey's Cane and South Toe Rivers. Land grants for former Cherokee lands were awarded to hardy pioneers as early as 1777. In 1797 John Gray Blount was awarded a blanket charter for land that eventually became Yancey County. Traders, entrepreneurs, and new settlers began to arrive. The new county, formed in 1833, soon became one of the busiest and most prosperous in the region. Burnsville, also established in 1833, had long been a stage stop.

Prosperity blossomed until the Civil War left its mark both emotionally and economically. The Scotch-Irish settlers who dominated the area had no use for a war they viewed as based on slavery, a practice that was little heard of in the hard existence of most mountain families. And the heavy taxes and conscription imposed by the government to finance the war were burdens for Yancey's citizenry. The discord and hard times resulted in the formation of new counties: Madison, Mitchell, and the area that later became Avery County, leaving Yancey County with 311 square miles by the war's end.

The pioneer heritage of Yancey County has been preserved in Burnsville, a charming town that is a fine illustration of a bygone era. The county's largest community and county seat, Burnsville is anchored by a classic town square with a

Mount Mitchell in Yancey County is the highest peak in the eastern United States, and it's a pretty sight, even though it is frequently foggy. Take N.C. Highway 128, off the Blue Ridge Parkway at milepost 355.4. On a clear day the stone observation tower at the top of the mountain affords a 70-mile view.

statue in honor of its namesake, Captain Otway Burns, a privateer during the War of 1812 and also a member of the North Carolina General Assembly. Life in the town still revolves around the square, and homes are nestled on the mountains rising on one side. A visit to coastal North Carolina in Beaufort will reveal many legends about Otway Burns; he is also buried there.

The county, with a population of 17,000, was economically distressed during the 1980s by crippling unemployment of 23 percent. But with the resilience of their ancestors, Yancey County citizens banded together to revitalize their homeland, and as a result they gained national attention and new industries. In 1980, when the comeback plan was launched, Yancey County placed an advertisement in the *Wall Street Journal* that included a group photograph of the unemployed workers of Yancey County with the caption, "We want to work for you." The bold move attracted *Fortune* 500 industries that are now part of Yancey County's growing industrial base.

Agriculture—tobacco, corn, dairy products, and cultivated berries—still plays a vital part in the county's economy, as it did in pioneer times. Ornamental shrubs and Christmas tree production have also gained a hold. Mining has always been important here: The excavation of mica and feldspar and sand and gravel operations are found in the northern part of Yancey County, near Mitchell County.

The proximity of Asheville, just 35 minutes away, is a plus for Yancey County.

Increasing numbers of retirees are settling here, and premier golf communities are springing up. The rich traditional local arts heritage has always drawn creative people, nurtured by the support of the dynamic Toe River Arts Council. The oldest summer stock playhouse in North Carolina is over 50; it is located in Burnsville.

Yancey County is blessed with seasonal changes and a topography that lends itself to outdoor recreation. The presence of the South Toe and Cane Rivers makes camping, tubing, canoeing, and kayaking easily accessible. The nearby Nolichucky River, flowing into Tennessee, is extremely popular with white-water enthusiasts. Hiking is favored due to the county's network of some 100 miles of trails of varying degrees of difficulty. The Black Mountain Range in Yancey County features Mount Mitchell, at 6,684 feet the highest peak east of the Mississippi. You can see this majestic peak from the Blue Ridge Parkway, which runs the length of Western North Carolina's mountains.

For more information contact the Yancey County Chamber of Commerce, 106 West Main, Burnsville, NC 28714; (828) 682-7413, (800) 948-1632; www.yanceychamber.com.

CENTRAL MOUNTAINS

Buncombe County

Sitting high on a plateau surrounded by mountains, Buncombe County, population 191,000, has enjoyed a history of good fortune due to its position as a geographical crossroads. Development historically follows the path of primary water sources, and so it did here along the mighty French Broad River.

Trade with the Cherokee Indians was established as early as 1673 along the well-worn Indian paths that crossed at the site of present-day Asheville. The natural riches of the region and the flow of commerce soon drew large numbers of settlers. Samuel W. Davidson and his family were the first to settle in the region in 1784, along Christian Creek in the Swannanoa Valley. Trade continued to boom, and the county was officially formed in 1791. The business of government brought in scores of new settlers, traders, speculators, and adventurers. With this influx of new citizens, the well-traveled Indian paths soon became thoroughfares for traders and stock drovers from Kentucky and Tennessee moving through the French Broad Valley on their way to the open markets in South Carolina. The construction of the Buncombe Turnpike from 1824 to 1828 further secured this steady stream of trade.

From the early 1800s to 1880, Buncombe County settled into a period of bucolic bliss. Recovery from the Civil War was slow, and it was not until completion of the railroad in 1880 that the county came into its own. The railroads brought the moneyed class, which was attracted by the healthful climate, crisp mountain air, and sparkling social atmosphere. One young visitor, George Vanderbilt, vowed to return, and when he did he changed the county forever. After purchasing 125,000 acres, he set about building a castle. The construction of his Biltmore Estate in 1895 brought a legion of artists and craftspeople whose legacy remains as an influence on the area's architecture.

The 1920s were Buncombe County's boom time. The architectural character of Asheville, the county seat, was formed during these glory days, giving it the unique cosmopolitan flavor that continues to attract visitors and newcomers alike. An exciting buzz has been developing about this city over the past few years. A magnet for professionals, artists, artisans, retirees, students, New-Agers, and alternative-lifestyle seekers, Asheville was named All-American City in 1997. This city of roughly 68,800 retains a small-town mountain charm wrapped in big-city sophistication. The noted American novelist Thomas

Wolfe was born here, bringing his native city unwelcome notoriety when he wrote of it in his coming-of-age novel, *Look Homeward, Angel.*

The city's geographic growth has always been limited by the mantle of mountains that surrounds it, but modern transportation links the county with nearby cities like Atlanta, Knoxville, and Charlotte that comprise the fastest growing region in the United States. Downtown Asheville boasts the finest collection of art deco buildings this side of Miami Beach, and restoration of these old gems is booming. Pack Square, historically central to the city, and Haywood Street form the cultural and commercial heart of downtown.

The county is framed at all points of the compass with interesting communities. Just 15 minutes north of Asheville lies Weaverville, a town of roughly 3,000 with a charming Main Street. Many retirees choose to live in Weaverville, along with a growing number of young professionals seeking the slower pace of country life (they reside in Weaverville or its outlying farmland and make the short commute to Asheville). The completion of the Interstate 19/23 connector to Tennessee, now titled I-26, has opened this area for non-stop traffic from Charleston, South Carolina, to Tennessee, Kentucky, and Ohio.

Ten more minutes north on the interstate will lead you to the area of Big Ivy, a pastoral mixture of bald hillsides, meadows, tobacco farmlands, and barns that connect the communities of Barnardsville and Dillingham. The pioneer Absolom Dillingham settled at the foot of the Great Craggies in the early 1800s, and his descendants continue to make it their home today. Several excellent examples of pre–Civil War and Civil War–era cabins remain in the area, with the Carson Cabin and schoolhouse restored to its former self. Carson Cabin, which is on Dillingham Road, is open on certain holidays for viewing.

Twenty miles east of Asheville, Black Mountain was established in 1893 as a quaint summer resort town known as Grey Eagle, attracting visitors looking for relief from the heat of the low country. Today much of its turn-of-the-century charm is still intact. It is known for its wealth of antiques shops and cultural events. Avant-garde Black Mountain College operated nearby from 1933 to 1956, and a museum capturing the school's glory is located in downtown Asheville.

The French Broad River divides West Asheville from Asheville, giving West Asheville its distinct personality. Before being incorporated into the city of Asheville, West Asheville was very much its own town. Haywood Road, the main thoroughfare in West Asheville, is reminis-cent of America in the 1950s or 1960s. A revitalization of the area today mingles new bakeries, organic markets, and coffee shops with secondhand shops, a phar-macy, gas stations, and old storefront offices. West Buncombe County still retains much rural farmland, old home-steads, and pastures dotted by grazing cattle. The Arden/Skyland area to the south is Buncombe County's fastest grow-ing section, populated by many young families attracted by the quality of life in the county. Buncombe County benefits from its closeness to the French Broad River, Pisgah National Forest, and the Blue Ridge Parkway, which form the northern and eastern edges of the county and offer outstanding recreational opportunities.

City and county economic develop-ment groups are working together to develop a plan for sustained industrial growth for the area without compromis-ing the unique flavor of this central mountain county.

For more information contact the Asheville Area Chamber of Commerce, 151 Haywood Street, Asheville, NC 28801; (828) 258-6101, (800) 257-1300; www.asheville chamber.org; www.exploreasheville.com. Or call the Black Mountain Chamber of Com-merce at (828) 669-2300, (800) 669-2301; www.blackmountain.org.

Henderson County

From almost any place you happen to be in Henderson County, you can see moun-tains, yet much of the land consists of rolling hills. There are also marshes here similar to those in the lowlands, and some of the rich river valleys are surprisingly flat. That's because the county rests on a high plateau between the Blue Ridge and the Great Smoky Mountains. Elevations here range from 5,000 feet on Little Pisgah Mountain down to 1,400 feet at Bat Cave.

Hendersonville, the prosperous county seat, sits at an altitude of 2,200 feet, almost smack-dab in the middle of the county. This bustling and ever-growing lit-tle city, with its pretty and very-much-alive downtown area, is just off I-26 and is actually closer to the Asheville Airport than Asheville is. It's long been one of Western North Carolina's most popular retirement areas. In 1838, when the 378-square-mile county was established out of a former section of Buncombe County, the Flat Rock community, just a few miles south of Hendersonville, was already a grand summer retreat for the wealthy citi-zens of Charleston, South Carolina.

Before the Revolutionary War, the land that makes up Henderson County was the hunting grounds of the Cherokee.

In 1787 William Mills received one of the first land grants west of the Blue Ridge and left his mark in many of the names he gave to the area: Mills River, Mills Gap, Sugar Loaf Mountain, and Bald Top, to list a few. Mills was a Loyalist who was wounded and left for dead during the Revolutionary War's Battle of King's Mountain in 1781. The night after the bat-tle, he made his escape in the darkness back to his home on the Green River in what was then Rutherford County. Tories were frequently hanged during those volatile days (see Polk County), so he con-tinued on up into the high country and hid in a cave in Sugar Loaf Mountain, which overlooked this rich plateau. He must have liked the land he saw stretched out below him, because he and his wife Eleanor eventually became the first white settlers in the area, and others soon followed.

More than 60 years later, in 1841, a vote was taken on whether to put Henderson County's seat of government in the little community of Horse Shoe (still a small and friendly place) or to situate it some 8 miles away near the Buncombe Turnpike close to the foot of Stoney Mountain. The voters chose the more centrally located turnpike site at what became Hendersonville. Charleston's Judge Mitchell King, who had a summer home in Flat Rock, gave the county a 50-acre tract on Mud Creek, known as Chinquapin Hill. Two other men donated an adjoining 29 acres. Streets were quickly laid out, and a courthouse was finished in 1842.

In 1847 Hendersonville, which already had several hundred residents, was granted its charter and grew slowly but steadily, with agriculture as its economic base. In 1879 the long, dusty trip up the turnpike was shortened considerably when the railroad came to town, bringing with it new growth and prosperity. The first train's arrival, it's said, prompted the greatest celebration to date held in North Carolina's mountains. In this century a number of well-known personalities have visited or established homes in Henderson County, including F. Scott Fitzgerald and Carl Sandburg. The Sandburg home in Flat Rock is now a National Historic Site open to the public. The lovable television legend "Howdy Doody" (a marionette) was in residence here until the death of his mentor, Buffalo Bob.

In the 1920s Florida's real estate boom reached up into Western North Carolina, as Sunshine State developers saw the potential for tourist dollars in all sorts of locales. Large hotels and resorts, some of them highly speculative, blossomed on ridges with grand mountain views. Many still dot the Western North Carolina mountains, but not all were so lasting. Nevertheless, many Floridians were introduced to Henderson County during this era, and the migration of residents from that state still occurs each spring, as they, like the Charlestonians more than 150 years ago, seek to escape lowlands' heat and humidity and to "escape the vapors."

Such part-time residents almost double the population of this and other Western North Carolina counties each summer. Today Henderson County has nearly 80,000 full-time residents. Hendersonville proper has a population of nearly 10,000, with approximately 30,000 in the Greater Hendersonville area. There are many reasons for this besides the area's climate, beauty, and recreational possibilities. The very fact that the county has been "a summer place" for so long allows visitors and new residents to feel welcome and to be quickly absorbed into community life. Its reputation for tolerance led a *New York Times* writer to describe Henderson County residents as "polished yet fleshy and down-to-earth," just like their famous apples. They certainly make good use of any talents newcomers want to share, which has resulted in a rich cultural environment. In the county, for example, you'll find the Flat Rock Playhouse (North Carolina's state theater), a number of amateur and semiprofessional theater groups, a symphony orchestra, and scores of talented writers, artists, musicians, and craftspeople.

Henderson County's economy is a diverse mix of light manufacturing, tourism, agriculture, and retirement. The county goes out of its way to fulfill the needs of its many senior citizens and anticipates future requirements as that population grows.

If there is a problem looming on the horizon, it's the rapid disappearance of good agricultural and undeveloped land. Subdivisions are filling the land, as more and more visitors and summer residents make the county their year-round home. A number of small towns, such as Mountain Home and Fletcher, are beginning to merge into a nearly unbroken strip of businesses.

A plethora of Web sites cover North Carolina's mountain communities. Among the most interesting are www. ncblueridge.com, www.highcountryhost. com, and www.freakinasheville.com (for Alternative Asheville information).

Many of the small farms that stretched along U.S. Highway 64 W. going toward Brevard are now broken up into large sub-urban plots or housing developments.

East of Hendersonville still remains "apple country," where approximately a million trees—a sight to behold during spring bloom—make the county the largest apple producer in the state and seventh in the nation. This glorious harvest is celebrated each September with a three-day Apple Festival, the largest and most popular of the many annual events held in Henderson County. Two of the most distinguished visitors in recent times were then-President George Bush and his wife Barbara. They actually had dinner with an Asheville family who had met them on a tour of the White House. When invited to join the local family for lunch, the Bushes accepted and attended the Apple Festival as well.

The drive through apple country is dramatic for reasons other than spring apple blossoms and the fall harvest. Just down the road from the center of fruit production at Edneyville (about 8 miles from Hendersonville), you'll cross the crest of the Blue Ridge. Then, for the next 5 miles or so, the highway takes a precipi-tous dive through perpendicular peaks to Bat Cave and Hickory Nut Gorge. It's a quick reminder that Henderson is, indeed, very much in the mountains.

For more information contact the Hendersonville Visitors and Tourists Travel Information Center, 201 S. Main Street or P.O. Box 721, Hendersonville, NC 28793; (828) 693-9708, (800) 828-4244; www. hendersonvillechamber.org.

Polk County

One might assume this county was named after the eleventh president of the United States, James Polk. This is not the case. Col. William Polk has been honored by the people of this region for his exemplary efforts in the Revolutionary War. He was wounded in 1775 and recovered in time to take his troops to join with George Wash-ington in the Jerseys in November 1776. The rest is history. He later served as a trustee of the University of North Carolina. He often hosted his friends Lafayette and Andrew Jackson.

Most of Polk County's 234 square miles lie within the Blue Ridge foothills. The western edge, the area that's covered in this book, is mountainous. In this sec-tion we present an overview of the county's three municipalities: Saluda, Columbus, and Tryon.

Saluda, with a population of approxi-mately 680, is on the county's western border at an elevation of 2,095 feet. It sits at the top of the steepest standard-gauge railroad grade in the eastern United States, known as the Saluda Grade. It's a small and winsome village that has long been a vacation and retire-ment spot and is home to quite a few artists and craftspeople. As in Henderson County, apples are the main source of farm income here.

Columbus and Tryon are "twin-towns," separated by I-26, which goes northwest to Hendersonville and Asheville and southeast to Spartanburg and Charleston. It also connects at this point to U.S. Highway 74, which is a four-lane highway to Charlotte.

Columbus, sitting at an elevation of 1,131 feet, is the smaller of the two towns. Its population is only around 1,000. It is the county seat amidst the township, which has a population of 4,000. Colum-bus was named for Dr. Columbus Mills of Mills Spring, which is a small adjacent community that still retains its pristine character. Dr. Mills's ancestor, Col. Ambrose Mills, had been a Loyalist like his son William Mills, the man who first settled Henderson County. Unfortunately Ambrose was not as lucky as William. After the British lost the Battle of King's Mountain, William was left for dead and escaped; Ambrose was captured by Patriots and hanged.

The county was established in 1854. In 1855 the North Carolina legislature appointed a committee to locate a county seat within 2 miles of the center of the county. That done, a 100-acre tract of land was purchased for $1.00. By 1857 Columbus's imposing courthouse of handmade bricks was finished. The town is now a mix of late-nineteenth-century homes, buildings, and churches, combined with condominiums, a modern hospital, high school, and a college campus. The county population is now approaching 17,000.

Neighboring Tryon has a population of 1,800 full-time residents, more than half of whom moved here from some other part of the country. These transplants are mostly writers, artists, educators, professional people, and industrial executives who have helped to magically transform the area into a cultural center that attracts even more of the same types of people. Tryon's original attraction was its climate, and for years the sick came here to improve their health. There's a well-publicized weather phenomenon in this area of the mountains known as the isothermal belt, or thermal belt, which provides a more equitable climate than other areas in the region. Caused by inversions of warm air, particularly in the spring and fall, this miniclimate enables apple growers in the region to produce abundant crops, and grapes and peaches thrive in the botanically rich Tryon area.

As settlers moved into this Cherokee land the relationship between the British and the Cherokee prospered. A peace treaty in 1730 resulted in a steady stream of British and American-born traders traveling up the old Blackstock Road from Charleston to exchange cooking utensils, cloth, and other items for furs and hides. Before too long, a sprinkling of trading posts and white families dotted the area.

The French and Indian War ended this "perpetual peace," and by 1756 forts were constructed in the face of the conflicts between the two cultures. The Block House, a fort near Tryon, still stands. Though it became a private home many years ago, the annual Block House Steeplechase was held there until the event became so popular that it was moved to the Foothills Equestrian Nature Center. (See our Recreation and Attractions chapters for more information on the event.)

The bloodshed was so heavy that, in 1767, Royal Governor William Tryon came in person to parley with the Cherokee. They established a boundary line that ran from a point near Greenville, South Carolina, to the highest point on White Oak Mountain, which was renamed Tryon Peak by the settlers. The peak towers over the area and is particularly dominant when seen from I–26 and as you travel north toward Columbus and Tryon: The mountain comes into view dead ahead right at the North Carolina–South Carolina state line. The boundary, however, meant little to land-grabbing settlers, and it wasn't until the Battle of Round Mountain in the spring of 1776, which the Cherokee lost due to the defection of an Indian named Skyuka, that the Indians gave up their claim to this attractive territory.

By 1839 a post office, also named for Governor Tryon, stood at the foot of Tryon Peak. The community that grew up around it became a favorite resting place for drovers transporting livestock from Kentucky, Tennessee, and the higher mountains of North Carolina to ports on the coast. Though Tryon is now Polk County's largest town, it wasn't incorporated until 1885, primarily to accommodate the rail line that runs through the center of town.

Today the Tryon area is well known to horse lovers all over the nation for its large equestrian estates, steeplechases, fox hunts, and miles of bridle trails. In this storybook-like town, you'll find a number of charming antique and gift shops and other family-owned businesses. The Tryon Theater on Trade Street was originally a 1920s vaudeville theater that now shows first-run movies and occasionally hosts theatrical performances.

Poet Sidney Lanier, who penned "Song of the Chattahoochee" and "The Marshes of Glynn," came to this area to try to cure the tuberculosis he contracted during five months in a Union prison camp during the Civil War. He had planned to stay in the Mimosa Inn in the little community of Lynn, but it was full, so he was given an upstairs room in the Lemuel Willcox house across the road, where he died on September 8, 1881. The Mimosa Inn is still in business (see our Bed-and-Breakfasts and Country Inns chapter). The Willcox house too still stands and is known as the Lanier House. Though the poet's stay in the area was brief, he has become a part of local lore. Nearby Lake Lanier was named for him, and Tryon's architecturally interesting and active public library is known as the Lanier Library.

As a point of clarification, the stately restored mansion of Royal Governor Tryon is not located here. It is on the eastern seaboard in New Bern, North Carolina, where the colonial government was established.

For more information contact the Polk County Chamber of Commerce, 401 N. Trade Street, Tryon, NC 28782; (828) 859-6236; or Polk County Travel and Tourism at (800) 440-7848; www.polkchamber.org.

Transylvania County

This county, with a population of 27,600, has the distinction of being the only one in America called Transylvania. The name naturally leaves the residents open to some teasing about vampires and makes for wonderful T-shirt slogans and Halloween festivals. However, the name, which comes from the Latin for "across the mountains/woodlands," is more than appropriate because 80 percent of this fair county's 378 square miles are covered by forests, almost half of which are managed by the U.S. Forest Service. Elevations in the county range from 1,020 feet at Horsepasture to 6,025 feet on Chestnut Ridge.

One of the most popular entrances to Pisgah National Forest, with all its beauty and recreational possibilities, is just outside Brevard, the county seat. From this entrance the two-lane U.S. Highway 276 climbs 16 miles to the Blue Ridge Parkway. Along that route you'll pass such alluring attractions as Looking Glass Falls, the Fish Hatchery, Sliding Rock (a natural water slide), and the Cradle of Forestry. (See our chapters on Waterfalls, Arts and Culture, and Forests and Parks.)

The county has more than 150 large waterfalls, hence its nickname, "The Land of Waterfalls." It could also be called "The Land of Music" because, in addition to the music of falling waters, rivers, and more than 200 miles of streams, it's the home of the international Brevard Music Festival (see our Arts and Culture chapter). Also, Brevard College, a liberal arts institution within the town limits, is known for its fine music department, and the college hosts numerous events in all the arts. This creativity is contagious: Performing groups, artists, writers, and talented craftspeople contribute to the area's cultural milieu of art and music festivals, craft shows, and other events that are an accepted part of daily life here. Most recently, an international film festival was added to the city's cultural scene.

For the Eastatoes, a band of the Cherokee that claimed this land until 1787, this area was mostly hunting grounds, where the Eastern buffalo was quite prevalent. At one time the Eastatoes had a small settlement near the present town of Rosman, where a hunting path crossed the headwaters of the French Broad River. Another well-used Indian trail came up from South Carolina near what is now Ceasar's Head State Park in South Carolina. It was this path, which came to be known as Douthit's Pass, that many settlers used when they migrated into the areas of Transylvania and Henderson Counties. As the settlers pushed into the area, the peaceful Eastatoes retreated farther up into the mountains.

John Douthit Jr. grew up near the Moravian settlement of Old Salem and in 1790 bought 1,000 acres of land at Table Rock Mountain in South Carolina near the beginning of this path. His sister, Jose Douthit, married Robert Orr Jr. and lived in Brevard. John Douthit was an early pioneer who cut many trails through this rugged territory.

Civil War battles came no closer to Transylvania than Asheville, though a number of its citizens fought and died for the Confederate cause. Others, loyal to the Union, helped smuggle Union sympathizers through an "underground" from Georgia to Tennessee and on to the north.

There was even a private war called the Walton War that took place here in 1811, fought between Georgians and North Carolinians when both states laid claim to this area. The federal government, which had gotten the land through a treaty with the Cherokee, gave the property to Georgia, and its legislature named it Walton County in honor of George Walton, a signer of the Declaration of Independence. North Carolina claimed that the disputed area was a part of what was then Buncombe County. Hostilities arose, and in 1811 the North Carolina militia was sent in to throw the Georgians out. Skirmishes took place 2 miles southeast of Brevard. Some lives were lost, and a few prisoners were taken in the Walton War, but the two states finally agreed that the 35-degree line of latitude was the official boundary. The issue was finally settled in 1813 when surveyors proved that the land belonged to North Carolina.

Transylvania County itself wasn't established until May 20, 1861—the same day North Carolina seceded from the Union—when it was carved out of an eastern section of Henderson County and a western part of Jackson County. Brevard, Transylvania's county seat, was incorporated in 1868 with only 70 residents and seven registered voters. The town was named after Dr. Ephraim Brevard, a physician and the author of the Mecklenburg Declaration of Independence, which preceded the national Declaration of Independence by a year. (The Mecklenburg Declaration, which was drafted at the Mecklenburg Council of Safety in 1775, was sent to the Continental Congress in Philadelphia, but it never arrived.) Dr. Brevard died in 1780 at the age of 37 while in a British prison in Charleston, South Carolina; his statue now stands on Transylvania's courthouse lawn in Brevard.

Brevard's first post office was in the Red House, which is now a bed-and-breakfast inn. From those humble beginnings, Brevard, with a population of nearly 6,000 full-time residents, has blossomed into a lovely flower of a town with an attractiveness that is still growing. Several years ago the *Rand-McNally Places Rated Retirement Guide* chose Brevard as the best of 107 locations in the nation to retire. It scored high in climate, terrain, leisure activities, and safety from crime. It was above average in housing, cost of living, and health care, and the town's friendliness and nearness to attractions was particularly noted. Brevard has continued to rate at or near the top of similar lists. A five-lane connector to I-26 and the Asheville Airport, less than 20 miles away, is bringing new life to Brevard and to Transylvania's other small municipalities of Rosman and Lake Toxaway, the latter having some of the highest-priced real estate in the mountains. In fact this already outstanding county is in the middle of a renaissance.

For more information contact the Brevard Chamber of Commerce, 35 West Main Street or P.O. Box 589, Brevard, NC

28712; (828) 883–3700, (800) 648–4523; www.brevardchamber.org, www.visitwaterfalls.com.

SOUTHERN MOUNTAINS

Cherokee County

Cherokee County, the westernmost county in this region, is bordered by both Georgia and Tennessee, with Murphy, its county seat, only 20 minutes from either state and just two-hour drives from either Chattanooga or Atlanta. The 1996 Olympic white-water canoe event was held at the Ocoee Venue just 31 miles from the town of Murphy. It's a rural county of fertile river valleys lined with glorious mountain ridges. One of the most beautiful is the 10-mile-long, 2-mile-wide Valley River Valley, with the Snowbird Mountains soaring on one side and the Valley River Mountains on the other. Cherokee County's other small municipality, Andrews, lies near the head of this valley. Both it and Murphy are surrounded by the Nantahala National Forest, which takes up 92,363 acres of the county's 300,100 acres, offering facilities for all kinds of outdoor recreation, including off-road vehicle trails. (See our Forest and Parks and Recreation chapters for more on the Nantahala.) Another 37,000 acres is under the control of the Tennessee Valley Authority. This includes the 22-mile-long Lake Hiwassee and its connecting and much smaller Appalachia Lake, which together cut diagonally across the center of the county. They were created when the Hiwassee River was dammed in 1936 for both electricity and flood control, providing the county with a source of water-based recreation.

In 1549 Hernando de Soto and his men, who were in search of gold, were the first Europeans to pass through the area. They stopped for a time at the Cherokee town of Guasili near present-day Murphy. Later Spanish adventurers mined here, as evidenced by old tunnels, shafts, coin molds, and Spanish cannonballs found in the region. However it wasn't until the early 1700s that the first English-speaking explorers ventured into this corner of North Carolina. They described it as a "hilly land where the soil is deep and rich and rivers promise an easy route to the heart of the continent—or even beyond." Nearly another half-century passed before the Baptist Church established a mission school and church at the Old Natchez town on the Hiwassee River in 1820. The French had thrown the Natchez Indians out of Mississippi, and some ended up in this area, merging with the Cherokees. Ten years later, Col. A. R. S. Hunter built an Indian trading post at the present site of Murphy and called it Huntersville; in 1835, when a post office was established, he changed the name to Huntington and made himself the first postmaster.

In 1838 Fort Butler was built here as headquarters for the removal of the Cherokees, who were to be relocated to Oklahoma. Once that tragic task was accomplished, settlers flooded into the area. In 1839 Cherokee County was formed out of a portion of Macon County, and a year later it had a population of 3,427 residents. In 1851 Murphy was incorporated as its county seat. A decade later, when the county had little more than 9,000 citizens, it was asked to send 1,100 men to fight for the Confederate cause. The last battle of the Civil War took place at Hanging Dog Creek, about 4 miles northwest of Murphy, near the site of the Nantahala National Forest's popular Hanging Dog Recreation Area, which offers camping and access to Lake Hiwassee. Today, Murphy's population is estimated at 1,650; Andrews has 1,550 residents; the county as a whole tops out at around 22,000.

The first of Cherokee County's four ill-fated courthouses, a brick structure built in Murphy in 1844, was burned in a raid near the end of the Civil War. A second was torn down and replaced; two more burned. Understandably concerned citizens, and especially the local lawyers, urged that the next courthouse be "as totally fireproof as possible." So the fifth—

a very beautiful structure—was built in 1927 of a regal blue marble found only in the Valley River Valley. You can visit the town of Marble (home of the blue marble) on N.C. Highway 141. The town prospered in the early part of the century but is now a ghost of its former self.

In 1891 the Southern Railroad reached Murphy from Asheville, and a logging boom began. Not much remains from the pioneer and antebellum days of 1838 to 1870, but Cherokee County has a substantial number of buildings and homes dating from the prosperous era that began in the 1880s. You can see examples of Greek Revival, Federal, Neoclassical, Victorian, and Queen Anne architecture here, and the residents have taken great pains to preserve this heritage. You'll also find an even larger slice of history preserved in the interesting Cherokee County Museum next to the courthouse. The cultural preservation and influence of the John C. Campbell Folk School at Brasstown on the line between Cherokee and Clay Counties can't be overestimated (see the Clay County listing following). Many festivals and fairs also take place in the region, including an old wagon train tradition, which is a highlight of the Fourth of July celebration in Andrews. This is also the area where Eric Rudolph, one of the FB.I.'s "Ten Most Wanted," hid out for five years and was subsequently apprehended in the town of Murphy, by rookie officer Jeff Postell, in 2003.

We think you'll love this rural and remote, but far from isolated, county, which its residents refer to simply as "God's Country." For more information contact the Cherokee County Chamber of Commerce, 805 Highway 64 W., Murphy, NC 28906; (828) 837–2242; www.cherokee_countychamber.com.

Clay County

If you tend to look back with nostalgia to a simpler place and time, you'll want to travel to Clay County, Western North Car-

olina's smallest county in the southwesternmost corner of the state. When trying to come up with words to describe the 213-square-mile area, quaint always comes to mind, along with time-warp, and Mayberry, that mythical North Carolina town featured on television's The Andy Griffith Show. (The actual site is Mount Airy in Stokes County, just beyond Alleghany County.) The rolling farmlands and mountain-ringed valleys dotted with cattle and picturesque barnyards full of foraging chickens look more like paintings than a real landscape, but Clay County is real all right, and down-to-earth, too.

The county is as uncluttered and unpolluted a place as can exist on this planet today while being two hours, more or less, from Atlanta, Chattanooga, and Asheville. Stretched along its southern border, you'll find beautiful, mountain-encircled Lake Chatuge and its 132-mile shoreline. It's called the crown jewel of the Tennessee Valley Authority's (TVA's) many lakes because of its lovely setting. The lake, which North Carolina shares with Georgia, is not only pretty to look at, it's also a prime area for fishing and other water sports. The county, with a population of 7,200, has 65,650 acres of federal land, 43,400 of which make up part of the Nantahala National Forest, including the Fires Creek Bear Sanctuary in the high mountains of the northeastern corner of the county.

Much of Clay County is at an altitude of 1,900 feet, but peaks here can soar as high as 5,400 feet. In 1830, eight years before the Cherokee were forced out of the area, a single white settler, John C. Moore, moved here from Macon County with his wife and son. He grooved together a cabin of poplar logs in the Tusquitee section and cleared land for planting. After the Cherokee removal, people began to settle around Fort Hembree, a mile west of the present-day county seat of Hayesville, which had been built to enforce that removal. But even up into this century, Clay was an isolated area. It didn't become a county until 1861, when it was separated from Cherokee County. Its first industry, in fact, was a tanning company that sold its tanned deer hides at 12.5 cents per pound. Local folk used the hides to make shoes because there was no market where they could buy footwear.

Once the site of the county seat was chosen, W. H. Hancock donated 20 acres, and chestnut logs were split into rails to fence the town, with gates at different points to let the traffic in and out. Hayesville was named after state representative George Hayes, who had helped establish the new county. Within a few years Hayesville had a courthouse and a log jail that stood where the old brick jail now stands. It continues as a captivating structure housing history archives as the Clay County Historical Museum. The red-brick courthouse at the center of town was built in 1888 and is on the National Register of Historic Places. The Licklog Players, a regional theatrical group, makes its home at Hayesville's state-of-the-art Peacock Playhouse.

Unlike so much of the rest of the area, the population of Hayesville continues to shrink. Some 20 years ago, the town had a population of 385; today 279 people live here. This lack of crowds and too-fast development is one of the county's main attractions. Despite its laid-back lifestyle, or perhaps because of it, Clay County's schools have continuously ranked among the top four districts in the state. The students exceed state expectations in all areas of achievement and performance, and Clay County posts one of North Carolina's lowest dropout rates, although the county spends only about 60 percent of the state's average local expenditure per student. According to the Child Advocacy Institute in North Carolina, Clay County has ranked as the best place in the state to raise a child and has been first on the Children's Index (used to rate such factors as prenatal care, child abuse rates, family violence, education, and income).

No place reflects the spirit of Clay County's magical preservation of some of the best aspects of the past better than the John C. Campbell Folk School at Brasstown. Both the school and Brasstown straddle the Cherokee-Clay county line and both counties claim it. The school, established in 1925, is not only one of the best craft schools in the nation, it also teaches music, dance, fly-tying, and gardening. The public is invited to traditional music concerts, dances, gospel sings, craft demonstrations, and other events. It's worth a visit. (See our chapter on Mountain Crafts.)

This homegrown, do-it-yourself spirit is obvious in other areas of life here, such as the Mountain Valley Farmers Market, which takes place every Saturday of the growing season from 7:00 to 11:00 A.M. on the square in Hayesville. Everything sold at this market is guaranteed to be home-grown or handmade, including vegetables, flowers, eggs, herbs, honey, ornamentals, baked goods, and crafts. It's also alive in the many festivals held on the town square. (See our chapter on Annual Festivals and Events.)

For more information contact the Clay County Chamber of Commerce, P.O. Box 88, Hayesville, NC 28904; (828) 389-3704; www.claycounty-nc-chamber.com.

Graham County

There are sections of any county in Western North Carolina that can be called "rugged," but in 1872, when this area became a county, it was described by early explorers as "the most rugged, isolated, inaccessible land in all Eastern America." This 274-square-mile county is literally walled off by the Snowbird Mountains, the Cheoah Range, the Yellow Creek Mountains, and the western range of the Great Smoky Mountains, called the Unicoi. Elevations in the county range from 1,777 feet to approximately 5,560 feet at the western end of the county, which adjoins eastern Tennessee.

Graham County, with a population of 8,000, is at the southwestern boundary of the Great Smoky Mountains National Park. Approximately 60 percent of the county is in the Nantahala National Forest, including the 3,800-acre Joyce Kilmer Memorial Forest of virgin timber. Here you'll find trees that are hundreds of years old and grow 150 feet tall. Some are 20 feet in circumference at their bases. This memorial forest is a part of the 14,000-acre Joyce Kilmer–Slickrock Wilderness Area, which offers more than 60 miles of wilderness hiking trails. A 27-mile portion of the Appalachian Trail also crosses Graham County.

In addition to other wildlife, the woods here are famous for their "Rooshians," German wild boars that were mistakenly thought to be from Russia. An English company that planned to establish a high-priced hunting preserve in the mountains shipped them, along with other exotic game, to America. The preserve was a failure. The boars escaped, multiplied, and are still hunted here and in other sections of the mountains where they are notorious for rooting up the native habitat. Graham also contains more than 100 miles of clear mountain streams and 14,000 acres of lakes, including the fjordlike Calderwood and Cheoah Lakes, 2,800-acre Lake Santeetlah, and 30-mile-long Lake Fontana. On the last you'll find Fontana Village, a former town for the workers who built Fontana Dam in the early 1940s, now a large and lovely resort. (See our chapter on Resorts.)

Graham County was the home of Chief Junaluska, the Cherokee leader who saved Gen. Andrew Jackson's life in the Battle of Horseshoe Bend in the War of 1812. Ironically the same Andrew Jackson, as president of the United States, issued the order to round up and send the Cherokee to Oklahoma. Junaluska walked all the way back to North Carolina from that territory and was ultimately successful in his struggle to keep the remaining Cherokee people in the mountains, thus maintaining the Eastern Band of the Cherokee. He was more than 100 years old when he died. His grave is in Rob-

binsville (population 777), Graham's quaint county seat. The first road into Graham County was built in 1838 for the specific purpose of removing the Cherokee from their native land. Now a number of excellent highways enter the area from south, east, and north. Graham County's borders are 79 miles from Knoxville, Tennessee, and 88 miles from Asheville.

For more information contact Graham County Travel and Tourism Authority, 427 Rodney Orr Bypass, P.O. Box 1206, Robbinsville, NC 28771; (800) 479-3790. Or call the Chamber of Commerce at (828) 479-3790; www.grahamchamber.com.

Haywood County

No one knows exactly when the first white settlers moved into the area that now makes up Haywood County, but some came more than 200 years ago, lending their names to many of the geographic points of interest here, such as Mary Gray Mountain. Others whose names stuck to the areas that they settled—Allens Creek, Francis Cove, Stamey Cove, and Ratcliffe Cove—have descendants whose names help fill the Haywood County phone book today.

Actually back then all the land that is now in Buncombe and Haywood Counties, plus all the territory west to the Tennessee line—including the present-day counties of Macon, Jackson, Swain, Graham, Clay, and Cherokee—were a part of Burke County. In 1792 Buncombe County was broken off from Burke, and in 1809 Haywood County was formed from a section of Buncombe and named for John Haywood, North Carolina's state treasurer from 1787 to 1827. Because the Cherokee moved west of the Tuckasegee River after the Revolutionary War, the new county was made up of 2,500 white residents. Land grants were given to numerous English, Scotch-Irish, German, and Dutch settlers.

Today Haywood County has approximately 50,000 residents and consists of 546 square miles of craggy mountains, rolling foothills, and deep valleys. The county is surrounded by the Great Smokies on the north, the Newfound Mountain Range on the east, the Pisgah Ridge on the south, and the Balsam Mountain Range on the west. Elevations range from 1,400 feet at Waterville on the Pigeon River to 6,621 feet on top of Mount Guyot. Nineteen peaks in the county are higher than 6,000 feet. This most noted is 6,030-foot Cold Mountain, the star of Charles Frazier's best-selling novel, *Cold Mountain.* Almost 40 percent of land is under the protection of the National Forest Service (Pisgah National Forest) and the National Park Service (24 miles of the Blue Ridge Parkway run through the county).

Interstate 40 and a number of other highways, including U.S. 19, U.S. 23, and U.S. 276, serve the county seat of Waynesville, 27 miles from Asheville. Haywood has three other incorporated towns: Canton, Clyde, and Maggie Valley. Waynesville is one of the county's oldest towns, established in 1809 as a voting precinct in an area that had been called Mount Prospect. When the county courthouse and jail were built here in 1810, the town's name was changed to Waynesville. A charming, arty town with its pretty Main Street, Waynesville is perched on top of a small plateau and has striking views in all directions. It has a population of nearly 10,000 full-time residents.

One of North Carolina's top 20 destinations is "Folkmoot," founded and hosted in Waynesville. This international extravaganza features the nations of the world every July with two weeks of street dances and performances conducted in Waynesville and throughout the mountains. (See our chapter on Annual Festivals and Events.)

Canton is the next largest town, with a population of 4,000. In 1861 there were only two houses where Canton now stands at the ford of the Pigeon River. After the Civil War, the hamlet known as Pigeon Ford grew to village size, and in 1881 the

railroad track crept up into the Blue Ridge Mountains and stopped here, and the name was changed to Buford in honor of the railroad's president. In 1891 Buford was renamed Pigeon Ford, and in 1893 it was given the name it goes by today.

Canton's major industry is the Blue Ridge Paper Mill. It is now employee-owned. It was its parent company, Champion Paper Company, that turned Canton into a boomtown. Champion deserves a huge "tip of the hat" for cleaning up the air and water pollution it created. The employees deserve the boasting rights of having kept this major industry alive by investing their earnings and lives to do so.

Lake Logan, the "watering hole" for employees and special guests of Champion, has now been acquired by the Boy Scouts of America Daniel Boone Council, the Episcopal diocese, and the National Forest Service. According to legend, the "Boojum" continues to find a home there as well.

Of the other two municipalities, Clyde, the home of the excellent Haywood Community College, has a population of 1,189; and Maggie Valley, named for the young daughter of its first postmaster, has just 354 people. However don't let Maggie Valley's small size fool you. This popular resort town 7 miles west of Waynesville draws thousands of visitors with its many attractions, music and dancing at The Stompin' Ground, and the Cataloochee Ski Area, North Carolina's oldest ski resort.

With its easy access to Asheville, the Blue Ridge Parkway, and the Great Smoky Mountains National Park, more and more people are noticing how nearly perfect Haywood County is.

For more information contact the Haywood County Chamber of Commerce, 107 Woodland Drive or P.O. Box 600, Waynesville, NC 28786; (828) 456-3021; and the Maggie Valley Chamber of Commerce, 623 Soco Road or P.O. Box 87, Maggie Valley, NC 28751; (828) 926-1686; www.haywoodnc.com.

Jackson County

Jackson County has a growing population of more than 28,000. Here the Blue Ridge Mountains, with their dramatically shattered and steep rock faces, roll in long, forested ridges toward the southwest. Elevations in the county range from 1,850 to 6,450 feet, with many 5,000-foot summits, and cool, high valleys that sit at 3,000 to 4,000 feet. Rainfall and waterfalls are abundant in the region and lend, along with the 28,000 acres of national forests, a lush beauty to the landscape.

The prehistoric hieroglyphics made by ancient Native Americans who long predate the Cherokee on Judaculla Rock, between Cashiers and Cullowhee, give mute evidence that the area has attracted humans throughout the ages. (See our Attractions chapter.) However, it wasn't until 1828 that the first white settlers moved into the area. Yet by 1850 there were enough people in this broad depression between two mountain ranges drained by the Tuckasegee River to warrant a new county. Both Haywood and Macon Counties consented to part with some territory to form a new one.

The county stretches between the Balsam and Cowee Mountains and runs from the top of the Blue Ridge on the south to the Great Smoky Mountains in the north. The new county was named for Andrew Jackson, seventh president of the United States, and its first seat of government, Webster, for Daniel Webster, the American statesman and orator. Its settlements, strung along picturesque Tuckasegee River, grew into rustic towns. Three of them—Sylva, Dillsboro, and Webster—are incorporated and three others—Cashiers, Cullowhee, and Whittier—are not.

Sylva, at 2,039 feet in the northwestern section of the county, has more than 2,000 full-time residents. Most of the area's businesses and industries are here. The courthouse, which is reached by climbing 107 steps, was built in 1914 when the county seat was moved to Sylva. From its hilltop vantage point, the courthouse overlooks the river and the bustling town that stretches down two long streets. Sylva is the county seat.

A mile away, Dillsboro, founded in 1884, has a population of only 150, but its 50 or more shops have become home to the works of hundreds of artists and craftspeople. Thousands of visitors come here to ride the Great Smoky Mountain Railroad's excursion trains and to shop and spend time in this pretty and creative place. The famous old Jarrett House Inn is also here. (See our chapter on Bed-and-Breakfasts and Country Inns.)

Webster, the former county seat and the site of a number of historic homes, has a growing population of 452. The town was built on an Indian mound, and the surrounding area offers sweeping views of the Tuckasegee River.

Cullowhee, situated in the scenic Tuckasegee River basin and surrounded by mountains, forests, and streams, is the home of Western Carolina University. It has a student body of 6,700, a faculty of some 325 professors, and is the center of arts and culture in the county. The university also has the Mountain Heritage Center, with its museum and programs that preserve and promote this region's unique heritage. The annual Mountain Heritage Day, a festival of traditional music, crafts, food, and fun that attracts thousands, is also held in Cullowhee.

Whittier lies at Jackson County's lowest elevation, 1,839 feet, in farming country on the border of Swain County. Dr. Clark Whittier of California, a relative of the Quaker poet John Greenleaf Whittier, established it. Nearby is the site of the Cherokee town of Stikohi or Stecoee, destroyed in 1776 in a preemptive strike after the Cherokee sided with the British at the beginning of the Revolutionary War. Later Col. William H. Thomas, white chief and friend of the Cherokee, established his home here and used treaty funds to buy land that became the Qualla Boundary, the home of the Eastern Band of Cherokee. (See our chapter on the Cherokee Indian Reservation.)

The deceptively small town of Cashiers actually has 1,250 residents, with several thousand more in the area surrounding it. The town sits high up in a mountain valley at an elevation of 3,478 feet, not far from spectacular Whiteside Mountain, whose sheer rock faces are the highest vertical drops in the east. Right outside town, you'll find the historic High Hampton Inn, which maintains its old traditions and a fine golf course. In the early 1900s several other inns were established in the area to serve Southern gentry escaping lowland heat and humidity. Many of these visitors ended up building summer homes, and the area has continued to attract vacationers and those who serve them. Nearby, for example, is Sapphire Valley, a huge community resort with all the amenities. Lake Glenville, right on the highway between Cashiers and Cullowhee—along with other small lakes in the Cashiers area—offers fishing, boating, canoeing, and other water sports.

A promotional writer once remarked that this area "is not only beautiful [to see]; it's a beautiful feeling, too." That's not hype.

For more information contact the Jackson County Chamber of Commerce, 116 Central Street, Sylva, NC 28779; (800) 962-1911 or (828) 586-2155; www.main.nc.us/jackson; and the Cashiers Area Chamber of Commerce, NC 107 S. or P.O. Box 238, Cashiers, NC 28717; (828) 743-5191; www.cashiersnorthcarolina.com.

Macon County

Somewhere back in time, American Indians built a mound known as Nik-wa-si along the banks of the Little Tennessee River. A town council house was built on its top, and the lodges of the city were spread up and down the valley. This site formed the government and spiritual center of the Middle Cherokee tribe. According to Cherokee tradition, the "Immortals" remain deep within the mound. They are the defenders of their people. A marker at the mound is now on East Main Street in Franklin, Macon's county seat.

It was here that Hernando de Soto came in search of gold in 1540; ironically his expedition totally overlooked the wealth of gemstones for which this area is now so famous. De Soto's visit, however, was relatively peaceful compared with what came later. In 1760 war broke out between the Cherokee and encroaching settlers, and the ancient town of Nik-wa-si was attacked by the British on several occasions and eventually destroyed. Finally, in the Treaty of 1815, the Cherokee gave up the land east of the Nantahala Mountains. Nantahala, meaning "land of the noonday sun," was so named by the Cherokee because only at midday does sunshine reach the bottom of the deep Nantahala Gorge.

This newly conquered territory became a part of Haywood County, and in 1817 Jacob Siler and William Britton journeyed from Buncombe County to set up a trading post, thus becoming the first white settlers in the area. They were not, however, the first to get to know it well. Botanist William Bartram had been hospitably received by the Cherokee during his stay at Nik-wa-si in 1777, and today's Bartram Trail, second in popularity only to the Appalachian Trail, actually passes through the city limits of Franklin. (See our chapter on Forests and Parks.)

Macon County was formed in 1828 and named after Nathaniel Macon, who served in the U.S. Congress for 36 years. The large territory that made up the original county was later broken up to eventually form all or parts of Cherokee, Jackson, Clay, Swain, and Graham Counties. Macon now covers 517 square miles and has a full-time population of about 26,000, though vacationers and second-home owners more than double that number every summer.

The town of Franklin, with a permanent population of around 3,000, was named after Jesse Franklin, one of the men who surveyed the town in 1820 and became governor of North Carolina within the year. The town was not incorporated until 1855. During the Civil War, Franklin was staunchly for states' rights and sent 1,000 of its 3,000 adult males to join the Confederate army. More than 50 percent of these men became casualties. As the war drew to a close, Col. George W. Kirk's Union regiment rode into Franklin and burned and looted the town.

Today Franklin sits at the convergence of three major highways—U.S. 441, U.S. 64, and N.C. 28—at an elevation of 2,800 feet. Elevations in Macon County overall range from 1,900 feet in the Little Tennessee River basin to 5,500 feet at Standing Indian Mountain.

Macon County's other town is Highlands, which sits atop a mountain plateau at 4,118 feet, making it the highest incorporated town east of the Mississippi. Driving the narrow, curving stretch of U.S. 64 along the Cullasaja Gorge that connects the two towns is an adventure in itself and offers some of the most-photographed waterfalls in the mountains, including Lower Cullasaja Falls, Bridal Veil Falls, and Dry Falls. Highlands was purposely created in 1875 by Samuel T. Kelsy and Clinton C. Hutchenson, who bought the land from the Dobson family of Horse Cove, a small community south of Highlands. A year later the two men sent flyers all over the country advertising the climate and altitude of the new "town," and by 1883 Highlands had 300 residents and was incorporated. Now its winter population hovers around 1,000, but that grows to from 20,000 to 25,000 during the summer, not counting all the visitors who arrive to shop and take in the attractions of the surrounding area.

Where Franklin is rich in gemstones, Highlands is rich in botanical treasures. Macon County as a whole gets 50 inches of rain a year, but Highlands averages 70. This contributes to its unique plant life and led to the establishment of one of the oldest research centers in the country, the Highlands Biological Station, where scientists from all over the world study the area's

Before you travel, contact the chamber of commerce or visitor centers of the areas you plan to cover. Most of them offer an informational kit that they will send you before you leave home.

flora and fauna. Highlands also has some of the most expensive real estate in the mountains. Summer residents support its fine shops, restaurants, and cultural events.

Macon County loves its visitors, and tourism is its leading industry, but the county is not solely dependent on it. Forestry products, farming, and ranching are still a large part of the local economy, and managers of new, nonpolluting industries are finding that this is an area where business and outdoor pleasure can be easily combined.

For more information contact the Franklin Area Chamber of Commerce, 180 Porter Street, Franklin, NC 28734; (828) 524–3161; and the Highlands Area Chamber of Commerce, Fourth Street or P.O. Box 404, Highlands, NC 28741; (828) 526–2112; www.highlandschamber.org.

Swain County

Swain County was created in 1871 out of parts of Jackson and Macon Counties and was named for David L. Swain, a former governor and president of the state university. The cabin in which he was born is in Asheville, incorporated in the Beaverdam Run condominium complex.

Eighty-five percent of the county's 553 square miles is federal land, which means it's mostly mountains, forests, streams, rivers, and wilderness. Yet this unspoiled, unhurried, unpolluted piece of paradise is just 60 miles from Asheville and 85 miles from Knoxville, Tennessee. The southern part of the Great Smoky Mountain National Park comprises 216,662 acres of the county; the Nantahala National Forest manages another 21,000 acres. And the Blue Ridge Parkway finally comes to an end—or originates, depending on which way you're traveling—in Swain County and takes up 709 acres of county land. In addition, 29,000 acres of the Cherokee Indian Reservation, including the town of Cherokee with its many diversions, is also within the county. The reservation is known as the "Qualla Boundary." The boundary begins in the north at Soco Gap, which connects into Maggie Valley. The town of Cherokee lies within that boundary. This includes the authentic Museum of the Cherokee and the Qualla Arts and Crafts Center. Leading from those centers are the directionals pointing the way to the outdoor theater where *Unto These Hills* drama is presented throughout the summer, and the 17th-century prototype of a living Cherokee village, Oconoluftee Village, stands.

The elevation at Bryson City, the county seat, is only about 1,800 feet, while just a dozen miles away, as the crow flies, the mountains soar to 6,643 feet at Clingman's Dome.

Some of the state's most scenic rivers—the Nantahala, Oconaluftee, and Tuckasegee—add their beauty and recreational possibilities to all the other attractions. The Nantahala River alone draws thousands of rafters and kayakers, and many white-water outfitters, including the well-known Nantahala Outdoor Center, are in or near Bryson City. Some great mountain biking trails in the area attract such events as Knobscorcher, one of the state's most popular series of mountain bike races. Fontana Lake stretches into the county just a few minutes west of Bryson City.

Bryson City, population 1,250, is a lively, attractive town on the banks of the Tuckasegee River, with parks both along the river and on its islands. It's a popular stop for passengers on the Great Smoky Mountain Railroad, which offers train excursions through the area. As if that weren't enough, annual riverfests, high-school band competitions, chili cook-offs, and other celebrations are held throughout the year. Needless to say, if you like the outdoors, you're going to love it here, because the 11,800 full-time Swain County residents have quick access to some of the largest expanses of wilderness areas in the eastern United States.

For more information contact the Swain County Chamber of Commerce, 16 Everett Street or P.O. Box 509, Bryson City, NC 28713; (828) 488-3681; www.greatsmokies.com.

GETTING HERE, GETTING AROUND

A natural charm and mystery surrounds many parts of the Western North Carolina mountains, still considered to be wild and remote. Over time, the paths traveled by the bear, mountain lion, deer, and elk became hunting trails for Native Americans. These trails became the dusty and muddy roads used by early settlers. As time flows with the tides of progress, the roads became paved, curvy two-laners. Today, the magnificent highways of America bring travelers into these mountains on beautiful scenic drives. Not the least of these is the Blue Ridge Parkway. Yet there's still a wealth of wilderness to be found. And within this wilderness there is access to nature preserves, waterfalls, hiking trails, and the area's other attractions. Their lure continues to bring millions of visitors here each year.

National and state highways now crisscross this ancient land of the Cherokees. The Blue Ridge Parkway winds its way southwest at an average elevation of 3,000 feet through the northern and central mountains, finally turning northwest in the southern mountains. It ends at Cherokee at the southern entrance to the Great Smoky Mountains National Park (see our Blue Ridge Parkway, Cherokee Indian Reservation, and Forests and Parks chapters). Two busy interstate highways—I-40 and I-26—intersect in Asheville, and just an hour or so south, I-26 crosses Interstate 85 at Spartanburg, South Carolina, on that interstate's busy leg between Atlanta and Charlotte.

Getting to many of the best hiking trails, the prettiest waterfalls, and some of the most beautiful areas of the woods can involve taking Forest Service (FS) or unpaved secondary roads (SR). Many of

these are steep, curvy, narrow, graveled, and often one lane with only small pullouts to get around oncoming traffic. Passing is mostly impossible and certainly inadvisable. But, if your vehicle is in decent shape and its tank filled with gas, we encourage you to explore these adventuresome byways. Don't, however, be in a hurry, and watch out for logging trucks. It's also a good idea to stop by the closest ranger station (the numbers are listed in the Forests and Parks chapter) and ask about road conditions. Bad weather sometimes washes out whole sections of these roads or creates landslides.

The Asheville Regional Airport, adjacent to I-26 and strategically located between Asheville and Hendersonville, is connected to Brevard by a five-lane highway. The jetport located at the Asheville Regional Airport handles corporate and private air traffic. The more metropolitan central mountain area is also served by the ever-growing Greenville-Spartanburg International Jetport. The Charlotte-Douglas International Airport, one of the nation's busiest air hubs, is just two hours southeast. Some of the southern mountains residents, however, find that it's just as convenient (and closer) to fly out of the Atlanta-Hartsfield International Airport or from Chattanooga or Knoxville, Tennessee. The mountains also have several general aviation airports.

When this wilderness first opened, few rail lines reached the region. Eventually the highest railroad point in the southeast was in North Carolina. Thomas Wolfe wrote of the nostalgia of hearing the train whistle at night. But alas, passenger trains into the mountains are now part of history. Today a number of railroads provide freight service to the mountains, and Amtrak serves

CLOSE-UP

The Interstate 26 Connector

After 11 years of planning and building, I-26 now connects Charleston, South Carolina, with the Ohio Valley, and what a road it is! In addition to underpasses for wildlife, there are run-off ramps for runaway trucks with special traps for containing hazardous waste spillage. An automated spray, triggered to de-ice the bridge approaching notorious Sam's Gap, which peaks at the North Carolina–Tennessee line, has been built as a winter safety feature. Even monarch butterflies have been given special consideration with the development of a special preserve filled with their favorite flowers and milkweeds high above the interstate.

A unique visitor center offers comfort and assistance as well as a gallery of traditional crafts native to the region. The center has vast picnic areas and offers great scenery. Photo opportunities abound all the way from Asheville north through Tennessee.

This new corridor connects directly with I-81 at Johnson City and provides access to the culturally rich town of Abingdon, Virginia, with its grandiose Martha Washington Hotel and the Abingdon Theatre.

Along the way on I-26 W., one encounters the college town of Mars Hill. Heading east on U.S. 19 just past Mars Hill, enter into Yancey County to the quaint town center of Burnsville, North Carolina. Located along U.S. 19 are the historic Penland School of Craft, the town of Spruce Pine, and the Appalachian State University town of Boone.

These mountains were opened by the forerunners of the Cherokee Nation, the Palo People, about 12,000 years ago. Their tracking of animal pathways became the thoroughfares of the Cherokee. In 1540 DeSoto and his Spanish conquistadors widened these paths in their search for wealth. French expeditions opened paths in their eastward explorations from the Mississippi, while the Scottish and English settlers widened the pathways to accommodate their westward movement from the Atlantic.

nearby Greenville and Clemson, South Carolina, but rail passenger service in Western North Carolina is limited to a railroad excursion company, the Great Smoky Mountains Railway. It is based in both Dillsboro and Bryson City, North Carolina (see our Attractions chapter).

DRIVING IN THE MOUNTAINS

While airports and interstate highways make arriving in the Western North Carolina mountains extremely easy, you'll be taking other highways and byways in order to enjoy all the scenery and attractions this region offers. And that brings up the subject of patience. Driving in the mountains can require abundant patience, but it's usually not the kind demanded by bumper-to-bumper traffic jams. In many areas you'll have the roads mostly to yourself, yet you may need to allow double the time it would normally take to drive a set distance. There are a number of reasons for this. The very nature of these steep-graded, twisting roads demands slower speeds. The top speed allowed on the Blue Ridge Parkway, for example, is 45 miles per hour, and some hairpin curves, even on major routes, require that you slow down to 15 miles per hour. In addition, sudden weather changes can bring blinding fog or downpours. In winter, unexpected ice, snow, and freezing rain can bring travel to a dangerous crawl.

Another thing that can—and probably should—cut into your traveling time is the incredible scenery you'll encounter along the way. Smoky mist curling out of a deep valley, a sunset turning a lake to rosy pink, a waterfall cascading down a mountainside, a highway pull-off offering a green-dappled vista that stretches for miles will tempt you to stop for a look. For those who enjoy the journey as well as the destination, the North Carolina Scenic Byways project covers 1,600 miles of picturesque North Carolina back roads, free of man-made eyesores. Each route was chosen for its particular attractions, based on historic significance or natural beauty, such as waterfalls, rivers, or land formations.

Here in the mountains of Western North Carolina, we are fortunate to have nine of these scenic byways, which cover 410 miles. You can identify the road you're traveling as a scenic byway from the distinctive white sign decorated with green mountains and blue waterways and the title NC SCENIC BYWAY emblazoned at the bottom. The signs have been in place along North Carolina's mountain roads since fall of 1994.

The North Carolina Department of Transportation has issued a helpful, 91-page guide booklet for the entire state system of scenic byways. You can get a copy at most North Carolina welcome centers and DOT offices, or you can write to Scenic Byway Program, NC DOT, P.O. Box 25201, Raleigh, NC 27611-5201. The publication is free, but in it you'll find an envelope that allows you to make a much-appreciated donation.

Even if your schedule forces you to pass by all this beauty, other motorists

The state maintains more than 77,000 miles of primary and secondary roads. North Carolina also has the largest state-maintained roads system in the United States. North Carolina is commonly called the Good Roads State.

may have traveled great distances just to enjoy the sights and passing them safely may be impossible for several miles—another time when patience can be a life-saver. In case you're the sightseer, remember to pull over, when you can do so safely, to let those who must hurry pass you by.

Pay attention and be ready to maneuver when driving through an area with FALLING ROCKS or ROCK-SLIDE AREA signs. (I-40 north of Asheville was closed for months in 1998 due to a huge landslide.) It's possible to come around a curve and find a fair-size boulder in your path. Likewise, be prepared to share the roads with pedestrians, bicyclists, horseback riders, and a variety of wildlife. The last is particularly prevalent at night.

At lower elevations flash floods are common. These sometimes send rivers and creeks flooding across bridges and low-lying roadways. Never try to cross such stretches. The water can be deceptively swift and deep.

Here are a few other rules you should be aware of:

• A new resident must apply for a driver's license within 30 days of moving here. Bring your out-of-state license, proof of insurance, and proof of residency to a driver's license office of the North Carolina Department of Motor Vehicles; you'll have to pass a written exam and an eye exam. Each county has a DMV office. Most offices are open from 8:00 A.M. to 5:00 P.M.; some close for lunch from noon to 1:00 P.M.

• New residents also must register their vehicles and purchase license tags within 30 days. The title of the car or

Most country roads have gas stations along the way, but fuel up before driving deep into the mountains. If you're visiting waterfalls or hiking areas off gravel roads, you won't want to chance being stranded in a remote area. Gas is generally cheaper close to town than it is in the countryside.

name of the lien holder, proof of insurance, and the odometer reading are required. Vehicles must also be inspected within 10 days of the registration date.

• The North Carolina Safe Roads Act forbids drivers to drink alcohol or to have an open container of an alcoholic beverage in the passenger area. All front seat passengers are required to wear seat belts. Children younger than four must ride in child safety seats. All children younger than 12 must wear seat belts. There is no longer an exemption for vehicles registered outside the state. Children younger than 12 may not ride in the open beds of pickup trucks except when an adult is present to supervise the child, or the child is secured or restrained by an approved seat belt. Other exceptions are if an emergency situation exists, if the vehicle is operated in a parade with a valid permit or in an agricultural enterprise, or if the vehicle is being operated in a county that has no incorporated area with a population greater than 3,500. The state requires that headlights be on whenever windshield wipers are on. Motorcyclists are required to wear helmets and use their headlights at all times. (The jury is still out concerning the use of handheld cellular phones while driving. The phone companies themselves are urging their customers to pull off the road when making or receiving a call. Mountain, as well as highway, driving deserves your utmost attention.)

COMMERCIAL AIRPORTS

Central Mountains

Million Air Asheville
New Airport Road, Fletcher, NC
(828) 684-6832
Million Air Asheville shares the runway with the Asheville Regional Airport. They offer 24-hour service for corporate and private aircraft. Tie-downs, fueling, flight instruction, and aircraft maintenance are available. The staff can arrange catering, car rentals, ground transportation, and hotel reservations. They offer complete services for the corporate and private flyer.

Asheville Regional Airport
708 New Airport Road, Fletcher, NC
(828) 684-2226
Western North Carolina's only commercial air service is centrally located on N.C. Highway 280, just 15 miles south of Asheville, and is easily accessed from I-26. The airport is tourist friendly and not far from all the most popular vacation destinations. Hendersonville is 8 miles from the Asheville airport; Brevard only 20; Waynesville, 36; Sylva, 57; Cashiers, 58; and Highlands, 69. This airport, the fourth largest in the state, sees about 27 flights a day. Four carriers—Comair, USAirways, Atlantic Southeast Airlines (ASA), which is a Delta regional carrier, and USAirways Express—carry passengers to hubs in Raleigh, Charlotte, Atlanta, Pittsburgh, and Cincinnati. Continental Airlines offers direct flights to Newark, New Jersey, and to Dallas, Texas. Northwest Airlines has started a new non-stop seasonal service between Asheville and Detroit, Michigan.

The 900-acre airport has a wide primary runway, 8,001 feet long and 150 feet wide, capable of serving large aircraft. A full-service, fixed-base operator caters to all corporate, private, and charter needs. A shuttle service is provided by Airport Ground Transportation, which is available for long or short distances. Also on hand are four auto rental services: Hertz, Avis, Budget, and National. (Alternate airport transfer services are listed at the end of this chapter.)

A special visual feature of the expanded 80,000-square-foot terminal is the 40-foot-high atrium running the width of the terminal, which opens up the existing space with welcome daylight. Four boarding gates on two levels, increased parking (including 190 short-term and 590 long-term spaces), a cafeteria, and a lounge provide a pleasant seating area for those seeking sustenance. A welcome center, a gift and periodicals shop, a full-service travel agency, an ATM machine, lockers, and the USS *Asheville* display round out the goods and services available on-site at the Asheville Regional Airport.

Asheville Regional Airport Ground Transportation
Airport Road, Fletcher, NC
(828) 681-0051
Transportation from the airport can be contracted at the facility located in the baggage claim area. There is no taxi stand at the Asheville Regional Airport, although taxis are available. Just check the yellow pages of the phone book. (Other transportation systems are listed at the end of this chapter.)

Asheville Regional Airport Welcome Center
Airport Road, Fletcher, NC
(828) 687-9446
Located within the Asheville Regional Airport, the Welcome Center provides a multitude of services to the traveler. Regional brochures and newspapers are available. Flight information and paging services are on tap. A wide selection of mountain crafts, including handmade quilts, walking sticks, and CDs and videos of mountain traditions are in abundance. The center also features a complete selection of books from pleasure reading to travel logs.

If you plan to fly your own plane, it would be a good idea to call the airports at which you intend to land and refuel. Smaller airports may not offer all the services to which you are accustomed.

Just across the court is their unique shelving of "Books for Less." These used editions can be purchased using the honor system. Even after closing hours, one can purchase a favorite book by simply depositing the amount noted on the book into the lock box located on the shelf.

GENERAL AVIATION
Northern Mountains

Ashe County Airport
639 Airport Road, Jefferson, NC
(336) 982-3713, (336) 982-3899 after hours
This public airport, which is off U.S. Highway 221, has a 4,300-foot paved and lighted runway. Tie-downs, fueling, flight instruction, and light aircraft maintenance are available. Rental cars are available from Ford and Chevrolet (336-246-8806) dealers in West Jefferson, 5 miles from the airport. The facility is open daily from 9:00 A.M. to 5:00 P.M.

Avery County Airport
U.S. Highway 19 E., Spruce Pine, NC
(336) 765-4564
The elevation of this public airport is 2,750 feet. It has a 3,000-foot runway; fuel, flight instruction, and aircraft maintenance are provided. Its hours are 8:00 A.M. to 5:00 P.M. Monday through Saturday and 1:00 to 5:00 P.M. Sunday.

Boone Airport
Bamboo Road, Boone, NC
(336) 265-3598
This airfield, though privately owned, is open to all visitors to the Boone area in

Watauga County. The field contains a 2,670-foot paved runway. Use is restricted to daylight hours only. Rental cars or taxis service the airport. Also available are maintenance, fuel, air tours, and flight instruction.

Elk River Airport
N.C. Highway 194, Banner Elk, NC
(336) 898-9791
Use of this private airport, which is in Avery County and has a 4,600-foot paved runway, is restricted to members and guests of the Elk River Club. No fuel is available, and the runway is not maintained (snow clearing, etc.).

Central Mountains

Hendersonville Airport
Shepard Street, Hendersonville, NC
(828) 693-1897
This private airport, which began in a pasture in 1936, is open for public use. It has a 3,000-foot paved and lighted runway that can handle a wide range of aircraft. The facility also has hangar space, rents aircraft, provides fuel and maintenance, conducts flight training, and offers scenic flights, including rides in vintage aircraft provided by the nearby Western North Carolina Air Museum.

Southern Mountains

Andrews-Murphy Airport
Airport Road, Andrews, NC
(828) 321-5114
Constructed in 1947, 2 miles from Andrews on U.S. 19/129, this Cherokee County facility has a 5,000-foot lighted, asphalt runway and provides fuel and operational-level maintenance. It also offers hangars, tie-downs, plane rentals, charter flights throughout the country, air ambulance service, flight instruction, and sightseeing flights, along with a pilot lounge. The air-

port is open from 8:00 A.M. to 6:00 P.M. seven days a week.

Jackson County Airport
Airport Road, Cullowhee/Sylva, NC
(828) 293-5156, (828) 421-5255,
(828) 586-0321
The Jackson County Airport sits just above Western Carolina University at Cullowhee about 2 miles northwest of town. The runway is 3,300 feet long. The elevation is 2,844 feet mean above sea level (MSL). The airport is operated under the Jackson County Airport Authority. It is currently unattended. Operating hours are from 9:00 A.M. to 6:00 P.M. seven days a week. It is equipped with pilot control lighting (PCL) and the fuel is on a self-serve basis twenty-four hours. They offer flight instruction, sightseeing flights, car rentals, and on-call mechanic service.

Macon County Airport
Airport Road, Franklin, NC
(828) 524-5529, (800) 435-9686
The lighted runway of the Macon County Airport, called "the biggest little airport in North Carolina," has been extended from 3,800 feet to 4,400 feet. The facility, which is about 3 miles northwest of town off N.C. Highway 28, provides both 100LL-octane gas and jet-A fuel. On-site car rentals, flight instruction, sightseeing tours, and hangar space are other services. The airport can do maintenance work on most general aviation aircraft.

BUS LINES
Central Mountains

Apple Country Transit
Hendersonville, NC
(828) 698-8571
Transportation operates from Hendersonville to surrounding areas, including Asheville Airport, with nominal fees. A monthly pass of $10 allows for unlimited rides.

Asheville Transit System
49 Coxe Avenue, Asheville, NC
(828) 253-5691
The main terminal is beside the downtown post office on Coxe Avenue. One way to get there is to walk from the corner of Pritchard Park on Patton Avenue to the traffic light at the corner of Patton and Coxe. Turn left and walk 2 blocks to the terminal. Schedules for buses to many areas of town are available at the terminal and by calling the number above.

Greyhound Bus Line
Tunnel Road, Asheville, NC
(828) 253-5353, general information;
(828) 253-8451, passenger agent
Seventh Avenue East, Hendersonville, NC
(828) 693-1201
Dellwood Road West, Waynesville, NC
(828) 926-2327
The Greyhound Bus Line is the only bus company providing long-range scheduled motor coach service from this area. The Buncombe County terminal is located east of the tunnel that connects downtown Asheville to Tunnel Road. The Waynesville terminal is located at the Red Barn convenience store, and the Hendersonville office is easily located in downtown Hendersonville.

These Greyhound facilities provide passengers and package service to all major U.S. destinations. The terminals open at 8:00 A.M., but closing times vary so call ahead. The toll-free number for Greyhound central reservations is (800) 231-2222.

TOURING COMPANIES

Whether you arrive by family vehicle, commercial jet, private jet, bike, kayak, canoe, or on foot, you can find opportunities for custom-made excursions through the following companies.

Asheville Blue Ridge Touring Company
(828) 275-1765
www.ashevilleblueridgetour.com

Touring service provided throughout Western North Carolina, including the Blue Ridge Parkway and Great Smoky Mountain National Park, for individuals and small groups. City tours are also available. Airport meeting and greeting is available throughout Western North Carolina, South Carolina, Tennessee, Virginia, and Georgia. Wedding parties and executive meetings may be served with first-class transportation. The company also offers step-on guide service.

Asheville Historic Trolley Tours
(828) 669-8046, (888) 667-3600
www.ashevilletrolleytours.com
See all Asheville by riding the historic trolley with a 70-minute narrated tour. The trolley schedules are posted throughout Asheville and at the Asheville Area Chamber of Commerce, hotels, and other public venues. The route includes major attractions, the Thomas Wolfe Memorial, and Biltmore Village. Passengers may disembark at any stop along the way and reboard the trolley using the same ticket. A minimum of four trips are scheduled daily beginning from the Asheville Area Chamber of Commerce at 9:30 A.M. The trolley can be chartered for family reunions, weddings, and other special occasions.

Asheville Touring Service
Asheville, NC
(828) 681-0051
Customized touring services are provided throughout Western North Carolina. Their service area includes Raleigh, North Carolina, to the east; Knoxville, Tennessee, to the west; Atlanta, Georgia, south; and north into West Virginia.

Dillingham-Richards International, Inc.
Pearson Drive, Asheville, NC 28801
(828) 253-3943
Riding and walking tours are led by Western North Carolina's premier historian, lecturer, tour guide, and winemaster-cum-coauthor Insiders' Guide's own Ken Richards.

Street parking in many small towns is often free, or else only a nominal fee of a few coins for a couple of hours is charged. Not so in Asheville. Parking at meters is strictly monitored, and if time runs out on the meter where you're parked, you'll be slapped with a ticket. Also, parking in private business lots around town means almost certain towing. So save yourself a lot of headaches and inconvenience and park in one of the three city garages centrally located downtown.

Pegasus Transportation
Asheville, NC
(828) 281–4600, (800) 462–4062

Pegasus can be scheduled for airport pickups and customized touring. Additionally they feature transportation to dinner events, to Biltmore Estate, and Grove Park Inn. Their services range beyond the Asheville area to Charlotte/Douglas International Airport and to Greenville/Spartanburg Airport.

Special Occasions Limousine
Asheville, NC
(828) 687–9918, (888) 288–9915

Their motto is "Anywhere, Any Time"; and they offer 24-hour service. Their variety of premium class vehicles range from sedans to vans, Black Car Service (black stretch limousines) to luxury stretch limousines.

Young Convention Services (YCS Group)
Grove Park Inn, Asheville, NC
(828) 251–9013, (800) 627–1185

With offices on Sunset Mountain in the Grove Park Inn, YCS Group provides guide and transportation services to local areas and beyond. Their services include transporting your group from your hotel and meeting you at airports throughout Western North Carolina, upstate South Carolina, and eastern Tennessee. They offer tours of historic Asheville, Cherokee (Qualla), Great Smoky Mountain RR, artisans of the mountains studios, and the Biltmore Estate. Dine-around—providing a variety of dining experiences throughout the area—is another of their featured tours. Additional offerings are available through your personal request and contacts.

Young Tours
Riverside Drive, Asheville, NC
(828) 258–0098

Through the creativity of Ralph Young Sr., this company became "people-movers" by bolting theater seats to a truck and transporting folks from Western North Carolina to the Chicago Exhibition in the 1930s, during the Great Depression when money was scarce. Again in 1982, with the World's Fair just down the road in Knoxville, Tennessee, the Young fleet was enlarged to provide transportation. Today they have a large fleet of minicoaches and highway coaches with seating for from 22 to 55 passengers.

They offer receptive tour services, shop services, and charter tours. Step-on guides are also available.

CLIMATE

The effort to capture the essence of these ancient, lush mountains in a word or phrase has been going on for centuries. The Cherokee, who managed to push the previous tribes out of the area before the Europeans came, referred to their home as Sa-koh-na-gas, which means "blue." It referred to the mountains' blue haze, which is created when sunshine and warm, humid air combine with the hydrocarbons produced by the region's thick forests. This single word was later elaborated into "the great blue hills of God" and "land of the blue mists."

The Great Smoky Mountains, on the other hand, were named for the fog that forms as a result of the temperature differences between the air and the mountains' many water sources. This cloudlike mist curls up from valleys and mountain peaks like smoke from a fire, particularly in the early morning, around sunset, and after rains.

This blue mist and curling "smoke" are integral parts of the landscape of both the Great Smokies and the Blue Ridge Mountains, as well as all the lesser-known cross ridges, such as the Graham, Nantahala, Snowbird, Balsam, and New Found Mountains.

The Land of the Sky, a more recent description, was culled from the title of an 1876 romantic novel set in this tranquil region. The phrase has remained popular ever since, perhaps because our eyes, indeed, our very beings, are forever tempted skyward by the many mile-high peaks found here. And what a sky it is! Washed year-round by frequent showers, its intense daytime hue—bracketed by rosy dawns and riveting, multicolored sunsets—has been given its own name: Carolina blue. And you seldom have to travel far, if at all, for a mountain-high view of brilliant star- and moon-studded nights scarcely dimmed by artificial light.

A PLACE FOR ALL SEASONS

Others herald the region as the Land of the Four Seasons, for it is the long-lasting springs and autumns, plus mild winters and summers, that have attracted tourists and new residents to the area for nearly two centuries.

Crocuses and daffodils start pushing up through the earth in late February, and the false spring that usually occurs around this time of the year can have you hiking or playing golf in your shirt sleeves. In March, tulip magnolias, yellow forsythia, and other early-spring flowers bravely brighten the landscape despite the real possibility of a late snowfall. By the end of April, dogwoods and silverbell trees are blooming everywhere. While in May, mountainsides are afire with flame azaleas, and the dense thickets of several species of native rhododendrons begin their bloom bursts, a show that lasts right into July. May is also the time when a large portion of the mountains' spring wildflowers reaches its peak, including pink and white mountain laurels that coat the slopes and overhang roadways, rivers, and boulder-strewn creeks.

By June, summer greens up the region with all the lush, ferny beauty of a rain forest. Daytime temperatures are mostly in the 70s and 80s, but as summer plays out, a week now and then can be hot and humid enough for air conditioners and

Temperature changes are drastic in the mountains. Always take a sweater or jacket when driving from low altitudes to higher ones. We once experienced a sunny, warm day in town, which turned into a windy, icy hailstorm only 2,000 feet higher at a picnic area on the parkway.

Some days the mountain vistas don't go on forever. Smog and haze are a growing concern in the Blue Ridge Mountains. Not only are views sometimes obscured by smog, but the pollution also poses a threat to people with asthma and other health concerns. The local newspapers and broadcast media give a daily "air quality" report with a scale that ranges from green to red. Those with respiratory concerns, the elderly, and pregnant women should stick to lower elevations and/or stay inside when levels reach high orange and red.

electric fans, at least until a cooling thunderstorm comes along. Even then, by early evening the thermometer drops into the 60s, cooler still at higher elevations, and it's an extremely rare night when it could be considered too hot to sleep.

At any time you can find vast temperature differences by a quick change in elevation. For example, you can stretch the spring by several weeks if you follow the bloom from the valleys to the tops of the mountains, and in the fall the color changes begin at the top elevation and slowly work their way downward. The first hints of the colorful autumn to come are seen tinting some of the leaves at higher elevations as early as late August. In October, visitors by the thousands arrive to enjoy the brilliant red, yellow, and gold foliage display (see our sidebar on autumn leaves in the Blue Ridge Parkway chapter).

By mid-November, the barren branches of deciduous trees give mountain ridges a crew-cut look, and previously unknown lodgings peer from their wooded perches enjoying "winter views." But, while nights may bring freezing temperatures, days can be pleasantly warm. It's usually not until Christmas that the first frigid Alberta clipper roars south out of Canada. On those occasions temperatures can plummet to zero or below for a short period of time, and from then until well into spring, short spurts of bitterly cold weather, along with occasional snow or ice storms, alternate with surprisingly pleasant winter days. In most places the average snowfall in a typical year is around one foot, and even heavy snows usually disappear in a matter of days.

Rain, on the other hand, is a year-round event. Slightly more falls in the summer than the winter. (Winter wet fronts, rising up from the Gulf of Mexico, actually warm things up.) In summer, rain often takes the form of sudden crashing, late-afternoon and evening thunderstorms, sometimes with damaging winds and lightning. While such storms can spoil picnics and other outdoor activities, most residents enjoy these natural light-and-sounds shows, knowing the mountains offer protection from destructive tornadoes and hurricanes found elsewhere.

On the average rainfall totals from 40 to 55 inches per year, depending on the location. But in the rain belt, which includes a large part of Transylvania County and the southern sections of Jackson and Macon Counties, 80 inches or more can fall in a typical year. All that water has to go somewhere, and much of it tumbles off cliffs and down mountainsides. Transylvania, which dubs itself the Land of Waterfalls, has more than 150 of these splendid water shows. Even so, the county hasn't cornered the waterfall market. Cascades and waterfalls, some of which plunge hundreds of feet, can be found in abundance throughout the region. (See our Waterfalls chapter.) So can springs, creeks, rivers, ponds, and lakes. In fact, homes with such water sources are almost more the rule than the exception, and real estate ads touting "bold streams" are common, even inside the boundaries of some towns.

A PEOPLE FOR ALL SEASONS

All in all, nature has done things beautifully right in this small corner of the world, and the people here are not far behind in their own accomplishments. While the stamp of the Cherokee and the original Scotch-Irish settlers have made a deep mark on the area, later arrivals brought—and keep bringing—a wonderful array of cultural diversity and talent to the region. The hills still resound with the sounds of dulcimers and bagpipes, but you can hear rock 'n' roll and classical symphonies too. Here in the mountains, star-studded concerts and homegrown festivals are likely to attract the same enthusiastic crowds, and high-tech industries and nationally known New Age spiritual centers thrive beside handmade crafts and old-time religion. The mix of Old World and contemporary lifestyles, played out against the dramatic backdrop of the mountains, makes this region irresistible to visitors and transplants alike.

Western Carolina, indeed, seems to have much of the best of the modern world and has managed to hold on to a great deal that is wonderful from its past. As a part of their old mountain heritage, neighbors tend to respect one another's privacy yet always seem to be there when they need each other. And, despite the influx of new residents from all over the country, the area maintains a thick overlay of old-fashioned Southern hospitality and friendly service. Menus range from Old South standards, such as biscuits and gravy, grits, fried catfish, and presweetened iced tea, to the finest of continental cuisine and the best imported and domestic wines and local vintages. (See our Biltmore Estate and Winery chapter.)

Best of all, it's still a place where fear is far from being a part of daily life. In most places you don't have to worry if you forget to lock up your house or car. So far, the cost of living is within reason too.

So there you have it: a mild climate, inexpensive, friendly, laid-back, and lovely.

RESTAURANTS

Mountain cooking brings to mind visions of fluffy biscuits, thick gravy, corn bread, soup beans, buttery grits, soft-cooked vegetables like okra and squash, fried chicken, molasses-based barbecue, and deep-dish pies of all assortments, of course. Certainly, there has been a history of mountain cooking from the early settlers onward: canning your own garden vegetables, wild berries, and fruits, and making any dough from scratch. You will find plenty of family-style restaurants specializing in this type of down-home cookin' throughout the region, but you will also find a number of fine cuisine and ethnic restaurants.

As our area grows, so too do the dining choices. You could easily plan a vacation around the culinary options in many of our towns and communities.

Much of the delight of taking to the North Carolina mountain back roads comes from stumbling across a marvelous old inn or hotel. Back when travel to the big city was not as easy and eating out was a rare treat, many people in the rural countryside made their way to these same establishments because they regularly set a table for a Sunday crowd. Today, these old inns and hotels are great gathering places, open to local residents and travelers alike, for sumptuous dining every day.

We have scoured the cities, small towns, and countryside in an effort to provide you with a variety of quality-rich epicurean experiences, unique to our area. Our selections, which are featured by region, may vary greatly in style, from the smallest coffee shop with the best biscuits, burgers, and chocolate malt in the area to the most elegant haute cuisine from a French master chef. Variety is the spice of life, after all. There are also plenty of fast-food and franchise restaurants throughout the mountains. We, however, highlight places that give you a taste of

the region and maintain a proven track record. As you make your way through North Carolina's mountains, we welcome your recommendations. If your personal dining favorites are not included here, tell us about them for the next edition.

PRICE CODE

Most of these restaurants will accept major credit cards for payment; we've noted those that do not. While menu changes may certainly affect the pricing of some restaurants, we've provided a pricing guide for an idea of what you can expect on the check for a basic meal for two (without desserts and alcoholic beverages). This table does not reflect tax or gratuities. Enjoy!

$	Less than $20
$$	$20 to $35
$$$	$36 to $50
$$$$	More than $50

NORTHERN MOUNTAINS

Alleghany County

Jubalo's/Tlaquepaque Mexican Restaurant $-$$
381 South Main Street , Sparta Square, Sparta, NC
(336) 372-5000
Jubalo's, a popular, fun-filled neighborhood grill and pizza place, is down at the east end of Main Street in the town's newest shopping center and now specializes in Mexican cuisine.

The pleasant, playful decor is an eclectic combination of modern styles. The wall covering serves as a backdrop for old movie stars' photos, and the dining room is filled with wooden tables and chairs and green plants. Order your pizza with the usual toppings or get a vegetarian pie. You can also get Mexican tacos, burritos, and more. Jubalo's serves imported and domestic beer, wine, and wine coolers and serves lunch and dinner. The restaurant is closed Mondays.

Marion's Old Homeplace $-$$
off N.C. Highway 21 S., Glade Valley, NC
(336) 372-4676

Just 10 minutes outside Sparta, you'll see the signs for Marion's Old Homeplace in Glade Valley, one of those pastoral crossroads that once had a country store, a community school, farmhouses with wide front porches, and a country doctor. The picturesque ghosts of the store and the school remain, and the old farmhouses grow lovelier with time.

Marion's Old Homeplace restaurant was built in 1921 as the 12-room home and clinic of Glade Valley's country doctor, G. F. Duncan. In 1927, as Dr. Duncan's health failed, the lovely old home passed to Glade Valley's Presbyterian minister, the Rev. Wayne Thompson. After his death in 1956, the house was purchased by Mr. and Mrs. J. Coke Marion. A longtime restaurateur, Mr. Marion parlayed his culinary expertise into a smoked-ham business, which he established next door. Marion hams were enjoyed in this northwest North Carolina and southwest Virginia region for decades. After J. Coke Marion's death in 1972, his son, Bud Marion, transformed the residence into an elegant country restaurant that offered hearty, family-style dining. Recently, Yolanda and Rodolfo Prito bought the restaurant, keeping the same menu and theme of good country food.

Marion's Old Homeplace has become a mecca for loyal diners within a 100-mile radius of Glade Valley and Sparta. Folks from Winston-Salem, Boone, Charlotte, and towns as far into Virginia as Pulaski regularly make the pilgrimage to the Old Homeplace for a favorite table in any number of rooms: the Sitting Room, the Sun Porch, the Bedroom, and other dining rooms that have been named for their original use.

Servers present you with a basket of homemade breads and a plate heaped with the all-you-can-eat tender country ham or old-fashioned fried chicken (it's your choice), homemade biscuits, and genuine red-eye or chicken gravy. Fresh vegetable selections change daily and include such old-time favorite side dishes as green beans, mashed potatoes, and pinto beans with relish. Baked apples, buttered corn, and homemade slaw round out the list. For dessert, you'll want to loosen that belt and order heavenly, fresh-baked blackberry or apple cobbler, served with a scoop of ice cream.

Marion's is open from the last weekend in April through the last weekend in October. Dinner is served on Friday and Saturday, and lunch and dinner are served on Sunday.

The Senator's House $$$-$$$$
360 North Main Street, Sparta, NC
(336) 372-7500

The Senator's House offers American cuisine in the 1916 renovated historic home of North Carolina State Sen. Eugene Transou. Although it's only open Fridays and Saturdays, the candlelit dinners of four or five courses are a special treat to end the week with. Breads and desserts handmade in the bake shop accompany each freshly prepared meal. And diners can usually choose from beef, chicken, pork, lamb, or seafood. Choose from a selection of wines and beers also.

Ashe County

Don's Mountain Aire Seafood
and Steak House $-$$$
Intersection of N.C. Highways 16 and 163
Glendale Springs, NC
(336) 982-3060

This friendly restaurant is a welcome sight after working up an appetite traveling the winding two-lanes of Ashe County. (Don's is just minutes from Holy Trinity Church, up the road in Glendale Springs, where you can see the exquisite Ben Long fresco of the Last Supper.) Don's Mountain Aire Seafood and Steak House is noted for its extensive selection of fresh seafood, delivered several times a week from the coast. Fresh stuffed flounder, salt-and-pepper catfish, and stir-fried shrimp are customer favorites. You can also order a substantial filet mignon, chicken strips (grilled or fried), and even such delicacies as frogs legs. Don't forget to try out the generous-size, homemade hush puppies—they're delicious.

Well-prepared, ample portions and excellent service have created a loyal clientele at Don's. The restaurant is open daily for dinner year-round (hours change with the season), and there's a Sunday lunch, too.

Glendale Springs Inn
and Restaurant $-$$$
7414 N.C. Highway 16, Glendale Springs, NC
(336) 982-2103, (800) 287-1206

Artist Amanda Smith is innkeeper and owner of this newly restored inn and restaurant in the 1892 structure of what once was a general merchandise store, a circuit courthouse, a post office, a chapel, a community center, a boarding house, and an inn. (Read more about the inn in our Bed-and-Breakfasts and Country Inns chapter.) Two wood-paneled dining rooms and one white and peach room offer guests plenty of seating, while side-porch dining by the garden is also available. Lazy fans spin overhead in the main dining hall, where creaking wooden floors and an old piano evoke visions of Saturday night country jamborees. Smith brings in a pianist or a country fiddler or two at times, but don't let the sounds of down-home music mislead you: The ambience and cuisine are quite sophisticated.

Tables are covered in crisp linens, and the menu offers delicacies whipped up by the resident chef. A seasonally changing menu offers sautéed bluepoint oysters, mushroom ravioli, bronzed spice-encrusted rib pork chops with goat cheese, mashed sweet potatoes, and green apple and leek ragout, to name only a few of the dishes and their complements that were on the menu when we were there.

For our summer luncheon we tried the marinated grilled chicken club sandwich—fresh, tender, and filling, and the fried salmon cake salad, with ratatouille, slim green beans, and napa cabbage served with crisp Vidalia onion rings and roasted red pepper remoulade, all accompanied by bread fresh out of the oven. A summer brunch offers everything from breakfast fare, such as poppy seed pancakes and poached eggs with chicken confit potato croquettes, to salads and hot entrees, such as free-range chicken and dumplings, coriander-encrusted salmon, and petite filet mignon with barbecued shrimp. Do call for evening reservations, but feel free to walk in for lunch.

Louisiana Purchase $$-$$$$
N.C. Highway 184, Banner Elk, NC
(828) 963-5087
www.lapurchasenc.com

If your heart belongs to the moss-draped avenues of New Orleans and the sultry tones of Bourbon Street, and your palate enjoys Cajun, Creole, or classic French cuisine, you'll want to try Louisiana Purchase in Banner Elk. Owner and chef Mark Rosse has created a classy restaurant with the flavor of old New Orleans here in the High Country, with a special emphasis on classic French. Murals of the Big Easy lend atmosphere to this casually elegant restaurant, and live jazz on weekends adds to the New Orleans ambience of Louisiana Purchase. The restaurant has an extensive wine list, too. Louisiana Purchase serves dinner Sunday through Saturday and stays open late on Friday and Saturday. Reservations are suggested.

River House $$–$$$$
1896 Old Field Creek Road off N.C.
Highway 16 N., Grassy Creek, NC
(336) 982–2109
www.riverhousenc.com

The River House restaurant, part of a lovely 1870 farmhouse bed-and-breakfast inn, is a destination for diners from across the country and abroad. The fare at River House is an unusual mix of European haute cuisine and down-home American style. Unlike the petite-sized servings you get in some restaurants, where presentation is the primary goal, generous portions are guaranteed at River House—and the presentation is impressive too.

At River House, start with a popular appetizer known as gyoza, a spicy, scallop-shaped, Japanese-style dumpling served with a lemon dipping sauce. Another tasty lead-in is roasted red peppers served with a mild, vinegar-based sauce. Homemade soups such as curried vegetable are always popular. There is a wide choice of River House specialties: medallion of beef tenderloin, baked tortellini and rotini, Southwestern vegetable lasagna, and rainbow trout, as well as luscious desserts, such as coeur a la crème, chocolate mousse cake, and chocolate bourbon cake. On Sundays a four-course menu pampers guests.

Avery County

Bear Trail Cafe $, no credit cards
3 Main Street, Newland, NC
(828) 733–7132

This little burger joint will give you a malt and a burger like you've never had! More than that, it's a fully functioning soda fountain, and the building itself was once a pharmacy. Sit at the black-top counter on a blue vinyl stool or at one of the wooden chairs and tables in the black-and-white-tiled locale. The young owner was working the grill like a Labor Day cookout as we sipped our thick chocolate malt, so rich it almost sufficed as lunch.

Homemade soups and chili complement the fresh salads. Deli sandwiches are piled high with a quarter-pound of deli meats, lettuce, tomato, and your choice of cheese. The Charbroiler provides various sizes of juicy burgers, while the chef on the grill can concoct a patty melt, Reuben, grilled ham and cheese, and even a Western omelette. It's too good to pass by such quality, simple food.

For dessert you have your choice of banana splits, ice-cream sundaes, giant cookie sandwiches, shakes, malts, and apple pie. Wander to the back with your root beer float and check out the old *Life* magazines, antique pharmaceutical equipment, and medicine bottles saved from the old drugstore.

The Corner Palate $–$$
N.C. Highway 184, Banner Elk, NC
(828) 898–8668

This is one of those delightful places that seems to have it all. The shake roof and cottagelike construction make it feel like home. Window boxes and lace curtains add that individual touch. Blue plate specials appeal to those who burn calories for a living, and pasta and stir-fries give the menu a contemporary flair. Add soups, salads, quiches, omelettes, quesadillas, jambalaya, steak, chicken, and fish entrees, and, well, what more could you want? A children's menu is also available. Lunch and dinner are served every day.

Famous Louise's Rock House
Restaurant $–$$, no credit cards
U.S. Highway 221, Linville Falls, NC
(828) 765–2702

You can dine in three counties and never step outside the door of Famous Louise's Rock House Restaurant, which is just 3 miles north of Linville Caverns. This quaint family-owned restaurant has the distinction of sitting directly on the spot where Burke, McDowell, and Avery Counties meet. Signs point the way to your dining location—and favorite county—or you can sit near the fireplace, the spot where all three counties come together! Your food

Caviar from Canton

Caviar from the mountains? It's not so unusual if you look at the early beginnings of fish farming: Dick Jennings founded Sunburst Trout Company in 1946 in the region of Pisgah National Forest. At first Dick supplied farm-raised trout, but then he began experimenting with smoked trout and trout pâté. In more recent years, working with his daughter, Sally Eason, who now heads the business, Dick has worked up the trout eggs, or roe, for eating. Eventually their caviar collection caught on in restaurants throughout the region. As in the case of the pungent mountain onion, the ramp, which found its way to the kitchens of New York chefs, so too has the rainbow trout caviar of the mountains of Western North Carolina caught on. Eason has even taken "coals to Newcastle" by traveling to Armenia, where sturgeon roe from the Caspian Sea reigns as king. She demonstrated to caviar collectors a better way to harvest the eggs. This caviar is best with poached trout or smoked trout, on salads, toasted bagels, or toast corners, and with cream cheese or butter.

will be cooked in Avery County, picked up by your waitress in Burke County, and very often served just over the line in McDowell County.

Famous Louise's serves bountiful lunch and dinner specials seven days a week: pork loin, country-style steak, roast beef, turkey with all the fixin's, fried chicken, and a full complement of side dishes that includes pinto beans, snap beans, and creamed corn. For seafood lovers, the Rock House receives deliveries from the coast three times a week. Leading the list of desserts is Famous Louise's spectacular strawberry rhubarb pie. Top this with a scoop of vanilla ice cream, and you're in dessert heaven.

This rock building has a somewhat checkered past that dates from the early part of the century when it was a Prohibition-era roadhouse, followed by numerous incarnations as mediocre restaurants. Famous Louise's was the restaurant magic that finally "took," due chiefly to owner Louise Henson, the original "Famous Louise," and her devoted family and loyal patrons. You can see Louise's personal photo gallery upstairs in the banquet room—that's her in one glossy framed photo from the 1950s, as a high school basketball star for Linville Falls! Take note of the set of unusual diamond, circle, square, and heart-shaped rocks built into the outside wall at the restaurant's entrance. As you leave, you can pay your check in Avery County. The Rock House is closed on Tuesdays.

Pineola Whistle Stop Café $
U.S. Highway 221, Pineola, NC
(828) 733-0080
Look for this little "drop in" restaurant just off the Blue Ridge Parkway. It is located high up in the land of Christmas trees and is open seven days a week. Tuesday through Saturday means an early break-

fast at 7:00 A.M. It closes at 2:00 P.M. for the staff to rest, but Whistle Stop reopens for supper at 4:00 and closes by 9:00 P.M. Even though the menus state lunch and dinner, we need to be clear that in the mountains, folks often refer to the noon-time meal as dinner and the evening meal as supper.

Stonewalls   **$$-$$$**
N.C. Highway 184, Banner Elk, NC
(828) 898-5550
This rustic stone building is home to a marvelous family restaurant that specializes in American cuisine, specifically well-turned steaks, luscious prime rib, and popular seafood dishes (the lobster is melt-in-your-mouth luscious). Stonewalls also has a superb salad bar. Stonewalls serves dinner only, seven days a week.

Tartan Restaurant   **$-$$**
31 Coffey Road, Linville, NC
(828) 733-0779
Here's a cozy, unassuming restaurant near Grandfather Mountain that serves a pleasing array of mountain favorites with Scottish flair. The menu offers breakfast, lunch, and dinner specialties, but the unique lunch sandwiches seem to be the place's calling card. The Cameron is a hearty construction of cold roast beef slices topped with Swiss cheese, grilled mushrooms, onions, and green peppers. You can make a meal of the Shad's Scottish Spud, a baked Idaho potato stuffed with ham, green peppers, mushrooms, onions, and American and Swiss cheeses, topped with sour cream and bacon bits. And since you're in Linville and in a Scottish mood, try the Loch Ness. In this dish, Nessie is disguised as a filet of flounder served with slaw and the Tartan's own tartar sauce. For dinner you can order steak, seafood, and barbecued ribs.

Tartan's is open every day for breakfast and lunch and in the spring and summer for dinner too.

Mitchell County

Cedar Crest   **$-$$**
311 Locust Street, Spruce Pine, NC
(828) 765-6124
On Locust Street, one of the two main thoroughfares of tiny Spruce Pine, you'll notice numbers of people making their way into an obscure doorway. Follow them. They're heading for the Cedar Crest, a popular local restaurant in an old storefront with a rustic interior. The ceiling still boasts the old pressed tin found in so many turn-of-the-century mercantiles. Cedar Crest has a menu of hearty selections. Summer and winter hours vary slightly, but breakfast, lunch, and dinner are served year-round. The restaurant is open every day.

Upper Street Café   **$**
198 Oak Avenue, Spruce Pine, NC
(828) 765-0622
This little boutique diner with mountain-friendly people closes at 2:00 P.M., but its 7:00 A.M. opening time means early breakfasts Monday through Friday. Owner Jeane Eskew came to town after operating inns and restaurants in major cities. She serves traditional mountain fare as well as contemporary cuisine.

Watauga County

Coffey's Restaurant & Bar   **$$-$$$**
179 Howard Street, Boone, NC
(828) 264-3663
This popular downtown place offers a snazzy variety of seafood, including oysters, tuna, skewered shrimp on polenta, mussels in white wine and garlic, and a classic bouillabaisse. Coffey's uses locally grown lettuce and vegetables and accompanies each meal with a crusty European-style bread. Artisan cheeses and fruit are not often found on menus in the area. Special modern touches of tomato jam

and creamy wasabi sauce, for example, set this place apart.

Crippen's $$$-$$$$
239 Sunset Drive, Blowing Rock, NC
(828) 295-3487
www.crippens.com

Part of Crippen's Country Inn & Restaurant, this dining room has a strong tradition in the mountains for fine dining. Written up in national magazines and newspapers, Crippen's still aims to please each diner with specialties like Marinated and Grilled Breast of Chicken with Coconut-Ginger Sauce, Sweet Plantain Mash and West Indian Pumpkin; Rosemary and Garlic Marinated Grilled Pork Tenderloin with Rosemary-Zinfandel Sauce, Sugar Snaps and Goat Cheese-Chive Mash. These two dishes alone say it all: great attention to detail, flavor, and unique groupings. A nice selection of fish entrees and specials are featured daily. This is a fairly formal dining affair, so plan ahead and make reservations.

After dinner in Blowing Rock, head over to Kilwin's Chocolates and Ice Cream in the middle of Main Street. It stays open until 10:00 P.M. and offers sundaes, malts, and a wonderful assortment of ice cream on cones or in dishes. During the daytime, candy cooks stir and cook the fudge on marble slabs right before your eyes.

Daniel Boone Inn Restaurant $-$$
130 Hardin Street, Blowing Rock, NC
(828) 264-8657
www.danlbooneinn.com

Since 1959, this old-fashioned, family-style restaurant has been drawing locals and visitors for hearty dining in a historic structure that was Boone's first hospital. For a fixed price big serving bowls and platters of food are brought to your table, including fried chicken, country-style steak, biscuits, mashed potatoes, green beans, slaw, corn, fresh-stewed apples, dessert, and beverage.

In the summer, lunch and dinner are served each day. In the winter, dinner is served at 5:00 P.M. Lunch and dinner are served on Saturday and Sunday starting at 11:00 A.M. A large family-style breakfast is served from 8:00 to 11:00 A.M. every Saturday and Sunday throughout the year. Children ages 4 to 11 receive discount meals, and meals are free for children 3 and younger.

Reservations may be made for groups of 15 or more.

The Gamekeeper Restaurant $$$-$$$$
Shull's Mill Road, Blowing Rock, NC
(828) 963-7400
www.gamekeeper-nc.com

The Gamekeeper is in a rustic lodge-style converted house built in 1926 near Yonahlossee Resort on Shull's Mill Road between Boone and Blowing Rock. This elegant restaurant, with starched linens, impeccable service, and unforgettable fare, accommodates guests in cozy private nooks warmed by a fireplace.

Dining here is a culinary experience: The menu is composed entirely of wild game—and not just venison either. Selections often include boar, antelope, and duck. The restaurant has a selection of fine wines to complement these exotic dishes.

From January through March the restaurant serves dinner Friday and Saturday only. It's open every day except Tuesday through the summer. Reservations are required.

Jackalope's View $$-$$$
Beech Mountain Parkway, Banner Elk, NC
(828) 898-9004

Jackalope's View, located in Archer's Inn on Beech Mountain, may indeed have the best view on the mountain, aside from the ski lifts that is. (See our Bed-and-Breakfasts and Country Inns chapter for more on Archer's Inn.)

Surrounded by lush flora, the restaurant faces the Grandfather Mountain ridge directly opposite. Open for dinner year-round, the restaurant and bar retain a familiar feel thanks to the individual attention of the proprietors. The hosts have created an eclectic menu of exquisitely crafted dishes, which changes seasonally. Wild game, including antelope steak, makes an appearance several times a year. Fresh herbs from the garden add bursts of flavor to the fresh brochette, thinly sliced toasted French bread with diced garlic, tomatoes, and fresh basil sprinkled over the top. Each entree, be it filet mignon, shrimp ziti, or tender crab cakes, shares the attractively presented dinner plate with fresh vegetables hand-picked from the local farmer's market by the chef. Do not miss the pommerey mustard vinaigrette on the garden salad served with the entree.

Ceiling fans turn slowly overhead as the lights begin to twinkle in the valleys below, and the time for dessert and coffee pulls nigh. The fresh homemade desserts are impossible to resist, complemented with several different coffees and espressos made in the beautiful brass machine looming over the bar. We were treated to an exhilarating strawberry sorbet, so pungent it literally burst into flavor in our mouths. A terrace provides for outdoor dining on warm summer evenings.

Jimmy's Java $-$$
611 West King Street, Boone, NC
(828) 265-3477
www.jimmysjava.com

Whether you're after a coffee fix, live music, or a variety of fresh sandwiches and innovative dishes, try Jimmy's Java, with long opening hours from 7:00 A.M. to midnight. Paninis, those wonderful stuffed grilled sandwiches, reign supreme here and fill a menu of wraps, smoothies, and of course, coffee drinks. A list of unique heartier dishes, including a Welsh-inspired supper, make Jimmy's ideal for both snacks and dinner.

Murphy's Restaurant & Pub $-$$
747 West King Street, Boone, NC
(828) 264-5117

Murphy's has been a landmark in Boone for the last nine years. Located in downtown Boone, the drawing card at this busy place is its imaginative menu, which attracts a lively crowd to its four dining venues. The traditional dining room is furnished with comfortable booths. The sunny deck out back is an option until the end of October, when temperatures start to dip in the High Country. The bar area is a friendly place for a quick bite to eat, a little liquid refreshment and a gander at a favorite sports channel on wide-screen TV, and an attached game room.

One of the best views in Boone can be found at Howard's Knob Park because it's at the highest elevation in the city. The 5.7-acre park's picnic tables are often used for peaceful lunchtime getaways from May through October. To find the park turn at the Daniel Boone Inn on King Street and then immediately turn right, following that road to the top of the hill.

Our Daily Bread $
627 West King Street, Boone, NC
(828) 264-0173

Our Daily Bread may become part of your daily routine after you try one of their sandwiches, homemade soups and chilis, and homemade pumpkin bread. The sandwiches are imaginative combinations, such as the Jamaican, a generous portion of turkey topped with pepper cheese and sweet relish on a roll; and the South of the Border, roast beef with pepper cheese and a spicy picante sauce. If you want a hot dog with a twist, you can order Our Daily Bread's Not Dog, a tofu-based vegetarian hot dog. But the most engaging items on the menu have to be the chilis (vegetarian chili is one choice) and homemade soups ladled into an edible bowl of scooped-out sourdough bread! Blue-and-white checkered tablecloths add a bit of color to this otherwise pleasantly plain locale. The simple good food and selection of imported beer and wines are calling card enough for the cafe.

Try the teas, juices, and those trendy flavored waters; you can also take home your own custom-ground gourmet coffees. The restaurant is closed Sundays.

The Red Onion Cafe $$
227 Hardin Street, Boone, NC
(828) 264-5470

Walk into this chic establishment and you'll think you've found an art gallery, until the tempting aromas and solicitous waitstaff confirm that, indeed, you've found the Red Onion Cafe. Sitting in the heart of the university district, the restaurant serves creative soups, salads, sandwiches, quiche, pasta, and specialty items.

Prints, paintings, and sculpture by local and regional artists surround diners, and all of the art is for sale. The plant-draped piazza outdoors is also a popular dining spot, weather permitting.

Culinary styles include Southwestern, Italian, and American. The Southwestern Wrap, a new twist on the traditional burrito, has sautéed vegetables blended with a black-bean sauce and cheddar cheese wrapped in a flour tortilla, served with tortilla chips and a spicy salsa. On the Italian side, fettuccine verde with shrimp is a mix of spinach fettuccine, fresh mushrooms, and diced tomatoes tossed with a creamy Parmesan sauce and served with six tasty tiger shrimp. The Red Onion Cafe's grilled steak Caesar salad is a combination of spicy, marinated grilled slices of New York strip served on a bed of mixed greens and tomatoes with croutons, Parmesan, and Caesar dressing, served with a whole wheat roll. The cafe is known locally for its bountiful salad bar and ample desserts, including the house specialty, the Horace cookie—a butterscotch brownie with pecans, warmed and served with vanilla ice cream. Wines, imported and domestic

beers, herb teas, and flavored waters head the beverage list.

The Red Onion is open daily for lunch and dinner.

The Speckled Trout & Oyster Bar $-$$
Main Street, Blowing Rock, NC
(828) 295-9819

Since 1986, the Speckled Trout Cafe has been serving hearty breakfasts, lunches, and dinners that everyone seems to love. A no-nonsense atmosphere allows diners to concentrate on any one of the house specialties made with the fresh or smoked rainbow trout from local waters. There's even trout for breakfast. The Big Daddy's Breakfast is panfried trout and two cheese-scrambled eggs, served with a biscuit or toast. Trout and oyster dishes dominate the dinner menu, but a classic selection of steaks can be chosen from as well, with interesting side dishes. Lunch is the tamer meal here, with standard sandwiches, soups, and salads.

The Village Cafe $$-$$$
Main Street, Blowing Rock, NC
(828) 295-3769

It is a rare experience when a restaurant can transfer you to distant shores, evoke forgotten memories, or fulfill long-sought-after daydreams. Step off Main Street in Blowing Rock and down the path beside Kilwin's. At its end you'll find a tree-shaded bower and the Village Cafe. It could be an English garden in Britain's Lake District, it could be a flowered courtyard in Provence, but we only have to travel within our own mountains to find this jewel. The restaurant is tucked into the Randall Memorial Building, a quaint, white-frame cottage on the National Register of Historic Places that housed a mountain crafts co-op in 1907. Later the building served as the Blowing Rock Village Library.

Today, with her culinary expertise and style, chef Annie Esposito has transformed this site into one of the premier dining destinations in the High Country. A constant stream of guests makes the pilgrimage down the path to the cafe for exquisite breakfasts and lunches and deliciously crafted desserts. The thoughtfully chosen menu makes use of the best in flavors and fresh ingredients. Imagine the soft sweetness of Belgian waffles made to order, garnished with plump, fresh raspberries, blueberries, strawberries, and an unbelievably light honey syrup.

Most memorable are the variety of fresh soups daily: mushroom and hazelnut, sweet corn and green-pepper sauce, tomato, and smoked gouda. A cafe specialty is the marvelous homemade Argentine fugasa bread, which you may also pick up to take home. Desserts were flowing out of the kitchen the sunny afternoon we spent there. Diners were not being shy with the bananas Foster and a warm pear-and-hazelnut crisp. . . a la mode. For refreshment choose a Mimosa, a delightful combination of freshly squeezed orange juice and champagne. Sangria, fresh fruit juices, cappuccino, espresso, and hot chocolate are also available. The delightful staff even picked fresh flowers out of the garden for a birthday bouquet gracing our table.

You may dine in the courtyard under the trees in fair weather. The Village Cafe is open seasonally, from late April to late October. Breakfast and lunch are served from 8:00 A.M. to 3:00 P.M. daily, except Wednesday.

The Wildflower $$-$$$
831 West King Street, Boone, NC
(828) 264-3463

This cheery cafe demonstrates that an eclectic menu is great fun. Grilled whole wheat flatbread seasoned with olive oil, garlic, and fresh herbs served with sun-dried cranberry-green olive caponata, creamy artichoke puree, and a curried-lentil humus show up on the appetizer side. The seared sashimi-grade tuna, salad with snow peas, and Musaka tossed with Asian vinaigrette and garnished with tempura green beans and lotus root is but one dish. Try the smoked seafood quesadilla served with a Granny Smith apple chipotle salsa and a chili sour cream. Bar-

becue salmon, pork, and steaks also show up in this repertoire. Attacking the menu is like reading a novella, with so many descriptions and ingredients.

Woodlands Barbecue and
Pickin' Parlor $
U.S. Highway 321 Bypass, Blowing Rock, NC
(828) 295-3651
www.woodlandsbbq.com

Woodlands has been a favorite High Country dining landmark for several decades. The menu features chopped and sliced pork and beef, ribs, chicken, and home-style Mexican food. Woodlands caters too. It's open for lunch and dinner seven days a week. There's also live acoustic entertainment with no cover charge.

Yancey County

Garden Deli $-$$
Town Square, Burnsville, NC
(828) 682-3946

Ed Yuziuk is a transplanted mountaineer from New York City. This former owner and editor of the *Yancey Journal* couldn't find a real New York–style deli like the ones he remembered as a boy, so he opened his own. Satisfaction at last! All deli-lovers who happen upon this great little spot couldn't be more satisfied. During the summer season many customers prefer to eat on the spacious outside deck shaded by wisteria vines and willow trees.

Ed and wife Carolyn prepare menu favorites the way they like to eat them, sending to New York for such authentic deli ingredients as Grossinger's rye or real New York cheesecake. They meticulously slow-smoke their own meat for barbecue, removing all visible fat and hand-chopping the meat, which is then blended with the Yuziuks' own barbecue sauce. Carolyn's three-bean chili, pastrami sandwiches, superthick subs, and unique Reubens are popular items. The Garden Deli Reuben is a New York–style blend of fresh corned beef, topped with Ed's family-secret, Ukrainian-style Kapusta kraut, then covered with melted Swiss on that famous Grossinger's rye bread.

The deli is open for lunch Monday through Friday all year and is open Saturday during the summer.

Nu-Wray Inn $$$
Town Square, Burnsville, NC
(828) 682-2329
www.nuwrayinn.com

The legendary inn, ca. 1833, opened its doors under the ownership of Mr. Wray, who married a Mrs. Ray. From that time forward it became known for its good housekeeping and family-style meals. The last of the Wrays to operate the inn was Rush Wray. Just as its founding family had its roots in England, the current innkeepers, Chuck and Rosemary Chandler, left East Anglia in the UK to settle in this area.

A touch of Victorian has been added to the reception room, with walls adorned by paintings of fox and hound hunting scenes. The dining room is handsome, with white linen cloths. Evening dining April through November takes place 5:30 to 8:00 P.M. by reservation. Roast beef and Yorkshire pudding, country ham, rainbow trout, salmon, and roasted chicken are samples of what one can find at this table. Friday is fish and chips day.

CENTRAL MOUNTAINS

Buncombe County

Berliner Kindl German Restaurant & Deli $$-$$$
20 Ball Street, Black Mountain, NC
(828) 669-5255

Originally from the land of the Oktoberfest and Stammtish, the owners of this comfy restaurant have recently expanded their location into three dining rooms that can accommodate an entire chorus of musicians. At the same time there are cozy nooks where two or three can enjoy hearty fare of sausages, schnitzel, sauerbraten (marinated pork), and other German fare. Beers are on tap and in bottles. German deli items and other wares are available at the check-out counter. The decor is adorable Bavarian kitsch.

Blue Moon Bakery and Cafe $
60 Biltmore Avenue, Asheville, NC
(828) 252-6063

Blue Moon is essentially a gourmet bakery that offers great stone-ground, organic grain breads and the lovely imported cheeses, olive oil, vinegars, jams, and pastas that accompany these heavenly loaves so well. But it is also a trendy lunch spot.

The aroma of fresh bread greets you at the door of the shop that's housed in one of those grand old renovated storefronts on the revived Biltmore Avenue. You can pick up your daily loaf quota and dawdle for a casual lunch with friends at intimate little tables, sampling Blue Moon's savory homemade soups and sandwiches. Round out your midday meal with pastries or maybe focaccia, the crisp and chewy Italian flat bread topped with rosemary. Cappuccino, espresso, and juices are in abundant supply. Do allow ample time for the ordering and serving process, as creative confusion reigns behind the counter.

Blue Moon is open Monday through Saturday for breakfast and lunch and Sunday for brunch. Bread runs out by 3:00 P.M., so be there early.

Cafe on the Square $-$$$
1 Biltmore Avenue, Asheville, NC
(828) 251-5565

This elegant cafe that opened in 1990 set the tone for the resurgence of Pack Square. At Cafe on the Square, at the corner of Biltmore Avenue and Pack Square, conversation sparkles at tables framed in the tall windows of this sophisticated turn-of-the-century building. The luncheon menu features salads, sandwiches, and entrees. For dinner you can choose from pecan chicken, fresh fish, duck, steaks, and more. Trying the daily specials may be the best option, because selections have been hit and miss as of late. In the warm season, however, you can't miss with the outdoor cafe, which sprawls out onto the cobblestone sidewalk. The cafe serves lunch and dinner daily, except Sunday.

Early Girl Eatery $-$$$
**8 Wall Street, Asheville, NC
(828) 259-9292**
This little cutie serves up organic dishes and comfort food favorites. Homemade sausage and jams, stuffed omelettes and pancakes are dished up for breakfast. The light airy design that overlooks the street is a winner for daytime and evening dining. Lunch features sandwiches and wraps, as well as salads with spring-fresh ingredients year-round. Dinner goes heavier, with duck breast over polenta and panfried chicken in addition to a menu of innovative specials. Sunday brunch finds a line forming at the door, so be sure to get there early, or be ready to wait.

Flying Frog Cafe $$-$$$$
**1 Battery Park Avenue, Asheville, NC
(828) 254-9411**
This exciting restaurant features creative interpretations of classical dishes by chef Vijay Shastri. This child prodigy had his own restaurant in this very spot when he was only 17 years old. Today, he and his father, Jay Shastri, have pooled the family's expertise to make this one of Asheville's most unusual—and delicious—restaurants. Vijay lends his special flair to the French Cajun, Indian, and Caribbean specialties.

For an appetizer try the Crawfish Cocktail or dahl, a traditional Indian lentil soup with ginger, herbs, and spices. Entrees range from Rasta Pasta, strips of spicy jerked chicken sautéed in fruity olive oil with garlic, bell peppers, onions, mushrooms, green olives, Parmesan cheese, and pasta to bouillabaisse, crab cakes, and, of course, frog legs. A whole page of Indian specialties features curry and spices in palate-pleasing combinations. The restaurant serves dinner Wednesday through Monday.

French Quarter Café $$-$$$
**203 East State Street, Black Mountain, NC
(828) 669-1989**
The two sisters who last lived in this quaint French-style cottage would be pleased with the hospitality and ambience of this welcoming restaurant. There are several rooms available for indoor dining and veranda service, as well. The cuisine follows a New Orleans style, even offering beignet as a dessert item. Crayfish, shrimp, and oysters are gently sautéed and served in light sauces over grits or rice. Knife and fork sandwiches are also on the menu, with choices ranging from roast beef to vegetarian. Its location directly beside the Black Mountain Chamber of Commerce and Visitors Bureau makes this ideal as a one-stop option. You'll want to dine here more than once.

The Grape Escape $-$$$
**1 North Pack Square, Asheville, NC
(828) 225-9463**
This wine bar and grill overlooks Asheville's main square and provides plenty of tables outside to do just that. Featuring 80 wines by the glass, the Grape Escape encourages the unique form of tasting by flights of four wines. Latch onto a favorite and order your full pour. But besides wines, a full bar and selection of ports accompanies the menu of French-influenced lighter fare like salmon mousse with toasted bread rounds or baked brie in crust and side salad. A full menu with aromatic lamb dishes, steaks, a splendid herb-rubbed grilled chicken, and fresh vegetables garnishes makes this stylish, if noisy, wine bar a must-see. Owners Michel and Vonciel Baudouin often visit tableside.

La Caterina Trattoria $$-$$$$
**39 Elm Street, Asheville, NC
(828) 254-1148**
Robbin and Victor Giancola arrived in Asheville several years ago. Like many, they were looking for that perfect place to get away from their former, hectic existence in California. When Victor, an

experienced chef at a top-rated restaurant in San Francisco, decided to put the brakes on the fast pace, he couldn't leave his first love, the restaurant business. The result was the Giancola version of a neighborhood Italian trattoria as he remembered it from his youth in the Bronx. He christened his restaurant La Caterina in honor of his mother, whose picture, a lovely sepia wedding photo of decades ago, hangs in the restaurant.

The flavorful menu is devoid of the usual heavy sauces most people expect with Italian cooking. These are true Southern Italian dishes, just like Victor's mother used to make.

"No spaghetti and meatballs here," says Victor. Instead, try dishes like roast chicken with rosemary, light pastas (the pasta is made fresh daily right in the front window), Italian greens such as arugula, and light desserts such as zabaglione, an Italian egg custard with fresh fruit topping. The salads are a delight—try the tender spinach strawberry salad or the mixed greens with walnuts, vinaigrette, and freshly ground gorgonzola. Preparation is the key here, light and spontaneous, just like the atmosphere. The cafe has an outdoor patio that seats 40. Whimsically decorated, the patio is enclosed with small cedar trees and a wrought iron fence. Be sure to peruse the extensive wine list, more than one hundred to choose from at quite economical prices.

Dinner is served seven days a week, starting at 5:00 P.M. La Caterina serves dinner only.

La Paz Restaurante-Cantina $-$$
10 Biltmore Plaza, Asheville, NC
(828) 277-8779
La Paz's owners constructed their distinctive cantina in Biltmore Village from the ground up. With its wraparound dining porch and patio, La Paz dominates the north corner near the old Asheville train station. The interior features brick walls and lovely hardwoods. The atmosphere is lively, and the upscale food an authentic blend of Mexican and Southwestern fla-

vors, prepared by an all-Hispanic staff led by master chef Juan Quiroz. The ample bar features Mexican drink specialties.

La Paz is open for lunch and dinner seven days a week.

The Laughing Seed Cafe $-$$
40 Wall Street, Asheville, NC
(828) 252-3445
Tucked into one of the bends of twisting Wall Street is the Laughing Seed Cafe, which specializes in international vegetarian cuisine. If you're not accustomed to an entirely vegetarian menu, you will be pleasantly surprised. Owners Joan and Joe Eckert are dedicated folks who strive to educate the dining public to the delicacies and flavors, not to mention the outright good health, that can be achieved with vegetarian cooking.

And this is not just rice and beans. We're talking about exotic and delicious dishes from Morocco to Thailand sharing the extensive menu with old favorites from closer to home. Try the Moroccan sweet and sour carrots, Tanzanian eggplant, *channa dal* from India (garbanzos stewed in fruit juice and spiced with curry, garam, and Marsala) or Mushroom Madness (a scrumptious pizzalike concoction). Order a combination of baked avocados, garden burritos, and black bean chili, or make a meal with one dish. If you choose to limit yourself to one dish, we recommend the Laughing Seed's Harmony Bowl: layers of brown rice, beans, steamed vegetables, plain tofu, and sesame ginger sauce mingle in one harmonious dish. The moss green Spirulina Sunrise is a delightful sweet fruit smoothie packed with vitamins.

Sunday brunch at the Laughing Seed is a real treat, too. Dishes such as poached eggs atop vegetable pancakes and whole wheat French toast complement the regular menu. Laughing Seed is closed on Tuesday.

The Market Place $$-$$$$
20 Wall Street, Asheville, NC
(828) 252-4162

Ever since this restaurant opened in 1979 in downtown Asheville, breaking bread has been a celebratory ritual here. Over the last two decades, the Market Place has become a world-class restaurant, acclaimed by publications ranging from the *New York Times* and *Food & Wine* to *Bon Appétit, Southern Living,* and *Wine Spectator.* In the heart of Asheville's renovated downtown, a sophisticated, urban look provides a backdrop for classic culinary traditions infused with imaginative, contemporary twists. The freshest fruits, vegetables, meats, and seafoods of the season guide the ever-evolving menu. Featured are over 150 wines with more than 20 served by the glass.

Reservations are suggested. Serving dinner Monday through Saturday, The Market Place is also open Sundays in October.

Rio Burrito $
11 Broadway, Asheville, NC
(828) 253-2422

Tom and Andrea, transplanted San Franciscans, were driving on the Blue Ridge Parkway when they dipped into Asheville and decided to stay. They saw the need for big burritos in this town and made Rio Burrito Asheville's busiest lunch locale. The restaurant is fairly small—and you can watch the cooking going on right in front of you—and many downtown office workers take out the giant roll-ups and eat them on the run. Even so, you get your suits, your hippies, your young mothers and kids, your high schoolers, and pretty much anyone else lining up for made-to-order burritos stuffed with succulent chicken, steak, seafood, vegetables, beans, and many combinations.

Rio Burrito closes early, so if you desire a burrito dinner, get there by 7:00 P.M. Rio Burrito is open for lunch and early dinner every day except Sunday and Monday.

Salsa $-$$
6 Patton Avenue, Asheville, NC
(828) 252-9805

This sassy little downtown restaurant is short on space but big on taste and innovative cuisine. Salsa is the creation of Hector Diaz, who brought the wonderful culinary heritage of his native Puerto Rico to this popular eatery.

This is not the usual quickie Tex-Mex joint. It's gourmet Mexican and Caribbean fare with pizzazz.

The menu includes herb chicken quesadillas and tacos made salsa style (fire-roasted pepper tacos and black bean and goat cheese tacos, both served with pico de gallo salsa, are two favorites). The Caribbean menu sparkles with unique ingredients, such as plantains with gazpacho salsa. Exotic root vegetables, unique to the Caribbean, as well as sweet potato and pumpkin are regular ingredients in the gigantic burritos and enchiladas. Piñonos, plantains stuffed with a variety of fresh herbs, meats, and vegetables, are always on the specials.

Whatever you chose, it's guaranteed to be an explosion of flavor. The hearty servings usually mean you have something for lunch tomorrow, as well. Salsa is a staple with locals, and since showing up in the *New York Times* and *Southern Living,* Salsa has gained a following with folks just visiting or passing through. Be prepared for a wait in the high season. Waiting diners mill around on the sidewalk in front talking about what they'll try *this* time.

Salsa is open Monday through Saturday for lunch and dinner.

Veranda Café & Gifts $-$$
119 Cherry Street, Black Mountain, NC
(828) 669-8864

Wandering down Cherry Street is a delightful treat in Black Mountain. It is adjacent to the historic archives and galleries, where Cherry Street and State Street meet. Antiques shops, bookstores, ice cream parlors, public rest rooms, restaurants, and more all lead to the gift shop in the old train depot at the foot of the street. Along the way find pizza and sandwiches in the various restaurants.

For some real mountain cookin'—bowls heaping with southern fried chicken, country ham, green beans, sweet 'taters, hot biscuits, pound cake, and nightly entertainment in the barn—pull up a chair at Pisgah View Ranch (828-667-9100). (For more information see our chapter on Recreation.)

Dining ambience surrounded with creative gift items at Veranda Café & Gifts provides a bit of all of the above. Dining tables are set up throughout the shop as well as on the back porch. The soups and sandwiches are unbeatable in creativity. Fluffy desserts grace the tea and coffee menu.

Weaverville Milling Company $$
Reems Creek Road off Old U.S. Highway 19, Weaverville, NC
(828) 645-4700

Set in a century-old mill, this charming restaurant is big on homey atmosphere and fine dining, served with down-home style. The French onion soup is a cheesy, savory favorite, and the menu has hearty entrees that include fresh rainbow trout, substantial beef stroganoff, and luscious prime rib. This is rib-sticking fare, and you'll be entertained just gazing around the lofty environs of the rustic Weaverville Milling Company interior and the antique mill structure, much of it still in place.

The restaurant has seasonal closings and hours that vary throughout the year. Call if you wish to make specific plans or for directions from Asheville. It's a short and scenic 15-minute drive.

Zambra $-$$$
84 Walnut Street, Asheville, NC
(828) 232-1060

Hector Diaz makes his mark again! The innovative chef and owner of Salsa has opened this snazzy Spanish/Moroccan-style bar and restaurant. The menu offers Spanish-style tapas—a menagerie of small portions of delectable dishes to be shared by the whole table. Calamari are fried to crisp perfection and served with divine lemony salad greens, curried lamb and mushrooms nestle in a bed of garlic polenta, and dozens of other dishes are simply too tantalizing to skip. You may end up with a table covered in small dishes, if you're not careful. More alarming yet . . . you're sure to finish them off in one go! Spanish and French wines, sherries, and ports tickle the tongue, while the Moorish interior dazzles the eyes. Entree-size meals are also available. On the weekends Zambra invites musicians to make music in the bar area, sometimes even featuring a pale belly-dancer or two. Zambra is open for dinner only.

Henderson County

Cypress Cellar $-$$
321 North Main Street, Hendersonville, NC
(828) 698-1005

Cypress Cellar is a local favorite, with its homey atmosphere below-ground and a patio that sits at the bottom of the stairs from Hendersonville's Main Street. The fair is simple and casual Cajun-style, with perennials like gumbo, jambalaya, red beans and rice, and little po' boy sandwiches, as well as a selection of salads.

Expressions $$$
114 North Main Street, Hendersonville, NC
(828) 693-8516

Expressions has been a well-loved fixture of simple elegance on Main Street for more than a decade, and award-winning chef Tom Young still takes as much care with the quality of his food as when he first won our hearts and palates. This is not only worth a stop, it is worth going out of your way for an upscale dining experience.

Chef Young's cuisine is beautifully and innovatively presented. To tell you that you can get seafood, beef, duck, quail, pork, and chicken here doesn't begin to tell the story of the subtle flavors that imbue the dishes. To accompany one of these splendid meals, you can choose from a list of more than 200 fine domestic and French wines. Reservations are recommended. Expressions also has a comfortable upstairs lounge that's perfect for unwinding after a busy day or for quiet conversations with old friends.

Hubert's $$
Laurel Park Shopping Village, U.S. Highway 64 W., Hendersonville, NC
(828) 693-0856

Hubert's tantalizes us with such dishes as shrimp Provençal (a stir-fry of jumbo shrimp, asparagus, tomatoes, mushrooms, garlic, and sherry) and veal scallopini Florentine (veal turned in eggs and Parmesan cheese and served on butter-leaf spinach). Your entree includes selections from the Accents Gazebo, which includes a splendid array of breads, cheeses, salads, and desserts. Or you can just skip the entree and head for the Gazebo.

Hubert's is open for lunch Monday through Friday and dinner Monday through Saturday. A family dinner is served from noon to 3:00 P.M. Sunday and a complete dinner from 3:00 to 8:00 P.M. Reservations are suggested.

The Samovar Cafe $
Heritage Square Mall, Hendersonville, NC
(828) 692-5981

For over 20 years, this enduring and endearing little luncheon establishment has served its customers a wide selection of homemade foods. You can choose from 24 hot and cold sandwiches, soups, quiches, crepes, 10 different salad platters, hamburgers, desserts, and frozen yogurt. Daily specials and beer and wine are also available.

If you aren't familiar with Hendersonville, you might pass the place right by. Keep an eye out; it's at the corner of Church and Barnwell Streets. The Samovar is open for lunch seven days a week.

Seasons at Highland Lake Inn $$$-$$$$
Highland Lake Road, Flat Rock, NC
(828) 693-6812

With much of the food grown right on the premises in organic gardens and greenhouses, which you're welcome to tour, you can be assured that the food here is some of the freshest you'll find anywhere. It's also some of the tastiest. While there's always the popular prime rib, you can also have seared grouper in almond crust with fresh chive and green herb butter, cheese tortellini with roasted red pepper cream, and Dijon hen stuffed with prosciutto ham, Dijon mustard, and fresh herbs.

At Sunday brunch you can select such dishes as poached whole blue trout over aspic with dill mayo dressing and cucumber or Alpine wheat crepes with Swiss cheese, ham, and asparagus (these brunches change themes frequently so that you can have Brunch Santa Fe one day and Brunch Orleans another).

Dinner is served Tuesday through Saturday. Attire is casual but nice. Spirits are served at all dinners and after noon on Sunday. Reservations are recommended. (For more information on Highland Lake Inn, see our Resorts chapter.)

Sinbad Restaurant $$-$$$
202 South Washington Street, Hendersonville, NC
(828) 696-2039

If you like well-prepared Middle Eastern cuisine and seafood—or even if you think you don't—you should try the dishes here. They are superb and served amid authentic Lebanese ambience. You can order Middle Eastern classics such as kabobs, curry, grape leaves, kebbeh, tabouleh, hummus, baba, and falafel or select from delicately prepared seafood, Sinbad's own creation, daily specials, or vegetarian dishes.

For those of you who are less adventurous, local dishes are prepared with a European flair. The bread alone would be worth coming for. Downstairs, a bar with a fireplace is an ideal place for small, private parties.

Sinbad's is open for lunch and dinner Tuesday through Saturday. The restaurant also serves beer, wine, and cocktails.

Woodfield Inn $$-$$$
U.S. Highway 25, Flat Rock, NC
(828) 693-6016

Three dining rooms await you in this historic 1850 inn, where you can have dinner or Sunday brunch surrounded by antebellum charm. Porch and patio seating is also available. Specialties include Morgan Mill trout, fresh seafood, including lobster dishes, and filet mignon. All dinners include a fresh garden salad, garden vegetables, and hot, homemade bread. Much of the produce comes from the inn's own gardens. Special items are on the menu for the health-conscious individual. (For more information on the Woodfield Inn, see our Bed-and-Breakfasts and Country Inns chapter.)

During the summer, Woodfield is open for dinner from Wednesday through Sunday and for a memorable brunch on Sundays. Winter hours are modified. Call for information during that season.

Polk County

The Orchard Inn $$$$
U.S. Highway 176, Saluda, NC
(828) 749-5471, (800) 581-3800

This lovely, plantation-type inn with its beautiful view of the Warrior Mountains has an elegant glassed-in dining area that stretches across the back and around one corner of its main building. The chef will carefully prepare your four-course dinner according to the seasonal food available.

"Freshness," she says, "dictates the menu." The day we dropped in she was preparing a curried carrot soup and a fresh tossed garden salad with classic bleu cheese dressing. Diners would also have their choice of a meat (perhaps rack of lamb or beef tenderloin), fish (mountain trout or maybe salmon), or poultry (which could be duck breast, Cornish hen, or quail), with vegetarian dishes on request.

Dessert the day we were there was a low-fat, chocolate-decadence cake. Prior to dinner the inn serves complimentary hors d'oeuvres. (Because this is a dry county, you are welcome to bring your own favorite alcoholic beverage.) The Orchard Inn is open year-round. Dinner is served Tuesday through Saturday by reservation.

Pine Crest Inn $$$$
200 Pine Crest Lane, Tryon, NC
(828) 633-3001

The dining room at Pine Crest, with its hunter green, burgundy, and deep blue decor, is reminiscent of an elegant English tavern. Both breakfast and dinner are served to the public here by reservation only, and the menu changes every day. If you're lucky, they might be serving cornmeal crusted catfish with citrus-horseradish reduction. All entrees are perfectly matched with fresh vegetable and various starches, such as chive mashed potatoes or creamed barley on mushroom risotto. The Pine Crest Inn's dining room is open Monday through Saturday.

Stone Hedge Inn $$$
300 Howard Gap Road, Tryon, NC
(828) 859-9114

A meal at this stately stone manor is an equally stately pleasure. Big picture windows cover one wall, so no matter where you sit in the dining room you have a stunning mountain view. After sunset, tables are illuminated with candles in crystal globes, and the ambience is romantic. Chef Thomas Dinsmore has designed an eclectic menu that offers contemporary cuisine as evening specials, along with traditional favorites such as broiled North Carolina mountain trout, Black Angus beef filet, veal piccata, and shrimp scampi. Entrees include homemade soup or salad, rice or potato or pasta, and rolls. A delectable selection of homemade desserts include the Chocolate Amaretto Passion Cake, rum cake, seasonal pies, cheesecake, and locally made ice cream.

The restaurant is open for dinner by reservation Wednesday through Saturday and for Sunday brunch.

Rutherford County

Lake Lure Inn $-$$$
U.S. Highway 64/74, Lake Lure, NC
(828) 625-2525, (800) 277-5873
This stately inn overlooking beautiful Lake
Lure has been a tradition in Hickory Nut
Gorge since 1927. The dining room is an
elegant setting for such gourmet offerings
as roasted vegetable and herb cheese ter-
rine, lobster ravioli with lobster sauce,
Rendang shrimp and scallops, or veal
medallion au poivre vert. For the little
ones who might have trouble pronouncing
these fancy dishes, Lake Lure Inn offers
chicken finger and hamburger platters
(and cheese tortellini in tomato sauce for
discriminating pint-sized palates).

Dinner is served April through October, and the restaurant offers a Sunday
brunch. Hours vary during the off-season,
so call ahead.

Transylvania County

Brown Trout Mountain Grille $$$
U.S. Highway 281 N., Lake Toxaway, NC
(828) 877-3474, (828) 226-1906
The Brown Trout Mountain Grille is a real
find. The twenty-minute drive from Brevard on U.S. 64 W. is filled with grandiose
views of the mountains. The air becomes
richer and cleaner to the senses. Car windows need to be opened and the air con-
ditioner shut down. Rounding the curve
on U.S. 281 N., less than a mile off of U.S.
64, you'll spot the restaurant on your right
and glimmering Lake Toxaway on the left.
On entering the grille, you truly walk into
a cavelike atmosphere because the Brown
Trout is cut back into the mountain.

Soft music creates a pleasant background and is served up live throughout
the evening. With luck, Donna Pimental
may be one of the servers. She is certain
to sing an aria or two from some of the
roles she has performed with the Asheville
Lyric Opera Company and other repertoire from past recitals.

When proprietor Cliff Singleton came
to this area, he knew that this was the
place. He immediately sent for Chef Daniel
Shaffer to join him. Packing up his apron,
chef's knives, pots, and pans, Daniel pulled
up stakes and brought his experience
from top restaurants in Savannah and
Hilton Head to this site.

Menu items range from thrown pizza
crust to sauces so light they need to be
eaten quickly so they won't float off the
plate. One specialty produced by Chef
Daniel is shrimp and grits with a cream
sauce laced with ham strips. The grits are
highly refined at a local stone gristmill.
Another is saddle of venison with a white
almond-based sauce, which almost defies
earthly description. Native mountain trout
is a must on the menu. The trout, and
other seafood, is served in a variety of
elaborate ways.

The wine list meets all needs and
beyond. The kids' menu, under $5.00, is in
addition to the extensive pizza menu. This
amazing kitchen produces some of the
most delectable food found in these
southern mountains. The staff is warm and
charming. Reservations are important as
many people have discovered this hideaway. Be assured, once you have visited,
you'll want to keep returning.

Should you wish to spend some time
in the area, Cliff can assist. Just 2 miles up
the road he has five cabins on the mountain side called the Cabins at Seven Foxes.
It's a secluded oasis on seven landscaped
acres. The Brown Trout Mountain Grille is
open year-round, every evening, with the
first seating at 5:30.

Cardinal Drive-In $, no credit cards
328 South Broad Street, Brevard, NC
(828) 884-7085
Here's a flash from the past: an honest-to-
goodness, old-fashioned drive-in right out
of the 1950s. Of course, you can eat in the
air-conditioned dining room, but who
would want to when you can get service
without getting out of your car? You can
also get a Cardinal Burger cooked fresh to

order; foot-long hot dogs; fresh, home-made onion rings; and fried chicken and shrimp dinners. If you'd like something a bit more health conscious, Cardinal can oblige with grilled skinless chicken breast in a sandwich or on a platter. But whatever you order, don't miss out on the fresh straw-berry, pineapple or banana shakes. To use an old '50s Campbell Soup slogan, they're mmm-mmm good! The place is open daily.

The Corner Bistro $
1 East Main Street, Brevard, NC
(828) 862-4746

This is the place to stop for a healthful, prettily prepared, inexpensive lunch or light dinner. There are more than a dozen "meat-wiches" and even hot dogs served here (we particularly liked the smoked salmon with horseradish mayo, capers, onions, tomato, and spinach on cracked wheat bread). There's an even finer array of salads and "vegi-wiches," such as a veggie tortilla made with spinach, sprouts, avocado, tomatoes, mushrooms, onions, carrots, and shredded cheddar, topped with balsamic vinaigrette and wrapped in the flour tortilla. All sandwiches are served with a choice of tortellini salad, rice and bean salad, or chips. And there are daily delicious dessert selections. The Corner Bistro is open Monday through Saturday. The hours vary from day to day so be sure to call ahead of time to make sure it's open at the time you want to eat.

Earthshine $$$
Golden Road Lake, Toxaway, NC
(828) 862-4207

This unusual resort takes pride in offering healthful, delicious foods prepared from scratch—"or pretty darn close"—and has opened its almost-red-meat-free, buffet-style lunches and dinners to the public. Though each meal is limited to a one-entree menu, these change frequently. You might, for example, be served a lunch consisting of everything you ever wanted for building your own Mexican creation: flour tortillas, refried beans, seasoned taco meat, sautéed chicken strips with onions and peppers, and Spanish rice—and that's just the hot stuff! Or you could be served chicken cordon bleu, Earthshine-style. You can be sure that lunch will include homemade bread and a fresh salad bar. Now you can go there for breakfast too.

For dinner you might get marinated swordfish chunks skewered with a variety of peppers and onions, Cornish game hens prepared with a lovely orange glaze, or lemon and ginger pork loin. All dinners include homemade bread, a fresh salad bar, a vegetable, potato, pasta or rice, and a dessert, such as fresh apples baked with brown sugar and oat topping, plus fresh whipped cream or vanilla ice cream. Or how about chocolate pecan pie?

To get to Earthshine, go west out of Brevard on U.S. 64 and follow the signs, or see our chapter on Resorts for more spe-cific directions and information. Earth-shine opens its dinner to the public on Friday and Saturday.

Essence of Thyme Coffee Caffe $, no credit cards
37 East Main Street, Brevard, NC
(828) 884-7171

Here's another fine place to relax after wandering in and out of Brevard's inter-esting shops. Essence of Thyme opened in December 1994 and was welcomed by Brevard's coffee lovers. Shoppers will get an energy boost after relaxing over a cup of cappuccino. Or how about a cafe latte, that great mix of espresso and steamed milk topped with foamed milk? To go along with these and other special cof-fees, you can treat yourself to a variety of freshly baked New York bagels, yummy cakes, and an array of fresh pastries. Lun-cheon specials, such as soups, sand-wiches, and salads, are also available. If you're lucky, you may find a really com-fortable spot in one of the limited number of upholstered chairs in the back of the cafe. And more and more, there is some good live music at Essence of Thyme, which is open daily.

The Falls Landing Restaurant $$
23 East Main Street, Brevard, NC
(828) 884-2835

When it comes to fresh seafood with a Caribbean touch, the owners of the Falls Landing, former longtime residents of the Virgin Islands, know how to do it right! Their Cajun mahi-mahi is done to a turn, too. When you come here, it's essential that you try the famous conch fritters (we bet you can't eat just one!).

Fresh nightly specials include lots of fresh seafood, steaks, pasta, and chicken. Friday night is lobster night. If you're lucky, you might be there when superb cheese soup is on the menu. The bar also mixes some excellent drinks. Lunch is served at the Falls Landing, located just across from the courthouse on Main Street, every day; it's open for dinner from Tuesday through Sunday.

Jordan Street Cafe $$
30 West Jordan Street, Brevard, NC
(828) 883-2558

This small, elegant, nonsmoking restaurant serving truly fine American cuisine has only been open for slightly more than a year, but it's already a favorite with locals with discriminating taste. For that reason reservations are recommended, particularly for Sunday brunch. When the weather permits, you can dine out on Jordan Street's outdoor patio. Brunch is served on Sunday from 10:00 A.M. until 2:00 P.M. The restaurant is open for dinner every evening except Tuesday.

October's End $-$$
115 U.S. Highway 64 W., Lake Toxaway, NC
(828) 966-9226

Even if the food here wasn't delicious—and it is—it would be worthwhile to stop in for a meal just to be able to enjoy a leisurely view of Toxaway Falls as it pours over its great granite dome into the valley below.

Here at October's End you can sit out on a wide, enclosed deck that overlooks the falls while you enjoy either American or Italian dishes. If the weather isn't con-

ducive to outdoor dining, you'll find the dining room, with its gas-log fireplace, cozy and friendly. For lunch, the restaurant offers Italian subs, gourmet pizza-for-one, and hot dishes, such as eggplant parmigiana and fried mozzarella served with a marinara sauce. You can also get such standards as hamburger platters and barbecue and other sandwiches.

For dinner we did an informal survey that seemed to break down by gender: Women preferred Chicken Piccata sautéed with white wine, lemon, and capers; men went for Veal October stuffed with cheese, spinach and prosciutto, and topped with fresh tomatoes, basil, and olives. You'll also find great seafood and a full-service bar and lounge.

October's End is open from May until the end of October—thus, the name. Hours vary, so call for a specific time.

Dining in can be a real treat when ingredients are made up of fresh, home-grown produce. During the growing season, most small towns here have farmers' markets once or twice a week, where local gardeners and farmers come to sell what they've harvested that morning. You can often find homemade jams, jellies, relishes, and the like here, too. Just ask around.

Rocky's Soda Shop & Grill $
36 South Broad Street, Brevard, NC
(828) 877-5375

Like the Cardinal Drive-In listed earlier, Rocky's offers another trip into "the old days" with its ice-cream concoctions, great shakes, real old-time hamburgers, and other treats hot off the grill. It's a nice complement to D. D. Bullwinkel's general store right next door. You can get breakfast, lunch, and dinner at Rocky's Monday through Saturday. It's also open on Sundays for lunch.

SOUTHERN MOUNTAINS

Cherokee County

The Oak Barrel Restaurant   **$$-$$$**
163 County Home Road, Murphy, NC
(828) 837-7803
You won't find a finer place to eat in this section of the country than this restaurant, housed in what was once an old home. In this lodgelike atmosphere, you'll find smoking and nonsmoking dining rooms, private dining rooms, and a covered porch where you can eat during spring, summer, and fall. You'll also find an extensive menu of gourmet continental cuisine, with five or six specials, including the chef's choice of hors d'oeuvres. Occasionally, the chef will prepare a "game table," laden with such treats as venison, duck, and the like. Another great favorite is the Oak Barrel's chateaubriand, but you can also order most any kind of steak you desire. There's also the catch of the day, and Cajun dishes are nice variations. The pub is available for private bookings. Reservations are recommended.

Clay County

Broadax Inn Restaurant   **$$**
Elf Road, Hayesville, NC
(828) 389-6987
This is a truly unique restaurant housed in the old Elf schoolhouse (see our Bed-and-Breakfasts and Country Inns chapter). The two former large classrooms, separated by an archway, can seat as many as 96 people, and the place is often filled because it's a popular spot for parties and banquets. Owners Roger and Ruth Young had thought that of all their menu items the excellent prime rib would be most in demand, but of late, they say the hit of the restaurant is crab-stuffed shrimp. We can recommend it, and the friendly Broadax too (it's closed in January and February).

The restaurant is open for dinner Wednesday through Sunday in the summer and Thursday through Sunday in the winter.

Haywood County

Cataloochee Ranch   **$$**
119 Ranch Road, Maggie Valley, NC
(828) 926-1401, (800) 868-1401
Cataloochee Ranch has endured and prospered in the same family for more than a half-century for many reasons, including its lovely location high on a mountain overlooking Maggie Valley. The food it serves has also played a big part in its popularity. These are family-style meals to which the public is invited by reservations only. And what feasts they are! Here's a sample menu, though they change regularly: potato and wild leek soup, smoked turkey breast served with cornbread dressing and giblet gravy, stuffed pork loin with spinach and black walnuts, cranberry chutney, sweet potato pie, sautéed sugar snap peas, freshly baked breads with homemade preserves, Chef Patsy's homemade desserts, and assorted beverages. The price is all inclusive.

The Cataloochee Ranch is open year-round, but meals are only served in the winter by special arrangement (for more information, see our Resorts chapter).

Grandview Lodge   **$$$**
466 Lickstone Road, Waynesville, NC
(828) 456-5212
Hearty fare awaits guests in the dining room at Grandview Lodge, which is open to the public by advance reservation only. All meals are served family style with guests seated around tables in groups from two to 10.

Breakfast consists of juice, fruit, hot and cold cereals, biscuits, eggs, bacon or locally made sausage, homemade jams and jellies, and a beverage of choice. Pancakes, waffles, French toast, or a cheese strata provide alternate fare.

The dinner menu changes daily and consists of an appetizer, salad, entree, five vegetables (most locally grown) or side dishes, homebaked bread, and beverage and desserts. Typical entrees are marinated pork roast, barbecued brisket of beef, beef burgundy, and chicken roasted in wine and orange juice. (For more information on Grandview Lodge, see our Bed-and-Breakfasts and Country Inns chapter.)

Lomo Grill $$$$
121 Church Street, Waynesville, NC
(828) 452-1704, (828) 452-5222
Brick walls, hardwood floors, a quiet elegance, and the sweet smell of the wood-burning Argentine grill enfold you when you enter the Lomo Grill. This is the place to come when you're in the mood for a relaxed, leisurely dinner.

In the true Italian and Mediterranean tradition, each selection is cooked to order with the finest natural ingredients available. You could, for example, start with an appetizer of Lomo Involtini de Melanzane, which is grilled eggplant, French goat cheese, sun-dried tomatoes, Parmesan cheese shavings, fresh basil, tomato sauce, and cumin yogurt sauce. Follow that with a Lomo Caesar salad and then choose from an extensive menu of entrees that include pastas, fish, poultry, veal, or beef. (Though the restaurant has only been open for around three years, its beef has already won awards.) To end this fine repast, we'd suggest the homemade flan with caramel spread and fresh whipped cream or homemade crepes stuffed with bananas and caramel. Lomo Grill is open for dinner daily except in the winter.

The Old Stone Inn $$$-$$$$
900 Dolan Road, Waynesville, NC
(828) 456-3333, (800) 432-8499
The rich warmth of wood envelopes you in the Old Stone Inn's guest lounge and dining room, and dinner here is a hearty affair. Entrees include such choices as beef tenderloin in puff pastry, Muscovy duck with apricot glas, and cedar-planked

salmon trout fillet. Your entree is accompanied by several vegetables, including fantastic vegetable casseroles, and freshly baked bread. Desserts include Grand Marnier Crème Caramel, and such ice cream delights as the Smoky Mountain Brown Bear Ice-Cream Coupe for Two.

Dinner is available here by reservation (for more information, see our Bed-and-Breakfasts and Country Inns chapter).

The Swag $$$$
Hemphill Road, Waynesville, NC
(828) 926-0430, (800) 789-7672
The Swag, an exclusive inn 5,000 feet up in the Smoky Mountains with 50-mile views, takes a limited number of outside guests by reservation only for its lunches Monday through Saturday, its sensational dinners seven days a week, and its unforgettable Sunday brunches. The chef-chosen dinners feature four-course meals of such favorites as tomato-basil soup, fresh salads, grilled rainbow trout or beef tenderloin, and desserts that might include lime mousse or Derby Pie.

The Swag is open from mid-May through October (see our Bed-and-Breakfasts and Country Inns chapter for more information).

Jackson County

Balsam Mountain Inn $$$
Off U.S. Highway 74/23, Balsam, NC
(828) 456-9498
Many people come to dine at the Balsam Mountain Inn for the older-era atmosphere captured by this turn-of-the-century inn, only to come back again and again for the great food. Both lunch and dinner are offered to guests as well as the public in its huge dining room. Lunches are light, consisting of sandwiches and salads, except on Sundays, when a full dinner menu is served. Dinners, from rotating menus, offer such entrees as trout, prime rib, ham with brown sugar–citrus glaze, or chicken in an artichoke, mushroom, and

white wine sauce. These are accompanied by a variety of fresh fruits, vegetables, and breads—with a choice of too-tempting desserts and an eclectic selection of beer and wine. (For more information on Balsam Mountain Inn, see our Bed-and-Breakfasts and Country Inns chapter.)

Balsam Mountain Inn's dining room is open to the public Tuesday through Sunday by reservation.

High Hampton Inn $$-$$$$
U.S. Highway 107, Cashiers, NC
(828) 743-2411, (800) 334-2551

The High Hampton Inn believes in tradition, right down to the food it serves. Many dishes you'll eat—served buffet style at the inn—are the same favorites you'd have found here 50 years ago: fried chicken, fresh local trout, and prime rib; a memorable cream of peanut soup; a cranberry Waldorf salad; Southern-style vegetables such as stewed corn; homemade bread, including sausage cornbread; and peppermint ice cream with chocolate syrup.

The High Hampton Inn is open April through November, and breakfast, lunch, and dinner are available to the public (for more information, see our Resorts chapter).

The Jarrett House $$, no credit cards
U.S. Highway 441, Dillsboro, NC
(828) 586-0265, (800) 972-5623

When R. Frank Jarrett owned this inn from 1894 until his death in 1950, he let his wife, "Miss Sallie," run the place (see our Bed-and-Breakfasts and Country Inns chapter). However, he cured the hams that were served, and the great platters of fried ham, red-eye gravy, hot buttermilk biscuits, and North Carolina's famous sourwood honey were said to make strong men weep because they were too full to eat as much as they wanted.

Great platters of food, which still include ham, gravy, and biscuits, load down the tables in the Jarrett House, and people still line up as they've done for more than a century to eat in the large dining room, which seats as many as 125.

You'll also still find other longtime favorites, such as fried chicken and mountain trout, along with all the fixins.

From November 1 through May 1, the Jarrett House serves lunch Tuesday through Thursday and dinner on weekends. The rest of the year, breakfast is served on weekends, lunch Monday through Saturday, and dinner seven days a week. No reservations are required except for groups of ten or more (for more information on the Jarrett House, see our Bed-and-Breakfasts and Country Inns chapter).

Lulu's Cafe $$
612 West Main Street, Sylva, NC
(828) 586-8989

Dining at Lulu's is a lovely adventure in eating. You can choose from a menu that includes really good vegetarian, Greek, Italian, Caribbean, Indonesian, and American food. For example, you can have a melt of provolone and feta cheese, Greek olives, tomatoes, onions, and pepperoncini (a spicy pepper) in a Greek pita bread, or perhaps island jerk chicken served with Caribbean black beans, jicama, saffron basmati rice, and grilled plantain. We were impressed with a delicious vegetarian black bean chili, accompanied by a glass of beer (wines are served here too). You can then follow your full-course dinner with an old-fashioned dessert. The restaurant's always unusual decor has a fresh new look. It consists of mulberry walls, moss green chairs, and floral tablecloths; black accents and burgundy ceiling fans set off colorfully matted black-and-white photos. Lulu's is open year-round for lunch and dinner Monday through Saturday.

The Market Basket $$
U.S. Highway 107 S., Cashiers, NC
(828) 743-2216

This is a highly unusual restaurant. During the day The Market Basket is a delicatessen, a caterer, and a gourmet grocery store with a full line of health food, fresh produce, meat, and seafood—all set in an atmosphere that includes a grand piano. At night it becomes a fondue restaurant without the oil, where you can sauté your own food on a 500- or 600-degree granite slab. But that doesn't begin to tell the story of this place.

Basically, it serves health-conscious cuisine, but that doesn't mean it's not exciting. For lunch there's an array of soups, hot foods, sandwiches, and salads. At night tables are put into the store's aisles (you might find yourself sitting next to the artichokes or the flour), and it becomes a super-popular cafe. In fact people are turned away all the time, even in winter, so we highly recommend you make reservations. You can start your dinner with an appetizer, such as baked garlic, smoked salmon, baked brie, or baby-back ribs, and move on to entrees that include lamb chops, filet mignon, fresh seasonal seafood dishes, an array of marvelous vegetarian dishes, and huge salads. Or you can try something from the hot-rock menu, which also includes vegetarian, chicken, beef, seafood, or a combination of them all. If you're the least bit Southern—or want to be—we suggest you try shrimp and grits, a mouthwatering, New Orleans–style dish.

The Market Basket is open for lunch Monday through Saturday. It's open for dinner Thursday through Monday; it's closed Tuesday and Wednesday. Guitarist/singer Cy Timmons usually entertains in the evenings, and there's live piano music for lunch on Friday and Saturday.

Macon County

The Gazebo Creekside
Cafe $, no credit cards
103 Heritage Hollow Drive, Franklin, NC
(828) 524-8783
This award-winning cafe is the perfect place to relax and unwind. Built around an old gazebo, the beautiful outdoor setting allows for creekside seating, while you enjoy the abundant North Carolina bird life. Open for lunch only, the homemade fare includes soups, salads, deli sandwiches, desserts, gourmet coffees, and

ice-cream delights. The Gazebo is open from April through October.

On the Verandah $$$
Lake Sequoyah, Highlands, NC
(828) 526-2338
The scenic dining setting overlooking Lake Sequoyah sets the tone for the exquisite menu at this restaurant, to which *Wine Spectator* magazine has given its Award of Excellence yearly since 1987. The food is prepared with fresh ingredients and is cooked to order.

For starters you can order roasted eggplant with fresh tomatoes, herbs, and goat cheese or flame-roasted shrimp with citrus soy dressing, followed by a Thai roasted-peanut salad with romaine lettuce, scallions, shredded carrots, and alfalfa sprouts. For an entree you could have, among other things, stir-fried scallops on angel-hair pasta with a peppered ginger-scallion sauce or sautéed lamb chops with a honey-roasted pecan and ancho chili crust, mint aioli, and lemon walnut couscous. Daily fresh fish and seafood specials are paired with complementary wines.

This family-owned restaurant offers a library of bottles of hot sauces from everywhere. They even bottle their own special recipe. It is offered as a take home sale item in a three pack.

In addition to dinner, On the Verandah offers a Sunday champagne brunch with soup, a salad bar, Mimosa cocktails or Kir Royale, and such entrees as poached eggs on crab cakes topped with fresh lime Hollandaise sauce. Piano entertainment is featured nightly at the wine bar—where you can choose from more than a dozen wines by the glass. On the Verandah is open daily for dinner from Easter through New Year's.

Ristorante Paoletti $$
440 Main Street, Highlands, NC
(828) 526-4906
Now entering their nineteenth season in Highlands, Arthur Paoletti and his family have made their restaurant a definite destination. Even Chef Wolfgang Green (see

Wolfgang's on Main) brings his guests here for dinner when he chooses not to cook. Because practice makes perfect, it might be said that the family "practiced" serving fine cuisine for 20 years at Delray Beach in Coral Gables, Florida. They've gotten it down really good now. They specialize in the freshest coast fish and seafood dishes. Their homemade pastas, breads, and desserts sing out, "Il Italiano." Veal chops with champagne cream, roasted rack of lamb, and dry aged Angus sirloin strip steak are just a few of the extensive offerings on their menu.

Their 20-page wine list provides a trip around the world without leaving the table. Their wine cellar has been designated by the *Wine Spectator* for an "Award of Excellence."

Wolfgang's on Main $$$
Main Street, Highlands, NC
(828) 526–3807

Wolfgang's is located in one of the oldest houses in Highlands, built in 1880. Whether dining inside by a fireplace on a handmade rhododendron table, outside on the awning-covered deck, or in the garden pavilion, you're in for a dining treat.

Wolfgang and Mindy Green are legends in their own time and in Highlands, N.C. Working the front of the house, Mindy is certain to offer a warm welcome, exuding a sense of hospitality.

Chef Wolfgang, former executive chef for the Brennan's Family Commander's Palace in New Orleans, is internationally acclaimed, having won numerous awards, including chef of the year in both Jamaica and Texas. His background brings a freshness and variety to a menu that's so attractive, it's really difficult to decide what to order.

New Orleans specialties include Wolfgang's Signature Soup, a shrimp and lobster bisque; Crawfish Étouffée; Maryland blue crab cakes served on a lobster cream sauce with pecan-crusted shrimp; Veal Medallions Wolfgang on a cabernet sauce topped with crawfish and béarnaise sauce; as well as many other selections.

Some favorites with locals are Chef Wolfgang's fresh mountain trout with pine nuts, Trout Cote D'Azur, and Trout Admiral. For unforgettable Bavarian fare try the Wiener schnitzel or rostbraten—a trimmed sirloin steak, pan-fried and topped with thinly sliced fried onions. For that special romantic evening in the mountains, try the chateaubriand for two, presented on a silver platter with an assortment of fresh vegetables.

Wine steward Billy Creswell has an extensive knowledge of his subject and offers subtle suggestions for wines to match your meal. Even though he could readily point out the $2,900 Petrus or a $2,450 Mouton Rothschild, he permits the wines of that caliber to present themselves. It is more likely that he will suggest those that begin in the $20 range, with an opportunity to select from an extensive wine list that includes wines to complement each meal, as well as over two dozen selections available by the glass. They are one of three restaurants in Highlands to have received the prestigious *Wine Spectator*'s Award of Excellence, beginning in 1999.

And to complete your meal, try Wolfgang's Apple Strudel made from a family recipe, Black Forest Torte, Strawberries Romanoff, the famous Bananas Foster, or one of the daily special desserts. Espresso, cappuccino, or one of a wide variety of ports and a cigar from the restaurant's humidor are delightful ways to finish a wonderful dining experience.

Wolfgang's is open for lunch and dinner every day except Wednesday. Throughout the year the gourmet and adventurer is offered other opportunities in Highlands for special events with Wolfgang heading a consortium of innkeepers and chefs to provide all-weather excitement in wining, dining, and culture (see our Annual Festivals and Events chapter).

Swain County

Hemlock Inn   **$, no credit cards**
Off U.S. Highway 19, Bryson City, NC
(828) 488–2885
The food at the Hemlock Inn, set on 65 wooded acres, 3 miles from the Great Smoky Mountains National Park, is so good that, at their guests' insistence, the inn put many of its recipes into a cookbook called *Recipes from Our Front Porch*. If you are not a guest here (see our Bed-and-Breakfasts and Country Inns chapter), you can still make a reservation for dinner Monday through Saturday. You'll be seated at a lazy-Susan table laden with native foods, including fruits and vegetables provided by the Hemlock's neighbors' gardens (in the summer, you may be offered corn on the cob picked

Are you hungry and want to know a great place to eat wherever you are? Strike up a conversation with a few of the local residents. Ask them their favorite places to dine. The result will probably be some excellent down-home cookin' at a great price.

just a few minutes before it's cooked and served). Entrees might include country ham and fried chicken, accompanied by homemade yeast rolls and biscuits with mountain honey. The delicious desserts are all made from scratch too.

The Hemlock Inn is open May to November. While you're here, make time to sit in a rocking chair out front and enjoy the view.

NIGHTLIFE

The appeal of life in the mountains is the love of the land, the fascinating variety of the people who live here, and the opportunity to control the pace of our lives. So you won't find too many dusk-to-dawn party venues here. Instead, the emphasis is on music—traditional, Old-Time, alternative, folk, singer-songwriter, country, Latin, reggae . . . and a whole lot more.

Our urban centers have seen an exciting growth in nightspots and locales, which lend themselves to socializing after the theater or concert. Asheville, for one, has become a beacon for sophisticated diners, theatergoers, and art aficionados. Live music is so popular here, you'll find a variety any night of the week, in several different venues. In Asheville, you will find a thriving downtown, both day and night. The people who live downtown, in the vast lofts with wooden floors and beamed garrets, grab their morning coffee and newspaper at the corner coffee shop, walk to Sunday brunch at several cafes with such offerings, and spend their summer evenings chatting over a glass of wine at the outdoor Italian trattoria.

Join them in sampling nightlife into the wee hours, dancing at a club, or listening to jazz in the intimate atmosphere of a New Orleans–type jazz bar. A downtown cinema features first-run foreign films and award-winning American movies. Poetry slams and original plays, evening exhibition openings at art galleries, and several excellent venues for daily live music and dance propel this area into the forefront of local entertainment. Asheville and a number of the smaller cities in the North Carolina mountains maintain brewpubs, manufacturing their own special flavors and types of beer and housing a dart-board or two, possibly even a pool table.

Mainstream nightlife here is generally found in the restaurant/bars in most larger mountain cities (see our Restaurants chapter). Not only can you enjoy a night out with friends over a great meal, you can also find first-rate musical entertainment. This ranges from piano mood music to mellow acoustic guitar, honky-tonk country to hot jazz, and pulse-blasting rock. The fine restaurants and cafes in Blowing Rock, Hendersonville, Boone, and other communities often offer live music.

Colleges and universities in the region contribute much to mountain nightlife (see our Arts and Culture chapter). We've got your typical raucous college pubs and bars found in any campus town, if that's what you crave. On the flip side, however, you can also find mellow, laid-back coffee-houses, featuring singer-songwriters, poetry evenings, author's readings, or even games of checkers and backgammon.

Major concert arenas are still out of our region, as far away as Atlanta, Charlotte, or Greenville, South Carolina, but Asheville's Civic Center is undergoing changes and working to book big-league names in entertainment. Local colleges and universities sporadically bring big-name groups to the area. And a number of intimate little clubs, especially in Black Mountain in the central mountains, have become springboards for local talent moving on to the big time. Other alternative clubs catering to the avant-garde, the bizarre, or performance art maintain a bit of Bohemia.

An average night out for the younger set often includes plowing through the

Need we say, "Don't drink and drive"? Especially with the curving mountain roads, you won't want to be behind the wheel with a couple of beers in you. Ask the manager of the bar or restaurant to call a cab for you or contact your hotel, which can dispatch a car to pick you up.

popcorn-and-nachos crowd at the local moviehouse. Megaplex cinemas are aplenty in the mountains. They are busy social gathering places for families, couples, seniors, and movie critics, so don't try to get into a sneak preview 30 minutes before show time. We also have film societies, film discussion groups, and film festivals.

But nightlife here can also be as basic as a Friday night high school football game, a Saturday night dance at the town hall, or listening to the chorus of crickets and tree frogs on a hot summer night.

In this chapter we present a number of representative nighttime entertainment listings in the mountains, including some of the restaurants that offer exceptional entertainment as part of the dining experience. Because of the trendy nature of nightlife, nightspots lend themselves to frequent openings and closings and changing of hands. Therefore we have noted the more established and highly recommended locales and urge you to check local newspapers for up-to-the-minute entertainment listings. Unless otherwise noted, don't expect a cover charge for the following locales.

NORTHERN MOUNTAINS

Alleghany County

Alleghany Jubilee
Main Street, Sparta, NC
(336) 372-4591
Start stompin' your foot and tappin' your toes—this is old-time music. Housed in the old 1930s-era movie theater on Main Street in Sparta, the Alleghany Jubilee provides a weekly stage for local country talent, old-time music, and lively square dancing. Other than high school football, the Alleghany Jubilee is Sparta's main attraction on the weekend.

The Jubilee square dance is held every Friday night from 8:00 to 11:00 P.M. The Jubilee old-time music livens up Saturdays again from 8:00 to 11:00 P.M. or whenever

the music stops. This is family entertainment, folks.

Admission is usually around $4.00 for adults and children get in free.

Be aware that some counties in North Carolina are dry. That means you won't get a drink there. Some restaurants will allow "brown bagging" and might charge a small corkage fee. ℹ️

Mountain Music Jamboree
Burgiss Barn, Laurel Springs, NC
(336) 384-4079, (800) 803-4079
www.mountainmusicjamboree.com
The old barn at the Burgiss Farm Bed-and-Breakfast in southern Alleghany County has found new life as a rollicking, good-time music hall with a worldwide reputation. Tom and Nancy Burgiss are the genial hosts of this rousing, regular weekend party dedicated to the preservation of traditional mountain music and dance, generally held on Saturday nights.

The barn, smartly dressed in an upscale Nashville Barn Dance decor, with feed-sack banners and a polished wooden dance floor, swells with good feeling to the sounds of 64 different local family bands. Two different bands play each week, spotlighting the creative talents of mommies and daddies, aunts and uncles. The Burgisses also serve up a delicious meal and enough tasty fixins to require at least one round off the dance floor.

Elk Knob Road is off N.C. Highway 18. Admission is $5.00 for adults, and children are admitted free. No smoking or alcohol are permitted in the barn.

Ashe County

Glendale Springs Inn & Restaurant
7414 N.C. Highway 16, Glendale Springs, NC
(336) 982-2103, (800) 287-1206
This restaurant and inn (covered in both

our Bed-and-Breakfasts and Country Inns and Restaurant chapters) also often provides live music on weekend evenings and on holidays. Usually local bluegrass and country music strummers or even a solo pianist will play for the dinner-and-dessert crowd in the wood-paneled dining room of the inn.

As Ashe County is a "dry" county, the restaurant is not allowed to sell alcohol, but brown bagging is permitted. Call ahead for a schedule of performers and restaurant hours, as they change by season.

Avery County

Beech Mountain Street Dances
Beech Mountain Highway, Banner Elk, NC
(800) 468-5506
In summer check out these lively monthly street dances in mile-high Beech Mountain. This unique recreational community offers fun every season of the year. Dates and times vary, so call ahead of time.

Watauga County

beansTalk
352 West King Street, Boone, NC
(828) 262-0999
This is one of the new wave '90s coffeehouses that thrives on mellow music and New Age individuality. This great little place

is on Boone's main thoroughfare downtown. The aroma of gourmet coffees and fresh pastries will make you want to linger.

Contra Dancing and Traditional American Folk Dancing
165 Morris Street, Blowing Rock, NC
N.C. Highway 194, Apple Barn, Valle Crucis, NC
(828) 297-1393
Enjoy the resurgence of these art forms of traditional folk dances. In winter dancers gather from 7:00 to 10:00 P.M. the second Saturday of the month at Blowing Rock Elementary. The summer schedule is the same, but groups meets at the Apple Barn at Valle Crucis. Newcomers are welcome!

Klondike Cafe
441 Blowing Rock Road, Boone, NC
(828) 262-5065
The Klondike Cafe is a diamond in the rough. This gutsy bar serves deli sandwiches, gourmet burgers, Mexican dishes, and imported and premium domestic beers. But the grub is not the attraction. Outside, the patrons claim spots at the long tables running the length of the building. Sitting like birds on a wire, Klondike's clientele, mostly college students, but also locals and hardy tourists, hang out and watch Boone go by on U.S. 321, the Blowing Rock Road. Inside, live entertainment keeps the place rockin', and sports on wide-screen TVs and weekly dart tournaments add to the mix. The place opens at 11:00 A.M. and closes when everyone goes home. You kind of figured that, didn't you?

Murphy's Restaurant & Pub
747 King Street, Boone, NC
(828) 264-5117
Murphy's has been a landmark in Boone for seven years. The drawing card at this busy place is its imaginative menu, which attracts a lively crowd to its four dining areas. Two bars offer a friendly place for a quick bite to eat, a little liquid refreshment, and a gander at a favorite sports channel on one of three wide-screen TVs.

(See our Restaurants chapter for more information on Murphy's.)

Regal's Litchfield Cinemas
210 New Market Center, Boone, NC
(828) 262-3800
This modern multiplex cinema on Boone's east side offers first-run features in seven theaters. The box office opens at 4:00 P.M. weekdays (1:00 P.M. Saturday and Sunday). If you go before 6:00 P.M., you'll catch the cheaper matinee rate.

CENTRAL MOUNTAINS
Buncombe County

Barley's Taproom
42 Biltmore Avenue, Asheville, NC
(828) 255-0504
Barley's Taproom is part of the renaissance of turn-of-the-century storefronts on Biltmore Avenue, just off Pack Square in downtown Asheville. Drawing on a grand mixture of the young professional crowd, visitors, good ol' boys, couples, rugby players, alternative types, and just about everyone else who lives in Asheville, Barley's offers forty beers on tap. On certain nights, jazz, acoustic guitar, and blues resonate over the convivial din. There is no cover charge.

Regional microbrewed beers are on tap from Highland Brewing Company, Asheville's first microbrewery, which is downstairs at Barley's.

The friendly staff, a combination of students, artists, actors, and jolly bartenders, will make you feel like a regular your first time there. This is the place where everyone comes before and after barhopping! But upstairs, Barley's has created its own new bar. This loft, where smoking is allowed, contains red pool tables, dartboards, and lots of young vivacious people. No food may be taken to this upstairs bar, so eat downstairs first before you go up to play.

Hungry after a late night out? In Asheville try Tupelo Honey Café on College Street or Akumi Sushi on Wall Street. Both stay open until 3:00 A.M. or 4:00 A.M. on the weekends.

Barley's is open from 11:00 A.M. to 2:00 A.M. daily. Lunch and dinner are served weekdays until midnight and Fridays and Saturdays until 1:00 A.M.

Beanstreets
3 Broadway, Asheville, NC
(828) 255-8180
Beanstreets is Asheville's preeminent coffeehouse. In addition to flavored coffees, cappuccino, lattes, and giant soup-bowl-sized hot chocolates, pastries, breads, and light sandwiches, the main thrust of Beanstreets is the atmosphere. The bizarre, eclectic clutter only enhances the acoustic guitar, Celtic sounds, and alternative poetry performances that accompany the gentle clank of coffee mugs. Local art and a hodgepodge of sofas, easy chairs, and whimsically painted tables and chairs seem to be popular with all walks of life: This corner coffeehouse is unlike anything in downtown Asheville.

Sit on a barstool at the large picture windows and watch the world go by or sit in the sunken "living room" for conversation or a game of chess, backgammon, or a board game or two. Watch local gurus plot astrological charts, students hunched over homework papers, couples discussing their romantic futures, businessmen and -women poring over data, and downtown residents grabbing their morning cup-a-joe.

In the summer outdoor tables attract a collection of dog owners and sun-worshippers. The staff and owners always have a kind word. Twirl the Magic Eight Ball at the cash register for the chance at a free cup of coffee.

Due to the erratic nature of nightclubs and bars, and their often quick turnover, we have listed the mainstays of various towns. Be sure to check the local papers of each town for an up-to-date listing. In Asheville the Mountain Express newspaper runs an excellent listing of concerts, locales, and movies.

Fine Arts Theater
36 Biltmore Avenue, Asheville, NC
(828) 232-1536
www.fineartstheater.com

Asheville's only downtown cinema is an ode to resplendent movie houses of the past. The Fine Arts Theater maintains a grand hall with art deco sconces, mauve stucco walls, and plush seats in the high-ceilinged main theater. Upstairs, another more intimate theater runs an alternate film offering. Fine foreign films, independents, and less-commercial American films are featured here.

Besides the usual sweets and popcorn, beer and hard ciders, coffee and biscotti are also sold. This cinema, a drama theater at its inception, and later an X-rated movie theater during a period of downtown Asheville decay, has been fully reconstructed and restored to lavish splendor. Go for the quality films, go for the atmosphere, go for the history!

Grey Eagle
185 Clingman Avenue, Asheville, NC
(828) 232-5800
www.greyeaglemusic.com

Located in the artsy River District, with working studios just a stone's throw away, Grey Eagle has a devoted audience. The club highlights singer-songwriters, regional bands, and top national acts like Arlo Guthrie, Doc Watson, Leo Kottke, and others. The bar serves local brews, and a cajun kitchen satisfies the hungry. It's the ultimate laid-back, quality music scene. If you're lucky, you can catch one of the occasional Latin dance evenings.

Jack of the Wood
95 Patton Avenue, Asheville, NC
(828) 252-5445

This English-style pub, which features darts, long wooden tables and benches, and a small raised stage, is a great drop-by nightspot for any season. Celtic music jams have people bringing their own instruments on certain nights of the week, while regular groups, ranging from folk to Celtic, to balladeers, to bluegrass take the stage on the weekends. Bring your Greenman Ale (made by Jack of the Wood's own brewers) outside to the benches, and you'll be sure to hear the tales of all sorts of interesting folks.

Magnolia's
26 Walnut Street, Asheville, NC
(828) 251-5211

This raw bar and grille turns into one big party when the sun goes down on the weekends. Sometimes Asheville blues legend Kat Williams takes the stage, or other bands play rousting cover tunes, while patrons push away tables and chairs on the enclosed patio to dance into the night.

The Metro
38 North French Broad Avenue, Asheville, NC
(828) 258-2027

This club complex actually includes two more venues: Patio Cabaret, with a cabaret drag show on Sundays, and Hairspray Cafe, with a long bar and pool tables. Metro, which is the largest space of the three, features a spacious dance floor and columned bar. Though it is billed as a gay club, it's not exclusive. So no matter what your proclivity, if you're dying for a night of shaking your booty with a fun crowd, look no further. Musically themed evenings feature Techno, Industrial, Jungle, Garage, Goth, and others.

Old Europe Coffee House
18 Battery Park Avenue, Asheville, NC
(828) 252-0001

In the warm weather this cafe, run by native Hungarian Zoltan Vetro and his wife

Melinda, doubles in size when tables and chairs spread out over the sidewalk. Patrons—regulars and tourists alike—enjoy the authentic European outdoor cafe atmosphere late into the evening. You can order from a number of beautiful and sumptuous tortes and desserts, coffee drinks, wines, beers, and liquors. The helpful staff will also box up goodies to go.

The Orange Peel
101 Biltmore Avenue
(828) 225-5851
theorangepeel.net

This is the music hall that Asheville has long been waiting for. A nonsmoking venue that can hold up to 1,000, it now pulls in national and international musicians but also has a steady stream of famed local and regional performers on any given week. Longtime nightclub owners Jack and Lesley Groetsch owned the Howlin' Wolf in New Orleans for more than 12 years. They've done the old Orange Peel (a famed music hall of yore in Asheville) justice with a juicy high-tech sound system, lighting, a grand stage, plenty of dancing room, and a long chrome bar. There's plenty to do besides dance . . . with a gallery called Ring-Dang-Do, featuring funky outsider art and eclectic collectibles, a counter for Orange Peel merchandise, and bar stool seating from which to view the dance floor.

Stella Blue
31 Patton Avenue, Asheville, NC
(828) 236-2424

This spunky club has come a long way. Although the decor is fluorescent paint against black with pool tables in the back, this music hall catches some great bands. The dance floor is adequate, though you practically have to walk through it to reach the bar on entering the club. Well-known regional bands play here, as well as eclectic groups from all over. Nationally known hip dance bands like Mandorico and Los Straitjackets seem to perform on a fairly regular basis.

Tressa's Downtown Jazz & Blues
28 Broadway, Asheville, NC
(828) 254-7072

The New Orleans–style jazz bar, a private club that welcomes guests for a nominal fee, has all the ambience, musical variety, and the spectacular patrons of a venue in a major cosmopolitan center. Nut brown walls, a long oak bar, original pressed-tin ceiling, and linen-covered individual tables, including two window tables, make up the foundation of Tressa's, which is in a building put up in 1913. The fully stocked bar, mirrored and framed with columns, offers exquisite martinis, spicy Bloody Marys, wines, champagnes, and many other cocktails.

Music ranges from blues and jazz to Latin groove, with a brigade of live bands every week. Co-owners Tressa and Terry stir up liquid concoctions while dressed in elegant evening garb. But you'll be sweating away on the crowded dance floor or straining to hear your date over the cheerful din. Call ahead for the music schedule and for information concerning membership if you'll be around for a while. The VIP Lounge and the Breathe oxygen bar at Tressa's upstairs is an elegant new addition to this place. First, it's nonsmoking; second, it's much quieter and less populated than the party downstairs. There's also plenty of seating either by the windows, overlooking Broadway, by the nifty fireplace, at the chic bar, or past the oxygen bar with intimate tables. Enjoy an oxygen boost with "flavored" mixtures for 10- to 20-minute intervals. It may look silly with neon tubes up your nostrils, but customers swear they're more energetic afterward. Upstairs is open Wednesday through Saturday and definitely worth a visit. This is one place where you will want

Often bars or dance venues will advertise themselves as "private clubs." Generally a member can sign you in as a guest, or you might be charged a nominal fee for "membership" at the door.

to toss on a silk scarf, a bevy of beads, a dress shirt—all without pretension, but for the fun of it.

Rutherford County

Lake Lure Tours
U.S. Highway 64/74-A, Lake Lure, NC
(828) 625-0077, (877) FUN-4-ALL
Lake Lure Tours offers twilight cruises beginning at 6:00 P.M. and dinner cruises departing at 6:00 and 7:00 P.M., seven days a week, March through November, weather permitting. Reservations are required.

Transylvania County

Earthshine
Golden Road, Lake Toxaway, NC
(828) 862-4207
When you have dinner at this resort, you get entertainment that alternates between folk sing-alongs and folk dance to interactive Cherokee programs and campfire tales (see our Resorts chapter). Reservations are required.

Essence of Thyme
37 East Main Street, Brevard, NC
(828) 884-7171
Entertainment at Essence of Thyme, a coffeehouse on Main Street, is very eclectic and often very fine. The musicians and other entertainers who perform here do so for no charge (there's a tip jar), so they tend to practice their arts here when they

Don't let the fear of encountering smoke-filled interiors prevent you from going to hear live music; some music and dance venues won't allow smoking or confine it to a particular room or outdoor area.

have a Friday or Saturday night free of a paying gig. Therefore the establishment often doesn't know who will be performing until the actual week of the event.

Things usually get underway around 7:00 or 7:30 P.M. and go on until about 9:00 P.M. in winter and until 10:00 P.M. in summer. When the entertainment is firmed up, it's posted in the front window.

Two-Step Junction
Henderson Highway (U.S. Highway 64), Pisgah Forest, NC
(828) 862-4051
This is the place for dancing of all kinds: swing, two-step, line dancing, round dance, waltz, and cha-cha. Lessons are offered Tuesday through Thursday from 7:00 to 9:00 P.M. Friday and Saturday nights a disc jockey plays the music for open dancing until around midnight. If you don't dance but would like to learn—or just want to improve your style—the Junction offers lessons. Call for more information.

SOUTHERN MOUNTAINS
Cherokee County/ Clay County

John C. Campbell School Dance Events
1 Folk School Road, Brasstown, NC
(828) 837-2775, (800) FOLK-SCH
Square and contra dances, clogging, and circle dances with live musicians and callers are held here both on weekends and during the week. You also can learn English country dances and Balkan and other folk dances. A free introduction to contra, square, and circle dances with recorded music is held every Tuesday night from 7:00 to 8:00 P.M. for folk school students and interested local residents. Community contra and square dances with live music are held twice a month, usually on the first and third Saturday from 8:00 to 11:00 P.M. Call for details.

ℹ️ *The view from Henderson County's Jump Off Rock stretches across the high plateau of Henderson and Transylvania Counties to the ascending peaks of Pisgah Forest. Jump Off Rock got its name more than 300 years ago when a young Cherokee chieftain and the woman he loved used to meet here. When he was called away to tribal wars, she would climb to this overlook to watch for his return, often singing an Indian love call—but there was never an answer. Finally, returning warriors brought news of her lover's death in battle.*

At twilight, it's said, she climbed to the rock, sang a few notes, and jumped off. Lore has it that on some moonlit nights you can still hear her song. To reach the rock from Hendersonville, drive out Fifth Avenue West, which turns into Laurel Park Drive, and follow the road until it ends at Jump Off Rock.

Cherokee Indian Reservation

Harrah's Cherokee Casino
777 Casino Drive, Cherokee, NC
(800) HARRAHS
Open seven days a week, 24 hours a day, this new and popular casino, three football fields big, has 2,300 video gaming machines, three restaurants, a gift shop, a child-care facility, and a 1,500-seat theater with big-name, live entertainment. Tribal Bingo is also available in Cherokee. (See our Attractions chapter for details.)

Haywood County

Bogart's Restaurant and Tavern
222 South Main Street, Waynesville, NC
(828) 452-1313
No matter what type of music you like, you'll eventually hear it if you drop into Bogart's for a couple of Friday or Saturday nights. A little bit of everything—folk, country, rock, and blues—is played here, though not every week. It's a fun watering hole, with a cozy upstairs loft area.

Carolina Nights
3732 Soco Road, Maggie Valley, NC
(828) 926-8822, (888) 622-7469
www.maggievalleyusa.com
Full-scale productions of country music, gospel, and pop, along with magicians and comedians can be enjoyed here every night from spring until fall and on weekends in the winter. Closed on Sunday. Tickets may be purchased for the dinner and show, or just the show.

Diamond K Dance Ranch
1 Playhouse Drive, Maggie Valley, NC
(828) 926-7735
Here you can enjoy country music and dancing on the fabulous 2,000-square-foot dance floor. Dancing lessons are offered on Friday evenings. They are open on Friday and Saturday evenings. Admission is under $10 for adults and no charge for children under 12. A snack bar is available, and no alcohol is served.

Maggie Valley Opry House
3605 Soco Road, Maggie Valley, NC
(828) 926-9336
From May through October, bluegrass, mountain music, and dancing take place beginning at 8:00 P.M. nightly. Maggie Valley is the home of Raymond Fairchild, five-time world champion banjo picker. He and his special guest performers are always dropping in to keep everyone's toes tapping.

Saratoga's Cafe
2723 Soco Road, Maggie Valley, NC
(828) 926-1448
You can enjoy great food and live music in the publike atmosphere of Saratoga's Cafe on Friday and Saturday nights. Wednes-

Bars here have a 2:00 A.M. last call, so night owls, start early!

day is jazz night with the famed house band. There is no cover charge, but do call for reservations.

Shephard's Thunder Ridge
2701 Soco Road, Maggie Valley, NC
(828) 926-9470
Thunder Ridge, next door to Saratoga's Cafe, is Maggie Valley's newest nightspot, presenting world-class country and rock bands. If you like this type of music, you'll enjoy it even more due to the club's spacious dance floor and excellent sound sys-

tem. Special guest bands frequently appear here. A DJ is always keeping it alive and jumping. Open on Thursday, Friday, and Saturday evenings.

The Stompin' Ground
3113 Soco Road, U.S. Highway 19,
Maggie Valley, NC
(828) 926-1288
www.stompingroundpresents.com
From spring through fall every Friday and Saturday from 8:00 to 11:00 P.M., The Stompin' Ground, going strong since 1982, offers music and dancing in "the mountain clogging capital of the world." No alcohol is served at this 100-seat music hall, so it's fun for the whole family. Just come in and stomp!

RESORTS ⛰

Resorts have been a part of this region for as long as some of the towns have been here. They weren't quite as fancy as some of the vacation spots we have now, but, just like today's, they drew flocks of visitors seeking the relaxing and restorative beauty of the mountains.

As early as 1827, when this area was still known simply as "The Wilderness," wealthy planters from Charleston were building large summer homes in Flat Rock, which would become Henderson County. They realized (though they didn't know why) that malaria, which plagued the coast, was not a problem here. Twenty years later, in 1847, a number of these folks built the Flat Rock Hotel, later called the Farmer Hotel, after its new owner, Squire Henry T. Farmer. Today it is known as the Woodfield Inn, an elegant place where people still relax in their rocking chairs on its wide veranda (see our Bed-and-Breakfasts and Country Inns chapter).

Similarly, two entrepreneurs purchased 839 acres in 1876 in Macon County for the sole purpose of establishing a town in what they thought would become the major population center of the mountains. In a brochure published that same year, these men claimed that there was "no better climate for health, comfort and enjoyment" than in what would become the upscale resort town we fondly know as "Heavenly Highlands." By 1879 they had opened the Smith Hotel to tourists here. It's still in business today, although it's now named Highlands Inn. Similar stories of countless old inns and resorts prevail throughout these mountains.

PRICE CODE

Most of the accommodations in these chapters will accept major credit cards; we have noted those that accept none. Rates are based on double occupancy.

$	$60 to $80
$$	$81 to $100
$$$	$101 to $120
$$$$	$121 and more

Amenities have changed with the times. Golf courses, swimming pools, Jacuzzis, and the like have been added, but such attractions can be found almost anywhere in the country. The unique allures of Western North Carolina's mountains as a resort area are the same as they have been for more than a century: a mild, healthful climate with four distinct and equally lovely seasons; botanical diversity unmatched in America; rock-strewn rivers and streams that'll sing you to sleep; mountains older than time stretching out to forever; more unspoiled wild areas than you could ever explore; and people who take the time to be polite.

In selecting the resorts for this book, we focused on those that could be "desti-nations." In other words, there is enough to do in these places that, if you so choose, you can arrive and not feel it nec-essary to seek diversions outside the resort for quite a while. With all the attrac-tions in the surrounding areas, you might be cutting yourself short, but that was our criterion. We think you'll like these selec-tions, but, as usual, there are others just as interesting around the bend. Let us know what you discover.

NORTHERN MOUNTAINS

Madison County

Wolf Laurel Resort   **$$$–$$$$**
Rt. 3, off U.S. Highway 23 N., Marshall, NC
(828) 680-9777, (800) 221-0409
www.wolfelaurelresort.com
Spread below 5,600-foot Big Bald Moun-tain, Wolf Laurel Resort is a 5,000-acre pri-

vate resort community about 15 minutes north of Mars Hill. The resort is also open to mountain vacationers. Play 18 holes of golf on a challenging mountaintop course full of ridges, hills, and winding curves. The ski slopes of Ski the Wolf are just next door. (See our Golf and Skiing chapters.) Two tennis courts provide sport and recreation, as does hiking in the surrounding areas. A portion of the Appalachian Trail passes just a mile away. Fish in a mountain stream, swim, or picnic in a wooded glade—this resort uses the surrounding environment to its great benefit.

If you'd like to visit Wolf Laurel, a variety of vacation lodgings are available, from privately owned rental units ranging from one- or two-bedroom condominium suites with kitchenettes to private homes with one to five bedrooms. A clubhouse restaurant is also available.

From Asheville take U.S. 23 N. and follow Wolf Laurel signs, which you begin seeing after the Mars Hill exit.

Watauga County

Chetola Resort $$$-$$$$
North Main Street off U.S. Highway 221, Blowing Rock, NC
(828) 295-5500, (800) 243-8652
www.chetola.com

Chetola is the Cherokee word for "haven of rest." And as you approach the resort lodge down the country lane that winds around serene Chetola Lake, you will understand the inspiration for the name.

This fine resort just outside Blowing Rock (off the N.C. Highway 321 bypass) has a long history. The estate was first purchased by Lot Estes back in 1846 for a mere $5.00. He called it Silver Lake. The property changed hands and served the next 50 years primarily as a way station for coach traffic. Then at the turn of the century, as roads improved, the inn became a fashionable accommodation for lowlanders escaping the oppressive heat of the Deep South. One such lowlander,

Alabama lumberman W. W. Stringfellow, fell in love with the High Country, purchased the Silver Lake property, renamed it "Chetola," and built the fine manor house that remains today. The property was sold once again, in 1924, to J. Luther Snyder, known as the "Coca-Cola King of the Carolinas." Snyder bought additional adjoining property and continued to improve the estate. He built houses on the property for his children and their families and added a swimming pool and bowling alley.

The estate found new life in 1982 as Chetola Resort. Local business people envisioned bringing the splendor of Chetola to the public. Developers of the present resort have been mindful of the tradition and history of Chetola, incorporating this legacy whenever possible. The marvelous manor house is now home to the Manor House Restaurant, its ambience enhanced by the rich architectural character of the structure. Snyder's Soda Shoppe features sandwiches, burgers, and ice-cream specialties. It is located in the recreation center. A 42-room Chetola Lodge and Conference Center includes spacious suites and professional meeting and conference space.

The resort offers a wide variety of diversions: boating on seven-acre Chetola Lake, hiking on the trails of Moses Cone Memorial Park just over the hill, cross-country skiing on the nearby Blue Ridge Parkway, and tennis on Chetola's five courts. Highlands Sports & Recreation Center at Chetola houses an indoor pool, a fitness center, whirlpool, sauna, massage therapy, body wraps, and regulation racquetball courts. Premier golf and skiing resorts are just minutes away in nearby Blowing Rock, Boone, and the Banner Elk area. You can fill your days and nights entirely with the luxury of Chetola. (See our Golf and Skiing chapters for more information.)

If you become enamored of your surroundings, you can make Chetola home. Condominiums are also available for purchase.

Green Park Inn & Resort $$-$$$
U.S. Highway 321, Blowing Rock, NC
(828) 295-3141, (800) 852-2462
www.greenparkinn.com

Green Park is one of the South's oldest luxury resorts. Established in 1882 and listed in the National Register of Historic Places, it's situated 4,300 feet above sea level in the Blue Ridge Mountains, affording guests an atmosphere of breathtaking splendor and relaxation. The inn has 85 guest rooms and offers numerous amenities. The furnishings and spaciousness reflect a time when heads of state, noted actors, playwrights, and business leaders were guests of the Green Park. Franklin Roosevelt, Calvin Coolidge, J. D. Rockefeller, and more recently Newt Gingrich, have brought their entourages to the Green Park for lavish galas.

Green Park's restaurant, the Laurel Room, serves a breakfast buffet seven days a week. The Divide Tavern, which features an extensive wine list, has the ambience of a classic English pub, complete with billiards and a sporting throw of darts. It's a popular spot for relaxing after a round of golf or tennis at the adjacent Blowing Rock Country Club, a private club where Green Park guests have privileges.

Only 2 miles from Blowing Rock, the Green Park Inn offers easy access to all the area's attractions: Hiking on the Blue Ridge Parkway or taking in a view from the town's namesake—Blowing Rock—are two options. You can reach the inn by heading south on U.S. 321 out of downtown Blowing Rock; it's just less than 2 miles on the left.

Suites and single guest rooms are available in several combinations.

Hound Ears Club $$$$
N.C. Highway 105, between Boone and Blowing Rock
(828) 963-4321
www.houndears.com

Cradled in a splendid valley of the magnificent northern mountains south of Boone off N.C. 105 S. is Hound Ears Club, which takes its curious name from a prominent rock formation on the ridge high above the club. You can reach the club on N.C. 105, 6 miles from Boone. (A large sign will alert you.)

A scenic, 18-hole golf course, complete with waterfalls, lakes, and streams, makes an interesting challenge for avid golfers. Tennis players can take to one of the six clay or two hard-surface courts here. Tennis instruction is available for all ages, or you can just enjoy a leisurely game with friends.

The swimming pool at Hound Ears is unique and secluded, tucked back into the mountain in a natural grotto. The huge rock grotto surrounding the pool and pavilion area creates a natural swimming spot with an important manmade comfort: The pool is heated to a constant 85 degrees.

If you like horseback riding, stables and bridle trails are just a few miles away at Moses Cone Memorial Park.

The long-range panoramic view from the balcony guest rooms in the Hound Ears lodge is incredible. The tastefully decorated double bedrooms provide all the amenities, including maid service. Modified American Plan rates and special golf and tennis package rates are available at various times of the year.

If you decide that a weekend is too short a stay, other long-term accommodations are available at Hound Ears. You can choose from Clubhouse Suites, privately owned condominiums, and chalets on the lovely wooded hillside near the golf course. You can also purchase property and make engaging Hound Ears your home year-round.

Westglow Spa $$$$
2845 U.S. Highway 221 S., Blowing Rock, NC
(828) 295-4463, (800) 562-0807
www.westglow.com

This is a year-round European-style spa set in an elegant, historic plantation-style mansion that looms over the highway on its green hill. The object here is to pamper, rejuvenate, and reenergize yourself. The spa's program includes a variety of treatments—body sloughing, aromatherapy, herbal body wraps, Parisian body polish, facials, foot reflexology, and body massage. Fitness programs are also a large part of the schedule. Weekly weight management programs that include nutrition and diet assessment are also offered.

A poolside buffet lunch is open to the public, but be sure and make a reservation beforehand.

Choose from a day sampler to all-inclusive overnight stays. Rates vary according to the kind of treatment and length of stay.

Yonahlossee Resort & Club   **$$$$**
226 Oakley Green, Boone, NC
(828) 963–6400, (800) 962–1986
www.yonahlossee.com
The emphasis at Yonahlossee is on horseback riding and tennis. Both recreations are taken seriously here, and this former girls' camp with its spectacularly lush, secluded 300 acres is the perfect setting for both. The tennis and equestrian community of Yonahlossee, Cherokee for "trail of the bear," is protected on three sides by Moses Cone Memorial Park. Property developers have taken great care to preserve the pristine quality of the land.

As a guest of the resort, you can indulge in a variety of pleasurable pursuits. The award-winning Racquet Club at Yonahlossee won the tennis industry's prestigious Court of the Year award in 1989. Six outdoor clay courts are surrounded by large viewing decks. Bad weather doesn't stall tennis enthusiasts here: Three indoor Deco-Turf courts with large climate-controlled viewing areas assure tennis play summer or winter, rain or shine.

Yonahlossee's Saddle Club continues over 60 years of tradition and accommodates the serious rider as well as the novice. A large 28-stall barn, spacious tack rooms, generously sized stalls, a lounge, and wash stalls provide all the necessary convenience any horse person (or horse!) could want. There are also miles of trails, an outdoor arena, and a cross-country jumping course. If you vacation with your horse, you can board him here while you visit. Year-round boarding is also available.

You can also take advantage of the outdoors at Yonahlossee's small lake, an ideal place for canoeing, fishing, and swimming. Or swim inside in the lovely 75-foot indoor swimming pool. Other golf and ski areas are about 20 minutes in either direction.

Accommodations include fully equipped, beautifully appointed cottage suites nestled in the woods of Yonahlossee. These casually elegant, rustic cabins have fireplaces and private decks. The resort also has two- and three-bedroom town homes in contemporary designs of wood and glass, many with long-range views of the surrounding mountains.

The Gamekeeper Restaurant is on the resort grounds and has a tempting menu studded with exotic wild game dishes and other fine cuisine (see our Restaurants chapter).

Yancey County

Clear Creek Guest Ranch   **$$$$**
100 Clear Creek Drive, Burnsville, NC
(828) 675–4510, (800) 651–4510
www.clearcreekranch.com
The Clear Creek Guest Ranch is truly a resort for the entire family. Don't expect to be lounging around the pool with cocktails at this resort. Owners Rex and Aileen Frederick have created so many fun-filled diversions that you probably won't even get to the heated pool until well after twilight.

Able to accommodate up to 50 people at a time in one- to three-bedroom units, the ranch welcomes families, couples, and groups, as well as individuals, because you won't be on your own here for long. You will have plenty of opportunities to join in group activities such as horseback riding, tubing, white-water rafting, hiking, barbecues, and other fun. The family-style seating in the dining room of the main lodge, a grand hall with a rustic adjacent living room area, ensures that you will get to know your neighbors over breakfast and other meals.

The atmosphere of Clear Creek is casual. Rex and Aileen stroll the grounds in jeans and make a concerted effort to make everyone feel at home. They are hands-on hosts and enjoy spending time with guests, be it at mealtimes helping plan guests' itineraries with them, over a game of checkers, or simply sitting out on one of the spacious front porches for a chat.

At an elevation of 3,000 feet, the ranch perches at the foot of a mountain range and offers a splendid view of Mount Mitchell and the Pisgah National Forest environs. The guest units, built of rough-hewn log siding, are spacious and modern, with porches and rocking chairs outside each door. Air-conditioning and ceiling fans in each room are perfect for sultry summer nights, and large pine beds, covered with fluffy pillows and patchwork-quilt comforters keep you toasty warm on cooler evenings. The Fredericks like to keep life simple, so you will only find one television and a telephone in the main lodge. There is cable, though, and a fax for those who need to do a bit of business anyway.

Most of your day will be spent on the trails, either riding (Western saddle) on the morning ride, afternoon ride, or all-day ride, led by experienced wranglers (also students, many from a college specializing in equestrian studies); tubing down the South Toe River; white-water rafting with one of the local outfitters; golfing at the nearby Mount Mitchell Golf Course; hiking some of the many trails of the Pisgah National Forest; or sightseeing.

The Fredericks arrange trips to local artisan studios and into the larger communities of Asheville, Spruce Pine, and beyond. If you plan on staying for several days, you will experience at least one, if not more, barbecues at the Toe River, where the Fredericks set up a large picnic dinner, replete with tablecloths and dishes, under a cozy wooded shelter at the South Toe River swimming hole. "Brunch on the Mountain" and grilling by the pool are also weekly features.

Counselors offer special activities for children between the ages of 5 and 12 during the summer. Ping-Pong, volleyball, pool, and video games are provided in a special building "just for kids."

The live-in chef and his helpers, usually college students from all over the country, whip up three hearty meals a day for guests, including homemade soups, breads, pastries, and main dishes. The chef will pack picnic lunches for guests to take with them on their outings, and after several hours of trail riding, tubing, or hiking, you'll be ready for lemonade, iced tea, fruit, and cookies provided in the dining room in the afternoon.

A constant supply of fresh coffee, hot chocolate, and juice in the main lodge came in handy after our evening swim under the stars. It gave us just enough energy to climb into the hot tub for a steaming soak, amidst vapor mixed with moonlight.

CENTRAL MOUNTAINS

Buncombe County

Grove Park Inn Resort & Spa $$$-$$$$
290 Macon Avenue, Asheville, NC
(828) 252-2711, (800) 438-5800
www.groveparkinn.com
The Grove Park Inn is one of the premier landmarks of the city of Asheville. Kings, U.S. presidents, inventors, golf legends, famous actors, and writers (Eleanor Roosevelt, Franklin Roosevelt, Harry Houdini, George Bush, Henry Ford, Thomas Edison, and Mikhail Baryshnikov to mention a few) have all passed through the massive stone portico of the Grove Park Inn.

The inn, built in 1913 from tremendous boulders blasted out of nearby Sunset Mountain, was an engineering marvel and the personal vision of dynamic entrepreneur E. W. Grove, who invented Grove's Chill Tonic, a drink claiming to have "medicinal" value for many aches and pains. He came to Asheville during the

CLOSE-UP

The Mystery of the Pink Lady

It's been said that there is a sad but gentle ghost residing within the gray granite walls of Asheville's historic Grove Park Inn, known as the Pink Lady. She has been seen, felt, and experienced by hotel employees and guests for more than a half-century. The mystery centers around Room 545 in the Main Inn, where employees, guests, and repair workers have seen or heard ghostly phenomena, including unexplained chills and rushes of cold air and the feeling of a presence of some type, prompting the hotel's engineering facilities manager in 1995 to write: "I was on my way back to check a recent bathtub resurfacing in Room 545. As I approached the room, my hair suddenly lifted from my scalp and stood on end on my arms. Simultaneously I felt a very uncomfortable cold rush across my whole body." His words echoed those of a painter who had worked in the hotel in the 1950s. Neither of these employees knew of the other's experiences.

Other employees as well as guests have mentioned that they have seen the luminous form of a lady dressed in pink party clothes, whisking around corners of the grand hotel. The legend dates back to senior employees' recollections of a young woman, dressed in pink, who fell to her death in the Palm Court Atrium around 1920, several stories below Room 545. The manager of the Grove Park Inn, who has seen the Pink Lady several times over the past five years, explains: "It's like a real dense smoke—a pinkish pastel that just flows. It's a real gentle spirit, whatever it is." And still to this day it remains an unexplained presence at the Grove Park Inn Resort.

city's turn-of-the-century boom period, attracted by the natural beauty of the area and the city's possibilities. With the Grove Park Inn, E. W. Grove left not only an architectural legacy to the city of Asheville, but, by example, a spirit of business foresight and daring that continues to define the unique character of our small mountain city.

The inn has had continuous success through the years. The Sammons Corporation acquired the Grove Park Inn in the 1950s, and the resulting growth and innovation spearheaded by this ownership continues in the Grove tradition. Two new wings, designed to maintain the architectural integrity of the original structure, have been added. The 202-room Sammons Wing, built in 1984, also houses a gallery of specialty shops. In 1988 the Vanderbilt Wing was completed. It has 166 rooms, 28 of which comprise the private guest rooms and suites of the Club Floor. The original stone edifice is composed of 142 rooms.

The inn is furnished with antique pieces in the rich oak texture and artistic line of the Arts and Crafts style, so popular in the early 1900s. The inn's Great Hall is dominated by fireplaces at either end. Measuring 6 feet deep, 6 feet high, and 12 feet wide, these hearths are truly room size in proportion. This majestic old inn with its distinctive red-shingled roof sits commandingly on Sunset Mountain. With the lush golf lawn spread out before it, it makes a stunning visual impression on the approach from Kimberly Avenue.

Open year-round, the inn is alive with activity. Golf has always played a major role in the history of the Grove Park Inn. The 18-hole course, designed in the 1920s by renowned golf architect Donald Ross, has hosted many of golf's greats: Bobby Jones, Arnold Palmer, Jack Nicklaus, Ben Hogan, Sam Snead, Fuzzy Zoeller, and Doug Sanders, to name a few. A comprehensive golf program is administered by the inn's golf professional. There is also a well-stocked sports shop for your convenience.

The recent addition of a 40,000-square-foot spa has added yet another dimension to the grand hotel. (See our Close-up.)

Other recreation at the inn includes an indoor and an outdoor pool, racquetball and squash courts, and three indoor and six outdoor tennis courts, two of them clay. A tennis pro is on staff to give instruction and lessons. The inn also has a health club for aerobics, weight training, sauna, and whirlpool treatments and massage. In 2001 the inn added a world-class spa, built partially underground between the two residential wings.

Forty-two meeting and conference rooms and 50,000 square feet of meeting space are available at the Grove Park Inn. Professional coordination and technical support serve numerous business, convention, and reunion groups. Other guest services include child care (with a children's activity program), laundry, valet, shoeshine, and room service.

Dining is an experience at the Grove Park Inn. The Blue Ridge Dining Room, near the Great Hall, is a family place. Good, basic American cooking, prime rib, chicken and pasta, wonderful soups, and other traditional entrees are available in a casual atmosphere. A scrumptious breakfast buffet is offered here seven days a week, and the famous Friday night seafood buffet is a winner.

Chops, the inn's elegant outdoor restaurant, needs no decor, only the colors of the evening sky. This new addition features all that is excellent in steak. Evening entertainment of jazz, pop, and classical music fills the air in the casual atmosphere of the terrace. For other fine dining, try Horizons at the Grove Park Inn. A pianist plays classical selections and light jazz for your pleasure. Reservations are required for Horizons and Chops.

There are a variety of accommodation packages at the Grove Park Inn, and any choice is an indulgence in this marvelous historic hotel. In addition to golf and tennis packages, Adventure Weekends offer planned events ranging from stand-up comedy to big band and jazz celebrations. Christmas is a 40-day Grove Park Inn celebration that starts the day after Thanksgiving and runs through a rousing celebration of the New Year.

Henderson County

Highland Lake Inn—A Country Retreat $$$
Highland Lake Road, Flat Rock, NC
(828) 693-6812, (800) 762-1376
www.hlinn.com
This country retreat offers an expanse of 180 wooded and pastured acres. Its award-winning restaurant offers breakfast, lunch, and dinner. Special events are offered monthly as well as a sought-after Sunday brunch. The *Wine Spectator*'s Award of Excellence is only one of the many accolades heaped upon the restaurant and the inn.

You can have your choice of accommodations. There are 20 rooms with private baths in the lodge, which has a spacious lobby with a large fireplace and an atmosphere that is modern and rustic at the same time. Each cabin duplex has one large room with a fireplace and one small room; each unit has its own entrance and private bath. The "inn" at Highland Lake has romantic rooms with fireplaces and whirlpools. There are also five cottages that range in size from two bedrooms and two baths to four bedrooms and two baths. They have lovely names: Waterlily, Honeysuckle, Periwinkle, Dogwood, and Azalea. And, yes, you'll find all these wonderful plants in profusion here, for Highland Lake is known for its gardens. Not only are they pleasing to see, but the organic plots, which include berries and herbs, also provide much of the food, including delicious salads and grilled vegetables, that has made the inn's healthful, gourmet meals some of the most popular in Henderson County (see our Restaurants chapter).

For recreation, you can choose from tennis, swimming in an Olympic-size pool or in a lake, canoeing, fishing, or playing volleyball, basketball, horseshoes, or beach ball games. A hundred acres of walking trails will take you through wildflower meadows and under venerable oaks. Just across the way, there's a nine-hole golf course and—remember this is "Historic Flat Rock"—the Carl Sandburg Home, St. John in the Wilderness Church, and the Flat Rock Playhouse are also just minutes away (see our Attractions and Arts and Culture chapters).

To get to the Highland Lake Inn—a perfect place for business conferences, group retreats, and family reunions as well as family or personal vacations—take U.S. 25 S. out of Hendersonville for about 5 miles and turn left onto Highlands Lake Road at the Pinecrest Presbyterian Church. The entrance to the inn is at the waterfall.

Rutherford County

The Chalet Club   **$$$$**
532 Washburn Road, Lake Lure, NC
(828) 625-9315, (800) 336-3309
www.chaletclub.com
This secluded mountainside resort offers a lodge and seven spacious cottages. Fabulous views can be enjoyed from the large balconies. This family-owned and -operated resort pampers its guests with three meals a day of contemporary southern cooking. The meals are served buffet style in the dining room. Available activities are fishing, boating, water skiing, tennis, swimming, and hiking on 7 miles of private trails.

Transylvania County

Earthshine   **$$$$**
Golden Road, Lake Toxaway, NC
(828) 862-4207
www.earthshinemtnlodge.com
The environmentally friendly simplicity makes Earthshine a wholly different kind of resort, but one that has gained national fame. Accounts of visits and articles on this unique destination frequently appear in the national media, and the L.L. Bean company has used Earthshine more than once as the setting for the photos in its famous catalog.

The cedar-log lodge, with its eight guest rooms and massive rock fireplace, was built by hand in 1988 by owners Marion Boatwright and Kim Mauer (with a little help from their friends) on the site of a 100-year-old homestead bordering Pisgah Forest. Each room has a private bath and a "little house on the prairie loft" that makes it large enough for a family. Sunrise Cottage, a classic chalet, is also available for guests.

But as fine and old-fashioned comfortable as the place is, the real attraction seems to be getting back to a simpler time and relating differently to the world and yourself. Earthshine's 70 acres adjoins Pisgah National Forest, and you can spend your time here hiking and horseback riding through forests and meadows. Or try challenging yourself on their high ropes course and then take on some real rock climbing. You can also learn homesteading skills, such as animal care and organic gardening. If you come in May, you can help shear sheep. Children can travel back through time 150 years when they work and play at Earthshine's pioneer homestead or its secret Cherokee hideout,

Transylvania County: The Pretty Place

This is one of those spots known more by locals than by tourists. Well-attended Easter sunrise services are held here, as are many weddings. The waves-of-mountains vista is framed by an open-sided chapel, called Symmes Chapel, with steeply sloping tiers of seats fitted to the side of the mountain. The view is—we aren't exaggerating—truly breathtaking.

To find the Pretty Place, which is part of the facilities of Camp Greenville, a summer camp, take U.S. 276 out of Brevard toward Greenville, South Carolina. Drive 12 miles until you see the turnoff at the YMCA CAMP GREENVILLE sign on the left. Follow the signs for about 4.5 miles, enter the camp, and drive to the chapel. It's a side trip well worth taking. However, no picnicking is allowed in the area.

where they'll learn ancient games, dances, work skills, and forest ways. They can also take a real wilderness trek—bushwhacking, creek hiking, and learning to build fires. On most Sunday nights kids can learn what it's like to camp out in a barn loft. Cowpokes who aren't quite ready for the trail can hone their skills taking ring rides.

In the evenings you can join in rousing sing-alongs, mountain dances, Cherokee ceremonies, games, and other entertainment. Or you can choose to simply relax in a hammock or rocking chair. Earthshine is also available for family reunions, weddings, training retreats, and seminars, and it operates a year-round outdoor education program for students in grade four and higher.

Rates include lodging and three mighty meals a day, prepared mostly from scratch (see our Restaurants chapter). There's an extra charge for horseback riding and the high ropes course.

To find Earthshine take U.S. 64 W. out of Brevard for about 11 miles. Turn right at Thorpe's Convenience Store (Earthshine signs will mark the way). Go almost a mile and turn left onto a gravel road for 1.6 miles. Turn right at Earthshine's drive and go up the hill.

The Greystone Inn $$$$
Off U.S. Highway 64, Lake Toxaway, NC
(828) 966-4700, (800) 824-5766
www.greystoneinn.com
When you really want to reward yourself or celebrate something simply wonderful, spend a weekend or a week or two at the Greystone Inn.

First, a little history: A hundred years ago, a group called the Lake Toxaway Company built a 640-acre lake in the high mountains between Brevard and Cashiers that they called "America's Switzerland." There they created a five-story, 500-room hotel out of the finest woods and with the most modern conveniences, such as electric lights, bathrooms, elevators, steam heat, refrigeration, and long-distance telephone and telegraph service. They offered European cuisine, full orchestras for dancing and lavish balls, and all those outdoor sports we enjoy today: tennis, horseback riding, sailing, fishing, and more.

Such a grand place attracted the likes of Henry Ford, Thomas Edison, John D.

When our long-lasting, colorful autumn season finally ends, and the leaves float from the trees, the best views of the mountains suddenly appear. Clean, picture-perfect streams sparkle along roadsides; waterfalls tumble over icicle-covered rocks, and with summer haze a thing of the past, Blue Ridge Parkway views, unhampered by foliage, stretch forever. Come and see!

Rockefeller, Harvey Firestone, the Wanna-makers, and the Dukes. It also attracted Savannah native Lucy Armstrong Moltz. In 1915 she moved into her "small summer place" on the lake—a magnificent six-level, 16,000-square-foot Swiss chalet that was indeed small compared to her 30,000-square-foot marble mansion in Savannah, which would one day become a home for Armstrong College. But only a year later, in July 1917, a devastating flood weakened Lake Toxaway's dam. The following August it gave way, wreaking havoc below the resort's lake all the way into South Carolina and exposing the huge dome of rock at Toxaway Falls (see our Waterfalls chapter). Faced with devastating settlements, the Lake Toxaway Company abandoned the property. The hotel was finally torn down in 1948. But despite the loss of the lake, Lucy Moltz loved the area and stayed.

"I have been around the world twice," she said, "and I've found there's no place more beautiful or special," she noted.

She lived to see a new dam constructed in 1960 and the area more than revived. Today homes in the Lake Toxaway development are valued up to $1 million or more, and land here, along with that in Highlands, ranks as some of the richest real estate in the North Carolina mountains. In 1985 the Moltz home, which is now on the National Register of Historic Places, was elegantly renovated and opened as the Greystone Inn.

Each of the 19 antique and period-reproduction bedrooms in the Mansion, as it's called, has its own unique character.

There are canopied beds, brass beds, fireplaces, private patios, and other charming touches that vary from room to room, but all come equipped with Jacuzzis. The Mansion's public rooms, which include a library, are the epitome of grace and elegance, yet are cozily comfortable and welcoming. The Lakeside Cottage, which was built in 1995, has two luxurious private suites with an adjoining door for families or couples traveling together.

Next door, the Hillmont Building (where 12 spacious, luxurious rooms have private balconies overlooking the lake) was built in 1988 in a manner that blends with the architectural style and furnishings of the Mansion. All these rooms have Jacuzzis, wet bars, sitting areas, and gas fireplaces.

The rates, which are reasonable considering what you get, are on a Modified American Plan that includes your room, an incredible High Country breakfast menu from which you can order anything you desire, and dinner with a varied menu. The rates include soft drinks and complimentary hors d'oeuvres; mid-afternoon tea, coffee, and cake served on a wicker-filled sunporch; a daily newspaper; water skiing, hydrosliding, and tubing with the boat, equipment, and driver provided; a daily champagne cruise on a canopied electric boat; use of a bass boat and fishing equipment; tennis court time; croquet, volleyball, and other outdoor sports; swimming in the pool or off the dock at the lake; and evening turndown service.

At the Spa, you can drop in for a sauna (terry robe and slippers provided) or, for an extra charge, choose from massages, body treatments, and skin and nail care.

Maps are available to spectacular waterfalls and hiking trails on the Lake Toxaway property, and the inn has six mountain bikes for guests' use. On Wednesdays, weather permitting, there's a mountaintop cheese and wine outing. Arrangements can be made for shopping excursions to Highlands, Cashiers, Brevard, and Asheville. The Greystone also owns memberships in the Lake Toxaway Country Club so that all their guests can make use of those facilities, including its 18-hole, par 71 championship golf course. During certain periods both green fees and golf carts are complimentary.

The Greystone Inn is a little over an hour from Asheville off U.S. 64 W. in Lake Toxaway. You'll see the sign.

SOUTHERN MOUNTAINS

Graham County

**Historic Fontana Village
Resort** $-$$$$
**N.C. Highway 28, Fontana Dam, NC
(828) 498-2211, (800) 849-2258
www.fontanavillage.com**
If you want solitude without boredom, this is the place to come. Fontana is more than a resort. It's actually a small, secluded, self-contained town that's a fascinating part of our nation's history. In December 1941 the Japanese bombed Pearl Harbor, and the nation knew right away that it was going to need new sources of electrical energy to power the war effort. Twenty-four days later, on New Year's Day 1942, the Tennessee Valley Authority (TVA) got the assignment to build a 480-foot-tall dam, the highest in the eastern United States, across the Little Tennessee River. Overnight a village for workers and their families sprang up; the village included a school, a 50-bed hospital, churches, and space to play. Work on the dam went on around the clock, seven days a week. On November 7, 1944, the project was complete; Fontana Lake's 10,600 acres filled with water, and electricity began to zip through the wires to Oak Ridge not far away over the mountains.

After the war there was power to spare for rural electrification, and the dam proved itself in flood control. Not long after that the village was transformed into a year-round resort and has been improving ever since. On the southern border of the Great Smoky Mountains National Park,

Fontana Village offers guided hikes, arts and crafts shops, three swimming pools (one indoor), a giant waterslide, an exercise spa, horseback and bike riding, miniature golf, volleyball, basketball, softball, tennis, a playground, a trout pond, a church, a post office, a village store, an ice-cream parlor, the Village Grill for hamburgers and pizza, the Peppermill Buffet House, a small museum, and a host of activities, including traditional Smoky Mountain dances and other entertainment. It also operates the Fontana Marina on Fontana Lake, where you can take a lake cruise or rent all kinds of boats. The fishing is great in both the lake and nearby trout streams (see our Recreation chapter).

As for accommodations, you're almost sure to find something to fit your budget and group size. There are rooms at the inn (some with fireplaces), cottages with kitchenettes (some as large as three bedrooms and three baths with a fireplace and whirlpool), and campground sites. (Camping costs $8.00 without hookup and $20.00 with.)

In addition to the previously mentioned eating establishments, the village also has a fine restaurant at the inn, and the village store has provisions for meals in your cottage and for cookouts and picnics. Special weekend getaways are available in winter, including a Holiday "Christmas at Fontana Village" package. Nearby residents can get season passes to use all the amenities, from the swim club and waterslide to minigolf. The resort

Most people only think of our mountain resorts as spring, summer, and fall playgrounds. But many visitors are finding them great places to celebrate the holidays. Fontana Village, for example, has a "Mountain Holiday Weekend" that includes tree-trimming, caroling, and seeing Santa. There are also hayrides, great food, and dancing under the holly and ivy.

Graham County's Maple Spring Observation Point is the highlight of a 900-foot loop trail, designed for wheelchair use, that includes a deck that opens to a sweeping view of mountain peaks and valleys. It is on Wagon Train Road (SR 1127) approximately 4.5 miles beyond the entrance road to the Joyce Kilmer Recreation Trail.

is approximately 95 miles from Asheville and 22 miles from Robbinsville on N.C. 28.

Haywood County

Cataloochee Ranch $$–$$$$
119 Ranch Drive, Maggie Valley, NC
(828) 926-1401, (800) 868-1401
www.cataloochee-ranch.com

For 64 years Cataloochee Ranch has welcomed guests to its 1,000-acre resort that's a mile high in the Great Smoky Mountains. In 1934, when the area was still a pristine wilderness, Tom and "Miss Judy" Alexander acquired what had been a rugged sheep and cattle farm and turned it into this mountain legend. Family members still run the ranch today, which borders the Great Smoky Mountains National Park.

The name Cataloochee comes from the Cherokee *ga-da-lu-sti,* which has been translated as "standing up in a row" or "wave upon wave," a reference, no doubt, to the range upon range of mountains—the Blue Ridge and the Smokies—that are visible here. The ranch itself has three major peaks: Fie Top, Moody Top, and Hemphill Bald, with elevations from 4,700 to 5,680 feet. There are accommodations for 70 guests. You can stay in one of 16 cabins that sleep two to eight people (two of the cabins were originally pioneer log homes). Laurel and Wintergreen each have a living room, two bedrooms, two baths, and a fireplace. Azalea, Rhododendron, Sourwood, Chestnut, and Crabapple—

one-bedroom, one-bath cabins—all have fireplaces. Four new cabins—Pond House, Willow, Dogwood, and Sassafras—each have fireplaces and Jacuzzi tubs. They are great for couples. In the Silverbell Lodge, you have many options, including one- or two-bedroom suites or individual cabins with fireplaces. Here, also, is the Balsam Room, a gathering place with a double fireplace that can be converted into a well-appointed conference room.

The historic main Ranch House, once a large barn, has six guest rooms, two dining rooms, the Big Room, a card room, and offices. The furnishings throughout the resort feature colorful quilts and primitive or classic antiques that reflect the ranch's pioneer heritage. At this altitude air-conditioning is not needed. In early morning and during the evening, even in summer, a fire in the fireplace is usually more desirable.

Daily rates include breakfast and dinner. These are family-style feasts you'll never forget (see our Restaurants chapter). There are also frequent outdoor cookouts and a beer and wine service. Other amenities include a trout pond, a twenty-foot heated swim-spa, horseshoe pits, Ping-Pong tables, a croquet court, and hiking paths.

But the real star here is horseback riding. These guided rides usually last two to three hours. Twice a year longer trips for experienced riders are offered. Call the ranch for more information.

Cataloochee Ranch is also the closest facility to the Cataloochee Ski Resort, just a mile over the hill, which has winter ski packages. Though no meals are served at the ranch at this time, stays here are very reasonably priced. Restaurant services are available at the ski lodge (see our Skiing chapter).

To get to the ranch, take exit 20 or 27 off I-40. Follow U.S. 19 S. through Maggie Valley to the west end and follow the directional sign. The ranch is 3 miles up paved Fie Top Road.

Maggie Valley Resort $-$$$
1819 Country Club Road, Maggie Valley, NC
(828) 926-1616, (800) 438-3861
www.maggievalleyresort.com

The mountains, as is typical in this particular area, soar almost straight up around the valley where this resort is nestled. They also shelter it from extremes in temperature. In summer the greenness of its forested slopes and well-cared-for grounds and gardens is totally soothing to the soul. One of this resort's main attractions is its golf course. It has been the site of four North Carolina Open golf tournaments, and *Golfweek* rates it as one of America's best. There is also a driving range and practice area, a pro shop, locker room, and a professional staff that offers clinic and private instruction (see our Golf chapter for more information). Two hard-surface tennis courts are adjacent to the golf course. There's also an oversize swimming pool surrounded by trees, flower and herb gardens, and relaxing scenery.

The Valley Room, the resort's restaurant, serves breakfast, lunch, and dinner, including popular theme buffets. On some evenings there's live entertainment and dancing, including a clogging show on Thursday nights. A full-service lounge called the Pin High Club overlooks the golf course. Rates are reasonable here, and the resort also offers money-saving golf packages that include greens fees, use of the tennis courts and pool, full country breakfasts, and dinner at the Valley Room. In the winter you can get ski packages that include lift tickets at the nearby Cataloochee Ski Area and a full country breakfast.

Rooms in the guest lodges are spacious, and each has its own balcony, cable TV, and coffeemaker. Guest villas are on the golf course's back nine. Each villa has a living room, dining area, and furnished kitchen, and both one-bedroom, one-bath and two-bedroom, two-bath units are available. Ask about special vacation and golf packages.

The Maggie Valley Resort is 35 miles west of Asheville. Take exit 20 off of I-40 onto U.S. 276. The resort is a half-mile from the intersection of U.S. 276 and U.S. 19.

Waynesville Country Club Inn $-$$$$
176 Country Club Drive, Waynesville, NC
(828) 452-2258, (800) 627-6250
www.wccinn.com

This may be a contemporary resort, but it's kept one very old tradition of mountain inns: rocking-chair hospitality. French doors lead from the modern lodge to the 270-foot-long main terrace that overlooks the manicured acres of its golf course. As in the old days, it's lined with rocking chairs—just one hint of the southern hospitality you'll find here.

Nestled between the Blue Ridge and the western ridges of the Great Smokies, this resort offers 27 picturesque holes of golf with fairways winding like ribbons through the mountain valley (see our Golf chapter). Accommodations are gracious and varied. Rooms in the main lodge or its Woodcrest wing offer panoramic views of the first tee. The Brookside or the Fairway lodges have porches or balconies within putting distance of the golf course. For a more private setting, you can stay in the Senator or Governor cottages, or the two-bedroom Country Villa, which features a kitchen and dining area. All accommodations have cable TV and air-conditioning. There is also a swimming pool and two tennis courts near the main lodge.

For meals you have your choice of the main dining room or a light to lavish lunch at the Tap Room. (The Tap Room is also open at night.) Golfers can also grab a bite at the Creekside Pavilion. "Good food," the managers say, "is as important as good golf." In testament to this, all the bread is freshly baked on the premises.

The Tower Lounge is the place to go to quench your thirst. The resort's nine meeting rooms will seat from 10 to 300 people. Numerous golf, holiday getaway, and special winter packages are available. Contact the inn for more information.

To get here, take exit 27 off I-40, follow U.S. 23/74 to the West Waynesville exit and follow the signs.

Jackson County

Fairfield Sapphire Valley $$-$$$$
70 Sapphire Valley Road, Sapphire, NC
(828) 743-3441, (800) 533-8268
www.fairfieldsapphirevalley.com
It all began back in 1896 with the opening of Fairfield Inn on Fairfield Lake. Although the inn is gone, the pristine scenery and a distinctive way of life remain. Nestled in the south Blue Ridge Mountains, Fairfield Sapphire Valley has become a 5,700-acre, four-season resort community.

A wide variety of on-site amenities will please every member of the family. Sapphire Mountain Golf Club, a par 70 championship course, is highlighted by its signature waterfall hole. The tennis center features eight Har-Tru courts, two all-weather courts, and a complete pro shop with instruction. The newly renovated recreation center features one indoor pool, two outdoor pools, miniature golf, an exercise room, Jacuzzi and sauna facilities, and a game room. Scenic trail rides are the pride of the equestrian center. Leisurely canoe and paddleboat rides are available in season. Fishing is abundant in the streams and lakes on the property. The recreation department also offers daily excursion to area attractions, a nature program, and hiking. Kids Kamp makes summer an adventure for children ages 3 to 14. Winter sports include skiing and snowboarding.

Accommodations range from hotel rooms to three-bedroom condominiums. Three- and four-bedroom homes are also available.

Often both large and small resorts keep substantial libraries for their guests. Feel free to grab a classic or a bestseller for poolside or fireside reading.

There are two on-site restaurants that feature fine dining in a casual atmosphere. Mica's Restaurant and the Library Club are open for lunch and dinner to resort guests. O'Connell's Pub and the Library Lounge are available to members.

Fairfield Sapphire Valley is approximately 60 miles southwest of Asheville between Cashiers and Lake Toxaway on U.S. 64 W.

The High Hampton Inn and
Country Club $$-$$$$
N.C. Highway 107 S., Cashiers, NC
(828) 743-2411, (800) 334-2551
www.highhamptoninn.com
In the early 1800s Wade Hampton II, a South Carolina upcountry planter and owner of Millwood, a Columbia, South Carolina, plantation that was the social center of Southern aristocracy, bought 450 acres in Cashiers. The property served as a farm and hunting preserve and provided escape from heat, humidity, and malaria. Hampton's son, Wade Hampton III, spent a lot of time here before he went on to become a general in the Confederate army and, later, South Carolina's governor and a U.S. senator.

In the 1880s the Hampton Place in the mountains, which by now had a seven-bedroom "cottage," a kitchen building, servants quarters, and outbuildings, was sold to Dr. and Mrs. Halsted (she was Wade Hampton III's niece). Her husband had been the first professor of surgery at John Hopkins Hospital, and she had briefly served as head of nursing. They called the place High Hampton, from the title of his ancestral estate in England, known as High Halsted. The couple gradually increased the property to 2,200 acres (see "The White Owl of High Hampton" Close-up). They are responsible for many of the lovely trees and shrubs that are still seen on High Hampton's current 1,400 acres.

After the Halsteds' deaths in 1922, E. Lyndon McKee of Sylva, the father of the present owner, William D. McKee, purchased the estate. A small inn was constructed on the site of the present

The White Owl of High Hampton

As we mentioned in the listing for High Hampton Inn, Dr. and Mrs. Halsted, the second owners of the High Hampton property, gradually increased their holdings by buying out adjoining farms. In the process Dr. Halsted made an offer for a 50-acre homestead owned by Mr. Hannibal Heaton and his wife. He wanted to sell, but Mrs. Heaton adamantly refused.

"I'll kill myself if you sell our home," she supposedly told her husband.

But Dr. Halsted must have made an offer that Hannibal felt he shouldn't refuse, so off he went to close the deal. But when he returned home with the bill of sale, he found his wife hanging from an oak tree, and the story goes that there was a white owl flying around her head screeching like a crying woman. Some said it was the spirit of the woman herself.

Shortly after his wife's death, Hannibal Heaton disappeared from the Cashiers area and was never heard from again. Mrs. Heaton, a woman of her word, was buried in the Upper Zachary Cemetery, just a short distance from where the High Hampton Inn stands today. And it's still said by some that the owls heard at night around High Hampton are Mrs. Heaton, still crying over the home she loved and lost.

building, but a fire in 1932 destroyed it and all the other buildings on the property. The present High Hampton Inn was completed in 1933, and to the pleasure of those who come year after year, time seems to stand still at this resort. "Nothing much changes here but the seasons," it's said. There are no televisions or telephones in the 120 rooms in the lodge and its cluster of cabins. And the accommodations are rustic rather than plush. You can also rent two-, three- and four-bedroom homes with fireplaces, kitchens, daily maid service, and resort privileges.

On its many hiking trails, on its lake, in its rocking chairs, and in its gardens, you can find all the peace of mind you might have been missing. Yet there are nearly as many activities happening here as you'd find on a cruise ship. Very popular, but only one aspect of this venerable resort, is the 18-hole, par 71 golf course that offers a sce-nic vista with every swing of the club (see our Golf chapter). The late George W. Cobb, who designed the course, said, "I've yet to see a course designed by me or others with greater natural beauty or one more enjoyable to play." There are also five fast-dry clay tennis courts, a red-clay court, and a complete tennis shop with regularly scheduled clinics and private lessons.

There are many hiking trails, guided walks, and a fitness trail. The 35-acre Hampton Lake is the center of swimming, sunbathing, sailing, canoeing, rowing, and pedal boating, and you can fish here year-round without a license. A playgroup is conducted for children ages 2 to 4, and a kids' club entertains children ages 5 to 12. There are teen activities, croquet, archery, and workshops, including seminars on golf, tennis, quilting, basket making, watercolor painting, bridge playing, fly-fishing, native wildflowers, trees, birds,

With so many fabulous dinners and snacks, resort guests find themselves putting on the pounds over a weekend. Be active and stroll the grounds before or after dinner and make use of the equipment or sports activities provided.

garden flora, and many other subjects. More than 150 kinds of birds have been spotted in the vicinity, making High Hampton a great area for bird-watching.

One of the most cherished traditions is afternoon tea served between 4:00 and 5:00 P.M. It's also traditional for the guests to gather before and after dinner in the Rock Mountain Tavern to meet other guests. After-dinner entertainment is offered each night. These events (movies, games, or other activities) are posted daily on the bulletin board. There are also special occasions, such as the Scottish Heritage Houseparty, July 4th Picnic, Teddy Bear Picnic for children and—the most traditional of all—the Thanksgiving Houseparty that closes down the inn for the season (High Hampton is open from mid-April through November).

Daily rates are on a Full American Plan, which includes three buffet-style meals a day. No gratuity or service charge will be added to your bill, and you are not expected to tip. There are extra but very reasonable charges for greens fees, golf carts, boats, and the kids' club and playgroup.

To reach High Hampton Inn, take U.S. 64 to Cashiers and turn south on N.C. Highway 107. The resort will be on your left a short distance out of town.

BED-AND-BREAKFASTS AND COUNTRY INNS

E veryone needs to get away from time to time to recharge and renew the spirit. Leave behind all the encumbrances of real life and get back to ourselves. Some of us like the anonymity of an obscure roadside motel, or the pure convenience of it, but then there are those times when a bit of real creature comfort and coddling wouldn't be too bad at all. In fact, for many, it's the only way to travel.

North Carolina's mountains are blessed not only with natural beauty but with scores of charming and graceful inns. These jewels can be found scattered all across the area and offer you pampering you probably don't even get at home. The memory of making new acquaintances, enjoying stimulating conversations, and experiencing gorgeous sights, sounds, and tastes will last long after the key has turned in your door back home.

Country inns abound in the Southeast United States. Bed-and-breakfasts hark back to the old English style of housing a traveler and fortifying him or her with a hot breakfast before the long ride onward. The establishments we recommend to you in this chapter are some of the finest examples of the bed-and-breakfast inns and country inns North Carolina's mountains have to offer. Some have lavish surroundings and interiors worthy of a museum estate, and some sport the more simple comforts of home. We've chosen each one—be it unique or traditional—because it offers the traveler a memorable stay. All are devoted to making your stay as pleasing as possible. We've given you the choice of large or small, elegant or rustic, in the heart of town or secluded in the countryside. Use this as a guide and strike out on your own to find out what's so special about Southern hospitality.

PRICE CODE

The average nightly rate for two adults at the facilities in this chapter is indicated by a dollar-sign ($) ranking in the following chart. Most businesses accept major credit cards for payment, but where no credit cards are accepted, we've noted that information.

$	$50 to $80
$$	$81 to $100
$$$	$101 to $120
$$$$	$121 and more

These establishments have varying policies concerning children, pets, and cancellation; please inquire about these when you call to make reservations.

NORTHERN MOUNTAINS

Alleghany County

Burgiss Farm Bed and Breakfast $$$
294 Elk Knob Road, off N.C. Highway 18, Laurel Springs, NC
(336) 359-2995, (800) 233-1505
www.breakfastinn.com
The Burgiss Farm Bed and Breakfast offers a rollicking good-time atmosphere and country hospitality, thanks to its genial innkeepers Tom and Nancy Burgiss.

A substantial addition to this 1897 farmhouse has created a house within a house. The addition, furnished with lodge-style comfort, has two guest rooms and a private bath, a massive great room with a stone fireplace rising the full height of the vaulted ceiling, a large Jacuzzi room, and even a mountain stream running through it. The complete privacy of these separate guest accommodations is very popular with honeymooners and families. Reservations are required and should be made as soon as you know your travel plans, as dates close out quickly. Also, an added goodie you might find in your room is complimentary wine from the small winery on the premises.

Room prices include your choice of breakfasts—served at the time you desire. Select items from Nancy's creative breakfast menu of such delights as Hawaiian pancakes, eggs Benedict, Canadian bacon, home fries, homemade breads, and baked fruit. A real favorite is Nan's Cream Cheese Eggs: two baked eggs in cream cheese sauce served on an English muffin, with a special double-baked fruit dish on the side—delicious! Kona coffee is the house specialty.

For lively entertainment check out the Burgiss Farm's Mountain Jamboree (see our Nightlife chapter). This bluegrass and old-timey mountain music community bash, which gets going every Saturday night in the restyled barn, provides great fun. The Burgisses also keep mountain bikes around at no extra charge, for those who like to take a spin down the country roads. Tom and Nancy will recommend a good trail for guests, according to one's abilities.

Doughton Hall Bed & Breakfast $$$
12668 N.C. Highway 18, Laurel Springs, NC
(336) 359-2341
www.doughtonhall.com
Less than a mile from the Blue Ridge Parkway's exit to rural Laurel Springs is Doughton Hall. Open year-round, this lovely Queen Anne–style home, built in the 1890s, was once home to former Congressman Robert L. Doughton, an influential figure in Congress during the 1940s. Doughton Hall, listed on the National Register of Historic Places, has been newly refurbished by innkeepers Pam and Ed Hall. We felt like part of the family the minute we stepped into the wonderful old entrance hall. The inn has marvelous woodwork, high ceilings, and old-fashioned

sitting rooms. The Halls have furnished the home with antiques, some of them original to the house. Photos of Congressman Doughton during his term in Washington decorate the sitting room walls.

You have a choice of three guest rooms, two with private baths that include Jacuzzis. One room has a splendid queen-size brass bed. The buffet breakfast is generous enough to serve a crowd—eggs cooked to order, several kinds of fresh bread, country ham, sausage, bacon, croissants, and more—even if the house isn't full of guests. Pam's mother, who frequently is responsible for preparing this bounty, explains that it's no trouble at all, because she's always cooked for a houseful at home.

You can fish from the creek at the end of the lawn, rock on the front porch, or have a cool drink in the gazebo.

Ashe County

Glendale Springs Inn & Restaurant $$$–$$$$
7414 N.C. Highway 16, Glendale Springs, NC
(336) 982-2103, (800) 287-1206
www.glendalespringsinn.com
This splendid inn is composed of two buildings: the original historic structure, whose foundations were built ca. 1892 and completed between 1902 and 1905; and the guest house across the country road. The main house has been used over the century as a general merchandise store, a circuit courthouse, post office and chapel, a community center, a boarding house, and a private home. It now houses three dining rooms, five guest rooms with private baths, and two parlors for relaxing. The guest parlors are peppered with owner Amanda Smith's family antiques, as well as those acquired later, including a Duncan Phyfe sofa upon which she remembers being courted, an old English sewing cabinet, a marble chess set, and a slender "lady's desk" made of burlwood. Pine and oak broad-beamed wood floors creaked underneath our steps as we

peeked into the cheerfully painted pastel bedrooms. Crisp sheets and comforters cover the one king- and four queen-size beds in the main house. Battenburg lace curtains surround the deep claw-foot tubs, and each bedroom has a television and air-conditioning.

Our favorite accommodation here is the cottage, with four large bedrooms with fireplaces and Jacuzzis. Country quilts cover these cherry high-poster king- and queen-size beds, and one room is furnished with an extra bed for a child. We especially like the butler pantry in the guest cottage, featuring makings for tea, coffee, and hot chocolate at any time of day or evening.

Rocking chairs on the front porch of the cottage and porch swings and white wicker furniture on the main house's front porch are perfect for watching the twilight curtain descend over Glendale Springs, as fireflies light up the evening. A full breakfast is provided for inn guests in the dining room, and lest you not stray too far from the office, fax and a photocopier are available for your use.

The inn is just a walk down the road from one of the Ashe County Frescoes. The Blue Ridge Parkway is also close-by.

River House   **$$$$**
**1896 Old Field Creek Road , off N.C. Highway 16 N., Grassy Creek, NC
(336) 982-2109
www.riverhousenc.com**
Remember as a child when you and your parents would take a Sunday drive? You marked the time by counting the cows in the pastures and the bridges over creeks and rivers. As the sun began to mellow, you'd round a hill and there would be the comforting sight of your aunt and uncle's farmhouse. A wonderful aroma would drift from inside, and you'd hurry upstairs to find your favorite room just as you remembered it. Recapture that feeling in remote northern Ashe County, at River House.

Innkeepers Gayle Winston and John Stewart have taken pains to re-create and maintain the gentler pace of a time past. No televisions or room phones disturb the tranquility of River House, an elegant 1870 farmhouse that was once home to a local physician. The home has been meticulously restored and tastefully furnished with period antiques. River House sits near the Virginia border on 125 beautifully rolling acres, a mile of which hugs the New River. The inn, open year-round, offers two guest rooms upstairs in the main house, each with a private bath and a choice of queen- or king-size beds. These two front bedrooms have views of the lazy New River, one of the oldest in the world, and the mountains beyond.

You also have your choice of two cottages, one a former doctor's office, behind the main house. These offer guests a wonderful sense of privacy. Each of the four cottage rooms includes a sitting area and a whirlpool bath. Two rooms have private porches with views of the river or mountains or both!

River House is also home to an exceptional restaurant with a unique menu prepared by chef Bill Klein of Hickory, North Carolina. Guests who discover River House return frequently, say its innkeepers, not only for the gracious service of this old-style country inn, but also for the magnificent fare of the River House restaurant. Regulars come from across the country and abroad. (See our Restaurants chapter.)

Avery County

Archer's Mountain Inn   **$$–$$$$**
**2489 Beech Mountain Parkway, N.C. Highway 184, Beech Mountain, NC
(828) 898-9004, (888) 827-6155
www.archersinn.com**
Archer's Mountain Inn, nearly 5,000 feet above sea level, offers views of Sugar and Grandfather Mountains and acres of fresh mountain air, lush foliage, and surrounding flower and herb gardens. With new owners, a new restaurant (Jackalope's View; see our Restaurants chapter), and new decor, the inn has captivated a youthful, inspired audi-

Many B&Bs and inns package their own coffee blends, jams, herbs, and other goodies. These small souvenirs make lovely gifts for friends, or the house sitter, back home . . . or for yourself as a reminder of a heavenly vacation.

ence. Guests enjoy the wood-paneled rooms, with high cross-beamed ceilings, the personal fireplaces, the views of the opposing mountain ridge, the private porches with rocking chairs—somehow you just don't want to leave your room.

Three buildings compose the inn. Two are for guest housing—one has eight guest rooms with knotty pine paneling and exposed beams. Each room has a queen-size bed, a stone fireplace, and small kitchenette, as well as private porches. The main building has six guest rooms, one with an outdoor hot tub on the broad balcony. All rooms have fireplaces, private baths, real down comforters, and coffee- and tea makers.

We love the Presidential Suite, a grand affair with 14-foot-high ceilings, a king-size four-poster bed, a large fireplace, a private balcony, and a glassed-in bathroom with a Jacuzzi. We sipped from the complimentary decanter of port until late in the evening, watching the lights twinkle in the valley below. When we opted for company, we sidled up to the bar in the inn's dining room where locals, the innkeepers, guests, and friends were watching the basketball playoffs. You won't be a stranger for long here.

The Hawk's View is another building offering spacious rooms decorated with structural cedar beams, a fieldstone fireplace in each room, kitchen efficiencies, and a broad porch for the unparalleled views.

The owners have built walking trails around the inn, which is perched on the edge of Beech Mountain, and a small waterfall flowing into the garden below the terrace, open for dining in the warm months. Candi prepares a breakfast for overnight guests, who select from a menu of omelettes, fluffy pancakes, French toast, fresh fruit, ham, sausage, bacon, and other offerings. Personal service, excellent food, and a homey but pampered atmosphere make it hard to leave Archer's Mountain Inn.

The Azalea Inn $$$–$$$$
149 Azalea Circle, Banner Elk, NC
(828) 898-8195, (888) 898-2743
www.azalea-inn.com

Originally owned by members of one of Banner Elk's founding families, the house has been restored with antiques, including Banner Elk's first claw-foot bathtub. From its elegantly furnished rooms to cozy porches, the seven-bedroom inn is a pleasing and restful escape.

In the heart of town, the inn is within walking distance of the village shops and many fine restaurants. A full breakfast completes your stay. Two new vacation rental cottages are now in the back of the property.

Banner Elk Inn Bed
& Breakfast $$$–$$$$
407 Main Street E., Banner Elk, NC
(828) 898-6223
www.bannerelkinn.com

This small, charming inn is convenient to Boone and the ski resorts of the northern mountains. The tasteful decor here has the flavor of both the Victorian era and Old World Europe. All five guest rooms have private baths. Ask about the third-floor Garrett Suite, which is perfect for honeymooners. It has a full bath with a tub for two, a view of the stone fountain in the English garden below, cable television, and a king-size bed.

Breakfasts including banana nut muffins, Parmesan omelette soufflé with cheddar cheese sauce, and pumpkin bread might be on the weekend menu. Weekday breakfasts are full service but a bit simpler. Enjoy gardens with a bubbling stone fountain in the spring and summer. Sugar Tree Cottage in back of the property is available for short-term rental.

Eseeola Lodge $$$$
U.S. Highway 221, Linville, NC
(828) 733-4311, (800) 742-6717
www.eseeola.com

This wonderful old inn is central to the history of Linville as well as to the development of the High Country as a tourist destination. The original Eseeola Lodge, destroyed by fire in 1936, had its beginnings at the turn of the century with the advent of the railroad in these long-remote mountains. As a result of the railroad's coming, Eseeola Lodge and Linville soon became a fashionable watering place for the wealthy of the Southeast. Golf became a passion at the lodge, and a premier 18-hole course designed by renowned golf architect Donald Ross was added in the 1920s. In those early years Eseeola Lodge was the center of community activity and lively entertainment for the village of Linville.

Today's lodge, with its distinctive chestnut bark siding, continues the tradition of that early Eseeola Lodge. There are 29 small, tastefully furnished guest rooms, most with private porches. They surround the warm, richly furnished, wood-paneled main gathering room. The fireplace at one end draws people to its comfortably stuffed armchairs and perhaps a lazy nod by the fire. Adjoining the main gathering room is the lodge dining room where breakfast and dinner are served; the price of meals is included in accommodations. The elegant dinner menu includes specialties such as crab mousse with red and yellow pepper sauce, poached Carolina flounder stuffed with spinach, and grilled loin of veal. Gentlemen are asked to wear a jacket and tie for dinner.

The manicured grounds offer a number of diversions: tennis on clay courts, a heated swimming pool, golf, and croquet. The clubhouse serves lunch. Eseeola Lodge is surrounded by 2,000 acres for hiking and fishing. The lodge provides a special children's recreation program.

Eseeola Lodge is open from mid-May to mid-October.

Linville Cottage $-$$$
154 Ruffin Street, Linville, NC
(828) 733-6551, (877) 797-1885

A whitewashed picket fence surrounds this restored, turn-of-the-century Victorian farmhouse, with its English cottage perennial and herb gardens. The rooms are filled with antiques and collectibles. The charm of the cottage is accented by the eight-gable tin roof, plank floors, and featherbeds. A breakfast room overlooks Grandfather Mountain and the Blue Ridge Parkway. The accommodations allow comfortable lodging with enchanting rooms filled with simple country antiques and collectibles, but very, very casual. Delightful English country-cottage perennial and herb gardens surround the inn. The innkeepers serve a deluxe full continental breakfast of homemade breads and baked goods served with jellies and jams preserved from the gardens. The inn also houses a small shop out back filled with antiques and collectibles.

Madison County

Baird House $$$-$$$$
41 South Main Street, Mars Hill, NC
(828) 689-5722, (800) 297-1342
www.bairdhouse.com

This fine old house was once the home of Dr. John Hannibal Baird, a medical doctor of the late 1800s, who served the people living in the mountains around Mars Hill. In appreciation for his dedicated service, local residents built this home in the 1890s for Baird, his wife, and their nine children. It was considered one of the grandest homes in the area. Dr. Baird continued his medical practice until his death in the 1920s.

The home then passed to Dr. Baird's son, John W. Baird, also a physician. At his untimely death, his grieving widow, Lexine, left the area for rural Harlan County, Kentucky. There, carrying on the family medical tradition, she became a nurse-on-horseback to the folks of that remote area. She did return to Baird House, however, many years later, renting rooms to students of Mars Hill College. They knew her kindly as "Ma Baird" or "Aunt Lex."

Today Yvette Wessel, a transplant from Connecticut, carries on the hospitality begun by the Baird family. She has furnished the home in 18th-century French, English, and American antiques, all chosen with a particular nod to history and many with stories of their own, such as the Wellington chests used by British naval officers or the wood-framed fanlight Yvette rescued from a building demolition in New York City.

Baird House contains five guest rooms, two with private baths. Two rooms have fireplaces. A full breakfast is served. Baird House is open year-round except December.

The Duckett House Inn & Farm $$–$$$
433 Lanee Avenue, Hot Springs, NC
(828) 622-7621

Hot Springs, once a fashionable destination for Victorians seeking the curative waters for which the town was named, continues to evoke that earlier charm. Always a popular stopover for hikers of the Appalachian Trail, which passes through town, Hot Springs is currently enjoying a renaissance of sorts, and The Duckett House Inn & Farm is part of that rebirth. With the inn as your base, you can enjoy white-water rafting, the Hot Springs Spa mineral baths, and hiking. This 1900 Victorian farmhouse has six guest rooms and a cottage that sleeps seven.

Room rates include a full vegetarian breakfast. Gourmet vegetarian dinners are available on weekends for an additional charge.

Marshall House Bed &
Breakfast Inn $–$$
150 Hill Street, Marshall, NC
(828) 649-9205

Marshall House is nestled in the hillside above the town of Marshall, about 30 minutes northwest of Asheville. Noted society architect Richard Sharp Smith built this home in 1903 as the private residence of James H. White, a prominent Madison County community leader and political figure. The distinctive pebble-dash exterior is typical of the homes Smith built in the Asheville area and the cottages of Biltmore Village, commissioned by George Vanderbilt.

Marshall House fosters the serenity of that simpler time, characterized by the town of Marshall itself, just below on the banks of the French Broad River. Choice antiques decorate the house. Two rooms have private baths; the others have shared baths. A sumptuous breakfast of pancakes, French toast or waffles, eggs, and homemade breads or bagels is served to guests in the formal dining room. From the veranda you can see the spectacular French Broad River and the village that hugs its banks. A resident cat and dog share the house with you.

Mountain Magnolia Inn
& Retreat $$$–$$$$
204 Lawson Street, Hot Springs, NC
(828) 622-3543
www.mountainmagnoliainn.com

The Rumboughs were the founding family of Hot Springs, which was originally called Warm Springs. The name emanated from the natural springs boiling from the ground. Confederate Col. James H. Rumbough built Rutland House in 1868 so that it had the space necessary to accommodate a family of 10. In the 1950s the last of the Rumboughs downsized Rutland by removing its tower and upper two floors. Pete and Karen Nagle of Charlotte, North Carolina, purchased the remains of this once-glorious estate in 1997, planning a minor renovation as their retirement home. But as the work got under way, they discovered that they had a mission to bring Rutland House back to its Victorian glory. They literally raised the roof, returning the upper floors and the tower to their former positions, and reclaimed the grounds from the overgrowth. Amidst this restored luxury, along with contemporary ventilation and heating, they offer five individual guest rooms, three two-bedroom suites, and one three-bedroom house. The inn is open year-round except for January. The dining room and porch are open to the public for Sunday brunch and nightly dining. Nearby are the hot tubs for dipping and massages. The Appalachian Trail crosses nearby at Max Patch, and trails of lesser mileage also crisscross this mountain valley paradise.

Mitchell County

The Switzerland Inn $$$-$$$$
Mile 334, off the Blue Ridge Parkway, Little Switzerland, NC
(828) 765-2153, (800) 654-4026
The Switzerland Inn is a landmark in the northern mountains. Perched high on a ridge, it straddles Mitchell and McDowell Counties and commands one of the most spectacular views in the region. In fact the view is so spectacular that the area derived its name from its resemblance to the equally beautiful mountain views of Switzerland, its European cousin. North Carolina State Supreme Court Judge Herriot Clarkson was the first to be inspired by the Swiss-like atmosphere of this knob, and he determined to make it his own, buying 1,100 acres in 1910. The charm of the place is its unchanging personality, remaining pretty much as it was 80 or so years ago.

It's no wonder that the Blue Ridge Parkway planners chose to guide the scenic highway along this route at its beginning in 1935. The exit at Little Switzerland is the only one on the parkway that leads to private land. The Jensen family, longtime seasonal residents who are now permanent mountaineers, purchased the inn in the 1980s. They have maintained the 55-room lodge and its surrounding grounds with the same devotion Judge Clarkson brought to Little Switzerland so long ago.

The Switzerland Inn is a veritable kingdom unto itself. Quaint lodging, fine dining, and unusual specialty shopping are all available here. The ambience is wonderful in this rustic, Swiss chalet–style lodge, and in particular in its great hall. Guests mingle here, playing a friendly game of checkers, relaxing by the fire, listening to the charming strains of a Victorian-era music box, or just burrowing into the comfortable armchairs to watch the mists roll in over the mountain ridge. For summer fun the Switzerland Inn has an outdoor swimming pool, a tennis court, and the pleasures of the magnificent Blue Ridge Parkway at your doorstep.

Shopping along the little avenue of specialty stores adjacent to the Switzerland Inn is a bit like visiting Santa's Main Street. You can find anything from sinfully rich fudge and homemade candies to mountain crafts, unusual toys, ladies' fine accessories, and one-of-a-kind gift items.

If you stay a night at the Switzerland Inn, you'll want to stay a week. Book early for visits during mid-October, which is the peak of the leaf season in the North Carolina mountains. The inn is open May through October.

Watauga County

Alta Vista—Gallery/Bed
& Breakfast $$$-$$$$
2839 Broadstone Road, Valle Crucis, NC
(828) 963-5247
This historic brick farmhouse in the heart of Valle Crucis cultivates more than just tasty breakfasts, gardens, and charming rooms—it also houses an art gallery on the first floor. With only three guest rooms, Alta Vista is a personable boutique B&B, much like any number of smaller pensions or guest houses in Germany or France. The rooms feature tasteful decor, antiques, queen-size beds, fresh flowers, and private tiled baths. The wonderful breakfasts here, set out on cafe tables in the spacious upstairs corridor, include a hearty breakfast quiche, cinnamon French toast, and home-baked muffins. The gracious hosts lay out homemade cookies on an antique sideboard each afternoon with

cold or hot beverages. Alta Vista's perennial gardens deserve an after-breakfast stroll, and you might consider walking on to the Valle Crucis Community Park across the street. It borders the Watauga River. Particularly engaging and unusual is the Alta Vista Gallery downstairs, which features more than 200 national and international artists. Originals as well as prints allow for an assortment of pricing. Owner Maria Santomasso-Hyde showcases her own impressionist oil paintings here, while you'll also find smaller items of glass, pottery, jewelry, and kaleidoscope crafts.

Watch out for the leaf season, usually all of October and the latter part of September. This is when most B&Bs and inns are completely booked, sometimes a year in advance. It's the perfect time to be in the mountains, but please, plan ahead for the most pleasurable and restful stay.

Gideon Ridge Inn $$$-$$$$
6148 Gideon Ridge Inn Road, Blowing Rock, NC
(828) 295-3644
www.gideonridge.com

What is it about this inn we like so much? Could it be the understated elegance of tasteful decor and magnificent family antiques throughout the house that enveloped us immediately into its fold? Was it the views from the rooms, porches, and gardens that spread over countless mountain ridges? Or was it the gardens themselves—paths running through graduated banks dotted with rich yellow black-eyed Susans, rhododendrons of pink and white and ivy, and a pergola under which to sit with our first cup of steaming coffee to gaze over the mountains? Perhaps it was just the small touches that captured our hearts. Afternoon tea was spread before us on the dining room island as we arrived. A pot of Earl Grey,

which the innkeepers import from England, sat beside plates of light homemade shortbread and finger sandwiches.

Made of cedar and the red stone of Grandfather Mountain, the building itself hugs the ridge. The nephew of Moses Cone, a textile magnate who built textile mills in Greensboro, North Carolina, with the money from his Cone Export & Commission Company in New York City, constructed the home as a mountain cottage in 1939. In front of the fireplace in the living room is a soft leather sofa, perfect for sinking into and reading the magazines and newspapers provided, and a wide leather hassock. The carpet was designed by William Morris. Several carpets and Central Asian kilims lend the hall and dining room their natural earthen warmth. The walnut dining table, a fourth-generation family heirloom, is surrounded by high-back chairs. Four Russian impressionist paintings in muted hues decorate the walls. The artist was a friend of innkeeper Cobb Milner and his wife, whom they met when they spent nine months in Minsk, Belarus, in 1993.

The butler's pantry is stocked for guests with cold juices and sodas, a kettle, and plenty of tea, coffee, and hot chocolate-making items. The 10 guest rooms are each unique—adorned with table and chair settings, a large bed, and decorative knickknacks—they seem almost like small apartments. Seven of them have fireplaces. Think mahogany four-poster beds, marble sinks, and antique furniture in every room. Our favorite is the Sunrise View, set apart from the others with its own private entrance. The king-size bed, piled high with thick pillows and quilts, offers a view out the picture window of the sun rising over 90 miles of mountain peaks. Under the beamed cathedral ceiling is a Franklin iron stove, an open whirlpool tub surrounded by a stone wall, and a bathroom designed with an exposed stone wall, in the shower. Each room has a private bath.

Breakfast, set at individual wooden tables in a glass-enclosed terrace above the gardens, can include stuffed French toast, cornmeal pancakes, muffins, waffles, sausage, and numerous other edibles, all attractively presented with fresh fruit. On our visit we were served genuine Vermont maple syrup and loved the added touch of apricots stewed with cinnamon sticks.

The Inn at Ragged Gardens $$$–$$$$
203 Sunset Drive, Blowing Rock, NC
(828) 295-9703
www.ragged-gardens.com

This grand old inn surrounded by a stone wall and lovely English cottage-style flower gardens is covered by the rustic chestnut bark siding frequently found on fine older homes in the High Country. Owners Jama and Lee Hyett have refurbished and reconstructed the inn to reflect an architecturally and decoratively succinct masterpiece. Built as a seasonal summer "cottage," the estate has been remodeled to accept guests all year long in its 12 distinctive rooms, all designed and decorated by a Charlotte interior decorator working in conjunction with the Hyetts. These rooms include five new suites designed in the Arts and Crafts period style. Each of these five suites has separate sitting areas, whirlpool baths for two, fireplaces, and balconies or patios looking into the formal rock-walled garden.

Our personal favorites are the Rock Garden Garret and the Evergreen Garret—soothing bedrooms under the eaves of the skylit roof. The Rock Garden is a suite with a king-size bed, a window seat, a whirlpool bath, and a giggling fountain in the reading nook. The Evergreen is resplendent with a unique handcrafted king-size bed, a corner fireplace, and a whirlpool bath with an old-fashioned dressing area—a lady's dream.

Another favorite is the Camelot Suite, a jewel-toned suite with soft ochre walls, a rock fireplace, wrought iron furnishings, and a Middle Eastern wall tapestry. The queen-size bed is adorned with a fantasia-like coat of arms, with arcs of richly draped fabric emanating from its center. The sitting room contains a twin bed and a love seat, separated from the bedroom by a pair of antique French doors. Other rooms—Monet's Garden, Moss and Lace, Blue Wisteria, and English Lavender—evoke floral garden visions as well. Four new rooms with various themes have been added recently. A very popular room has proved to be the new Lee & Ann's Treehouse, situated privately on the third floor of the new wing and fashioned after a tree house lover's fantasy.

The central focus of the Ragged Garden Inn is its magnificent stone staircase in the grand hall. Another excellent touch is the butler's pantry on the second floor, always furnished with sodas, juices, coffee, tea, mints, hot chocolate, and rich home-baked cookies present under a glass dome. If the cookies haven't spoiled your breakfast appetite, pull close to the lace-covered table and Jama and Lee will cook up eggs to order, fresh fruit cups, omelettes, pancakes, waffles, and sausage, only after you have helped yourself to the buffet of muffins, bagels, and breads. Candles glow on the mantel on misty cool mornings, while summer days allow for breakfast out on the porch overlooking the brilliant variety of flowers of the Ragged Gardens.

The Inn at Taylor House $$$$
N.C. Highway 194, Valle Crucis, NC
(828) 963-5581

This lovely, two-story farmhouse with double chimneys and a wraparound porch was built in 1911 for the family of C. D. Taylor. Today it has been transformed into a sophisticated European-style inn with farmhouse flair. Innkeeper Carol "Chip" Schwab runs her inn as an extension of her home, offering much more than an overnight stay. Guests also enjoy the inn's mountain escape for family reunions, wedding and anniversary celebrations, special luncheons or dinner parties, art shows, cooking classes, and flower shows.

The Inn at Taylor House is decorated with a mix of European and American country antiques, Oriental rugs, and original art work. There are 10 spacious rooms in the inn, all offering private baths and goose-down comforters. Three of the rooms are suites, complemented by comfortable sitting rooms. A gourmet breakfast is included and usually includes seasonal fruit, pancakes, fresh vegetables, and specially prepared egg dishes.

The inn's old milkhouse has been converted into a charming gift shop that offers unusual items, garden accessories, and specialty foods. A private massage parlor is located on the property, and a masseuse is on call for massages, manicures, and pedicures.

Lovill House Inn $$$$
404 Old Bristol Road, Boone, NC
(828) 264-4204, (800) 849-9466
www.lovillhouseinn.com

This historic home, built in 1875, was the residence of Capt. Edward Francis Lovill, a decorated Confederate officer, North Carolina state senator, and a founding trustee of the Appalachian Training School, later Appalachian State University. In fact it was in the front parlor of Lovill House, the captain's occasional law office, where he and B. B. Daugherty drafted the papers establishing the university. The home continued as a Lovill family residence well into the 1970s.

Innkeepers Scott and Anne Peacock discovered Lovill House and transformed this elegant residence and its 11 wooded acres on the edge of Boone into one of the premier bed-and-breakfast inns in the High Country. Personal service and attention to detail are the secrets of their success.

You'll wake to the rich aroma of home-baked muffins and coffee outside your door. Enjoy a full gourmet breakfast, including seasonal fruit, home-baked breads, Belgian waffles, eggs Benedict, garden vegetable strata, and omelettes, accompanied by country ham, sausage, or bacon. The informal evening social hour is popular with guests of Lovill House. Groups gather outside by the stream, in the rockers on the front porch, or around the cozy front parlor fireplace.

You can hike the trails on the lovely grounds, or the innkeepers can recommend the best local restaurants. Restoration of the grounds and outbuildings continues, with plans for additional accommodations in the future.

The inn is furnished in a casually elegant country style, with a mix of antiques and quality reproductions. The wormy chestnut paneling was discovered during restoration and supplemented by matching refinished wood recovered from old, abandoned barns. The inn offers five guest rooms, each with a private bath, television (discreetly tucked away in a wooden cabinet), and telephone. Beds at the Lovill House are spread with down comforters. The innkeepers encourage you to let them know if you have special dietary requirements, if you'll be celebrating a special occasion, or if you require any other service to make your visit more enjoyable.

Maple Lodge $$$-$$$$
152 Sunset Drive, Blowing Rock, NC
(828) 295-3331
www.maplelodge.net

This charming inn reflects the simplicity and grace of the 1930s and '40s. Named for the maple tree in the front yard, this pleasant two-story frame home was built as a boarding house for tourists. Staying at Maple Lodge reminds us of visiting the elegant, treasure-filled home of a favorite aunt, one who greets you warmly at the door, offers delectable goodies served on fine china and hot cider from her sunny kitchen out back, and ushers you to a more-than-perfect guest room. In short, you feel at home.

Maple Lodge has 11 guest rooms, each named for a garden flower. These rooms, with twin-, full-, queen-, or king-size beds, all have private baths. Some beds have lovely crocheted canopies.

A hearty buffet breakfast that includes homemade muffins, breads, a variety of egg dishes, and fresh fruit is served every day from 8:30 to 10:00 A.M. in the pleasant sunroom overlooking the flower garden.

Main Street, Blowing Rock is just a stone's throw from Maple Lodge, convenient to restaurants and shopping. Blowing

Rock Stage Company performs just down the street in summer.

Mast Farm Inn **$$$$**
SR 1112, off N.C. Highway 105, Valle Crucis, NC
(828) 963-5857, (888) 963-5857
www.mastfarminn.com

The Mast Farm Inn has been a landmark and vital part of the history of the High Country since 1885. It was operated as an inn by Finley Mast and his wife, Josephine, in the early 1900s. The Masts were known far and wide for their mountain hospitality, not to mention the bounty of their table. And it's still possible to find someone, as we did, with personal memories of that early Mast Farm. The gracious lady we encountered, who was visiting from Pulaski, Virginia, recalled the pleasure of her visit to the Loom House of Mast Farm more than 60 years earlier as a student from Appalachian State University in Boone.

In 1972 the Mast Farm Inn was included on the National Register of Historic Places. It remains one of the best examples of a self-contained mountain homestead in the state. The rambling 18-room Victorian farmhouse is the center of the inn and is open year-round. The main house has nine guest rooms, all with private baths. All rooms have queen- and king-size beds. Original outbuildings—the Blacksmith Shop, the Woodwork Shop, and the Loom House—have been converted to additional, comfortably furnished guest quarters.

The Raspberry Hill Cabin is the newest accommodation here. Built from white pine logs and featuring a cathedral ceiling, it is both rustic and spacious. Sit on the porch and rock for a while—you'll feel as though you own the valley. The cabin features two full bedrooms (one king, one queen), two bathrooms (one with a whirlpool tub), a loft with a double futon, a great room, and a fully equipped kitchen.

The Loom House, the log cabin originally built by David Mast in 1812, was Finley and Josephine Mast's first home. Here Josephine gloried in her weaving, at which she was expert. Some of her work has been featured in exhibits at the Smithsonian Institution. Today the Loom House is a special guest cottage with a kitchen, sleeping loft, and fireplace. The combination of period farmhouse antiques and modern conveniences at the Mast Farm Inn allows guests to easily enjoy the charm of turn-of-the-century mountain life in North Carolina.

Rates include a bountiful breakfast. Breakfast offers something different on the menu every day, but it always features scrumptious homemade breads, fresh fruit and jams, jellies, and preserves.

Wanda Hinshaw and her sister Kay Hinshaw Philip took over the inn three years ago and have made many changes since then. Changing the dining from family-style country cooking to fine dining a la carte is perhaps the most noticeable.

Dinner is served six nights a week from May through October and on weekends the rest of the year.

Yancey County

Nu-Wray Inn **$$-$$$$**
Town Square, Burnsville, NC
(828) 682-2329, (800) 368-9729
www.nuwrayinn.com

It seems as if the town of Burnsville grew up around the Nu-Wray Inn. The recorded heritage of this venerable accommodation dates back to 1833. It was long known as a stagecoach stop for weary travelers making their way through the rough country of North Carolina's mountains. From the wide, covered front porch to the second-floor balcony or topmost third-floor aerie, the Nu-Wray Inn is a special place. One of the distinct pleasures of the inn is wandering its wonderfully creaky floors and twisting stairways. The inn passed from the Wray family after the death in the mid-1980s of family scion Rush Wray.

Noted writers Thomas Wolfe of Asheville and O. Henry, master of the classic short story, stayed here. It was here at the inn, an hour's distance from Asheville, that Thomas Wolfe retreated in 1937 to avoid a dubious welcome after the publication of *Look Homeward, Angel,* the thinly disguised portrayal of Wolfe's boyhood home and its less-than-pleased citizenry. Faithful fans often request the room that housed a celebrity of a slightly more recent era, the King himself, rock 'n' roll legend Elvis Presley.

Terrell House Bed and Breakfast $$-$$$
109 Robertson Street, Burnsville, NC
(828) 682-4505
www.terrellhousebandb.com

A little off the beaten path in the friendly township of Burnsville, historic Terrell House is surrounded by mountains, offering its guests vistas of the Blue Ridge Mountains, the Bald and Unakas Ranges, and Seven Mile Ridge. The nearby Black Mountains are capped by the majestic Mount Mitchell. The inn is about 30 minutes from Asheville.

The 1900 Colonial-style home was built as a girls' dormitory for the Stanley McCormick School. You can choose from six lovely guest accommodations, each with its own personality and furnished with a queen- or full-size bed. Each room has a private bath with shower.

Make yourself at home in the parlor, where the company of other guests adds to the pleasant stay here. Or seek out the tranquility of the garden swing or the wicker-furnished back patio.

You will awake to the aroma of freshly brewed coffee, and a sumptuous breakfast is served in the dining room.

CENTRAL MOUNTAINS

Buncombe County

Black Mountain Inn $$-$$$$
718 Old Highway 70, Black Mountain, NC
(828) 669-6528, (800) 735-6128
www.blackmountaininn.com

Hidden away from the passage of time and nestled within the forest, the Black Mountain Inn embraces its guests with long-forgotten romance and charm. The house was built originally as a stagecoach stop approximately 160 years ago. At the turn of the 20th century, the home was owned by Martha Mallory, who operated the inn as a TB sanitarium until her untimely death. She was killed on the railroad tracks on her way home from town. The house fell into ruin and became a squatter's camp, complete with cows stabled in the dining room! The property was purchased by Mary Aleshire and Daisey Erb in 1940. Mrs. Aleshire was the manager of the Norton Art Gallery in Palm Beach, Florida. She restored and updated the historic property and two years later opened the house as The Oak Knoll Art Studio, which served primarily as a summer retreat for Mrs. Aleshire and her many famous guests. Ernest Hemingway, John Steinbeck, Norman Rockwell, and Helen Keller were among the guests attending the garden parties that were common events all summer long. In 1989 the house, badly in need of further restoration and updating, began its new life as the Black Mountain Inn.

The hosts of the Black Mountain Inn, June and Godfrey Bergeron, welcome you to this inn, which is perfectly situated on a knoll in the Swannanoa Valley. With three acres of wooded property, it's an ideal location for guests who travel with pets. Seven comfortable guest rooms and one suite—the Artist Loft—are decorated in casual old-fashioned furnishings. Each room has its own private bath.

The Artist Loft is a restored art studio with more than 1,000 square feet of private sanctuary with wonderful views. Peter's Room rests among the trees. Throw open the seven windows and wake up with the birds. Fern's Room is one of the pet-friendly rooms. This large, first-floor room is capable of sleeping four and is perfect for families with young children. Emily's Room features a 7-foot, claw-foot tub.

Breakfast at the Black Mountain Inn is a sumptuous buffet featuring June's famous homemade granola. Fresh fruits,

CLOSE-UP

Mount Pisgah

Mount Pisgah is the highest peak on the Asheville Plateau. Standing at 5,700 feet, this mountain overlooks western Buncombe County. Nudging it from the south is "The Sleeping Rat." On its north face, after a fierce snow, one can see "The Bride and Groom."

Some folks believe Pisgah is a Cherokee word, but it is found in the Old Testament in Deuteronomy 34:1: "Then Moses went up from the plains of Moab to Mount Nebo, to the top of Pisgah . . . from there he saw the promised land." Assumedly the early settlers of this wilderness of Western North Carolina must have hoped they had reached the promised land after all the hardships they faced in carving trails and homes out of it. They were either Bible-believing people or as survivors became such—thus naming the symbol of their hope, Mount Pisgah.

---

homemade breads or biscuits, and a main egg course, along with special blend coffee or tea, greet you each morning.

The dining room is decked for the holidays with all white linens, lights, and flowers.

Black Walnut Bed and
Breakfast Inn $$-$$$$
288 Montford Avenue, Asheville, NC
(828) 254-3878
www.blackwalnut.com

New owners, Peter and Lori White, have operated specialty bakeries at Marthas Vinyard and in West Palm Beach, Florida. They are certain to provide many tantalizing breakfast moments for their guests. The Black Walnut Inn stands out significantly from its surroundings as a Shingle-style house built in 1899 by architect Richard Sharp Smith. It was restored as a bed-and-breakfast in 1992.

Only a short walk from downtown, the inn is surrounded by a lushly landscaped garden of flowers, black walnut trees, conifers, ivy, and perfectly trimmed shrubbery. Four guest rooms in the main house and a loft in the garden cottage echo this perfection.

We enjoy cozying up to the fireplace in the graceful living room. A large front porch with rockers allows you to enjoy a balmy summer evening in this mountain town. The innkeepers are pet friendly, but do book your pet in advance.

Cedar Crest $$$$
674 Biltmore Avenue, Asheville, NC
(828) 252-1389
www.cedarcrestvictorianinn.com

Less than a mile north of the entrance to Biltmore Estate sits another Victorian beauty. Rising from a flower-bedecked hill on lower Biltmore Avenue, Cedar Crest commands the ascent from Biltmore Village. The traffic scurries uphill toward downtown Asheville, but this exquisite bed-and-breakfast seems forever poised in the Gilded Age.

The opulent Queen Anne–style home was built in 1891 for prominent Asheville businessman William E. Breese. Breese played host to Asheville society, but as the century passed and the prosperous 1920s waned, Cedar Crest fell into disrepair. Through the years the home took on the guise of a sanitarium and, much later, a boardinghouse. Then the founding innkeepers answered an ad in *Preservation News* and came all the way from Wisconsin to rescue this lovely, faded lady. Careful restoration followed, much of it just removing decades of grime and ill-conceived decoration. What emerged was the amazing beauty of rich oak woodwork, intricately carved mantels, and solid Victorian construction. The inn has been lavished with period antiques: claw-foot tubs, delicate lace, brass beds, and Victorian collectibles.

Ten guest rooms are available at Cedar Crest, described by its innkeepers as "a passage to 1890." All rooms are air-conditioned and have telephones and private baths; some rooms have working fireplaces. The upper two floors also feature a sitting area, and guests can sit on the wide veranda. A separate guest cottage, built in 1915, adjoins the main house and is wonderful for vacationing families. The inn is open year-round, and its four acres are planted so that something is in bloom every season. (And there is even a croquet court.)

Chestnut Street Inn $$-$$$$
176 East Chestnut Street, Asheville, NC
(828) 285-0705
www.chestnutstreetinn.com
Enjoy a candlelit breakfast at Chestnut Street Inn in this historic district. Late afternoon tea and Friday evening social hour allow you to meet other guests in the antique-filled parlors. Artworks by local artists provide extra interest. Large four-poster beds satisfy the need for downy comfort, as does the fluffy bathrobe provided for your stay. A chocolate on your pillow ends the day with the luxury in which you began it.

The Hawk & Ivy $$$
133 North Fork Road, Barnardsville, NC
(828) 626-3486, (888) 395-7254
www.hawkandivy.com
Wake up gazing over a country meadow, take a morning walk to the fish pond or an afternoon stroll through the wildflowers, or even pick a bowl of berries for your

breakfast with innkeeper Eve Davis at this country bed-and-breakfast retreat. Eve and her husband James, an ordained minister and licensed contractor, wear many hats at the Hawk & Ivy. To give you an idea of the inn's many fine touches, let us mention that Eve's gardens and floral designs in Atlanta were featured in national magazines, books, and television. Eve's organic garden here grows a bounty of berries, produce, and flowers, all of which find their way into your sojourn at the inn. She also maintains a tiny craft gallery on the grounds, carrying small crafts from friends and local artisans, as well as her own crafts and dried flowers.

Set in 24 acres of wildflower fields, this farmhouse built in 1910 is only 20 minutes from Asheville but is completely in the country. You can choose between the main house bedroom or three bedrooms in the cottage across the way. The former has its own private bath and an heirloom four-poster bed covered in fine linens and down comforter. Two bedrooms (one has a double bed, the other two twins), a large shared bath, full kitchen, and living room with fireplace, sofa, television, and phone compose the first floor of the guest cottage. Of course Eve's flower arrangements embellish these charming quarters, as do the fine watercolors on the walls. A second-floor suite completes the cottage, taking up the entire light-filled loft space, and including a full kitchen, bathroom, extra-long double bed, single bed, and queen-size pull-out sofa. The private deck overlooks a valley, mountain ridges, and the small lake. In case the view is not enough entertainment, there is also a television. Both kitchens are supplied with fresh-ground coffee and tea, creamers, and condiments.

Both Eve and James cook up incredibly innovative and fresh breakfasts, usually beginning with a bowl of fresh raspberries or other seasonal fruit from the garden. Guests dine at the long family table in the dining room, surrounded by early American Impressionist paintings. If weather permits, breakfast is served on the veranda. Breakfast might include a combination of several of the following: fresh baked goods, asparagus omelette, melons with strawberry puree, coffee cakes, baked vanilla French toast, or cheese grits casserole with jalapeños, all served on delicate family heirloom china.

The Davises encourage guests to stroll around the property and will recommend hikes close by. In the field above the farmhouse, a large festival "barn" is the setting for many a wedding, wedding reception, and family reunion. Two knolls have served as locations for nuptials, with live music and buffet tables elegantly arrayed in the rustic wooden structure. On occasion Eve teaches flower arranging and drying and herb preparation workshops out of the barn or in her art studio.

The Inn Around the Corner $$-$$$
109 Church Street, Black Mountain, NC
(828) 669-6005, (800) 393-6005

The Inn Around the Corner features five lovely guest rooms in a restored 1915 Four Square Victorian House. The upstairs porch, with porch swings and rockers, slows time to a standstill. All rooms are sold with private baths on a first-come, first-served basis. Adjoining rooms may be available as suites—just ask and the innkeepers will gladly accommodate you. Four of the rooms are on the second floor, and one room is on the first floor with a private bath. Quilts on the beds, soft colors, hand-stitched samplers, and floral arrangements mark Grandma's Room, while Beau's is decorated in muted country colors with a patriotic theme. Available only as a suite with Beau's room, Ashley's is a lovely old-fashioned room, located on the second floor with full-size canopied bed. The Spring Garden bears soft yellows, greens, and mauves, which carry out the botanical theme in this wicker-filled room with a full-size bed and single bed. A full-size bed is also available on the porch. A lovely view of the mountains awaits outside the private entrance to the second-story porch. A bountiful breakfast is served to guests in the dining room or on one of the porches, weather permitting. The innkeepers are amenable to special dietary requirements or requests, but be sure to tell them ahead of time.

The inn is close to Black Mountain's quaint downtown shopping area, with a variety of dining possibilities. The inn is also a short distance from a walking trail around Lake Tomahawk.

Hiking, kayaking, rafting, and fishing trips will gladly be arranged by the innkeepers for your enjoyment.

The-Inn-on-Mill-Creek $$$
1407 Mill Creek Road, Ridgecrest, NC
(828) 668-1115, (877) 735-2964
www.inn-on-mill-creek.com

The Inn-on-Mill-Creek provides guests a relaxing mountain bed-and-breakfast just 20 miles east of Asheville. Secluded among mountain laurel near the top of the Ridgecrest Pass, seven scenic acres are hidden in the Pisgah National Forest between the historic villages of Black Mountain and Old Fort. The Carillons (Jim, Aline, Jeffrey, and Kate) are your nurturing hosts.

The inn features four guest rooms or suites, each with private baths and many unique amenities. Also enjoy a two-story great room with a piano corner, a soapstone wood stove, and cozy river-bed stone hearth. A library nook in the upstairs balcony for quiet reading is lit by a historic cathedral chandelier. The innkeepers provide two choices for your breakfast seating: a warm and open dining room with its own wood stove hearth and great view of the lake, or a south-facing solarium overlooking the dam and waterfall. The solarium also provides a hot tub for evening stargazing or relaxing. Be sure to check out the creekside deck for sunning yourself as you listen to the waterfall or for enjoying a family cookout.

Enjoy the family fish lake, waterfall, and dam, which powers Andrews Geyser in the valley. A sunny deck overlooks the lake and the Long Branch of Mill Creek. The plentiful breakfasts are made with seasonal fruits and berries from the Carillons' own orchard.

The Lion and the Rose $$$$
276 Montford Avenue, Asheville, NC
(828) 255-ROSE
www.lion-rose.com

The Montford Historic District is home to some fine examples of Victorian architecture. The Lion and the Rose, one of these homes, is listed on the National Register of Historic Places. This handsome bed-and-breakfast inn is a simplified Queen Anne/Georgian-style residence, built in 1898, that celebrates the English style. And this stately mansion certainly seems "to the manor born."

The innkeepers have furnished all five faithfully restored guest rooms with period antiques and Oriental rugs. High embossed ceilings, oak woodwork, and leaded- and stained-glass windows are just a few of the architectural details that give distinction to the Lion and the Rose. Each room has a private bath.

Monte Vista Hotel $$
308 West State Street, Black Mountain, NC
(828) 669-2119, (800) 441-5400

The Monte Vista is one of those fine, old boardinghouse inns that used to dot the landscape of the South, particularly areas like Black Mountain, which grew up as a tourist retreat. Today the Monte Vista sits like an elegant dowager queen, still beautiful and still most interesting. The minute you enter the spacious lobby with its roaring fireplace, lofty ceiling, ornately carved Victorian settees, and overstuffed armchairs, with an army of family photographs and vintage prints decorating every available space, you know you've passed the threshold of time.

This is America in the early 1920s and '30s, when gasoline cost pennies a gallon and motoring was an adventure. You can just imagine an excited vacation party arriving at the Monte Vista, children bounding up the grand old staircase to a pleasantly appointed room, then back downstairs for a buffet meal in the cheery dining room.

Today visitors come from all over the country, perhaps remembering this lovely old hotel from childhoods long ago. The distinct character of the Monte Vista has long drawn creative types—writers and artists—seeking the inspirational seclusion of the inn.

Monte Vista Hotel has been owned and operated by the same family for generations. Third-generation innkeeper Rosalie Johnston works to make your visit a memory you'll share with your own children. The 55 guest rooms are furnished in a comfy collection of 19th-century antiques and Depression era pieces. Rooms have quaint private baths, no telephones, and no televisions—they've pulled the plug on the hectic pace of the new millennium.

Red Rocker Inn $$$-$$$$
136 North Dougherty Street, Black Mountain, NC
(828) 669-5991
www.redrockerinn.com

The measured pace of the red rockers on the enormous porch overlooking the lovely gardens of this elegant inn gives you a feel for its relaxing atmosphere. Tucked away in a quiet residential neighborhood in the quaint village of Black Mountain, just 14 miles east of Asheville, the Red Rocker Inn is determinedly slow-paced. Innkeepers Craig and Margie Lindberg have elevated this calm to an art form.

The inn was a boardinghouse known as Dougherty Heights back in 1927. It became the Red Rocker Inn in 1964. The tranquility of the place is its hallmark, and the 17 exquisite guest rooms (each with private bath) reflect this search for inner peace. The warm fireplace and lovers' window seat in Elizabeth's Attic, the inspired stained glass of the Preacher's Room, and the white lace canopy bed in the romantic Anniversary Room are just a few of the Lindbergs' thoughtful efforts to give visitors an island of calm. The inn is centrally heated and air-conditioned.

The dining room is a celebrated spot for guests as well as the community. With the generous bounty provided by the innkeepers, the dining room seems to be the only place where guests might exhibit a lack of self-restraint in this peaceful domain. The family-style meals, served on lace-clothed, candle-lit tables, are robust and hearty Southern selections heaped on in generous proportions. The desserts are decadently delicious confections, such as "Heath Bar" pie or X-rated triple layer chocolate cake. Where's that rocker when you need it?

The Red Rocker Inn is open almost year-round (February through December). Spectacular season's specials are offered during the winter, spring, and early fall.

Richmond Hill Inn $$$$
87 Richmond Hill Drive, Asheville, NC
(828) 252-7313, (888) 742-4536
www.richmondhillinn.com

Sitting on a promontory overlooking the French Broad River a short distance from downtown Asheville is this sparkling jewel known as Richmond Hill Inn. This magnificently renovated 12-room mansion, built in 1889, was the private residence of former congressman and international diplomat Col. Richmond Pearson and his wife, Gabrielle.

This elegant home faced the wrecking ball in the early 1970s when it was propitiously rescued by the Preservation Society of Asheville and Buncombe County, which worked to have the mansion placed on the National Register of Historic Places. This designation was achieved in 1972, and by 1981 the society had purchased seven acres of adjacent land on which to move the mansion, should the need arise. Circumstances favored the society, which purchased Richmond Hill for $1.00 from North Carolina Baptist Homes, Inc., with the provision that the home be moved from the original site. By 1984, with funds secured, the Preservation Society moved this grand old Queen Anne structure 600 feet to the east.

Richmond Hill had its rebirth in 1987, when the Preservation Society sold the mansion to Albert Michel, a Greensboro-based businessman and president of the Education Center. Michel and his wife Margaret were preservation advocates and took to the Richmond Hill project with gusto. The Michels began a mammoth, three-year renovation that necessitated the purchase of 40 additional acres from the original estate; the completion of a 900-square-foot, octagonal ballroom for meetings; the design of a glass-enclosed porch to complement dining; and the renovation of five third-floor guest rooms.

The richly paneled grand entrance hall features a portrait of the beautiful Gabrielle Pearson. The 12-foot ceiling rises to 23 feet as you ascend the wide staircase with its hand-turned spooled balusters. The 12 original guest rooms of the main house are dressed in Victorian splendor and richly furnished with Oriental rugs, period antiques, and private baths as well as modern amenities. Second-floor rooms are all named for Pearson family members, and the recently renovated third floor honors noted authors from Asheville or those having Asheville connections. Downstairs, the library has more than 200 books, many of them first editions, from Mr. Pearson's personal collection. The world-class restaurant at Richmond Hill is named in honor of Gabrielle Pearson, who was a gracious hostess here and abroad during her husband's diplomatic career.

The Croquet Cottages, designed to complement the mansion's Queen Anne-style architecture, were built in 1991. Each of the nine cottages is individually decorated in a style reminiscent of a Victorian country estate, with pencil-post beds, fireplaces, spacious baths, and a porch with rocking chairs. Modern amenities such as televisions, telephones, and refrigerators have been added. The Garden Pavilion, added in 1996, is a lovely U-shaped structure overlooking a parterre garden and waterfall. It houses 15 additional guest rooms, a banquet dining room, and a gift shop.

The improvements at Richmond Hill are like a string of pearls added to a natural beauty. As the Michels reclaim the

With so many B&Bs in the area, we are hard pressed to mention them all. Therefore we urge you to explore on your own at the Asheville Bed & Breakfast Association Web site, www. ashevillebba.com, the association has 21 member inns. Or call (877) 262-6867 to order a variety of brochures before your visit.

mountain around the mansion, they also reclaim the glory that once crowned this lovely Asheville landmark.

Richmond Hill Inn is open year-round.

Sourwood Inn $$$$
810 Elk Mountain Scenic Highway, Asheville, NC
(828) 255-0690, (828) 253-2785
www.sourwoodinn.com

Located just off the Blue Ridge Parkway on 100 acres, this is what a country inn is all about. Walking trails crisscross the forested land, but even just sitting in your room looking out over the mountain through the dense foliage below, you will know you have truly "gotten away from it all." Sourwood Inn is finely constructed of cedar trimmed with stone. The entire structure sits on hilly terrain at an elevation of 3,200 feet. Easily accessible to downtown Asheville, it is nonetheless in the countryside and can feel like wilderness, with densely growing trees and birdsong all around.

Each of the inn's 12 guest rooms has a private balcony overlooking the Reems Creek Valley, a wood-burning fireplace, and a tub with a view! When you turn on your faucet to draw a bath, you will be amazed with the ensuing waterfall, thanks to Scandinavian faucetry. The French doors that open onto the guest room balconies let mountain breezes drift in at night. Decorated in muted forest and meadow colors, the rooms are as peaceful within as the idyllic countryside outside.

The inn also maintains numerous public areas—porches with rocking chairs, a

lobby with plush chairs in front of a crackling fireplace, and a library stocked with books for your leisure time. There's also a game room downstairs with a billiard table. Susan and Jeff Curtis, who live on the premises, are innkeepers with Susan's parents Nat and Anne Burkhardt.

Sassafras Cabin is nestled in the woods 100 yards from the main inn. Complete with a screened-in porch, the cabin has two full baths, a fully equipped kitchen, a living/dining area, and a bedroom loft. There's a wonderful variety from which to choose at Sourwood Inn. You may never want to leave. Sink back into those chairs, admire the perfectly designed and built carpentry work and decorative touches, grab a good book from the library of Nat's favorites, kick up your feet in front of the fire, and plan a walk in the crisp fresh mountain air after dinner.

Tree Haven Bed & Breakfast $$-$$$
1114 Montreat Road, Black Mountain, NC
(828) 669-3841, (888) 448-3841
www.treehavenbandb.com

A gracious welcome brings you back to a more relaxed, timeless serenity in this 1908 restored home, surrounded by mature oaks, hickory, pine, hemlock, and chestnut trees. Centrally located just outside the gates of Montreat, only a mile from downtown Black Mountain, Tree Haven is ideally situated for both the casual stroller and the serious hiker. Return home to sit on the porch and watch the fireflies light up the night skies, or stroll the grounds bordered by a gently flowing creek. Innkeeper Carol Redmond has traveled the world as a delegate for the sport of synchronized swimming after being honored as a member of the Helms Swimming Hall of Fame. Previously from the West Coast, she has found Black Mountain to be a perfect place for rest and relaxation amidst nature's wonderland. International guests, especially, will find a helpful, if not bilingual, resource for local travel. Carol, an avid hiker herself, will help you find those hidden mountain trails when you can tear yourself away from the homey surroundings of the inn. Private baths, a whirlpool tub, air-conditioning, and a smoke-free environment ensure your comfort at Tree Haven. You can chose from rooms with king or queen beds. Vegetarian breakfasts are also available.

WhiteGate Inn & Cottage $$-$$$$
117 East Chestnut Street, Asheville, NC
(828) 253-2553
www.whitegate.net

The first thing you'll notice about this 1889 inn are the unique gardens and greenhouse that surround it. Deliciously landscaped with lush foliage, waterfalls, a koi pond, and a patio with a gas log fire pit, the WhiteGate Inn makes it hard to want to come inside. But once you do, delight in the large rooms decorated with elegant antiques and oriental rugs. Saunter down to breakfast, after reading the complimentary morning paper, to a three-course breakfast in the dining room. Monogrammed robes and down comforters have allowed you to revel in comfort the night before. A guest refrigerator remains stocked, and a library has a selection of videotapes, books, and CDs.

Henderson County

Apple Inn $$-$$$$
1005 White Pine Drive, Hendersonville, NC
(828) 693-0107, (800) 615-6611
www.appleinn.com

Situated on three acres just 2 miles from downtown Hendersonville, this lovely home with its large wraparound porch was once the summer residence of a South Carolina lawyer and his family. Surrounded by dogwoods, azaleas, and 100-year-old oaks, poplars, and maples, it provides a quiet retreat conveniently close to all the many attractions of this popular area. Two fine restaurants and a number of interesting shops are within walking distance at the Laurel Park Shopping Center.

The inn, in one of the nation's largest apple-producing counties, offers five bright and comfortable rooms with private modern baths, each named after a

different apple. They have been furnished charmingly with antiques and adorned with fresh flowers. In addition there is the Apple Branch, a two-bedroom, two-bath cottage that sleeps six. It has a full kitchen, dining area, and living room area, front porch, color cable TV, a private phone, and a private driveway. It's available by the week, month, or with a two-night minimum.

Each morning a delightful, home-cooked breakfast of fresh fruits, quiche, strudel, or French toast and tasty breads or muffins awaits you on the patio, accompanied by gourmet coffees and teas. Though relaxation is a favorite occupation at the inn, you can also choose a game of billiards, badminton, croquet, or numerous board games. It also has a corporate membership at Oak Hills Racquet Club, where you can swim or play tennis.

To reach Apple Inn take the U.S. 64 exit off I-26. Go 4 miles until you see a Hardee's on the right and an Exxon station on the left. Turn left here onto Daniel Drive and take the first right at a four-way stop onto White Pine Drive. The inn's driveway is the first on the left.

The Claddagh Inn $$$
755 North Main Street, Hendersonville, NC
(828) 697-7778, (800) 225-4700
www.claddaghinn.com

The regal old Claddagh Inn was Hendersonville's first bed-and-breakfast establishment. Built around the turn of the century by an ex-mayor of Hendersonville, W. A. Smith, it was sold in 1906 and became the Charleston Boarding House, since it largely served Charlestonians escaping the heat of the coast for mountain coolness. In 1985 it was renamed the Claddagh (pronounced CLAW-da), a Gaelic symbol that represents love and friendship. The hospitality of its owners, Gerri and Augie Emanuele, lives up to the name.

Here you'll have a choice of 14 uniquely decorated, air-conditioned rooms, all with private baths, telephones, and televisions. Each has its own individual, old-fashioned and charming flavor.

The inn also offers a very large parlor and a cozy library with books, games, and a piano. Full—indeed, gigantic—breakfasts in the attractive dining room are included in the rates. The facilities are also available for small catered parties or meetings.

Echo Mountain Inn $$-$$$$
2849 Laurel Park Highway,
Hendersonville, NC
(828) 693-9626, (800) ECHO-INN
www.echoinn.com

This massive stone-and-frame inn 3 miles from Hendersonville was built in 1896 on a mountainside that overlooks the whole area—a spectacular view that's visible from many of the guest rooms and the dining room, which is open to the public for dinner. (See our Restaurants chapter.) The view is particularly pretty at night with the city lights twinkling below. The inn's 23 rooms, many with fireplaces, are decorated with antiques and reproductions. There is also one cottage and an annex with 10 suites, some with kitchenettes. All accommodations have cable television and telephones, and some have air-conditioning, although with an elevation of 3,100 feet, the last is seldom needed.

On the grounds you'll find shuffleboard courts and a swimming pool. Although the atmosphere at Echo Mountain is casual and leisurely in keeping with the nature of an authentic country inn, dinners here are quite exquisite and definitely gourmet.

To reach Echo Mountain Inn, drive west on Fifth Avenue in Hendersonville; this street will turn into the Laurel Park Highway.

Flat Rock Inn $$$
2810 Greenville Highway, Flat Rock, NC
(828) 696-3273, (800) 266-3996
www.bbhost.com/flatrockinn

The Flat Rock Inn is across U.S. 25 from the Woodfield Inn and just as convenient to all local attractions. This elegant but homelike bed-and-breakfast was built in 1888 as a summer retreat by Charleston's R. Withers Memminger, a son of C. G. Memminger, the first secretary of the treasury for the Confederate states. Known locally as Five Oaks, the home was skillfully renovated in 1992, and its new owners, Dennis and Sandi Page (in their own words, "corporate dropouts from Dallas"), opened its doors to the public in 1993.

Currently the Flat Rock Inn offers four rooms with private baths, each elegantly Victorian but with beautifully different atmospheres. Two of the rooms have private, second-floor porches; a third offers a six-foot tub in an alcove behind lace curtains. Flat Rock Inn also offers splendid, family-style, Texas-size breakfasts with such gourmet items as eggs Benedict or cherry blintzes, as well as those country favorites: buttermilk biscuits topped with local jams and jellies.

Flat Rock Inn is open almost year-round, closing only during the first two weeks in January.

Melange Bed & Breakfast $-$$$$
1230 Fifth Avenue W., Hendersonville, NC
(828) 697-5253, (800) 303-5253
www.melangebb.com

Luxuriously cosmopolitan best describes this B&B, just a 15-minute walk from downtown Hendersonville. The mansion, complete with a pony barn and a dollhouse with six-foot ceilings, was designed and built by North Carolina's famous architect, Erle G. Stillwell, in 1920. In the 1960s its owner added marble mantles from Paris, crystal chandeliers from Vienna, and hand-painted porcelain accessories from Italy.

The old grandeur is still represented by the 11-foot, ornamented ceilings, the ornate mirrors, and marble fireplaces, now graced by contemporary comfort, fine tiles, Turkish rugs, books, candles, and flowers. Four guest rooms occupy the second floor, and a full-floor suite with two bedrooms is on the third. Each is named after its predominant color scheme: Rose, Pearl, Cinnamon, Green, and Red. And each has a private bath or

Jacuzzi, hardwood floors, air-conditioning, a TV and VCR, and a private telephone. A large collection of video films and books are available for guests.

Depending on the season, a gourmet breakfast is served on the rose garden patio, on a Mediterranean porch, or in the formal dining room. It includes fresh fruits, an egg entree, coffee cakes, and thick, crusted bread served with self-prepared, compound butters and delicious pre-serves. The yogurt here is homemade.

Special services are offered at an additional fee, such as fruit plates, champagne or special chocolates in your room, an elegant high tea, or a five-course candlelight dinner. You can also order a relaxation spa, a therapeutic massage, or a reflexology session from a certified therapist.

Hendersonville's Fifth Avenue is just 1 block over from U. S. 64 W. Drive 0.8 mile from Main Street to Blythe Street. Turn left. On Fifth Avenue, Melange is on the left behind a hemlock hedge. The driveway is after the Melange sign.

The Waverly Inn $$$
783 North Main Street, Hendersonville, NC
(828) 693-9193, (800) 537-8195
www.waverlyinn.com

For a stay in pretty Historic Downtown Hendersonville, you can't find more handy accommodations than at the three-story Waverly, the oldest surviving inn in town, which is listed on the National Register of Historic Places. It's a 2-block walk from the Waverly to Hendersonville's dynamic downtown with its wonderful shops and restaurants and frequent art shows and festivals. Open year-round, the Waverly is a large and gracious inn, even though it now faces a street whose steady stream of traffic reflects the popularity of the town.

You'll get a good view of all this activity from the inn's long, wide veranda, which holds about 20 rocking chairs; there are almost that many on the upstairs porch, too. Polished wood, four-posters and turn-of-the-century fittings fill the 14 guest rooms and one suite, all of which come with private baths, cable TV, and telephones. There are sitting rooms on all three floors.

In their rates innkeepers John and Diane Sheiry and Diane's sister Darla Olmstead include a hearty breakfast cooked to order—and that means all you can eat. There's also a social hour between 5:00 and 6:00 P.M. If hunger hits you anytime, we were told to just raid the cookie jar for one of Darla's famous delectables. That's a special delight for children, who are welcome at the inn. To find the Waverly turn north on Hendersonville's Main Street.

Woodfield Inn $$$$
U.S. Highway 25 S., Flat Rock, NC
(828) 693-6016, (800) 533-6016
www.woodfieldinn.com

Every time we drive up to the Woodfield Inn, we feel we should be in a carriage rather than a car. This impression has something to do with the elegant way this old establishment sits proudly back on its spacious grounds, immediately setting the tone of a more leisurely lifestyle.

The Woodfield Inn was built in 1847 by a group of prominent men who wanted to create "a good, commodious tavern on or near the Main Saluda Road." Their Flat Rock Hotel, as it became known, was a great success. Eventually Henry T. Farmer, a relative and ward of Charleston's Charles and Susan Baring, the original "founders" and social leaders of fashionable Flat Rock, bought it. One of Squire Farmer's most outstanding contributions to the inn was the creation of a style of black walnut rocking chair that didn't creep annoyingly across the floor when rocked. These Flat Rock Rockers were so well liked that Farmer opened a furniture factory to produce them. The factory closed down, however, during the Civil War, and although the inn's present rockers are still favorites with the guests, Squire Farmer's rocking chairs have never been duplicated.

Fortunately the Southern congeniality for which the inn was so famous has been handed down. Full of history and antiques, the Woodfield's 18 guest rooms have been redecorated by the inn's owners, Rhonda and Michael Horton. Likewise they have restored the outside of the inn to its historic colors of white and Charleston green.

The Woodfield is a popular place anytime, but it's particularly busy during the Flat Rock Playhouse's season late May through early September (the theater, which is the official state theater of North Carolina, is practically next door). So is the Carl Sandburg Historic Site (see our Arts and Culture chapter). The inn is also a favorite spot for weddings and other special events.

The Woodfield is open all year and serves dinner and Sunday brunch to the public. It's 2.5 miles from Hendersonville on the U.S. Highway 25 S. (Greenville Highway). If you're coming from town, the inn will be on your right.

Polk County

The Foxtrot Inn $$$, no credit cards
800 Lynn Road, Tryon, NC
(828) 859-9706, (888) 676-8050
www.foxtrotinn.com

Though Foxtrot is in Tryon's city limits, this 1915 home set high on six wooded acres is a quiet and elegant escape. It was purchased several years ago by Wim Woody, a Tryon native who grew up in the house next door. Graciously proportioned and traditionally furnished, the inn has four air-conditioned guest rooms (two are suites with sitting rooms). Each room has a private bath. You can also stay in the two-bedroom guest house, which has a fully equipped kitchen, one and a half baths, a deck, air-conditioning, cable TV, and mountain views.

Wim and his wife, Tiffany, begin each day with a beautifully presented gourmet breakfast after which you can go for a walk in the woods or lounge by the pool. Evenings often find guests playing games in the card room or sitting by a roaring fire in the living room. A 50 percent deposit is required for reservations. The

inn is in Tryon just off N.C. Highway 108, which leads to I-26.

The Mimosa Inn $$
Mimosa Inn Drive, Tryon, NC
(828) 859-7688, (877) MIMOSAINN

This pretty, rambling bed-and-breakfast inn with its column-lined veranda has 200 years of history behind it. In the 1700s King George granted John Mills 90,000 acres of land in this area. He and his son operated Mill's Inn here along the trading trail that would become Howard Gap Road. After the Civil War, a Pennsylvania Presbyterian minister named Dr. Leland McAboy bought the inn, named it the McAboy House and, like the Millses, became known as a hospitable host. In 1903 Aaron French and David Sterns bought and modernized the property with innovations such as gaslight and hot and cold running water, added a casino/bowling alley, and renamed it The Mimosa Inn. Fire destroyed most of the building in 1916, sparing only the casino/bowling alley, which was remodeled into the current Mimosa Inn.

The Mimosa Inn has 10 guest rooms, many with mountain views, and serves a hearty breakfast on the veranda or in the dining room. From I-26 take the Tryon/Columbus exit (exit 36) and follow N.C. 108 W. for 2 miles. The marked entrance drive is on the left beyond the mansion.

The Oaks Bed & Breakfast $$$
Greenville Street, Saluda, NC
(828) 749-9613, (800) 893-6091
www.theoaksbedandbreakfast.com

Built by a local banker as a private residence in 1894, this interesting, turreted house was a boarding home from 1905 until the 1940s. Tall trees set off the exterior, which features a wraparound porch with seasonal hanging baskets, wicker furniture, and a swing. Inside you'll discover an inviting library with a fireplace and a large, airy living room. The center of the house is the gracious dining room where delicious gourmet breakfasts are served family style.

CLOSE-UP

Polk County: White Oak Mountain

Polk County's topography varies from rolling foothills to level plains on one side and high timber-clad mountains on the other. You can see a great example of all this from what has been called "the greatest view east of the Rockies." Drive east on N.C. 108 for just less than 5 miles to Houston Road (SR 1137). Turn left and drive a half-mile to a fork. Bear right for just more than a half-mile, turn left onto White Oak Mountain Road, and drive 2 miles to "The Brow," fronting the White Oak Condominiums near the top of Shunkawaken Falls. From this height of 3,000 feet on a clear day, you can see fields and farmlands stretching for 50 miles, and it's very pretty at night with all the lights twinkling below. Another great vista lies across the relatively flat mountaintop westward to the base of the last incline of Tryon Peak, which is the highest of a number of summits on the White Oak Mountain massif. It's called Sunset Rock, and it's a popular Polk County picnic spot with a view of rugged, steep mountain ranges flowing into each other.

Each of the inn's four distinctively decorated guest rooms has a private bath and cable TV. You have your choice of the Blue, Gold, Green, or Red Room, each of which contains a four-poster queen-size bed, an extra-long, full-size bed, or three single beds.

The property also has a separate and self-contained guest house, The Acorn, which boasts a nice view of the ivy-filled woods below.

The Oaks, which is open year-round, is just a short walk from the antiques, arts, crafts, and old-time stores of Saluda. To find this comfortable bed-and-breakfast, go to Saluda and take Greenville Street in the center of town. Drive a half-mile; the Oaks will be on your right. The Oaks is open April through mid-December.

The Orchard Inn   **$$$$**
N.C. Highway 176, Saluda, NC
(828) 749-5471, (800) 581-3800
www.orchardinn.com
Simply ascending the winding drive to the Orchard Inn will make you feel that you're arriving somewhere special—and you are.

The inn, sprawled with plantation-like elegance on a ridge, was built by the International Brotherhood of Railway Clerks and Engineers as a mountain getaway in the early 1900s, near the terminus of the steepest railway grade east of the Rockies. That engineering feat is a marvel even today, and a stay in this tranquil place is just as marvelous.

In addition to the nine guest rooms in the imposing main building, there are three remodeled cottages with fireplaces, whirlpool baths, and private decks. Each room and cottage has a personality of its own, from the delicate patterns on the wallpaper to its paintings, prints, stenciling, and quilts. The entire guest quarters are furnished with period pieces and antiques. Wide porches and a shaded deck hold swings, rockers, ferns, and blooming plants. You can relax on swings out on the grounds, too.

The Orchard Inn is a place of leisure, where a naturalist guides morning walks on nearby nature trails. The dining area is an airy, glassed-in porch that runs the length and along one end of the inn. From here a stunning view of the mountains stretches all the way into South Carolina. Full breakfasts and French Provincial dinners "with a country flair," say the hosts, are served, and dinner is open to the public by reservation. Complimentary hors d'oeuvres are offered prior to dinner. The chef will also prepare an insulated strapbag hiker's picnic, a romantic picnic basket, or a box lunch for your journey home. You do need to keep in mind that Saluda is a "dry" town as far as alcoholic beverages go, but you may bring your own spirits. There's ice in the rooms.

The Orchard Inn, which is open yearround, is a short distance outside of Saluda on the way to Tryon.

The Pine Crest Inn $$-$$$
5 Pine Crest Lane, Tryon, NC
(828) 859-9135, (800) 633-3001
www.pinecrestinn.com
In 1918 a hotel owner from Michigan, Carter P. Brown, created the charmingly rustic Pine Crest Inn. Later, in the 1920s, Brown played a leading role in establishing the Tryon Riding and Hunt Club that helped make Tryon the equestrian center it is today.

Pine Crest Inn is still thriving. It's full of fireplaces, wide porches, tranquil gardens, bright lawns, and wooded grounds. The inn has 35 air-conditioned rooms, most with fireplaces and all with telephones, televisions, and nice robes for guests. Rates include a full continental breakfast and complimentary sherry or port in the rooms. Both suites and cottages are available, along with a gourmet restaurant. (See our Restaurants chapter.)

The complex also has a lovely conference center available for retreats, seminars, or other gatherings. To get there turn off of Trade Street onto Market Street and follow the signs to the inn's entrance at the top of the hill.

Stone Hedge Inn $$$
222 Stone Hedge Lane, Tryon, NC
(828) 859-9114, (800) 859-1974
www.stone-hedge-inn.com

The Stone Hedge Inn is on a 28-acre estate just 3 miles from Tryon town center. The inn property includes the main house, a guest house, and a poolside cottage, all surrounded by gardens, wooded walks, and rolling meadows. Each building is a unique fieldstone structure exhibiting the character of its 1930s vintage architecture. All six rooms are large with private baths, air-conditioning, cable television, and a telephone. Two rooms possess rich pine-paneled walls and ceilings, with a fireplace for a rustic feel, while those in the main house have highly decorative sculptured ceilings and antiques for a more formal ambience.

A full breakfast is served in the dining room, where large picture windows offer mountain views. The dining room, open to the public, serves dinner with an eclectic mix of contemporary specials and traditional favorites. Owners Thomas and Shaula Dinsmore bring a fresh lightheartedness to the inn's peaceful atmosphere.

Stone Hedge is open all year. To get to the inn, which is about 2.5 miles from Tryon, take N.C. 108 to Howard Gap Road.

Rutherford County

Lake Lure Inn $$$$
U.S. Highways 64/74, Lake Lure, NC
(828) 625-2525, (888) 434-4970
www.lakelureinn.com
This stately inn overlooking beautiful Lake Lure has been a tradition in Hickory Nut Gorge since 1927. In its early days F. Scott Fitzgerald, President Franklin D. Roosevelt, and Emily Post came to Lake Lure Inn. Today the inn, with 50 guest rooms, has been renovated and attracts scores of vacationers.

Guests may choose from a variety of chambers—standard rooms with two double beds or one queen, deluxe rooms with a king, or rooms with king- or queen-size bed and a pullout sofa in a large sitting area. There are also two suites, and all rooms are furnished with antique historic inn furniture. All rooms have color cable

TV, phone, and a private bath. The spacious lobby runs the width of the hotel and is furnished with sofas, soft chairs, and area literature and newspapers to help plan your local sight-seeing. Fresh flowers and old photographs of famous former guests complement the decor. Cozy up to the fireplace in the main dining room for the complimentary continental breakfast, which includes cereal, breads, bagels, muffins fresh from the inn's kitchen, juices, coffee, and tea.

If you are lucky enough to be staying over for Sunday, a champagne brunch, served mid-March until mid-November, can be your meal of the day. This lavish buffet features a cutting station with prime rib and ham, omelette bar, waffle station, and a table of hot dishes and side dishes, including chicken, fish, and vegetables. A salad bar and pasta varieties round out the main course, but don't forgo the dessert selection, which often features homemade cobblers and pies. The dining room also serves dinner Wednesday through Saturday year-round; Tuesday dinner is added in peak season. Check with the front desk about the varying lunch schedule.

The inn's outdoor pool has a sundeck, and a shaded veranda with benches and chairs allows you to look out over Lake Lure at the front of the inn. Tennis courts are available next door. Chimney Rock Park and the Bottomless Pools are nearby.

Lake Lure Inn is open year-round; seasonal rates are available.

Transylvania County

The Inn at Brevard $$-$$$
410 East Main Street, Brevard, NC
(828) 884-2105
www.innatbrevard.8m.com
This elegant, columned inn, listed on the National Register of Historic Places, is within easy walking distance of all the great shops and restaurants in downtown Brevard, and the Silvermont Mansion (see our Arts and Culture chapter) is just down the street. The inn has a distinguished his-

tory. It was built in 1885 as the private home of Mrs. Woodbridge, a wealthy widow from Virginia who entertained the nobility of the Victorian era here, including her good friend, Lady Astor. Woodbridge bequeathed the house to her only daughter, Rebecca, who married William E. Breese, a prominent attorney and mayor of Brevard. In 1911 Breese hosted a reunion of the Confederate troops who served under Stonewall Jackson (Jackson's widow attended).

The house was sold in the 1940s and operated as the Colonial Inn for many years. There are five nonsmoking rooms in the main house, three with private baths. Ten cabin-style rooms with private baths are in the adjacent lodge. A full breakfast is included in the tariff.

When entering Brevard on U.S. 64, turn east onto U.S. 276 at the courthouse in the center of town. The inn is just a few blocks away on the left.

Key Falls Inn $-$$
151 Everett Road, Pisgah Forest, NC
(828) 884-7559
www.keyfallsinn.com
A quiet and restful stay can be yours in this large Victorian farmhouse built between 1868 and 1869. Formerly known as the Patton House after its original owner, John Patton, this bed-and-breakfast has four guest bedrooms and a two-room suite furnished with antiques. All have private baths. The house's porches are popular for reading, relaxing, and enjoying the view. A sumptuous breakfast is included in the price, and complimentary refreshments are served in the afternoon.

On the inn's grounds you'll find a tennis court with a view of Pisgah Ridge Mountains and a cookout and picnic area, where you may want to fry up some of the bass or bream you've caught from the inn's pond. Key Falls Trail begins on the grounds and climbs up to Key Falls, one of the many waterfalls in Transylvania County. The French Broad River borders one side of the property, which is just 2

CLOSE-UP

The White Squirrels of Brevard

In 1986 the Brevard City Council declared the city a squirrel sanctuary because some of the squirrels around here are super-special—they're white! We enjoy our gray squirrels, too, but the white variety, which you can see darting throughout the town, have become a symbol of Brevard. These squirrels are not albinos, as they have normal dark eyes and a dark stripe down their backs. In the last few years, probably because of Brevard's increased urbanization, they are migrating to the countryside around the town.

---

miles from Brevard. Children 12 and older are welcome.

The Red House Inn and Bed and Breakfast $-$$$
412 West Probart Street, Brevard, NC
(828) 884-9349

Four blocks from the center of town and on the road next to the Music Center, you'll find Brevard's oldest house. It was built as a trading post in 1851 after the first house, which was built in 1848, burned. The house survived years of neglect and several attempts to destroy it during the Civil War. It even managed to remain in the same family until some 20 years ago, when it was finally sold. The trading post closed in 1861, and the structure then became the W. P. Poor Tavern, which had four rooms for boarders. The street at that time was also called Poor Street, but the residents understandably didn't cotton to that! Hence the name was changed to Probart Street, after Poor's middle name, and so it remains today.

Since its days as a tavern, the building has been used as a residence, a railway station, the county's first courthouse, Brevard's first post office, a boardinghouse, a hotel, and briefly as a school. It's been added to and altered over the years, but the original foundation is still firm, and its four-corner chimneys are still functioning. The inn still has four guest rooms with private or shared baths, plus a small efficiency cottage with a queen-size bed. Stay for a week and your seventh night is free.

And, yes, the house is painted red—the trim on its wide upstairs and downstairs porches is a bright contrast in white. The story goes that in the days when the streets had no numbers, the houses all had names. As the New England branch of the family had several homes, each called Red House, the family in Brevard decided to use that name too.

The Red House is open all year. To reach it, turn off Caldwell onto Probart Street; the inn will be on your right.

The Sassy Goose $$-$$$$
Reasonover Road, Cedar Mountain, NC
(828) 966-9493
www.sassygoose.com

The Sassy Goose, owned and operated by Bette and Bob Vande Weghe (pronounced *vanda way*) and daughter Linda, is really a miniature resort. The country-style lodge on a 50-acre site 10 miles from Brevard has three sunny guest rooms, each with a private bath and TV. Common space includes a library with a fireplace, a breakfast room, and a deck overlooking the lake. Two new log-cabin suites with queen-size beds are tucked back in the woods. Each suite has a sitting room, a kitchenette, and a screened porch or a deck. There is a two-bedroom, two-bath cottage, complete with living room, kitchen, dining room, and sunporch, available as a weekly rental.

There are also a six-acre lake for swimming, fishing, and boating and a small par 2 golf course where you can practice your chip shot. Several regular golf courses are nearby. Bocce, croquet, horseshoes, and hiking are also available on-site. The continental-plus breakfast consists of melon and berries, cereal, and a bread basket of good things to put in the toaster oven.

The Sassy Goose is open May through October. There is a two-night minimum on weekends, and reservations are required.

From Brevard take U.S. 276 south to Cedar Mountain. Turn left on Cascade Lake Road and immediately turn right on Reasonover Road. It's another 2 miles to Sassy Goose. No credit cards.

Twin Streams Bed & Breakfast $$$
Twin Ponds Lane, Lake Toxaway, NC
(828) 883–3007

It's hidden away off U.S. 64 and offers only three guest rooms—but they are something worth seeking out. Each room in this pretty, contemporary structure is on a different level. French doors lead out to covered decks that overlook a cascading stream. The Woodlands Room is furnished in elegant period antiques and features scenes from the surrounding mountains. The Falls Room has antique country furnishings and artwork depicting some of the many waterfalls in the surrounding area. The light and airy Wicker Room, as the name implies, has Southern wicker furnishings, which lend the charm of a bygone era. King-, queen-, and twin-size beds are available. The rooms have private baths and are air-conditioned.

Twin Streams' large main deck overlooks a duck pond. Rates include a full gourmet breakfast and afternoon tea. The inn is open year-round.

The Womble Inn $-$$$
301 West Main Street, Brevard, NC
(828) 884–4770
www.thewombleinn.com

At the opposite end of Main Street from the Inn at Brevard is the Womble Inn, which has been under the friendly care of Steve and Beth Womble since 1974. This well-kept, large structure with wrought-iron-railed upper and lower porches has six guest rooms furnished with antiques. A continental breakfast can be enjoyed in the dining room or on the porch. At an additional cost, you can order a full American breakfast.

The gathering room is the place for watching television, listening to music, and having conversation in front of a crackling fire on cool days. The inn will also prepare generous picnic baskets from varied menu suggestions. It's only ½ mile from here to the Brevard Music Center, and you might want to order one of these for a Music Festival dinner-on-the-lawn (orders should be placed 24 hours in advance). In addition Beth Womble, who has long provided a catering service for many of Brevard's special occasions, has now started serving exquisite lunches to the public.

SOUTHERN MOUNTAINS

Cherokee County

Hawkesdene House $$$
381 Phillips Creek Road, Andrews, NC
(828) 321–6027, (800) 447–9549
www.hawkbb.com

Nestled on 20 acres in a mountain cove adjoining the Nantahala National Forest, Hawkesdene House combines the simple elegance of an English country house with the rustic beauty of the mountains. Children also love playing with the two resident dogs, Gigi and Tigger, and Smoky, the cat. For an extra cost, guests can venture out on llama treks with a packed lunch at dinner. Hiking treks with a meal also take place.

The Walker Inn   **$-$$**
39 Junaluska Road, Andrews, NC
(828) 321-5019

A lot of history comes along with a visit to this old inn, which more than deserves its place on the National Register of Historic Places. The Cherokee Indians had barely been forced into Oklahoma when, in 1839, William Walker and his partner, Col. Waugh, received a 295-acre tract in an area called Old Valleytown. It's said they took down Chief Junaluska's home (see our Attractions chapter) and used the logs to construct a store that, in 1846, became the area's post office. Because those logs were burned for fuel in 1926, we don't know if they really were from Junaluska's house. At any rate after Walker married Margaret Scott in 1844, he built a two-story log home that he eventually expanded into an impressive, 11-room, colonial-style classic known as the Walker Inn.

The Walker Inn became a vital stopover on the Asheville-to-Murphy turnpike. During the Civil War, however, drunken bushwhackers wrecked the house and forced an ailing William Walker away with them. He was never seen again, leaving a grieving Margaret to raise their five sons, which she did by becoming one of the finest innkeepers in the mountains.

Today much still remains from Margaret's time: hinges, latches, beams, bubble-glass window panes, a grand piano, a stagecoach stepping stone, heirlooms, and other memorabilia. The long, outside kitchen is now a dining room, and there's still a slave cabin on the grounds. Many of the inn's trees are at least 200 years old—one oak may be twice that old. There are five guest rooms, three with private baths. But despite modern conveniences, it's the past that's the attraction here. Just to the east of Andrews on U.S. 19 Business, turn right onto Junaluska Road. The Walker Inn is about ½ mile down the road.

This wonderfully historic inn is open April to November, and the superreasonable rates include breakfast.

Clay County

Broadax Inn Bed and Breakfast   **$$**
982 Elf School Road, Hayesville, NC
(828) 389-6987, (888) 515-0554

Roger and Ruth Young run this unique inn, which is in the old Elf Schoolhouse outside town. The redbrick building on five acres was built in 1928 and was used as a public school until 1968; the Youngs bought it in 1991. The Broadax is not only a bed-and-breakfast inn with the Broadax Restaurant on the premises, it practically operates as the town's community center because the Youngs have turned the old auditorium with its stage into a much-in-demand place for parties and other social events. The local high school, for example, holds its proms and Christmas dances here. In the past such country greats as Minnie Pearl, Roy Acuff, Mac Wiseman, Lester Flatt, Earl Scruggs, and the like performed on its stage.

The inn has five distinctive guest rooms, four furnished with queen-size beds and one with twin beds. There is also a two-bedroom, one-bath cottage. Breakfast is practically cooked to order, though Ruth says her standard offerings of oven French toast, breakfast pizza, and hot cakes are most in demand. There are also such items as eggs, potatoes, grits, sausage, bacon, ham, and homemade muffins.

The Broadax Restaurant, open to the public, is housed in two former classrooms separated by an archway. The restaurant can serve 96 people; a bar with an adjoining porch (with rockers!) can hold 20 to 30 more.

The inn is closed from January 1 until April 1. It's on Elf Road, which dead-ends off of N.C. Highway 175. There is no sign to direct you to the inn because this is a scenic highway where new signs haven't been allowed. And no one, by the way, knows why the school was called "Elf"—not even a man in his late 90s who used to own the property.

Graham County

Snowbird Mountain Lodge $$$$
275 Santeetlah Road, Robbinsville, NC
(828) 479-3433, (800) 941-9290
www.snowbirdlodge.com
Back in the 1940s brothers Arthur and
Edwin Wolfe of Chicago built this fine
lodge high on a mountain near the Joyce
Kilmer Memorial Forest (see our Forests
and Parks chapter). In 1993 the lodge was
added to the National Register of Historic
Places in recognition of its distinctive
characteristics of type, period, and
method of construction. The lodge is built
of native stone and chestnut logs—that
wonderful tree that a foreign blight took
from our forests. A massive stone fireplace dominates the main lodge room,
which is paneled in butternut, and
another warms up the dining room, paneled in cherry.

Thirty rooms—the lodge has a capacity for 50 guests—are paneled in a variety
of native woods, with furniture to match.
Handmade quilts, many in-room amenities, and private baths complete the comfort. None of the rooms have televisions
or telephones.

From its spacious flagstone terrace,
the inn offers a panoramic view of the
Snowbird Mountain Range, and in the valley below are glimpses of Lake Santeetlah
and the homes and fields of the Snowbird
Indians. The lodge has an interesting
2,500-volume library. There are 2.5 miles
of hiking trails on the property. You can
swim in a mountain pool fed by a cool
stream or spend the day fishing in any
number of blue-ribbon trout streams
nearby. Canoes and kayaks are available
for rent at the lodge and are a great way
to explore nearby Lake Santeetlah.

Evenings sometime include bluegrass
music entertainment on the front porch or
a slide presentation given by a resident
botanist, herbologist, or wildflower expert.

The rates at Snowbird are on the full
American plan, which includes a fine buffet-
style breakfast, a hearty picnic lunch, and
an exquisite full-menu dinner prepared by

the staff with fresh, seasonal ingredients.
There is a three-night minimum on holiday
weekends and all stays during October.
The lodge is open from April through
November. Snowbird is 10 miles northwest
of Robbinsville.

Haywood County

Grandview Lodge $$$
466 Lickstone Road, Waynesville, NC
(828) 456-5212, (800) 255-7826
www.bbonline.com/nc/grandview
Grandview has nine year-round guest
rooms and two two-room apartments
available in the spring, summer, and fall.
The rooms look out on two-plus rolling
acres of landscaped grounds graced by
apple orchards, grape arbors, and a
rhubarb patch. Comfortable rockers line
the porch.

All guest rooms have a king- or
queen-size bed and a second bed, a pri-
vate bath, color cable TV, and daily maid
service. The three lodge rooms also have
gas-burning fireplaces. A common room
with a piano and other amenities will
make you feel at home.

Full breakfast and dinner are included
in the rates, and both are sumptuous
meals planned around seasonal harvests
of locally grown fruits, vegetables, and
herbs. Linda, the lodge's chef and a grad-
uate home economist, prepares all dinner
breads, breakfast muffins, and biscuits; the
jellies, jams, and relishes are homemade,
too. Meals are served family style, and
Linda can accommodate special dietary
needs if she is notified in advance. The
public may dine here by making advance
reservations.

When you're ready to explore the
area, there's plenty to see. The lodge is a
short drive to white-water rafting, area
golf courses, tennis clubs, outlet shopping,
and attractions at Maggie Valley, the
Cherokee Indian Reservation, and the Bilt-
more House and Gardens. The Blue Ridge
Parkway and the Smoky Mountains
National Park are readily accessible.

Herren House $$-$$$$
94 East Street, Waynesville, NC
(828) 452-7837, (800) 284-1932
www.herrenhouse.com

Many B&Bs are converted from private homes, but Herren House has been known for its hospitality since 1897, when it was a boarding house named "Savannah." (It takes its present name from its second owner, Mollie Herren, who owned the house early in the last century.) Current owners Jackie and Frank Blevins continue this gracious tradition. Six spacious guest rooms, one equipped for wheelchair accommodations, are full of vintage furnishings, complemented by modern amenities, such as central air-conditioning. Each room has its own sitting area and private bath. There's even an octagon-shaped bedroom with a turn-of-the-century, 48-pane window.

Breakfasts delight with seasonal fruit topped with orange-maple sauce, herb-baked eggs, gingery pancakes, apricot scones, and pineapple muffins, along with homemade chicken sausage. (You'll be asking for the recipes.) Afternoon refreshments include chocolate delectables, homemade tea cakes, nut breads, cookies, a variety of teas, and freshly ground coffee.

Best of all, all this home comfort sits below soaring mountains on a quiet residential street just 1 block from Waynesville's captivating Main Street, full of irresistible shops and great places to eat. When you've worn yourself out enjoying Waynesville and all its nearby attractions, you can relax on Herren House's sprawling porches or in its fragrant garden. It's open all year, except for two weeks after New Year's Day.

Mountain Creek Bed & Breakfast $$
146 Chestnut Walk Drive, Waynesville, NC
(828) 456-5509, (800) 557-9766
www.bbonline.com/nc/mcbb

Set on six acres at 3,500 feet, just 5 miles from the Blue Ridge Parkway and from downtown Waynesville and 15 minutes from Cataloochee's ski slopes, this year-round establishment offers four rooms and two suites. All four bedrooms in the main house have a private bath with a shower and two have a soaking tub. The interior walls are knotty pine and the closets are cedar-lined. The two upstairs rooms have their own private balconies overlooking a spectacular mountain view. Two suites are located in the original carriage house just next door. Each has its own private porch, queen-size bed, and Jacuzzi tub. The large common area features a huge fireplace along with 40 feet of floor-to-ceiling windows.

A full breakfast is served every morning, and guests can dine in or out on the 1,600-square-foot deck that wraps around the west side of the house with a view of the creek, trout pond, and mountains. Menus include such items as egg truffles, banana- or strawberry-stuffed French toast, or ham-and-cheese strudel. During winter holidays Hylah and Guy will cook dinner for you. And because the two are avid tandem and mountain cyclists, they'll be happy to share their local cycling knowledge with you or arrange guided tours.

The Old Stone Inn $$$$
109 Dolan Road, Waynesville, NC
(828) 456-3333, (800) 432-8499
www.theoldstoneinn.com

If you're looking for a fine place to stay—or dine—near the wonderful shopping in downtown Waynesville, you can't beat the Old Stone Inn, formerly known as Heath Lodge. Built in 1946 out of stone and poplar logs, the inn consists of a number of buildings. The main lodge houses two guest rooms and the cozy guest lounge and restaurant centered around a large stone fireplace. Wendell's Attic, on the second floor of the building, with its wood-burning stove, is a more intimate room for drinks and conversation. Several other structures surrounding the main lodge house the balance of the inn's 22 rooms. Most of these neat, clean, and rustic-feeling quarters have been recently restored and updated and have private baths, ceiling fans, cable TV, and porches with rockers.

This in-town, country lodge sits on a heavily wooded hillside thick with large rhododendrons and mountain laurels.

A full gourmet breakfast is included in your room rate. Dinner and light appetizers are available to both inn and outside guests. Hours vary by season. The Old Stone Inn is open from April through December. To get here from N.C. Highway 23, exit onto U.S. 276 S. and continue to Dellwood Road (the second stoplight). Turn right and proceed less than ½ mile to Love Lane. Turn right and drive up the hill to Dolan Road. Turn left, and you'll find the Old Stone Inn on your left.

The Swag $$$$
2300 Swag Road, Waynesville, NC
(828) 926-0430, (800) 789-7672
www.theswag.com

When the innkeepers at the Swag, which refers to a dip in a ridge, call theirs a mountaintop inn, they mean it! This inn sits on 250 acres at 5,000 feet on a private mountain with 50-mile views. After negotiating the rather narrow gravel road and the 2.5-mile private drive, you might be tempted to think, "I'm obviously driving up to the end of the world, and what then?"

"What then" is a nationally known first-class inn with the types of amenities you expect of a fine hotel. Yet, when you ask many longtime residents if they've ever been to the Swag, they might respond, "The what?" Somehow this place has mostly remained a secret except to those who travel hundreds, if not thousands, of miles to stay here. Certainly it seems better known outside the region than it is here. Dan and Deener Matthews built what was to be a private family retreat using native stone and hand-hewn logs from old buildings, including a century-old church. They ended up turning the retreat into this highly praised inn.

The Swag's handmade quilts, woven rugs, and unique pieces of North Carolina art create an atmosphere of rustic elegance. Sixteen guest rooms all have private baths (some with whirlpools or steam showers, all with terry robes), and

Maggie Valley Accredited Reservations (828-926-3786) is open year-round to help families and groups locate lodging. For more information write to P.O. Box 866, Maggie Valley, NC 28751.

many feature balconies to bring that 50-mile view right indoors. Some rooms have fireplaces, but not small ones you might expect—these are impressive to say the least! There are also three cabins with separate sitting rooms and private porches and an extensive library to satisfy most literary tastes. One cabin has a billiard room and a hot tub. Outside a split-rail fence marks the boundary of the Great Smoky Mountains National Park with its many hiking trails, reached by the Swag's own private entrance. At the inn itself hammocks are handy places for a snooze, but for the more active, you can play racquetball on the indoor court, badminton and croquet outdoors, or swim in the secluded spring-fed pond.

A two-night minimum stay is required. The rates include three meals a day for two people, prepared by gourmet cooks and served atop 12-foot-long, handmade walnut tables (many of the inn's beds are also handmade and oversize). There are several private tables available, and a few outside reservations are accepted. Just remember that the inn is in a dry county, so bring your own spirits if desired.

Well, the Swag may have been a secret in this region once, but not any longer!

Windsong Mountain Inn
& Llama Farm $$$$
459 Rockcliff Lane, Clyde, NC
(828) 627-6111, (800) 838-1246
www.windsonginnbb.com

Windsong is a romantic, contemporary log B&B with a special flair, romance, and seclusion. It's located on 24 acres at 3,000 feet with fabulous views, where the gentle mountain breezes flowing down the mountain and through the many wind chimes inspired its name. One can be lazy here, sitting in the hot tub watching the hawks circling or perhaps lounging beside the swimming pool gazing at the flower and herb gardens. For the more active there's tennis and hiking or visiting in the pastures with the llamas and pygmy goats. For the ink-black, starry nights, there's a telescope for stargazing. In the morning you feast on an ever-changing gourmet breakfast served on fine English china. Innkeepers Russ and Barbara Mancini settled here after living many years in Bavaria, London, Berlin, and Budapest. They have put together a unique blend of European antiques and art, as well as African, Southwestern, and Alaskan art. You may find a Sioux Indian picture next to a 200-year-old English clock.

Guest rooms feature queen-size beds, wood-burning fireplaces, and private baths with tubs for two. Each has unique decor. Rooms are equipped with a TV/VCR, and there's a large collection of videotapes available.

In addition to the Main Inn, there's the Pond Lodge with two-bedroom suites, great for families or those desiring privacy. Each suite has a living/dining room with a pot-bellied stove, a fully equipped kitchen, and a bath with a tub for two. Here you can sit on the deck and barbecue on the grill while watching the animals in the pasture. An extensive continental breakfast is provided for Pond Lodge guests.

The Yellow House $$$$
89 Oakview Drive, Waynesville, NC
(828) 452-0991, (800) 563-1236
www.theyellowhouse.com
The Yellow House sits at 3,000 feet on top of a hill looking out to the ever-changing colors of the Blue Ridge Mountains. Located just a mile from Waynesville, it has been likened to a grand old duchess on a throne. One thing is for sure, when you arrive at this more than 100-year-old home, surrounded by three acres of lawn, garden, and ancient pines, prepare to be pampered. There are no televisions or other distractions in this quiet rural setting.

There are eight rooms total. All are charming and each has a fireplace, but

our favorite is the E'staing Suite with both rooms opening on a private upstairs porch. From here, there's a pine-framed view of the mountains and town, particularly fine at night when lights twinkle below and stars twinkle above. An adjacent cottage contains a French country kitchen. It offers two bedrooms, two baths, two fireplaces, and a view of the pond from every room.

The rates include your choice of a breakfast served in your quarters, in the dining room, or on the front veranda. Other amenities include appetizers and conversation in the evening and a refrigerator stocked with soft drinks. All rooms have coffee service, terry robes, and controlled music. For an extra charge a licensed massage therapist is available on request, and you can also order a French Country-, Mediterranean-, or American-style picnic hamper. Also ask about the Yellow House's special packages that include fly-fishing, guided nature hikes, mountain memory photo tours, golf, and trips to the Biltmore Estate.

Jackson County

Applegate Inn Bed
& Breakfast $$-$$$
163 Hemlock Street, Dillsboro, NC
(828) 586-2397, (800) 353-0377
www.applegatebed-breakfast.com
There are lots of sights to see in the beautiful countryside around the Applegate Inn, but you might just want to stay put in this quaint country home and enjoy the peace and quiet. With the village of Dillsboro as its backdrop and Scott's Creek just across the way, you don't have to go far to see the scenery that brings people to these mountains.

But if you do decide to wander, the Great Smoky Mountains Railway Depot and the town's 50 unique shops and restaurants are just a footbridge away. The inn is also within a few miles' drive of the Great Smoky Mountains National Park, Maggie Valley, Nantahala Gorge, and other sights.

This one-story inn has five large guest rooms and three minisuites. Each room has a queen-size bed and private bath with charming decor to make you feel at home. Air-conditioning and cable TV are other amenities.

A full country breakfast served on old-fashioned Currier and Ives china includes apple pancakes, one of the inn's many specialties.

Room rates include breakfast. The inn offers special weekly rates, too.

Balsam Mountain Inn $$$-$$$$
off U.S. Highways 73/23, Balsam, NC
(828) 456-9498
www.balsaminn.com
This magnificent 1908, neoclassical Victorian inn owes its life to its delightful innkeeper, Merrily Teasley. Gracing 26 acres, the three-story structure with its two-tier, 100-foot-long porches sits at 3,500 feet and is surrounded by 6,000-foot peaks. It was once the popular destination of passengers on the old Southern Railway, but in recent years the 50-room beauty had fallen into disrepair until Merrily bought it in 1990 and lovingly and authentically restored it. She also sets the happy, relaxed tone of her entire staff.

Today you'll have a choice of large rooms with private baths (including a few suites and bed/sitting rooms), graced with flowery prints, 10-foot wide hallways, a wicker- and plant-filled lobby, a fine library, a gift shop, a nature trail on the property, and easy access to Pisgah Forest hiking and the Blue Ridge Parkway. You'll also be very pleased with the inn's restaurant. Wonderful breakfasts are included in the rates, but you'll also want to enjoy the exceptional lunches and dinners offered to guests and by reservation to the public.

Innisfree Victorian Inn $$$$
N.C. Highway 107, Glenville, NC
(828) 743-2946
www.innisfreeinn.com
As the name implies, this is a gabled Victorian. Wide porches run around two floors of this superb building overlooking Lake Glenville.

The nine guest rooms are named in keeping with its era, such as the Prince Albert Suite, with French doors leading to a private veranda; the sensuous Cambridge Room, which has a parking place next to its private entrance; the cheerful Canterbury Room, with a bay-windowed love seat that affords a view of flower gardens and mountains; and the Windsor Room, which looks out on a fountain and has a roomy shower with a built-in seat, plus an Italian lavatory with gilded dolphins for faucets. Then there's Victoria's Grand Suite, which may be the most luxuriously romantic suite in the mountains. From its bay window you have a view of the lake and mountains that stretches for miles, and its elegant furnishings and art were gathered from around the world. A Jacuzzi is in the bathing chamber that also comes with a splendid view.

The Garden House, which follows the style of the main house, has two feminine boudoirs—the Elizabeth Barrett and Emily Bronte Suites—each with a four-poster bed made up in French lace, a private veranda, and two fireplaces, one in the bathroom. The Charles Dickens Suite is opulent with jade green walls and dark wicker, and its fireplace faces the two-person garden tub that actually has a view of the gardens. The secluded Robert Browning Room has its own entrance, fireplace, and private garden. All the accommodations in the Garden House have wet bars, TVs, and private phones.

Rates include the candlelit breakfast in the Tower, a 5:30 P.M. hospitality hour with hors d'oeuvres served on the sweeping upper veranda, and Irish coffee and hot chocolate by the parlor fire each evening. The Innisfree has gift certificates.

The Jarrett House $
100 Haywood Street, Dillsboro, NC
(828) 586-0265, (800) 972-5623
www.jarretthouse.com
Not only is the Jarrett House one of the oldest inns in Western North Carolina, it's practically a tradition. William Allen Dills,

There is a 3-mile, round-trip hike in Jackson County that takes you through a lovely mile-high meadow with superb views of the Pisgah National Forest. It is not a difficult hike. For part of the walk, you will be on sections of the Mountains-to-the-Sea Trail. Be sure to take a sharp left at the trail junction about 15 minutes from the start of your walk. To reach the trail drive to the Bear Pen Gap parking overlook at milepost 427.6 on the Blue Ridge Parkway in Jackson County. The trail begins at the lower end of the parking lot.

founder of the town of Dillsboro, built it in 1882, just two years after the railroad came through. Because the train from Asheville stopped here at noon, the Mount Beulah Hotel, as The Jarrett House was called then, became the place for passengers and railroad employees to eat lunch. By 1894 the hotel was serving "comers and stayers" from great distances away, including two women from Edenton, North Carolina, who were the first females to be seen smoking cigarettes in these parts. As Mrs. Minnie Dills Gray, one of William Dill's daughters, recalls in her *History of Dillsboro*, the two smokers "set the countryside agog and gave zest to the neighborhood gossip."

Dill sold the hotel to R. Frank Jarrett of Franklin in 1894. Jarrett, capitalizing on a sulfur spring that bubbled up into a soapstone basin at the rear of the hotel, renamed the place the Jarrett Springs Hotel. However the busy owner left the running of the hotel mostly to his wife, Miss Sally. After his death in 1950, a hotel operator from Gainesville, Georgia, bought the hotel and renamed it The Jarrett House. It has changed hands a number of times since then but has never changed its policy of serving copious and delicious country cooking.

The hotel, which is on the National Register of Historic Places, has 18 guest rooms with private baths and four with shared baths. While they're nothing fancy, they are loaded with atmosphere and the whole place is like a step back to the turn of the century. The Jarrett is open year-round. To find it, just go to Dillsboro—you can't miss it. No credit cards.

Macon County

4½ Street Inn $$$
22A 4½ Street, Highlands, NC
(828) 526-4464, (888) 799-4464
www.4andahalfstinn.com

We don't know what it is about the ambience of this bed-and-breakfast tucked away on large lot on a quiet street in Highlands, but when we visited one afternoon in early October, walking through the doorway felt like coming home at Christmas time. A fire crackled in the fireplace, music played softly, and great smells wafted from the kitchen at the back of the house. It's a place where we think you will feel at home just enjoying the sun and shade in the side yard or in a rocking chair on the large wraparound porch. A wide deck extends off the back of the house, where there's a hot tub for soaking. The 10 guest rooms, each with a private bath, are retreats for watching TV or reading a good book. Most rooms have king- or queen-size beds.

The innkeepers traditionally host their families for a pre-opening in April before the crowd begins to arrive. Rick's family comes for one week and Helene's for another. Not only is this an opportunity for their family reunions, but it also serves as a shake-down to make certain that everything is up and running. Then the inn opens to the public for the season.

The innkeepers offer bikes, canteens, backpacks, trail maps, and advice. They know the trails and the best routes for the greatest views.

The inn is about a ½-mile stroll from Main Street through a pretty residential area, where the houses are hidden behind giant rhododendrons. In addition to the gourmet breakfast, the rates include afternoon refreshments in the parlor and the use of the hot tub. There's a two-night minimum on weekends and a 10 percent reduction for stays of five nights or longer, excluding holidays and October. The 4½ Street Inn is open March through December. To find the inn from Main Street, take U.S. 64 E. toward Cashiers, turn right on Chestnut Street, and then left on 4½ Street.

Blaine House $$$
661 Harrison Avenue, Franklin, NC
(828) 349–4230, (888) 349–4230
www.blainehouse.com

Though this beautifully restored and professionally decorated 1910 home has just four rooms and a cottage for guests, innkeepers Suzy Chandler and Karin Gorboff like it that way. By being small and intimate, they feel they can pamper their guests. Here you'll find an elegant spacious room, Mildred's Suite, that offers a king-size bed, sitting area, and private bath/shower. Annie Mae's Suite is more romantic, with a queen-size bed and a spacious adjoining bath inviting you to relax in a 1925 pedestal foot tub. Minnie's Room offers a cozy country French motif with a gabled ceiling and pickled knotty pine walls, a king-bed (or twins), dressing room, and private bath/shower. Charles' Room is a delightfully decorated provincial room with original knotty pine walls and offers a queen-size oak bed with an adjacent cozy reading room enticing you to relax and read a book after an adventurous day. This room has a private bath/shower. All rooms have cable TV and air-conditioning. Finally there's the two-story Blaine House Cottage, a fully furnished, one-bedroom, with a living/dining area, full kitchen, daily linen service, TV, air-conditioning, and a small balcony.

You'll enjoy the touch of elegance and warm hospitality Blaine House provides. To find it follow U.S. Highway 441 Business to N.C. 28 N. The Blaine House is 1 mile north of Franklin's Main Street on the right-hand side. There is a private off-street parking area.

The Chalet Inn $$$
285 Lone Oak Drive, Whittier, NC
(828) 586–0251, (800) 789–8024
www.chaletinn.com

In 1979 George Ware came through the North Carolina mountains on his way to Fort Bragg and fell in love with the area. In 1985 while stationed in the Netherlands, he met and fell in love with his future wife, Holland-born Hanneke. When they decided to open a bed-and-breakfast inn, George wanted it to be in our mountains. After working in restaurant management and for a season at High Hampton Inn and Country Club, they started building The Chalet Inn according to an authentic Swiss-German design in the fall of 1990. The posts and beams and overhanging roof create a touch of Europe in North Carolina.

Nestled on 22 acres in a mountain cove, The Chalet provides gracious lodging and combines the traditions and congeniality of an Alpine *gasthaus* with rustic surroundings. A spring-fed brook curls around the inn on its way to the valley floor. The guest rooms have private balconies with carved wood railings festooned with flowers. European furnishings and German-Swiss windows continue the theme. The Wares even commissioned an award-winning German artist-blacksmith to make a traditional wrought iron sign. From the Chalet's great room, you can view Doubletop Mountain, which dominates 19 miles of forested ridges. The inn is twenty minutes from the Great Smoky Mountains National Park and the beginning of the Blue Ridge Parkway.

The Chalet's four lovely rooms, one romantic suite, and one family suite offer comfortable lodging for couples looking to spend some time alone and for families with older children who are exploring the mountains. All rooms and suites have private baths and air-conditioning. The Romantic Suite has a sitting room with a fireplace and whirlpool tub, a private entrance, and a private patio. Honeymooners and couples alike enjoy the ambience and relish the seclusion of the inn's cove. Guests at the Chalet Inn can

If you don't feel like making conversation with strangers over early morning breakfast, tell your hosts beforehand. They may be able to seat you more privately if you prefer.

enjoy its hiking trails, lawn games, and picnic area with a grill. A candlelit breakfast is served in the dining room or on the covered patio along the brook. It's a breakfast that satisfies all tastes: For the health conscious there's always plenty of fresh fruit, juices, and low-fat yogurt; for the world traveler with a hearty appetite longing for memories of the Alps, the German-style meats are fresh and German whole-grain breads and Swiss muesli are imported. Also included are a variety of cheeses, fresh-baked brotchen (rolls), and soft-boiled eggs or an egg casserole. The less adventurous can opt for cereal, home-baked pastries, and fruit compotes.

The Chalet is open from late March through New Year's Day and Valentine's Week.

Colonial Pines Inn $$$
541 Hickory Street, Highlands, NC
(828) 526-2060
www.colonialpinesinn.com

Large pillars framing a gigantic colonial American flag, and a porch that stretches across the front of the house is a statement of eloquence and grace. This quiet country guest house was once home to several original Highlands families. Innkeepers Chris and Donna Alley portray the very essence of hospitality. Within the inn is the warmth of knotty pine, antiques, and an eclectic mix of books, accessories, a playable grand piano, and a cozy fireside for chilly mountain evenings. The inn is surrounded by two acres of giant old rhododendron, hemlock, maple, and oak. Mountain views are spectacular from all rooms. There is also a guest house apartment on the property and a private cottage known as "Miss Rebecca's Cottage," which is a short distance away. The cottage is very special, sleeping two to six in three bedrooms, and it has two baths.

The lush berry bushes on the grounds are Chris's pride. Usually you'll find freshly made jams from these berries on your table. Breakfast for guests in the main inn is sumptuous and gourmet. Donna has a pleasant surprise for you when she serves maple syrup in a special maple leaf container. The coffee is always on and goodies are available in the guests' pantry.

The 1891 Stewart House $$-$$$
425 Hickory Street, Highlands, NC
(828) 526-8067

The 1891 Stewart House is nestled in a five-acre rhododendron and hardwood forest. It is just a short walk to downtown Highlands from here. The rooms are furnished with antiques. All bedrooms have featherbeds and private bath/shower. Seasonal fruits form the basis of a gourmet breakfast. Not to be missed are homemade jams and marmalades and assorted breads. A full porch affords great garden views. And to add sparkle to your stay and day is to have innkeeper Barbara Werder and her mother pop in and spin some tales of yesteryear.

Should you need some gardening hints, your innkeeper, Barbara, is an expert. Through her caring and teaching many gardeners have developed a vital concern for landscaping to protect what nature has provided.

Heritage Inn Bed and
Breakfast $$-$$$
43 Heritage Hollow Drive, Franklin, NC
(828) 524-4150, (888) 524-4150
www.heritageinnbb.com

This B&B is in the Heritage Hollow, a private village within the town of Franklin, with restaurants, antiques, and mountain craft shops within walking distance. Each of its five immaculate bedrooms (two are available with kitchenettes) is decorated with antiques, collectibles, and quilts in a country-comfortable theme. For added privacy each room has its own entrance, porch, and shower bathroom. There is a

Gathering Room with fireplace, cable TV, and phone, as well as a good selection of reading materials and videos. Most guests, though, end up in a rocking chair on the veranda enjoying the mountain scenery and serenity. Breakfast is hearty and homemade; early risers can have coffee on the veranda. Snacks and some refreshments are available throughout the day.

There is also a fully furnished, self-contained, one-bedroom apartment with a fireplace at the inn available for rent with a three-night minimum. (Breakfast is not provided with this rental.)

The inn is open year-round.

Hummingbird Lodge $$$
1101 Hickory Knoll Ridge Road, Franklin, NC
(828) 369-0430
www.hummingbirdlodge.com

The Hummingbird Lodge is a lovely log cabin on a mountaintop just 6 miles south of Franklin. Because woodlands surround it, hiking trails abound, including the Appalachian Trail. With advance notice the lodge will provide a picnic lunch for hikers or those out enjoying the scenery. Hummingbird has a large living room with a stone fireplace, a great porch with a hammock, a swing, and rocking chairs. There are three guest rooms, each with its own bathroom and each decorated with a different theme. The Garden Room is lined with a white picket fence, and has a king-size bed and a garden tub, with a view of the mountains. The Appalachian Room has a king-size bed and also has a mountain view and is decorated in local arts and crafts. The third room is adorned with Native American art from the Cherokee Reservation. The bed here is queen size, and the bathroom has a garden tub as well as a shower.

A full gourmet breakfast is included in the price and is served in the dining room or on the porch, weather permitting. Evening wine and hors d'ouevres are a wonderful way to end the day in this beautiful part of the world.

Kelsey & Hutchinson Lodge $$$$
450 Spring Street, Highlands, NC
(828) 526-4746, (888) 245-9058
www.k-hlodge.com

This lodge is named for the two men who founded Highlands. According to legend, it was in 1875 that Samuel Truman Kelsey and Clinton Carter Hutchinson drew two lines on a map: one was from New York City to New Orleans and the other from Chicago to Savannah. The intersection of these lines, they predicted, marked the spot that would become the nation's center of commerce. Well Highlands may not have accomplished that object, but this area does provide a respite from commerce, trade, and the hard facts of the daily business world.

The modern lodge was designed to preserve the property's rich historic past and blend it with the comforts of the present. There is charm everywhere. You might choose to stay in the elegance of the main inn, Lee House, or you might prefer the rustic charm of the Cottage Rooms or the Terrace and Garden Rooms. There is also Chestnut House for families, and let us not forget the all-important family member, the faithful canine. Be it Fido or Fifi, there are accommodations, with the family, for your pet. There is even a special walking area, and special arrangements can be made for canine dietary needs.

The inn's newsletter highlights events at the inn and in the area.

The Main Street Inn $$$-$$$$
270 Main Street, Highlands, NC
(828) 526-2590, (800) 213-9142
www.mainstreetinn.com

The Main Street Inn, built in the Federal Farmhouse style in 1885, has welcomed guests with Southern hospitality for more than a century. Formerly known as the Phelps House, it was restored to its original luster in 1998. The original hand-hewn beams in its adjacent Guest House were exposed through the addition of cathedral ceilings, and many of the original sand-forged windows were saved and reinstalled in the rooms as interior windows for the enjoyment of guests.

The inn, which is next door to all that wonderful Main Street shopping, features 20 cozy rooms, all with private baths, individual heating and air-conditioning, direct-dial telephones, and cable TV. Some rooms have sitting areas or balconies. Room rates include a hot country breakfast and afternoon tea. The inn is open from April through December, and advance reservations are preferred.

The Old Edwards Inn $$$
Corner of 4th and Main Streets, Highlands, NC
(828) 526-9319
www.oldedwardsinn.com

The two hotels sitting across from each other are almost as old as the town of Highlands itself, which was established in 1876. The Old Edwards Inn opened in 1878 and the Highlands Inn in 1880. Both are on the National Register of Historic Places. They were jointly owned but now have separate owners.

The decor throughout has been carefully researched and restored in the "county manner" with colonial wall colors, wall coverings, and stenciling by master artist Donna Feltman. Outstanding pieces of antique furniture and other decor add charm to every room. The inn offers numerous nonsmoking rooms, and for golfing guests, special arrangements can be made to play at several challenging courses nearby.

Adjacent to this huge brick structure is Central House, a part of the original wooden structure. The restaurant is in this section of the hotel and flows into the gardens. Surrounded by a hedge that wards off traffic noise and passersby on Main Street, cascading waterfalls and a koi pond provide an idyllic atmosphere for relaxation and dining. To conclude your day in town, on the golf course, or hiking the area, wine and cheese is served each evening.

The Old Edwards Inn can't accommodate cribs or cots nor meet the special needs of the handicapped, so it's suitable only for ambulatory adults. All the rooms have private baths, and the rates include a full hot breakfast. Weekly and monthly rates are also available. If you drive into Highlands on U.S. 64, the Old Edwards Inn is at the east end of Main Street.

Snow Hill Inn $$-$$$
531 Snow Hill Road, Franklin, NC
(828) 369-2100
www.bbonline.com/nc/snowhill

Snow Hill Inn perches on 14 acres high above the gem-rich Cowee Valley on a mountaintop. It's the place to come if you want to get away from city sounds and stress. The two-story home no longer looks like the old schoolhouse that it was in 1914, but in one of the rooms, the traces of students' names carved in the wall can still be seen. Each of the eight guest rooms has its own private bath, air-conditioning, and in-room phone. The 12-foot ceilings give an added dimension of spaciousness to all of the large guest rooms. There are two or more big windows in each room offering spectacular mountain views.

If you want to relax, this bed-and-breakfast is the place to do it. Sit on the covered front porch, sip your coffee, and enjoy the panorama of eleven different mountain peaks floating above the morning mist. If the afternoon is more to your liking, enjoy the incredible views from the sundeck of different mountain peaks. If you feel more active, you can play croquet or badminton on the lawn.

Snow Hill provides a sumptuous hot breakfast from 8:20 to 10:00 A.M. in the glass-enclosed dining room. Owners and innkeepers George and Rita Sivess's Southern hospitality is sure to make your stay here memorable.

Toad Hall $$-$$$
Highway 64, Frankline Road, Highlands, NC
(828) 526-3889
www.toadhallb-b.com

Toad Hall is located on Lake Sequoyah and is somewhat tucked away off the main road, as it is bordered with rhododendron on the highway side and the lake on the other. A separate lodge is adjacent to the main inn. It has all amenities necessary to enjoy a secluded rendezvous and respite.

Swain County

Charleston Inn $$-$$$
208 Arlington Avenue, Bryson City, NC
(828) 488-4644, (888) 285-1555
www.charlestoninn.com
This 1920s Victorian-influenced house has five rooms, each with private bath, while the Inn next door has 14 rooms, each with a queen- or king-size bed and a porch or private balcony. An additional two-bedroom Gingerbread Cottage can accommodate couples, large groups, or families, though everyone retires to the parlor in the evenings to gather by the cozy fireplace. The TV room completes the lovely gardens with a gazebo and fountains. Your hosts serve a full breakfast in the dining room or outdoors on the veranda.

Fryemont Inn $-$$
Fryemont Street, Bryson City, NC
(828) 488-2159, (800) 845-4879
www.fryemontinn.com
Two generations of Browns have served as innkeepers at this comfortable 37-room inn that sits on a mountain shelf overlooking the Great Smoky Mountains National Park. Everything about the inn, a tradition in hospitality here since 1923, is "woodsy": its rustic exterior, and lustrous hardwood floors; its chestnut-paneled bedrooms; the mountainous view from its tree-top, rocking-chair porch; its lovely 80 degree swimming pool nestled in a grove of hemlock, dogwood, and poplar. The large lobby is more than matched by a giant stone fireplace that can hold logs 8 feet long. There is also a full-service lounge and a library.

All rooms have private baths, but no two are alike, except for their many-paned, pocket windows that slide back to let in the mountain air. Adjacent to the main lodge are cottage suites, each with a living room, a bedroom with a king-size bed, a wet bar, and a working fireplace. Some suites have loft bedrooms; others have private decks.

Fryemont Inn's rates are reasonable and include both a hearty breakfast and dinner. The public can enjoy these wonderful meals by reservation. Fryemont Inn is open from April through November, but the cottage suites are open year-round.

Hemlock Inn $$$$
off U.S. Highway 19, Bryson City, NC
(828) 488-2885
www.innbook.com/hemlock
This is an unpretentious place, but there's nothing unpretentious about the view. Hemlock Inn is built on a small mountain that overlooks three valleys, backed up by big mountains. Sitting on the front porch with a steaming cup of coffee in hand and watching the sunrise is something worth getting up early for! The inn opened in 1952 with nine rooms; its popularity grew, and the owners added 12 rooms and four cottages to meet the demand. The growth stopped there, because owner-innkeepers Elaine and Morris White and their guests like the informality and personal attention of a small inn.

The rooms and cottages (one very secluded and popular with honeymooners) are furnished in antiques and pieces made by mountain craftspeople. The rates include family-style breakfasts and dinners and all gratuities. Meals for the public are by reservation only. And, since the innkeepers always feature fresh foods native to the area, what good meals they are!

Hemlock Inn sits on 45 acres 3 miles from the Deep Creek area of the Great Smoky Mountains National Park, between Cherokee and Bryson City. Take U.S. 74 to Hyatt Creek Road (exit 69). Turn right on Hyatt Creek and drive 1.5 miles, then turn left on U.S. 19. Drive 1.5 miles to the Hemlock Inn sign and turn right. The inn is 1 mile on the left. It's open mid-April through October.

OTHER ACCOMMODATIONS

In the preceding chapter we listed a number of inns and bed-and-breakfast establishments, and even at that, we barely scratched the surface of the area's many intimate and often historic establishments that have thrown open their doors to travelers. But such places are not for everyone—or not for everyone all the time. They certainly don't reflect all the accommodations we have in the mountains. There are dozens of reasonably priced, family-owned motels and cabins in and around our towns, and all the big chain hotels are represented throughout the region at locations very convenient to our attractions. Even in a small city like Hendersonville, there are more than 60 places to stay, with more opening all the time. Cherokee, a popular resort, has some motels and 110 cabins from which to choose, plus 27 campgrounds with more than 2,200 sites.

For this chapter we have chosen just a few of the larger, better-known establishments, plus some special smaller places you'll want to know about. But keep in mind that this is a guide, not a directory. For every listing we have here, there are many more similar types of accommodations in the same area. In short—except perhaps during the fall foliage season when the region is jam-packed with leaf-lookers—finding a great place to spend the night or an extended vacation is never a problem. The average nightly rate for two adults at the facilities in this chapter is indicated by a dollar sign ($) ranking in the chart below. Most businesses accept major credit cards for payment, but we note those establishments that don't accept credit cards.

PRICE CODE

$	$50 to $80
$$	$81 to $100
$$$	$101 to $120
$$$$	$121 and more

NORTHERN MOUNTAINS

Alleghany County

Alleghany Inn $-$$
341 North Main Street, Sparta, NC
(336) 372-2501, (888) 372-2501

If you get off the Blue Ridge Parkway at milepost 217 at its junction with N.C. Highway 18 and drive about 15 minutes west to Sparta, you'll find the Alleghany Inn, a nice, reasonably priced family stopover. This 64-room, pleasantly furnished modern motel is open year-round. The inn offers cable TV, queen- and full-size beds and king-size waterbeds. One efficiency is also available. A conference center is a recent addition to the inn. Smoking is permitted.

Bluffs Lodge $$-$$$
Mile 241, Doughton Park, NC
(336) 372-4499

Bluffs Lodge sits on a broad hilltop on the Blue Ridge Parkway with expansive, long-range mountain views. Here, rangers provide interpretive talks around an outdoor fireplace in the patio area. The accommodations are comfortable, with lots of amenities like private baths and large closets in each room. The Bluffs Lodge Coffee Shop is just across the road.

Ashe County

Best Western Eldreth Inn $$-$$$
829 East Main Street, Jefferson, NC
(336) 246-8845, (800) 221-8802
Some people consider rocking chairs a way of getting fit. Others want something a little more heart pumping. This 48-room inn features both—rooms with a view of Mount Jefferson, complete with rocking chairs on the balconies, and a well-equipped fitness center. It also offers a range of room sizes with double-, queen-, and king-size beds. Nonsmoking rooms are available. The inn's restaurant serves home-style meals for breakfast, lunch, and dinner (except Sunday night). Should you want to sample something different, Eldreth Inn is within walking distance of six restaurants. It is also next door to a shopping center and is only a short drive from the Ashe Country Frescoes (see our Arts and Culture chapter), canoeing on the New River, and local golfing.

Greenfield Resort $-$$
1795 Mount Jefferson Road, off U.S. Highway 221, West Jefferson, NC
(336) 246-9106, (336) 982-3381 (after hours)
Greenfield Resort is spread over approximately 100 rolling acres of pasture, originally part of the Rufus McNeil farm, ca. 1847, at the foot of Mount Jefferson. The McNeil homestead has been converted into a lively family-style restaurant. Greenfield also has a banquet room that seats 300; a convenience store with crafts, ice, and produce; eight rustic rental cabins; camping facilities; three fishing ponds stocked with bass and bluegill; and miles of hiking trails that wind around Mount Jefferson. The cabins sit on a ridge opposite Greenfield restaurant at the base of spectacular Mount Jefferson (see our Restaurants chapter). These units offer either one bedroom with a loft and shower or a two-bedroom efficiency with shower. There is also a large recreation room with cooking facilities. A bunkhouse-type cabin holding up to 22 people is also available.

The campground has 138 sites and can accommodate both RVs and primitive tent camping. Tent sites are $14 per night; for RV sites a full hookup costs $17.

Greenfield features buggy rides, Civil War reenactments, and two rodeos a year, making the resort more than a tourist stop—it's a community gathering spot.

Jefferson Landing Lodge $$$-$$$$
N.C. Highways 88 and 16, Jefferson, NC
(336) 982-4149, (800) 292-6274
Jefferson Landing Lodge is a superb addition to this premier golf community. The tastefully decorated facility has 17 units and numerous amenities, including a full-service lounge. The lobby has a vaulted ceiling and large windows that offer a breathtaking view of the golf course. Jefferson Landing Lodge is open year-round, and town home rentals and golf packages are also available. The Manor House has seven bedrooms.

Nation's Inn $$
107 Beaver Creek School Road, West Jefferson, NC
(336) 246-2080, (800) 801-3441
This 52-room, two-story hotel near N.C. Highway 221 opened in November 1994. The rooms, all with outside entrances, feature king-size or double beds. Complimentary continental breakfast is served from 6:30 to 10:30 A.M. Nation's Inn also has a meeting room that accommodates 25. It also offers smoking and nonsmoking rooms.

Avery County

Beech Alpen Inn $$-$$$$
700 Beech Mountain Parkway, Beech Mountain, NC
(828) 387-2252
Beech Alpen Inn is a country inn under the same management as its neighbor, Top of the Beech, just down the road. The Beech Alpen Inn is open year-round, offering a cool retreat in the summer and ski opportunities in the winter. Some of the rooms in this rustic, European-style inn have fire-

Call ahead if you need a refrigerator in your room for picnic food or leftovers if you'll be staying a while. Not all hotels have them in every room.

places and balconies, and all rooms have exposed-beam ceilings as well as great views of the mountains and ski slopes at nearby Ski Beech. King- and queen-size beds are available. The Beech Alpen restaurant offers a menu of fine dining, featuring New York strip, filet mignon, superb crab cakes, and mountain trout prepared by their award-winning chef.

Holiday Inn of Banner Elk $$-$$$
1615 Tynecastle Highway 184, Banner Elk, NC
(828) 898-4571, (800) HOLIDAY
This classic Holiday Inn is less than a mile from the entrance to Sugar Mountain Ski Resort and only 6 miles from Ski Beech. The motel has 102 rooms (some nonsmoking), king-size beds, and cable TV with free HBO. Also, enjoy use of the newly constructed business center. Summer visitors can use the outdoor pool, volleyball court, horseshoe pits, and Ping-Pong tables.

You can dine at the Elk Cafe, the inn's full-service restaurant, which hosts buffets on the weekends. Meeting and banquet facilities are also available.

Humpback Hollow $$$$
U.S. Highway 221, Linville Falls, NC
(828) 766-6555, (888) 263-3632
Each of these unique cabins has a fully equipped kitchen, including microwave and charcoal grill. If you'd like to relax indoors after all-day hiking, there's a VCR and great selection of videos. All the cabins are decorated with antiques and country charm. Hosts Tom and Karen Acheson provide all linens, complimentary wood for the woodburning fireplace, and morning coffee. There are three cottages in all: The 200-year-old historic log cabin Sunalee, with all the modern conveniences. It has a

deck and covered porch, two full baths, a large bedroom, and loft. The Conner Cottage has been built entirely of wormy chestnut and contains a gas-log fireplace and porch, also two bedrooms and one bath. Fiddlesticks is the newest log cabin with a gas-log fireplace and air-conditioning. With one bedroom and one bath, it's an ideal romantic getaway for couples. The large covered porch serves as a wonderful lounging area.

Parkview Lodge $$-$$$
U.S. Highway 221, off Blue Ridge Parkway at Mile 317, Linville Falls, NC
(828) 765-4787, (800) 849-4452
This attractive lodge right off the Linville Falls exit of the Blue Ridge Parkway is a pleasant place with a friendly atmosphere. In addition to its 16 rooms, the complex has two cottages with kitchenettes and a suite on the picturesque grounds that back up to the parkway. You'll find plenty of wooded privacy and a swimming pool banked by cultivated wildflower beds. Parkview is popular with the parkway's hikers and campers, who occasionally stop in for a dose of civilization, especially hot showers. Parkview Lodge is open year-round and serves a complimentary continental breakfast. A craft shop and wine and beer shop are also on the premises. Satellite television includes HBO and Disney channels in addition to network programs.

Pineola Inn and Pineola Motel $-$$
U.S. Highway 221, Pineola, NC
(828) 733-4979
Just at the head of the North Cove area on U.S. 221 going up the mountain to Linville and Boone is the tiny crossroads of Pineola. The Pineola Inn and the Pineola Motel, both owned by the same family, are very simple accommodations with reasonable rates. They're just a few minutes south of the major ski areas of Sugar Mountain, Ski Beech, and Hawksnest. The High Country Ski Shop and Pineola Country Store, also part of the complex, offer gifts, souvenirs, and ski gear. Ski equip-

ment rentals and cross-country ski instruction are also available at the ski shop. You can ski cross-country on the nearby Blue Ridge Parkway. Ask the proprietor of the High Country Ski Shop about cross-country instruction and the best access to locations for this winter sport. Don't miss the Indian artifact museum at the rear of the Country Store. This amazing lifetime collection of Avery County's Dellinger family is one of the largest private collections of Native Indian artifacts in the area.

Sugar Top   **$$$-$$$$**
303 Sugar Top Drive, Banner Elk, NC
(828) 898-6211, (800) 764-2786
If brilliant views, every modern amenity, and sleek contemporary decor top your list of must-haves at a vacation spot, then perhaps you should be staying at Sugar Top. Perched atop Sugar Mountain, this 10-story condominium resort offers arresting views from an elevation of 5,140 feet. The east side has a view of Grandfather Mountain, while the west side overlooks the Sugar Mountain ski slopes. All suites are approximately 1,100 square feet, with two bedrooms, two baths, dining area, living room with fireplace, private covered balcony, refrigerator, dishwasher, and wet bar. Amenities include an indoor pool, sauna, steam room, whirlpool, fitness center, 24-hour security, and front desk service.

Top of the Beech   **$$-$$$$**
Beech Mountain Parkway, Beech Mountain, NC
(828) 387-2252
This Swiss-style ski lodge caters especially to—who else?—ski enthusiasts. The lobby, with a beamed cathedral ceiling, is dominated by a huge stone fireplace. The rooms, with two full-size beds, have wonderful views of the slopes of Ski Beech, just a half-mile away. You can get a "supersaver" discount rate Sunday through Thursday, and a complimentary continental breakfast is served each morning. An on-site conference room seats 50.

Madison County

Comfort Inn-Mars Hill   **$$**
167 J.F. Robinson Lane, Mars Hill, NC
(828) 689-9000
This Comfort Inn has the good fortune of being close to Wolf Laurel ski slopes. There's also an outdoor pool for use, as well as cable TV and free HBO for guests. A free continental breakfast can be taken in the dining room with an exceptional view of the mountains.

Mitchell County

Big Lynn Lodge   **$$$-$$$$**
N.C. Highway 226A, Little Switzerland, NC
(828) 765-4257, (800) 654-5232
Just off the Blue Ridge Parkway milepost 332.5 is delightful Big Lynn Lodge, a welcome sight after a long drive. This rustic inn is a combination of individual rooms and cottages in a woodland setting. Some rooms offer a spectacular view of the valley below. An exceptionally nice feature here is the complimentary inclusion of breakfast and dinner with all accommodations. There's an early-bird discount if you make reservations prior to the busy fall season. Enjoy a fireplace and player piano in the living room.

Pinebridge Inn   **$$-$$$$**
101 Pinebridge Avenue, Spruce Pine, NC
(828) 765-5543, (800) 356-5059
The Pinebridge Inn has a history of hospitality. This school property, constructed in the early 1920s, was converted to the area's premier hotel and conference facility in 1985. The sturdy brick hotel houses 44 spacious rooms and suites, a deluxe apartment with Jacuzzi bath, and assembly and banquet space for small and large groups. Another accommodation on the grounds is a three-bedroom cottage with fireplace. The high ceilings and tall windows in these former classrooms provide a view of the beautifully landscaped courtyard. An extensive continental break-

fast is served each morning. Pinebridge Inn is open year-round and offers group specials and discounts for area attractions.

Guests can also take advantage of the Pinebridge Center, located just across the parking lot. This recreational and fitness center offers numerous recreational diversions including seasonal ice-skating in one of the South's largest rinks, indoor heated pool, whirlpool, sauna, steam room, and plenty of fitness equipment. A lighted 410-foot-long footbridge spans the Riverside Park and connects the facilities to downtown Spruce Pine. This is a 3-Diamond-rated AAA hotel.

Watauga County

The Alpine Village Inn $$-$$$
297 Sunset Drive, Blowing Rock, NC
(828) 295-7206
The Alpine Village Inn is in the heart of Blowing Rock, within walking distance of Main Street and all the shops and restaurants. This attractive motel offers many of the detailed amenities of a bed-and-breakfast inn: 100 percent cotton towels, percale sheets, magazines and flowers in the rooms, individual heat and air-conditioning controls, cable TV, and complimentary newspapers and morning coffee. Antique furnishings and collectibles complement the homespun decor. Room refrigerators are available. The rocking chairs in the gazebo on the grounds are an invitation to take it easy. A room with a hot tub and fireplace is also available.

Brookside Inn $$
7876 Valley Boulevard, Blowing Rock, NC
(828) 295-3380, (800) 951-6048
Brookside Inn is a small inn with 19 guest rooms and three villas situated on two landscaped acres, with a brook, lake, gardens, and orchard. Guest rooms and villas are furnished in a Victorian cottage motif, with quilts, comforters, wicker chairs, and painted furniture. In the center of the inn

is Brookside Gallery, which exhibits and sells the works of regional artists. It is in the bright gallery with high ceilings that the owners serve a complimentary continental breakfast of homemade bread, coffee, tea, and juice each morning. Rooms, most with two double beds, each have a private bath, telephone, and cable television.

The real drawing point of Brookside Inn is the park surrounding the establishment; only a short walk from downtown shopping and restaurants, you have lush gardens with 50-year-old apple trees, a rock Meditation Garden, resident ducks on the pond, and scads of flowers and plants. All guest rooms face the quarter-acre lake. Three villas contained in one building behind the inn each have kitchen facilities, and two have gas-log fireplaces.

The Broyhill Inn &
Conference Center $$$-$$$$
775 Bodenheimer Drive, Boone, NC
(828) 262-2204, (800) 951-6048
This inn on the campus of Appalachian State University features seven suites and 76 guest rooms. There are 22 meeting rooms for small- to medium-size meetings and the Trillium Ballroom for as many as 850 guests. Support services for conferences and meetings include a full catering service for meals and receptions, audiovisual equipment, and the services of professional technicians. The inn's dining room serves up a spectacular mountain view with every breakfast, lunch, and dinner. Duggins Lounge, a quiet and relaxing getaway, is open in the evenings.

The Cottages of Glowing Hearth $$$$
171 Glowing Hearth Lane, Valle Crucis, NC
(828) 963-8800
The term *cottage* is a great misnomer here, because we are speaking of 1,500-square-foot houses with 18-foot white pine tongue-and-groove ceilings, 100-gallon double spas, king-size four-poster beds, imported Mexican terra-cotta tile flooring, a private driveway, and a parking

area for each domicile, and 25 windows per "cottage" so as not to miss any of the spectacular views.

A fully equipped kitchen, a 30-foot-long front porch, and a stone fireplace and hearth enable you to feel quite at home on your vacation. Of course it's not only the professionally designed interiors that make each of the Cottages of Glowing Hearth a dream vacation home but the small touches as well. Hand-painted ceramic tiles decorate the dining island, a video library with 500 titles can easily distract you, and a full concierge service for reservations, tee times, and other needs provides a near-perfect vacation experience. All you have to do is sit back and enjoy.

The proprietors live on the property and maintain a fax, copier, and computer in the office if you must keep in contact with the outside world. The property is a non-smoking environment and is open year-round. Weekly rental rates are discounted.

Days Inn—Blowing Rock $$–$$$
U.S. Highway 321 Bypass, Blowing Rock, NC
(828) 295-4422, (800) 329-7466
Here's a good bargain for families. Deluxe king and oversize rooms are among the 118 guest rooms available. An enclosed atrium has a heated swimming pool and hot tub. The coffee shop serves a full breakfast only. Days Inn has ski packages and discounts for senior citizens and tour groups.

Fall Creek Cabins $$$–$$$$
off Highway 421, Fleetwood, NC
(336) 877-3131
Surrounded by miles of lush forest on all sides, a gurgling creek, and a small waterfall, Fall Creek Cabins seem far removed from civilization. But open the front door to your two-story cabin and you will soon realize that all your creature comforts have been taken care of. The cabins, built from a fragrant western red cedar, house two bedrooms, two baths, a living room, loft, and kitchen. The full kitchen, with dishes, blender, corkscrew, silverware, and washer and dryer, enables you to be com-

pletely self-sufficient once you've done your initial grocery shopping.

Proprietors Tim and Beverly Thompson have truly thought of everything— including adjustable dimmer lighting and thermostats in every room—to create just that perfect individualized atmosphere for whatever the occasion. Stacks of newspaper for getting a good blaze started have thoughtfully been placed in a basket by the stone fireplace. An enormous stack of firewood sits just outside the cabin, and a gas grill on the front porch means grilling those steaks and sausages will be a snap, leaving more time for outdoor activities or a longer soak in the hot tub on the covered porch, whichever your inclination may be. You can find a VCR, videos, and board games for the whole family in each cabin. During the day be sure to explore the extensive hiking trails, streams, waterfalls, and a trout stream stocked by the state. You'll have to purchase a fishing license for about $10, which you can find at any hardware store, fishing and bait shop, or even large superstore.

The Thompsons have built six cabins with their own personal preferences in mind. Having traveled the country and spent many a vacation wishing for the perfect mixture of rustic comfort, they have finally realized their dream and now wish to share it with you. The lofty cathedral ceilings in each cabin convey a sense of light and breeze. Light streams into the dining room windows as well as through the sliding glass doors into the living room. Each cabin is decorated in a different unobtrusive style, with country flavor and clean lines. Cabins are far from one another, so you will have no problem imagining you are the only ones on the mountain, but with all possible amenities at your fingertips.

Graystone Lodge $$–$$$
2419 Highway 105, Boone, NC
(828) 264-4133, (800) 560-5942
The gray stone exterior of this four-story inn links it to the Scottish influence of

Linville, just south on the same highway. Built against the hillside, the inn's first two floors offer parking lot entrances.

The 100 rooms of the Graystone Lodge have a number of comfortable variations that include luxury suites with king-size beds, parlors, and vaulted ceilings. Continental breakfast is free and served from 6:45 to 10:00 A.M. All rooms have cable TV, and you can rent a VCR. The inn also features an indoor heated pool. Special discounts are available.

Hemlock Inn $$
134 Morris Street, Blowing Rock, NC
(828) 295-7987
For those of you who don't like to fool with the intimacy of a bed-and-breakfast, who prefer to be left to your own devices, or who prefer to spend your money on sightseeing, gifts, and food rather than your accommodations, then the Hemlock Inn is for you. This motel-style inn is just off Blowing Rock's main street. It offers tidy rooms with double, queen- or king-size beds, air-conditioning, private baths, and the added plus of a kitchenette in every room. A microwave, coffee pot, and refrigerator enable you to be quite independent in your travels here. Or if you plan on heavy-duty cooking, suites are available with fully equipped kitchens. You also have the choice of nonsmoking and nonallergenic rooms.

High Country Inn $$-$$$
1785 N.C. Highway 105 S., Boone, NC
(828) 264-1000, (800) 334-5605
Built against the side of the mountain, High Country Inn takes advantage of its scenic wooded surroundings. This inn of native stone provides a variety of comfortable to luxurious accommodations.

All 120 rooms have been recently refurbished. You can indulge yourself in a suite, such as the deluxe Appalachian Room with a king-size bed, a whirlpool tub, and a cozy fireplace. This is a popular honeymoon destination, but it also draws skiers, golfers, and other groups interested in the High Country Inn's numerous

discount packages. High Country Inn has facilities for conferences, receptions, and banquets.

Geno's Sports Restaurant is open daily for breakfast and dinner in season, while Geno's Sports Lounge is good for a drink and a nibble. Guests also can use the indoor/outdoor pool, hot tub, sauna, and fitness center.

Hillwinds Inn $$-$$$
315 Sunset Drive, Blowing Rock, NC
(828) 295-7660, (800) 821-4908
This delightful little motel-style inn offers a relaxing respite from a day of shopping and dining. Choose from a variety of rooms with two double beds, or queen- or king-size bed, private bath, and telephone and TV. No pretensions here—it's relaxed and close to shopping and restaurants in downtown Blowing Rock, so the inn is the choice for business travelers, as well as those who don't like a lot of fuss, but do like privacy. Hillwinds' upstairs suite is a favorite with honeymooners, but we like it too—a comfortable bedroom with four-poster bed, plus a living room with television, wet bar, stereo entertainment system, and fireplace.

Just beyond the inn's gazebo, filled with rockers for late-evening chats, is a small guest house with mirror-image rooms; if two families or several friends are traveling together, you can share the cottage and still have thorough privacy. Containing a bath, bedroom, and lounge area, the guest house also has a full kitchen in each suite that may be used for a slight surcharge. Flowers and benches decorate the exterior of the inn, and maintain cozy seating in the lobby for sorting through the vast amount of information on the surrounding area, provided by the owners.

Holiday Inn Express $$-$$$$
1855 Blowing Rock Road, U.S. Highway
321 E., Boone, NC
(828) 264-2451, (800) SEE-MTNS
The location is convenient—between Boone and Blowing Rock—and amenities are plentiful at this Holiday Inn Express,

one of the national chain's new stream-lined facilities. Recently renovated, this motel features comfortable rooms plus free daily breakfast bar, free local calls, a fitness center, and an outdoor pool.

The Meadowbrook Inn $$-$$$
U.S. Highway 321 Bypass, Blowing Rock, NC
(828) 295-4300, (800) 456-5456

This gracious inn offers numerous ameni-ties in elegant surroundings. Rooms and suites are furnished in a traditional decor, and deluxe accommodations include fire-places and oversize whirlpool baths. A serene pond is bordered by landscaped grounds. The Meadowbrook Inn has an indoor, heated pool and whirlpool and a fitness center. A glass-enclosed room adjacent to the pool area is used for meetings, conferences, and private dining. The Artist's Palate overlooks the garden and pond. A seasonal menu features fine wine and American cuisine.

Quality Inn Appalachian $$-$$$$
Conference Center, 949 Blowing Rock
Road, Boone, NC
(828) 262-0020, (800) 228-5151

Only minutes away from Appalachian State's campus, area businesses, and recreation, this modern hotel offers big-city conveniences and amenities. Guests enjoy spacious suites, king and connecting rooms, an indoor/outdoor pool, a fitness center, a restaurant and lounge, and cable television. Full-service banquet facilities include catering, several meeting rooms, and a 3,750-square-foot ballroom. A com-plimentary morning paper is a nice touch. Smoke-free and wheelchair-accessible rooms are also available.

Smoketree Lodge $$-$$$$
N.C. Highway 105 S., Foscoe, NC
(828) 963-6505, (800) 422-1880 in N.C.

The Smoketree Lodge is tucked away off N.C. 105 leading directly into Boone, just a few minutes away. This hidden delight is sheltered by a canopy of trees that do much to give Smoketree its sense of pri-vacy so near to bustling Boone. The lobby

is graced by a massive fireplace that rises to the full height of the vaulted ceiling.

The comfortable rooms at Smoketree each have kitchenettes, and laundry facili-ties are available on the first floor. The complex also includes a game room, an indoor pool, a hot tub, a sauna exercise room, and gas and charcoal grills out back for picnic fun on the hill behind the lodge.

The Blowing Rock area has an array of small, clean, and cozy motels too numerous to mention here. If you prefer the independence of a motel to a bed-and-breakfast and the price to larger resorts and inns, then take a drive through Main Street and the streets branching off this thoroughfare. Most of these smaller motels are happy to take walk-ins if you are not quite sure of your travel plans beforehand.

Swiss Mountain Village $$-$$$$
2324 Flat Top Road, Blowing Rock, NC
(828) 295-3373, (888) 785-1188

The mountain cabins and chalets of Swiss Mountain Village offer the homey charm of a bed-and-breakfast with the privacy of your own home away from home. Set on lovely landscaped grounds, surrounded by a forest filled with native rhododendron and mountain laurel, Swiss Mountain Vil-lage has log cabins built from rough-hewn timbers. Each authentic Swiss-style chalet has a loft and stairway over a native-stone fireplace, and each comes furnished with everything you'll need to feel at home, right down to the towels, linens, stoneware, pots, and utensils. A washer and dryer are also included in each unit, so you could stay for days and only bring one suitcase. Hiking trails and a fishing pond are on the property for your out-door recreation.

The variety of accommodations at Swiss Mountain Village is a plus, especially if you have a big family or a large group of vacation-minded friends. Studio and one-, two-, and three-bedroom units are available, each with queen-size beds and queen-size sleeper sofas. Some have extra twin beds or bunks, so bring a crowd.

Yancey County

Alpine Village   **$$-$$$$**
200 Overlook Drive, Burnsville, NC
(828) 675-4103
Alpine Village is a unique animal. It has the individuality of a bed-and-breakfast, the serenity of a retreat, and the variety of a small resort. Yet it is highly affordable and a splendid alternative for large families or groups on the road for summer fun.

Set high back in the mountains in the shadow of spectacular Mount Mitchell, Alpine Village is a cluster of private one- and two-bedroom, chalet-style condominiums with all the amenities of home, each accommodating from four to six people. Most cabins are equipped with a kitchen, a dishwasher, a washer/dryer, a telephone, a whirlpool bath, linens, private decks, cable TV, and gas grills. A heated pool and a tennis court are on the grounds, and golf is available at a special discount to guests at nearby Mount Mitchell Golf Club. You can rent these cabins by the night, week, or month. A two-night minimum stay is usually required.

Blue Ridge Motel   **$-$$**
204 West Boulevard, Burnsville, NC
(828) 682-9100
The unusual interior wood paneling of the rooms at the Blue Ridge Motel is one of the attractions of this small family-owned motel, situated just a few minutes west of Town Square and U.S. 19 E. This pleasant two-story, redbrick motel, built in the 1950s when wood paneling was not the life savings' investment it is today, boasts a distinctive variety of wood interiors, from apple wood to pine, walnut, and oak. Some of the furniture was also handmade during that early period. You can sleep on a bed with a delightful handmade ash, oak, wal-

nut, or maple headboard. All rooms have private outside entrances, and the motel is within easy walking distance of shopping and a number of local restaurants.

This motel is popular with skiers, since Wolf Laurel is about 40 minutes away. Group rates and senior citizen discounts are available.

CENTRAL MOUNTAINS

Buncombe County

Best Western Central   **$$-$$$**
22 Woodfin Street, Asheville, NC
(828) 253-1851
Just off I-240, which loops around the city, Best Western Central is convenient to attractions at all points of the compass. This hotel has 144 guest rooms, a swimming pool, meeting rooms, and a restaurant and lounge.

Comfort Inn—River Ridge   **$$-$$$**
800 Fairview Road, Asheville, NC
(828) 298-9141, (800) 228-5150
This hotel is in the eastern part of Asheville, off I-240 at the River Ridge Outlet Mall. Accommodations are moderately priced, and the hotel has 178 guest rooms, including a number of luxurious two-room suites with large whirlpool garden tubs, king-size beds, a living room, kitchen and dinette areas, and private balconies. A fax and a copier are in the lobby, and a continental breakfast is served by the fireplace in the large sitting area adjacent to the lobby. The Comfort Inn also has a pool, a playground, and volleyball and basketball courts. You can walk down the hill to the Outlet Mall from Comfort Inn.

Comfort Suites   **$$-$$$$**
890 Brevard Road, Asheville, NC
(828) 665-4000, (800) 228-5150
Comfort Suites caters to the corporate business traveler. The hotel contains 125 spacious rooms, each with a full- or queen-size bed, sleeper sofa, coffee pot,

and refrigerator. Two thousand square feet is devoted to meeting space that can accommodate gatherings of up to 100 people. Complimentary deluxe continental breakfast, free airport shuttle, an exercise and hot-tub room, and an outdoor heated pool are some of the amenities provided by Comfort Suites. The hotel is next to the Biltmore Square Mall.

The Doubletree
Biltmore Hotel $$$-$$$$
115 Hendersonville Road, Asheville, NC
(828) 274-1800, (800) 222-TREE
Since its construction several years ago, the Doubletree Biltmore Hotel in Asheville has become one of the prime fixtures in the southern end of town. The hotel's brick-and-stone exterior is a modern blend of the angles and lines and stately presence of the turn-of-the-century architectural opulence characterized by its neighbor, Biltmore Estate. The light wood-paneled interior and dramatic lighting of the hotel lobby complement the elegance of the lush furnishings.

The hotel has 160 guest rooms, including 20 suites. All rooms have cable TV with HBO, valet and room service, and electronic door locks. A gift shop and fax machine are in the lobby. This hotel also caters to corporate business, with several flexible meeting rooms and on-site advance coordination of catering, audiovisual equipment, and entertainment.

Forest Manor Inn $$-$$$$
866 Hendersonville Road, Asheville, NC
(828) 274-3531
South of Biltmore Village toward Arden is Forest Manor Inn, an oasis on four wooded, beautifully landscaped acres that at one time were considered to be out in the country. The lovely stone structure that now serves as the office was once a private residence, built in 1926. It has a curiously colorful history: During Prohibition the sons who inherited this lovely home turned it into a rowdy roadhouse. As years went by it became a somewhat subdued restaurant. Then it caught the

eye of a nefarious local character who turned it into a gambling operation during the 1940s and '50s. Eventually this check-ered existence subsided, and the elegant old home took on respectable status as the pleasant motor lodge it is today.

Five cheerful, canary-yellow buildings surround the stone lodge. The inn's 21 guest rooms are either delicately papered or paneled in knotty pine. Parking is just outside your door. King-size beds, smoke-free rooms, and continental breakfast are other amenities. A private, landscaped pool area is open during the summer season.

Great Smokies SunSpree
Resort $$-$$$$
1 Holiday Inn Drive, Asheville, NC
(828) 254-3211, (800) 733-3211
This 120-acre resort caters to corporate and tourist groups. The individual traveler, however, may also find this an enjoyable resort conveniently located three minutes from downtown Asheville. An 18-hole golf course sprawls over rolling green hills and a fully stocked pro shop supplies all your sports needs. The resort's 10,000 square feet of meeting space accommodates a wide variety of functions, including ball-room banquets, sunset receptions, and boardroom meetings. All rooms feature balconies or patios and, of course, some fairly incredible views. Recreational amenities include tennis, a jogging trail, several swimming pools, an on-site exercise room, or a nearby full-service health club. Also available are children's programs and a game room so you can enjoy a peaceful meal while the kids play.

Hampton Inn—Asheville $$-$$$$
1 Rocky Ridge Road, off I-26, Asheville, NC
(828) 667-2022, (800) HAMPTON
Southwest of the city, the Hampton Inn of Asheville has 121 nicely appointed guest rooms, a fully equipped fitness center, an indoor heated pool, a sauna, and a hot tub. Free airport transportation, nonsmoking rooms, and meeting facilities are also available. The Biltmore Square Mall, the Movies at Biltmore Square, and several fast-food

restaurants are nearby. You can also ask them about their new Tunnel Road Facility, which is close to Asheville Mall.

Haywood Park Hotel $$$-$$$$
1 Battery Park Avenue, Asheville, NC
(828) 252-2522, (800) 228-2522

The Haywood Park Hotel was a prominent flagship in the resurgence of downtown Asheville. A full-service hotel in the heart of downtown was a risky business a decade ago, but the renovation of the historic Ivey's Department Store at the corner of Battery Park Avenue and Haywood Street into the sleek Haywood Park Hotel was backed by strong business commitment. The success of this undertaking brought a level of sophistication to the inner city that set the tone for the upscale mood and cultural renaissance enjoyed by downtown Asheville today.

The hotel renovation is an interesting use of space, opening up and reshaping the former boxy retail building. The adjoining atrium space, which houses shops, restaurants, and offices, brings the sky inside the heart of this city block with its vaulted ceiling, skylights, and gleaming glass elevator.

The Haywood Park Hotel has 33 exquisitely appointed guest rooms, some with great views of the architectural richness of downtown Asheville. Meeting rooms are also available, and the superb restaurant, the Flying Frog Café, a chic gathering place, makes the Haywood Park Hotel a popular dining spot for downtown business professionals and visitors alike. This fine

---

Haywood Park Hotel in downtown Asheville has two secrets. One is the third floor. It is the most recently renovated in lovely greens and golds. The Haywood Atrium and hotel lobby maintains a fine selection of boutiques, a fine art gallery, flower shop, and a cafe, without any markup because of location.

---

hotel has also hosted a number of celebrities, whose photos line the lobby walls.

Holiday Inn—Tunnel Road $$-$$$
201 Tunnel Road, Asheville, NC
(828) 252-4000, (800) HOLIDAY

This Holiday Inn has been a fixture on Tunnel Road for a good while, undergoing major renovations in recent years. It is a popular site for corporate groups, reunions, and senior citizen groups. It's an easy walk from here to the Asheville Mall and numerous restaurants along Tunnel Road. The 131 guest rooms feature double and king-size beds, cable TV with free HBO and ESPN, and room service. The inn has an outdoor pool, and you can purchase tickets to Biltmore Estate here.

Mountain Springs Cabins
& Chalets $$$
N.C. Highway 151, Asheville, NC
(828) 665-1004

Tucked back in the mountains as cabins and chalets are wont to be, Mountain Springs Cabins & Chalets are off U.S. 19/23; turn onto N.C. Highway 151 and follow signs for 5 miles to Mountain Springs. You will find them almost adjacent to the Blue Ridge Parkway. A mountain stream meanders past the cabins.

All are furnished in fine country antiques and have modern baths, fireplaces, and cable TV, with swings and rockers on the porches. Flowers decorate the window boxes and grapes dangle from arbors. Fragrant herbs grow outside in the herb gardens—all the better to use in your cooking in the charming kitchens. The cabins range in size from one bedroom to two bedrooms with loft. There are lots of places to stroll, swim, birdwatch, and hike in the most enchanting acreage that surrounds the cabins and chalets. Or you can just while away the time in a hammock under the trees. A true retreat for lovers of nature and seclusion, Mountain Springs accommodations can be rented on a daily or weekly basis. Children are welcome.

Ramada Plaza Hotel-West $$-$$$$
435 Smoky Park Highway, at I-40 and
U.S. Highways 19/23, Asheville, NC
(828) 665-2161, (800) 228-2828
The six-story lobby atrium with a cozy
fireplace is the focal point of the 166-
room Ramada Inn West. The hotel has
Lisa's Restaurant and the Eagle's Nest
Lounge, and local crafts are highlighted
at Ann's Gifts. Guests may use the hotel's
health club, sauna, hot tub, and indoor-
outdoor pool.

Rennaissance Asheville
Hotel $$$-$$$$
31 Woodfin Street, Asheville, NC
(828) 252-8211
The 12-story Rennaissance Asheville Hotel,
a prominent feature on the skyline of
downtown Asheville, provides guests with
a breathtaking view of the city and the
mountains beyond. This modern award-
winning hotel has 275 guest rooms and
seven suites, all decorated in an elegant
Queen Anne style with all the amenities.
Concierge service and health club privi-
leges are available to guests, and there
are nonsmoking floors.

The lobby contains a gift shop and a
new restaurant known as Orchards. The
hotel also has 14 flexible meeting rooms
with state-of-the-art conference planning
and support. An 8,100-square-foot ball-
room is also at your disposal.

The Rennaissance is within walking
distance of Pack Square, fine restaurants,
shopping, and downtown galleries.

Sleep Inn—Biltmore $$-$$$
117 Hendersonville Road, Asheville, NC
(828) 277-1800, (800) 62-SLEEP
This Sleep Inn in Biltmore Village opened
in the fall of 1994. It offers upscale quality
accommodations at a reasonable price.
Attractively furnished, this hotel offers a
number of pleasing amenities: queen-size
beds, smoking and nonsmoking rooms,
connecting rooms, free continental break-
fast, and free local calls. A fax and copier
are also available for busy working travel-

ers. The Biltmore Estate entrance is just a
few blocks away.

The Renaissance Hotel in Asheville is a
stone's-throw from the center of town.
It's also right beside the Thomas Wolfe
Memorial and the Urban Trail. Find the
bronze shoes and throw rug in front of
the Wolfe House—these represent the
famous author's actual size 13 shoes.

Willow Winds $$$
39 Stockwood Road, Asheville, NC
(828) 277-3948
Only minutes from Biltmore Estate, these
individual homes on 40 acres of land
give you the full luxury experience of
staying in a fully furnished domicile,
including washers, dryers, equipped
kitchen, televisions, VCRs, and your own
phone line. From one-bedroom homes to
three-bedroom homes with two stories,
these beautifully furnished residences
also contain Jacuzzi tubs inside and hot
tubs outdoors.

If you haven't bought your groceries
yet, not to worry, you'll be supplied with a
gift basket containing fresh fruit, cookies,
coffee, and wine. A stocked pond on the
property enables you to fish for your own
dinner if you care to. Houses may be
rented for as few as two nights in the off
season and a minimum of five nights during high season.

Wingate Inn $$-$$$
11 Rocky Ridge Road, Asheville, NC
(828) 665-4242, (800) 228-1000
The Wingate Inn provides everything for
the traveling businessperson. Free Internet
access in every room means being truly
connected while you're on the road. Guest
rooms also feature a coffeemaker,
microwave, refrigerator, safe, hair dryer,
and iron and ironing board. Meeting
rooms are also available, and a fitness
center lets you blow off steam at the end
of the day. A complimentary, expanded

continental breakfast nourishes the hungry before it's time to hit the road.

Henderson County

Hampton Inn $$
155 Sugarloaf Road, Hendersonville, NC
(828) 697-2333, (800) HAMPTON

Hampton Inn, right off the junction of I-26 and U.S. 64 (take exit 18A going to Batcave), has 117 rooms and two suites. Amenities include cable television with HBO, free local phone calls, an outdoor swimming pool, health club privileges, senior discounts, and a free deluxe continental breakfast. Nonsmoking rooms are available, and third and fourth guests stay free of charge. From here, it's just a hop, skip, and a jump to Wal-Mart, the Blue Ridge Mall, and a number of familiar chain restaurants. A bit farther on is Hendersonville's historic Main Street, with its abundance of shops, restaurants, and galleries.

The Quality Inn and Suites $$
201 Sugarloaf Road, Hendersonville, NC
(828) 692-7231, (800) 4-CHOICE

This large facility is also at the junction of I-26 and U.S. 64 (exit 18A). In addition to air-conditioned corporate, spa, and two-room suites, the inn has an excellent restaurant court and lounge overlooking an indoor, Olympic-size, heated swimming pool. The motel offers a full range of amenities, including a fitness room, sauna, free newspaper, local phone calls, banquet facilities, room service, a hot tub, and meeting rooms. All the sites of Main Street Hendersonville are nearby.

Rutherford County

Fairfield Mountains Resort $$$-$$$$
747 Buffalo Creek Road, Lake Lure, NC
(828) 625-9111, (800) 829-3149

This resort offers efficiencies, condominiums, rentals, and time-shares for travelers wishing to enjoy the scenery of Lake Lure

and Chimney Rock and the recreation of two golf courses on the 2,400-acre Fairfield Mountain Resort property. Several of Fairfield's 100 units sit on the banks of the lake, opposite the town of Lake Lure. Others offer views of mountain ridges and foliage. Efficiencies include efficiency kitchens, telephones, TV, and air-conditioning. Larger two- and three-bedroom units also contain these amenities, but with a full kitchen.

Because many of the units are actually second homes that are rented out by the resort, you will find the interiors decorated to the individual tastes of the owners. This lends a delightfully homey and distinct atmosphere to each rental. Some homes maintain a two-day rental policy, but many allow for anywhere from a one-night's stay to several weeks or months.

If you don't feel like cooking, two restaurants located at the resort can provide pleasant dining. Legends Bar and Grill serves breakfast, lunch, and dinner, and Lakeview Restaurant serves dinner.

Polk County

Days Inn $$
I-26 at Exit 36, Columbus, NC
(828) 894-3303, (800) 329-7466

Situated between the twin towns of Tryon and Columbus, this facility offers many extras, such as an outdoor pool, suites with whirlpool baths, cable television with HBO, nonsmoking rooms, free continental breakfast, AARP discounts, mountain views, and 24-hour desk and wake-up services.

Transylvania County $
Brevard Motor Lodge, U.S. Highway 64
and Caldwell Street, Brevard, NC
(828) 884-3456

While staying here, you'll be across the street from Brevard College's picturesque campus, within walking distance of downtown Brevard, and just minutes away from the Brevard Music Center. This small motel—all its rooms are on the ground floor—offers individual heating and air-conditioning, a small refrigerator in each room, a heated pool, and fax and copier service.

Hampton Inn $$
800 Forest Gate Center, Brevard, NC
(828) 883-4800, (800) HAMPTON

In 1995 this 81-room Hampton Inn opened just off the main entrance to Pisgah Forest outside Brevard near the intersection of N.C. Highway 280 and U.S. 64. The facility offers two conference rooms and continental breakfasts. There is no restaurant on the premises, but you'll be within walking distance of quite a few places to eat. Shopping, too, is at your front door in the Forest Gate Shopping Center.

Imperial Motor Lodge $$
U.S. Highways 64 and 276 N., Asheville Highway, Brevard, NC
(828) 884-2887, (800) 869-3335

Situated between downtown Brevard and the entrance to Pisgah Forest, Imperial Motor Lodge is Transylvania County's largest motel. Each of its 92 rooms has individual heating, air-conditioning, and cable TV with HBO. Every room has a refrigerator. There is also a large sundeck and pool. Smoking and nonsmoking rooms are available, and a continental breakfast is served in season.

Pisgah Inn $$
Mile 408.6, Blue Ridge Parkway, NC
(828) 235-8228

The Pisgah Inn is a landmark on the Blue Ridge Parkway. From late April until early November, this inn's location at 5,000 feet and just a hike down a trail from Mount Pisgah itself offers you the opportunity to explore nature's unspoiled mountain seasons—and you barely have to step outside to do it. In addition to two double beds, a private bath, and color television, each room at Pisgah Inn has its own private porch or balcony directly overlooking Pisgah Ledge and the ever-changing play of lights and shadows on the mountain peaks below. A restaurant serves excellent food at very reasonable prices, and the view from the dining room is spectacular.

If you want to get out in all this beauty, you can hike on a number of trails—interconnecting with many other Pisgah Forest trails—that begin practically at the inn's door. This is a popular place so advance planning is important. You might be able to simply drop in and get a room, but it's wiser to make reservations. During fall-foliage days, early reservations are essential.

Many hotels and motels have Internet access right in the rooms. Some even have high-speed LAN lines, so be sure to carry your cable along if you want to hook up.

Rainbow Lake Resort $$$
East Fork Road, Brevard, NC
(828) 862-5354

This serene mountain valley just across the road from the trout-filled headwaters of the French Broad River is perfect for those who want a quiet stay in the mountains. The 12 rustic cottages have front porches with porch swings and rockers. They are sprinkled throughout the woods overlooking a three-acre lake. Their simple board-and-batten exteriors belie the elegance within. The tastefully decorated interiors include original works of art, hardwood floors, fine furnishings, and fully equipped kitchens. Each has a private phone, cable TV, and air-conditioning. Some have fireplaces. You can choose from one, two and three bedrooms. Here you'll find trails, boating, fishing, badminton, horseshoes, volleyball, streams, waterfalls, hammocks, quiet reading nooks, tranquility, and a summer symphony of crickets and frogs to sing you to sleep. Rainbow Lake is the perfect place for holding seminars and family reunions. Well-behaved, flealess pets are accepted with prior arrangements. Rainbow Lake Resort is located 8 miles from Brevard. Take either U.S. 64 W. or U.S. 276 S. out of Brevard for about 3 miles. Signs will tell you where to turn.

SOUTHERN MOUNTAINS
Cherokee County

**Cherokee Hills Golf and
Country Club**   **$$$-$$$$**
**Harshaw Road, Murphy, NC
(828) 837-5853, (800) 334-3905**
If you like to golf, this is the place to stay in Murphy (see our Golf chapter). The complex has 12 units available in the club's lodge that feature fully equipped efficiencies, including two queen-size beds, a bath with a tub and shower, kitchens, cable television, daily maid service, and air-conditioning. Spacious two-story town houses are available for rent at little more per night than you would pay at a fine hotel. Golf packages bring down the price even more. Rentals also include access to the pool, tennis courts, a restaurant, a golf course, a driving range, and a putting green.

Comfort Inn   **$$**
**114 U.S. Highway 64 W., Murphy, NC
(828) 837-8030**
Murphy's Comfort Inn, which is open all year, has 55 rooms, 10 of which come with whirlpools and refrigerators. One really nice attraction here is the heated indoor pool with a sunroof. Other amenities include a conference room, cable television and movie rentals, and free continental breakfasts.

Clay County

Chatuge Mountain Inn   **$**
**U.S. Highway 64, Hayesville, NC
(828) 389-3873, (800) 948-2755**
This facility is east of Hayesville on U.S. 64 going toward Hiwassee, Georgia. It has 14 clean, comfortable rooms, including one efficiency unit. All rooms have air-conditioning, cable television, and telephones.

Graham County

Thunderbird Mountain Resort   **$-$$**
**U.S. Highway 129 N., Santeetlah, NC
(828) 479-6442, (800) 479-6442**
Built on one of the many little peninsulas that poke out into Lake Santeetlah, Thunderbird Mountain Resort, about 6 miles from Robbinsville, has 32 rooms with lake views, plus cottages, lake swimming, and a good restaurant. The seclusion of this comfortable resort is synonymous with a relaxing vacation. Right next door is the Santeetlah Marina with seventy slips and all kinds of boats and watercraft for rent, including a giant water tricycle. You can buy fuel, bait, tackle, hunting/fishing licenses, boat registrations, ice, and snack food here, too. The marina also has a water ski shop and a ski instructor for private lessons.

Haywood County

Best Western   **$$**
**3811 Soco Road, U.S. Highway 19,
Maggie Valley, NC
(828) 926-3962, (800) 528-1234**
Best Western, formerly the Mountainbrook Inn, on the busy highway that cuts though the center of this highly developed resort town, is within walking distance of many Maggie Valley attractions. Even so, you can relax on the rocking chairs here while you view mountains right from the front porch of your room. Or, during the summer season, you can unwind in a heated pool and large whirlpool spa. The grounds include a picnic area with grills. The large motel-type rooms contain two queen-size beds. There are full baths and showers, a couple of upholstered chairs with a small table, cable television with free HBO, and—probably best of all for the budget-conscious—a microwave, a refrigerator, and in-room coffee. There is no charge for

children 17 and younger staying in the same room with a parent. Cribs are available at no cost. A continental breakfast is served each morning.

Best Western Smoky Mountain Inn $$
330 Hyatt Creek Road, Waynesville, NC
(828) 456–4402, (800) 218–2121

At the Best Western Smoky Mountain Inn, you're within an hour's driving distance of some of our most famous attractions, including the Biltmore Estate, the Great Smoky Mountain Railroad, the Blue Ridge Parkway, the Cherokee Indian Reservation, and Ghost Town in Maggie Valley to name a few. The inn's 58 modern, spacious, and comfortable rooms feature large picture windows revealing gorgeous mountain views. King-size, handicapped-accessible, and nonsmoking rooms are available on request. Microwave, minirefrigerators, and color TVs are standard. Complimentary continental breakfast is served each day. Daily newspaper, magazines, and reference books are available in the lobby. This inn is 5 miles north of the Blue Ridge Parkway on U.S. 23/74. Take the West Waynesville exit 95.

Chalet Motel and Apartments $$
Soco Road, U.S. Highway 19, Maggie Valley, NC
(828) 926–2811, (800) 371–8587

Nestled up and off U.S. 19 in a secluded and quiet spot, Chalet Motel rents apartments, efficiencies, and rooms. These vary in the types of accommodations offered. One efficiency, for example, has a king-size bed and a kitchenette; another has a queen-size bed and a full kitchen. The average apartment has a living-dining room combination, a bedroom with two double beds, and a separate full kitchen. They have heat and air-conditioning, cable television with HBO, AM/FM radio, and private patios with pretty mountain views. The lawn is flat and expansive and has shade trees, picnic tables and grills; there are trails and trout streams close by.

Twinbrook Resort $$
230 Twinbrook Lane, Maggie Valley, NC
(828) 926–1388, (800) 305–8946

Set on 20 acres, this four-season facility features 14 one-, two-, three-, and four-bedroom, individually crafted cottages with fireplaces, phones, and cable TV. The cottages are scattered among tall hemlocks. On site are an indoor pool, a hot tub, a game area, horseshoe pits, a volleyball court, and a playground.

Jackson County

Comfort Inn
U.S. Highways 23/74, Mile 86, Sylva, NC
(828) 586–3315, (800) 654–3315

All rooms at Sylva's Comfort Inn have phones and cable television. The inn also has a swimming pool, serves a complimentary continental breakfast, and has other services and discounts you'd expect from a motel chain such as Comfort Inn. This one is near Sylva and Dillsboro on the highway to Waynesville.

Cottage Inn $$-$$$$
off U.S. Highway 64, Cashiers, NC
(828) 743–3033

Since 1932 the year-round Cottage Inn has been a mountain hideaway for quiet, lovely vacations. Each of the 14 air-conditioned cottages has a fireplace, kitchen, color TV, full bath, and deck and porch. In addition to the cottages is the new Knolltop Lodge Bed-and-Breakfast with four guest rooms each with a private bath, air-conditioning, a common parlor with a TV and a fireplace, and a full breakfast daily.

The nine-acre complex also has an enclosed heated pool, a tennis court with a basketball goal, a nature trail, a picnic pavilion, swings and hammocks, laundry facilities, and the Heathstone room for meetings.

Mountain Brook Cottages   **$$$**
208 Mountain Brook Road, Sylva, NC
(828) 586–4329
Midway between Sylva/Dillsboro and
Franklin, these 12 brookside cottages offer
fireplaces and equipped kitchens. Some
have bubble tubs/saunas and king-size
beds. There is also a spa/sauna bungalow.
In addition Mountain Brook offers a game
room, a stocked trout pond, and a nature
trail. Wedding and honeymoon packages
are available.

Mountain Creek Cottages   **$$–$$$**
2672 Dicks Creek Road, Dillsboro, NC
(828) 586–6042
The sounds of rushing water will lull you
to sleep at this beautiful creekside setting.
Accommodations for two to six people
have full kitchens, DSS TV with HBO, and
private cookout areas. There's a lot to do
in this area of the mountains, but you
might just opt for hanging out in a ham-
mock by the cascading stream.

Macon County

Hampton Inn   **$$$–$$$$**
Highway 106 and Spring Street,
Highlands, NC
(828) 526–5899, (800) HAMPTON
This newest of Hampton Inns sits on an
overlook affording great views. It is
upscale offering complete amenities.

Heritage Cottages and Villas   **$$**
97 Heritage Hollow Drive, Franklin, NC
(828) 369–2028
Because it sits on seven acres filled with
rhododendrons, dogwoods, and towering
pines, this complex right in the heart of
Old Town Franklin can offer amazingly
quiet lodgings. You have your choice of
villas or cottages. The villas, which can
sleep from two to six people, have one or
two queen-size beds, a bath with a separate dressing room, a full kitchen, and a
living/dining area with a fireplace. Each of
the cottages, which are for two to three

people, has a queen- or king-size bed, a
sofa, eating areas, and efficiency kitchens.
All units have air-conditioning, cable TV,
an electric toaster, and a coffeemaker.
Even the dishes, cooking utensils, and
linens are furnished. You will be within
walking distance of downtown Franklin
with its shops, museums, and restaurants.
A bakery and a creekside cafe are practically on the premises.

Highland Suite Hotel   **$$$$**
200 Main Street, Highlands, NC
(828) 526–4502, (800) 221–5078
Just where the shopping stops on Main
Street, you'll find the Highlands Suite
Hotel, where all rooms are suites, each
with individual climate control, whirlpool
spa, two telephones, two cable TVs, VCR,
microwave oven, wet bar, and refrigerator.
In addition each living room has a queen-
size convertible sofa bed, and each bedroom offers a choice of either one
king-size or two extra-large twin beds.
Many suites have gas-log fireplaces.

There are also complimentary continental breakfasts and evening wine and cheese,
free parking in a covered garage, and free
local phone calls. Nonsmoking rooms and
walk-in closets are available options.

Skyline Lodge   **$$$**
Flat Mountain Road, Highlands, NC
(828) 526–2121, (800) 5–SKYLINE
At an altitude of more than 4,000 feet,
Skyline is housed in a Frank Lloyd
Wright–designed, tastefully furnished
building with 50 acres of grounds that
have streams, lakes, waterfalls, and nature
walks. Other attractions include a swim-
ming pool, tennis courts, a gourmet
restaurant, and a spa with a sauna, a
steam room, and a whirlpool. The facility
also offers facials, full-body massages, and
foot- and hand-care sessions, along with
guided fitness walks, aerobics, yoga, and
seminars on healthful living (seminars are
offered only to guests participating in the
lodge's "Holiday Health" specials). Skyline
Lodge is open year-round.

Swain County

Best Western Great Smokies Inn $$
U.S. Highway 441, at Acquoni Road, Cherokee, NC
(828) 497-2020, (800) 258-1234
Right across the street from the 8,000-square-foot Great Smokies Convention Center, this Best Western has 152 extra-large rooms with cable TV with a free movie channel; it also has a swimming pool. Myrtle's Table Restaurant at the facility serves breakfast, lunch, and dinner.

Hampton Inn of Cherokee $$
U.S. Highway 19 S., Cherokee, NC
(828) 497-3115, (800) HAMPTON
The 67 rooms here each have an inside entrance, temperature controls, and cable TV with free movie channels. Half the rooms are designated nonsmoking. Children younger than 18 stay free in a parent's room. A free continental breakfast is available from 6:00 until 10:00 A.M., and a full-service restaurant is right next door.

Harrah's Cherokee Casino
and Hotel $-$$$$
777 Casino Drive
(828) 497-7777, (800) 427-7247
www.harrahscherokee.casinocity.com
An enterprise of the Eastern Band of Cherokee Indians, this newly opened luxurious hotel has an indoor heated pool, whirlpool, fitness center, Selu Garden Café, Club Cappuccino, and a 10,000-square-foot conference center. The 252 rooms include eight suites.

Holiday Inn Cherokee $$
U.S. Highway 19 S., Cherokee, NC
(828) 497-9181, (800) HOLIDAY
Facilities here include 154 rooms with cable TV with a free movie channel, banquet facilities to accommodate up to 200, both indoor and outdoor pools, a whirlpool, and a sauna. The Chestnut Tree Restaurant serves breakfast and dinner. This Holiday Inn received the Top Ten Customer Service Award and has earned a superior rating for seven consecutive years.

Mountain View Log
Cabin Rentals $$$$
off U.S. Highway 441, Cherokee, NC
(828) 497-9552, (800) 392-1003
Here you'll find peace and quiet within minutes of bustling downtown Cherokee and the recreational opportunities of the Great Smoky Mountains National Park. These newly built cabins feature microwave-equipped kitchens, mountain-stone fireplaces, color cable TV, private indoor hot tubs, king-size beds, phones, all linens, and porches with rocking chairs and swings. The Mountain View Log Cabin office is at the Discount Souvenirs gift shop on U.S. 441 N., about a mile from the entrance to the Great Smoky Mountains National Park. There is a maximum of four people per cabin.

Pioneer Motel and Cottages $$
U.S. Highway 19 S., Cherokee, NC
(828) 497-2435
Situated on 16 waterfront acres a ½ mile from downtown Cherokee, Pioneer offers one-, two-, or three-bedroom cabins with full modern facilities overlooking the Oconaluftee River, or you can choose a spacious room in the motel. All rooms are air-conditioned and have cable TV. Other recreational amenities are fishing (with a tribal permit), basketball, horseshoes, a pool, and a picnic area on the premises.

SHOPPING DESTINATIONS

Besides memories and photographs, often the best memento of a certain place is that handwoven scarf, a vase from the little antique shop on Main Street, the earrings from the gem mine, the humidor from the wood-carvers. Americans are big shoppers; no tour is planned without the "shopping day" figured in. Thankfully, we can travel at our own pace in the mountains and stop off for any little shopping expedition we please.

Each of the three geographical regions identified in this book is anchored by a major shopping location or group of locations: Boone in the Northern Mountains; Asheville, Hendersonville, and Brevard in the Central Mountains; and Waynesville, Highlands, and Dillsboro in the Southern Mountains. Fanning out from these cities are towns and country crossroads that add to your shopping options. The shops in our larger cities sell just about anything you could want: museum-quality mountain crafts, English antiques, international imports, fine art, and upscale decorative items for your home, for starters. Furniture reproduction showrooms, factory-direct stores, and upscale outlets are good places to stretch your dollars. And then there are the malls, where America's retail giants do business side-by-side with local shopkeepers.

If you prefer a gentler pace, and want to really "know" a town, take a stroll down the "Main Street USA" of North Carolina's small mountain towns during midday lunch. The well-ordered rows of storefronts with their enticing shop windows are also often carefully preserved examples of early twentieth-century architecture. And don't miss the buys waiting for you out in the countryside, where a turn down a back road can put you at the door of a charming country store. Once the backbone of our rural economy, these simple shops are often treasure troves of Americana. If you are an antique aficionado, you may be amazed at the great buys you can find in the middle of nowhere—a country community may have Saturday yard sales, for example. What looks like an old farmhouse with junk out on the front porch may actually be an "antique barn," where you can find fascinating old farm tools, cupboards, tables, dishes, and scads more.

NORTHERN MOUNTAINS

Ashe County

GLENDALE SPRINGS

Up in the beautiful and remote countryside of Glendale Springs in Ashe County, you won't find scads of shops and malls: There's not a chain store in sight, but you will hit upon a few choice gift shops.

Greenhouse Crafts
248 J.W. Luke Road, Glendale Springs, NC (336) 982-2618
The place is booming despite its remote location, apparently proving the old saw, "If you build it, they will come," or rather, "If you paint it, they will come." And paint they do. Greenhouse Crafts sits across the road from the Holy Trinity Episcopal Church, where noted North Carolina artist Ben Long completed his fresco of The Last Supper in the early 1980s. (The other of the two Churches of the Frescoes is St.

Mary's Episcopal, about 12 miles away near West Jefferson, off U.S. 221.)

Greenhouse Crafts has tastefully complemented the frescos' religious theme with angel statuary, inspirational art, literature, and an array of music. The shop also has traditional mountain crafts, collectible figurines, and unusual functional and whimsical pottery, such as a playful set that depicts Noah's Ark. Handmade jewelry, including silver rings and bracelets made in the area, can be found here, along with stained-glass lamps, gorgeous wooden dulcimers, and other smaller gift items. The owner might even play a tune or two for you on the delightfully seraphic-sounding dulcimer. We can't begin to encompass all the items in the shop in a few words, so make it a definite stop and see for yourself when you're in the area.

JEFFERSON

Jefferson and West Jefferson, only a few miles apart, are towns so small and ubiquitously 1950s America that they could well be part of a Hollywood movie set. Instead they are real places, which we are privy to stop at and stroll down the eerily quiet main streets. But quiet doesn't mean lifeless—in both of these towns you will find "five and dimes," secondhand shops, and even a gallery or two. Don't expect much in terms of quantity of shops, but do look into the few shops you will find. The shopkeeper will always be a wealth of local information.

Country Charm & City Elegance
314 East Main Street, Jefferson, NC
(336) 246–4846
This gift shop features hand-painted birdhouses, traditional teddy bears, and other small items.

Sugar 'n Spice
205 Long Street, Jefferson, NC
(336) 246–4279
This little shop will whip you up a gift basket in no time, taking from the candy-

by-the-pound, boxed chocolates, candy bars, and many other sweets available. You can also make your own, choosing from the variety of little stuffed animals and other gifts to accompany your tasty selections, or just buy a handful of jawbreakers and taffy.

TODD

Todd General Store
N.C. Highway 194, Todd, NC
(336) 877–1067
As you wend your way along scenic N.C. Highway 194 in Ashe County, you'll come upon the charming crossroads community of Todd, originally named Elkland, that's halfway between Boone and West Jefferson. Sixty years ago this was a thriving lumber town where the railroad was king, but once the region was lumbered out, the community seemed to heave a great sigh and disappear. Where once there were two hotels, a bank, a post office, a buzzing mill, nine stores, and doctor and dentist offices that served mill workers and railroad men, there is now only tough little Todd General Store, on the banks of the New River. The store is the heart of the tiny community and a reminder of its glory days.

Its interior has been restored, but in a leisurely way. The collectibles and genuine antiques that cover the two stories seem like they've always been there. Folks still gather on stools and straight-back chairs around the potbellied stove, which is fired up in cold weather. Simple wooden shelves hold groceries, staples for a community that would rather come here to shop than drive north to Jefferson or south to Boone. And you can still buy home-baked goods here, prepared by the women of the valley. Penny candies (well, close to a penny) are crammed beneath vintage glass-front store cases.

A lunch counter is also open at the General Store, where you can get a hearty barbecue sandwich and monstrous pickles—no skimping on portions either. The store sells gift items, antiques, collectibles, and souvenirs of your ramble here.

Avery County

BANNER ELK

The Shoppes of Tynecastle is an attractive grouping of specialty shops at the junction of N.C. Highways 105 and 184. Sports shops, galleries, home furnishings shops, and others are anchored by a distinctive stone tower that makes this destination easy to spot.

Head north on N.C. 184 to the town of Banner Elk and its attractive new upscale shopping complex called the Village at Banner Elk.

This cluster of shops features the following:

Almost Rodeo Drive
Suite 101, N.C. Highway 184, Banner Elk, NC
(828) 898-4553
This is a boutique for ladies' and children's clothing (the other location is on Main Street in Blowing Rock). The pieces are fairly unique and of natural fabrics.

BEECH MOUNTAIN

Beech Mountain is primarily a ski resort community, but there is a hardy contingent that lives here year-round. We've included a few of the places where year-rounders shop.

Fred's General Mercantile Company
501 Beech Mountain Parkway, Beech Mountain, NC
(828) 387-4838
This store has stepped in to fill the void for the brave few who live here year-round, as well as for the legion of tourists who continually make the pilgrimage to mile-high Beech Mountain. Fred Pfohl and his colorful, old-fashioned store anchor the community. Among Fred's inventory are groceries, ski accessories, warm clothing, crafts, toys, even hardware and toothbrushes.

Stay and have lunch at—yep, you guessed it—Fred's Backside Deli (828-387-9331) at the rear of the store. And you can't miss, nor would you want to, Wildbird Supply (828-389-4838), also inside Fred's General Mercantile Company. The company's motto is, "Wildbird's supplies everything but the birds," and that includes seed, feeders, books, and nature guides. In back of this store you can watch birds, squirrels, and chipmunks romp and munch on the feed left in the landscaped forest-garden plot. Fred's motto reads, "If we don't have it, you don't need it."

The Wizard's Toy Shop
503 Beech Mountain Parkway, Beech Mountain, NC
(828) 387-4848
Next door to Fred's is a great shop for the kids that specializes in educational and creative toys, including Playmobil, Sanrio, and Brio toys, erector sets, puzzles, games, and electric trains.

Watauga County

BLOWING ROCK

This quaint mountain village about 15 minutes from Boone is a shopper's paradise. Its short, very walkable Main Street is an easy stroll from almost every accommodation in town, so you don't have to worry about parking. Irresistible specialty and antiques shops line this main thoroughfare. We've described some of the most interesting ones here.

Appalachian Rustic Furnishings
1085 North Main Street, Blowing Rock, NC
(828) 295-9554
Owned by Bill Fitch, this shop displays incredible handmade furnishings and objects for home, lodge, camp, and cabins. We fell in love with the birch-bark lamps and picture frames. Mirrors made of wood and moss brought out our primal instincts for house and home, and who wouldn't want a handmade rocking chair or table from the finest wood in the Blue Ridge?

Fitch's workshop is a few miles down the road in the countryside, so you won't get to see any on-site working, but he

Avery County: Beech Mountain

You'd expect a mile-high mountain to offer spectacular views, and Beech Mountain won't disappoint you. Take U.S. 184, which turns into Beech Mountain Parkway, and look for Pinnacle Ridge Road, which you follow until you come to Sunset Park. There are several overlooks going up the mountain beyond the park as you pass through residential areas. Small turnouts with decks allow you to stop and take a look. If you go at night, you can see the glow of Boone's city lights behind the mountains.

does maintain photographs around the shop of various pieces being handcrafted.

Bless Your Heart
1009 Main Street, Blowing Rock, NC
(828) 295-9133
This cottage-style gift shop caters to "the romantic at heart." Garden items, freeze-dried flower arrangements, and specialty gift baskets are among the gifts at the charming shop.

Bob Timberlake Gallery
946 Main Street, Blowing Rock, NC
(828) 295-0008
On the corner of Main Street and U.S. 221, Bob Timberlake carries a collection of popular furniture lines and original artwork.

Cabin Fever
915 Main Street, Blowing Rock, NC
(828) 295-0520
Cabin Fever offers a complete collection of log cabin and vacation home furnishings. Choose from unique and distinctive furniture, lighting, kitchen items, bed-and-bath decor, hardware, gifts, and more. Cabin Fever is a family-owned business with its largest store located in downtown Blowing Rock.

Hanna's Oriental Rugs & Gifts
Main Street, Blowing Rock, NC
(828) 295-7073
Another fine shop on Main Street, Hanna's sells imported items of exceptional quality, including Oriental and Central Asian rugs, exquisite Austrian Swarovski crystal, Lladro porcelain figurines and cloisonné, jade, and ivory pieces from around the world.

Martin House
Main Street, Blowing Rock, NC
The Shoppes of Martin House is an assortment of shops all in one place. This former residence, built on Main Street in the late 1800s, and adjoining cottages showcase all kinds of pretty and practical things: clothing, candy, toys, gourmet coffees, gems, candles, vintage reproduction photographs, and Victorian floral arrangements.

Some of the fine shops in the area include the Chicory Suite Martin House (828-295-4231), a quaint cottage off the Martin House courtyard in back that sells gourmet coffees and kitchen items. It smells wonderful too! G. Whiliker's & Co. Martin House (828-295-9549) has a jumble of whimsical toys, games, puzzles, and books to tickle any child's fancy. Follow your sweet tooth to Sweet Rosie's Martin

House (828-295-9318), where you can fill a brown bag with old-fashioned candies and nuts (you can also buy gourmet pet treats here).

Bookstores may well be the first place you should look for information on a town. Whether you are moving to the area, vacationing, or looking for something interesting to do, check out the bulletin boards at the local bookstore. Places to rent, job opportunities, writer's conferences, literary evenings, concerts, items for sale—you will undoubtedly feel like an Insider once you are clued into this information.

Pleasant Papers
105 Village Shoppes, South Main Street, Blowing Rock, NC
(828) 295-7236

One of our favorite shops tucked back into an alcove on South Main Street is Pleasant Papers. Here you can find any number of beautifully embossed notecards, cards with elegant floral and gold borders, or even with Southwestern and Impressionist motives—anything for wedding invitations, baby showers, New Year's party invites, and the list goes on. You can also order writing paper specially engraved with your own logo or initials, and certainly you will find the perfect pen here for your correspondences. Writing the folks back home has never been so thrilling!

Serves You Right!
Southmark on Main Street, Blowing Rock, NC
(828) 295-GIFT

Serves You Right! by Karyn Kennedy Herterich, a Blowing Rock seasonal resident from Florida dedicated to offering unique gifts and essentials for the kitchen, dining room, and bar, with particular emphasis on tableware, party, and entertainment acces-

sories. Key vendors in this 1,000-square-foot store are Bernardaud/Limoges, Faberge, Battersea, Herend Porcelains, Lynn Chase Designs, Mariposa, Penzo of Africa, Royal Worcester, Vietri, and other quality lines. The shop also maintains a variety of whimsical gifts, such as Extendible Forks, which allow you to eat off others' plates, and other fun gift items. Styles and designs for trays, placemats, serving accessories, and paper goods number in the hundreds in this charming store. Serves You Right! also has another store in Biltmore Village in Asheville.

SouthMark
Main Street, Blowing Rock, NC
(828) 295-3700

SouthMark was the first new shopping development on Main Street in over 50 years, when the landscaped shopping center opened in 1992. Inspired by Blowing Rock's turn-of-the-century thriving resorts, their distinctive Victorian-influenced structures of towers and gables serve as a gateway to the south entrance of town. English gardens display summer topiaries of swans, lions, and rabbits, making South-Mark a unique place to shop. Eight of the area's most upscale shops are located here, with an additional six all-weather seasonal pavilions, which open in May. Shoppers may find Herend and Faberge china here—or even paint their own pottery next door. Ladies' and children's apparel have a home in two shops here, as do high-end crafts, a sports collectibles shop, and a bookstore. The seasonal pavilions offer additional merchandise from wellness products, flowering baskets, and plants to pizzas and salads.

Windwood Antiques
1152 South Main Street, Blowing Rock, NC
(828) 295-9260

For English country pine and the cottage look, visit this shop across from Blowing Rock Realty. You can also find reproduction pieces, such as those popular antique armoires that have been converted into entertainment centers.

BOONE

Boone and the nearby towns of Blowing Rock, Foscoe, Banner Elk, and Valle Crucis create a beehive of tourist shopping activity. Specialty shops, outlet sites, crafts and fine art galleries, and antiques shops abound here.

DOWNTOWN BOONE

Shopping in downtown Boone gives you a chance to see the town's revived main thoroughfare, King Street. To find this historic street from N.C. 105 as you enter the city, turn left at the intersection of U.S. 321, and wind your way through the university district. The shops on West King Street sell quality clothing, jewelry, gifts, fine art, and pottery—a bit of everything in one place. With so many students around, you can count on funky clothing and accessories shops, along with lots of music and dorm-decor stores.

If you're looking for an unusual card or book, need a pen or sketch book, have a sweet tooth, want to find a special toy or game to keep your young backseat driver busy, or would like to buy a CD with music as inspiring as the mountains, Boone's downtown shops can accommodate you.

Ad-Lib
611 West King Street, Boone, NC
(828) 264-0010
Ad-Lib (also in downtown Asheville on Biltmore Avenue) is a women's clothing store that emphasizes natural fabrics and a casual but very elegant style—definitely the fashion trend for any time of year. Here, you will find fabulous richly hued cotton sweaters, silk skirts, linen shirts, and racks of scarves. Unique jewelry, beads, choice candleholders, and picture frames make this an emporium for fine gifts as well as fine additions to your own closet.

Blue Planet Map Company
240 Shadowline Drive, Boone, NC
(828) 264-5400
You can travel around the globe and never leave Boone, or so it will seem, when you walk into Blue Planet Map Company. If you love maps, you must visit this shop. They sell raised relief maps, travel guide books, world and state atlases, reproductions of antique maps, USGS topographical maps, geographic games, children's books, globes, calendars, and even jewelry, clothing, and gifts on the map theme. Oh, and they have lots of compasses, too. You'll never get lost again.

Candy Barrel
624 West King Street, Boone, NC
(828) 268-0666
You'll be sorry if you pass up the decadently rich fudge and handmade candies in this nineteenth-century-style sweet shop. It carries more than 500 varieties of candy.

Dancing Moon Earthway Bookstore
553 West King Street, Boone, NC
(828) 264-7242
This tiny shop offers those unique books, cards, and posters you can't find at a chain store. It also carries incense, candles, and other items. (See our Close-up on Bookstores.)

Farmers Hardware
661 West King Street, Boone, NC
(828) 264-8801
This is an old-fashioned, authentic, full-service hardware store, started as Boone Hardware Company in 1924. Patrons step back in time as they walk the aisles along creaky wooden floors.

Service is friendly and prompt, and you can buy nearly any kind of tool or supply you need for electrical, construction, painting, yard and garden, and outdoor work, plus birdfeeders and more. The company also operates Farmers Lawn and Power Equipment Store, 678 N.C. 105 Extension, (828) 264-6044, for sales, repair, and rentals.

So, you've been shopping all day, your feet are sore, and you're near collapse.... Why not revive yourself with an espresso or some soothing tea? Some area bookstores have cafes that serve snacks. Flip through a magazine or novel and let yourself be momentarily transported to another place and time.

Farmers Hardware Ski Shop
140 Depot Street, Boone, NC
(828) 264-4565

One of the area's premier ski shops, located behind Farmers Hardware, this store has served the Southern skier since 1969. The year-round shop sells high-quality ski equipment, clothing, accessories, and outdoor gear, such as hiking boots and backpacking equipment. The full-service snowboarding and skate shop, carrying snowboard equipment, in-line skates, and ice skates, is a newer addition to the shop.

Top quality merchandise for the skier includes skis by Rossignol and Dynastar; boots by Nordica, Lange, and Tecnica; and clothing by Columbia, the North Face, Helly, Hansen, Nils, and Solstice. The shop is in Boone's oldest commercial building, constructed in 1911 to house a Ford dealership. Note the rustic, timbered interior that was renovated in 1976 but retains its yesteryear elegance.

Footsloggers
533 Depot Street, Boone, NC
(828) 262-5111

Footsloggers carries all the stylishly rugged, top-quality clothing and footwear for those who like the outdoors or just the outdoorsy look. This is also the place to go in Boone for all kinds of camping, hiking, and outdoor gear (see the "Outfitters" section of our Recreation chapter for more information).

Grapevine Music
641 West King Street, Boone, NC
(828) 264-7168

Celtic tunes and New Age music seem to be appropriate anthems for the mountains, and Grapevine Music has sounds that soothe the spirit. You can find mountain bluegrass on the rack, too.

Mast General Store
630 King Street, Boone, NC
(828) 262-0000

If you're looking for wool socks and flannel, down-filled, and general mountain attire, this is the place. Just like its sister stores in Valle Crucis and other spots in this area, Mast General Store in Boone stocks quality leisure clothing, hats, belts, and other leather accessories.

We like the seasonal sale bins! The Boone store is a two-story, turn-of-the-century-style department store in the restored 1913 Boone Mercantile at the corner of King and Depot Streets. Boone's Mast Store also carries shoes, housewares, and gifts and has departments for children and maternity needs (see the Mast entry under Valle Crucis).

The candy shop adjacent to the clothing section is one step over the threshold into sugar heaven. Sold by the pound, the candy is stocked in barrels. Just carry your little basket around and start filling it up with old-fashioned horehound candy, peppermints, taffy, and imported hard coffee candies, mints, and other tooth-rotting goodness!

Old Boone Antique Mall
631 West King Street, Boone, NC
(828) 262-0521

This is a storehouse of American and European antiques spread over three floors and 27,000 square feet. Here you'll find antique jewelry, furniture, linens, decorative items, prints, and family china from more than 75 dealers. Take your time browsing. Each vendor has set up almost an entire store within the allotted space.

Purveyors of Art and Design Materials
499 West King Street, Boone, NC
(828) 265-0209

This is where you can stock up on art materials, instruction books, and frames—the expert staff will dole out free advice.

The Stonehinge
535 King Street, Boone, NC
(828) 262-1950
This is the place for distinctive jewelry, treasures of nature, and unique gifts.

Wilcox Warehouse Emporium
161 Howard Street, Boone, NC
(828) 262-1221, (828) 265-3973
Enjoy shopping and dining under one roof in historic downtown Boone at the Emporium. The renovated building still smells of the herbs that once were brought here by mountain people.

In 1944 Charles Wilcox built the warehouse for Wilcox Natural Products, a botanical company that gathered and sold herbs worldwide. Now, with its original hardwood floors and open-beam ceilings, the building houses shops, galleries, offices, a food court, and a microbrewery. Visitor parking is off Rivers and Howard Streets.

From Boone to Blowing Rock,
U.S. Highway 321
This busy highway serves as the primary link between Boone and Blowing Rock—and it is here that you might fulfill a great deal of your shopping needs if you take the time to stop.

Blowing Rock Antique Center
U.S. Highway 321 Bypass, Blowing Rock, NC
(828) 295-4950
This is one of those fun warehouse-style antiques centers that's stocked by independent dealers. Here you can observe the history of popular culture in America. *Eclectic* is the word for this place, where you can find a 19th-century trunk next to a 1920s dining table set with 1950s Fiestaware and handmade linens. You might find an old Beatles album mixed in with turn-of-the-century sheet music or even a Brady Bunch lunch box like the one you had in the fifth grade. Browsing is half the

fun! A second location is open in downtown Boone (828-264-5757).

Country Farmhouse
U.S. Highway 321, Blowing Rock, NC
(828) 295-9914
This gift shop across from Chetola Resort (there's a second shop in Valle Crucis, 828-963-4748, across from the Mast General Store) stocks gift items that include baskets, twig furniture, folk art, face jugs, quilts, birdhouses, afghans, and even duck decoys.

The Incredible Toy Company
3411 U.S. Highway 321 S., Boone, NC
(828) 264-1422
Toys, toys, toys! The kids will see this one before you do, so you might as well be prepared to stop and enjoy this fun place between Boone and Tweetsie Railroad. It offers a large selection of educational toys, games, books, puzzles, science kits, and the well-known Brio and Playmobil sets.

The Mustard Seed Market
U.S. Highway 321, Blowing Rock, NC
(828) 295-4585
You might miss this little stand if you blink. This unassuming roadside market on U.S. 321 at Aho Road, 2 miles north of Blowing Rock, is open daily and is much more than a produce stand. English garden statuary, unusual perennial flowers, honey, herb vinegars, hand-painted gifts, and custom-made flags share the space with the fresh fruits and vegetables.

Tanger Shoppes on the Parkway
U.S. Highway 321, Blowing Rock, NC
(828) 295-4444, (800) 720-6728
This well-landscaped outlet center provides a delightful shopping experience while you're visiting the area. The center features 32 name brand outlets—some the best known in the industry—such as Gap, Nautica, Polo Ralph Lauren, Coach, Bass, Izod, Royal Doulton, Jones New York, Kaspar, Jockey, Big Dog, and Geoffrey Beene. Cooks will especially enjoy Corning Revere

and Kitchen Collection, which feature every gadget a cook needs. The center also features a full-service restaurant, Parkway Cafe, and well-known Kilwins, serving locally made gourmet ice cream, candy, and fudge. Relax in the courtyard and enjoy a meal or a treat. Since being purchased by the national outlet industry giant Tanger Factory Outlets, the center has added amenities such as wheelchairs and strollers, as well as a centrally located office that sells gift certificates and disperses information about Tanger's 33 centers.

Tanner Factory Store
U.S. Highway 321 Bypass, Blowing Rock, NC
(828) 295-7031
This shop sells quality Doncaster fashions at attractive outlet prices. A second store is located near the entrance to Sugar Mountain in Avery County (828-898-6734).

FOSCOE

Where N.C. 105 passes through Foscoe, south of Boone, you'll find a corridor known for antiques shops. Classic English, French, and American 18th- and 19th-century pieces are displayed by the community's many professional antiques dealers. The Foscoe area is a hot destination for Western North Carolina innkeepers and bed-and-breakfast proprietors.

Going hand in hand with the sale of antiques in Foscoe are galleries of fine art, traditional crafts, and unique specialty shops along N.C. 105.

DeWoolfson Down
9452 N.C. Highway 105, Foscoe, NC
(828) 963-4144, (800) 833-3696
Did you ever wonder where innkeepers get those sumptuous down comforters for your nightly lodging at some of the Boone area's best bed-and-breakfast inns? Well, the secret's out. . . it's DeWoolfson Down, 9 miles south of Boone on N.C. 105.

But there is so much more here: down pillows hand-stuffed to your order, silk comforters from China, Egyptian cotton sheets designed in France, crisp damasks from Germany, and silky Jacquard sheets from Italy—with up to 590 threads per inch. Clear out the trunk of your car before you come because you won't go home empty-handed.

Green Mansions Village
N.C. Highway 105, Foscoe, NC
Across from the entrance to Seven Devils on N.C. 105 (there's a large sign indicating the turn for Seven Devils) is a complex of antique, specialty, and women's clothing shops. Finder's Keepers Green Mansions Village (828-963-7000) displays substantial antique English furniture: 18th-century chests, baronial tables, and estate artifacts are among the treasures. Dreamfields Green Mansions Village (828-963-8333) has an eclectic selection of modern international decorative items and European antiques, as well as international fine art and unusual sculpture. The Country Gourmet, Ltd. (828-963-5269) is a shop that reminds us of a cook's home—one where the cook loves to try every recipe that comes along. You can find scores of specialty kitchen tools, attractive functional stoneware, unusual cookbooks, and items for the family hearth.

Staffordshire Antiques
8599 N.C. Highway 105, Foscoe, NC
(828) 963-4274
Anglophiles, take note! This is one of two shops on N.C. 105 that imports directly from the British Isles. Eight miles south of Boone, this shop concentrates on 18th- and 19th-century antique furniture imports. Two red English phone booths stand outside the shop. You can't miss them.

VALLE CRUCIS

The Ham Shoppe
N.C. Highway 105, Valle Crucis, NC
(828) 963-6310
Up N.C. 105, just as you turn toward scenic Valle Crucis, is the Ham Shoppe. This is a store for jams, jellies, homemade breads, pies, dry pasta, and other staples for your kitchen. Even better though, are its made-

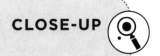
Bookstores

When you're on the road, bookstores are almost as important as gas stations. They offer you a connection to the community through books on local legends, maps of trails and tours, and cards of nearby places of beauty. Many include works by local authors who wax poetic about the mountains, drawing inspiration from the region. The following is a list of some of the region's stores.

NORTHERN MOUNTAINS

Blowing Rock

Pleasant Papers
South Main Street, The Village Shoppes, Blowing Rock, NC
(828) 295-7236
More than a bookstore, this fine shop also includes quality papers, greeting cards, and specialized gifts.

Boone

Blue Planet Map Company
240 Shadowline Drive, Boone, NC
(828) 264-5400, (800) 810-6277
www.blueplanetmap.com
Wanderlust to your heart's content with the wide range of local and worldwide travel books and a broad selection of atlases: road, travel, DeLorme topo, United States, world, and historical. They even stock CD-ROM map software.

Dancing Moon Earthway Bookstore
553 West King Street, Boone, NC
(828) 264-7242
www.thedancingmoon.com
Dancing Moon specializes in books and magazines of the healing and spiritual arts. This small shop also carries unique travel books, cards and posters, musical cassettes, candles, and even incense and oils. In other words, everything you might want to embellish your reading environment.

Waldenbooks
1180 Blowing Rock Road, Boone Mall, Boone, NC
(828) 264-4084
Waldenbooks is one of the country's leading chain bookstores featuring regional and outdoor books.

Spruce Pine

Blue Moon Books
271 Oak Avenue, Spruce Pine, NC
(828) 766-5000
www.bluemoonbookstore.com
The uncluttered space offers a sofa and table for browsing as well as a small cafe in the corner for sipping coffee and trying a muffin or giant cookie.

Located in the old Day's Drugstore, the red-and-white tiled floor and high tin ceiling make this more than a bookstore, it's a gathering place as well. Blue Moon features a large children's book section, regional book selections, and an array of handpainted notecards.

Used books are in the back, and a selection of major U.S. papers help keep you up with national news.

A children's story hour gathers here on the first Saturday of each month, and occasional live music keeps the shop open on certain evenings. Call for details.

CENTRAL MOUNTAINS

Asheville

Accent on Books
854 Merrimon Avenue, Asheville, NC
(828) 252-6255
www.accentonbook.com
This store has a good selection of quality magazines, cards, and children's books in addition to a good selection of books on the great outdoors and the culture of the region.

B. Dalton Bookseller
3 South Tunnel Road Asheville Mall,
Asheville, NC
(828) 298-7711
800 Brevard Road Biltmore Square Mall
Asheville, NC
(828) 667-1293
B. Dalton is well-known throughout the country for its broad selection of books. This chain store includes many books of regional interest.

Barnes & Noble
83 South Tunnel Road, Asheville, NC
(828) 296-9330
The mammoth bookseller has hit the mountains, too. But this B & N maintains a large regional books section all about the area, including wonderful photo books. In addition, the store features local author readings as well as bringing in folks from outside. The Starbucks coffee from the cafe wafts throughout the store, and the gelato (just as good as in Italy) is worth standing in line for.

Blue Ridge Parkway Bookstore
Mile 382, Folk Art Center, Asheville, NC
(828) 298-0495
Small but well stocked, this bookstore offers the best selection in nature books, trail maps, books on regional culture, and beautiful wildlife cards. (There are 11 other bookstores like it along the parkway.)

Book Rack
485 Hendersonville Road, Asheville, NC
(828) 274-5050
Book Rack has a great selection of half-price used paperbacks that are sold and traded in a fresh and friendly environment.

Books-A-Million
736 South Tunnel Road, Asheville, NC
(828) 299-4165
This store bills itself as "a novel bookstore of epic proportions," and they aren't kidding. The megastore includes an excellent selection of regional and travel books as well as out-of-town newspapers. There's also a cafe and an area for frequent book signings by authors.

Downtown Books and News
67 Lexington Avenue, Asheville, NC
(828) 253-8654
You can usually buy hard-to-find newspapers, periodicals, and obscure books at this excellent and interesting combination news-stand/used-book store. Foreign magazines, obscure fashion magazines, computer, food, art, photography, and alternative living are only some of the many subjects of magazines you will find here.

Some of the area's bookstores, like Malaprop's Bookstore/Cafe in Asheville, have cafes where you can read, rest, and sip coffee or tea. PHOTO: CONSTANCE E. RICHARDS

Malaprop's Bookstore/Cafe
55 Haywood Street, Asheville, NC
(828) 254-6734
www.malaprops.com

Malaprop's is simply an Asheville institution. We remember sipping our hazelnut coffee in the cafe, hunched over our high school homework, dreaming of literary travels, while ethereal music provided the background sounds for this haven of learned tranquility in the then-decayed Asheville downtown.

Owner Emoke Bracz, a writer, poet, and translator of Hungarian poetry and literature, fine-tuned the art of the book trade in the 16-year life span of this once-small bookstore and cafe. Now two doors down from its original cramped-but-cozy space, Malaprops boasts shelves of fascinating fiction, alternative nonfiction, prose, and poetry, as well as a large section with works of local authors and books on the region. Coffee table gift books, stationery, cards, journals, and artistic calendars make this one-stop shopping for all your literary gift needs.

And then there's the cafe! Author signings, prose readings, poetry readings, singer-songwriter evenings gather hoards of literati of all types into the spacious adjoining cafe. Local art and photographs adorn the walls, and cafe tables spill out onto the broad sidewalk in front of Malaprop's, where an amalgam of adopted Ashevillians and visitors sip coffee and herb teas and snack on fresh bagel sandwich combinations, muffins, cookies, and cakes. Malaprop's will order any book for you they don't already have and sends out a seasonal newsletter filled with poetry, artful sketches, and literary news.

You can spend hours delving through the shelves of a good bookstore, like Malaprop's in Asheville. PHOTO: CONSTANCE E. RICHARDS

Once Upon a Time
7 All Soul's Crescent, Asheville, NC
(828) 274-8788
This is more than a bookstore. It offers the area's largest selection of children's fiction and nonfiction, books, games, and tapes. It recently added children's clothing.

Waldenbooks
800 Brevard Road Biltmore Square Mall, Asheville, NC
(828) 665-1066
This respected chain bookstore offers a wide choice of books of interest to the traveler and the resident.

Brevard

The Book Nook
15 South Broad Street, Brevard, NC
(828) 883-9745
The Book Nook has new and used books, that, as its proprietor proclaims, "contain only natural ingredients: sex, murder, adultery, joy, sorrow, passion, and mayhem." If you don't see what you're looking for, they'll be happy to conduct book searches for you.

Cradle of Forestry in America Interpretive Association
100 South Broad Street, Brevard, NC
(828) 884-5713

This nice store is stocked with nature-related books, gifts, prints, forest maps, literature, and National Forest information. This nonprofit organization puts the money it makes right back into our area's magnificent national forests. It oversees another bookstore in the Cradle of Forestry itself in Pisgah Forest.

Highland Books
409 North Broad Street, Brevard, NC
(828) 884-2424

Highland carries the latest in new paperbacks and hardbacks in fiction and nonfiction and a wonderful, large selection of greeting cards and gifts. The staff welcomes browsers. It has extensive gardening and children's sections and travel and regional books, including nature books, field guides, and maps.

There's a comfortable reading area, where you can peruse a book or preview some of the videos of local interest. Highland also has a wonderful selection of greeting cards and gifts.

Hendersonville

Mountain Lore Books
555 North Main Street, Hendersonville, NC
(828) 693-5096

Mountain Lore has books for all ages and interests. In addition to popular best-sellers and paperbacks, this independent bookseller specializes in regional, gardening, nature, and children's books.

Waldenbooks
1800 Four Seasons Boulevard, U.S. Highway 64 E., Blue Ridge Mall, Hendersonville, NC
(828) 692-4957

This popular chain store's books cover almost any subject that might interest you.

SOUTHERN MOUNTAINS
Cashiers

Chapter 2
U.S. Highway 64 E., Ingles Shopping Center, Cashiers, NC
(828) 743-5015

Chapter 2 carries new and used books and has a large selection of cookbooks, books of regional interest, and children's books. Its real forte is, however, fiction.

Dillsboro

Time Capsule
N.C. Highway 441, Riverwood Oaks Gallery, Dillsboro, NC
(828) 586-1026

This shop specializes in used, rare, and out-of-print books, but it also has a good selection of hiking, flower, and other nature books pertinent to the region. With more than 10,000 volumes, plan to stay a while. It's across the railroad tracks from Front Street.

Highlands

Cyrano's Bookshop
390 Main Street, Highlands, NC
(828) 526-5488

Cyrano's describes itself as "cozy but complete." It's also defined by customer service, and the staff promises to track down hard-to-find titles.

Sylva

City Lights Bookstore & Cafe
3 East Jackson Street, Sylva, NC
(828) 586-9499
www.citylightsnc.com
City Lights offers new and used books, including great regional and children's sections, as well as cards and calendars. Enjoy your book purchase with a specialty coffee, soup, sandwich, salad, and/or dessert either in the store or at the outside seating area. On Friday and Saturday evenings, acoustic and folk musicians provide live entertainment.

Waynesville

Waynesville Book Company
184 North Main Street, Waynesville, NC
(828) 456-8062
At the corner of Haywood and Depot Streets, this full-service bookshop is housed in a tobacco warehouse built in the 1780s. In business since 1978, it has a broad range of new books with large sections of children's books, cookbooks, and regional books. It also carries greeting cards, books on tapes, and some delightful storytelling tapes. The shop's a great place to relax, browse, and visit with the store's two aging but friendly dogs: a golden retriever and a poodle. There's also plenty of parking, which is sometimes a problem in the summer in Waynesville.

to-order takeouts. Touted as "Ham Sweet Hams," the mouthwatering honey-glazed, spiral-cut baked hams are the obvious house specialty. But there is so much more to feast on here: strawberry-rhubarb pie, ham spread, cinnamon buns, preserves and fresh-baked sourdough bread. Use the Ham Shoppe as your special corner grocer or as a deli—it serves this dual purpose well.

Mast General Store
N.C. Highway 194, Valle Crucis, NC
(828) 963-6511

The ultimate shopping destination once you reach Valle Crucis is the historic Mast General Store on N.C. Highway 194. Built in 1882 by Henry Taylor, the store was sold around the turn of the century to W. W. Mast. Over the next 70 years, the Mast family business established a tradition in the region for offering "everything from cradles to caskets." The interior of the store remains very much the same as it was a century ago. The old post office, still in service, is at one end, and the store's classic potbellied stove, an asset in these snow-prone hills, is still a central element.

You'll delight in a ramble around this old-time mercantile. Sit out on in the porch swings or rockers on the back porch. This is where you should be sipping your ice-cold A & W or hot-and-spicy ginger ale. It certainly revved us up after lunch for more sight-seeing. Next door is the Annex, which was built in 1909 as a rival general store but is now part of the Mast Store. This place has quality seasonal apparel and camping and fly-fishing gear. A deli in the Annex provides light refreshments that you can enjoy outdoors, and a candy store offers barrels of taffy, jawbreakers, horehound candy, licorice, and about a hundred other sweets sold by weight. Just take your basket around and fill it up.

Yancey County

BURNSVILLE

The small-town charm here adds to the fun, especially if you're looking for a break from malls and megamarts.

needle me this
112 West Main Street, Burnsville, NC
(828) 682-9462

The region is famous for its fine handcrafts, so you will not want to miss the display of finished quilts at this little shop. You can order a custom-made quilt here, too. For do-it-yourselfers, the shop carries fabrics and notions and offers sewing and quilting classes.

Something Special
102 West Main Street, Burnsville, NC
(828) 682-9101

This is a place where the country crafts and gifts are abundant and unique. The shop carries pottery, wooden shelving, prints, and home-decorating items.

CENTRAL MOUNTAINS

Buncombe County

ASHEVILLE MALLS AND SHOPPING CENTERS

The Asheville area has long been known for its tradition of crafting talent and resourcefulness. Entrepreneurship is alive and well here also, and it's been aided by an influx of newcomers in the last 20 years who have added fresh ideas and culturally diverse backgrounds to an already interesting mix of creative people. Asheville has become a proving ground for individuals who have a business concept and a dream. The tourism-based economy here has spawned new growth and the revitalization of Asheville's downtown.

But if you hunger for megaparking lots and busy shopping malls, we've got you covered. There are two large malls in the area: the Asheville Mall, 3 South Tunnel Road, (828) 298-5080, anchored by Sears, JCPenney, and Montgomery Ward; and Biltmore Square Mall, 800 Brevard Road, (828) 667-2210, anchored by well-known retailers such as Belk, Dillard's, and Proffit's. And there are also bustling community shopping centers and other specialty shops at all points of the compass from Asheville.

One busy area shopping center east of Asheville, River Ridge Outlet Center, 800 Fairview Road, (828) 298-9785, devotes its entire 40 stores to outlet shopping. You can easily reach River Ridge from exit 8 off Interstate 240, which loops around the city, or by taking exit 53B off Interstate 40. Don't overlook the shops along the main streets of the area's small towns for some quaint alternatives. Some nearby towns have developed their own shopping districts that draw outside visitors. One of these is the village of Black Mountain, 15 minutes east of Asheville, which has become known as a haven for antiques (see details in the Black Mountain section in this chapter). And if you look, you're apt to find a favorite shop out in the county that's noted for its special wares, personal service, or both.

Another not-to-be-missed shopping experience is the North Carolina Farmers Market, 570 Brevard Road, southeast of Asheville (see our Attractions chapter). It's 36 acres of fresh produce, quality plants and garden supplies, crafts, and just about everything you'd expect to find at an old market square.

DOWNTOWN ASHEVILLE

The renaissance of Asheville's inner city as a shopping destination is well-known and

Souvenirs for friends, family, or the house sitter back home can be as simple and delightful as a jar of local jam or honey. Check out the Western Carolina Farmer's Market in Asheville or any number of small tailgate markets on Saturday mornings.

Wait until dark, when the lights of Asheville begin to twinkle, and drive along Town Mountain Road up the crest of the mountain. Start at Old Toll Road, which winds along behind Grove Park Inn and through residential areas and runs into Town Mountain Road. As you climb higher, you'll be able to see the lights of Asheville below, the view widening as you ascend the ridge. Soon the other side of the ridge will open up so that the lights of Marion appear in the distance.

has been touted in magazine and newspaper articles nationally. What is particularly pleasing to Asheville's visitors and residents alike is that the downtown has become a very pedestrian-friendly place. There are several municipal parking garages downtown, one on Biltmore Avenue south of Pack Square and the other on Rankin Street off Patton Avenue, west of the Square. There's also a city parking garage behind the Asheville-Buncombe Library at 67 Haywood Street near the Asheville Civic Center. If you're an energetic shopper, you'll want to make a day of it, with lunch at one of Asheville's charming downtown restaurants and bistros. The visual appeal of the city's architecture is an added bonus. Unique shops are aplenty in downtown, and we could fill the chapter on Asheville's antique shops alone; so please do take he time to stroll around and discover your own favorites.

You can start with the so-called Renaissance Corridor of Biltmore Avenue near Pack Square. What was once a decaying, questionable area lined with X-rated movie houses and blank storefronts only 15 years ago is now a thriving avenue of upscale shops, art galleries, and other venues. The sudden, unexpected growth of Biltmore Avenue set the tone for further downtown efforts and was a vital link to the revival of Pack Square as the elegant heart of the city it had been.

At the south end of Haywood Street is the intersection of Battery Park Avenue, anchored by the historic and architecturally interesting Flat Iron Building, constructed during Asheville's boom period in the 1920s. This building also helps to shape what is known as Wall Street, the narrow, twisting alley behind the Flat Iron Building that has long been the address for interesting and artistically inclined entrepreneurs.

Ad-Lib
40 Biltmore Avenue, Asheville, NC (828) 285-8838
This is a sister store to the one in Boone, featuring women's clothing that emphasizes natural fabrics and colors. A collection of hats hangs on one wall, and one section of the shop is devoted to unique leather shoe styles. Comfort and quality are of the utmost importance here. Sweaters, jumpers, dresses, shirts, skirts, and pants in silks, linens, cottons, and wools in an array of magnificent natural colors set this clothing store apart from others. Ad-Lib also sells artistic jewelry, candleholders, and one of a kind picture frames.

Amore
36 Battery Park Avenue, Asheville, NC (828) 236-0072
Unique also in that it stays open late, Amore maintains a variety of tasteful, small gift items, including home decor and bijoux jewelry items, soaps and lotions, fancy cocktail napkins, wind chimes, and more.

Asheville Antiques Mall
43 Rankin Avenue, Asheville, NC (828) 253-3634
You could spend a day in these shops alone, which are stocked by independent dealers with an amazing assortment of furniture, decorative and household items, antique prints, paintings, jewelry, and books. Some friends who just moved from Vienna, Austria, couldn't believe the assortment of wonderful antique furnish-

ings. It was all we could do to drag them out of the place before they had committed their life savings.

Asheville Wine Market
65 Biltmore Avenue, Asheville, NC
(828) 253-0060
You can take home an exquisite sampling of the grape from the Wine Market. Winemaster Eberhard Heide is the proprietor and will assist you in your choice of premium international wines and beers. The array is staggering, so you might be wise in choosing Eberhard's famous Wine Samplers, six international vintage wines specially priced and packaged. You can also buy specialty items for the wine connoisseur at the Asheville Wine Market.

Bloomin' Art
60 Haywood Street, Asheville, NC
(828) 254-6447
This is more than just a florist. Besides fragrant bouquets, baskets, and unusual items of floral artistry, you'll find plant holders and flowerpots.

Celtic Ways
14 Wall Street, Asheville, NC
(828) 254-0644
Vivid tartans drape the windows of Celtic Ways, a shop with a true Scot's heart. Tartan kilts, shawls, scarves, tams, gloves, and some jewelry—all can be found at this ethnic treasure chest.

Craven Handbuilt Porcelain
111 Roberts Street, Asheville, NC
(828) 232-1401
The Cravens' work has been exhibited in major galleries all over Europe—Marbella, Madrid, Paris, Munich, and other major cities—and more recently in the United States.

The couple has worked together since 1972, and for most of that time they've lived in southern Spain, where they developed their distinctive style and colors, moving to the Loire Valley of France for three years before settling in the North

Carolina mountains. Working exclusively in porcelain and using antique lace for imprinting, Jo Lydia designs and builds the pieces, and Ian fires them using a glaze-on-glaze technique.

Downtown Books and News
67 Lexington Avenue, Asheville, NC
(828) 253-8654
Toward the funkier north end of Lexington Avenue, you'll find this excellent book and magazine store. (See the Close-up on Bookstores in this chapter for more details.)

The Earth Guild
33 Haywood Street, Asheville, NC
(828) 255-7818
Its gorgeous storefront is a good indication of the quality of handcrafts you'll find inside. Weaving, pottery, handmade jewelry, and other lovely wares are all visible behind large streetfront windows. You can also find supplies for the making of your own crafts here.

Enviro Depot
18 Haywood Street, Asheville, NC
(828) 252-9007
This great place teems with toys, games, puzzles, books, posters, and scientific activities for the avid naturalist and the environmentally conscientious. It also offers lotions and potions made of natural ingredients, and our favorite, Burt's Beeswax Chapstick, among other items.

A Far Away Place
11 Wall Street, Asheville, NC
(828) 252-1891
This is more than a store: Part gallery, part shop, it's a total experience. The talents of artisans from more than forty native cultures are represented in this gallery/shop. Exquisite ancient artifacts hang alongside the work of present-day artists. An excellent array of music native to faraway lands is also on display. You'll find jewelry, clothing, hats, bags, stationery, and books here, devoted to lands beyond our hemisphere.

Grove Arcade
1 Page Avenue, Asheville, NC
(828) 252–7799

One of America's shopping arcade jewels, the Grove Arcade reopened in 2002 after years of renovation after the previous tenants, the National Climactic Data Center, moved out with the construction of the new Federal Building. The Arcade houses an open market for produce and poultry, freshly roasted coffee beans, herbs, and dry goods, as well as individual shops and antiques stores. Cafes, delis, and restaurants also fill the venerable space that was loving brought back to its original splendor by experts around the country. An outdoor market on the south side of the Arcade features crafts, plants, local honey and jams, and artwork during the warm months.

As in many other parts of the country, you can usually find any item you're looking for at about one-tenth the retail price by traveling around to garage sales. There are hundreds happening here every week. Pick up a local paper to find out where they are.

Kress Emporium
19-21 Patton Avenue, Asheville, NC
(828) 281–2252

An architectural landmark, the Kress building in downtown Asheville was built in 1918 as a five-and-dime. Constructed of rich ceramic tile, the Kress building is only one of the many brilliant examples of art deco in the city. For years the building fell into disrepair and its first floor was used for various flea markets. Today this restored space is a showcase for over 80 artists, artisans, sculptors, hatmakers, jewelry designers, and many others devoted to artistic endeavors. Artists rent booths, decorate the walls, and add their works, so you are essentially strolling through 80 galleries under one roof.

Everything from Turkish kilims, heirloom stitched children's clothes, handmade dolls, and shimmery velvet hats to paintings, hand-carved furniture, antique tools, black-and-white art photos, glass sculptures, and much, much more is on display in this high-ceilinged bright hall.

Lexington Park Antiques
65 West Walnut Street, Asheville, NC
(828) 253–3070

Another fine sampling of the Asheville antique district, Lexington Park Antiques specialize in. . . everything!

The L.O.F.T.
53 Broadway, Asheville, NC
(828) 259–9303

This eclectically funky shop, filled with a menagerie of distressed furniture, paper lamps, candles, natural soaps, stationery, frames, handmade journals, and other gift and decorative items, is truly a local favorite. Handmade paper, beeswax soaps, picture frames, mirrors, sketchbooks, plush furniture, flowerpots, and so much more grace this home designer's dream of a shop. "L.O.F.T." stands for Lost Objects, Found Treasures.

Lorraine's Antiques
26 Battery Park Avenue, Asheville, NC
(828) 251–1771

Originally from South Africa, Brian and Lorraine Pottow bring with them a unique sense of taste for eclectic and traditional European and American antiques in this three-story shop. Everything from large armoires and sofas to small jewelry items, sculptures, and paintings dress this store.

Malaprop's Bookstore/Cafe
55 Haywood Street, Asheville, NC
(828) 254–6734

Fascinating books, gifts, gourmet coffee, and stimulating conversation mingle at Malaprop's new location, just a few doors down from the old one. This bookstore is one of the mainstays of downtown Asheville and a popular stop for visitors and locals. Visiting authors, special events, poetry readings, and the spacious coffee-house make Malaprop's much more than just a place to buy books. (See our Close-up on Bookstores.)

Tops for Shoes
27 North Lexington Avenue, Asheville, NC
(828) 254-6721

This is another of those gutsy establishments that survived the decay of downtown and persistently worked to make the area a viable business district again. For more than 20 years, Tops has been known for quality footwear for the whole family, and the shop has a reputation for its service and large inventory. If you're shopping at Tops, parking is free at the city parking deck on Rankin Avenue.

T. S. Morrison
39 North Lexington Avenue, Asheville, NC
(828) 258-1891

An Asheville institution since 1891, the building is itself an architectural antique. This refurbished general mercantile store maintains a period atmosphere and has Victorian-era memorabilia and specialty gift items displayed in original store's cases. You can also find a variety of stamps and stamping accessories, stationery, crockery, baskets, glass gift items, and much, much more. Traditional candy bins allow you to pick out your own sweets, which are sold by the pound. The store also carries some old-fashioned hair tonics, powders, and soaps, so if nostalgia is what you are after, you may just find it in these interesting items. Spicy ginger ale, root beer, and cherry drinks are sold by the bottle. T. S. Morrison is more than just a gift shop, it's part of Asheville history, and yes, the old drawers still contain hardware store items for sale, like nails, fasteners, and nuts and bolts.

Woolworth Walk
25 Haywood Street, Asheville, NC
(828) 254-9234

This former Woolworth's, originally constructed in the 1920s, was brought back to life after renovation and the infusion of booths and wall spaces featuring the work of local and regional artists and crafters. Decorative art, jewelry, glass, pottery, textiles, painting, metal sculpture, photography, and other imaginative art and crafts make this a lively emporium of gifts. Several artists maintain working studios on the lower level.

BILTMORE VILLAGE

Moving along to the south end of Asheville, near the entrance of Biltmore Estate, reached by taking Biltmore Avenue or McDowell Street south, you will find Biltmore Village. Geographically in Asheville, this junction of cobblestone streets and old buildings is an "incorporated town" (see our Area Overviews chapter). Therefore we're discussing the village separately.

When George Vanderbilt constructed his mansion in 1895, it was obvious that such a grand place would need a town at its gate to supply it. Vanderbilt didn't have to start from scratch; he merely purchased the existing village of Best, a good distance from the mansion on the outskirts of Asheville. Construction of suitable lodging for his craftspeople gave the new village a distinctively English-hamlet look that it has retained. The original cottages, which have the pebble-dash exterior used in some Asheville homes of the period, today form a cluster of specialty shops, restaurants, and galleries. The creative spirit, it seems, has survived the century. Mr. Vanderbilt would be pleased.

Biltmore Village's cobbled sidewalks along such streets as Angle, Swan, and All Souls will lead you past a delightful assortment of shops.

Bellagio
5 Biltmore Plaza, Asheville, NC
(828) 277-8100

This is a most unusual shop devoted to wearable art. Richly colored, sensually textured fabrics are transformed into exquisite garments and then complemented by handcrafted jewelry. Unique handbags, shoes, and jewelry make this well worth a stop.

Interiors Marketplace
2 Hendersonville Road, Asheville, NC
(828) 253-2300
This market is 1 block north of Biltmore Village, near the former Asheville Train Depot. Asheville is one of only a handful of cities in the nation where this shopping concept, much like an Old World bazaar, has been brought to such successful fruition.

Interiors Marketplace, with its upscale pizzazz, has numerous vendor vignettes—merchandise artfully arranged in harmony as you might find it in your own home. Items generally are one-of-a-kind imported pieces, unusual handcrafted work, fine art, and skillfully chosen domestic and imported antiques.

New Morning Gallery
7 Boston Way, Asheville, NC
(828) 274-2831
This gallery and shop occupies two stories and is surrounded by urban landscaping. This is one of the South's premier arts and crafts shops, displaying the work of some of America's finest artists and craftspeople. New Morning Gallery has expanded into a lavish show space for handcrafted furniture as well.

Once Upon a Time
7 All Souls Crescent, Asheville, NC
(828) 274-8788
This is a splendid bookshop that will please your child with its thousands of books, toys, children's music, story tapes, artwork, and more. (See our Bookstore Close-up.)

Vitrum Gallerie
10 Lodge Street, Asheville, NC
(828) 274-9900
This is North Carolina's only gallery dedicated to the fine art of studio glass. A colorful and creative selection of glass art jewelry, vases, goblets, paperweights, and sculpture sparkle in this sunny, 2,000-square-foot gallery.

BLACK MOUNTAIN

Only 15 minutes east of Asheville is Black Mountain, a picturesque village that is an antiques lover's delight. In the historic district anchored by Cherry Street, near the town's old train depot, is a cluster of shops that have fine antiques and collectibles. Black Mountain is an extremely walkable shopping town where everything from handcrafts, artwork, collectibles, and antiques are available within a few tiny blocks. State Street is Black Mountain's main artery.

Black Mountain Antique Mall
105 Sutton Avenue, Black Mountain, NC
(828) 669-6218
The BMAM has Southern primitives, folk art, and vintage linens and displays an antique quilt collection. It is one of the older, more-established antique malls here, and it offers many cases of small items for browsing as well.

The Cherry Street Antique Mall
139 Cherry Street, Black Mountain, NC
(828) 669-7942
This antique mall sells items from many dealers. It's a great place to spend time browsing. Two floors house the wares of 18 dealers, with items as small as jewelry trinkets to large pieces of furniture. The mall also sells antique craft pottery.

Howard's Antiques
121 Cherry Street, Black Mountain, NC
(828) 669-6494
This shop sells those hot collectible antique toys and sturdy oak furniture. Especially fun are the inventive toys (compare these unique pieces with modern action figures and the other plastic stuff in malls today!).

Song of the Wood
203 West State Street, Black Mountain, NC
(828) 669-7675
Follow your heartstrings to the melodies of Song of the Wood. The talented musicians here play lively tunes on handcrafted

hammered and mountain dulcimers and other traditional musical instruments. Selling instruments and tapes and CDs of their own music is a side business.

Henderson County

FLAT ROCK

Hand in Hand Gallery
2713 Greenville Highway, Flat Rock, NC
(828) 697–7719

Located in the historic Flat Rock area, the shop offers works of porcelain artist Avid Voorhees and jeweler Molly Sharp. Works of other artists in a variety of media range from handmade glass-bead jewelry to hand-forged wrought iron work. It is just past the Carl Sandburg house on U.S. 25, which is also known as the Greenville Highway.

Secret Garden
2720 Greenville Highway, Flat Rock, NC
(828) 697–1331

It's worth the short drive down the Greenville Highway (U.S. 25 S.) in order to pay a visit to this special shop—particularly if you or a loved one loves gardening and garden themes. In addition to flowers and plants, the shop is filled with small, decorative garden sculptures and plaques, small fountains, garden flags, garden books, small framed flower prints, T-shirts, hats and tote bags with garden themes, and flowery doormats, just to name a few items found here.

For children there are stuffed critters like raccoons, turtles, and insects found in the garden. Then there's a whole selection of floral scents, soaps, and candles. Make sure, too, that you don't miss the downstairs shop. Besides a flower-bedecked patio, there's a "kitchen/dining" area with floral- and fruit-painted china, unique wine racks, canisters, and so on. Another room holds tapestries, plant stands, and fabulous rayon-chenille throws.

The next driveway south of the shop takes you to a cutting garden where you can select and cut fresh flowers and pay by the stem.

HENDERSONVILLE

Over two decades ago, when main streets in most small towns were dying due to competition from big malls and discount stores, Hendersonville, which didn't even have a mall at the time, was taking steps to keep its downtown vital. The facades of historic buildings were exposed and refurbished, and Hendersonville's wide Main Street became a serpentine drive lined with trees and blooming plants. Park benches, too, became a permanent part of the Main Street scene. They are fine spots for resting tired feet, chatting with a friend, or eating takeout in the sunshine while you watch the world go by. Few weeks pass without a downtown festival, art show, or other event taking place here.

If there's any problem with downtown, it's that the very popularity of the area sometimes makes finding a parking spot difficult. But if you don't mind walking a block or two, that problem can usually be solved by going to one of the large metered parking lots on Church or King Streets, which run parallel to Main Street, 1 block away in either direction. There are also parking areas on Fifth and Sixth Avenues between Main and King. Though there are no meters on Main Street or its side streets, watch your 15-minute or two-hour limit if you want to avoid a ticket, because, again, due to the downtown's popularity, the limit is strictly enforced. That's a pity, in a way, because a couple of hours is never enough time to browse through all the places you'll want to visit, much less shop and enjoy lunch in one of the area's good restaurants.

Here's just a sampling of some of the places you might find interesting in Hendersonville.

508 Main Street
508 Main Street, Hendersonville, NC
(828) 692–8506

The diverse items you'll find inside this shop are as elegant as its green-and-gold exterior. These include, among many other things, seasonal florals and silk flowers, gold and sterling silver jewelry, decorative

Many towns around the mountains show their hospitality by providing visitors with centrally located public rest rooms. In Hendersonville, you'll find them in Iron Gate Marketplace, at 318 North Main Street between 3rd and 4th Streets and at Henderson County Travel & Tourism, 20 South Main Street located between Barnwell Street and Allen Street.

garden items, home-decor flags, pen-and-ink drawings, stationery, a locally made card line, and locally made chocolates. The shop also carries the Aromatique home fragrance line and Maralyce Ferree's line of Berber and fleece coats and drizzle-wear.

Bunny, the shop's owner, also creates gift baskets of local foods and fragrance that are delivered anywhere in Henderson County and shipped nationwide.

Assembly Required
Village Square on N.C. Highway 191, Hendersonville, NC
(828) 692-9677, (800) 486-2592
This full-service brew shop has all the equipment, books, kits, and ingredients that you need for making your own beer, wine, liquors, cheese, vinegars, and sodas. If you also need advice, owners Jack and Marilyn Bradt can provide plenty of that, too.

Banana Moon
338 North Main Street, Hendersonville, NC
(828) 697-1941
This is by far our favorite clothing store on Main Street, and one of our favorite sections is the selection of outfits made of flax. In addition to all the dresses, sweaters, hats, and handbags, there's everything wonderful for the bath and oodles of charming jewelry. Be prepared to buy.

Barbara's Antiques
421 North Main Street, Hendersonville, NC
(828) 697-1550, (877) 793-7476
Antiques and fine china exquisitely displayed is a hallmark of this lovely shop. China, in fact, is owner Barbara McCoy's

specialty. Here you'll find beautiful examples of Wedgwood, Bavarian, Prussian, English, and other fine china fit for the most elegant dining room.

Beehive Resale Shop
451 North Main Street, Hendersonville, NC
(828) 692-8882
For nearly two decades the popular Beehive Resale Shop has provided top-quality women's clothing at affordable prices. It carries some terrific brand-name women's fashions and accessories at a fraction of the regular retail price, and the inventory changes daily.

Blue Ridge Mall
1800 Four Seasons Boulevard, Hendersonville, NC
(828) 697-1745
Anchored by Belk, JCPenney, and Kmart, this mall is full of boutiques and specialty shops and is the site of a number of special events, such as craft shows put on by the Henderson County Crafters Association.

Carolina Mountain Artists
444 North Main Street, Hendersonville, NC
(828) 696-0707
One of the first things you notice about this artist co-op is the variety and high quality of the skills displayed here. The guild is made up 32 artists, whose talents range from painting on canvas, wood, clay furniture, gourds, floor cloths, and other fabrics to woodworking (including fine doll furniture), needlework, lovely quilts, wearable art, stained glass, pottery, jewelry, watercolors, baskets, bird and butterfly houses, silk flower arrangements, and greenery. We were particularly taken with both the quality and the affordability of the fabric-decorated plates. In fact the prices on much of this original art are very reasonable.

The Consignment Gallery
411 North Main Street, Hendersonville, NC
(828) 697-7712
By visiting these two North Main Street shops, owned by Tippy and Arthur D'Amato, you could furnish and decorate an

entire home with quality antiques and still be able to adorn yourself or a loved one with some incredible estate jewelry.

Past-'N-Present is the place to go for a single piece or for whole sets of furniture. Although the shop specializes in mahogany and oak, you also can find Victorian couches, marble-top chests, player pianos, antique telephones, mirrors, clocks, and lamps. You can also buy excellent wall decorations. In addition to paintings, there are prints, including those by Salvador Dali and second-edition Audubon prints.

The Antique Consignment Gallery has some furniture pieces but concentrates more on china, glass, and collectibles. Here you'll find modern and antique jewelry, china by top names, sterling silver plates, figurines by Lladro, Hummel, and Armani, and much more. And Arthur, who writes a column on antiques for a local paper, will be happy to give you some tips on distinguishing the real antique from the fake.

The Curb Market
**221 North Church Street, Hendersonville, NC
(828) 692-8012**

The Curb Market started out on Main Street in 1924 with eight merchants selling their wares beneath umbrellas. It has mushroomed to 137 selling spaces, many staffed by third- and fourth-generation sellers. Merchants here are required to be Henderson County residents and to make or grow all items they sell. Among these are fresh vegetables, fruits, flowers, dairy products, baked goods, jams, jellies, pickles, relishes, and handmade gifts of all kinds, including afghans, aprons, booties, dolls, folk toys, pillows, quilts, rag rugs, table linens, walking sticks, woodwork items, and wreaths.

Dancing Bear Toys, Ltd.
**418 North Main Street, Hendersonville, NC
(828) 693-4500**

In addition to almost every toy currently popular with children today, Dancing Bear carries a good selection of delightful puppets, costumes, puzzles, and educational toys and books.

A Day in the Country
**130 Sugarloaf Road, Hendersonville, NC
(828) 692-7914**

This store, just off I-26 at the Hendersonville exit, has one of the area's largest selections of unique and unusual gifts, including afghans, collectibles, gourmet foods, tapestries, antique and French country furniture, silk floral arrangements, and more.

Days Gone By
**Gifts and Collectibles, 303 North Main Street, Hendersonville, NC
(828) 693-9056**

Until a few years ago, this was downtown's oldest business, Justus Pharmacy, established in 1882. Retaining all its old-time flavor, it's now a place where you can find drugstore/soda-fountain collectibles. Afterward sit down for an old-time ice-cream soda or sundae at the Old-Fashioned Soda Parlor.

The Goldsmith by Rudi, Ltd.
**324 North Main Street, Hendersonville, NC
(828) 693-1030**

Rudi Haug has been doing business in Hendersonville since 1975 and is now helped by his son and daughter. This large, full-service jewelry store is so popular for new purchases, custom designs, and jewelry repairs that there are five full-time jewelers working to fill the orders. The store does mounting, engraving, and restyling.

At Rudi's, in addition to the finest in all kinds of jewelry, you can buy clocks, fine Swiss watches, a great line of pen sets, and silver picture frames. There's also a fabulous array of gold and silver charms, including a popular Hendersonville charm that comes in three sizes in gold or silver.

Honeysuckle Hollow
**512 North Main Street, Hendersonville, NC
(828) 697-2197**

Romance and nostalgia fill the air at Honeysuckle Hollow. Vintage clothing, linens, lace, scarves, fragrances, glassware, candles, antiques, and jewelry turn this shop into an exciting treasure hunt. It's the place to go, too, for wonderful cards and relaxing contemporary, classical and traditional tapes and CDs.

Jane Asher's Fourth and Main Antique Mall
344 Main Street, Hendersonville, NC
(828) 693-0018
The antique and collectible lover will find 5,000 square feet of friendly, one-floor shopping here put together by 25 dealers. Though this is certainly the place to come if you like European clocks (you can get your clock repaired here, too), this store also carries a tempting array of fine china, glassware, art glass, dolls, Victorian quilts, toys, beaded Victorian bags, religious artifacts, costume and fine estate jewelry, old-fashioned sewing tools, and lots and lots of buttons. Prices on the whole are moderate, but you can find the rare and expensive piece here, too.

Mast General Store
527 North Main Street, Hendersonville, NC
(828) 696-1883
True to its atmosphere, this beautifully restored 1905 emporium is chock full of old-time mercantile items, but you can also find quality outdoor gear, footwear, and traditional clothing for all four of our seasons. The original Mast General Store opened in Valle Crucis in 1883.

Mehri & Company
501 North Main Street, Hendersonville, NC
(828) 693-0887
Opulence describes this unique store. Mehri & Company carries estate and antique jewelry, unique gifts, custom silk arrangements, and antique furniture, tapestries, and collectibles. You'll also find wonderful table linens, plushy pillows, and unique picture frames. If it's not of high quality, you won't find it here.

Mountain Lore Books
555 North Main Street, Hendersonville, NC
(828) 693-5096
While specializing in regional, gardening, nature, and children's books, Mountain Lore has all the best-sellers and a wealth

of new paperbacks. (See our Bookstore Close-up in this chapter.)

The Paintin' Shed
442 North Main Street, Hendersonville, NC
(828) 698-8088
This is the place to come for arts and craft supplies and advice. You can take any number of classes here, including decorative tole painting, working in sculpting clay, lampshade cutting and piercing, pen-and-ink drawing, and much more. All the items sold here are handcrafted locally.

Purple Sage
416 North Main Street, Hendersonville, NC
(828) 693-9555
This is the place to go if you're a gourmet cook, know one, or would like to become one. You'll find pots, pans, knives, kitchen gadgets, coffee, cookbooks, gifts, and imported and domestic wines. There's a wine cellar downstairs, and Purple Sage also holds periodic wine tastings and cooking classes. The award-winning chef/owner of Expressions Restaurant has added Purple Sage to his library of culinary enterprises.

Somewhere in Time
514 North Main Street, Hendersonville, NC
(828) 693-5900
You lose track of time in this shop's vast array of Victorian and country collectibles and antiques. It's the perfect place to browse and browse and, of course, buy. Be sure to check out the items on the "half-price table."

Sweet Memories
430 North Main Street, Hendersonville, NC
(828) 692-8401
The focus here is on regional fine crafts, including a distinctive selection of Southeastern art glass, functional and decorative pottery, jewelry, wood, fiber, metalwork, china painting, and handcrafted gifts.

Touchstone Gallery
318 North Main Street, Hendersonville, NC
(828) 692-2191

We never go to Hendersonville without dropping in to see what beautiful art and whimsical creations are displayed at this gallery, which specializes in contemporary American art and exceptional craft items. We seldom leave without being creatively inspired ourselves.

Village Green Antique Mall
424 North Main Street, Hendersonville, NC
(828) 692-9057
It will take you a while to see all the quality antiques and collectibles here. The mall contains 12,000 square feet full of inventory brought in by 35 dealers from six states. Shipping and delivery service is available.

Wickwire Gallery
330 North Main Street, Hendersonville, NC
(828) 692-6222
This fine art/folk gallery displays both established and emerging artists. (See the "Visual Arts/Henderson County" section of our Arts and Culture chapter.)

NAPLES

Crystal Visions
5920 Asheville Highway, Naples, exit 13
(828) 687-1193
This unique shop is a bookstore, and much more. Its product line offers all things for spiritual growth resources. Among these items are fountains, crystals, candles, chimes, angels, music, prisms, fairies, jewelry, pyramids, and aromatherapy. Hours are Monday through Friday 10:00 A.M. to 6:00 P.M. and Saturday 10:00 A.M. to 5:00 P.M.

Rutherford County

CHIMNEY ROCK/LAKE LURE

Most folks visit the Chimney Rock/Lake Lure area to see the Chimney or to boat and swim in Lake Lure. Another good reason to visit this thermal belt is for the rest and relaxation afforded by the many lodges, motels, cabins, and RV sites. There are those who make it a destination for fine dining as well.

Esmeralda Inn even offers a chef's table that takes you beyond the already extraordinary dining experience in their dining room. The chef's table is a glassed in air-conditioned area situated directly in the kitchen. The room can accommodate up to eight persons. You participate in the meal by observing the chef prepare your four courses. He interacts with you as he brings the meal to your table.

Shopping at Chimney Rock Park Sky Lounge takes you back to the days of penny arcades and yesteryear in America, when everyone brought home souvenirs of salt water taffy, items embossed with the name of the town or site visited, spoons, postcards, and other memorabilia. In addition you can find walking sticks, T-shirts, caps, and videotapes of the film made there, *Last of the Mohicans*.

The road going through Chimney Rock/Lake Lure was once a main route from Asheville to Charlotte, North Carolina, via Rutherfordton. This two-lane road is known by at least three names: Highway 64/74-A, Lone Star Memorial Highway, and Andrew Jackson Highway. Just prior to entering the town of Chimney Rock from the west, you have crossed the eastern Continental Divide, leaving Henderson County and entering Rutherford County. The shops lining the road are self-explanatory as tourist destinations. You can find novelties, sandwiches, fudge, and ice-cream cones. Pick and choose based on your interest. Permit us to suggest two that we have found of special interest.

Edie's Good Things
Highway 64/74-A, Chimney Rock Village, NC
(828) 625-0111
Edie offers fine crafts, most of which are handmade by artisans of the mountains. Pottery from the Barking Spider of Penland area is available. Jewelry by the four-generation-old firm of Stuart Nye of Asheville can be found here. An entire section is metalwork of menorahs and

other religious symbols. Wood, glass, and clay have been sculpted and turned into objects of art. Although small, the shop does have a first and second floor, and a roof with spectacular views. Edie is certain to invite the shopper to go up on the roof for a grand view of Chimney Rock. If you are looking for fine crafts, this is the place.

Julie's Gourmet Market and Specialties
2402 Memorial Highway (64/74-A),
Lake Lure, NC
(828) 625-2990

Julie's is a half-mile east of the lake and has been an oasis since 1996. She offers something special for the discerning palate with her large selection of wine and cheese. For the camper who wants a quick meal already prepared, Julie can supply it. These range from smoked salmon pâré to pasta and other Italian specialties. She even carries prime steaks, poultry, fresh fruits, and vegetables. If you need a gift basket for someone back home, Julie can assist you in selecting the items and then ship it for you. These quality items are reasonably priced.

Transylvania County

BREVARD

A few years ago the heart of downtown Brevard was struggling to find itself. Many people predicted doom for downtown commerce after Kmart and Wal-Mart opened in separate shopping centers at about the same time and took Belk and other downtown businesses with them. Quite the opposite has happened. Brevard's central district is vitally alive as the heart of Transylvania County's social life.

Shopping here is more attractive than ever. Brevard is perched on top of a high hill and is graced by an old, redbrick courthouse where Main and Broad Streets meet. Lovely views of the mountains of Pisgah National Forest rise in the west. Here you have a choice of festivals, art shows, and entertainment all year long.

On summer weekends there's nearly always music on the courthouse lawn, including programs by musicians from the Brevard Music Center. And an array of shops and restaurants, both new and old, have turned this into a delightful place to roam and enjoy.

Businesses stretch up and down Main and Broad and spill over onto all the side streets. Merchants and restaurateurs have even moved into some of Brevard's interesting old houses, transforming them into enticing shops and eateries. We've included a sampling of stores you can find in downtown Brevard. It's best to simply follow your nose in and out of all the pretty and fun shops. Stop in, too, at the Transylvania County Arts Co-op, 7 East Main Street, across from the courthouse, to view original works by local artists. Down the street the Chamber of Commerce, 35 West Main Street, (828) 883-3700, is loaded with visitor information, and it has an art gallery too.

Anytime you get tired or hungry, there are any number of convenient places where you can drop in, sit down, and get a bite to eat. (A few of these, but by no means all of them, are listed in our Restaurants chapter.) There are also some park benches scattered along Main Street where you can sit and take in the passing scene.

Brevard Antique Mall
57 East Main Street, Brevard, NC
(828) 885-2744

Brevard's largest antique shop has 20,000 square feet of quality antiques and collectibles, featuring 60 booths on three floors. There are always really beautiful pieces here with enough room to display them properly.

Celestial Mountain Music and Folk Art
16 West Main Street, Brevard, NC
(828) 884-3575

You're likely to find people making music when you walk into this store, and you're sure to encounter a fascinating array of musical instruments, such as handcrafted mountain dulcimers, Celtic harps, guitars, dobros, mandolins, autoharps, and crystal flutes—and you can schedule lessons to learn how to play them. The shop also records traditional music and makes instrument repairs.

D. D. Bullwinkle's
38 South Broad Street, Brevard, NC
(828) 862-4700

This unique shop, which specializes in Southern products, is practically impossible to describe—you'll have to see it for yourself. The shop sells dozens of kinds of penny candy, gourmet coffee, gifts, books, beautiful handmade furniture, jams, jellies, relishes, T-shirts (some with local logos), and—our favorite—very funny horse swings made from old tires.

Adjoining the shop is Rocky Soda Shop, where you can enjoy an old-fashioned milkshake, meal, or snack (see our Restaurant chapter for more information on Rocky's).

The Forest Place
100 South Broad Street, Brevard, NC
(828) 884-5713

This shop is a real find. It brings the forest into the city. Educational manipulatives, books, CDs, and all sorts of nature-oriented items are available. Maps, compasses, backpacks, water bottles, and sweats are on the shelves. This is just one of the many outlets across the United States that serve as a retail conduit for our forest system. All profits go to the support of environmental and forestry programs.

The Frame-Up
4 West Main Street, Brevard, NC
(828) 883-2385

This is the place to go for fantastic archival framing. The store also carries one-of-a-kind jewelry, wood turnings, handmade furniture, and beautiful (framed, of course) prints, as well as blown glass, porcelain, and pottery.

Heritage Antique Mall
15 West Main Street, Brevard, NC
(828) 883-4323

Fifteen or so carefully chosen dealers bring everything from the finest antique furniture to vintage comic books, all beautifully displayed. Here's the place to look for a rare book. If you've been looking for a special, specific something, put your desire on file with owners Greg and Sandy Wagner; they'll try to locate it for you. The mall specializes in antique fishing gear.

Jeanie's Boutique
112 South Broad Street, Brevard, NC
(828) 884-9573

For superfeminine fashions at prices so low you won't believe the tags, go to Jeanie's. The shop sells stunning Indian clothing at a cost that's often less than you'd pay at discount dress stores. Stay a while and chat with the shop's interesting owner.

Not only do our local thrift stores support excellent local charities, they can dress you in style. Four like-new silk blouses were a steal for 25 cents each at a sale in Brevard's Humane Society Thrift Shop on East Main Street.

Main Street Ltd.
224 East Main Street, Brevard, NC
(828) 884-4974

Housed in a grand, two-story white house, this shop is filled with exquisite surprises, including gift baskets, home accessories, and camp care packages for the many children who attend summer camps in the area. The store's unique gift wrapping turns any purchase into a celebration.

O. P. Taylor's
2 South Broad Street, Brevard, NC
(828) 883-2309

This store is a world unto itself. It carries, among other things, some beautiful, high-quality casual clothes. But the main attractions are the toys that fill its second floor, and flow down the stairs, sometimes right out on the sidewalk. It's a place that delights children and adults alike.

The Pink Flamingo
35 East Main Street, Brevard, NC
(828) 883-4515

If you have a special party to attend or are feeling flamboyant, stop by the Pink Flamingo. You'll find super-stylish—sometimes a little outlandish—ladies' fashions at surprisingly low prices. The store stocks some very pleasing jewelry and accessories, too.

We always check "the backroom" for items on sale, and almost every week there will be a special half-price sale on, for example, "any dress with yellow in it" or "any article with sequins." You won't believe the buys!

Beware before you buy: Some smaller shops may have strict return policies or "no return" policies. Be sure to clear the issue with the manager before your purchase if you may have to return or exchange the item.

The Proper Pot
44 East Main Street, Brevard, NC
(828) 877-5000

You'll find just the thing for the cook in your life. In addition to kitchenware, the Proper Pot sells linens, gift baskets, and gourmet teas and coffees.

The White Squirrel Shoppe
2 West Main Street, Brevard, NC
(828) 877-3530, (888) 729-7329

This wonderful shop's jam-packed with collectibles; odds and ends of small, wonderful pieces of furniture; lamps; statues; and gifts and crafts. There are also a number of its namesake white squirrels in all sizes and shapes. These make great souvenirs of the area because there really are white squirrels in Brevard (see the White Squirrel Close-up in our Bed-and-Breakfasts and Country Inns chapter).

SOUTHERN MOUNTAINS
Haywood County

WAYNESVILLE

Where downtown Brevard is built on a hill, Haywood's county seat sits on a high plateau. This affords mountain views in all directions. And like Hendersonville, Waynesville, with its turn-of-the-century buildings, brick sidewalks, park benches, and plants, has made its charming downtown one of the most popular shopping spots in the county. There's an interesting mix of more than 50 stores here: boutiques, galleries, specialty shops, family and service stores, and restaurants. Here, too, is the place to find festivals and fun events, such as Razzle-Dazzle (a children's street festival) and the International Festival, which is a day of music, dance, food, and crafts held in association with Folkmoot, the International Dance Festival (see our Annual Festivals and Events chapter).

Twice a month on Friday evenings in July and August, the street is blocked off in front of the courthouse for dances with live bluegrass bands, clogging demonstrations, and dancing instruction, all free of charge. On Wednesday and Saturday in late summer and fall, when the harvest comes in, a farmer's market is set up downtown.

Even without these events, you can spend several hours or perhaps a full day browsing and eating—and probably still miss an interesting little place or two tucked in a side street or upstairs over another shop.

We've never had a problem finding a parking spot on Main Street, but if you do, there's free parking on Montgomery and Wall Streets, both of which run parallel to Main Street, 1 block in either direction. From Wall Street, a couple of walkways lead right down to Main. While you're here, take time to visit the Shelton House (828-452-1551), just off Main Street, home to the Museum of North Carolina Handicrafts (see our Mountain Crafts chapter).

If you don't shop yourself out in Waynesville, you should travel another 10 or 15 minutes to Maggie Valley. Here, along a 3-mile stretch of U.S. 19, you'll find a bonanza of craft and souvenir stores. There is lodging, RV parks, camping, restaurants, and other attractions (see our Attractions, Other Accommodations, and Nightlife chapters).

Blue Owl Studio and Gallery, Inc.
11 North Main Street, Waynesville, NC
(828) 456-5050
Hand-painted antique graphics of North Carolina's mountains are the mainstay of this gallery, but you'll find other interesting items here, too. (See "Visual Arts, Haywood County" in our Arts and Culture chapter.)

Candy Barrel
55 North Main Street, Waynesville, NC
(828) 452-0075
Its name explains it all. Barrels and baskets brimming with candies line the walls and run in a great aisle down the center, assailing you with scents of sweetness. Anything you find here sells for $4.59 a pound, so you can mix the flavors to your taste buds' content. If that wasn't enough, there's a soda fountain in the rear, and you can enjoy its treats there or at the tables on the store's "front porch." There are various kinds of homemade fudge, too.

Chloe & Co.
117 North Main Street, Waynesville, NC
(828) 452-7792
Housed in a small stone building that was Waynesville's first library, the selection at this upscale boutique is not large, but the items here are ever so tempting! There are stylish ladies' fashions and accessories and a number of excellent pieces of fine antique furniture.

Earthwork's Environmental Gallery
110 North Main Street, Waynesville, NC
(828) 452-9500
Earthwork's brings together arts and crafts of this county and Mexico's Native Americans. Africa is also represented. (See "Visual Arts, Haywood County" in our Arts and Culture chapter.) The Earthwork's Frame Gallery (828-456-3666) is at 152 South Main Street.

Gatekeepers
4 North Main Street, Waynesville, NC
(828) 698-5466
Excellent taste is reflected in the home accessories, gifts, and furniture found here. And the old building with its squeaky wooden floors and tin ceiling is almost as interesting. There's a fine garden shop in the rear.

Home-Tech: The Kitchen Shop
5 North Main Street, Waynesville, NC
(828) 452-7672
The items here can make cooking an adventure. This kitchen shop offers all that is necessary to make a cook a chef. In addition to cookbooks, it has fine German-made cookware, small appliances, Burton burners and stove-top grills, gourmet coffees and all the items needed to brew them, handmade cutting boards and butcher-block tables, gift baskets made to order, and much more.

Mast General Store
63 North Main Street, Waynesville, NC
(828) 452-2101
In addition to selling outdoor clothing and gear, this store also serves as a ticket office for local cultural events. The original fixtures of this early 20th-century store are still in place, including rocking chairs for its customers. Old-time housewares and other unusual items are stocked on the mezzanine. Periodic demonstrations by well-known regional craftspeople are also held here.

O. P. Taylor's
162 North Main Street, Waynesville, NC
(828) 452-7212
O. P. Taylor now has a branch of his toy store in Waynesville. (See the Brevard listing in this chapter.)

Ridge Runner Naturals
33 North Main Street, Waynesville, NC
(828) 456–3003, (800) 525–3009

Ridge Runners carries nature-inspired gifts for all ages: birdfeeders, wind chimes, nature puzzles, T-shirts, books, games, walking sticks, maps, and much more.

Slow Lane
71 North Main Street, Waynesville, NC
(828) 456–3682

If you need to decorate a home, this is not a bad place to start. Although you won't find sofas and beds and the like at Slow Lane, you will find wonderful solid oak furniture made by craftspeople who live within 100 miles of town.

This big store also offers all kinds of gifts, including clocks, baskets, lace, tons of teddy bears, large gold-framed prints of a nostalgic nature, furniture throws, place settings, and table linens.

If you are shopping for a gift, remember that some shops offer creative or unique gift wrapping and specialty boxes.

T. Pennington Art Gallery
15 North Main Street, Waynesville, NC
(828) 452–4582

To see Teresa Pennington's amazing skills at reproducing mountain scenes with colored pencils is worth the trip to this gallery. (See "Visual Arts, Haywood County" in our Arts and Culture chapter.)

Turnabouts
142 North Main Street, Waynesville, NC
(828) 456–4766

This eclectic coffeehouse/gift shop with charming taste is a great place to stop, rest, and feed the senses. While you sip a cappuccino, one of 20 varieties of coffees, or something from the finest selection of teas, you can browse through a wonderfully wry collection of greeting cards, shop for a lovely natural fiber nightgown, buy some

European linens or Czech crystal, purchase aromatherapy products and candles for your bath, select a gift for a special child, add to your gourmet food supply, or select a gourmet food basket. You can order a gourmet picnic basket, too.

Turnabouts is planning to hold "Wine Nights" on Thursday, Friday, and Saturday evenings. Look for cheeses, pâtés, and fine desserts.

Twigs & Leaves
98 North Main Street, Waynesville, NC
(828) 456–1940

David Erickson and his wife, potter Kaaren Stoner, whose studio is in this craft gallery, call their shop "an adventure into the art of Nature," and it certainly is! Kaaren's leaf-enhanced pottery, arches and outdoor seatings made of twigs and branches, nature photos and handmade fountains, meditation pools and organic plant vessels, whimsical lizards and many, many other artists' nature-related items, plus reasonable prices, make it nearly impossible to leave this shop without making a purchase. For us, it wasn't possible at all.

Whitman's Bakery & Sandwich Shop
18 North Main Street, Waynesville, NC
(828) 456–8271

Whitman's is one of the busiest stores in town. The wonderful smells wafting out the door tend to lure you right in. And believe us, the sandwiches layered between freshly baked bread are hard to beat! It's another great place for sweet tooths, too.

Jackson County

DILLSBORO

Sylva is the county seat of Jackson County, and it's a bustling town stretched out along two busy one-way streets graced with a number of very nice shops and restaurants. But it's the tiny, doll-like town of Dillsboro, just a mile down Business U.S. 19/23, that's the real shopping mecca for tourists and area residents alike. It's also one of the stops made by excursion trains of the Great Smoky Mountain Railroad, which brings even more visitors to Dillsboro.

With a shopping area approximately 2 blocks long and two streets wide (plus the railway that runs through the middle of town), you wouldn't think there could be so much to see, but there is. The following are only a few of nearly 50 shops and restaurants you'll find in this village. Most are open March through December, giving many of the crafters who supply and often own the shops here time to craft and restock during the winter months.

Dillsboro's is a delight at any season, but the fantasy finish to the Dillsboro shopping season takes place on the first two Fridays and Saturdays in December when the Christmas Luminaries is held. Thousands of candles light the way to extended evenings of musical entertainment and complimentary refreshments.

Here's just a brief sampling of the treats in Dillsboro.

Bradley's General Store
Front Street, Dillsboro, NC
(828) 586-3891
When you've visited all the stores listed here and a great many others, you'll find respite at Bradley's General Store, which has country gifts, home furnishings, and—best of all—an antique, but working, soda fountain.

CJ's
Front Street, Dillsboro, NC
(828) 586-3198
For collectibles and gifts, most of them American made, take a look at CJ's. They have an extensive inventory of figurines and decorative items for the true collector.

Dogwood Crafters
90 Webster Street, Dillsboro, NC
(828) 586-2248
Housed in a large, renovated log building around the corner from Front Street, this is one of our favorite stores in Dillsboro. We are particularly taken with the lovely, artistic cornhusk dolls, but there also are hundreds of contemporary and traditional handicrafts on display, including pottery, pillows, art, and toys.

If you are shopping for something unique or for certain types of products, save yourselves some time by calling the local chamber of commerce for stores that might carry the items on your list.

Duck Decoy Inc.
Front Street, Dillsboro, NC
(828) 586-9000
Some of the best duck woodcarvers in the country live in North Carolina, and Duck Decoy displays some of their works along with other distinguished gifts, such as handmade oak tables and benches, backpacks, an array of knives, gourmet jellies, tin signs, and T-shirts.

Enloe Market Place
78 Front Street, Dillsboro, NC
(828) 586-3603
Housed in an historic old home, Enloe carries fine gifts, prints, and home accessories and offers a children's corner full of items to delight the kids. Want to impress your friends? Pick up a few bars of monogrammed soap.

Front Street Company/Yarn Corner
64 Front Street, Dillsboro, NC
(828) 586-0089
Needleworkers will love the variety they'll find at this shop. Gifts, fine yarns, hand-painted needlepoint, and cross-stitch supplies are sold here. You can also take a class or receive assistance on your latest project. And for a respite before more shopping, you can dine at the Front Street Cafe or out in the courtyard. Front Street Company is a great place to purchase delectable gourmet items like teas and

Want to relax? Try some of the reading areas and reading rooms that book-stores provide for their customers to enjoy books. Comfortable chairs or sofas are often a part of the experience.

coffees, plus jams and jellies, which make great gifts or personal indulgences.

Gallery Z
Front Street, Dillsboro, NC
(828) 586-3383

The mountains are becoming world famous for studio glass, and at Gallery Z you can see some samples of it in the form of candleholders, lamps, vases, and perfume bottles.

Maple Tree Gallery
Front Street, Dillsboro, NC
(828) 586-8021

Here's a gallery that not only sells gems, jewelry, and specimens but will also do gem mounting and repairs while you wait. The handmade wire-wrap jewelry, custom designs, and gem cutting make this an interesting stop.

Mountain Pottery
Front Street, Dillsboro, NC
(828) 586-9183

At Mountain Pottery you can see pottery being made in an open studio. It's also got the town's largest selection of handmade porcelain, stoneware, and raku. The pottery is supplied by more than 75 crafts-people from the region.

The Nature Connection
Front Street, Dillsboro, NC
(828) 586-0686

This is a delightful store for both adults and children. It's full of home and garden accessories: fountains, metal sculpture, clocks, blown glass, and birdhouses and feeders. Nature themes are also found in the books, guides, T-shirts, music, educa-tional items, and toys. And this list doesn't begin to cover what you'll find here.

Riverwood Pewter Shop
N.C. Highway 441, Dillsboro, NC
(828) 586-6996, (800) 580-2547

The Riverwood Shops developed around a hand-hammered pewter business estab-lished in 1930. The Riverwood Pewter Shop is still here making hand-hammered pewter on the premises. You'll find the shop 1 mile south of U.S. 74/23.

Riverwood's Oaks Gallery
N.C. Highway 441, Dillsboro, NC
(828) 586-6542

Right next door to the Riverwood Pewter Shop, this cooperative of more than eighty Appalachian craftspeople is a showcase of weaving, jewelry, glass, wood, wearables, and pottery.

Southern Traditions
Front Street, Dillsboro, NC
(828) 586-3943

For a different kind of time travel, visit this charming old country home that's really a shop. At Southern Traditions you can look for antiques, gifts, home accessories, and counted cross-stitch supplies. The shop will gladly ship your purchases anywhere you like.

Village Studio
Front Street, Dillsboro, NC
(828) 586-4060

The talents that flower in these mountains are beautifully showcased in this gallery. It's filled with paintings and prints by area artists, handmade dulcimers, gifts, and cards. The gallery-style shop also displays decorative accessories for home and office. The studio also does professional framing.

Macon County

HIGHLANDS

"There's just no place like Highlands," is a comment heard frequently. It's true, and the town has gone out of its way with rules and regulations to make sure that its small but busy downtown stays as nice as it is now. Highlands is also well named. Its elevation of 4,118 feet provides pleasant summertime temperatures for roaming its Main Street and surrounding shopping areas. If you've never been to Highlands before, you might want your first stop to be at the Visitor Information Center, 386 Oak Street, (828) 526-2112, just above Town Hall on U.S. 64. Not only will the staff give you the scoop on the whole area and a shopping guide that includes a map, but there are also public rest rooms here.

On Main Street you can spend hours roaming in and out of the shops, where you'll find a wide variety of clothing, jewelry, art, gifts, handicrafts, toys, bird and bat houses, food, furniture, flowers, and so on. If there's one overriding theme, it's quality. The residents who occupy some of the most expensive real estate in the mountains expect it, and if the droves of shoppers who come here from other areas are any indication—the friendly merchants of Highlands aim to please.

Any first-time Highlands' shopper will be immediately drawn to Main Street's diverse shops. But don't stop with Main Street. Highlands has a number of distinctive shopping areas, including quite a few of its side streets. One example is Fourth Street: Shops here are referred to as "on the hill." Other small Highlands shopping centers (all within walking distance of downtown) include Wright Square, Oak Square, and Mountain Brook Square. There are also some great shops on the main roads leading into town.

Just keep in mind when contemplating a Highlands' shopping spree that some of these stores close after October or December or are open only on weekends. At this high an elevation, where winters can be bitter cold, a lot of residents and some storeowners spend the colder months in warmer climes.

Bryant Art Glass Studio
260 Franklin Road, U.S. Highway 64,
Highlands, NC
(828) 526-4095

Some shops you encounter here will agree to ship ungainly or breakable objects to your home. Inquire before you buy.

Everything glass is made here by fusing together pieces of glass at 1,500 degrees in a kiln. Ground enamels are used for colors and crochet doilies or stencils for the designs. Awarded commissions include the cobalt and clear-glass plates designed for the Charlotte Mint Museum of Craft and Design. (See our chapter on Arts and Culture.)

Highlands Wine and Cheese Co.
Mountain Brook Center, U.S. Highway 64,
Highlands, NC
(828) 526-5210
This wine and cheese shop offers pâré, imported cheese, a large selection of imported and domestic wines, deli trays, and gift baskets.

House of Lord
Main Street, Highlands, NC
(828) 526-9147
Long an elegant fixture on Main Street, House of Lord is the place to go for fine jewelry and art. The lines carried here are by internationally known designers.

I'm Precious Too!
Main and Leonard Streets, Highlands, NC
(828) 526-2754
As this store's name implies, it carries simply precious antiques, delicate linens, collectibles, and some fine clothes.

Find something unusual you'd love to give as gifts on different holidays? Don't hesitate to buy several at once; you may never be back to that particular little place and will regret it later.

Many shops now have Web sites. It's a splendid way to keep tabs on what your favorite new find will be keeping in stock.

Juliana's
Main Street, Highlands, NC
(828) 526-4306

Antiques and decorative accessories are featured in this shop. You will find specialties such as majolica, Victorian silver plate, and other gift items.

McCulley's
Fourth Street, Highlands, NC
(828) 526-4407

McCulley's, with another shop in Aspen, Colorado, specializes in Scottish cashmere knitwear for women and men.

Mirror Lake Antiques
Fourth Street, Highlands, NC
(828) 526-2080

This full-service antique store has a large selection of estate jewelry. It's the place to look for semiprecious stones, mineral specimens, gold jewelry, jewelry design, and remodeling.

Stone Lantern
Main Street, Highlands, NC
(828) 526-2769

This is one of our favorite shops in Highlands. It's not just the beautiful, well-chosen items from Asia found here. It's the wonderful way in which they're displayed. Expect some high prices, but the quality is worth the cost.

Tiger Mountain Woodworks
N.C. Highway 106 S., Highlands, NC
(828) 526-5577

Shopping for a rustic look? This shop sells handcrafted furnishings, including custom lodge furniture and country reproductions, including beds, tables, dressers, and other items for the entire house.

The Toy Store
Main Street, Highlands, NC
(828) 526-9415

We never go to Highlands without dropping in at the Toy Store to see the latest in toys and games. Here you'll find old and new favorites, plus stuffed animals, dolls, and so much more.

Whiskers
Main and Third Streets, Highlands, NC
(828) 526-3612

Whiskers specializes in gifts for pets and their people. You'll find collars, catnip toys, biscuits, decorative leashes, bones, bowls, T-shirts, and all manner of things pet lovers can't do without.

Cherokee County

If you go any farther west in North Carolina than Cherokee County, you'll be in Tennessee. If you go south from there, then welcome to Georgia. So with just about 20 miles within the North Carolina state line, you can still have your "last cup of coffee" before leaving the state. The Daily Grind coffee shop in Murphy advertises just that idea. You can find quaint, old-timey Southern town centers in Murphy and in Andrews. There is also the opportunity to pick up a big chunk of folklore while you are here.

The Mountains to the Sea Trail begins in this corner of North Carolina. By following a meandering line you can make it to the sea by crossing over Mount Mitchell, the Appalachian Trail, the Blue Ridge Parkway, and plenty of cities and towns all the way to Manteo, North Carolina, and the Atlantic Ocean. The highway distance is about 550 miles. The meandering footpath is about twice that.

So tuck into a B&B or tie-down your RV and enjoy the ambience of this special corner of North Carolina.

OUTDOOR SAFETY

Beware the unprepared hiker. Remember that nature, as spectacular as it can be, is also a powerful force and should be respected as such. There are basics of common sense and courtesy that are important to remember whenever you venture into the national parks and forests, as well as other wilderness areas. Be aware when you enter a primitive environment that you will be faced with the challenge of being entirely self-sufficient for whatever time you remain there, and for a lost hiker that could run into days. Invariably, every year a hiker or two is lost in the mountains, requiring rescue teams to scour the area. Often there will be no shelters, campgrounds, water spigots, or rest rooms, and wilderness trails are maintained to the most primitive standard. There will be few blazes or signs, so a compass and topographic map and knowledge of how to use them are essential.

Observe all park regulations. These rules are designed to protect not only the natural environment but also the health and safety of park visitors. Park officers are empowered to enforce the federal regulations on which these rules are based. You can look over a copy of these at park offices throughout the region (see the listings in our Forests and Parks chapter).

Careful planning is a must when you visit our national forests, the Great Smoky Mountain National Park, or the Blue Ridge Parkway. Know what you want to do and what your visit will require; know your surroundings and be aware of our often-changing weather. The mountains have much to offer enthusiasts of all ages, from beginners to experienced outdoors people. The following are reminders and tips in cases of emergency. Do take an interest in researching your outings further. These are the basic safety rules to follow, but educating yourself and training will allow you to enjoy the wilds all the more.

DRIVING

When traveling by car on the Blue Ridge Parkway or the back roads of the national forests, make sure you observe all traffic regulations and drive a vehicle that's in good working order. Breaking down in some of the remote regions can spell disaster (or at least great inconvenience). Have enough gasoline to take you to your destination and back again, because gas stations are few and far between on the Parkway and can seem a world away when you're sitting by the wayside on a dusty back road. Bring along necessary auto tools and a good spare tire and make sure your brakes and headlights are in good working order. (These mountains often have steep grades to negotiate, and the Blue Ridge Parkway's 27 tunnels require the use of headlights.)

When packing the car for the trip, include the following items: a first-aid kit, flashlight, blanket, light jacket or sweater, and a change of clothing, in case the weather changes (see our chapter on Climate). In case of a total breakdown, there's always AAA. For emergency road service, call (800) 477-4222; in Asheville you can call (828) 253-5376. This is also the number of the local AAA travel office. (Nonmembers will be charged, but they will be helped in an emergency.)

WHAT TO PACK

For any extended hiking or camping activities, something that will be longer than just a stroll to a waterfall, always have these essentials with you: a map, a compass, a flashlight/headlamp with extra batteries and bulbs, extra food, extra clothing, sunglasses, first-aid supplies, matches in a waterproof container, and fire starter.

When taking off into the woods, don't forget to take along a respect for the land and your own personal safety. Before you step foot on the trail, study a map of the area. (Maps are often available at visitors centers and ranger stations or posted on a bulletin board near park entrances.) Know where you're going and don't stray from the trails, many of which are clearly marked. It's easy to become disoriented in deep woods, and steep drop-offs covered by foliage can mean sudden disaster. If you get lost, stay put; you're easier to find that way. It's good to have a pocket whistle when hiking. Use three blasts on the whistle to alert those in search of you. If you get lost near a stream or creek, follow the water downstream; it will most likely lead to a community.

Dress properly for the season and wear sturdy worn-in shoes with thick, absorbent socks to prevent blistering. This helps in terms of comfort as well as navigation of rough terrain. Changes in elevation make for unpredictable weather. Be aware of the potential for change and be prepared.

When hiking or camping, never go alone. Always tell someone your route (you are required to sign in with a park ranger for overnight hikes in national parks). And always make your whereabouts and intentions known to others.

Carry plenty of water. Streams may look sparkling and your thirst may be great, but, unfortunately, the water can be contaminated.

TRAILS

Trails are rated by difficulty level, steepness, how obvious the trail is to follow, and the roughness of the tread. Markers indicating difficulty are provided by the forest service and are usually at the beginning of the trail. The easiest trails have obvious routes and easy grades, with some pitches up to 20 percent maximum and a relatively smooth tread. They are indicated by a green mark with a slight curve. More difficult trails are marked with a curving blue line and have routes that are usually recognizable but are somewhat challenging with moderate grades, with some pitches up to 30 percent maximum and a smooth to rough tread. A most difficult trail may not be recognizable, requiring a high degree of skill, and may have a steep grade with some pitches greater than 30 percent and rough tread. The hardest trails will have markers with a black zigzag on them.

You should not leave any trail unless you have the equipment and survival skills to meet any condition of terrain, climate, or exertion. Mechanical forms of transportation are not allowed in some wilderness areas. Although most trails are open only to hikers, some are designated for horse use in the Southern Nantahala and Shining Rock Wildernesses. Mountain bikes are not permitted, and you may not hike with a group of more than 10 people. Check in at the ranger station before your hike.

FOOD AND COOKING

It's a good idea to bring a camp stove if you have one (or can borrow or rent one). They have improved in size and utility. If you must have a fire, make sure you control it. Use existing fire rings when possible. Make sure the fire is dead before leaving, using sand or water to douse the smoldering embers thoroughly. Fires are prohibited in the Shining Rock Wilderness and Middle Prong Wilderness Areas; therefore you must carry a backpack stove if you wish to cook in this area. Bring plenty of energy-rich, protein-packed edibles. You'll be exerting a great deal of energy while hiking, swimming in mountain pools, or rafting and kayaking. Any type of "bar"—be it granola, fruit, oatmeal—packs easily and staves off hunger on the trail. Homemade trailmix with raisins, dried fruits, nuts, a few carob or chocolate chips, and sunflower seeds is fairly free of additives and added sugars. A handful can keep you going on those uphill climbs.

Carry plenty of water (squeeze bottles are the most easily accessible) and drink often, even when not thirsty. You may become dehydrated before you feel the urge to quench your thirst. Good foods to prepare over campfires or stoves include beans, pasta, couscous, instant soups, instant oatmeal, and hot cereals. Throw in any fresh vegetables you have brought along with you. If you have aluminum foil, steam fresh legumes by double-wrapping them with herbs and place them in the embers of your fire. In 10 minutes enjoy steamed veggies. For breakfast throw a handful of your trailmix in with the instant oatmeal or hot cereal. It can make a world of difference if you're camping for several days.

WHAT TO DO WITH WASTE

Remember the rule of seasoned campers and hikers: "Pack it in—pack it out." Leave no trace of your time in the woods, not only for the sake of future generations but also for the benefit of the true residents of the woods—the wildlife. Use thoughtful methods of sanitation. Bury all human waste and toilet paper in a hole 6 inches deep and at least 100 feet away from any water source. Tampons and pads should be carried back out with you in sealed containers—the scent of blood could attract bear or other wild animals. Do use biodegradable soap and a wash pan; scatter your wash water away from creek banks. Obviously you should take all trash back out with you. Carry resealable bags that can be shut almost airtight for your food waste.

WILD ANIMALS

Be aware of your intrusion into the animals' woodland home. Leave all wild animals alone. Bears come out occasionally in the mountain park lands, particularly in the southern mountains near the Great Smoky Mountains National Park. Do not approach bears. They may look cuddly, but they can be dangerous. If one approaches your car, stay inside with the windows rolled up. Make noise on the trail or at your campsite—bears won't be interested in investigating foreign clamor. Before you sleep, take all food out of your tent. Seal your edibles as securely as possible in a backpack and hang it from a tree several yards from your sleeping area.

Snakes seldom bite unless disturbed or teased, but be aware of them and be able to identify poisonous snakes. Rattlesnakes and copperheads thrive in these parts. Dry conditions tend to bring snakes to water sources. Take note: Rattlesnakes do not always rattle their tails before striking and can strike from any position, in any direction. If you are struck by a poisonous snake and have no suctioning kit, seek help immediately. Immobilize the limb and keep the wound below heart level at all times. Try to identify the markings on the snake, so medical personnel will know which antivenin to administer. Not every bite will require antivenin, but every bite does need medical evaluation.

Rabies can be carried by the common raccoon, another cute, cuddly looking creature you don't want to approach. The

ⓘ

It's true, raccoons and other small animals are cute, and those that have been fed by humans often seem friendly. However, it's best, as with all wild animals, to give them their space. Every year a few hundred rabies cases are reported.

1997 summer produced a rabies scare; squirrels and even a domestic kitten were affected by the disease. A rabid animal will generally foam at the mouth, act aggressively, and have wild eyes, often rolling back into the head. Stay far away from such animals. If bitten, seek medical treatment immediately.

INSECTS

Ticks can be a problem in the warmer months. Infected ticks can cause Lyme disease. (Should a tick bite you, leaving a red spot that takes on the looks of a bulls-eye, itches, and is accompanied by a fever, see a doctor as soon as possible. These are the indications of Lyme.) Check yourself after being in the woods and follow these tips: Wear light-colored clothing so you can quickly spot ticks on you, tuck pant legs into socks; use insect repellent with DEET, and do not remove ticks with your fingers. Use pointed tweezers or splinter pickers. Lightly grasp the body of the insect, gently and slowly pull the body straight out, so as not to leave the head behind. Do not squeeze the tick, as this could push its bacteria directly into the victim's bloodstream. You should save the tick and take it with you when you seek medical help, enabling the physician to analyze it and prescribe prophylactic antibiotics if necessary. Mosquitoes can flourish in the damp woods, so bring plenty of repellent.

West Nile virus has arrived in the mountains and has claimed its first human victim. So be particularly vigilant about protecting yourself from mosquitoes: use insect repellent even over clothing, and wear long pants, socks, and long sleeves in heavily infested areas. Mosquitoes are most active from dusk to dawn, so consider avoiding outdoor activities during the early morning or evening hours.

According to the Centers for Disease Control, most people who are infected with the West Nile virus will not have any type of illness. It is estimated that 20 percent of the people who become infected will develop West Nile fever: mild symptoms, including fever, headache, and body aches, occasionally with a skin rash on the trunk of the body and swollen lymph glands.

The symptoms of severe infection (West Nile encephalitis or meningitis) include headache, high fever, neck stiffness, stupor, disorientation, coma, tremors, convulsions, muscle weakness, and paralysis. It is estimated that one in 150 persons infected with the West Nile virus will develop a more severe form of disease.

PLANT LIFE

Foliage is abundant on the trails. One of these plants, poison ivy, a common bush, causes an itchy rash and more severe reactions in those allergic to it. It grows as a vine or short shrub with three glossy light-green leaves per stalk. Avoid it. If you feel you have been in poison ivy, wash your skin thoroughly with soap and warm water after contact. The oily sap this plant emits, known as urushiol, can cling to pets' fur, clothing, shoelaces, even gardening tools for an extended period and plague you months after. Wash everything that may have come into contact with the plant. Don't burn green plants—some may be poison ivy, which rendered a Waynesville singer voiceless for months after inhaling the noxious smoke.

HUNTING

Also, be aware of hunting season. If you hike trails during hunting season, always wear bright "hunter-orange" for your protection. Deer season runs from early to mid-October and again from late November to mid-December. Bear season runs from mid-October to early November and again from mid-December to early January. These are very general time frames. Be sure to call for specific dates each year.

You can call the 24-hour phone line at the North Carolina Wildlife Resources

Commission (919–662–4381), for information on hunting and fishing seasons and regulations in this region of North Carolina.

WATERFALLS

Waterfalls are another deceptively beautiful lure of nature here in the mountains. They have a magnetic quality, but they can be deadly. Each year someone thinks the view must be better from the top of the falls—a fatal mistake. There have been numerous deaths in the past few years due to slipping and falling from the tops or even sides of waterfalls. The rocks in any of our mountain streams are moss-covered and slippery, and the water rushing over the falls is swift and cold. One misstep can be the last. View these wonderful waterfalls at the proper distance and from the bottom, looking up. Do not attempt to climb them. Use that zoom lens to get a closer look.

HYPOTHERMIA

Hypothermia, the condition that causes a potentially fatal drop in body temperature, is a term you need to know. And contrary to popular belief, you don't have to be stranded in a snowstorm to experience this life-threatening condition. Whenever cold, moisture, and fatigue persist, it takes only a few hours to bring on the fatal results of hypothermia. Poor food intake, improper clothing, and alcohol can contribute to the problem.

Symptoms of hypothermia include exhaustion, uncontrolled shivering, confusion, loss of motor coordination, slurred speech, irrational behavior (like trying to disrobe in the cold), and unconsciousness. A victim of severe hypothermia, which occurs when the body core temperature falls below 92 degrees Fahrenheit, shivers in waves, cannot walk, curls into a fetal position to find the last remnants of warmth in the body, and has rigid muscles. All forms of hypothermia must be treated immediately by drying and warming the victim.

For mild hypothermia add more layers of clothing, put on dry clothes, increase physical activity, and seek shelter.

For moderate hypothermia add food and fluids, heat the victim with body contact, and get the victim in a sleeping bag with another person who is wearing light clothing (to transfer body heat).

For severe hypothermia create a shell of total insulation around the victim and surround the victim with dry clothing, blankets, and multiple sleeping bags. Wrap all of the above in plastic to prevent heat loss to prevent the core temperature rises and pushes warmer blood toward the extremities. Feed the victim warm sugar water a bit at a time.

Urinating will help conserve heat by emptying the bladder and concentrating body heat on the contracted inner organs. Do not expose the hypothermic victim to extremes of heat. Extremes of heat will burn the victim or can shock the heart. Remember that even a 50-degree day can bring on hypothermia if conditions are wet and windy. Keep your head covered in this kind of weather. Body heat may quickly be lost without a hat.

All victims of hypothermia should get medical attention.

HEAT EXHAUSTION AND HEAT STROKE

In warm weather the sun can be intense at these higher elevations, especially in the summer months. And it's getting hotter. Local weather announcers say we're breaking records every month with record highs. Bring along enough sunblock for all exposed skin. We also recommend sunglasses to cut the glare, and a sun hat. Bring plenty of fluids along and drink them, whether you're thirsty or not. You may become dehydrated even before you feel the urge to quench your thirst. Heat exhaustion, which can lead to heat stroke, must be taken care of immediately. A major increase in the body core temperature can kill a victim within minutes.

Signs to watch out for are sweating, increased pulse, weakness, dizziness, nausea, and thirst. Signs of heat stroke are hot skin, either very pale skin or very flushed skin, decreased urine output, increased temperature, and a change in mental status—disorientation and incapacity to reason or make judgments. Try to help relieve these symptoms immediately.

For heat exhaustion rest in the shade, replace fluid loss with a water-and-salt solution (a teaspoon of salt per quart of water), remove all but the most necessary articles of clothing, and refrain from further physical activity for the day.

For heat stroke move the victim to a cool spot. Remove the victim's clothing and pour water on the extremities. Then fan him or her, increasing air circulation and evaporation, or cover the victim with cool, wet cloths and fan him or her. You can also immerse the victim in cool (but not cold) water. Do not allow the heat-stroke sufferer to become cold or the body will begin shivering to produce more heat. Also make sure the person refrains from all physical activity, then seek medical help.

FINAL THOUGHTS

Nature can be formidable, but it can also inspire. Don't be afraid of challenging yourself, but do enter into your outdoor endeavors armed with knowledge, preparation, and training. If you're a wilderness novice, read outdoor magazines before your trip. Brush up on basic first-aid preparation with books specifically designed for the hiker and camper. We are fortunate in Western North Carolina to be surrounded by a wealth of natural beauty. If we remember to respect that natural environment, our visits to these wood and park lands will be memorable for all the right reasons.

RECREATION 🍀

Leisure time reigns supreme here in the mountains. The quality and diversity of recreational opportunities are unparalleled. After you've been swept along in a white-water raft, gone aloft in a hot-air balloon, come close to nature—and a backpacking llama—on a scenic hiking trail, and reeled in a trophy trout on a mountain lake, you're still not finished. Whether you prefer the tamer environs of a city park or the wild river adventure just over the ridge, you'll find just what you're looking for in these hills.

Our mountains have the perfect places to fish from a boat on a peaceful lake, dive off a houseboat into crystal clear waters, take to tumbling waters in an inner tube, zip along behind a ski boat, canoe through placid or swift rivers, or race over rapids in a kayak or a raft. (See our section on outfitters at the end of this chapter for canoeing and rafting outfitters. Swimming pools are included under "City and County Programs and Areas.") The suggestions that follow are just a few of the recreation possibilities.

This chapter begins by highlighting the various city and county park areas and their accompanying recreation programs. Then we give you an overview of the Lakes, White-water Rafting and Kayaking, the Rivers, Canoeing, Fishing, Hunting, Mountain Biking, Rock Climbing, Hiking, Camping, Horseback Riding, Off-Road Vehicle Trails, and Other Recreation (like Airborne Rec, Llama Treks, and Bowling). Listings of a few of the region's guides and outfitters are at the chapter's end. For a list of ranger stations and National Park Service visitor centers see our Forests and Parks chapter for contact information.

COUNTY AND CITY PROGRAMS AND AREAS

When time allows, we mountain folk tend to head for the fabulous recreation offered by the 1.5 million acres of public lands in our area (see our Forests and Parks chapter), often overlooking the many recreational opportunities right in our cities and towns. In this section we describe some of those recreational possibilities. And we haven't even attempted to include the ever-so-many private clubs and spas that abound in the region.

Northern Mountains

ALLEGHANY COUNTY

Crouse Park
Grayson and Cherry Streets, Sparta, NC
This city park provides a playground and covered picnic areas on the grounds of the Crouse House, the former home of one of Sparta's leading citizens. Basketball, volleyball, and horseshoes are also popular here.

ASHE COUNTY

Ashe Park
off Old Highway 16, Jefferson, NC
Centered in a lush green valley, Ashe Park is well equipped for fun with two tennis courts, two baseball fields, two covered picnic areas, a barnlike covered building that can house groups up to 75, four bathrooms, plenty of parking, and a breathtaking view of Mount Jefferson. It's also home to the county's Old Time Fiddler's Convention celebrated each year. (See our Annual Festivals and Events chapter for more on the convention.)

West Jefferson Park
Church Avenue West, Jefferson, NC
West Jefferson's city park is a pleasant, grassy expanse on the rolling hills behind Main Street. Picnic tables are scattered by the creekside, and a basketball court crowns the hill.

AVERY COUNTY

Banner Elk Town Park
Highway 194, Banner Elk, NC
This city park is behind NationsBank, just north of the stoplight in Banner Elk. A few benches, flowers, and a walkway add pleasant touches to this small city park.

Sunset Park
Beech Mountain Parkway, Banner Elk, NC
This intimate little memorial park on a half acre gives visitors a lovely place to stop and reflect on the incredible natural beauty of mile-high Beech Mountain.

MITCHELL COUNTY

Mitchell Family YMCA
Summit Avenue, Spruce Pine, NC
(828) 765-7766
The Mitchell Family YMCA serves a three-county area. The focal point of the complex is a large ice-skating arena that draws school and camp groups from the region. Junior ice hockey, swimming, basketball, a fitness center, gymnastics, and a variety of sports programs are also offered. Hours of operation vary seasonally.

WATAUGA COUNTY

Blowing Rock Memorial Park
Main Street, Blowing Rock, NC
Picnic tables, a children's playground, and tennis courts fill this picturesque public park in the center of tiny Blowing Rock. Just off the main street, the park lends itself to outdoor lunches and ice-cream cone breaks. The park is also the center of village cultural events.

Boone Greenway Pedestrian Walking and Biking Trail
Boone, NC
The access point for this ambling trail is adjacent to the university parking lot on Dale Street and the Watauga County Parks and Recreation Complex on Complex Drive.

Broyhill Park
off Main Street, Blowing Rock, NC
This serene, beautifully landscaped city park, highlighted by a small, placid lake, is just behind Main Street in Blowing Rock. A walking path, beautiful gazebo, and ducks gliding across the water make this pleasant little park a favorite of local residents and visitors alike. A hiking path actually calls for some hearty climbing on the way back, during which you will pass leafy rhododendrons, a little waterfall, and forestation.

Watauga County Parks and Recreation Department
1012 State Farm Road, Boone, NC
(828) 264-9511
The county parks and recreation department oversees a number of this area's recreational attractions. Countywide schools are home to a number of park facilities, such as lighted tennis courts, lighted athletic fields for football and soccer, outdoor basketball and volleyball courts, and numerous children's play areas.

The Watauga County Swimming Complex on Complex Drive (828-264-0270) is a popular High Country recreation spot. In an area where winter can bring a definite chill, the indoor, heated 25-meter pool, diving pool, and adjoining children's pool are welcome entertainment. It is open daily, year-round, and the public is welcome. Modest fees vary according to age. Season passes are available. A changing schedule of Red Cross swimming instruction, aquacise, senior exercise, and scuba classes is available on request.

Tot Lot Park, in front of the Watauga County Swimming Complex, is a play area for all children. A picnic shelter, volleyball court, and rest rooms are nearby.

An outdoor county pool with a capacity for 60 swimmers is open seasonally from Memorial Day through Labor

Day at Green Valley School off N.C. Highway 194 E. Hours are noon to 6:00 P.M. Tuesday through Saturday and 1:00 to 6:00 P.M. on Sunday.

Howard's Knob Park, open from April 1 to October 31, is at the highest elevation in the city of Boone. To get to this pleasant little park, head west on King Street, turn right across from the Daniel Boone Inn, and proceed to the top of the hill. You'll find picnic tables, wildflowers, and a great view of Boone at this five-acre park.

Central Mountains

BUNCOMBE COUNTY

Asheville Parks and Recreation
Asheville City Hall
(828) 259-5800

Asheville's parks and recreation facilities are scattered throughout the city and provide a multitude of recreational activities and cultural programs for all ages. Many of these are play areas, some with picnic tables and other amenities. The sites are open daily from 6:00 A.M. to 10:00 P.M. and can be used free of charge. Maps of park locations are available from the office of city parks and recreation.

Outdoor public swimming pools are found in Malvern Hills (Sulphur Springs Road) and also on Walton Street. They are open June through August and charge a moderate admission. The pools offer Red Cross Learn to Swim classes, fitness, and lifeguard certification training. Approximately 20 public tennis courts dot the city for year-round use on a first-come, first-served basis. Some of these hard-surface courts are lighted for evening play.

Buncombe County Parks and Recreation
205 College Street, Asheville, NC
(828) 250-4260

This comprehensive county recreation program includes a multitude of services and recreation sites throughout Buncombe County. Athletics is a big part of the program. Softball, soccer, and tennis are available through a number of leagues, teams, and associations in cooperation with or sponsored by the department.

The Aston Park Tennis Center on Hilliard Street (828-255-5193) offers memberships, clinics, private lessons, and regular tournament play. The court facility is free to use and is open beginning in April Monday through Thursday from 9:00 A.M. to 9:00 P.M. and Friday through Sunday from 9:00 A.M. to 7:00 P.M. After Thanksgiving, the center is open Saturday, Sunday, Tuesday, Wednesday, and Thursday from 10:00 A.M. to 6:00 P.M.

Lake Julian District Park off Long Shoals Road is a thermal lake, used as a cooling agent for the CP&L electric facility on its shore. The lake, south of Asheville in the Skyland area, is a family recreation park open year-round for fishing, canoeing, paddleboating, and outdoor games. A children's play area and picnic shelters are also available. Fishing is allowed from shore or by boat for a rental fee. Patrons must provide their own electric motor—gas motors are not allowed. North Carolina fishing laws are enforced, and a local lake permit is required. Hours are 8:00 A.M. to 6:00 P.M. October to March, in April from 8:00 A.M. to 8:00 P.M., from May through August 8:00 A.M. to 9:00 P.M., and in September from 8:00 A.M. to 8:00 P.M.

The Buncombe County Parks and Recreation Department operates a variety of recreational park sites along the French Broad River and at numerous other points in the county. There are also many athletic fields, community centers, and public pools.

The parks and rec department also sponsors a variety of county-wide enrichment classes in the arts and Red Cross swimming instruction. Call the main number provided earlier for more information.

Lake Louise
Lake Louise Drive, Weaverville, NC

Just under a mile from Main Street in this small town north of Asheville is Lake Louise, a humanmade lake developed in 1911. The park once sported a dance pavilion on an island in the middle of the lake.

Back then, a daily trolley line from the big city of Asheville brought dapper gentlemen and ruffle-skirted young ladies to Lake Louise for evening dance socials.

Today, Lake Louise, with its central 40-foot-high fountain, is enjoying a new generation of visitors of all ages. Walkers on the popular lake path can observe an assortment of tree species cultivated by the Tree Board of the Town of Weaverville. You can identify more than 34 kinds, including sycamores, river birch, Japanese maples, flowering cherry, sugar maples, weeping willow, sweet gum, redbud, and Virginia Pine. This place is popular with local school groups with junior botanists in tow.

Lake Louise also offers a children's playground, an outdoor exercise facility, public rest rooms, and picnic shelters for visitors. Hours are 7:00 A.M. to 11:00 P.M. daily year-round.

Lake Tomahawk Park
South Laurel Circle Drive, Black Mountain, NC
(828) 669-2052
This lovely little lake and 20-acre park in a residential area of picturesque Black Mountain was a WPA Depression-era project. Visitors can enjoy the scenic water view, well-trod walking path, landscaping, and resident waterfowl. A community center, public pool, and play areas are part of Lake Tomahawk Park. The park opens around 5:00 A.M. and closes around midnight.

HENDERSON COUNTY

Boyd Park
Main Street, Hendersonville, NC
(828) 697-3079
This city park is within walking distance of downtown. It has a miniature golf course and an activity building used for meetings and events, such as local cat shows. There are also two tennis courts that are open until 11:00 P.M. year-round.

Dana Park
Dana Road, Dana, NC
(828) 685-3546

Dana Park's six acres contain a softball field, a children's playground, and a community building with a fireplace and a complete kitchen, making it a popular spot for family reunions and gatherings. Classes in clogging, fitness and aerobics, and other types of instruction also go on here. Call the park for more details on the classes. This park is 8 miles from downtown Hendersonville.

Edneyville Park
off U.S. Highway 64 E., Edneyville, NC
You'll find this four-acre park tucked behind the Edneyville Volunteer Fire Department off U.S. 64 E., about 10 miles from downtown Hendersonville. It has two tennis courts, a basketball court, a children's playground, a covered picnic shelter, and rest rooms. The Edneyville branch of the Henderson County Library is also here.

Jackson Park
Glover Street or Harris Street, Hendersonville, NC
(828) 697-4884
Jackson Park's 212 acres on the southeast edge of Hendersonville make it the largest county park in Western North Carolina. It has four lighted tennis courts, eight lighted softball/baseball fields, a soccer field, three playgrounds, rest rooms, four covered picnic shelters for 50 to 150 persons, and 20 woodland picnic tables that overlook the playing fields.

There's usually a lot of playing to watch in this heavily used recreation area. The adult softball program usually involves around 76 men's and women's teams, totaling 1,200 participants. The youth soccer, softball, and baseball programs take place here, too, along with the Four Season Senior Games. A summer day camp that includes crafts, organized games, and planned activities is operated at Jackson as well as at other county parks for children ages 5 to 11. Call for more information.

A 1.5-mile nature trail meanders through part of the park. This pretty, peaceful path takes you through hard-wood and pine forests and wildflower and wetlands meadows. Dogwoods and silver-bells bloom in the spring, and sourwoods bloom in the summer. Self-guiding brochures that help with plant and tree identification are available.

The park also hosts a number of special events: On Easter weekend 10,000 eggs are hidden for the children to find. Fourth of July is celebrated with softball and horseshoe tournaments, children's games, music, food and an impressive fireworks display after dark. On the first Saturday in October, Farm-City Day brings city and farm folks together here. There are displays of antique and modern farm equipment (including draft horses), tractor pulls, live-stock exhibits, a petting zoo, a Civil War reenactment, chainsaw carving demonstra-tions, live mountain music, and much more. On the weekend before Halloween, a scary "Haunted Trail" winds through the woods, and there are games, treats, and a costume contest. In December the park is decorated with luminarias. (See our Annual Festivals and Events chapter or call the park's num-ber for more information.)

The entrance gate is also accessible from Four Seasons Boulevard by turning onto Harris Street, or you can turn onto Glover Street from the Spartanburg High-way (U.S. Highway 176) to reach the park's Glover Street entrance. The park is open daily from 7:30 A.M. to 11:00 P.M.

King Memorial Park and Green Meadows Park
Seventh Avenue, Hendersonville, NC
(828) 697-4968

The combined facilities of these two parks include the Mud Creek Nature Walk, a playground, a softball field, covered bas-ketball courts, and the Green Meadows Activity Building, which hosts community meetings, pet shows, and the like.

Patton Park
off Fourth Avenue, Hendersonville, NC
(828) 697-3081

The main attraction here is an outdoor Olympic-size swimming pool operated by the city. In May the pool opens on week-ends only; the regular schedule begins in June and runs until November. There is a small admission fee.

Stoney Mountain Activity Center
Stoney Mountain Road, Hendersonville, NC
(828) 697-4722

Activity is the right word for this center. All kinds of classes are taught here, including dance, tumbling, fitness, and aerobics. To find the center drive north out of Hendersonville on U.S. 25, turn left onto Stoney Mountain Road, and drive a mile; the entrance will be on the right.

YMCA
810 Sixth Avenue W., Hendersonville, NC
(828) 692-5774

Just a few blocks from downtown, this complex is one of the more popular places in Hendersonville. It includes a gymnasium, four lighted tennis courts (two are Har-Tru composition courts), and a weight-training/wellness center with free weights and Nautilus and aerobic equipment. There is also a five-lane, 25-meter, heated indoor swimming pool as well as a whirlpool and sauna. The Y offers classes and activities for both chil-dren and adults.

POLK COUNTY

Polk County Recreation Department
Park Street, Columbus, NC
(828) 894-8199

The Polk County Recreation Department, which is dedicated to serving citizens of all ages, offers programs in aerobics, youth basketball, youth volleyball, line dancing, men's basketball, and stretch-and-strengthen exercises at Stearns Gym on Walker Street. Gibson Park on Park Street boasts a baseball field and swim-ming pool. The pool, open from June through August, offers family passes, swimming lessons, and water aerobics.

TRANSYLVANIA COUNTY

Brevard College
400 North Broad Street, Brevard, NC
(828) 883-8292
Many of the recreation facilities at Brevard College, including the indoor swimming pool, are open to the public through inexpensive continuing education classes that include aerobics, water aerobics, beginning rock climbing, and even golf. The campus is also a popular place for runners and walkers.

Champion Park
Rosman, NC
(828) 884-7977
The swimming pool here in Rosman is open from early June until September seven days a week until dark. Champion Park also offers a softball field, a multipurpose court, a playground, a picnic shelter, and a river access site.

Franklin Park
Lakeview Drive, Brevard, NC
(828) 884-6959
Brevard's public swimming pool, open in the summer, is within walking distance of downtown, just 1 block off East Main Street. You'll also find a fine new playground with slides, swings, modern monkey bars, and a special area for younger children.

Silvermont Park
East Main Street, Brevard, NC
Open seven days a week from 8:30 A.M. until 10:00 P.M., Silvermont has two lighted basketball courts, three tennis courts, a playground, a picnic shelter, and a walking path located on the grounds of a historic mansion. Mountain Music Night with a live local artist is free of charge every Thursday from 7:30 until 10:00 P.M. (See our Arts and Culture chapter for more on Silvermont.)

South Broad Park
South Broad Street, Brevard, NC
The small picnic area found at this arboretum is a lovely place to bring a lunch.

It's right next to a large multipurpose playing field.

Transylvania Activities Center
1150 Ecusta Road, Brevard, NC
(828) 884-3156
Headquarters of the Transylvania Parks and Recreation Department, this park also contains a gymnasium, two lighted softball fields, two soccer fields, a playground, and a concession area with rest rooms.

The park's program includes organized sports and fitness, including a children's soccer program, a softball league in the fall, aerobics and jazz-aerobics, kung fu classes, a ballroom dance club, senior games and silver arts, volleyball, and children's tumbling and gymnastics. The county also sponsors youth dances, ballroom dances, and summer day camps, as well as Holiday Crafts Week and Halloween Fest.

Southern Mountains

CHEROKEE COUNTY

Andrews Recreation Park
Andrews, NC
(828) 321-2135
Andrews Recreation Park has a beach volleyball court, basketball and tennis courts, a softball field, playground equipment, and an area for horseshoe games. In addition there is a Little League baseball field, picnic areas, swimming pools, and the Andrews Community Center, which contains a large room with a stage, a smaller meeting room, and kitchen and rest room facilities. The park is wheelchair accessible.

Ferebee Park
Bristol Avenue, Andrews, NC
(828) 321-2135
This park provides a quiet and restful picnic area, playground, and rest rooms just up from Main Street.

Hall Memorial Park
First Street, Andrews, NC
(828) 321-2135
Right next to the Andrews Chamber of Commerce, this new park and its gazebo play host to summertime country and gospel concerts and many other events. The Valleytown Cultural Arts Center built the park.

Hiwassee River Park
Murphy, NC
(828) 837-6617
The colorful displays of flowers, bushes, and trees were planted and are maintained by volunteers with Cherokee County CARE. It features a walking path, benches, and picnic tables.

Konehete Park
103 Konehete Street, Murphy, NC
(828) 837-6617
This large city park offers a swimming pool, four lighted tennis courts, and four baseball/softball fields (three with lights). There are also areas for fishing, volleyball, two soccer fields, and outdoor basketball courts.

Organized activities include swim teams, football, basketball, baseball, softball, and soccer leagues for children, youth, and adults. Wrestling, gymnastics, aerobics, line dancing, basketball, and other events are held in the park's Old Rock Gym. Runners and walkers can use the trail or sidewalks throughout Konehete Park or use the running track at the Murphy High School.

Murphy Garden Club Park
Murphy, NC
(828) 837-6617
You'll find this park next to the Valley River near the post office. Its convenient location, picnic tables, and barbecue stands make it a favorite spot to enjoy lunch or to just sit in a car and watch the river flow past.

Valley River Park
Andrews, NC
(828) 321-2135
On the banks of the Valley River right within the city limits of Andrews, this park offers fishing, a softball and baseball field, and a picnic area.

CLAY COUNTY

Clay County Recreation Park
N.C. Highway 175, Hayesville, NC
(828) 389-3532
This popular public park, not far from the 140-foot-high Chatuge Dam, is on N.C. 175 on Lake Chatuge (see our information on this lake in the Lakes section of this chapter). The park has 25 campsites, picnic and swimming areas, a boat launch, and a ballpark.

GRAHAM COUNTY

Graham County Recreation Complex
Knight Street, Robbinsville, NC
(828) 479-7983
The county has a large complex formed by the elementary and middle schools, the public library, and the community and senior citizens center. All the buildings are located in the same area.

This complex also contains tennis courts and a swimming pool. The pool is open from June through August; there is a small admission fee.

HAYWOOD COUNTY

Town of Canton Recreation Park
Penland Street, Canton, NC
(828) 646-3411
This city park, roughly 17 acres in size, contains three picnic sheds and numerous outside picnic tables, two outdoor basketball courts, four lighted tennis courts, play equipment both for small children and teenagers, and two Little League baseball fields. The park's swimming pool and wading pool are open from the middle of May until the first of September; admission for

kids 17 and younger is 50 cents; 18 and older, $1.00. Concessions are available at the pool.

Canton also has an entertainment shelter and bandstand where summer programs are held. Around the park is a 1-mile walking and jogging trail along the banks of the Pigeon River. The parks department uses the sports fields at area public schools for team sports.

Town of Waynesville Recreation Park
128 West Marshall Street, Waynesville, NC
(828) 456-9541, (828) 456-8577
There's plenty of action at this park, which consists of six hard-surface tennis counts, two outdoor basketball courts, a swimming pool, two picnic areas with shelters, a playground, three softball/baseball fields, two sand volleyball courts, a modified golf driving range, soccer fields, shuffleboard, a quarter-mile track and fitness trail, a horse-show ring, and a recreation building. The City Parks and Recreation Department, which runs the complex, also sponsors all kinds of youth and adult team sports and special events that include an open tennis championship, a trout fishing festival, an Easter egg hunt, and judo and bridge tournaments. For senior citizens there are craft and exercise classes, trips, health programs, and meals (see our Retirement chapter). There's a full complement of fitness, hobby, and education classes for other adults and children, too.

JACKSON COUNTY

The Jackson County Parks and Recreation Department (828-586-6333) operates eight facilities. With 12 full-time staff members and an annual budget of around $250,000, it is able to offer lots of activities year-round. Use the central phone number to get more information on the following areas:

Caney Fork Creek Park
Caney Fork Road, Caney Fork, NC
You'll find this little park 7 miles up Caney Fork Road next to the Caney Fork Commu-

nity Center. It has a lighted basketball court, a softball field, shuffleboard courts, horseshoe pits, and a picnic shelter and tables.

Cashiers Community Center
off U.S. Highway 64, Cashiers, NC
(828) 743-9990
This small park and complex has a lighted ballfield, lighted tennis courts, an indoor basketball court, and an outdoor swimming pool (open from June through August; admission is $2.00). Senior citizens' meals are served in the community center building, which is also available for meetings. The complex also includes the Cashiers Child Development Center, which provides day care for 35 children ages 2 months to 5 years.

Cullowhee County Park
off N.C. Highway 107
Cullowhee, NC
This 30-acre park has four soccer fields, two baseball fields, outdoor basketball courts, picnic shelters, a playground, a creek walk and nature trail, and a park's administration building that will also house a recreation center and gymnasium.

Dillsboro River Park
Dillsboro, NC
Canoers and kayakers can access the Tuckasegee River through this one-acre park. The park has picnic tables.

East LaPorte River Park
N.C. Highway 107 S.
The seven acres that form this park on the Tuckasegee River include river access for tubing, canoeing, and swimming; rest rooms; picnic shelters; a multipurpose basketball court; a beach volleyball court; and a greenway for free play and hiking trails.

Fairview Youth Complex
Fairview Road, Sylva, NC
Three youth baseball fields, a concession stand, rest rooms, a score tower, and picnic facilities make up this complex between Sylva and Cullowhee.

Mark Watson Park
Old School Road, Sylva, NC

This county park has four lighted tennis courts, two adult softball fields, a double-size asphalt basketball court, a play-ground, horseshoe pits, a picnic shelter, and a fairly large greenway for free play.

Ralph J. Andrews County Park
Glenville, NC
(828) 743-3923

Built on land near the Glenville dam donated to the county by the Nantahala Power Company, this 78-acre park offers full RV hookups, tent camping, picnicking, hot showers, and boat ramp access to Lake Glenville. To reach it go about 1.5 miles north of the Glenville Post Office until you come to Pine Creek Road on the left. Follow the signs to the park entrance, approximately 2 miles down the road.

Sylva Swimming Pool
Municipal Drive, Sylva, NC
(828) 743-9715

This outdoor, 185,000-gallon pool has high and low diving boards. It is open from June through August. Admission is $2.00 for those older than 12 and $1.00 for children 12 and younger.

Western Carolina University
N.C. Highway 107, Cullowhee, NC
(828) 227-7317

Recreation facilities at the university include the Reid Health and Physical Education Building, Breese Gymnasium, A. K. Hinds University Center, and Ramsey Regional Activity Center. Among the indoor and outdoor sports available here are tennis, volleyball, basketball, swimming, bowling, handball, racquetball, softball, badminton, table tennis, and archery. The university also promotes extensive student intramural and athletic programs and offers Tiny Tot and Youth Swim programs in the summer. The swim program is open to the public. Also open to the public are continuing education courses in yoga, t'ai chi ch'uan, hydrorobics, and other fitness classes.

MACON COUNTY

The Arrowood Pool
SR 1310, Franklin, NC
(828) 524-4446

This pool, open to the public, is at the LBJ Civilian Conservation Center. To get there, go west out of Franklin for 3 miles and turn right at the LBJ JOB CORPS/WAYAH BALD sign. Take the first left onto Wayah Road (SR 1310).

Highlands Recreation Park
U.S. Highway 64, Highlands, NC
(828) 526-3556

The recreation center here is open to the public from 8:00 A.M. to 10:00 P.M. Monday through Saturday and noon to 6:00 P.M. on Sunday. It offers swimming (admission is $2.00), a Nautilus room ($5.00 a visit, $20.00 for a month), tennis courts ($1.00 per person per hour; courts may be reserved one day in advance), and aerobics ($4.00 a class). You can join a cardiovascular program or play softball, baseball, volleyball, basketball, bridge, and duplicate bridge here. Classes are taught in tumbling, rappelling, and wrestling. There is a picnic shelter with a playground nearby. The parks department also sponsors a Fourth of July Celebration, com-

---

As viewed from the Macon County Osage overlook, the mountains seem to go on forever in shifting hues of blue and green. At certain times during the year, the mountains are totally shrouded in blue, which gives both the mountains and the Blue Valley Overlook its name. For a view you won't forget, drive 5.5 miles south of Highlands on N.C. Highway 106. Just a bit farther down this same highway, you'll come to the Osage Overlook with another great view of the Blue Valley.

---

plete with a parade and fireworks, as well as a summer playground program, various bazaars, and a craft festival.

Macon County Recreation Park
U.S. Highway 441 S., Franklin, NC
(828) 349-2090
The many attractions at this large and well-maintained park include softball fields, indoor and outdoor basketball courts, shuffleboard and tennis courts, horseshoes, a children's playground, a loop walking trail, a gymnasium, a swimming pool, two outdoor picnic shelters, and four conference/party rooms. The community building here is open from 8:00 A.M. to 5:00 P.M. daily.

SWAIN COUNTY

Alarka Community Park
Alarka Road, Alarka, NC
A few years ago, when an old school building burned in this community west of Bryson City, the town used the land as the site for a fire department and a park with a playground, a picnic area, a nice jogging trail, and a pavilion.

The Bryson City Island Park
Access on Island Street, Bryson City, NC
As early as 1890 the editor of the *Swain County Herald,* the county's first newspaper, urged the county commissioners to strike a bargain for Island Park, as he called the seven-acre island in the Tuckasegee River, "where citizens may find a pleasant rendezvous far from the noise and bustle of city life." However it wasn't until 1986, almost a century later, that Bryson City's downtown island, reached by a swinging bridge, finally became a park.

A lot of history has happened here. It's said, for example, that one of Jesse James's gang members lived on the island for a while (see Iron Foot Island Close-up).

A lighted trail circles the island, and tags identify many of the native plants and wildflowers along the trail. Boy Scouts

who used the island for a camping site and headquarters in the 1930s and 1940s built the interpretive center. Island Park has a launching site for canoes and kayaks and areas for picnicking and fishing.

River Front Park
Island Street, Bryson City, NC
This half-acre park that runs along the Tuckasegee is the site of the town's Riverfest (see our Annual Festivals and Events chapter). It also has a picnic area, including a covered pavilion and a walking trail. Another of Bryson City's parks, the small Ela River Park, also on the Tuckasegee, is used mostly for picnicking and fishing.

Swain County Recreation Park
West Deep Creek Road, Bryson City, NC
(828) 488-6159
This attractive 34-acre park has a lighted field for baseball and softball, four lighted tennis courts, a basketball court, two playgrounds, shuffleboard and volleyball courts, horseshoe pits, a pavilion and picnic area, and a jogging trail. There is also an outdoor swim complex with an Olympic-size pool, an intermediate pool, and a kiddie pool. The pools are open June through August for a small admission price. Season tickets are available.

The list of organized activities includes several softball leagues, volleyball, soccer, aerobics, line dancing, tennis, and swimming lessons. Youth programs feature karate, winter ski instruction, ball programs, and a billiards league. The parks department also sponsors events such as the Christmas Extravaganza.

Plans for the next decade include the construction of a community center that will house an eight-lane bowling center, an Olympic-size indoor swimming pool, a double gymnasium, a teen center, racquetball courts, a fitness center, a commercial kitchen, a large multipurpose room, arts and crafts classrooms, a large conference room, and a walking track.

Iron Foot Island

Iron Foot Island, Bryson city's seven-acre island park, is just downstream from the Cherokee's Old Mother Town of Kituhawa. Several Cherokee battles with other tribes and whites were fought in the island's immediate vicinity.

The most famous battle occurred in the 1700s and involved the Shawano, a tribe the Cherokee had fought for many years. A noted Shawano leader, Tawa-li-ukwanun, led a raid on the town of Tikwal-itsi, near the present site of Bryson City. A Cherokee conjurer named Dead-wood-lighter forecast that the raiders would set an ambush on the island. Some of the

Cherokee warriors took his advice and forded the river above the island, entering the site from the rear. But some didn't listen and went straight up the north bank of the river, where they were taken "like fish in a trap." After several bloody encounters, the Shawano were driven up Deep Creek and over the Smokies at Clingman's Dome.

The island was named for Ralph Clark, alias, "Iron Foot." while riding with Jesse James, tradition has it, one foot had been shot off during a train robbery. To equalize his gait an iron stirrup was attached to the limb with the missing foot. Clark lived on the island as a hermit.

THE LAKES

Most of our mountain lakes are found in the central and southern mountains. Some of the smaller ones are private or in residential resort communities. Here we've listed some of the more popular lakes that have public access areas.

Central Mountains

BUNCOMBE COUNTY

Lake Julian
Overlook Road extension access off N.C. Highway 146

Lake Julian is a thermal lake used as a cooling agent for Carolina Power and Light. Therefore the lake is deliciously warm, often reaching a scorching 95 degrees in summer! You might find the power plant that looms over one side of the lake a bit disconcerting, but the water never goes below 50 degrees in winter—the best time for fishing here is between October and March.

Several covered picnic areas make this a favorite spot for family reunions and company gatherings. Picnic shelters range in size from four to 10 picnic tables and can be rented for about $20 and $35 for Buncombe County residents. Nonresidents pay roughly $35 and $45. A children's playground, volleyball court, and horseshoe pit provide some free landlubber entertainment. Paddleboats, fishing boats, or canoes for can be rented for under $10 an hour if you are a county resident. If not, then expect to pay about double. If you bring your own boat, there is a launch fee of under $5.00 per day. When there's room, a boathouse and dock can hold your sailboat for approximately $120 (residents) and $180 (nonresidents) per year. The lake is well stocked with bass, crappie, catfish, brim, and talapia, and the price for fishing is nominal.

Lake Julian Park is open from 8:00 A.M. to 9:00 P.M. April through August, 8:00 A.M. to 8:00 P.M. in September, and 8:00 A.M. to 6:00 P.M. October through March. It is closed on Thanksgiving, Christmas, and New Year's Day. For more information, call the ranger station at (828) 684-0376.

Lake Powhatan Recreation Area
FR 3484
(800) 280-CAMP

Lake Powhatan is a popular destination with a lot to offer besides the pretty little lake for fishing (it also has a swimming beach and a lifeguard on duty). There are 96 sites for tents and trailers (no hookups), a trailer dump station, picnic tables with grills, rest rooms with flush toilets, hiking trails, information hosts, and a central supply of drinking water. The campground is open from mid-April through October, and the Forest Service provides numerous activities during the summer season. (See the "Camping" section in this chapter.)

Powhatan is in the Bent Creek Experimental Forest with a system of hiking trails that can get confusing, so pick up a map from the campground office at the entrance to the area. The Western North Carolina Arboretum with its 10 state champion big trees is near Lake Powhatan.

RUTHERFORD COUNTY

Lake Lure
U.S. Highway 74

This sparkling jewel is one of the most picturesque lakes you'll find anywhere—Chimney Rock Park and other spectacular mountains tower over it, and its 1,500 acres include 27 miles of shoreline. You'll find a number of marinas here, but before you haul your boat to the lake, you should be aware that launch fees have been set high to lessen lake congestion. Also, because of its beauty, the shoreline here is quite developed. Still, you'll find a protected, sandy beach area for public use. It

is in the center of the Lake Lure Recreation Area, across from Lake Lure Inn.

Lake Lure Fun Center is filled with opportunities. It is located directly on the public beach. There is an admission charge that provides access to the swimming area. Within the Fun Center are climbing areas for kids, slides into the lake, and many other activities. You can rent a snappy little scooter from Hickory Nut Cycles and explore the roads of Lake Lure/Chimney Rock area. Helmets are required and supplied. You must have a valid driver's license.

A water shuttle service operates between the Resort Marina and the Lake Lure Marina. From the Lake Lure Marina, you can easily walk to the Fun Center and the beach. Exploratory boat excursions of Lake Lure are available through Lake Lure Tours. Their toll free number is (877) FUN-4ALL.

Southern Mountains

CHEROKEE COUNTY

Cherokee Lake
Access off N.C. Highway 294

Operated by the Tennessee Valley Authority, this small lake, about a mile in circumference, is fed by the backwaters of Lake Hiwassee. Its new pier is a great place to take children fishing, and the pier is designed for easy access for disabled individuals.

Lake Hiwassee
Access off U.S. Highway 64

Built in 1935, the TVA's 307-foot-high, 1,376-foot-long Hiwassee Dam is the highest overspill dam in the United States. It blocks the Hiwassee River to form the center of recreation and fishing in Cherokee County—the 22-mile-long, 6,090-acre Lake Hiwassee. Its 163-mile shoreline is almost completely surrounded by the Nantahala National Forest. In 1955 a second generating unit was added to the dam, along with the world's largest electric motor and reversible pump-turbine, which enable water from the dam to be used to generate electricity during peak hours. During off-hours, the water is then pumped 205 feet back into the Hiwassee reservoir for reuse.

The lake is known for its smallmouth bass and walleyes, but fishermen will also find largemouth bass, bluegill, and crappie here.

The Hanging Dog Recreation Area is less than 4 miles northwest of Murphy off U.S. 64. The area features a 26-site campground, a picnic area, hiking trails, and a boat launch ramp. (See "Camping" section for more information.) There are also a couple of marinas in the area.

CLAY COUNTY

Chatuge Lake
Access off U.S. Highway 64
Stretching from Clay County into Georgia, Chatuge Lake, with its gradual 132-mile shoreline, backed up by high mountain peaks, reminds us of a Swiss alpine lake. It provides endless hours of water sports and fishing and presents some of the most beautiful views in the county. Thirty-two species of fish have been caught here; smallmouth and largemouth bass, spotted bass, and sunfish are the important sport catches. Striped/white bass hybrids are also stocked annually to control the gizzard shad population, and threadfin shad are stocked periodically to augment the prey bass.

Built in 1941 by the Tennessee Valley Authority, Chatuge has been called the crown jewel of the TVA system because of its picturesque setting. It is also one of the most developed of those lakes, with more than 76 miles of shoreline in private hands. There are three commercial marinas in the area.

The popular Clay County Recreation Park, not far from the 144-foot-high Chatuge Dam, sits on the reservoir 6.2 miles from Hayesville on U.S. 64 (turn

right onto N.C. 175). Here you'll find 25 campsites, picnic shelters, a ballfield, a swimming area, and a boat launch ramp.

Another good facility on the lake, this one in the Tusquittee Ranger District of the Nantahala Forest, is the Jackrabbit Mountain Recreation Area. It is on a pine-wooded peninsula that has three camping loops with 103 campsites, a swimming beach with shower facilities, hiking trails, two picnic areas, and a boat launch ramp. To get to the Jackrabbit Mountain Recreation Area, drive 2.5 miles down N.C. 175 from U.S. 64; turn right on SR 1155.

GRAHAM COUNTY

Cheoah Lake
Access along N.C. Highway 28
This long and narrow Graham County lake is just a few miles west of Fontana Lake. Lying tranquilly between steep green hills, it is reminiscent of a Scandinavian fjord. The water is so clear, you can usually see right down to the bottom. A turn onto U.S. 129 from N.C. 28 will bring you to the 225-foot Cheoah Dam, which was built between 1917 and 1919 on the Little Tennessee River. In 1930 the Calderwood Dam farther down river in Tennessee formed Calderwood Lake, which is contiguous to its twin, Cheoah.

Santeetlah Lake
Access off U.S. Highway 129 N.
This emerald-green lake in the center of Graham County is popular with both motorboaters and canoeists. Santeetlah has a reputation as one of the best bass-fishing lakes in the area, and pike and crappie are also plentiful. Three public boat ramps are located along its shores. A popular one is at Cheoah Point off U.S. 129 N., just outside Robbinsville near the ranger station (see the list of ranger stations in our Forests and Parks chapter). Cheoah Point also has a campground with 26 campsites, water, flush toilets, a picnic area, and a boat ramp. It is open from April 15 until October 31. (See "Camping"

in this chapter.) To get to Cheoah Point, take U.S. 129 N. for 7 miles, turn left at the sign, and go 0.8 mile.

JACKSON COUNTY

Lake Glenville
N.C. Highway 107

Lake Glenville Dam, 4 miles north of Cashiers, was built on the Tuckasegee River in Jackson County in 1941. It was renamed Lake Thorpe in 1951 after Nantahala Power's first president, J. E. S. Thorpe. Today it's marked as Lake Thorpe on many, but not all, maps, but it's still Lake Glenville to most people in this area. The 6-mile-long lake covers 1,462 acres and offers 26 miles of shoreline. At an elevation of nearly 3,500 feet, it's the highest major lake in the eastern United States. Lake Glenville is a great place to cruise, canoe, swim, ski, and fish. Mountain trout, walleye, brim, pike, and largemouth and smallmouth bass are the fish you can expect to catch here.

Three marinas in the Glenville community rent pontoon, fishing, and ski boats. These are well marked by signs on N.C. 107. The Ralph J. Andrews County Park also provides boat access to the lake. This reservoir is the source of water for a hydroelectric plant at the 1,200-foot level, said to be one of the highest facilities in the East. To visit it, turn off of N.C. 107 onto Pine Creek Road and drive about 2 miles past the Ralph J. Andrews County Park to the power plant. The beach area near the dam is a favorite spot for swimming and sunbathing.

MACON COUNTY

Cliffside Lake Recreation Area and
Vanhook Glade Campground
Access off U.S. Highway 64 W.

Cliffside—a pretty and popular little lake in the Nantahala National Forest—is a great place to picnic, swim (the water is cold!), boat, hike, and fish (mostly for rainbow and brook trout). Here you'll find 17 picnic tables, two picnic shelters, a bathhouse with cold-water showers and flush toilets and the Clifftop Vista Shelter.

There are numerous hiking trails in the area, including an interpretive loop around the lake. Cliffside Vista trail climbs 3 miles to an overlook of the lake. Tent camping used to be allowed here, but all camping has now been moved to the nearby Vanhook Glade Campground, though campers may use Cliffside Lake and showers. (See our "Camping" section in this chapter for more information on the Vanhook Glade Campground.)

There is a $3.00 day-use parking fee at Cliffside from May 1 through October 31.

Nantahala Lake
Access off Wayah Road

This large lake, which provides electricity for the Nantahala Power and Light Company, is in a remote area of Macon County, reached by the paved-but-very-windswept, two-lane Wayah Road (SR 1310). The regular releases of water that supply the fast rides for rafters and kayakers on the Nantahala River cause the lake's water level to vary widely. Nevertheless fishing is good here. In fact Nantahala Lake is the only lake in the state that contains Kokanee salmon, a freshwater hybrid of the sockeye salmon. There are two public access sites: Rocky Branch, on the east side of the lake just off Wayah Road; and in the Choga area on the lake's western arm, off FR 440. There's a school and a volunteer fire department in the nearby Nantahala Community but no stores to speak of, so stock up ahead of time with what you need for an outing here.

SWAIN COUNTY

Fontana Lake
U.S. Highway 129

At an elevation of 1,710 feet, this deepwater lake reaches 30 beautiful miles into the mountains, covering 10,530 acres when full. Much longer than it is wide (it has a 240-mile shoreline), Fontana runs east and west with the Great Smoky Mountains National Park on the north and the Nantahala National Forest on the south.

The lake was created in the 1940s by the Tennessee Valley Authority's Fontana Dam (see the Fontana Dam listing in our Attractions chapter). It's great for boating, waterskiing, fishing, and exploring. You'll find public boat launches on Fontana's south shore. There are also boat docks at the Fontana Village Resort (see our Resorts chapter), along with sight-seeing cruises and boat rentals, including Wave Runners, bass boats, houseboats, pontoon boats, and ski boats. The lake is home to abundant smallmouth and largemouth bass, native trout, and walleye. You'll also find white bass, muskie (some 4 feet or more in length), and a number of panfish.

WHITE-WATER RAFTING AND KAYAKING

Western North Carolina and its adjoining states have some of the country's most thrilling white water. We've described some of the most popular rivers for rafting and kayaking in this section, listing them in alphabetical order.

Trips on all these rivers can be booked though any number of white-water rafting companies that provide guides and instruction. Children must weigh at least 60 pounds before being permitted to raft (because that's how big they've got to be to fit into a life jacket safely). Some companies also rent rafts, canoes, and kayaks and offer canoe and kayak clinics. Individual rates for rafting trips range from around $25 to $50. Rates are cheaper on weekdays and for groups. An overnight trip on the Chattooga that includes camping out on the river and four meals will run about $125. The following are just a few of the white-water runners in the region. Some run trips in other states and other countries. (Also see our section at the end of this chapter for other outfitters, many of which include white-water rafting in their services.)

Blue Ridge Rafting
U.S. Highways 25/70, Hot Springs, NC
(828) 622-3544, (800) 303-RAFT

Carolina Outfitters Rafting
12121 U.S. Highway 19 W., Bryson City, NC
(828) 488-6345, (800) 468-7238

Nantahala Outdoor Center
11044 U.S. Highway 19 W., Bryson City, NC
(828) 488-2175, (800) 232-7238

Wahoos Adventures
3385 U.S. Highway 321, Boone, NC
(828) 262-5774, (800) 444-RAFT

THE RIVERS

The Chattooga River

The Chattooga, made famous by the movie *Deliverance*, can produce some of the best white water in the Southeast and is one of our personal rafting favorites. Designated as a Wild and Scenic River by Congress in 1974, the Chattooga has its headwaters in the North Carolina Mountains and flows south to form the boundary between South Carolina's Sumter National Forest and Georgia's Chattahoochee National Forest. There is a 6-mile "floating section" from an access point on S.C. Highway 28 about 1.5 miles from its border with Georgia. This stretch is also open to canoers and tubers, and while it can be a real challenge, it's great for family rafting trips with children or for youth groups.

One section of the Chattooga has been designated as Section IV. It provides a really exciting raft ride. You'll get great wilderness scenery, steep and technical rapids and frequent ledges and waterfalls, such as the super-rush of Five Falls. Check with the guide companies for more information. Enjoy the outdoors, but don't venture beyond your capabilities.

The French Broad River

The French Broad is one of the world's oldest rivers, and you seem to keep running into it or one of its many forks—including the North Fork, the East Fork, the West Fork, and the Middle Fork—almost anywhere you travel in the valleys of the central mountains. It was not named, as some think, after a Parisian lady. The French Broad got its name in the seventeenth century when explorers realized that unlike the area's other rivers, this one flowed to the west toward the land claimed by the French. To the Cherokee, it was the "Long Man," and its many forks were called "Chattering Children."

Longer, warmer, and wider than many mountain rivers, the French Broad offers rapids that range from class II to class V. Class II offers slow moving waters good for floating and drifting. The river becomes more active as the nomenclature increases. Class V rapids, therefore, require more expertise in the fast moving water. How challenging the river is depends on the amount of rainfall and the season. High water and big waves occur most often in the spring and early summer; in midsummer and fall it's usually a more gentle river that's better for canoeing and family outings.

The Nantahala River

Because the Nantahala River is a controlled-release river from the Nantahala

When white-water rafting for the first time, pay attention to everything your guide says. Try not to panic if you get in trouble. Always remember the most important thing—if you fall in, keep your feet up and float. Do not try to stand— you may get caught in the rocks and drown in as little as three feet of water, under the rushing force of the current.

Dam upstream, it has usually consistent white water from spring until fall. Its clear and quite cold waters rush the rider for 9 miles through the spectacular Nantahala Gorge in the Nantahala Forest. This is one of the most heavily used white-water rivers in the region, with a constant flow of rafters and kayakers who are fun to watch even if you don't care to join in the sport. Typical raft trips include class III rapids at Nantahala Falls.

The New River

The New River is one of the few north-flowing rivers in America. This river runs through the geographically remote Alleghany and Ashe Counties. Though one of the oldest rivers in the world, the New River was named by surveyor Peter Jefferson (Thomas's father) who was surprised to find this "new" river behind the mountains. The North and South Forks of the river flow over 100 miles through forested mountains and valleys. They join just south of the Virginia state line, and the river continues through Virginia. Because of its scenic beauty and recreational value, a 26-mile stretch of the South Fork has been designated a National Scenic River.

The headwaters are shallow with a few mild rapids, allowing for easy paddling. This river is ideal for family fun—for large groups and less-experienced canoers and kayakers. Tubing is great on this river; it allows you to meander downstream at a relaxed pace. Children love tubing, and many outfitters can supply you with dual tubes, allowing Mom or Dad to share the tube with a smaller child. Fishing and swimming are also excellent in this river.

The Nolichucky River

The Nolichucky River that runs through a gorge in the Pisgah National Forest in North Carolina and the Cherokee National Forest in Tennessee has few rivals in the

East during the high waters of early spring. Calm pools along the way allow you to catch your breath from some of the adrenaline-pumping rapids you'll have come through. The rafting season here is from March through October.

The Pigeon River

The Pigeon River in the heart of the Smokies near Gatlinburg and Pigeon Forge, Tennessee, has been considered a "dead" river for nearly 40 years, due to pollution and electric power generation. Now new regulations are restoring its health and requiring the power company to pump 1,200 cubic feet of water per second through the gorge. The upper part of the Pigeon offers exciting class III and class IV rapids; the lower section is better suited to the inexperienced and to families with children.

CANOEING

Mountain lakes, including most of those mentioned earlier, are excellent places to go canoeing. Experienced canoeists also like to paddle "white-water rafting and kayaking" rivers. (No canoeing is allowed, however, on the Chattooga until it crosses the Georgia-South Carolina line.) The New, Davidson, and Green Rivers are also popular, but the French Broad, along with its many tributaries, is probably the favorite and has been designated as a canoe trail by the state. This river forms near Rosman, where the North, West, Middle, and East Forks of the French Broad meet; then it gathers force and below Asheville becomes a wide, sweeping waterway that at times can demand some solid canoeing experience.

If you are inexperienced or simply want assistance with your trip, several companies in the area are outfitters specifically for canoeing. Consult our Outfitters section at the end of this chapter.

French Broad River Access Areas

Blantyre River Park, Old Blantyre Road

This four-acre park on the western boundary of Henderson and Transylvania Counties off U.S. 64 has river access and a canoe landing ramp. Future plans call for picnic tables and an open recreation area.

Buncombe County River Parks

There are several river parks in Buncombe County. South of Asheville, three parks—Hominy Creek River Park, Bent Creek River Park, and Glen Bridge River Park—hug the French Broad along N.C. Highway 191 and offer easy access. The Ledge River Park is north of town off N.C. Highway 251. Water picks up speed here.

Champion Park
U.S. Highway 64

You can put your canoe in at this park or access the river just west of Rosman, where U.S. 64 W. crosses the North Fork of the French Broad. These accesses put you in the quieter stretch of the French Broad as it meanders through woods and farms.

Hap Simpson Park
U.S. Highway 276

From Island Ford it's 13 miles to this park, just south of Brevard. It's a small, pleasant park with picnic tables and river access. A 15-mile paddle from here will take you to the Blantyre River Park, mentioned earlier.

Island Ford Access Area
off U.S. Highway 64 W.

To reach this area 13 miles downstream from Champion Park, turn off U.S. 64 W. onto Island Ford Road just a short distance outside Brevard. There's a large sign marking the site at the bridge across the river on Island Ford.

Tracking Station
off N.C. Highway 215

During the spring and after a rain, sections of the North Fork of the French Broad are runnable, but only by the very experienced canoeist. Cutting through a gorge on the eastern edge of the Nantahala National Forest, the trip is 7.2 miles from the access point by the bridge at the old tracking station just off N.C. Highway 215 (SR 1326) to the access point on U.S. 64 at Island Ford Road near Brevard mentioned in the Island Ford description earlier. In that distance the river drops 390 feet with a difficulty factor generally of 4 to 5 (two areas rate a 6). Before you attempt this run, make sure that the river gauge on the south side of the bridge at U.S. 64 is at least three inches above 0. You need that much water for a reasonably safe journey on the North Fork.

ℹ️ *White-water rafting, canoeing, mountain biking, or horseback riding can all be so much fun that you keep at it a little too long. When aching muscles or sunburns act up, check out the Health Care chapter for medical facilities to help you get back to normal. First aid can often be obtained from your outfitter or guide, but don't count on them having much more than the basics.*

Westfield River Park
Fanning Bridge Road

There are plans to further develop this 19-acre park, which now has river access, a canoe landing camp, and a recreation area. Fanning Bridge Road is off N.C. 280 at the northern boundary of Henderson and Buncombe Counties.

FISHING

No matter where you are in the Western North Carolina Mountains, you're never more than a few miles from a fishing lake, a trout pond, or one of our hundreds of miles of trout streams. However, with the exceptions noted below, North Carolina State fishing licenses and permits are required for all residents and nonresidents older than 16 who want to fish. Anyone younger than 16 may use a parent's or guardian's license. Licenses and permits are available at most discount stores, such as Wal-Mart and Kmart. The cost will range from $20 to $40 depending on the duration of the license and whether or not you are a state resident.

Fishing in National Forests

Fishing in National Forest lakes is allowed year-round, but fishing in the forests' rivers and streams is regulated and sometimes restricted. To fish in state-designated trout waters, anglers will need a North Carolina fishing license and trout permit. Streams located on game lands require a special-use permit as well.

Brook, brown, and rainbow are the dominant species of freshwater trout in the area, and for management purposes public mountain trout streams are designated as Wild Trout Waters (high-quality waters that sustain trout populations by natural reproduction) and Hatchery Supported Waters (waters that must be stocked periodically to sustain fishing and are usually closed in March). These are further classified as Catch and Release/Artificial Lures Only, Catch and Release/Artificial Flies Only, and Delayed Harvest Waters. These designations are marked with specifically colored signs along the watercourses, but these colors can vary from area to area, so acquaint yourself with them.

Because regulations, including catch limits, change according to where you're fishing, it's up to you to know the rules. So before baiting a hook, contact the North

Carolina Wildlife Resources Commission (919–662–4373) for full information or pick up a copy of *N.C. Inland Fishing, Hunting, and Trapping Digest* where licenses are sold.

THE CHEROKEE INDIAN RESERVATION

The Cherokee Indian Reservation has 30 miles of regularly stocked streams. State records for a brown trout (15 pounds, 8 ounces) and a brook trout (7 pounds, 7 ounces) were caught in these waters. To fish in tribal water, you need no state license, North Carolina or otherwise. All you need is a Tribal Fishing Permit, available at nearly two dozen Reservation businesses.

The permit sells for $5.00 and is valid for one day, with a creel limit of 10 fish. Permits for longer periods, such as three or five days, are also available. Children younger than 12 don't need a permit as long as they are with someone with the proper permit. Fishing is permitted on the reservation from a half-hour before sunrise to a half-hour after sunset. Most of March is closed to fishing, with the annual season opening the last Saturday of March and continuing until the last day of February the following year.

Over 400,000 rainbow, brook, and brown trout are added to the existing fish population each year, so some streams are closed on Tuesday and Wednesday for stocking. The reservation's "Fish and Game Management" brochure, which is readily available almost everywhere, gives the schedule for which streams are closed for stocking. If you'd prefer pond fishing, you'll find three well-stocked trout ponds on Big Cove Road in front of the KOA campground. A tribal permit is required to fish in ponds and streams.

THE GREAT SMOKY MOUNTAINS NATIONAL PARK

The Great Smoky Mountains National Park has more than 600 miles of streams full of rainbow and brown trout. Some of the

more popular ones include Deep Creek, Noland Creek, and the Oconaluftee River and its tributaries. Remote Forney, Hazel, and Eagle Creeks, all very good fly-fishing streams, can only be reached by boat over Lake Fontana, by horseback, or by long treks through the park. In the park you must have either a valid North Carolina or Tennessee fishing license; fishing stamps are unnecessary. Make sure you check park regulations at a ranger station or visitor center before you fish.

Possession of any native brook trout is prohibited. That's because that fish's range in the Smokies has declined by 70 percent since 1900 due to unsound logging practices before the park was established and from competition with the rainbow and brown trout that were introduced into the waters.

Trout Ponds

Other places where you don't need a state fishing license are the more than 35 trout farms scattered throughout the region. You can contact the North Carolina Agricultural Department (919–733–0635) or a local North Carolina Cooperative Extension Service for a trout farm brochure that lists the names, addresses, and phone numbers of members of the North Carolina Trout Growers Association and includes a map to help you find the farms. Recreational trout fishing in these ponds requires no elaborate equipment, and there are no limits to the catch. Many places will clean your fish free of charge.

Rates at trout farms vary. You might pay $2.00 or $3.00 per pound or perhaps $10.00 per day with a catch limit.

HUNTING

Among the species of game available to hunters in North Carolina's mountains are deer, turkey, bear, squirrel, grouse, raccoon, wild boar, red and gray fox, rabbit, dove, and waterfowl. The North Carolina

Wildlife Resources Commission (919–733-0635) schedules such seasons as deer (bow and arrow), deer (gun), deer (muzzle loading), black bear, squirrel, grouse, quail, wild boar, and wild turkey.

To hunt in national forest game lands, you must have a hunting license and a game-lands use permit. A big-game license is required for hunting deer, turkey, bear, and wild boar. Hunters entering game lands from the Blue Ridge Parkway must have a hunter parking and crossing permit, which is good for a one-year period and obtained in person from a park ranger (see the list of ranger stations in the Forests and Parks chapter). However you must have a hunting license to get a parking and crossing permit.

Licenses and permits can be purchased at most discount stores, such as Wal-Mart, and at other sports-oriented places, such as gun shops or camping supply stores. To help you with regulations, pick up a copy of *N.C. Inland Fishing, Hunting, and Trapping Digest* where licenses are sold.

MOUNTAIN BIKING

Rugged root-covered forest floors, gradual but devastating hillside climbs, lush trails near rushing creek beds—this is the biking environment you will encounter in this region. Mountain biking is one of the fastest-growing sports in the mountains, and while the Nantahala National Forest and the Great Smoky Mountains National Park have their share of great riding trails, Pisgah Forest is gaining a reputation as the place to go for this sport. There are more than 400 miles of marked trails in Pisgah Forest alone, and the rugged and often difficult terrain on many of these paths makes them a sporting challenge even for the experienced biker. Not all trails, however, are that bad (or good, depending on how tough a biker you are!).

Some of the trails on our public lands are gated forest service roads that are closed to motor traffic and have good riding surfaces. Some are single-track forest trails with a great variety of rigorous turf. However, because such trails are shared with hikers, some of the more popular hiking trails, such as the Pink Beds Loop in Pisgah Forest, are only open to bikers from October 16 to April 14, when there are fewer hikers.

A list of biking trails is available from any of our national forest offices, and you can buy a number of good books on mountain biking that give detailed overviews of the trails and rate their difficulty. Some good sources are Lori Finley's series, *Mountain Biking the Appalachians,* published by John F. Blair, which covers the Highlands-Cashier and the Brevard-Asheville-Pisgah areas. One of our favorites is *Off the Beaten Track,* volumes I and II, by Jim Parham (WNC Publishing, P.O. Box 158, Almond, NC 28702).

We want to stress that mountain biking is not a sport without danger. You should always wear a helmet, and when riding alone, always let someone know what trail you'll be taking and when you expect to be back. Jim Parham also stresses that you carry your bike over wet and boggy areas, stepping stones, and steps and avoid skidding or spinning out on steep grades. Occasionally trails can be confusing, so equip yourself with a good trail map and take water along to keep from becoming dehydrated. Finally watch out for and yield to the hikers and horses that may be sharing the trail with you. Be especially careful when going around blind curves.

Ski resorts are taking advantage of their slopes in the warmer months by opening them up to mountain bikers. Beech Mountain Ski Resort (800–468-5506) offers a variety of competitions throughout the warm weather, and Wolf Laurel in Madison County (828–689–4111)

Even if you didn't bring along your bike or your canoe, there are many recreational equipment rentals available in North Carolina's mountains.

is open most days during the summer and weekends after school starts. Call for exact times and an events schedule.

Some of the outfitters listed at the end of this chapter run bike trips into the mountains. These usually include the use of a 21-speed mountain bike, helmet, and water bottle; an experienced tour leader; and transport service to and from trails. Half-day tours cost approximately $40; an all-day biking trip runs about $65. There is usually a discount when you bring your own bike, and group rates are available. Four days of touring—including all the above and accommodations, meals, and more—will run more than $500. Bike rentals usually cost about $25 a day. Euchella Mountain Bikes give bike tours and can be contacted at (800) 446-1603 or (828) 488-8835, for Nantahala Forest tours.

ROCK CLIMBING

Rock climbing is not for the faint of heart, but for those intrepid few who have taken to this sport, the rewards can be exhilarating. North Carolina's mountains offer some spectacular granite outcrops, sheer cliffs, and steep gorges that make for rock-climbers' heaven. Some of the experts even practice ice climbing in the region.

This high-risk sport requires knowledge, practice, and focus. Bouldering, a good first start, allows you to apply climbing moves just a few feet off the ground. Anything more advanced should be done in the company of an expert rock climber.

The staff at a number of outdoor outfitters will lead rock-climbing expeditions to favorite climbing spots here in the North Carolina mountains (see the "Outfitters" section at the end of this chapter). Below we have listed several rock climbing spots favored for their ease (or difficulty, depending upon your experience). Obviously there will be many more throughout the mountain region, so ask around, especially at the outfitter shops.

For rock climbers who want to seek out even more sites, we suggest you get a copy of *The Climber's Guide to North Carolina* by Thomas Kelley, who works at Black Dome Mountain Sports, an outfitter. This company offers a rock-climb guide service, too.

Northern Mountains

There are several climbing spots in the Linville Gorge area.

SHIPROCK MOUNTAIN

Just outside Blowing Rock and behind Grandfather Mountain, Shiprock Mountain can be accessed off the Blue Ridge Parkway at milepost 303, Rough Ridge parking area (do not park along the side of the parkway). It offers a range of climbing for all levels and is a more traditional crack climbing area that does not require bolts.

TABLE ROCK

There are four access sites at Table Rock. To get there from Asheville, take U.S. 221 N. to Linville Falls. At the Rock House Restaurant, turn right onto N.C. Highway 183, which turns into N.C. Highway 181. Follow the signs to Table Rock parking and picnic area. Paths will lead you down to the rock area. Another path from the parking/picnic area leads to three popular climbing faces: North Carolina Wall, the Amphitheater, and the Chimneys. Don't try to climb around the waterfall, though; it's forbidden and dangerous.

Central Mountains

DEVIL'S COURTHOUSE

Off the Parkway at milepost 422.4, this smaller rock face is a good climb for those just getting started. The climb is predominantly easy to moderate. Access is via a paved trail that leads up the mountain from the parking lot. Just before you get to the top, look for a rather obscure side trail that leads off to the right, travels back downhill through underbrush, and ends at the base of the rock face.

SNAKE DEN

Snake Den is north of Asheville in Barnardsville. Take U.S. 19/23 N. to the Barnardsville exit. Drive several more miles to town, where you take the Dillingham Road to the right. At the end of Dillingham Road, take a left. The pavement ends within 2 miles. Continue on a twisting, winding road that is a Forest Service road. Go about 5 more miles on this Forest Service road until you reach the rock face on your left, within 2 feet of the road. You can't miss it.

HIKING

Hiking is a wonderful, easy, inexpensive way to enjoy the outdoors. You don't need much gear, and the rewards are priceless. Hiking, in its fundamental simplicity and solitary function, seems to evoke a primordial human connection with the forces of nature. Hiking in a peaceful wood with the gurgle of a mountain stream, a bird on the wing overhead, the comfort of a well-trod path, and the vista before you can have a profound effect on the human psyche. Best of all, most of our trails are easily accessible. No driving for hours; just a few minutes drive and you are up in the mountains ready for a few hours or an all-day hike.

Here in the North Carolina Mountains, we are blessed with an amazing array of beautiful places to explore on foot. There's the spectacular Blue Ridge Parkway that runs almost the entire length of Western North Carolina, and our proximity to major national forests such as Pisgah and the Great Smokies brings hiking possibilities virtually to our back doors. The Appalachian Trail runs right through our mountains. Numerous state and memorial parks in the region also have marked hiking trails. But be alert: The blazes on some trails are becoming faded and more difficult to see.

Safety should be foremost on your mind as you set off on a hike. Learn in advance about the topography you'll be covering and let someone know your plans. Don't invite trouble: Hike with a friend. Be prepared with appropriate clothing and walking shoes or boots suited to the terrain and take water and food along if you'll be traveling any distance into a remote area. Be aware of the sudden weather changes that can occur in these mountains. It's a good idea to carry a small flashlight and a whistle in case you get lost. If you do get lost, stay put. Three periodic short bursts on your whistle will help alert others to your location (see our chapter on Outdoor Safety).

In this section we point out just a few of the top hiking destinations, but you can find your own favorites by just heading toward the horizon or along a dusty country road that runs through a forgotten wood. Numerous excellent books on the subject are available, including *Hiking North Carolina* by Randy Johnson, *North Carolina Hiking Trails* by Allen de Hart, *Walking the Blue Ridge* by Leonard M. Adkins, and *Waterfall Walks and Drives in the Western Carolinas* by Mark Morrison. And be sure and take advantage of

The Sierra Club reminds its members that deer gun season (which usually runs from November to December) is the most dangerous part of the hunting season. Therefore it's wise to stay out of both public and private game lands during such times. The game lands include the Pisgah and Nantahala National Forests and the Shining Rock, Middle Prong, Linville Gorge, and Southern Nantahala Wilderness Areas. The club's advice: "Go to the Great Smoky Mountains National Park, where there is no legal hunting allowed. If you must go into the woods, wear blaze orange that is visible from all directions."

another valuable resource: ranger stations in your area. (See our Forests and Parks chapter for a listing.)

Northern Mountains

Hiking in the northern mountains is centered around the Blue Ridge Parkway and the popular trails of Cumberland Knob, the 30-mile trail system of Doughton Park, the mist-shrouded trails of Mount Mitchell (see our chapter on Forests and Parks), or the family-outing trails of Moses Cone and Julian Price Memorial Parks (see our chapter on the Blue Ridge Parkway).

Grandfather Mountain, near Linville, is another popular hiking area; a permit and fee are required (see our Attractions chapter). The 3,000-acre preserve is laced with nine trails designated by the National Park Service as National Recreation Trails that vary in length and levels of endurance.

Glen Burney Trail skirts the cascading New Year's Creek in Blowing Rock, as the stream falls into the John's River Gorge south of town. The 1.5-mile foot trail is steep—it descends some 800 feet below Blowing Rock—and provides breathtaking vistas of two substantial waterfalls: the 45-foot Glen Burney and the 55-foot Glen Mary. Take Laurel Lane off Main Street to the Annie Cannon Park parking area where a wooden trail map marks the trailhead.

Central and Southern Mountains

Even in the more urban central mountain region surrounding Asheville, there are plenty of easy-to-get-to hiking opportunities. Head out on the Blue Ridge Parkway where many trails intersect with parking and overlook areas or stroll along the paths that follow the Swannanoa River on the Warren Wilson College campus just east of Asheville. The North Carolina

Arboretum also features many miles of wildflower-rich, wooded trails in its 426-acre park.

U.S. 276 from the Blue Ridge Parkway down to Pisgah Forest is a hiker's paradise. Some of the favorite trails originating off this highway include North Cove, Pilot Mountain, Art Loeb, Coon Tree, Looking Glass Rock, Cedar Rock, and Black Mountain Trails. Stop by the ranger station/visitors center just a mile inside the forest's boundary for maps and information. There is also a 0.6-mile Pisgah Ecology Trail behind the center. (For other great hiking trails, see Three Famous Trails Close-up.)

If you're hiking alone, let friends know where you are going, which trails you might be taking, and how long you will be gone. A cell phone is often a lifesaver in unusual circumstances.

CAMPING AND CAMPGROUNDS

You can pitch a tent in the woods, down a creek prong of a wilderness area, or within a designated forest campground here in the mountains of North Carolina.

Blue Ridge Parkway

Crabtree Meadows
Mile 339.5
(828) 675-5444

Seventy-one tent sites and 22 RV sites lie close to large grassy clearings. The lawn of wildflowers runs up to the forest edge, with mountains visible in the distance. The campground has the requisite picnic tables, grills, tent pads, but no showers. Water fountains and hand water pumps are centrally located.

This is a quiet, peaceful area awash with rhododendrons and hardwood trees

Three Famous Trails

The Appalachian National Scenic Trail

This legendary trail runs through 14 eastern states from Mount Katahdin in Maine to Springer Mountain in Georgia and takes an average of four to five months to hike. As far as we know, close to 2,000 people have made this journey, but thousands of others have enjoyed shorter sections of it.

Almost 302 miles of the Appalachian Trail pass through our mountains. The trail crosses the Georgia–North Carolina line near Bly Gap in Georgia, runs through the Nantahala National Forest, crosses into the Great Smoky Mountains National Park at the Fontana Dam, cuts diagonally across the length of the park and weaves its way along the North Carolina–Tennessee border, exiting our state near Elk Park. It is blazed with white rectangles and a chain of shelters are spaced 8 to 12 miles apart throughout the entire trail.

You can access this famous trail at many points throughout its journey through North Carolina. Any good trail map of the region will show you where. You can also get detailed guidebooks at district offices or from the Appalachian Trail Conference, P.O. Box 807, Harpers Ferry, WV 25425-0807. For more information, call toll-free (888) 287–8673.

The Mountains-to-the-Sea Trail

This relatively new trail, which was begun in 1985, will eventually run from Clingmans Dome, the highest point in the Great Smoky Mountains National Park, to the state's lowest elevation on the Outer Banks at Nags Head. This will be a travelway with various sections open to hiking, mountain biking, horseback riding, and/or canoeing. It will cover almost 700 miles and is scheduled to be completed in the year 2020. However, 216 miles already cross our mountains from Blowing Rock on the Blue Ridge Parkway south to Balsam Gap, where the parkway crosses U.S. 19 north of Sylva.

This trail will take you through just about every ecosystem found in the Southern Appalachian Mountains, from

and a good base camp for hiking in the Pisgah National Forest; trails lead to scenic falls on Crabtree Creek. Crabtree Falls Trail, a strenuous 2.5-mile loop, begins near the campground entrance. A camp store, gas station, and restaurant/gift shop are also nearby.

Doughton Park
Mile 239.0

No reservations are needed here. It's first come, first served; about $10.00 per adult, $5.00 for Golden Age Passport holders, and youths younger than 18 stay for free. One hundred ten tent sites, including tent pads, picnic tables, grills, and lantern posts, are scattered in wooded areas and around a grassy hillside. A smaller area with 25 RV sites lies across the road, though none of the sites have hookups.

Rest rooms and water spigots are available but no showers. This is camping as it was meant to be! The park itself covers approximately 6,000 acres in high-elevation grass balds to cove hardwood forests and from mountain ridges to thickets of rhododendrons. It is generally blazed with three-inch white dots, except in areas such as the Middle Prong Wilderness, where routed wood signs point the way. Though mainly a foot trail, there are some sections open to mountain bikes. Contact the Pisgah District Ranger (the number is in our Forests and Parks chapter) for more information and maps.

The Bartram Trail

From 1773 until 1777, William Bartram, a Philadelphia naturalist, traveled throughout the Southeast, writing exact and vivid descriptions of the plants and animals he saw and of the Native Americans he encountered. He published the writings in 1791 as *The Travels of William Bartram,* and they are still wonderful to read today.

Now a memorial trail follows as closely as possible his original route across South Carolina, Georgia, and the Nantahala National Forest of North Carolina. When finished, it will be around 100 miles long. The trail enters the state just south of Highlands, near Rabun Bald, curves in a north-to-west direction

through Western North Carolina and will eventually link up with the John Muir Trail in Tennessee. Currently it climbs from the Georgia line to the crest of the Blue Ridge Mountains before descending to the Little Tennessee River Valley south of Franklin. Here a canoe trail down the Little Tennessee River to Franklin is under consideration. At Franklin it turns west and ascends the Nantahala Mountains to Wayah Bald, which at 5,385 feet is the highest point on the trail. It joins the Appalachian Trail briefly and descends to Nantahala Lake. Continuing mainly on private lands, it reaches Appletree Campground in the upper Nantahala Gorge then climbs up and over Rattlesnake Knob before reaching the "put in" on the Nantahala River. From the river it ascends Tulula Gap and continues along the crests of the Snowbird Mountains. The trail has been constructed as far as Porterfield Gap, south of the Joyce Kilmer Memorial Forest.

To learn more about this trail, order maps or to become a member of the society that is establishing the trail, write to the North Carolina Bartram Trail Society, Route 3, P.O. Box 406, Sylva, NC 28779. Maps are also available from the NFS.

Alleghany and Wilkes Counties and is the largest park on the parkway. It was named after Robert Lee Doughton, a U.S. representative who served from 1911 to 1953 and who was an advocate for the construction of the parkway.

Julian Price
Mile 297.0
(828) 963-5911
Reservations aren't required for Julian Price. Like Doughton Park, it's first

come, first served; about $10.00 per adult, $5.00 for Golden Age Passport holders, youths younger than 18 free. This campground sprawls across both sides of the parkway near Price Lake. One hundred twenty-nine tent sites lie fairly close together, divided by blossoming rhododendron bushes. Sixty-eight RV sites are also available, though with no plug-ins. Tent pads, picnic tables, grills, and spigots provide adequate comforts.

There are rest rooms but no showers; firewood can be purchased nearby. The park is marked by mild terrain, covered by a dense hardwood forest. Poplars, chestnut trees, and maples make a pleasant canopy for hikers and campers. Canoes may be rented at the lake, and hiking trails nearby lead to two smaller lakes and creeks.

Linville Falls
Mile 316.3
(828) 765-7818
Fifty-five tent sites and 20 RV sites are available in the campground of this 440-acre wooded park. Tent site 15 is the most secluded. The surrounding forest seems almost primordial with moss-covered trees and waterfalls that plunge through the granite walls of Linville Gorge. Fishing in the nearby Linville River is allowed, and a visitor center and bookstore provides campers with plenty of area information.

Mount Pisgah
Mile 408.6
(828) 235-9109
The entrance to Mount Pisgah Campground with its 70 tent sites and 70 RV sites lies directly across from Pisgah Inn on the parkway. Small sites, close together are arranged in three landscaped loops. A dense forest adds privacy. There are no showers, but central hand water pumps and individual picnic tables, grills, and lantern posts are provided. Maps of the area, including hiking trails, are available at the camp. A picnic area lies in a meadow bordered by rhododendron.

Great Smoky Mountains National Park

Of the 10 developed campsites in this national park, five are in Tennessee and five are in North Carolina. All have tent sites, picnic tables, fireplace grills, and bathrooms with cold water and flush toilets but no showers. There are a limited number of trailer sites but none of them have hookups. Sewage disposal stations are located at the Smokemont, Cades Cove, Deep Creek, and Cosby Campgrounds and across the road from the Sugarland Visitors Center about 5 miles south of Gatlinburg, Tennessee on U.S. 441. The stations aren't available for use in winter.

Three of the campgrounds—Elkmont and Cades Cove on the Tennessee side and Smokemont on the North Carolina side—take reservations from May 15 through October 31, which can be made by calling (800) 365-2267 up to five months in advance. All other campgrounds are on a first-come, first-served basis.

No more than six people may occupy a site (two tents or one RV and one tent). Group camping sites are available at Big Creek, Cades Cove, Cataloochee, Cosby, Deep Creek, Elkmont, and Smokemont. Reservations at group camps are required and can be made by calling (800) 365-2267 or (423) 436-1266.

There is a seven-day limit at any campground between May 15 and October 31 and a 14-day limit between November 1 and May 14. Pets are allowed in the campground as long as they are on a leash or otherwise confined.

The following list of camping areas shows the number of campsites, fees per night, open/close dates, and maximum RV lengths. To locate these camps, pick up a map or ask for directions at any of the park visitors centers listed in our Forests and Parks chapter, which also contains additional information on the Great Smoky Mountains National Park.

Abrams Creek
Abrams Creek Road
There are 16 camping sites at the Abrams Creek campground on the northwestern edge of the park. It is reached from U.S. Highway 129 as it circles the eastern end of the scenic Chilhowee Reservoir in Tennessee. Some sites will take RVs up to 12 feet long and are open from March 21 to November 3. The cost is $10 a night.

Balsam Mountain
Balsam Mountain Road

When you camp here be sure to have a sweater handy even in the summer, because at 5,310 feet it's the highest and coolest of the park's developed campgrounds. To reach it, turn off the Blue Ridge Parkway onto Balsam Mountain Road. Here you'll find 46 sites (some will take 30-foot RVs) and a 1-mile, self-guided nature trail through alpine woods. Balsam Mountain is open from May 23 though September 29 and costs $12 a night.

Big Creek
Big Creek Park Road

This campground, which costs $10 a night, is just 2 miles off I-40. It has a ranger station, 12 campsites, and is open from May 21 through November 3. A very narrow, graveled, one-lane road leads from this area to the Cataloochee campground some 15 miles away, but should the Cosby Campground be full, don't attempt this road with trailers or RVs or in the dark. In fact no RVs are allowed at Big Creek.

Cades Cove
Campground Road

One hundred fifty-nine sites capable of handling 35-foot RVs are available at this popular campground in Cades Cove, home to 700 people in the last century. (See our Forests and Parks chapter.) A few of these early buildings are still preserved, and the areas they originally cleared for farming are wonderful places to spot all kinds of wildlife, particularly in the early morning and late evening.

This campground is open year-round, and the fee is $12 to $15 per night.

Cataloochee
Cove Creek Road

This is another campground in the area of two pioneer communities, Little Cataloochee and Big Cataloochee. With a combined population of 1,200 people, it was the largest settlement in the Smokies. Some buildings are still there (see our Forests and Parks chapter), and this area, too, is a good place to see wild turkey and deer.

The pretty campground, tucked into tall evergreens, has 27 sites and will take some 31-foot RVs. To reach it take partly paved/mostly graveled Cove Creek Road off of U.S. 276 for nearly 12 miles. We think you'll find the rather rough trip and sharp curves worth it. Cataloochee is open from March 21 through November 3 and costs $10 a night.

Cosby
Cosby Park Road

Even if you don't want to camp, this is a good place to go to hike. In addition to a self-guiding nature trail, there are trails that will take you through lovely woods and to waterfalls. (Ask folks at the camp office for some suggestions.)

If you do want to camp, you are likely to find room at one of the 175 campsites here when other campgrounds are full. You can reach Cosby Campground by taking U.S. 321 and cutting south on Tenn. Highway 32. Turn onto Cosby Park Road. The campsites will take 25-foot RVs; cost is $12; and Cosby is open March 21 through November 3.

Deep Creek
Deep Creek Road

The Deep Creek campground, just outside Bryson City, rests on the site of yet another pioneer community and is a great place to go even if you don't want to camp here. It's only a short walk from the campground to Toms Branch, Juneywhank, and Indian Creek Falls. In addition Deep Creek is a popular place to go tubing.

The campground has 189 sites, some of which are suitable for 26-foot RVs, and the fee is $12 per night. In the summer programs that are advertised on the camp's bulletin board are offered at the camp's amphitheater. The campground is open from April 11 through November 3 but is open to picnickers and hikers year-round.

Elkmont
Elkmont Road

The Elkmont campground lies 1 mile off Little River Road, one of the easiest (except for the traffic) and most popular drives in the park. Early in this century Elkmont itself was a summer resort with dozens of cottages. Today it has 120 campsites, some suitable for 32-foot RVs, at $12 to $15 per night.

There is a self-guiding nature trail here, and park rangers offer programs for campers and noncampers alike. Elkmont is open from March 21 through December 1.

Look Rock
Foothills Parkway

Look Rock, named for Look Rock Mountain, is a campground just off the Foothills Parkway. This is an 18-mile drive that follows the crest of Chilhowee Mountain between U.S. 321 and U.S. 129 on the western side of the park.

Look Rock has 92 sites, some of which will take 35-foot RVs. It costs $12 per night and is open May 23 though November 3.

Smokemont
Newfound Gap Road

The site of this popular campground was once a small pioneer settlement and then a booming logging village. It was operated by Champion Fibre, which owned 93,000 acres of timber here prior to 1931. Today, second-growth timber has hidden old lumbering scars, but a stroll from the parking area will bring you to Mingus Mill, where corn has been ground into meal since 1886.

There is a short, self-guided nature trail along the stream in the campground that contains 140 sites, some suitable for 27-foot RVs. Smokemont is open year-round and costs from $12 to $15 per night.

Backcountry Camping

A free backcountry permit is required for all persons spending the night in the park's backcountry. (Day-hikers are not required to register or to obtain permits.) Backcountry permits are available at most park campgrounds, ranger stations, and at the Sugarlands and Oconaluftee visitor centers. Registration areas at ranger stations and campgrounds are accessible 24 hours a day. Visitor center registration stations are open from 9:00 A.M. to 5:00 P.M.

Camping is permitted only at designated sites and shelters. The few backcountry campsites and all shelters require advance reservations. A Great Smoky Mountains Trail map for backcountry campsite locations and information is available at visitor centers for $1.00. To make a reservation call (423) 436-1231 from 8:00 A.M. to 6:00 P.M. seven days a week.

(For more information on the Great Smoky Mountains National Park, see our Forests and Parks chapter.)

National Forest Camping

Most national forest campgrounds have no hookups, but all developed campgrounds have at least one 25-foot parking spur, and many campgrounds have one or more campsites that can accommodate a large motor home or trailer that's 35 feet long or longer. Some sites provide pull-through drives. Primitive camps that are scattered all over the forests, including the wilderness areas, are for tents only. A few of those that offer some amenities, like drinking water, are listed below.

In addition to these listed campgrounds, there are also 10 group camps designed for organized groups of from 25 to 100 people: Rattler Ford in the Cheoah District; Apple Tree and Kemsey Creek in the Wayah District; Kuykendall, Cove Creek, and White Pines in the Pisgah District; Silvermine and Harmon Den Horse Camp in the Appalachian French Broad District; Briar Bottom in the Appalachian Toecane District; and Boone Fork in the Grandfather District. Group camps are available only by reservation through the district office where the site is located. (See our list of district offices in the Forests and Parks chapter.) The exceptions are the campgrounds located in the Pisgah District. Call toll-free (877) 444-6777 at least 10 days but no more than 360 days in advance for group camping and no more than 240 days in advance for family camping. The cost of a group camp ranges from $15.00 to $80.00. There is a $16.50 service fee charged per group reservation.

NANTAHALA NATIONAL FOREST CAMPING

Cable Cove
FR 520 off N.C. Highway 28 E., Cheoah District
(828) 479-6431
Near Fontana Lake, this camping area that's open from April 15 through October 31, offers 26 sites, rest rooms with flush toilets, a picnic area, water, fishing, trails, and a boat ramp. The fee is $8.00 per night.

Cheoah Point
off U.S. Highway 129 N., Cheoah District
(828) 479-6431
At this area on Santeelah Lake, you'll find 26 sites, rest rooms with flush toilets, water, a picnic area, a boat ramp, swimming, fishing, and trails. It is open from April 15 through October 31, and the fee is $8.00 per night.

Hanging Dog
N.C. Highway 1326 W.
Tusquitee District
(828) 837-5152
A popular camping area on Hiwasee Lake, Hanging Dog has 67 sites, a picnic area, flush and vault toilets, water, a boat ramp, fishing, and trails. The fee is $8.00, and it is open from April 15 through October 31.

Horse Cove
FR 415
Cheoah District
(828) 479-6431
Located almost 17 miles from Robbinsville

and open from April 15 through October 31, Horse Cove has 18 sites, water, flush and vault toilets, fishing, and trails. The fee is $8.00 per night. There are also five sites open in winter at no fee, but there is no water available at that time.

Hurricane Creek
FR 67, Wayah District
(828) 524-6441
This is a primitive camp with undesignated sites and no drinking water. However it offers vault toilets, fishing, and horse and hiking trails. It is open from March 15 through January 1, depending on the weather, and the fee is $4.00 per night.

Jackrabbit Mountain
SR 1155, Tusquitee District
(828) 837-5152
Open from May 1 through October 31, this large camping area on Chatuge Lake has 103 sites and provides a dump station, a picnic area, flush toilets, amphitheater, showers, drinking water, swimming, a boat ramp, fishing, and hiking trails. There are evening programs in season. The fee is $12 per night.

Standing Indian
Old U.S. Highway 64, Wayah District
(828) 524-6441
There are 84 campsites at this campground located on the Nantahala River, along with a picnic area, rest rooms, an amphitheater, shows, drinking water, and hiking trails. Standing Indian is open from March 31 through December 1, and the fee is $10.00 per night. The charge for day use is $2.00 per car.

Tsali
FR 521, Cheoah District
(828) 479-6431
Made up of 42 campsites on Fontana Lake, Tsali has a picnic area, flush toilets, showers, drinking water, a boat ramp, fishing, and hiking, biking, and horse trails. Campsites are $15.00 a night. There also is a $2.00 trail-use fee in this popular area. It is open from April 15 through October 31.

The Legend of Standing Indian Mountain

Many years ago, say the Cherokee, a great winged monster swooped down and carried off a child playing near the village and took him to a cave high in the cliffs of a nearby mountain. Frightened people from all around came together and prayed to the Great Spirit for help in getting rid of the huge beast. After days and nights of prayer, a dazzling lightning bolt and a booming thunderclap came out of a clear sky and shattered the mountain, killing the creature and its offspring.

The lightning was so powerful, though, that it destroyed all the trees on the mountain's summit, producing the bald top that it has to this day. It also turned a warrior, who was posted on the mountain to keep an eye on the beast, to stone. Some said it was his punishment for being a poor sentry. Over the hundreds of years since this event occurred, this standing Indian has been worn away to a pillar of stone with an ill-defined head on top. In fact you may even have some trouble distinguishing the stone pillar from the jumble of rock that surrounds it, but you will be able to see the cliffs that were torn asunder by the Great Spirit's lightning bolt.

Vanhook Glade
off U.S. Highway 64, Highlands District
(828) 526-3765
Since Vanhook is located just off picturesque and popular U.S. 64 near Highlands and all its attractions, you might have to be a little lucky to get one of the 20 sites in this campground in high season. It has flush toilets, drinking water, and hiking trails. Campers also have access to adjoining Cliffside Lake and can use the showers there. Vanhook is open from May 1 through October 31. The fee is $10.00 per night. Day use at Cliffside Lake is $3.00 per car.

PISGAH NATIONAL FOREST CAMPGROUNDS

Black Mountain
FR 472, Appalachian District,
Tocane Station
(828) 682-6146
This very attractive campground on the South Toe River has 46 sites, flush toilets, drinking water, an amphitheater, fishing, and hiking trails. It's open from April 14 through November 1. The fee of $12 includes guided activities in season.

Boone Fork
FR 2055, Grandfather District
(828) 652-2144
On Boone Fork this 15-site campground has a picnic area, rest rooms, drinking water, and hiking trails. Open from April 1 through December 31, the fee for the campground is $3.00.

Carolina Hemlocks
N.C. Highway 80, Appalachian District,
Tocane Station
(828) 682-6146
Here you'll find flush toilets, drinking water, swimming, fishing, hiking trails, and 32 campsites. There is also a picnic shelter that is available by reservation. The area is open from April 14 through November 1, and the fee is $12 per night.

Curtis Creek
FR 482, Grandfather District
(828) 652-2144

This tents-only campground has no-charge, primitive, undesignated sites. There are, however, drinking water, vault toilets, a picnic area, fishing, and hiking trails. It is open from April 1 through December 31.

Davidson River
U.S. Highway 276, Pisgah District
(828) 877-3350

One of the most popular campgrounds in North Carolina's mountains, Davidson River (situated along the beautiful river of the same name) has 161 campsites and is just 1.3 miles inside the Brevard entrance to Pisgah Forest. It offers a dump station, flush toilets, an amphitheater, showers, drinking water, fishing, and hiking trails. There are also guided activities in season. It's open all year, and the fee is $15 to $18 per night. Reservations are available—and advisable—by calling toll-free (877) 444-6777.

Lake Powhatan
FR 806, Pisgah District
(828) 877-3350

This is another extremely popular campground on Lake Powhatan; it's less than 8 miles from Asheville and has 98 sites, a dump station, a picnic area, flush toilets, showers, drinking water, swimming, fishing, and hiking trails. A lifeguard and guided activities are offered in season. Lake Powhatan is open from April 7 through November 1, and the fee is $14 to $17 a night. You can also make reservations at this campground by calling (877) 444-6777.

Mortimer
N.C. Highway 90, Grandfather District
(828) 652-2144

Mortimer has 23 sites, a picnic area, vault toilets, drinking water, hiking trails, and fishing for a fee of $4.00 per night. In win-ter there is no fee, but there is also no drinking water.

North Mills River
SR 1345, Pisgah District
(828) 877-3350

Located on North Mills River, this campground has 28 sites, a dump station, a picnic area, flush and vault toilets, drinking water, hiking trails, and fishing. It is open from April 1 through November 15, and there is a 50 percent reduction in the $8.00 to $11.00 fees during the off-season.

Rocky Bluff
N.C. Highway 209 S., Appalachian District, French Broad Station
(828) 622-3202

This campground on Spring Creek has 30 sites, a picnic area, flush toilets, drinking water, an amphitheater, hiking trails, and fishing. It's open from May 1 through October 31, and the fee is $8.00 per night.

Sunburst
N.C. Highway 215, Pisgah District
(828) 877-3350

Based at the site of an old logging town, Sunburst has 14 sites, a picnic area, flush toilets, and drinking water. It's open from April 1 through December 30, and the cost is $7.00 per night.

HORSEBACK RIDING

This is true "horse country." Beautiful horse farms—many specializing in Arabians, Appaloosas, Tennessee Walkers, or other breeds—beautify our mountain landscapes. Riding stables and riding schools are scattered throughout. Many children have horses for pets instead of dogs or cats, and two horses in a pasture seem almost as common as two cars in a garage. WATCH FOR HORSES signs dot the secondary roads, and somewhere in the region nearly every weekend, a horse show takes place.

Where to Ride

Part of the reason for the popularity of horses here is that there are so many places to ride. In addition to private trails, fields, and pastures, there are many quiet dirt and paved roads that are used for horseback riding. There are also designated riding trails in the Pisgah and Nantahala National Forests and in the Great Smoky Mountains National Park. These are clearly marked with a horse sign, and you're not allowed on any other trails, though horses are permitted on many Forest Service roads.

The Tsali Recreation Area in the Nantahala National Forest (see our earlier Fontana Lake entry) is one of the premier riding areas in the Southeast. As of 1997 there is a $2.00 trail fee charged. There is access to more than 18 miles of bridle trails, but be forewarned: Mountain bikes are also allowed here, and although hikers and bikers should yield to horses, riders should always yield to motorized vehicles. Meandering through pine and hardwood forests, the trails cover terrain as varied as wide-packed dirt paths and rocky ones that overlook the lake.

In the Pisgah Forest two of the longer trails are the 12-mile South Mills River Trail in the Pisgah District and the rugged 18.4-mile Buncombe Horse Range Trail in the Appalachian Toecane District. The latter trail is suitable for overnight rides; on Community Hill, at 5,782 feet, you'll find a trail shelter with 10 wire bunks, a picnic shed, a horse corral, and a nearby spring.

Although most horse trails in the Pisgah District are for day rides or for primitive camping along the trails only, there is more developed camping at the South White Pines group campsite and the Harmon Den Horse Camp (tents only, open year-round). For more information contact the Pisgah District office at (877) 444-6777 or see "National Forest Camping" in this chapter.

Rider Etiquette

To lessen the impact on trails, the park service staff asks that horseback riders travel in groups of six or fewer and that they stay on designated pathways, because cutting across switchbacks tramples plants and can cause severe erosion. Try to avoid tying your horse to a tree, but if this becomes necessary, use a rope or a tree-saver hitch to avoid damage. It's better to picket or hobble your horse and move stock periodically to reduce trampling and prevent overgrazing.

To protect water quality keep horses at least 200 feet from water sources and carry a water bucket and weed-free feed with you. Scatter manure and fill in pawed holes, especially when breaking camp. Horseback riders are required to yield to motorized vehicles, but bikers and hikers are supposed to yield to horses. Because trails are often narrow and some horses are skittish, it helps if you tell hikers where to wait while you pass.

Riding Stables

Perhaps your involvement with horses only goes as far as wanting to take a trail ride. You can do that easily enough. There are many places in the mountains that rent horses and most also provide a guide.

One-hour riding lessons cost between $20 and $30; one-hour rides are about $15 to $25; half-day trips are between $32 and $55; all-day trips range between $65 and $75; and a three-day, two-night camping trip by horseback costs around $300. Most riding stables are open from mid-April until the end of October. Most have age requirements for children.

We've described a few of the stables in our mountain area.

NORTHERN MOUNTAINS

Arrowmont Stable and Cabins
1157 Pine Creek Road, Glenville, NC
(828) 743-2762, (800) 682-1092
Arabians, Appaloosas, and Tennessee Walkers are featured here. There are five trails that offer a range of views, from mountaintops to picturesque valleys and streams. Lessons and a guide are included in the cost. The stables are closed on Sundays.

Blowing Rock Stables
N.C. Highway 221, Blowing Rock, NC
(828) 295-7847
Blowing Rock Stables is almost a mile outside the town of Blowing Rock. Guided trail rides pass near Bass Lake and around the Manor House at beautiful Moses Cone Memorial Park. You can ride daily from April through December. The cost is $20 an hour ($35 for two hours) per horse. Boarding is offered at $300 per month seasonally and $250 a month yearly. Prices are subject to change.

CENTRAL MOUNTAINS

Earthshine Lodge
Rt. 1, P.O. Box 216 C, Lake Toxaway, NC
(828) 862-4207
Earthshine specializes in two- and three-hour Western-style horseback and mule rides. There's a two-rider minimum, a five-rider maximum, a minimum age of 12, and reservations are required.

Free corral kiddie rides are offered at scheduled times for guests.

Pisgah Forest Stables
Avery Creek, Pisgah National Forest
(828) 883-8258
Explore the forest on half-day or full-day trail rides or excursions that last three days and two nights (four-person minimum). For rides of more than an hour, there is a two-person minimum. Reservations are required two days in advance. Children must be 6 years old to ride alone.

Pisgah Forest Stables offers a three-hour waterfall ride.

When horseback riding, always wear long pants and boots with a separation between shoe sole and heel. Wearing shorts on a leather saddle will chap and blister your thighs in no time. Shoes without any type of heel may cause your entire foot to slip through the stirrup, and you could be dragged under the horse if thrown.

Pisgah View Ranch
Rt. 1, off N.C. Highway 151, Candler, NC
(828) 667-9100
Set in the shadow of Mount Pisgah, this ranch offers breathtaking views and 2,000 acres of fields and forests. Horseback riding across this picturesque acreage is only $12 an hour for guests of the ranch and $18 for visitors. The ranch is open May 1 through November 1 and features delicious home-cooked meals in a large old-fashioned dining room. Reservations are required. Watch for the signs.

SOUTHERN MOUNTAINS

Cataloochee Ranch
Rt. 1, P.O. Box 500, Maggie Valley, NC
(828) 926-1401
Two-hour and all-day accompanied rides are available for adults and children older than 6. Reservations are required.

Chunky Gal Stables
10981 U.S. Highway 64 E., Hayesville, NC
(828) 389-4175
This stable offers horseback riding, horse training, riding instruction, and long- and short-term boarding. You can choose between one-, two-, and four-hour rides. Arena riding is also offered for children and beginners. Chunky Gal is located 11 miles east of Hayesville. Trail rides are also available.

Fontana Riding Stables
Highway 28, Fontana Dam
(828) 498-2211

How would you like to give both your-self and your horse a vacation in the mountains? You can at Las Praderas Sta-bles and Cottages. Located on See Off Mountain Road, off U.S. Highway 276 approximately 7 miles south of Brevard, Las Praderas has trails, but it doesn't rent horses. Call (828) 883-3375 for more information.

Horseback rides can be around the village (one hour), up a trail with lake views (one hour), or a journey to waterfalls (two hours).

Hemphill Mountain Campground
off Maggie Valley Road
Waynesville, NC
(828) 926-0331
Here you can get hourly or day rides, including trips into the Great Smoky Mountains National Park. There are also pony rides for children.

Sapphire Valley Riding Stables
4000 Highway 64 W., Sapphire, NC
(828) 743-9574
Sapphire Valley has miles of scenic trails, and trips leave on the hour at 11:00 A.M. and noon, and 2:00, 3:00, and 4:00 P.M. There is a minimum of two riders, who must be at least 8 years old and weigh under 250 pounds.

Utah Mountain Riding Stables
1200 Utah Mountain Road, Waynesville, NC
(828) 926-1143
Explore hundreds of acres of trails on one- to three-hour rides. Children must be older than 5 to ride. Younger ones may ride double with an adult.

CLUBS, SITES, AND EVENTS

Although horses are a part of the lifestyle in all areas of the Western North Carolina, the heart of horse country is in the Central Mountain, particularly in Polk County around Tryon. In fact it's the top area in

the state for steeplechases and other equestrian activities. Below are just a few horse-lover activities. (Check out our chapter on Annual Festivals and Events for others.)

Central Mountains

Biltmore Estate Equestrian Center
Biltmore Estate
(828) 277-4485
Guests can expect to find guided trail rides on some 100 miles of trail through-out the Biltmore Estate. The new Eques-trian Center offers riding for children and adults as well.

Foothills Equestrian Nature Center
3181 Hunting Country Road, Tryon, NC
(828) 859-9021
The Foothills Equestrian Nature Center, or FENCE, presents more than 18 various equestrian events during the year and provides interpretive nature study for adults and children (see the FENCE listing in our Attractions chapter). The 330-acre preserve has equestrian facilities with sta-bling, a steeplechase course, three show rings, a cross-country course, and access to the Foothills Equestrian Trails Associa-tion (FETA) trail system.

Tryon Riding and Hunt Club
Tryon, NC
(828) 859-6109, (800) 438-3681
For half a century the Tryon Riding and Hunt Club has hosted the Spring Block House Steeplechase held on the next-to-last Saturday in April, and the Tryon Horse Trials, where horses perform dressage, stadium jumping, and cross-country, held in October.

The Western North Carolina Agricultural Center
1301 Fanning Bridge Road, Fletcher, NC
(828) 687-1414
There's a horse show here nearly every weekend, and most are free. The free shows start at 8:00 or 9:00 A.M. and finish

around 9:00 P.M. There is a charge for the occasional rodeo and gaited horse shows, which start at 6:00 or 7:00 P.M. Admission for gaited shows is usually $2.00 to $5.00.

OFF-ROAD VEHICLE TRAILS

The late 1980s locked the Forest Service in conflict with the owners of off-road vehicles. Jeeps, four-wheelers, motorcycles, and other all-terrain gadabouts were racing through the forests, creating erosion that polluted streams and endangered some trophy-trout waters, including the Lower Tellico.

Today, the Forest Service, off-road vehicle (ORV) owners, environmentalists, and landowners whose property was being harmed have worked out a plan that sanctions areas for the sport and establishes rules and regulations to govern it. At this time an individual does not need a permit to use an area set aside for ORVs (or ATVs, all-terrain vehicles), but that could change. A fee is charged for groups or commercial events. You don't even have to have a valid driver's license, but minors who operate these vehicles must be under the direct supervision of adults.

Trails in these areas range from a 15 percent pitch to a 50 percent pitch. You must know your vehicle and have good driving skills, and you should wear a sturdy helmet to lessen your chance of head injuries. Other tips for riders: Protect against erosion and stay on the road or trail, don't cut across switchbacks, and avoid wheel spin and wet trails. The following ORV areas are marked with symbols that show what kind of vehicles are allowed. Some old routes are badly eroded and have been closed to heal—don't ride on them.

BROWN MOUNTAIN

Brown Mountain has one four-wheel-drive trail in this area west of Lenoir. The other trails are open to ATVs and dirt bikes. There is no user fee.

ROY A. TAYLOR ATV TRAIL SYSTEM

This trail, in the Wayhutta section, east of Sylva, is open only to ATVs and dirt bikes. Trucks and jeeps are not allowed. User fee is $3.00; a season pass costs $20.00.

UPPER TELLICO

North of Murphy, Upper Tellico is open to all ATVs, dirt bikes, and four-wheel-drive vehicles. User fee is $3.00; a season pass costs $25.00.

OTHER RECREATION

There are other things to do with your leisure time in the mountains, including some activities that could be considered a bit unusual.

Airborne Recreation

Mount Pisgah Balloons
1410 Pisgah Highway, Candler, NC
(828) 667-9943
This operation began more than 15 years ago when ballooning was just catching on. Mount Pisgah Balloons, 30 minutes from Asheville, conducts pleasure tours over the mountains for around $110 per person. The company has found that hot-air travel attracts all ages: Its oldest balloonist was a local man in his 90s whose ride was a birthday gift from his children.

Transylvania Balloon Rides
40 Pole Miller Road, Brevard, NC
(828) 884-5821, (877) 500-0506
To find the right conditions, most hot-air balloon flights begin just before sunrise or sunset, catching the mountains at their most spectacular. Flights usually leave from a field between Brevard and Hendersonville and last about an hour, often passing over Henderson County apple country. There's a champagne toast at the end of the flight, and everyone is pre-

> *Going for a hot-air balloon ride? It's an experience you won't forget. Make it enjoyable by asking the operator what kind of weather to expect and clothing requirements, and ask about cameras and binoculars. Don't forget a hat, sunglasses, or gloves as they may prove to be useful.*

sented with a flight certificate. The cost is $125 per person; the maximum capacity is two passengers and the pilot. They will also take on advertising promotions.

Transylvania Balloon is open weekends. Though summer is the busiest season, the visibility in winter is usually better.

Llama Treks

WindDancers Lodging and Llamas
1966 Martins Creek Road, Clyde, NC
(828) 627–6986
If you've never met a wooly llama, here's your chance! Soulful eyes, a dignified demeanor, and personality make forming an attachment easy, especially during a long trek when the animals—much less damaging to the environment than other beasts of burden—not only carry your gear but become companions.

From April through November, WindDancers' llamas will tote the gourmet fixings for a lunch or dinner trek, served by talented guides. Overnight adventures into Pisgah Forest are also available, with overnight camping in a rustic shelter on top of the mountain. Reservations and a four-person minimum are required.

Bowling

Tarheel Lanes
3275 Asheville Highway, Hendersonville, NC
(828) 253–2695, (828) 692–5039
Western North Carolina's largest bowling center, featuring 32 lanes, is 2 miles north of downtown Hendersonville. It's a modern facility that also has a billiard and video game room, a pro shop, and a snack bar. Tarheel Lanes hosts local, state, and regional bowling tournaments. Summer hours are 11:00 A.M. to 11:00 P.M.; winter hours are 9:00 A.M. to 11:00 P.M.

OUTFITTERS

The North Carolina mountains are filled with recreation outfitters who provide services for outdoor enthusiasts. These services can be as comprehensive or specialized as you want, depending on the outfitter and what you want to do. Recreational clothing, customized adventures, specialty bike parts, and canoeing supplies—these are some of the stock in trade at the region's outfitters, which are divided into two basic types: retail and full-service.

In most North Carolina mountain counties, you'll find retail outdoor outfitters that supply the fundamentals for fun but not guide services. These businesses have the gear for the outdoor types or people who just want to look that way. The shops can clothe you in sturdy foot gear, jackets, pants, and vests to protect you from the elements, and they carry packs, from overnight frame backpacks to roomy day packs. Retail outfitters can provide hiking and camping food supplies, including a dehydrated five-course meal and the packable Sterno stove on which to cook it. And they have maps—detailed USGS topographical maps or basic day-hike trail maps—plus compasses and safety gear to get you there and back. Don't hesitate to ask questions. These people make a business of supplying recreation needs and can put you in touch with professional guides or just recommend a local day hike, fishing spot, or swimming hole.

The popularity of mountain biking and river canoeing has created a demand for superior service and products for these two sports, and specialty shops have sprung up in some mountain counties to fill the void. These places concentrate on service and repair, but the owners, more often than not, know their merchandise from longtime experience. Rentals are usually also available, as are tours.

A full-service outfitter does it all, supplying everything from gear to guided treks. These businesses usually have top-of-the-line gear, safety equipment, food supplies, and major recreational vehicles, from bikes to kayaks. And a few even offer mail-order service. You get more than basics here: Your purchase can become a learning experience. For example, while you're being fitted for those incredible, molded rock-climbing shoes that seem to become part of your foot, you can get tips on top climbing spots. Or get advice on the best telemark skis and cross-country areas in the mountains. You can discuss the purchase of a kayak with someone who has taken one out more than once or select a pack sturdy enough to withstand the Alps. These people have been out there and can offer you expert advice and memorable guided trips.

But let's say you're one of those gung-ho, let-'er-rip outdoor types looking for a heart-pounding thrill. You can find instant gratification here with adventure expedition services. The primary focus is group adventure, often including the entire family in the white-knuckle thrills of whitewater rafting, canoeing, caving, or rock climbing, depending on the outfitter. Safety is given paramount consideration and detail. Gear is available as a sideline, or you can rent it for the trip.

Below, we've listed some of the well-known outfitters and adventure services here in North Carolina's mountains.

Northern Mountains

Appalachian Adventures
Grade Road off Highway 194, Todd, NC
(336) 877–8800
This company outfits for canoeing, kayaking, tubing, and mountain biking on and along the New River. It is also a retail outlet for wilderness kayaks. Appalachian Adventures is based at an old train depot built in 1888. The landmark structure brims with a variety of gifts from the arts and crafts arena.

In spring, mid-April through mid-May, the outfitters are open weekends only. Beginning mid-May it's open seven days a week. All reservations require a 50 percent deposit. Call for a range of prices. Biking adventures take you through the back roads of Historic Todd and into green pastures, past old farms, and by the New River. The outfitters provide premapped routes, ranging from flat easy to ride pavement to more advanced rugged gravel and hilly terrain.

Boone Bike and Touring
899 Blowing Rock Road, Boone, NC
(828) 262–5750
This full-service bike shop near Appalachian State University offers high-quality models, accessories, repair service, and rentals.

Edge of the World Snowboard Shop and Whitewater Rafting
Highway 184, Banner Elk, NC
(828) 898–4464, (800) 789–EDGE
Edge of the World guides rafting and canoeing tours on a portion of the Watauga River in the northwest part of the county. They also supply caving and rock-climbing equipment. But here in the High Country of Watauga County, where skiing is king, no other outfitter covers the snowboarding scene as well as Edge of the World. The best quality equipment and advice are at your disposal here.

Footsloggers
553 West King Street, Boone, NC
(828) 262–5111
This upscale outdoor retailer in downtown Boone is popular with both students and tourists in the High Country of the northern mountains. It carries a full array of high-quality outdoor clothing, hiking boots, rock-climbing and hiking equipment, and

camping gear (see our Shopping Destinations chapter for more details).

High Mountain Expeditions
Main Street, Blowing Rock, NC
(828) 295-4200, (800) 262-9036

For information and guide service for overnight camping, caving, trips, family float trips, and white-water rafting on the Nolichuckey and Watauga Rivers and Wilson Creek Gorge, High Mountain Expeditions is one of the best places to go. When you stop for lunch, you will enjoy a gourmet feast by the river. All meals are prepared fresh daily by the Speckled Trout Cafe in Blowing Rock. They also outfit other popular mountain sports and offer kayak clinics, packages, and specialty trips.

Magic Cycles
208 Faculty Street, Boone, NC
(828) 265-2211

Magic Cycles is a specialty bicycle shop that also carries a large line of accessories. The staff repairs all types of bikes; rentals are also available.

New River Outfitters & General Store
10725 U.S Highway 221 N., Jefferson, NC
(336) 982-9193

The historic New River General Store in Ashe County is the site of this well-known river outfitter, a seasonal adventure operation focusing on family tubing and canoeing along the New River. Camping and fishing areas are nearby.

Riverside Canoe and Tube Rentals
Garvey Bridge Road, Chestnut Hill, NC
(336) 982-9439

Riverside offers canoe trips by the hour, day, or weekend. Prices include paddles, life jackets, and shuttle service. Inner tubes of all sizes are also available. At the facility itself, enjoy other recreation, including basketball, volleyball, and horseshoes.

Rock & Roll Sports
280 East King Street, Boone, NC
(828) 264-0765, (800) 977-ROCK

Rock & Roll is a full-service bike and rock-climbing shop, offering sales, service, rentals, and tours. They also offer equipment for ice climbing.

Wahoo's Outdoor Adventures and Canoe Outfitters
3385 U.S. Highway 321, Boone, NC
(828) 262-5774, (800) 444-RAFT

Wahoo's—you can almost feel the whitewater spray in your face—is an apt name for this adventure-trek outfitter that emphasizes whitewater rafting. During the summertime Wahoo's conducts rafting adventures down the Nolichucky River in nearby eastern Tennessee, several sections of the Watauga River, the French Broad and Pigeon Rivers near Asheville, and the Ocoee in southeastern Tennessee, which was the site of the '96 Olympic Games canoe and kayak competition.

Zaloo's Canoes
3874 N.C. Highway 16 S., West Jefferson, NC
(336) 246-3066, (800) 535-4027

Zaloo's is one of the oldest adventure operations in the High Country. These people know the New River like the back of their hand. For 15 years Zaloo's has guided canoeists along the pastoral turns of the New River, one of the world's oldest and one of the few north-flowing rivers in America. Canoe season runs from mid-March to late October. Individual canoes and tubing rentals are also available.

Central Mountains

B. B. Barns Inc.
831 Fairview Road, Asheville, NC
(828) 274-7301

B. B. Barns is an upscale, outdoor retail shop with a quality line of recreational clothing. It also sells topographical maps, books, and some gear. The shop, which has a complete greenhouse, also caters to home gardeners.

Black Dome Mountain Sports
**140 Tunnel Road, Asheville, NC
(828) 251-2001, (800) 678-BDMS**

Black Dome is one of those shops that does it all. In operations since 1993, this outfitter store has an expert staff and nationally known brands of gear and outdoor clothing for mountain sports as well as bikes and kayaks. You can also make your purchases through the shop's mail-order service.

Black Dome's local mountaineering guide service offers an array of adventure trips throughout Western North Carolina. Rock climbing is a specialty here, and the company's special-use permits allow excursions into Pisgah National Forest, not only for climbing, but also for caving, backpacking, and day hiking. Linville Gorge, Table Rock, and Wiseman's View are featured destinations. Also offered are guided flatwater trips for those who want to canoe.

ClimbMax Mountain Guides
**43 Wall Street, Asheville, NC
(828) 252-9996**

Obviously this outfitter's specialty is climbing. Experienced guides offer craggy rockface climbs to chilly ice cliffs. Climbing is taught in an indoor facility at the downtown Asheville location. Educational clinics and classes are continued in the field for those who want to move beyond "bouldering."

ClimbMax offers customized guided backpacking, hiking, and rock-climbing trips to various destinations around Western North Carolina. This outfitter reaches even beyond our borders, with trips to the American Northwest and volcano climbing in Mexico.

Davidson River Outfitters
**U.S. Highways 64, 276 and N.C. Highway 280, Pisgah Forest, NC
(828) 877-4181**

Specializing in fly-fishing, this outfitter can supply all the clothing and equipment you'll want for this sport. They also have fly-tying material, rent fly rods and reels, and fly-fishing lessons and instructional trips are available.

Headwaters Outfitters Inc.
**Intersection of U.S. Highway 64 and N.C. Highway 215, Rosman, NC
(828) 877-3106**

Headwaters provides canoeing, kayaking, and tubing adventures. It specializes in trips on the French Broad River but will also provide canoeing on other rivers by appointment. Trips range from 10 to 20 miles. Expect a 10-mile trip to take three to four hours and a 20-mile trip to last six or seven hours. A favorite place to go tubing is on the North Fork of the French Broad. Headwaters provides a drop-off, and the lively mountain waters will take you right back to their shop. The company also offers a full-day "sea" kayak adventure on Lake Jocassee with an instructor/guide, transportation, and a very nice lunch as another option. It can also arrange fishing trips, waterfall tours, and other outdoor excursions. Headwaters is open from April through October.

Hearn's Cycling & Fitness
**34 Broadway, Asheville, NC
(828) 253-4800**

Hearn's is a tradition in downtown Asheville. Since 1896 the name Hearn has been synonymous here with bicycles. From the turn-of-the-century elegance of bicycle touring to the mad dash and rugged individualism of mountain biking of 100 years later, Hearn's has seen it all. This versatile shop has a wide variety of bikes, parts, and accessories. They offer custom design and complete repair.

Liberty Bicycles
**1987 Hendersonville Highway, Arden, NC
(828) 684-1085, (800) 96-BIKES**

This full-service specialty bike shop is rated a Top 100 Dealer in the United States by the Bicycle Dealers' Showcase.

Just south of Asheville, they offer sales, repair, and custom frame work as well as a large selection of clothing, parts, accessories, maps, and exercise equipment. The shop also rents mountain bikes.

Looking Glass Outfitters
U.S. Highways 64, 276 and N.C. Highway 280, Pisgah Forest, NC
(828) 884–5854
Billed as an "outdoor shop," this store offers clothing, footwear, and equipment for rock climbing, backpacking, and hiking. It is a retail store, but also offers some canoeing trips and hiking tours.

Zippy Boat Works
U.S. Highway 25, Arden, NC
(828) 684–5107
About 20 minutes south of Asheville is Zippy Boat Works, where you can buy canoes and kayaks. The shop also has rentals, instruction, paddling gear, and guide books. The staff provides guided trips and paddling clinics on the French Broad River. The knowledgeable staff can also recommend solo trips to local lake sites and rivers.

Southern Mountains

Nantahala Outdoor Center
13077 U.S. Highway 19, Bryson City, NC
(828) 488–2175, (800) 232–7238

NOC, a long-established, employee-owned company, deserves its good reputation. The center can arrange food and lodging, and provide canoe and kayak instruction, white-water rafting, custom-designed programs, bicycle tours and rentals, and foreign and domestic adventure travel. It also has an outfitters store.

Slickrock Expeditions Inc.
P.O. Box 1214, Cullowhee, NC 28723
(828) 293–3999
Slickrock specializes in recreational and educational backpacking, camping, and canoeing trips in the southern wilds. The company's trips in the southern Appalachians include North Carolina's Joyce Kilmer/Slickrock Wilderness, Big Snowbird Wilderness, Bonas Defeat Gorge, and Panthertown Valley. Slickrock also ran a number of canoeing trips throughout the Southeast, including ones in Georgia's Okefenokee Swamp and on the Big South Fork National River in Tennessee. The latest offerings are canoe trips on the Rio Grande Wild and Scenic River in Texas and backpacking trips in Oregon's Strawberry Mountain Wilderness. Trips are completely outfitted and led by a professional wilderness guide. Call or write for a brochure.

SKIING

It's been only 40 years since Western North Carolina's first ski resort opened at Cataloochee in the Maggie Valley area of Haywood County. That same year Blowing Rock Ski Lodge became the first ski resort in the mountains' High Country. On its heels was Hound Ears, also in Blowing Rock, which opened during the winter of 1964–1965, followed in the winter of 1966–1967 by Seven Devils, now known as Hawksnest Golf and Ski Resort.

Beech Mountain Ski Resort opened in 1968–1969, creating a new type of larger ski operation that would incorporate an Alpine village atmosphere. In the late '60s, the Blowing Rock Ski Lodge became Appalachian Ski Mountain. In the early '70s, Sugar Mountain Ski Resort, in Banner Elk near Boone, and Wolf Laurel, in Madison County about 45 minutes north of Asheville, were launched. Skiing in the mountains had finally arrived. Unfortunately the industry stalled due to unseasonably warm winters and a downturn in the economy in the late '70s.

However, thanks to the latest advances in snowmaking technology and some cold winters, skiers are back with a vengeance to enjoy the ski season, which generally runs from mid-November through March.

Lift tickets for area resorts usually run between $20.00 and $30.00 on weekends, depending on the resort, and drop by as much as $8.00 to $10.00 during the week. Ski rentals and lessons will add to that cost. Resorts have also learned to diversify, offering a wide variety of package deals, attractions, discounts, and one-stop vacation planning. They also cater to newer trends such as snow-boarding, which is currently taking the slopes by storm. Some resorts have incorporated snowboard parks to accommodate these slope surfers. Tubing, or sliding down a hill on a large inner tube, akin to sledding, has also been introduced by several resorts. This is a great activity for the kids and folks who want to come along for the trip but don't necessarily want to ski this time.

As families increasingly take more long weekend trips instead of lengthy vacations, these cool slopes within a few hours of most of Western North Carolina look extremely inviting. Cross-country skiing, another popular slant on the sport, is enjoyed along country roads and forest trails with every heavy snowfall. It's found mostly, however, in the High Country of the northern mountains, usually on restricted routes along Blue Ridge Parkway areas, such as Roan Mountain (along the Tennessee and North Carolina border), Doughton Park (on the parkway just outside the town of Sparta), and other parkway links. There's also some cross-country skiing on private trails at Beech Mountain Ski Resort. For more information on cross-country skiing, call the rangers' office of the Blue Ridge Parkway (828–295–7591). For a complete overview of skiing in the mountains of North Carolina pull up Web site www.skinorthcarolina.com.

NORTHERN MOUNTAINS

Avery County

Hawksnest Golf and Ski Resort
1800 Skyland Drive, Banner Elk, NC
(828) 963–6561, (888) HAWKSNEST
(828) 963–6563 (snow report)
www.hawksnest-resort.com

This resort maintains 14 slopes: two beginner, six intermediate, and six advanced, with a peak elevation of 4,819 feet. The vertical drop is 619 feet. Their newest slope, Top Gun, a.k.a. Ski Challenge of the South, is reported to be the best new slope in the Southeast. Two double-chair lifts and two surface lifts get you to the top. The facility offers a restaurant and lounge, cafeteria, lockers, equipment and clothing rentals, ski lessons, and a snowboard park. Kiddy Hawk is a great program available for children ages 5 to 12. Nighthawk, however, is way past their bedtime; this program gives avid skiers the opportunity to ski under the stars on Friday and Saturday until 2:00 A.M. On these evenings live music entertains guests in the Nest lounge. Discount rates are available for groups of 20 or more.

Sugar Mountain Ski Resort
1009 Sugar Mountain Drive, Banner Elk, NC
(828) 898–4521, (800) SUGARMT (after Nov.)
www.skisugar.com

Sugar Mountain Ski Resort sits at 5,300 feet above sea level. Among the 20 slopes at Sugar are 7 beginner, 10 intermediate, and 3 expert runs. The vertical drop is 1,200 feet. The mountain is serviced by five chairlifts and three surface lifts. Sugar Bears is Sugar Mountain's ski program for children. The resort also offers equipment rentals, ski lessons, a tubing run, lockers, a nursery, game room, two cafeterias, lounge restaurant, deck grill, and club called the Last Run Lounge. The resort offers discounts for groups of 15 or more. To get to Sugar Mountain follow N.C. 105 N. to N.C. Highway 184; after 1 mile you will reach the turn for the resort.

Madison County

Wolf Laurel
Wolf Laurel Road, Rt. 3, Mars Hill, NC
(828) 689–4111, (800) 817–4111 (after Nov. 1)
www.skiwolflaurel.com

Wolf Laurel is just north of Asheville, a drive of about 40 minutes via U.S. 19/23. The highways split about 20 miles from Asheville; follow U.S. 23 north and watch for signs that lead to the Rt. 3 (Wolf Laurel Road) turn-off.

This resort is the newest of Western North Carolina's ski areas. Students from nearby Mars Hill College find it a convenient alternative to the resorts farther north, as do a number of Asheville's city dwellers.

The Wolf offers 54 acres of skiable terrain, in the form of 16 slopes for beginners as well as more advanced skiers. Elevation is 4,600 feet, with a vertical drop of 650 feet. Three lifts and one high-speed, quad chairlift service the mountain. Ski lessons are offered hourly every day until 7:00 P.M. The lodge provides a ski shop, clothing and equipment rentals, and a grill. Snow-tubing has taken the Wolf by storm, and the new Snow-Tubing Park allows for all day and evening tubing. Even better, tubers don't have to hike back up the hill, but rather they can hook their tubes up to a lift and ride their tubes back to the top, while enjoying the view. Lessons, season passes, discount packages, night skiing, and a children's Wolf Cub program (for children five to seven) are also offered at Wolf Laurel.

Accommodations are available at the Wolf Cave Inn, within walking distance of the slopes. Special packages and group rates are available.

Watauga County

Appalachian Ski Mountain
940 Ski Mountain Road, Blowing Rock, NC
(828) 295-7828, (800) 322-2373 (snow report)
www.appskimtn.com

This family-owned ski resort, begun in 1962, continues to be a popular destination for vacationers. Appalachian Ski Mountain offers nine slopes: two beginner, four intermediate, and three advanced, with a peak elevation of 4,000 feet. The vertical drop is 365 feet. You can get up the hill on two quad chairlifts, one double chairlift, one rope tow, and one handle-pull tow.

A Bavarian-style 45,000-square-foot lodge with a giant fireplace overlooks the slopes, housing a cafeteria, ski shop, and gift shop. A 200-foot observation deck allows for generous views. Lockers and clothing and equipment rentals are available, as are adult lessons and a SKIwee instruction program for youngsters 4 to 12.

The second weekend in December marks Appalachian Ski Mountain's anniversary, which is always celebrated with 1962-vintage ski rates—a bargain in anybody's book. Appalachian is also the home of the French-Swiss Ski College, one of the finest ski schools in the country.

Another fun celebration at Ski Mountain is the New Year's Eve fireworks display against the backdrop of a snow-covered slope. Two recent additions to the fun are the refrigerated outdoor ice-skating arena and snow skating. Billed as America's newest winter sport, snow skating uses shoes with skilike bottoms for skating or skiing down the slopes.

The only in-season closing times for the slopes are Christmas Eve night and all day on Christmas. The ice-skating arena is open from Thanksgiving until the end of the ski season, including Christmas. And on Valentine's night, after skiing, a grand fireworks display takes place. Group rates for fifteen or more people are available on request. The reservations department can book skiing and lodging for you.

To get to Appalachian Ski Mountain, take U.S. 221/321 from Blowing Rock to Boone. You'll see a sign for the resort about 1.5 miles onto U.S. 221/321. Turn here on to Edmisten Road and drive 2 miles to the resort.

Beech Mountain Ski Resort
1007 Beech Mountain Parkway, Beech Mountain, NC
(828) 387–2011, (800) 438–2093
www.skibeech.com
At 5,505 feet above sea level, Beech Mountain is the highest ski area in eastern North America. Established in 1969, the ski resort provides the complete winter sport experience from A to Z. Central to the resort is Beech Tree Village, a complex of facilities designed to anticipate the skier's every need. Its shops and services include equipment and clothing rentals, several gift shops, ski schools, a variety of restaurants, a nursery, video game facility, ski lessons, ski patrol, and even an outdoor ice-skating rink.

Beech Mountain has 14 slopes: three beginner, seven intermediate, and four advanced. The vertical drop measures 830 feet. The mountain is serviced by one high-speed detachable quad chairlift, one J-bar, and one rope tow, and every slope is within reach of the snow-making machines. A half-pipe run designed for snowboards was recently added along with snowboard rentals.

Through the resort rental offices, a variety of accommodations are available, including 650 privately owned town homes and chalets, four inns, and a bed-and-breakfast. You can come to Beech Mountain for your vacation and never have to leave the resort. Multiday packages and group rates are available.

SOUTHERN MOUNTAINS
Haywood County

Cataloochee Ski Area
1080 Ski Lodge Road, Maggie Valley, NC
(828) 926–0285, (800) 768–3588
(800) 768–0285 (snow report)
www.cataloochee.com
Cataloochee, North Carolina's first ski resort, has long been one of the region's

---

If the mountain weather fails to cooperate, and you find more grass than snow in the mountains on your trip, don't be disillusioned. The mountains in winter are excellent for hiking! Check with any local chamber of commerce or the National Forest Service for some easy trails, dress warmly, and go out for a hike, weather permitting. The leaves that obscure many views in other seasons will be gone, and a frozen winterland can be yours for the viewing at the meandering pace of a hike, rather than a fast downhill run.

---

favorites. Its mile-high location provides fine conditions for making and keeping snow. Omigosh, the area's longest advanced slope, plummets 2,200 feet from the very top of 5,400-foot-tall Moody Top Mountain and joins up with the 1,800-foot Lower Omigosh, an intermediate slope. These along with seven other advanced, intermediate, and beginner runs offer skiers plenty of options to match their skills. There are two double chairlifts and one surface lift, and night skiing is offered from Tuesday through Saturday. Snowboading began at Cataloochee in 1984. There are now nine trails, and snowboard clinics are offered seven days a week, five times a day.

You can contact Cataloochee for discounted stay-and-ski packages with accommodations in the Maggie Valley area. After you work up an appetite on the slopes, the lodge provides hot, home-cooked meals, or you can enjoy a toddy around the circular fireplace or on the deck that overlooks the ski runs.

Jackson County

Sapphire Valley Ski Area
4350 Highway 64 W., Cashiers, NC
(828) 743-1164
www.skisapphire.com
Sapphire Valley Resort, which bills itself as "a resort for all seasons," has its own ski area for its property owners and resort guests, in addition to such outdoor sports as golf, tennis, horseback riding, canoeing, fishing, swimming, and hiking. The ski area is composed of a novice hill with a rope tow and intermediate and advanced slopes served by a chairlift. There's a base lodge that contains a ski shop and rental shop; a ski school is housed in a separate building.

Night skiing is available but cross-country skiing is not. Snow-boarding came to Sapphire in 1995 with two trails and clinics available. After a workout on the slopes, skiers can relax at the resort's health club with its indoor pool, Jacuzzi, and sauna.

Macon County

Scaly Mountain Ski Area
7420 Dillard Road, Scaly Mountain, NC
(828) 526-3737, (800) 929-SNOW
www.scalymountain.com
The southernmost of the state's ski areas sits a few miles south of Highlands on N.C. 106. Its elevations range from 3,800 feet to 4,025 feet. We think Scaly is perfect for beginners and children. In fact, at 1,800 feet its beginners slope is actually its longest. The intermediate slope is 1,600 feet long, and Scaly's advanced slope, which makes up in steepness what it lacks in length, is only 1,200 feet. Served by one chairlift and a rope tow, these slopes are lighted for night skiing from Thursday through Saturday. Snowboarders will find four trails for their use, and clinics are available. Snow-tubing is allowed Thursday through Sunday.

Though rates are subject to change, they're moderate when compared with many other areas and even cheaper when scheduled by a group of 25 or more. You can also get a good price by buying a rental equipment, instruction, and lift-ticket package. Designed with families in mind, Scaly Mountain's lodge, which contains a huge, custom-made wood-burning stove, has windows that allow parents to keep an eye on the kids no matter which slope they are skiing. There is also a deck for outdoor viewing and a cafeteria for warm drinks and food.

GOLF

ool summers and mild winters divided by long rejuvenating springs and lingering, colorful autumns make "mountain golf," as it's commonly called here, a year-round pleasure. During the dog days of summer, you can head for one of the higher-altitude courses—up at 3,000 feet or more—for a decided drop in degrees. Or later in the year, if a particular day seems too chilly for a game, you can play one of the courses in the warmer "thermal belt" down around Tryon in Polk County, where the elevation is only 1,100 feet.

Wherever you play, you'll be surrounded by beauty and challenged by courses sculpted around undulating hills, deep mountain valleys, rivers, lakes, waterfalls, and majestic rock formations, all kept lusciously green by some 50 inches of rainfall spread relatively evenly throughout the year. Because of the hilly nature of many of the courses, golf carts are popular. Some courses require them.

There are dozens of public, semipublic, resort, and private courses scattered around the region. Some resort courses are open only to guests, but many offer reasonably priced golf packages that include accommodations and, often, meals. Others are open to the general public, but most require advance reservations. Here we give you a taste of the variety offered at our favorite courses that allow some public play.

North Carolina rates second only to Florida in the number of deaths caused by lightning. It's not that we get more strikes than other states, it's just that people here don't seem to respect lightning as much as they should. So take shelter at the first approach of a thunderstorm—but do it indoors, not under a tree.

Contact the Great Smoky Mountains Golf Association, P.O. Box 18556, Asheville, NC 28801, or the chambers of commerce of individual Western North Carolina counties for more detailed information.

NORTHERN MOUNTAINS

Alleghany County

New River Golf and Country Club
611 Golf Course Road, Sparta, NC
(336) 372-4869
New River Golf and Country Club is an 18-hole, par 71 rolling terrain course featuring front and back nines as different as night and day. The front nine is like a flatland course, whereas the back nine is a true mountain course, with many hills. Yardages are 5,601 and 5,741 (women's and men's tees). The club is open to the public daily, and greens fees are $20 weekdays and $28 weekends, including cart. To get here, turn at the sign after Twin Oaks General Store on U.S. 221 S.

Ashe County

Mountain Aire Golf Club
1104 Golf Course Road, West Jefferson, NC
(336) 877-4716
This well-established public course offers 18 holes on well-maintained fairways complemented by the natural, rugged beauty of the Appalachian Mountains. Greens fees range from $25 to $39 per person including cart. Amenities include carts, club rentals, and a driving range. Lessons and seasonal memberships are available, as are group rates. The club pro is Mark Hagel. The developers here also offer homesites in an adjacent golf course community called Fairway Ridge (see our Relocation chapter).

Avery County

Blue Ridge Country Club
U.S. Highway 221 N., Linville Falls, NC
(828) 756-7001
This relatively new semiprivate championship golf course sits in a beautiful valley with wonderful mountain views. Four tee boxes allow for various skill levels and playing options. Yardage for this challenging mountain course ranges from 4,800 to 6,900. The course features subtle elevation changes, gentle terrain, and mountain vistas. Ongoing development is enhancing the course's lovely North Cove Valley location. It costs $39 to play on Mondays through Thursdays and $48 to play on the weekend. The costs include carts.

Memberships are available. The Lodge at Blue Ridge operates as a 12-suite facility with all rooms including a private riverfront deck and a stone fireplace. Conference rooms are also available.

If golf is one of your main means of exercising, you may be tempted to bypass golf carts in favor of walking. On many of our hilly courses, that's likely to result in more exercise than you counted on.

Hawksnest Golf and Ski Resort
2058 Skyland Drive, Banner Elk, NC
(828) 963-6561
Located off N.C. 105, Hawksnest Golf Course is nestled high in the Blue Ridge Mountains. This par 72 course with large bentgrass greens offers the challenge of a true mountain course to golfers of all abilities. The thrill of playing this championship course is surpassed only by the majestic views from every hole (and the cool High Country weather). Facilities also include a well-stocked golf shop and full-service snack bar. Yardage is 4,799 and 5,953. Weekend play costs $39 before 1:00 P.M.; weekday play costs $39 before 1:00 P.M.

Madison County

Wolf Laurel Resort
Rt. 3, Mars Hill, NC
(828) 680-9772, (800) 221-0409
Wolf Laurel Resort offers an 18-hole championship course adjacent to "Ski the Wolf." Just 35 minutes north of Asheville, it offers many extras: a clubhouse and conference facility, pool, tennis, dining, putting greens, and a croquet lawn. The course offers magnificent views. Golf and ski packages are available.

Wolf Laurel is on Route 3, 10 miles north on U.S. 23 from the U.S. 19/23 divide. Costs are $40 per person and $14 for cart rental (which is a must).

McDowell County

Old Fort Golf Course
off I-40, Old Fort, NC
(828) 668-4256
This nine-hole, semiprivate course, established in 1962, lies southeast of Old Fort and is easily accessed off I-40. This rolling course has a small lake, a few streams, and a difficult dogleg on the third hole. The facility contains a driving range, pro shop, and snack bar. Individual yearly memberships are available for $350. Public greens fees are $12 and $16 for weekends and holidays. These fees are good for up to 27 holes of play.

Mitchell County

Grassy Creek Golf Club
2360 Swiss Pine Lake Drive, Spruce Pine, NC
(828) 765-7436
This semiprivate championship 18-hole, par 72 course is just 4 miles from the Blue Ridge Parkway. A new 8,000-square-foot clubhouse includes a restaurant, meeting space, and pro shop. There is also a driving range on site. Greens fees are $35 weekdays and $40 weekends and include carts. Yardage is 6,277 and 5,744.

Watauga County

Boone Golf Club
Fairway Drive off U.S. Highway 321,
Boone, NC
(828) 264-8760

This 18-hole course designed by Ellis Maples is a par 71. Level and gently rolling fairways and large bentgrass greens are features. Yardage is 6,400. The club is open daily to the public and features electric carts and a restaurant. Monday through Thursday costs are $39; during the weekends it costs $44 in the low season. Memorial Day through Labor Day, those costs change to $45 and $49, respectively, and include carts.

Willow Creek Golf Course
Bear Creek Road, Boone, NC
(828) 963-6865

This challenging nine-hole, par 27 course is set in a valley. The course features a great deal of variety and offers senior citizens and student discounts during weekdays. Yardage is 1,351 and 1,574. The golf course is 3 miles outside Boone, coming from Banner Elk on N.C. 105. Nine holes cost $9.00 walking, and 18 holes cost $15.00. With a cart the costs are $15.00 and $24.00, respectively.

Yancey County

Mount Mitchell Golf Club
7590 Highway 80 S., Burnsville, NC
(828) 675-5454, (828) 675-4923 (rentals)

This perfect vacation course is cradled in the valley below Mount Mitchell, the highest peak east of the Mississippi. Vacation rentals—privately owned houses and town houses—are available around the perimeter of the course. Renters pay $44 weekdays for greens fees and cart rental. Regular greens fees are $50 weekdays and $64 weekends and holidays. This fee includes a cart. It is a lovely, scenic location. Yardage ranges from 5,500 to 6,500.

CENTRAL MOUNTAINS
Buncombe County

Black Mountain Golf Course
18 Ross Drive, Black Mountain, NC
(828) 669-2710

This public course, operated by the town of Black Mountain, about 20 minutes east of Asheville, boasts one of the country's longest par 6 holes at 747 yards. The course offers not only challenging fairways but marvelous views of the surrounding mountains. The quaint town of Black Mountain, noted for its antique shops, restaurants, and musical tradition, is nearby.

Greens fees are $35 and $40, including the cart, for weekdays and weekends, respectively. This friendly, community golf course offers a multitude of discounts for senior citizens, Black Mountain residents, junior golfers (18 and younger whose parents are not members), and families. A pro shop and snack bar are also available.

Henderson County

Crooked Creek Golf Course
764 Crooked Creek Road,
Hendersonville, NC
(828) 692-2011

This 18-hole, 6,636-yard, par 72 championship course, situated just 1.5 miles from Hendersonville, is close enough for residents to take off for a quick game on a long lunch hour. Open to the public year-round, the course has a wide-open feel with Bermuda grass fairways and bentgrass greens. There's a practice green, range, snack bar, and pro shop. Crooked Creek provides both riding and push carts

Due to frequent showers, it's wise to get a covered cart and stick an umbrella in your golf bag.

as well as lessons from a pro. Rates run $15 for 18 holes when walking and $25 with a cart; 9 holes are $10 walking and $15 with a cart.

Cummings Cove Golf and Country Club
3000 Cummings Road, Hendersonville, NC
(828) 891-9412
Designed by Robert E. Cupp, former on-site golf architect of Nicklaus Design Company, this Scottish-style course has been rated as one of the top 50 in North Carolina by *GolfWeek* magazine. Embankments flank many of the greens of this challenging 5,288-yard, par 70 course, and woods border the entire course. Amenities include a modern clubhouse, pro shop, tennis courts, and pool.

Cummings Cove is 8 miles from Hendersonville off U.S. 64 W. and is open to the public seven days a week. Tee times are required, and cart and green fee costs, which are subject to change, currently run $32 from Monday through Thursday and $38 from Friday through Sunday and on holidays. (A seniors rate of $22 is offered Monday through Thursday for those over 55.) Nine holes are $17 Monday through Thursday and $20 Friday through Sunday and on holidays. These prices include taxes.

Etowah Valley Country Club and Golf Lodge
U.S. Highway 64 W., Etowah, NC
(828) 891-7022, (800) 451-8174
Conveniently situated halfway between Hendersonville and Brevard in the small community of Etowah, this semiprivate, 27-hole championship course, designed by Edmund Ault and beautified by horticulturist Jean-Claude Linossi, has bentgrass greens measuring up to 9,000 square feet. Its three 9-hole courses and four tee positions allow for a variety of 18-hole combinations. For example, the rather flat south course plays from 2,822 to 3,507 yards (par 36); the west course, with its large greens and bunkers, from 2,800 to 3,601 yards (par 36); and the open, rolling north course from 2,615 to 3,404 yards (par 37).

Other amenities include modern lodges, lighted putting greens, a driving range, heated swimming pool, clubhouse, bathhouse, fitness center, pro shop, restaurant, lounge, and meeting and banquet facilities for groups of up to 200.

For a different sort of challenge—or for nongolfing family members—Etowah provides a full-size, bentgrass greensward for croquet players and offers croquet packages along with a variety of golf packages. For example, a spring-through-fall, three-night weekend getaway golf package runs $327 per person, double occupancy, and includes lodging, breakfast, dinner, club storage, and unlimited greens fees. Cart rentals, which cost $30 for 18 holes for two people, are not included in the package price.

Nonguests can play 18 holes for $49. (The price includes a golf cart.)

Orchard Trace Golf Club
942 Sugarloaf Road, Hendersonville, NC
(828) 685-1006
Night doesn't bring an end to golfing at this 18-hole, 2,139-yard public course nestled in the heart of Henderson County's apple country. Seventy-two floodlights illuminate its entire 34 acres, making it the first fully lighted links in Western North Carolina. The course is made up of bluegrass fairways and bentgrass greens meandering around a small pond and two winding creeks. Hole distances vary from 81 to 212 yards. Greens fees for 18 holes are $16.50 with a motorized cart, $11.50 with a pull cart, and $10.00 for walking players. The clubhouse features a snack bar and a pro shop. (Seniors rate offers a $2.00 discount until 5:00 P.M. Monday through Friday.)

Polk County

Red Fox Country Club
2 Club Drive, Tryon, NC
(828) 894-8251
The Red Fox Country Club, designed by architect Ellis Maples and opened in 1966, was quickly recognized as one of the top

100 championship courses in the country. Situated less than 2 miles from I–26, its 18 holes are serenely set amid mountain streams that wind to a 30-acre lake. Here you'll find wide fairways; large, sloping greens; a practice green and range; locker room; snack bar; rental clubs; and pro shop.

For many years Red Fox was operated as a private club, but it became semipublic in the mid-1980s. Memberships range in price from $1,000 to $4,000 per year, but the public is also permitted to play at a cost of $30 from 7:30 A.M. to 3:00 P.M. and $20 after 3:00 P.M. Monday through Friday. On weekends the cost runs $35 until 3:00 P.M. and $25 after 3:00 P.M. Prices include a required golf cart. Golfers who enjoy competition can sign up for Red Fox's mailing list and will be invited to play in its open golf outings held throughout the year.

Rutherford County

Cleghorn Plantation Golf & Country Club
183 Golf Circle, Rutherfordton, NC
(828) 286–9117
This 18-hole golf course is in the foothills of the Blue Ridge Mountains. All fees include cart. Weekdays the fee is $25 and weekends, $31. Senior rate for weekdays is $18.

Lake Lure Golf & Beach Resort at Fairfield Mountain
112 Mountain Boulevard, Lake Lure, NC
(828) 625–3016, (800) 260–1040
A 27-mile shoreline of Lake Lure and the surrounding mountains create an idyllic experience on this 18-hole course. Additionally there are three restaurants, a fitness center, a marina, tennis courts, and three pools. To add even more interest, the movie *Dirty Dancing* was filmed at this site. Contact the resort for fees and other inquiries.

Meadowbrook Golf Club
1211 Meadowbrook Road, Rutherfordton, NC
(828) 863–2690, (866) 863–2690

This 6,400-yard course was built on the historic Deck family farm. It continues to be family owned. The 18-hole course runs up hills and down, through meadows, and along two creeks, creating challenges on both nines. All rates include carts. Monday through Friday rates are $25 and $19 for seniors. Weekend rates are $30 for everyone.

Transylvania County

Glen Cannon Country Club
Wilson Road, Brevard, NC
(828) 883–8175
Glen Cannon, a semiprivate course, is just 3 miles from downtown Brevard. This is one of the more established golf courses in the area, having been here for 33 years. Beautiful scenery surrounds this club, which offers a well-maintained 6,270-yard, 18-hole championship course that's open year-round. There's even a picture-perfect waterfall on no. 2. Amenities include tennis courts, a clubhouse, and swimming pool.

Though it is a semiprivate course, area visitors who live outside a 50-mile radius of Brevard may play on a per-day basis for $54, including a cart.

Sherwood Forest Golf Club
N.C. Highway 276 S., Cedar Mountain, NC
(828) 884–7825
Sherwood Forest, a 1,000-acre community resort, sits on a high plateau in the Blue Ridge Mountains, 8 miles south of Brevard on NC 276. Its 18-hole, par 54 golf course, open to the public, has Pencross bentgrass greens and stream-caressed fairways, bordered with the area's marvelous rhododendrons and mountain laurel. A river runs through the course, whose relative flatness makes it one of the few mountain courses

Does your golf game improve in the mountains? Some players swear their shots travel higher and farther here due to the thinner atmosphere.

where you don't have to ride. The front nine is heavily wooded, and the back nine is wide open. Water hazards are on eight holes. In winter greens fees are $11.00 during the week and $12.00 on weekends; in summer they're $12.00 during the week and $13.00 on weekends. Students can play for $9.00 during the week.

SOUTHERN MOUNTAINS
Cherokee County

Cherokee Hills Golf Course and Country Club
Harshaw Road, Murphy, NC
(828) 837-5853, (800) 334-3905
Semiprivate Cherokee Hills, with its 18-hole championship golf course, lies in a picturesque mountain valley 3 miles east of Murphy. In addition to a 12-unit lodge, this community resort offers town houses for rent or for sale, along with homesites, tennis courts, a pool, restaurant, and complete pro shop. Golf packages start at $75 per night, per person, double occupancy and include lodging and golf with a cart. Greens fees for nonguests are $15.00, and cart rentals are $10.60.

Clay County

Chatuge Shores Golf Course
Myers Chapel Road, Hayesville, NC
(828) 389-8940
This very attractive 18-hole, par 72 course serves the residents of several surrounding counties including Clay, Cherokee, and Graham. Yardage is 6,687. For residents of this area, annual family memberships are $340. Membership includes the use of the swimming pool and tennis courts. Cart fees for members are $5.00 per person for 9 holes and $9.00 for 18 holes. Cart fees for nonmembers are $6.50 for 9 holes and $11.00 for 18 holes. During the week nonmembers pay green fees of $12.00 for 9 holes and $18.00 for 18 holes;

on weekends and holidays it's $12.00 for 9 holes, $22.00 for 18 holes. There is a charge of $2.00 to use the pool.

Haywood County

Lake Junaluska Golf Course
756 Golf Course Road, Waynesville, NC
(828) 456-5777
This attractive golf course is directly across the highway from the Lake Junaluska Conference Center. Several holes provide panoramic views of the 200-acre lake and surrounding mountains. Reasonable prices are offered. Call for rates.

Maggie Valley Resort & Country Club
1819 Country Club Drive, Maggie Valley, NC
(828) 926-1616, (800) 438-3861
This nationally acclaimed, 18-hole, par 72 course has been the site of four North Carolina Open Golf Tournaments and numerous other tournaments. *GolfWeek* rates Maggie Valley as one of America's best, and its bentgrass greens have been ranked among the top 15 in the nation. It's diverse and challenging: The first nine holes run through the rolling terrain of the valley, while the back nine winds through the mountains.

Accommodations include cozy guest rooms and mountainside villas surrounded by more than 35,000 square feet of well-tended gardens. There is a heated pool, a restaurant, and a pub that offers resort-style nightlife. Call for special package rates.

Springdale Country Club and Resort
200 Golfwatch Road, Canton, NC
(828) 235-8451, (800) 553-3027
Springdale is another community resort centered around its excellent golf course. Eleven miles from Canton, not far from its entrance to the Blue Ridge Parkway, and surrounded by the grandeur of the Great Smoky Mountains, the course measures a challenging 6,812 yards from the championship tees. The 429-yard, par 4 no. 4, for example, has you punching your second

shot through a narrow opening up to a trap-protected green. On the flatter and shorter back nine, the 417-yard, par 4 no. 15 doglegs left and calls for a second shot across a pond.

But, while the golf may be exciting, this family-owned resort is casual and relaxed. Because golf is the name of the game here, you won't find pools, spas, tennis courts, or fancy dress codes. You'll find family-style, home-cooked meals served overlooking the 18th green and cozy cottages with rocking chairs, a view, and television. Other amenities include a practice green, range, chipping green, two restaurants, rental clubs, and pro shop. Package tours include accommodations, breakfast, dinner, unlimited golf cart, and unlimited golf. For permanent stays one- and three-acre homesites and town houses are for sale.

Cost for nonresidents is $45 per round, including a cart.

Waynesville Country Club Inn
Country Club Drive, Waynesville, NC
(828) 456-3551, (800) 627-6250

Here 27 holes of golf blend with mountain streams, ponds, and the ever-present mountain views. The links, made up of lush fairways and picture-perfect bent-grass greens, consist of three separate and distinct par 35, nine-hole courses that start and finish at the clubhouse. Each hole offers four sets of tees, thus ensuring a pleasurable experience for golfers at all levels of play.

Guests can choose from lodge rooms, cottages or villas, and several restaurants. You'll also find tennis courts, a pool, and a pro shop. Be sure to ask about Waynesville's special Getaway Holiday Packages as well as daily golf packages that start as low as $35 per person, double occupancy, during the uncrowded winter season. For nonresidents the cost will run around $48 for 18 holes, including a cart. (See our Resorts chapter for more information on the inn.)

Jackson County

High Hampton Inn & Country Club
N.C. Highway 107 S., Cashiers, NC
(828) 743-2450, (800) 334-2551

Sitting at 3,600 feet, this 1,400-acre estate with its private 35-acre lake surrounds a historic country inn and its nearby cottages. All of these are just steps from the 18-hole, 6,012-yard, par 71 golf course designed by George W. Cobb that provides a scenic mountain view. The cost, including a cart, is $55 (subject to change), $48 if you are a guest at the resort. In addition to the course, there are two putting greens and an excellent practice range with the tee area covered for protection against rain. High Hampton also offers a series of three- and four-day golf schools from April through October designed for beginners, intermediates, and more advanced players. Each year there are two tournaments, one in June and one in September, for seniors (age 50 to 64) and superseniors (age 65 and older).

Facilities include tennis courts, a play area, an archery field, and sports fields. An excellent children's activity program is offered from June 1 through Labor Day. There is also a well-equipped exercise room. The lake is popular for swimming,

---

The top of Whiteside Mountain in Jackson County offers a fantastic view of Cashiers Valley, the upper Chattooga River watershed, and the surrounding Blue Ridge Mountain peaks. A fairly easy 1.5-mile loop circles the summit with a 0.5-mile side trail to Devil's Courthouse. From Cashiers, take US 64 W. for 5 miles to Whiteside Mountain Road (SR 1690). Turn left onto this road and continue for about a mile until you reach the Whiteside Mountain parking area on your left. There is a $2.00 per vehicle parking fee (see our Forests and Parks chapter).

---

sailing, canoeing, rowing, and pedaling boats. You'll also find an exercise trail and several walking trails, with guided walks weekly. All meals are served buffet style, and High Hampton's famous afternoon tea is offered from 4:00 to 5:00 P.M. (See our Resorts chapter for more information.)

Sapphire Mountain Golf Club
50 Slicer's Avenue, Sapphire, NC
(828) 743–1174, (800) 533–8268

This challenging 6,147-yard golf course, with water hazards on 9 holes, plus a waterfall hole, is a part of the 5,000-acre, all-season Sapphire Valley Resort that grew around the old Fairfield Inn, built in the late 1890s. This is the perfect place to go with nongolf-playing family members, because while you're out on the links, they can entertain themselves with horseback and canoe rides, fishing, swimming, hiking, and tennis and join in supervised pro-grams for children. A recreation complex offers a heated indoor pool with sauna and whirlpool, an exercise/weight room, table tennis and pool tables, game machines, and minigolf.

Nonresidents can play here for around $55, including a cart. (See our Resorts chapter for more information.)

Macon County

Mill Creek Country Club
U.S. Highway 64 W., Franklin, NC
(828) 524–4653, (800) 533–3916

Bordered on three sides by the incredible natural beauty of the Nantahala National Forest, the main attraction at this 380-acre community resort is still the 18-hole championship golf course. Rolling terrain, rippling creeks, and thick stands of pine and willow trees interweave with the lush fairways and carefully manicured greens. As interesting as it is beautiful, this course can challenge players of any skill level. Half- and three-quarter-acre home sites and single-family homes are for sale. Two-day, weekly, and monthly rentals of deluxe villas also are available. Greens fees with a cart are $43 per person weekdays. Prices vary with the season. Golf packages are available. Please call for rates.

Swain County

Smoky Mountain Country Club
1300 Conley Creek Road, Whittier, NC
(828) 497–2772, (800) 474–0070

In 1996 Swain County finally got a golf course that proved worth the wait. Since then the county-owned course, set in the beauty of the Smoky Mountains, has gone through several cosmetic changes to increase both its attractiveness and playa-bility. The course was designed by J. Porter Gibson and modified by Brassie Gold Corporation. Each designer used the natural mountain terrain to develop a challenging place to play, and the result-ing par 70, 6,500-yard championship course, with its change in elevation approaching 1,000 feet, gives each hole a different and delightful view of the moun-tains. Each hole also offers unique chal-lenges. From the par 3's to the par 5's, no player is likely to get bored.

You'll find this fine golf experience a lit-tle more than a mile from the Smoky Moun-tains Expressway (U.S. 74) and 7 miles from both downtown Bryson City and Cherokee. There are a number of pricing options that allow anyone to play at a reasonable rate. Many local hotels offer golf packages and a multiplay package can be purchased at the golf course clubhouse. Yearly memberships are also available.

For a stunning view of the town of High-lands in Macon County, drive to the nature center on Horse Cove Road just outside town. It's a 20-minute, moder-ate hike from there to the Sunset Rocks Overlook. In addition to Highlands, you'll be able to see the whole of his-toric Horse Cove. A sign, RAVENEL PARK, marks the trailhead.

FORESTS AND PARKS

If we had to pick one reason why we love living in Western North Carolina, it would be its vast system of public lands. Few of us have to travel even an hour in order to be in a wild, natural, government-protected environment. For most residents it's a matter of minutes. Even an avid outdoors person could spend a lifetime here and probably never see all that there is of these great natural treasures. If you could accomplish such a feat, you'd have to do it three more times, because even the same place is vastly different when altered by the dramatic changes brought on by fall, winter, and spring.

Western North Carolina is home to more than half of the Great Smoky Mountains National Park and two huge national forests. The Pisgah National Forest and the Nantahala National Forest combined cover more than a million acres scattered over several tracts. In addition the National Park Service oversees the large section of the Blue Ridge Parkway that crosses this region of the state (see our Blue Ridge Parkway chapter). There are also three very diverse state parks to be enjoyed: New River, Mount Jefferson, and Mount Mitchell, plus two state forests: DuPont State Forest and Holmes Educational State Forest. There also are the rugged 10,000 acres that make up the Green River Game Lands.

In this chapter you will find a number of hiking and recreational possibilities, but there are many other suggestions in our Blue Ridge Parkway, Recreation, and Waterfalls chapters for getting out and about in our parks and forests. Detailed camping information can be found in our Recreation chapter. As a handy reference, we have included here a special section that lists all ranger stations, their loca-

tions, and phone numbers. They are a great source of information on forest trails, camping, plant life, wildlife, etc.

So let's jump right into some brief overviews of these mountainous public spaces as well as some of their, excuse the pun, high points.

THE GREAT SMOKY MOUNTAINS NATIONAL PARK

This national park, with 276,063 acres in North Carolina and 244,345 acres in Tennessee, hosts nine million visitors annually, making it the most heavily used national park in the country. Congress authorized it in 1926, but because the land was difficult to acquire from both individuals and timber companies, it wasn't dedicated by Franklin Roosevelt until 1940—and just in time, too! During the latter part of the 19th century, and even more so in the early part of the 20th, loggers were stripping these mountains bare, taking, at first, the most easily accessible trees from land that was later included in the park.

Lucky for us the loggers hadn't gotten around to some of the steeper and more remote areas. As a result we still have approximately 110,000 acres of old-growth forest within the 520,408-acre park. Some of these trees, such as poplar and spruce, are over 400 years old. However, in the more than half a century since cutting stopped, second-growth trees have made such a good comeback that most of us can't tell which areas are old growth and which are second growth.

As important as the park's trees are— and there are more than 130 species here—they are only one part of the area's

Because Great Smoky Mountains National Park is next to Cherokee, Pisgah, and Nantahala National Forests, visitors need to pay attention to where they are. A perfectly legal activity in a forest may get you cited before a court of law if you do the same thing in a park.

unique ecosystems, which contain 1,500 varieties of flowering plants, 300 kinds of mosses and 2,000 different fungi. Among the wildlife that makes its home here are 200 species of birds, 60 species of fur-bearing animals, 48 different kinds of fish and 38 species of reptiles. Of the last, the only two poisonous species are the timber rattlesnake and northern copperhead, the venoms of which are seldom lethal. Of the 27 species of salamanders that make the Smokies the salamander capital of the world, two of the most notable include Jordan's salamander, a subspecies found only here, and the hellbender, which can grow up to 2½ feet long. Reintroduction efforts are bringing back the red wolf and river otter. Just this past year a herd of eastern elk were returned to the park. Another herd will be brought in yearly for the next several years. The American bison that once roamed these mountains can only be found on farms today in Western North Carolina.

The most famous inhabitant here is, of course, the black bear. Around 1,700 make these mountains their home, giving it one of the country's highest bear densities. It's likely, therefore, that if you spend much time in the area, you'll come across a bear or two. To help make such an encounter fortunate instead of frightening, read *Bear Aware: Hiking and Camping in Bear Country,* by Bill Schneider.

Except for some fishing it's against the park rules to disturb any of the plants and animals in this wildlife sanctuary. The park, however, is here to be enjoyed, and its diversity can accommodate everyone

from the casual tourist and the weekend hiker to the person searching for a true wilderness experience. Despite its many visitors you can still find solitude by getting just a little off the beaten track or by visiting the area in the winter.

The Great Smoky Mountains National Park has 17 peaks more than 6,000 feet high. The highest in the park is 6,642-foot Clingmans Dome, which is accessible by trail and by car. Some 250 million years ago, these mountains, some of the oldest on earth, stood more than 15,000 feet tall, but time and erosion have worn them down to the beautiful and often-dramatic forms they take today. The park is also enhanced by 700 miles of fishing streams. Many provide rainbow and brown trout all year long, but possession of any brook trout, our native trout, is prohibited. A Tennessee or North Carolina fishing license is required, but trout stamps are not. Check out the regulations at a ranger station or visitor center before you fish (see our Recreation chapter for more on fishing regulations).

For general information on the park, call (865) 436-1200. You can call or write to get a free catalog of books, maps, hiking guides and videos that you can purchase. Park headquarters is at 107 Park Headquarters Road, Gatlinburg, TN 37738. In these days of budget cuts, it's particularly important to call ahead as services are changing and the folks at headquarters can keep you up to date.

Getting Around by Vehicle

One hundred and seventy miles of paved roads and 100 miles of gravel roads penetrate the park, some of them built by settlers in the 1800s, but there are no gasoline or automobile services, and speed limits are 45 mph or slower. U.S. 441, which is closed to commercial vehicles, is the only highway that goes completely through the park. There are numerous scenic pullouts all along this route through Newfound Gap, and a 7-mile spur road (closed in winter) goes out to Clingmans Dome. Efforts are made to keep the highway open all year, but always check at the nearest visitor center for winter road conditions. Sometimes the road is closed due to snow or ice, and sometimes only vehicles with chains are allowed. Although snow is fairly uncommon in the valleys, Newfound Gap receives an average of more than 5 feet a year.

Under normal weather and traffic conditions, it should take about an hour to cross the park on U.S. 441 if you don't make any stops, but during the peak visitor season from May until October or in bad weather, it can take much longer. There are other spur roads, some of them unpaved and some of which are closed in winter, that lead to special areas of interest or campgrounds in the park. These "back roads" offer access to less visited areas and are often scenic in their own right. Most are one way and can accommodate two-wheel-drive vehicles. Check on the conditions of these roads, however, before attempting them. A flash flood or mudslide sometimes makes them impassible.

Most park roads are open to bicycles. No off-road vehicles of any kind are allowed anywhere in the park.

Getting Around by Foot

The park's vast area is crisscrossed by over 850 miles of hiking trails, more than half of which are in North Carolina. Many of these trails were converted from old logging railroad grades or old logging roads. There are 51 official hiking trails and 11 self-guiding nature trails. You can pick up a leaflet about each nature trail as you enter it. For visitors just passing through, there are several trails right off of U.S. 441 that are marked by signs.

A relatively level trail in this area, the Kephart Prong Trail, is 9 miles north of Cherokee. It begins by crossing the

There are over 270 miles of road in the Smokies. Most are paved, and even the gravel roads are maintained in suitable condition for standard two-wheel-drive automobiles. Travel times on most roads will average 30 miles per hour or slower.

Oconaluftee River on a footbridge and will take you 4 miles to the Kephart Prong shelter and back, passing the remains of a 1930s Civilian Conservation Corps camp along the way. The longest trail in the park is the 69 miles of the Appalachian Trail between Fontana Dam and Davenport Gap. (You must obtain a free backcountry overnight permit to camp at shelters along the Appalachian Trail, but no permits are necessary on those sections of the trail outside the park boundaries.) The second-longest trail is the 43-mile Lakeshore Trail on the north shore of the Fontana Dam.

If U.S. 441 is open, you can cross-country ski on the Clingmans Dome Road as well as on other roads that are closed in winter. Horseback riding is permitted on designated trails. Saddle horses are available from about April 1 to October 31 at Cades Cove (865–448–6286), Smokemont (828–497–2373), Deep Creek (828–497–7503), Smoky Mountain (865–436–5634), and McCarter's (865–436–5354), near the park's headquarters at the Gatlinburg entrance to the park. Call these numbers for more information and rates.

Pets, on leashes or otherwise contained, are permitted in the park but are not permitted on trails or cross-country hikes. There are two exceptions: the Gatlinburg Trail and the Oconaluftee River Trail.

Places to Stay

Aside from the hundreds of motels, inns, cabins, bed-and-breakfasts, RV parks, and campgrounds that offer accommodations

CLOSE-UP

Reintroducing the Elk

Great elk once roamed the region of the Great Smokies and much of North Carolina's mountains but were rendered nearly extinct by overhunting and loss of habitat. The last elk in North Carolina was believed to have been killed in the late 1700s. In Tennessee, the last elk was killed in the mid-1800s. By 1900, the population of elk in North America had dropped to the point that hunting groups and other conservation organizations became concerned the species was headed for extinction.

An experimental release of elk into Great Smoky Mountains National Park began in February 2001 with the importation of two dozen elk from the Land Between the Lakes National Recreation Area along the Tennessee–Kentucky border. In 2002 and 2003 the Park Service imported more of the animals from Canada.

All elk are radio collared and are being monitored during the five-year experimental phase of the project. Project partners include the Rocky Mountain Elk Foundation, Parks Canada, Great Smoky Mountains Natural History Association, Friends of the Smokies, the U.S.G.S. Biological Resources Division, and the University of Tennessee.

The majestic elk do appear in the Park, with the early morning and late evening being the best time to see them.

---

just outside the park (some can be found in our Accommodations and Bed-and-Breakfasts and Country Inn chapters), there are 10 developed campgrounds within the park itself. Five of them are on the North Carolina side (see our Recreation chapter). From mid-May through October nature walks and evening programs are offered at most developed campgrounds.

To camp in the backcountry, you need a permit. You can pick one up free of charge from any park ranger station, campground, or at the Oconoluftee and Sugarlands Visitor Centers. However some backcountry campsites and shelters are so heavily used that they require reservations. Call the Backcountry Reservation Office (865-436-1231), open 8:00 A.M. to 6:00 P.M. daily, a month in advance if possible. You can only stay one night in a

shelter and three nights in a backcountry campground.

For a map and guide of park trails, backcountry campsites, and regulations, ask at a visitor center or send $1.00 to the Great Smoky Mountains Natural History Association, 115 Park Headquarters Road, Gatlinburg, TN 37738, (865-436-7318), and allow two weeks for delivery. This association has also put out an excellent book called *Hiking Trails of the Smokies*, available at visitor centers or by calling the association. (See the "Organizations" section of this chapter for more information about this association.)

LeConte Lodge, on 6,593-foot Mount LeConte, is the only lodge in the park. It's open from mid-March to mid-November and is accessible only by trail. The shortest trail to the lodge is nearly 5 miles one way, and reservations are required over a year in advance due to its popularity. Call or write LeConte Lodge, Gatlinburg, TN 37738, (865) 429–5704.

Some Points of Interest

CLINGMANS DOME

At 6,642 feet, this is the park's highest peak, the third highest in eastern America, and the highest point on the Appalachian Trail. It can be reached by a 7-mile-long spur road off U.S. 441 at Newfound Gap. From the parking lot a fairly steep half-mile trail takes you to an observation platform, which offers an incredible panoramic view.

In addition to the Appalachian Trail, there are other nearby trails you can pick up at Clingmans Dome. One easy trail for a family hike is the 2.2-mile (4.4 miles round-trip) Andrews Bald Trail. Look for the marked hiking trail at the west end of the parking lot. After about 1,000 feet the trail will fork. The right fork goes to Silers Bald. The left fork to Andrews Bald will take you downslope through a spruce fir forest to a grassy bald with excellent views to the south toward Fontana Lake. It's especially nice when the flame azaleas bloom in late June or early July. This trailhead is not accessible by car from December 1 through April 1.

CADES COVE

When these mountains were turned into a park, many of the people on small farms and in the communities had to leave. Restored log cabins and barns in a number of areas remind us of these hearty settlers. Few places, however, are as beautiful and well preserved as Cades Cove, which contains more pioneer structures than any other location in the park. Pastures, old buildings, and open vistas are a photographer's dream. And if you are in Cades Cove very early in the morning, you'll likely see deer and other wildlife feeding in the cove. There's an 11-mile, one-way loop that circles this scenic

mountain valley and many of its historic buildings. Numerous ranger-led walks and lectures on a variety of subjects are held in Cades Cove every day of the week during the summer season.

There are also numerous hiking trails in the area, many leading to lovely waterfalls. (Because many of these are in Tennessee, they are not included in our Waterfalls chapter.) One, Abrams Trail, begins in the back of Cades Cove loop road and is a moderate 5-mile, round-trip hike. Abrams Falls has the largest water volume of any of the park's falls and is among the most photogenic. The 2-mile Cades Cove Nature Trail is great for families wanting an hour's outing. Pick up a brochure explaining the Cove's cultural and natural history before you take this hike. Surprisingly few people use this convenient trail.

To reach Cades Cove take the Little River Road, a winding but relatively flat road that follows the Little River, from the Sugarlands Visitor Center on U.S. 441 near Gatlinburg. (See our listing of visitor centers in this chapter.)

ROARING FORK MOTOR NATURE TRAIL

Three miles from Gatlinburg, you can take this 5-mile, one-way loop through rich hardwood forests and past historic buildings and rushing mountain streams. To get to it turn onto Airport Road in Gatlinburg. Enter the park and follow the Cherokee Orchard Road to the Roaring Fork Motor Nature Trail. No RVs, trailers, or bicycles are allowed on this route.

CATALOOCHEE VALLEY

The most rugged peaks in the southeastern United States surround this 29-square-mile secluded valley, many of which are over 6,000 feet tall. The valley was once the largest and most prosperous settlement in what is now the park with a population of about 1,200 residents. The churches, a school, and several houses and barns remain. Once known for its farms and orchards, today it's famous for its dense wildlife.

Cataloochee Valley is definitely off the beaten track and requires a 10-mile drive on a winding, narrow, mostly gravel, relatively well-maintained road that seems much longer than it is. To reach it take U.S. 276 toward I-40. Just before it dead-ends into the interstate, turn left onto Cove Creek Road and follow the COVE CREEK MISSIONARY BAPTIST CHURCH signs. There is a ranger station in the valley where you can get more information on the area. There is also a campground with 27 sites that is open from April to November. (See our Recreation chapter for more information on camping.)

Any time you visit the Cradle of Forestry take the camera for spectacular views of Looking Glass Falls on U.S. Highway 276; take bathing suits and burlap sacks for riding down Sliding rock.

MOUNTAIN FARM MUSEUM

From May through October you can walk through a collection of southern Appalachian farm buildings, located at the park's southern entrance at Cherokee, with park interpreters who explain life as it existed here generations ago. These buildings, including a chestnut-log farmhouse, barn, apple house, springhouse, and blacksmith shop, were built in the 19th century and assembled for various locations throughout the park in the 1950s. Admission is free.

MINGUS MILL

Mingus Mill is ½ mile north of the Mountain Farm Museum on the Newfound Gap Road. Built in the early 1800s, it's an excellent example of a water-powered gristmill, and it's still grinding corn. Hours vary, but the mill is usually open daily in the summer and on spring and fall weekends.

Organizations

Great Smoky Mountains Natural History Association
115 Park Headquarters Road, Gatlinburg, TN 37738
(865) 436-7318
This nonprofit organization is for people who care about the park and want to know more about its natural and historical resources. Authorized by Congress, it supports the park's educational and scientific programs in a number of ways, including producing publications, such as a trail guidebook; funding special educational programs; purchasing river otters for the park; and funding visitors center exhibits and artifact collections. Members receive the association's newsletter, discounts from other park associations (such as those at Yellowstone and Yosemite), a subscription to the park's quarterly newspaper, and a chance to participate in annual meetings that include guided walks, guest speakers, and entertainment as well as the annual guided day hikes to interesting destinations within the park. Members also have the satisfaction of helping promote the association's goals. Annual and Lifetime Family memberships are available. Contact the association for more information.

The association also sponsors the Great Smoky Mountain Institute at Tremont, which provides photo workshops and environmental education programs in subjects such as Cherokee Earth Skills for everyone from school children to Elderhostel groups. Tuition, meals, and lodging are provided for a minimal fee. Call (865) 448-6709 for more information.

Friends of the Smokies
160 South Main Street, Waynesville, NC
(828) 452-0720
www.friendsofthesmokies.org
Over 60 years ago a group of people joined together to establish a national park here to preserve and protect the natural wonders of the region. This organization is still dedicated to fund-raising and

to restoring, preserving, and enhancing the park. For an extra fee, a special license plate for North Carolina may be purchased to support the Smokies. For more information and an application call the above numbers. If you love the Smokies, this is a great organization to join.

NATIONAL FORESTS

As we mentioned earlier, the Nantahala and Pisgah National Forests cover more than a million acres in the North Carolina mountains, including a number of wilderness areas. These vast forest lands of rivers, lakes, waterfalls, spectacular views, wild-life, and the richest plant life in the country can be accessed by federal and state highways, forest roads, and trails. You'll find that they can easily be explored by car, on foot, by kayak or canoe, and in designated areas, by horseback, mountain bikes, and off-highway vehicles. (See our Recreation chapter for more information on some of these outdoor sports and camping.)

You will find the maps and information you need to explore this vast region at the ranger districts listed in this chapter (and our chapter on Outdoor Safety will help to keep you well and happy while you're doing it). Because it will take a few lifetimes to get to know these two forests well, you should begin this delightful quest as soon as possible. It's your land. Enjoy it!

Nantahala National Forest

This national forest, in the southwestern part of our mountains between Waynesville and Murphy, contains more than 516,000 acres, sometimes taking in huge chunks of land and sometimes consisting of relatively small plots. When you travel in this part of Western North Carolina, you're constantly entering and leaving the

Driving in the mountains presents new challenges for many drivers. When going downhill, shift to a lower gear to conserve your brakes and avoid brake failure. For cars with automatic transmission, use L or 2. Keep extra distance between you and the vehicle in front of you, and watch for sudden stops or slowdowns.

forest. Although this might not make managing these public lands easy, it certainly makes for a lot of diversity.

Elevations in the forest range from a high 5,800 feet at Lone Bald in Jackson County to a low 1,200 feet in Cherokee County along the Tusquitee River below the Appalachian Lake Dam.

To get a better handle on this vast area, which is the largest of the four national forests in North Carolina, it's best to break it down into its four districts.

Cheoah Ranger District
U.S. Highway 129 N., Robbinsville, NC
(828) 479-6431
The Cheoah Ranger District is made up of 120,000 acres in Graham and Swain Counties that adjoin four large reservoirs (Lake Fontana, Lake Santeetlah, Lake Cheoah, and Calderwood Lake) and offer a network of 225 miles of hiking trails, including a 27-mile section of the Appalachian Trail. The Cheoah Ranger Station, adjacent to Lake Santeetlah on SR 1116 and 2 miles north of Robbinsville, is built on the site of a Civilian Conservation Corps campsite and contains an interpretive trail and a fine overlook of the lake. Here you can get forest information and maps.

Sitting to the southwest of the Great Smoky Mountains National Park, this part of the Nantahala Forest is often overlooked by visitors, but the slightly off-the-beaten-track district provides some incredibly beautiful places. First off, there is the 3,800-acre Joyce Kilmer Memorial Forest, which, maintained in a primitive state, has one of the nation's most impres-

CLOSE-UP

Cherohala Skyway

For a beautiful perspective on our lovely mountains, travel the new, 51-mile Cherohala Skyway that connects the Tellico Plains in southeast Tennessee to Robbinsville, North Carolina. (In Tennessee, take Tennessee Highway 165 and in North Carolina take North Carolina Highway 143.) Called a mini-Blue Ridge Parkway, it travels through some of the best scenery of the Cherokee and Nantahala National Forests, thus the name which is a combination of Cherokee and Nantahala.

Much of the two-lane blacktop in North Carolina looks down on the Snowbird, Slickrock, and Joyce Kilmer Forests. On clear, unhazy days you can see into the Great Smoky Mountains National Park. Rest rooms, picnic areas, and scenic overlooks are constructed along the way. Spirit Ridge, a lookout just east of Hooper Bald, is wheelchair accessible and offers one of most expansive views along the route.

sive remnants of old-growth forest. The Gennott Lumber Company, which started timber operations in the area in 1890, once owned the timber here, but—lucky for us—these trees were never cut. Now this memorial forest is a part of the 14,000-acre Joyce Kilmer-Slickrock Wilderness Area and contains magnificent examples of more than 100 species of trees, including yellow poplar, hemlock, sycamore, basswood, dogwood, beech, and several species of oaks. Many of them are hundreds of years old, and some are more than 20 feet in circumference and more than 100 feet high. The area was set aside in 1936 as a memorial to Joyce Kilmer, the soldier-poet and author of the poem "Trees," who was killed in France during World War I.

The Joyce Kilmer National Recreation Trail is an easy 2-mile loop that takes you past some of these great giants, many felled by age or lightning. In some areas the tree canopy is so thick that sunlight never reaches the ground. You'll also find a picnic area here and an outstanding

variety of vines, ferns, and early-spring wildflowers and shrubs, such as mountain laurels, rhododendrons, and flame azaleas. No plants, living or dead, may be removed from this area. Wildlife is abundant in this undisturbed forest. The adjoining Slickrock Wilderness Area, with 13,100 acres in North Carolina, contains 60 miles of hiking trails that meander along streams and climb high ridges. It's home to bears, bobcats, and nonnative, environment-uprooting wild boars and has a number of dispersed, primitive, no-fee campsites. (See our Outdoor Safety chapter for tips on camping in such areas.)

For those who want more comforts, such as picnic tables, rest rooms, and water taps, there are two campgrounds, not very far from the memorial forest. Horse Cove Campground, which charges $8.00 a night, has 18 units, and is by a rushing mountain stream called Little Santeetlah Creek. Rattler Ford campground nearby is reserved for groups.

To get to the Joyce Kilmer Memorial Forest, take U.S. 129 out of Robbinsville to

SR 1127 and follow the signs. Both the Horse Cove and Rattler Ford camp-grounds are off SR 1127.

There are two forest recreation areas near Lake Fontana. The Tsali Recreation Area has 41 camping units with showers and flushing toilets, a boat-launching area, and 38 miles of biking and horseback-riding trails. The popular trail network here now charges a nominal fee for horses and bikes. The Cable Cove Recreation Area also offers camping and hiking, with boat-ing access on Fontana Lake. It's 4 miles from Fontana Dam, the Appalachian Trail, and the entrance to the Great Smoky Mountains National Park. The area also has a mile-long nature loop trail marked with placards that will help you identify the plants and trees growing along it as well as some historical features. There is a small camping fee. On Lake Santeetlah, the Cheoah Point Recreation Area has developed camping, picnicking, fishing, and boating facilities. There is an $8.00 camping fee but no charge for day use. Nearby the Wauchecha Bald Trail provides access to the Appalachian Trail (see our Recreation chapter for more information on all these recreation areas).

Of all the outstanding wild places in the Cheoah District, two great favorites with anglers, hunters, and primitive camp-ing enthusiasts are the Big Santeetlah Creek area and the 10,000 or so acres that encompass the headwaters of Big Snowbird Creek. The latter was one of the last areas to be settled by whites in North Carolina, and it was here in 1836 that a number of Cherokee Indians fled to escape exile in Oklahoma. For more infor-mation on these two areas, contact the Cheoah Ranger Station.

Highlands Ranger District
2010 Flat Mountain Road, Highlands, NC
(828) 526-3765

The Highlands Ranger District covers more than 105,000 acres in Macon, Jack-son, and Transylvania Counties. Within it you'll find the 39,000-acre Roy Taylor For-est, which has some off-road vehicle trails

(see our Recreation chapter) and Jackson County's rugged Tuckasegee Gorge.

The Highlands District also contains two national and wild scenic rivers, the Chattooga and the Horsepasture. The Chattooga, on which the movie *Deliver-ance* was filmed, is very popular with white-water rafters, but only after it passes the South Carolina/Georgia border (see our Recreation chapter). No canoeing is permitted on either river within the dis-trict. The Horsepasture River is noted for its five waterfalls. Other famous waterfalls in this district include Whitewater Falls, Glen Falls, Dry Falls, and Cullasaja Falls. (See our Waterfalls chapter for more information on all of these. Also remem-ber that people die at such waterfalls every year. Please stay on trails and away from the water at the top of the falls.) Some of these cascades are found along the Cullasaja Gorge, another unbelievably rugged gorge in the area. You'll pass har-rowingly close to it when you take U.S. 64 from Highlands to Franklin.

One of the most famous mountains in the Nantahala Forest is Whiteside Moun-tain, between Highlands and Cashiers off U.S. 64 on the eastern Continental Divide. Said to be one of the oldest mountains on earth, it rises more than 2,100 feet from the valley floor to an elevation of 4,930 feet. Its spectacular north and south faces contain sheer cliffs ranging from 400 to 750 feet in height. They were formed of metamorphic rock commonly called Whiteside granite, gneiss containing a high content of feldspar, quartz, and mica, along with such minerals as pyrite and rare monazite. The white streaks seen on its south face are feldspar and quartz. These don't show up on the north face due to lichens and mosses that cover the stone. The Cherokee called the mountain Sanigilagi, "the place where they took it out," referring to where lightning "took out" the projecting rock on the mountain's western summit. What remained was said to have formed part of the great bridge a mythical monster named Spearfinger tried to build across the valley.

CLOSE-UP

Ranger Stations

The offices of the National Forests in North Carolina are at 160-A Zillicoa Street, Asheville, NC, (828) 257-4200. To reach them, take the UNCA exit off U.S. 19/23.

You can contact the U.S. Forest Service for help and information in the following areas:

NANTAHALA NATIONAL FOREST

Cheoah Ranger District
U.S. Highway 129 N., Robbinsville, NC
(828) 479-6431

Highlands Ranger District
2010 Flat Mountain Road, Highlands, NC
(828) 526-3765

Tusquitee Ranger District
201 Woodland Drive, off U.S. Highway
64 E., Murphy, NC
(828) 837-5152

Wayah Ranger District
90 Sloan Road, Franklin, NC
(828) 524-6441

PISGAH NATIONAL FOREST

Appalachian Ranger District, French Broad Station
88 Bridge Street, Hot Springs, NC
(828) 622-3202

Appalachian Ranger District,
Tocane Station
U.S. Highway 19 E. Bypass, Burnsville, NC
(828) 682-6146

Grandfather Ranger District
At exit 90 (Nebo/Lake James exit), off
I-40, 9 miles east of Marion
(828) 652-2144

Pisgah Ranger District
1001 Pisgah Highway, U.S. 276, north of
Brevard
(828) 877-3265

A 2-mile loop trail, designated as a National Recreation Trail, runs on the top of the mountain. It offers unparalleled views of the east, south, and west, where you will see at least 27 other peaks, the Cashiers Valley and the upper Chattooga River watershed. To reach the mountain drive 6.9 miles from the main Highlands intersection on U.S. 64 going toward Cashiers and turn onto Whiteside Mountain Road (SR 1600). From Cashiers the turn is just past the Jackson-Macon county line. After about a mile, you'll arrive at the mountain's parking area and the trail that follows the edge of the cliffs. Use extreme caution here with pets and children. This is a popular place for rock climbing, but it's only suitable for experts. The rock face is closed to climbers from February 15 through July 15 to protect nesting peregrine falcons.

Cliffside Lake and the Van Hook Glade Recreation Areas, off U.S. 64 between Highlands and Franklin, form one of the district's most popular camping, swimming, and fishing areas. Camping here is

$10.00 a night, and day use is $3.00 per car. This popular area fills up quickly, but there are also a number of primitive camping areas in the district. You can get information and maps at the district office off U.S. 64 just outside of Highlands or at the Highland Visitor Center in downtown Highlands. The visitor center is open daily from May through October; the office is open year-round from Monday through Friday.

Tusquitee Ranger District
201 Woodland Drive, Murphy, NC
(828) 837–5152

Elevations in the 158,579-acre Tusquitee Ranger District range from 1,200 feet to 5,499 feet at Standing Indian Mountain. It's most famous for its "chain of lakes"—Appalachia Lake, Hiwassee Lake, and Chatuge Lake—which offer opportunities to boat, water ski, fish, and swim. You can stay right on Hiwassee Lake at the forest's Hanging Dog Recreation Area, which has a large campground, a picnic area, hiking trails, and a boat launching ramp. At Chatuge Lake, the Jackrabbit Mountain Recreation Area has 103 camping sites, a swimming beach with shower facilities, hiking trails, picnic areas, and a boat launching ramp. (See our Recreation chapter for more information on these lakes and camping areas.)

Just to the north of Chatuge Lake, you'll find the Fires Creek Bear Sanctuary, a 14,000-acre block of land that's been set aside as a haven for black bears. This area offers excellent trout, fishing, picnicking, hiking, and camping. The most famous hiking trail in the area is the 25-mile-long Rim Trail, which follows the ridge around Fires Creek over several high-elevation balds that provide super-scenic vistas. There are several primitive camping areas here that include Huskins Branch, Hunter Camp, and Bristol Fields.

The Leatherwood Falls Picnic Area provides picnic sites near Leatherwood Falls, plus a wheelchair-accessible trail for wheelchair fishing along Fires Creek (see Leatherwood Falls in our Waterfalls chapter for more information). Another inter-

esting place to visit in this district is the Beech Creek Seed Orchard west of Murphy off FR 307. This nursery supplies the southern Appalachian forests with genetically improved seeds of white, shortleaf, and Virginia pines for reforestation. The orchard also has extensive hardwood clones banks of black cherry, oak, and yellow poplar. You can get district information and maps at the district office off U.S. 64 east of Murphy.

Wayah Ranger District
90 Sloan Road, Franklin, NC
(828) 524–6441

This Wayah District (wayah means "wolf" in Cherokee) is centrally located in the Nantahala National Forest. Its 134,000 acres are adjacent to the Cherokee Indian Reservation in the north and extend all the way down to the Georgia border on the south. Within these boundaries you'll find the Nantahala River Gorge, with opportunities for white-water rafting and kayaking; two famous national trails, the Appalachian Trail and the Bartram Trail, which meet on Wayah Bald (see the Three Famous Trails Close-up in our Recreation chapter); the Standing Indian Basin; and the Southern Nantahala Wilderness Area.

The 25,515-acre Southern Nantahala Wilderness Area, created in 1984, is managed by the Nantahala National Forest (10,900 acres are in North Carolina) and by the Chattahoochee National Forest in Georgia (where the remaining acreage is located). Elevations here range from 2,400 feet to 5,499 feet on Standing Indian Mountain, with numerous peaks higher than 4,000 feet. The terrain, cut by streams, is steep and rugged. The forests are often dense, but there are grass-heath balds along many of the high ridges. All of the developed trails within this wilderness are rated "more difficult" to "most difficult." The Georgia portion of the wilderness has no developed trails. However, old roadbeds, which have been closed to vehicles, are suitable for hiking. Many of these old roads connect with trails in North Carolina. Several trails are open to

CLOSE-UP

The Whiteside Mountain Legends

There was once a wicked ogress in these mountains who could pick up big boulders and meld them together by striking one against the other. Her skin had the appearance and feel of stone; any arrows or spears shot at her would just bounce off. Her name was Utlunta, but the Cherokees called her "Spearfinger" because of a very long forefinger that was shaped like a spear. Except for this finger she was capable of appearing as a harmless old woman, and she would use this disguise to lure young children to her. Then she would use her spearfinger to stab them in the back of the neck or through the heart and dig out their livers—her favorite food.

One day she began building a huge bridge from a point on the Hiwassee River (some 4 miles from the present Georgia line). First she built a treelike rock, which even today looks like a tree, and then she started extending her bridge toward Whiteside Mountain with her rock-melding technique. But lightning destroyed it, scattering the rocks all along the ridge, where they too can still be seen. Finally the Cherokee trapped her by digging a pit across a trail that she used. But again weapons were useless against her, until a chickadee lit on her finger, pointing out to its Cherokee friends her weak spot—the equivalent of an Achilles' heel. Thus the arrow they shot into it went straight to her heart, killing her.

Another myth says there is a cave in Whiteside Mountain where the devil had his throne. Others say it was in the nearby Devil's Courthouse—not to be confused with the Devil's Courthouse near the Blue Ridge Parkway. The one near Whiteside Mountain is considered to be the "supreme" throne room. The other is just a secondary "hall of justice."

---

horse travel. These are clearly marked by horse-with-rider signs.

Standing Indian Basin is a horseshoe-shaped drainage basin for the Nantahala and Blue Ridge Mountains. It's rimmed by several peaks that are more than 5,000 feet in elevation: Albert Mountain, Big Butt, Little Bald, and Standing Indian Mountain. There is an abundance of wildlife and recreational opportunities here, particularly hiking. The nicely landscaped Standing Indian Campground, which is open from March 31 to December 1, has 84 camping sites, picnic areas, water, and sanitary facilities for a fee of $10 a night. The Nantahala River, which flows right through the campground, offers fine trout fishing. No reservations are required.

Hikers and backpackers will find a special parking area at the Backcountry Information Center on FR 67, less than a half-mile from the campground and picnic area gate. The Appalachian Trail curves around the south and east ridge of the basin with various trails ascending off it. Trail heads can also be found all along FR 67, including the John Wasilik Memorial Poplar Trail that takes you to the second-largest yellow poplar in the United States (see our Attractions chapter).

The Big Indian Loop is a good horseback-riding trail—also shared with hikers, hunters, and fishers. It begins at a wildlife field off FR 67 about 4 miles beyond the Backcountry Information Station and meanders through extensive rhododendron and birch thickets with good views of Big Indian Creek. Just follow the orange blazes.

And while you're here, you'll probably want to climb Standing Indian Mountain. To do so take the Kimsey Creek Trail that begins at the Backcountry Information Center off FR 67, where there's a bulletin board containing information about the area's many trails, then follow the blue blazes to the road bridge in the campground. Immediately after crossing the bridge, take the Park Creek Trail to the first blue-blazed trail leading to the left. This is the Kimsey Creek Trail, a moderately difficult trail that follows Kimsey Creek upstream, crossing it several times. Along the way you'll go through three wildlife fields where you may see deer, grouse, or other wildlife. When it ends at Deep Gap, you can tun left on the Appalachian Trail and continue a little more than 2 miles to Standing Indian Mountain. Backtrack (about a 7.5-mile round-trip) or return downhill on the rather strenuous Lower Ridge Trail, another popular but steeper trail that's also used to get to Standing Indian Mountain (about a 10-mile hike). You can also drive to Deep Gap on FR 71, thereby cutting the hiking distance to the summit to just more than 2 miles—a 4-mile round trip.

Among the other interesting hiking possibilities—and we've only mentioned a few—are trails to both Mooney Falls and Big Laurel Falls, which can also be reached from FR 67 (see our Waterfalls chapter). Speaking of water, the 9-mile stretch of the Nantahala River that runs from Beechertown to Fontana Lake is nationally known as a world-class white-water river (see our Recreation chapter).

Area businesses situated along U.S. 19 offer a variety of services, including outfitting and guiding, boat rentals, instruction and clinics, restaurants, and overnight accommodations. Finally visitors can drive through the Coweeta Experimental Forest to see forest management practices in silver culture, hydrology, and engineering. A self-guiding brochure is available at the station office, which is open Monday through Friday from 7:30 A.M. until 4:00 P.M. It's on U.S. 441, south of Murphy. This unit of the Forest Service's Southern Research Station was established in 1934.

Pisgah National Forest

In 1886 George Vanderbilt came to this area and, like the authors of this book, fell in love with it. He bought several thousand acres of abused farmland near Asheville and built his famous Biltmore Estate, which still belongs to his family but is open to the public (see our Biltmore Estate and Winery chapter). To reclaim this used-up land, he hired Gifford Pinchot, a young American who had gotten his degree in scientific forestry in France. America had no schools of forestry at that time, so the studies could only be pursued in Europe.

When the opportunity arose, Vanderbilt also began to buy up acreage in what is now Pisgah Forest. His dream, and that of Pinchot, was to create a vast estate where forest resources could be conserved for a continual supply of goods. Eventually he owned 125,000 acres and named this vast tract after Pisgah Mountain, a prominent peak on his land. (In the Bible, Pisgah was the mountain from which God showed Moses the Promised Land. The Asheville area's 5,721-foot mountain is thought to have been named by Rev. James Hall, a chaplain who accompanied Gen. Griffith Rutherford on his punitive strike against the Cherokee in 1776.)

Pinchot left Biltmore Estate at the request of Theodore Roosevelt to establish what would become the United States Forest Service. Vanderbilt replaced him with a German forester, Dr. Carl A. Schenck, who eventually started Amer-

Know the rules of the park before you enter. Each park has a set of rules for the protection of guests as well as plant and animal life in the park.

ica's first school of forestry in the Pink Beds, a 20,000-acre parcel known for its lovely mountain laurels and other flowering plants. The area where the school stood is now a National Historic Site called the Cradle of Forestry. It still retains many of the school's structures, some of which were former buildings of the settlers who lived in the Pink Beds. The Cradle also offers guided trail walks and a great visitors center with a wealth of exhibits (for more specific information see our Close-up, The Cradle Keeps Rocking).

In 1914 George Vanderbilt died at the age of 52 of complications from appendicitis. Shortly after that, his widow, Edith, wrote a letter to the secretary of agriculture that began, "Sir: I now confront the question of what disposal I shall make of Pisgah Forest, which, under the terms of my late husband's will, has passed to me without qualifications or condition." What she did was pass on 80,000 acres of the land to the Forest Service that her husband's former employee, Gifford Pinchot, now headed.

Over the years other tracts have been added to this glorious forest so that it now contains 495,979 acres, which is more or less split across the middle by the Blue Ridge Parkway. It contains three wilderness areas: Shining Rock, Linville Gorge, and Middle Prong. The Appalachian Trail runs along its border with Tennessee, and the relatively new Mountains-to-the-Sea Trail crosses through the forest (see the Three Famous Trails Close-up in our Recreation chapter). There are many other popular attractions here, such as the Fish Hatchery, the Pisgah Center for Wildlife Education, Roan Mountain Gardens, and Sliding Rock. (There are small parking fees at both Roan Mountain and Sliding Rock, with season passes also available.)

Pisgah Forest surrounds the East's tallest mountain, 6,684-foot Mount Mitchell, a state park unto itself. Pisgah has some 40 recreational areas that offer fishing, camping, hiking, and so on. Some have developed campgrounds, but some provide only primitive camping in order to protect the environment, because this forest is a botanical wonderland. For example, the whole state has 55 species of orchids, and 39 of them are found in Pisgah. More than 200 species of plants grow on Roan Mountain alone. Pisgah is more of a whole piece than the Nantahala National Forest, but it still has some scattered boundaries and is divided into four districts. The most used, with more than five million visitors a year, is the Pisgah District, heavily composed of the land that was originally owned by the Vanderbilts.

Appalachian Ranger District, French Broad Station, U.S. Highways 25/70, Hot Springs, NC (828) 622-3202

This is an area of Pisgah Forest that can almost guarantee you solitude. Mostly in Madison County with a little bit of the northeast section of Haywood thrown in, it contains 79,292 acres of some of the Appalachians' most isolated and craggy terrain. Many peaks here are more than 4,000 feet, the highest being Camp Creek Bald at 4,844 feet. This area is rich in botanical surprises, including a number of threatened or endangered species.

The district's only developed campground is the Rocky Bluff Campground and Picnic Area, on a tree-covered ridge a little more than 3 miles south of Hot Springs on N.C. Highway 209 S. There is also a primitive campground at Harmon Den, and there are picnic areas at Murray Branch and Big Creek.

The district includes some 25 trails covering 127 miles, including 3 horse trails. Nearly 85 miles of the Appalachian Trail travels the mountain ridge forming the North Carolina-Tennessee state line. The famous trail can be accessed in many places, including on Max Patch Mountain

(4,629 feet), where there are extraordinary views from its grassy summit. To reach Max Patch by car, drive south from Hot Springs on N.C. 209 S. for 7.3 miles. Turn south on SR 1175 and drive 5.3 miles to SR 1181. Three miles on this gravel road will take you within a half-mile of the top. There you can take a 1.4-mile loop trail across its summit or a 2.4-mile trail around the top for great views from all sides.

For more information contact the French Broad District Ranger Station listed in this chapter.

Appalachian Ranger District, Tocane Station
U.S. Highway 19 E. Bypass, Burnsville, NC
(828) 682–6146

The 74,458-acre Tocane Station is full of history. Even the name dates back to the Cherokees, because it comes from the Toe and Cane Rivers that are in this area. According to legend, Toe was the nick-name of an Indian princess, Estatoe, who wanted to marry a young brave from another tribe. Her people not only rejected the marriage proposal, but they killed the young man, after which the princess drowned herself in the river that came to be called Toe.

In 1913 the National Forest Service purchased the first 25,000 acres that make up this district on the slopes of the Black Mountains. More than 55 miles of the Appalachian Trail meander in and out of North Carolina and Tennessee along a ridgeline to the north. The Craggy Mountain Scenic Area (not to be confused with Craggy Gardens on the Blue Ridge Parkway) is in the southwestern section of the district, where you'll find Douglas Falls (listed in our Waterfalls chapter).

One of the most renowned spots in this district is Roan Mountain Gardens, or simply "The Roan," as it's called around here. This 6,286-foot bald summit is the highest point of the Unaka Mountains, a range that forms a high barrier between eastern Tennessee and Western North Carolina. Even when it was nearly inaccessible, Roan Mountain was famous for its scenic beauty. In 1877 Gen. Thomas Wilder built a 28-room log inn on its summit and replaced that in 1885 with the 166-room Cloudland Hotel. His ads read: "Come up out of the sultry plains to the 'land of sky,' magnificent view above the clouds where rivers are born, a most extended prospect of 50,000 square miles in six different states, 100 mountain tops over 4,000 feet high in sight."

The hotel was abandoned after 1900 and burned just before World War I. After that the old stands of spruce and balsam fir trees were cut, and the root-stock of the lovely purple rhododendrons that grew here was sold to nurseries, leaving only a few straggling bushes. But nature prevailed, and the flowering shrubs came back in neat clumps rather than in dense thickets, though some of these bushes grow from 15 to 20 feet tall and produce up to 800 blooms each. Today, like the guests of the Cloudland Hotel, you can enjoy the far vistas, stunning sunrises and sunsets, and full-circle rainbows, plus 600 acres of rhododendron gardens and 850 acres of Fraser fir. The deep magenta-pink flowers are usually in full bloom during the last two weeks of June. You can learn much more about these and Roan Mountains' other wonderful plants on a self-guided trail through the gardens.

The name of the mountain is a mystery. Some say it came from a roan horse left on the summit by Daniel Boone. It may be from the red-berried "roan tree" that grows on its crest. Another mystery is the strange "music" heard there from time to time that sounds like the humming of thousands of bees. Scientists think that electrically charged air currents swirling by each other near the peak might cause it.

The gardens are on N.C. Highway 261, 13 miles north of Bakersville. The road to the gardens is open from approximately May 1 through October 31, depending on the weather. There is a $3.00 parking fee.

There are two family campgrounds in the Tocane District: the Carolina Hemlocks Recreation Area and the Vlock Mountain

Recreation Area (see our Recreation chapter for more information). There are areas for picnicking, fishing, swimming, and hiking. A mile-long Hemlock Nature Trail begins at the swimming beach. Two others, Colbert Ridge Trail and the Buncombe Horse Range Trail, start nearby.

Three miles on up N.C. Highway 80, turn right on FR 472 and drive 3 miles to reach the Black Mountain Recreation Area. The Briar Bottom Group Camp (reservation required) is in the same area. From the group camp's gate, the 1-mile Briar Bottom Trail loops the campground, crossing two footbridges in the process. Both hikers and bikers use it. Another short trail goes up Setrock Creek to a waterfall. Both the Mount Mitchell and Lost Cove Ridge Trails are accessible from the campground. (See our Recreation chapter.)

Grandfather District
Rt. 1, exit 90 (Nebo/Lake James exit) off of I-40, 9 miles east of Marion (828) 652-2144

This very scenic district's 186,735 acres cover parts of Avery, Burke, Caldwell, and McDowell Counties. Very near its center is the 10,975-acre Linville Gorge Wilderness Area, where you can still find virgin forests in deep coves and four different species of rhododendrons.

There are two campground/picnic areas in the district: the primitive, tents-only Curtis Creek Campground and the Mortimer Campground. The area also has two primitive camps in the Wilson Creek area at Chestnut and Kawana, and there are other picnic sites at Barkhouse on N.C. 181 and at Mulberry, north of Lenoir. (See our Recreation chapter for more information.)

The Linville Gorge Wilderness Area offers a well-worth-it challenge to hikers and rock climbers. Here the Linville River drops 2,000 feet in a 14-mile series of cascades between steep escarpments. Camping in the gorge is limited to three days and two nights. To control the numbers a free camping permit that you can get from the Forest Service (828-257-4203)

is required on weekends and holidays from May 1 through October 31. You can get permits at the rangers office off I-40, 9 miles east of Marion or at the Linville Falls Visitor Center (828-765-1045; milepost 316 at Linville) on Kistler Memorial Highway, which is open from 9:00 A.M. to 5:00 P.M. from April through November.

Famous Linville Falls is not a part of the Linville Gorge Wilderness Area. Just off the Blue Ridge Parkway, it's under the management of the National Park Service (see our Blue Ridge Parkway and Waterfalls chapters).

The Grandfather District has around 70 hiking trails, but many are not blazed or well maintained, so be sure to get information and good maps of the area before setting out. The one exception is the Mountains-to-the-Sea Trail, 46.5 miles of which run through this forest.

Pisgah District
1001 Pisgah Highway, U.S. Highway 276 (828) 877-3265

This district's 156,103 acres take in parts of Buncombe, Haywood, Henderson, and Transylvania Counties. It contains more than 275 miles of hiking trails that range from easy to very strenuous as well as horse trails and trails open to mountain bikes. The most challenging and the longest trails are the 31.7 miles of the Mountains-to-the-Sea Trail that runs through the district and the heavily used 30-mile Art Loeb Trail. The Pisgah District also has four campgrounds, plus three group campgrounds. Among the most popular are the Davidson River Campground right on the beautiful Davidson River, just 1.5 miles from the Brevard entrance to the forest on U.S. 276, and Lake Powhatan (see our Recreation chapter) on FR 3884 about 13 miles south of Asheville.

Definitely the most popular and used part of Pisgah Forest is the 16-mile stretch of U.S. 276 from the Brevard entrance to the Blue Ridge Parkway. This route brings you to the Davidson River Campground, the Pisgah District Ranger Station, the Fish Hatchery, the Pisgah Center for

Deep Gap Trail

One of our favorite hikes, which includes places where you pull yourself up by rocks and tree roots, is Mount Mitchell's Deep Gap Trail. This excellent but strenuous 8-mile round-trip hike covers four knobs on Mount Mitchell, the highest peak on the eastern seaboard at 6,684 feet. You'll see incredible wildflowers and coniferous forests, as well as ferns and lush mosses. To reach the trail entrance in this state park on N.C. Highway 128, off the Blue Ridge Parkway at milepost 355.4, leave your car in the picnic area parking lot. Walk directly through the picnic area until you reach a gravel trail with marker Deep Gap Trail. This is a rough hike that will bring on a quick sweat with its straight uphill climbs: pack plenty of water and a snack. It gets very chilly (so bring a jacket) in this high elevation, and much of the trail is the solid granite of the mountain. A walking stick and dependable shoes are a good idea. This is one of the most challenging hikes of the area.

Wildlife Education, famous Looking Glass Falls and Sliding Rock, a natural waterslide (see our Waterfalls chapter), and the Cradle of Forestry next door to the Pink Beds picnic area. All along this route, you'll find picnicking spots by the Davidson River and numerous hiking trails. One very popular one is Looking Glass Rock Trail, a strenuous 6.2-mile round-trip hike to the top of a huge granite dome, which dominates the area and is very popular with rock climbers. Also try Moore's Cove, a 1.4-mile easy hike that ends at a lovely waterfall that you can walk behind (see our Waterfalls chapter).

Two of Pisgah Forest's three wilderness areas are also in the Pisgah District: the 18,500-acre Shining Rock Wilderness and the 7,900-acre Middle Prong Wilderness. Unfortunately wilderness areas in this part of the country are in danger of "being loved to death." Certainly, if you are seeking solitude, these are not the places to find it. They have become so popular, and the impact of visitors on these areas is becoming so damaging, that you would do much better to visit other sections of the forest, where you occasionally might see some signs of past logging but can certainly have vast, beautiful areas of the woods almost totally to yourself.

STATE PARKS

Gorges State Park
Located on the NC-SC state line, access off U.S. Highway 64 just east of N.C. Highway 281 S., Sapphire, Transylvania County, NC
(828) 966-9099
This newest of state parks in North Carolina offers a primeval experience. It can be reached from Sapphire off N.C. Highway 281. Bring your own water and sandwiches. There are no facilities. You will find the splendor of plunging waterfalls, rugged river gorges, sheer rock walls, and one of the greatest concentrations of rare and unique species in the eastern United States. The surrounding forest is a virtual rain forest collecting more than 80 inches of rain per year with an elevation that rises some 2,000 feet in only 3 to 5 miles.

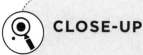

The Cradle Keeps Rocking

On a sun-filled day legendary Congressman Roy Taylor spoke at a celebration of the Cradle of Forestry.

With his unique mountain humor, Congressman Taylor chided the organizers for putting him on a shaded stand with the participants standing in the blazing sun. "By now you'd think that reason, mountain logic, and just plain common sense would tell you to put the speaker in the sun and the congregation in the shade if you desire a short oration and to the point." Being acutely aware of his constituency, even though retired, his comments were emphatic and to the point. He next introduced the heir to Biltmore Estate and great grandson of George Vanderbilt, Bill Cecil Jr. The crowd applauded both men for the wisdom they shared as both Roy Taylor and William Amhurst Vanderbilt Cecil Jr. vowed that the creative forestry program begun at the Cradle, which was the foundation upon which the U.S. Forestry Service began, is a legacy that would endure and continue. The Biltmore Forest School of Dr. Albert Carl Schenck, supported by the wealth of George Vanderbilt, had its "campus" and the beginnings of American forestry here.

A devastating fire had destroyed the building of the Cradle and all that was stored in it during the winter months.

This occasion celebrated both the history and the future of the Cradle with its reopening. Still intact were two trails. One could view the historic buildings of America's first foresters by following one trail. The other trail was lush with forest growth, a historic portable sawmill, and the 1915 Climax logging locomotive, whose bell children love to ring.

The new Forestry Discovery Center opened as a new and exciting chapter for the Cradle. It doesn't matter if you're an adult or child, if the weather is bad or good, if you have an hour to spend or a whole day, the Cradle of Forestry can enrich, delight, and enlighten you. The trails, the Forest Discovery Center, and the exhibits are all wheelchair accessible.

In April 1997 18 new exhibits opened in the center. One lets you climb a replicated hillside, complete with rocks, trees, wildflowers, and animals, through the different levels of a forest. Below the hill you can crawl through a 30-foot, underground tunnel with roots for handholds to observe the creatures living there. A "Water in the Forest" exhibit teaches the dynamics of a watershed, from raindrops to faucet. You can play with interactive tumbling blocks to learn "The Habitat Game" that is so important to wildlife survival. Interactive computers let you manage a forest ecosystem and show you the consequences of your actions. A "Global Connections" exhibit and video focuses on issues facing forest managers throughout the world.

A highlight is the "Fire-Fighting Helicopter Simulator," a sensory journey using visuals, sound, movement, and smells, a flight into the depths of a wildfire to drop retardant to quench the flames. Even the simulated pilots bob about with the buffeting of the helicopter. And you are there with them.

Here, also, you can view an 18-minute movie that recounts the history of the first forestry school, dine at the Forest Bounty Café, and browse through an excellent gift shop full of charming toys and a fine selection of regional and outdoor books. Outside two separate trails, which you can take with a guide or on your own, lead to some of the old buildings built by both early settlers and Dr. Schenck for his school and forest rangers. Modern-day craftspeople with 19th-century skills can often be found on the Biltmore Campus Trail: You might see a toy maker crafting a Gee Haw Whimmy Diddle, or a weaver, a basket maker, and a skilled open-hearth cook.

In addition to all this, there are many special programs and events that take place throughout the Cradle's season, which runs from mid-April through the end of November. These include the Appalachian Spring Celebration, which lasts from the end of April through the end of May; concentrates on the diversity of wildflowers, birds, and waterfalls; and includes a wildflower photography contest. Bugs, Bogs, and Beavers runs for over a week mid-July and offers guided hikes and ponds and streams explorations. Smokey the Bear's Birthday Party draws droves of children for all kinds of skits, games, music, a puppet show, birthday cake, and of course, Smokey; Forest Festival Day in early October brings over 50 crafters to the Cradle to demonstrate their skills at turning nature's bounty into art. At this festival you can learn to fly fish, try your hand with a crosscut saw, meet live animals, and speak with archeologists who have uncovered artifacts in the Cradle area dating back 5,000 years.

During the haunting season of Halloween, the Cradle staff calls on sleuths to join them in solving the mystery of the missing forestry student. Kiddies delight in this venture entitled, "The Legend of Tommy Hedges." Check with the Cradle staff for dates and times.

The Cradle is located on U.S. 276, 4 miles south of the Blue Ridge Parkway at milepost 412, or 11 miles from the intersection of U.S. 64 and 276 and N.C. 280 at the Brevard entrance to Pisgah Forest. It's open from 9:00 A.M. until 5:00 P.M. Admission for adults is $5.00; students 4 to 17 years old are admitted for $2.50; children ages 3 and younger are admitted free. Gold Age Passports are honored. For more information call (828) 877-3130 or (828) 884-5713.

CLOSE-UP

A Bass of a Fish Tale

Lake Jocassee, just inside South Carolina, is not only one access to North Carolina's newest park, Gorges State Park, but it has also produced the fourth-largest small-mouth bass ever caught in the entire United States. And at nine pounds and seven ounces, it beat the old South Carolina record as the largest ever taken from Lake Jocassee.

It all happened on a dark and calm night when Rosman, North Carolina, resident Terry Dodson took his rod and reel to the lake to gather a supply for the Old Toxaway Baptist church fish fry. He knew that something big had hit when the pole bent and the line started running. Claiming that it wasn't that much of a fight, he landed the big fellow and by the next morning of May 3, 2001, the South Carolina state biologist confirmed that this was a record-breaking catch.

This lake, sitting plumb on the state line, offers canoe and boating opportunities in addition to fishing.

Put this all together and it spells a bounty of waterfalls.

There are numerous trails that follow the Horsepasture River (National Wild and Scenic River), Toxaway River, Bearwallow Creek, and Windy Falls. Some of the mountains to be hiked are Chestnut, Grindstone, and Misery Mountain.

Backpack camping is permitted at traditional sites along the Foothills Trail. Horses and mountain bikes are permitted on the following roads: Auger Hole Road from Frozen Creek Road to Turkey Pen Gap on the western boundary of the park. Unlicensed ATVs are prohibited by state regulations throughout the state park system. Licensed four-wheel-drive vehicles are permitted on Auger Hole Road for access to WRC gamelands during hunting season.

A parking area with rest rooms and picnic table is planned for N.C. 281 S. and also in the Frozen Creek Road access area. Boat access to Lake Jocassee is currently available through Devil's Fork State Park in South Carolina.

New River State Park
Alleghany County access: by river only near Sparta, SR 1549 and SR 1308
Ashe County access: near Jefferson, SR 1590 (Wagoner Road) and U.S. Highway 221 off N.C. Highway 88 E.
(336) 982-2587 (for both counties)
The New River, around which this state park is framed, is reported to be the oldest river in North America. It cuts a deep, twisting groove from the state boundary with Virginia and flows like a curling, satin ribbon through Ashe and Alleghany, the two northernmost counties of Western North Carolina. The beauty of this primeval river was almost lost 30 years ago when the Appalachian Power Company applied for a license to dam the New River and build reservoirs along its length. Fortunately citizen opposition gained momentum, and in 1975, after extensive hearings and litigation, the North Carolina General Assembly acted to preserve a 26.5-mile stretch of this historic river—from its confluence with the Dog Creek to

the Virginia line—officially naming it a State Scenic River. The next year the secretary of the interior moved to designate the same stretch as a part of the National Wild and Scenic River System, and Congress followed suit to affirm the action, thereby prohibiting the construction of dams and reservoirs on the river.

Thus the New River State Park was born. The park covers not only a scenic and tranquil waterway, but three designated parkland areas as well. The pastoral fields and forests along the New River also have their own historic interest: Indian activity here has been documented from 10,000 years ago by archaeological excavations that uncovered pottery shards, arrowheads, stone axes, and other artifacts. This area of the New River Valley appeared to have served as a hunting ground for several neighboring tribes, Cherokee, Shawnee and Creek Indians, on their way north to hunting lands along the Ohio River.

Today, New River State Park is a popular destination for outdoor recreation. You can picnic at the river's access areas and at tables sheltered by a grove of trees or beneath a bona fide roof. Camping is facilitated at all three access points, but the Wagoner Road access off N.C. Highway 88 is the largest public area, offering rest rooms, hiking trails, campsites, picnic areas, and put-in points for canoeing. The New River's placid waters are perfect for canoeing, which makes it an extremely popular sport here. In fact the Alleghany County access area near the Virginia border can be reached only by canoe. This remote spot is bordered on one shore by an imposing rock face and on the other by a primitive camping area. Canoeing campers at this site must register at designated boxes or with a park ranger. Canoes may also be launched from the Wagoner Road access, the U.S. 221 access in Ashe County to the south, and from numerous bridges that cross the New River.

You'll probably see more than one fisherman hip-deep in the well-stocked waters of this river. Area natives claim these waters provide some of the best bass fishing in the state. Anglers do need a license and should also be aware of fishing regulations of the North Carolina Wildlife Resources Commission. Check with park rangers for more information (and see our Recreation chapter).

The park is home to 14 species of endangered plants, including Carolina saxifrage, rattlesnake root, and purple sage. Visitors are encouraged to help in the effort to protect this delicate fauna. River wildlife such as otters, beavers, muskrat, mink, and raccoon abound along the shores.

A note of caution: During heavy rains, be aware that the New River is subject to heavy flooding. Canoeists are encouraged to wear flotation devices and to portage around all low-water bridges to avoid entrapment. Most importantly, know the river section you plan to traverse. Park information and maps of the river's course are available at ranger stations. (See the Ranger Station Close-up in this chapter.)

Park hours are 8:00 A.M. to 6:00 P.M. November to February; 8:00 A.M. to 7:00 P.M. in March and October; 8:00 A.M. to 8:00 P.M. during April, May, and September; and 8:00 A.M. to 9:00 P.M. June through August.

Mount Jefferson State Park
Jefferson County access: SR 1149 from N.C. Highway 163 to SR 1152
(336) 246–9653

Mount Jefferson sparked interest as a park area in the 1930s when the Works Progress Administration constructed a rough 2-mile road to the summit of the mountain. It took another 20 years of local interest and persistence to reach state park status, which Mount Jefferson achieved in 1956.

Mount Jefferson is positioned geographically between the north and south forks of the New River and was once part of a broad plateau that formed much of the region. The drainage line formed by these two water sources played an important part in the formation of the mountain itself. Eons of weathering and erosion ultimately created Mount Jefferson, the majestic

Boojum and Hootin' Annie

The folks at Haywood County's Lake Logan know for certain that the Boojum walk these mountains. There's an inscription in a cave at that site that tells the story.

This large creature has roamed these mountains since time began. The Boojum was apparently on friendly terms with the giant folks of the Cherokee. (They are buried in the Indian mound in Franklin, North Carolina, but that's another story.) As folks began to settle these parts, the Boojum was curious and watched their every move. With the arrival of newborn babies and livestock, the Boojum danced around the mountains with great delight. Some folks mistook the dancing for thunder.

The Boojum was misunderstood. He didn't mean to cause trouble, but being a big old ramblin' sort, he just kind of messed things up. Without meaning to, he'd trampled crops, especially after a hailstorm, for example. So folks began to chase him away. This made him terribly distraught, and he formed lots of mountain streams with his big sad tears.

One day a sweet mountain girl named Annie happened upon the Boojum while he was sleeping. His great snoring was creating an infernal roar in the mountains, and his wheezing after each snore stirred up the biggest wind ever. Annie loved everyone and everything, so she had nary a fear of the big fellow.

"Howdy!" she said. The Boojum was used to folks throwing stones and sticks, so he tried to hide himself. This young gal wouldn't stand for that, however, and ran after him. Finally, possessing one of the best sets of lungs ever having come from Spivey,* Annie set up the sweetest hooting, which melted the heart of the Boojum. He slowly peeked out to see what it was all about.

The Big Boojum and sweet Hootin' Annie became the closest of friends as

promontory that rises 1,600 feet from the rolling meadows and valleys below.

The drive up the mountain provides spectacular views, particularly at sunset, and you can see three states from the top (Tennessee is to the west and Virginia to the north.) There are overlooks along the way and two moderately difficult trails at the top. The Summit Trail is just a fraction of a mile from the highest point on Mount Jefferson, and the 1.1-mile Rhododendron Trail that begins at the terminus of the Summit Trail is a delightful, self-guided, moderately difficult trek through the forest with stops at numbered stations. The lush beauty of the purple Catawba rhododendron makes this trail a delight in early June. This trail also passes by a rock outcrop called Luther Rock, made up of a volcanic amphibolite rock that gives Mount Jefferson its dark cast. The trail circles back to the picnic area parking lot below the summit.

Visitors to the High Country can still see evidence of the once-abundant American chestnut in the building materials of area homes and rustic lodges that predate the 1920 blight that devastated the species. And on Mount Jefferson you can see American chestnut seedlings that

any two critters could be. Every day Annie would hoot for the Boojum. Every day he would come to her, and the two of them would dance from one mountain top to another. They'd start off at the Pisgahs, and the Boojum would whirl and jig until they got to the Balsams. They'd circle their partner and find their way to the Black Mountains. One day they even got as far as one could go dancing from the Grandfather all the way to the Great Smoky Mountains.

When they danced, the Boojum would roar with laughter. Annie would hoot with joy, and her clogging shoe taps would shoot sparks off the flint of the mountain. Not knowing any better, the folks in the valley thought they were besieged with thunder and lightning.

This tale saddened quickly when more folks moved into the mountains. Trains came through, big roads were built, and then everyone came. The Boojum went deeper into the mountains to escape all this. Annie would commence hootin' while looking for him. More and more she had to hoot longer and louder . . . until one day the Boojum didn't answer her. So she went deeper into the mountains on her search and she was never seen again.

Some folks claim that you can still hear them dancing, hootin', and roarin' with Annie's taps striking off the flint.

One other thing. Folks are strange. Even though they drove off the Boojum and Annie, whenever they get together for a good time in these parts, they fill tables with mountains of mouthwatering food, they fiddle and strum, and dance and sing . . . and they call it a "Hootin' Annie." Now doesn't that beat all!

*Spivey is for Spivey Corners located in the eastern part of North Carolina, where a "Hollerin" contest is held annually.

continue to sprout in profusion. Sadly the insidious blight continues to claim the trees before they can reach any significant height. Red maple, basswood, tulip trees, and yellow birch also fill these woods, and you can spot a stand of big-toothed aspen below Luther Rock on the northern slopes of Mount Jefferson (only one other North Carolina county, Haywood, in the central mountain region, has these aspen trees).

Picnicking is popular at Mount Jefferson, which has a tree-shaded area with 32 tables and nine grills near the summit.

Rest rooms and drinking water are available nearby. There is no camping available here. Canoe-in and walk-in camping is available at nearby New River State Park.

Park hours are 9:00 A.M. to 5:00 P.M. November to February; 9:00 A.M. to 6:00 P.M. in March and October; 9:00 A.M. to 7:00 P.M. April, May, and September; and 9:00 A.M. to 8:00 P.M. June through August.

Rangers urge you to call ahead before visiting Mount Jefferson during the winter. The weather in these northern mountains is often unpredictable, and roads can quickly become impassable.

Mount Mitchell State Park
N.C. Highway 128, off the Blue Ridge Parkway, Mile 355.4
(828) 675–4611

At 6,684 feet Mount Mitchell is the highest peak in the eastern United States, and it also carries the distinction of being the site of North Carolina's first state park. The park covers part of the rugged Black Mountains, which were formed more than a billion years ago and soar higher than the nearby Blue Ridge range or the Great Smokies of Tennessee. This extreme elevation creates a climate more like that of Canada's, and many of the plants and animals found here are also more akin to their northern cousins than their neighbors down the hill.

Mount Mitchell State Park was formed in 1915, a reaction mainly to the effects of overcutting by the logging industry that had come into prominence at the turn of the 20th century in North Carolina. The disappearance of much of the forests in the Black Mountains prompted Gov. Locke Craig, backed by concerned citizens, to preserve the last vestige of natural lands in this range.

Mount Mitchell is named in honor of University of North Carolina science professor Elisha Mitchell who, in 1835, made the rugged trek into the Black Mountain Range to verify his conclusions that peaks here were indeed higher than Grandfather Mountain. Grandfather had long been thought to be the most prominent peak in the region. Mitchell, on a subsequent trip to the Black Mountain Range in 1857 to verify his measurements, which had again come under dispute, unfortunately fell from a cliff above a 40-foot waterfall, where he was knocked unconscious and drowned in the pool below.

This park has a marvelous array of 1,677 acres of woodlands, wildlife habitat, majestic views, trail systems, and public camping and picnic areas. Because of the alpinelike climate, the weather here is always cooler, even in summer, than that in other parts of the state. It's a good idea to keep an extra jacket handy. The mists that roll over Mount Mitchell are a constant reminder of the extreme elevation and have historically been a hazard to small aircraft.

Mount Mitchell's summit has great sight-seeing possibilities. On a clear day the stone observation tower at the top of the mountain affords a 70-mile view. Dr. Elisha Mitchell is buried at the base of the tower, and a marker honors his work. A small nature museum that once stood halfway up the trail from the parking area to the tower has been closed. In the spring of 2001 the new museum was opened adjacent to the parking area. It is wheelchair friendly. In this rustic structure dioramas and recordings give you a feel for the mountain's special plants and wildlife, and you can easily imagine the extremes of weather often found on lofty Mount Mitchell. You will also be greeted by Big Tom Wilson, the mountain man who found the body of Dr. Mitchell and then petitioned for his body to be removed from Riverside Cemetery in Asheville where he had been buried to the summit of the peak that bears his name. The life-size statue of Big Tom was carved from a tree trunk by his great-great-great grandson, world class wood-carver, David Boone of Pensacola, N.C. David is also a direct descendant of Daniel Boone. A new gift shop has also opened in the same building as the museum.

The parking area at the base of the summit is surrounded by a 40-table picnic area with stone grills and drinking water. Two sites have fireplaces under shelter and are often used for group picnics. Hiking trails branch off in several directions from the parking area. Look for the white-tailed deer that on occasion venture close to this area.

Stop at the ranger station at the entrance to the park for information on hiking, camping, and maps of trail areas both along the ridge and down the mountain. At Mount Mitchell you can camp family style with a rustic ambience at the nine-site campground that's open May 1 through October 31. This is tent camping only, no RVs. Rest rooms are nearby, but no showers or hot water are available.

For day visitors who crave sustenance at this mile-high peak, try the concession stand at the summit for light snacks. For a more substantial meal and an inspiring view, you can dine at the park's restaurant a half-mile from the ranger's office. The sturdy stone-and-timber, lodgelike restaurant serves breakfast on weekends and holidays and lunch and dinner daily during park hours. Both food service locations have rest rooms.

Hours at Mount Mitchell State Park are 8:00 A.M. to 6:00 P.M. November through February; 8:00 A.M. to 7:00 P.M. in March and October; 8:00 A.M. to 8:00 P.M. April, May, and September; and 8:00 A.M. to 9:00 P.M. June through August.

Stone Mountain State Park
Located in Alleghany & Wilkes County, 7 miles southwest of Roaring Gap (336) 957-8185

From U.S. Highway 21 take SR 1002 4.5 miles to Traphill. Turn north on John P. Frank Parkway for 2 miles.

This area is a delight for the rugged outdoor types who scale mountains and face windstorms. Weathering action over eons of time has created a mini-moonscape on this dome-shaped granite mass. Climbers are invited and must register when entering the park. Bring your ropes and use the available bolts, but leave your metal gear at home as it is not permitted to drive new bolts into the rock.

Of the nine hiking trails most are noted as strenuous. They include the 4-mile Stone Mountain Loop, Summit Trail to the top for 0.75 mile, and the 2.5-mile Widow's Creek Trail. And now we find two that are listed as moderate. They are the Self-Guided Nature Trail for 0.5 mile and Middle Falls/Lower Falls Trail at 0.75 mile.

Bikes are not allowed, but horses are. There's a 5-mile Bridle Trail leading into the park. There are many comfort zones in the park as well: 75 picnic tables each with a grill, 3 picnic shelters with Chestnut having 8 tables, Dogwood with 8 tables

also, and Hemlock with 12 tables. Pig cookers and portable grills are also permitted at the shelters, but in the grassy areas only. Some group camping is allowed through prearrangements. Toilet facilities are available, and drinking water can be obtained from the forest ranger. Backpack camping is permitted, and you can even roll in your RV in the tent/trailer area, but no water or electric hookups available. Clear flowing streams lure the angler who must possess a current fishing license and trail stamp. "Fish for Fun" is offered at Bull Head Creek. It is a catch-and-release area. A fly rod, reel, barbless hook, and a net are required.

The park is open year-around with seasonal adjustments for openings and closings. Give the ranger a call for more details and to register for the many opportunities.

STATE FORESTS AND GAME LANDS

Dupont State Forest
Sky Valley Road, Hendersonville, NC (828) 251-6509

This is Western North Carolina's newest state forest. Its 7,600 acres in Henderson and Transylvania Counties were purchased in 1996 and 1997 from DuPont after the company sold its industrial operation and 2,700 acres of surrounding land holdings to Sterling Diagnostic Imaging. A recent acquisition has enlarged the forest to 10,300 acres. The forest is situated in an upland plateau of the Little River Valley with elevations that range from 2,300 to 3,600 feet. Its gently rolling land is bordered by moderately steep hills and mountains that are topped by exposed granite slabs and domes.

Soon certain forest trails will be opened for horseback riding and bicycling. For now a special permit is needed for these activities. Registered as North Carolina gameland, hunting in season is by lottery only, and no hunting is allowed on Sundays. For fishing, streams here are

CLOSE-UP

Big Tom Wilson

In 1835, University of North Carolina Professor Dr. Elisha Mitchell announced that his barometric measurements indicated that a mountain (which in time would bear his name) was the highest peak in the Appalachian chain. The measurement of 6,674 feet stood until 1857, when Thomas Clingman claimed that he had found a higher peak. Clingman and his team measured the peak, which stands on the North Carolina and Tennessee line. The summit is in Tennessee and is known as Clingmans Dome. But it proved to be at least 40 feet lower than Mount Mitchell.

Eventually Mt. Mitchell was found to be even higher than Dr. Mitchell thought. Officially it stands at 6,684 feet. It is the highest point in the entire Eastern United States.

In response to Clingman's claim, Dr. Mitchell ascended the mountain alone to measure it. He did not return to his base camp at Black Mountain on schedule. After a search party failed to find any trace of Dr. Mitchell, they called upon Big Tom Wilson. Tom was known for his skill, knowledge, and prowess in the mountains. He was already legendary as a young man who had killed more than 100 black bears, which were a main staple in the life of the mountaineers.

Big Tom conducted the search with the help of a young lad of about 14 who carried a huge rope. As they ascended,

classified as "wild." (Contact the North Carolina Wildlife Resources Commission, 512 North Salisbury Street, Raleigh, NC 27604-1188, (919) 733-3391, for more details on both hunting and fishing in this forest.) ATVs are forbidden in the forest.

At present the land is open for hiking, and there are nearly a dozen interesting trails that range from easy to strenuous. (A detailed, hand-marked color map is available at the Henderson County Travel and Tourism office, 201 South Main Street, Hendersonville, for $7.00.) For a short hike to 13-foot Hooker Falls, the site of a former gristmill, take DuPont Road (off Crab Creek Road) for about 3 miles until you see the Little River bridge at the bottom of a long hill. Park near the gated Hooker Falls Road on the right just before the bridge. Walk around the gate and along

the dirt road, bearing left at the fork, and continuing parallel to the river. In a few minutes you will approach the top of Hooker Falls. Continue straight on the path to a good viewing location at the pool below. You won't want to miss the other three waterfalls: Triple Falls, High Falls, and Bridal Veil Falls.

If it's a hot day, and you'd like to cool off, continue on up DuPont Road for another 2.6 miles until it dead ends into Cascade Lake Road (Buck Forest Road on some maps). Drive almost a mile to a wide parking spot on the right. Walk across the road and go around the gate on the marked Corn's Mill Road and continue on the road. Walk past the intersection of Big Rock Trail to a crossing over Tom's Creek. Continue on the graded road to a fork. Take the right fork, and after a short dis-

the "smoke" of the Smokies, which some people might call fog, crowded in on them. Big Tom never faltered. Although he couldn't see through fog, there were folks who thought he could. Big Tom pointed out footprints of Dr. Mitchell that seemed to be going steadily up the mountain.

Approaching the summit and nearing the top of the waterfalls, Big Tom pointed out where Mitchell had mis-stepped. His footprints showed that he had stumbled on a rock or slipped off a log, evidenced by moss scraped off a rock, where Dr. Mitchell apparently tried to steady himself.

Reaching the top of the waterfall, the searchers saw brambles and brushes at the foot of the falls with a large, dark object floating underneath the mass. Big

Tom lowered the boy with a rope, and the lad called up that indeed there was a body. He secured the rope to the body, and Big Tom pulled Dr. Mitchell from the pool and carried his body down off the mountain.

Mitchell is now buried at the summit of Mt. Mitchell.

Big Tom has been immortalized by his great-great-great grandson, world class wood-carver David Boone. Standing in the museum at the parking lot on Mt. Mitchell is the 6-foot 4-inch wood carving created by Boone. You can hear the story from Big Tom himself by pressing a button on the cabin wall beside Big Tom. Years prior to carving this image, David Boone created the Big Tom Walking Stick, with an image of Big Tom on it.

tance, take the left fork (you'll still be on Corn's Mill Road) until you reach a gentle waterslide and popular ford on the Little River where local residents have enjoyed swimming for years.

There are multiple ways to get to this mecca of land and forest so ring up the forester to obtain directions that suit you.

Green River Game Lands
Big Hungry Road, SR 1802,
Hendersonville, NC
(919) 733-3391

Over 10,000 rugged acres in Henderson and Polk Counties make up these state-owned gamelands. There are 15 miles of beautiful trails here ranging from easy to strenuous, but because of the nature of the terrain, it's recommended that you don't hike here alone. It's also wise to

avoid the area during hunting seasons. Some of the trails offer great views of Tryon Peak and the Green River Gorge to the south. Others take you on a ridgeline next to the steep and dangerous Loobie Cliffs or for a view from Pace Cliffs. No vehicles or horses are allowed here. A brochure with a map and descriptions of the trails can be found at visitor centers in the area or contact the North Carolina Wildlife Resources Commission, 512 North Salisbury Street, Raleigh, NC 27604-1188, (919) 733-3391. It is also your source for information on hunting here.

Holmes Educational State Forest
Crab Creek Road, Hendersonville, NC
(828) 692-0100

Well-tended trails loop through 235 acres of mountain forests at this pretty state forest. One of the most delightful, and educational, things about it is the Talking Trees Trail, which features different hardwood trees that, at the touch of a button, tell stories about themselves, their sites, and the forest history. Two new trails include the Soil and Water Trail, featuring a 300-foot boardwalk over a wetland area, and Crab Creek Trail, spotlighting firefighting equipment displays and a walk through a pine stand. (Crab Creek Trail was built with wheelchairs in mind.) There is also a Forest Demonstration Trail that teaches actual forest practices. The Forestry Center houses audiovisual exhibits, and a natural amphitheater is available for special sessions or groups.

Holmes also has picnic tables and a group picnic shelter with a massive stone fireplace. For the hardy there are walk-in tent sites in the forest that can be reserved with a phone call. This pleasant state forest is open from mid-March through mid-November. It is 8.5 miles from Hendersonville on Crab Creek Road (SR 1127).

ATTRACTIONS

Most of the "attractions" in these mountains are the mountains themselves. There's not much of a need for artificial diversion, what with the natural activities inherent to this area. But if you tire of hiking, tubing down mountain streams, fly-fishing, mountain biking, kayaking, antiquing, and scouring the farmer's market for homemade preserves and string beans, then head over to these more organized attractions of the mountains.

It doesn't matter if rain is pouring through the treetops or sunshine is bursting over the rugged terrain, you'll always find something to do in North Carolina's mountains. We've included attractions in this chapter that can keep a whole family busy without costing a bundle—some are even free. One of the most alluring attractions in our mountains is the palatial Biltmore Estate in Asheville, to which we've dedicated an entire chapter. Other popular destinations, such as the Carl Sandburg Home in Flat Rock, have been included in other chapters. Details on the famous poet's lovely Connemara farm, where he spent the final 22 years of his life, can be found in the Arts and Culture chapter. The Annual Festivals and Events chapter is a good source of ideas for pleasurable outings, as are the Resorts, Rockhounding, and Waterfalls chapters. So pick your pleasure. But remember, these are only a few of the spontaneous, special ways to enjoy a ramble through the North Carolina highlands. Prices and times of operation are always subject to change, so do give a call before you head out.

NORTHERN MOUNTAINS
Ashe County

Ashe County Cheese Factory
106 East Main Street, West Jefferson, NC
(336) 246-2501
Did you know that it takes 10 gallons of milk to make one pound of cheese? That's one of the facts you'll learn as you watch cheese being made in this factory founded in 1930. The only cheese factory in North Carolina, it makes several varieties, including cheddar, Colby, and Monterey Jack. Guides escort groups through a viewing room, explain the process, and answer questions. Sample your favorites and take a few home from the company cheese shop across the street from the factory. The plant is open 8:30 A.M. to 5:00 P.M. Monday through Saturday. Admission is free.

Avery County

Grandfather Mountain
U.S. Highway 221, outside Linville, Mile 305, a mile off the Blue Ridge Parkway
(828) 733-2013, (800) 468-7325
The rugged outline of this ridge that takes on the appearance of a bearded face—the "grandfather"—gives this mountain its name. Grandfather Mountain is the highest in the Blue Ridge chain. It is part of the International Network of Biosphere Reserves, "a special place where man and nature thrive in harmony." Of the 324 existing Biosphere Reserves, Grandfather

is the only one privately owned. This wonderful oasis allows you to come close to the natural wildlife habitats of black bears, cougars, deer, eagles, and river otter.

The nature museum offers valuable information. If you have no fear of heights, you might attempt the exhilaration of the famous Mile High Swinging Bridge (keep remembering to look at the view).

Work off those wobbly knees with 12 miles of hiking trails. The Grandfather Trail is a favorite, a rugged but beautiful trail traversing 2.3 miles. The mountain also offers meandering footpaths and scenic walks for novice hikers. Once you've relaxed, spread a picnic and enjoy this majestic place, a reminder of the fragility of our relationship with this earth. The site is open daily except Thanksgiving and Christmas from 8:00 A.M. to 5:00 P.M. in winter, 8:00 A.M. to 6:00 P.M. in spring and fall, and 8:00 A.M. to 7:00 P.M. in summer. Ticket sales stop at 6:00 P.M. A gift shop and restaurant are on the site. Children younger than 4 are admitted free.

Madison County

Hot Springs Spa
315 Bridge Street, Hot Springs, NC
(828) 622-7676, (800) 462-0933
Does arthritis or rheumatism plague you? Do you seek relief from stomach, liver, or gallbladder ailments? Historically these mineral springs, maintaining a natural 100-degree temperature year-round, have provided relief for visitors as early as the turn of the 20th century. That was the heyday of this once-fashionable health resort. With the passage of time and a changing world, the springs fell into disuse, and the population dwindled away. But in 1990 the famous hot springs came into new ownership and are now back in business, offering a modern version of "taking the waters."

Jacuzzis filled with the curative waters are available for hourly rates, determined by the number of people in your party. These run from roughly $15 per hour for one person to $7.50 per hour per person for more than one in a tub. Several resident massage therapists are available by appointment for a thirty-minute session costing $35 or a one-hour session for $55.

The friendly employees at the spa make you feel like a long lost relative. The word *spa* may be a misnomer, though. This is a very casual place—don't expect luxury—but do expect to commune successfully with nature (leafy trees and the sky are your canopy), while some tubs have plastic "bubbles" so they can be used in inclement weather. Tubs are set alongside the rushing French Broad River and Spring Creek. A log fire in the central yard is perfect for lounging and communing with friends.

The Hot Springs Spa is open year-round. Rates increase for evening sessions (after 7:00 P.M.). Lodging facilities are available in the RV park and campground, for which options include electric, water, and sewer hookups and tent sites. There is also a facility for hot showers. Primitive camping cabins are also available, as is one fully furnished log cabin with a Jacuzzi on the back porch, fed from the natural spring. When camping, children 6 or younger stay free. Special discounts and group rates are also available for the campground.

If you're going to Hot Springs Spa, why not make a day of pampering yourself inside and out? Call for reservations and reserve at least two hours in the tub for a good soak. Venture down the road a bit to the Bridge Street Cafe (featured in our Restaurants chapter), where a canopied deck overlooks Spring Creek for wonderful outdoor dining. Try the crisp Pinot Grigio with a "gorgonzola, caramelized onion, and fresh rosemary open-fire grilled pizza." Superb!

McDowell County

Linville Caverns
U.S. Highway 221, between Linville and Marion, 4 miles south of the Blue Ridge Parkway
(828) 756-4171, (800) 419-0540

These limestone caverns with marvelous stalactite and stalagmite formations were first explored in the late 1880s by H. E. Colton and his local guide Dave Franklin. However the Indians had known about the caverns since 1822. Found deep inside Humpback Mountain, these caverns were also hideouts for army deserters from both sides during the Civil War.

Today, in the company of experienced guides, you can take a path that leads along an underground stream filled with trout whose life in perpetual darkness has resulted in blindness. The limestone formations, suspended like jewels, have developed over eons into interesting shapes, such as the Frozen Waterfall, Natural Bridge, and Franciscan Monk. Did you ever wonder what absolute darkness looks like? You'll get your chance deep in these caverns.

This must be the guides' favorite part—switching off those lights! You literally can't see your hand in front of your face.

The temperature underground is a constantly cool 52 degrees, so come prepared with a sweater or jacket. A gift shop is well stocked, and items are reasonably priced.

Admission is $5.00 for adults and $3.00 for children ages 5 to 12. Seniors pay $4.00, and children under 5 are free. Group rates are available. The caverns are open 9:00 A.M. to 6:00 P.M. June 1 through Labor Day; 9:00 A.M. to 5:00 P.M. April, May, September, and October; and 9:00 A.M. to 4:30 P.M. November through March. They're open on weekends only in December, January, and February and are closed Thanksgiving and Christmas.

Mitchell County

The Orchard at Altapass
Mile 328.4, Blue Ridge Parkway, near Little Switzerland
(828) 765-9531

This historic orchard features fresh apples and peaches from May to November and is open only during these months. You can pick your own or just buy the already-picked baskets and brown-paper bags of juicy fruits. Tours of the orchard are free. Come enjoy music, stories, and hayrides on Saturdays. The Orchard is open seven days a week.

Watauga County

The Blowing Rock
off U.S. Highway 321, Blowing Rock, NC
(828) 295-7111

Fanciful tales about this beautiful spot are as interesting as the facts. This rocky granite outcrop is swept by a constant updraft from Johns River Gorge 3,000 feet below. Those are the facts.

The most familiar romantic legend of the Blowing Rock is that a beautiful Indian maiden was taken from the plains to Blowing Rock by her father, a Chickawaw chieftain who was fearful of a white man's adoration of his daughter. The daughter met an Indian brave wandering below the Blowing Rock and shot an arrow in his direction to capture his attention. They fell in love, but a reddening of the sky brought them back to the rock. It was a sign of trouble to the brave, commanding his return to his tribe on the plains. With the maiden's entreaties not to leave her, the brave, torn by conflict of duty and heart, leapt from the rock. The maiden prayed to the Great Spirit every day until one evening, a gust of wind blew her lover back onto the rock and into her arms.

The Blowing Rock claims a panoramic view of Mount Mitchell, Hawksbill, Grandfather, and Table Rock Mountains in the distance. Blowing Rock is just outside the town of the same name and is open daily from March through November; it's open weekends in winter months, weather permitting. Hours are 9:00 A.M. to 5:00 P.M. March, April, and November; 9:00 A.M. to 6:00 P.M. May through August; and 8:00 A.M. to 7:00 P.M. September through October. Admission fees are $4.00 for adults, $1.00 for children ages 6 to 11, and $3.00 for seniors and groups of 20 or more.

For those Doubting Thomases out there who have to see for themselves why they call it Grandfather Mountain, head south on N.C. 105 from Boone. In the heart of Foscoe, look toward the mountain on your left, and lo and behold, there he is, sleeping on his back. You can almost hear him snore!

Daniel Boone Native Gardens
651 Horn in the West Drive, off N.C. Highway 105 and U.S. Highways 321/421, Boone, NC
(828) 264-6390
The stone gatehouse bids you welcome as you enter the gardens through the handsome wrought iron gate, a gift made by Daniel Boone VI, a direct descendant of the great pioneer. Adjacent to Horn in the West, these beautiful gardens include an extensive collection of native plants covering six acres, informally landscaped with trails, split-rail fences, and a reflection pool at the Squire Boone Cabin. Many plants, such as bloodroot, dogtooth violet, yellow lady slippers, and maidenhair fern, are marked. A spring trickles through the enormous boulders of the Rockery, while a statue of St. Francis stands in the center of the secluded prayer retreat. There's even a meditation sanctuary that lets you pause and give thanks for such beauty. The gardens are open daily May through

August and weekends in October 10:00 A.M. to 6:00 P.M. (until 8:00 P.M. when Horn in the West is running). A small admission is charged, but those under 16 are admitted free.

Hickory Ridge Homestead
591 Horn in the West Drive off N.C. Highway 105 and U.S. Highways 321/421 Boone, NC
(828) 264-9089, (828) 264-2120
You'll swear you just saw Daniel Boone, but it was one of the costumed interpreters at Hickory Ridge Homestead on the grounds of Horn in the West. This living museum offers a glimpse into 18th-century mountain life and culture through a variety of activities, including regular demonstrations in weaving and candle making, as well as presentations of other crafts. Try your hand at weaving on a 180-year-old loom, spinning wool, or participating in other hands-on activities. A nominal admission helps support the museum and its projects. Hours vary with the seasons, so call ahead. And while you're at it, ask about the intensive living history weekends and workshops.

Horn in the West
591 Horn in the West Drive
off N.C. Highway 105 and U.S. Highways 321/421, Boone
(828) 264-9089, (828) 264-2120
This outdoor drama, one of several in this region, depicts the lives of North Carolina's early settlers—Daniel Boone among them—and their struggle for independence from Britain. This production, set in pre-Revolutionary 1771, lasts about two hours and is a one-of-a-kind experience: history and excitement all rolled into one. Remember, this is an outdoor production. Summer evenings can be cool, especially at this elevation, so bring a light jacket just in case. The season is mid-June to mid-August, and the drama begins each evening at 8:00, with reserved seating. There are no performances on Mondays. Admission is $12.00 for adults and $6.00 for children 12 and younger.

Mystery Hill
off U.S. Highways 321/221 between
Boone and Blowing Rock
(828) 264-2792
Mystery Hill explores the relationship of
science, optical illusion, and natural phenomena. (See our Kidstuff chapter for a
complete description.)

Tweetsie Railroad
on U.S. Highways 321/221, between
Boone and Blowing Rock
(828) 264-9061, (800) 526-5740
Take a trip back to the Old West, where
there's plenty of old-fashioned fun for the
whole family. This 30-year-old theme park
features a 100-year-old locomotive, a petting farm, a Ferris wheel, and musical
shows. (See our Kidstuff chapter.)

CENTRAL MOUNTAINS

Buncombe County

Asheville Tourists Baseball
McCormick Field, off Biltmore Avenue
Asheville, NC
(828) 258-0428
Professional baseball at McCormick Field
has been a fixture in Asheville since 1924.
Many of the all-time greats of the game,
such as Babe Ruth, Ty Cobb, Jackie
Robinson, Pete Rose, and Nolan Ryan,
played here en route to the majors. The
Asheville Tourists are currently in their
fifth year of affiliation as a farm team with
the National League's Colorado Rockies.

The new McCormick Field, a much-
improved facility, was completed in 1992.
The old McCormick Field, with all its well-
worn charm, was actually famous for a bit
part as background in some of the final
scenes for the popular baseball movie *Bull
Durham* with Kevin Costner. The new stadium is grand, but it's Asheville's baseball
tradition that keeps folks coming to
McCormick Field to cheer on the Tourists.

The Tourists baseball season begins in
April and runs through the first week in
September. The Asheville team, a member

of the South Atlantic League, plays about
seventy-two home games. Box seats are
$7.00 for adults and $6.00 for children; general admission seats are $5.00 for adults
and $4.00 for children ages 3 through 12.
These prices are subject to change.

The Asheville Urban Trail
Locations in downtown Asheville
(828) 259-5800, ext. 4000
Asheville's formative period, the boom
time from 1880 to 1930, left an indelible
imprint on the character of the city. This
was the era of George Vanderbilt (Biltmore Estate), E. W. Grove (Grove Park
Inn), and George Willis Pack (Pack
Square), men whose taste for elegance
produced a stunning blend of architectural styles that remains today.

To highlight and pay homage to this
remarkable period in Asheville's history,
the city has commissioned the development of the Urban Trail. This series of 30
stations is marked by plaques, sculptures,
mosaics, murals, and other interpretative
visuals created by world-class artists from
Russia, Italy, and the United States, that
bring the area's history to life. The open-
air museum runs 1.6 miles around downtown through five themed paths. The trail
is almost complete. The walking benefits
of the trail are free, along with the pleasure of the path. Regularly scheduled
guided tours of the Urban Trail are run

*Before shopping at the Farmer's Market
outside of Asheville, try the Moose Cafe,
just above the market's entrance, for a
hearty country breakfast. Steaming hot
biscuits grace your table before you
even order and can be slathered with the
honey, molasses, or homemade apple
butter already provided. Lunches and
dinners are traditional Southern fare; the
menu includes a daily special and a four-
vegetable plate. Prices are reasonable.
Soak in the local atmosphere, try a piece
of deep-dish pie, and buy a jar of apple
butter to take with you.*

from April to November, the second Friday of each month at 4:00 P.M., the third Sunday of each month at 3:00 P.M., and other special group tours as requested. The two-hour tour meets in front of Pack Place at the marquee sign, on the southeast corner of Pack Square in downtown Asheville. Tours will be on schedule except in extreme weather conditions. A $5.00 donation per person is suggested (no charge for children under 12 accompanied by an adult).

Touring the Asheville Urban Trail on your own is made easy with the aid of "Artful Asheville—Along the Urban Trail," a comprehensive take-along guide with maps and informative history about each of the 30 stations (sculptures and plaques) around the city. The booklet is available at bookstores and museum shops in Asheville.

The Botanical Gardens
151 W. T. Weaver Boulevard, Asheville, NC
(828) 252-5190
This wonderful 10-acre garden oasis in the middle of bustling north Asheville is adjacent to the campus of the University of North Carolina at Asheville. The gardens were begun in 1960 by the Asheville Garden Club and designed by Doan Ogden, a noted landscape architect, to preserve the heritage of native mountain plants and flowers. Today this mature garden has a wealth of beauty around every bend in the path and within every leafy bower. A bonus is the proliferation of birds and other small wildlife that have made this wonderful garden their home. You may spot a few rabbits at dusk; squirrels and chipmunks abound in the daylight hours. A meadow for sunning, a gazebo for lounging, and a cool creek make this an oasis close to the city, perfect for those after-dinner walks. Many of the trees and other flora are marked with small tags for

identification. This site receives support from volunteers, donations, and memberships. A botany center offers nature-related gift items. Admission is free. No pets are allowed.

The Folk Art Center
Mile 382, off I-70 east of Asheville
(828) 298-7928
The Folk Art Center is home to the Southern Highland Craft Guild, an educational nonprofit organization founded in 1930 to give economic support and development to the craftspeople of the Appalachian region. The guild serves nine states and has a membership of more than 700 craftspeople who work to preserve and perpetuate the Appalachian heritage as well as develop the contemporary face of craftsmanship.

The center's century-old Allanstand Craft Shop offers for sale the work of guild members throughout the nine-state region. There is also a fine crafts gallery on the upper level and a 250-seat auditorium that is the scene of workshops, programs, and lectures by the guild and National Park Service. Craft demonstrations are held April through December in the foyer of the center. Clay Day and Fiber Day are two of the special events also sponsored by the guild at the Folk Art Center each year (see our Annual Festivals and Events and Mountain Crafts chapters for more information on the guild). Admission is free.

North Carolina Arboretum
1000 Frederick Law Olmsted Way,
Asheville, NC
(828) 665-2492
This 426-acre facility boasts a 25,500-square-foot Visitor Education Center, the Horticultural Support Facilities and Greenhouses, the Plants of Promise Garden, and the mile-long Natural Garden Trail, all of which are open to the public. The Core Area Gardens include the Stream Garden, Spring Garden, Outdoor Events Garden, Appalachian Quilt Garden, Blue Ridge Court, and Grand Promenade. Numerous

woodland trails lace the forested areas and follow the path of Bent Creek. Guided tours are available for groups if you call ahead. Educational lectures, tours, and workshops are scheduled throughout the year. A cafe and plant retail shop are welcome recent additions.

A car fee of $6.00 per vehicle is required at the gate. Nominal fees apply for educational programs. The outdoor areas are open seven days a week from 7:00 A.M. to 7:00 P.M. The Visitor Education Center is open Monday through Friday from 8:00 A.M. to 5:00 P.M. and Saturday from 9:00 A.M. to 5:00 P.M. The greenhouse is open 8:00 A.M. to 4:00 P.M. Monday through Friday. The second and fourth Sunday of the month feature an open house from 1:30 to 4:30 P.M.

Turn off U.S. Highway 191 to the Blue Ridge Parkway. The arboretum entrance is directly before you enter the parkway.

Western North Carolina Farmer's Market
570 Brevard Road, Asheville, NC
(828) 253-1691

It's been described as shopping at a 36-acre roadside stand. The WNC Farmer's Market, southeast of Asheville, offers a bounty of fresh produce and quality plants, shrubs, trees, and garden supplies. The retail area is reminiscent of an old market square with wooden tables overflowing with goods, fresh vegetables, crafts, and other gifts from the farm. The garden center is operated by several generations of garden specialists, Jesse Israel & Sons, supplying every gardening need.

The restaurant, The Moose Cafe, is on U.S. 191 just south of the main entrance and serves good, basic home cooking. The truck stands are a feast for the eye and food for the soul, too. The conversation from the back of the truck gives as much pleasure as the brown-paper sack of red Delicious apples you carry home with you.

Sections of the market are open 24 hours daily, and the retail buildings are open from 8:00 A.M. to 6:00 P.M. daily in summer and 8:00 A.M. to 5:00 P.M. in winter.

Western North Carolina Nature Center
75 Gashes Creek Road, Asheville, NC
(828) 298-5600

From the moment you step through the door and a three-dimensional, full-size diorama of woodland creatures greets you, you know you are indeed crossing that bridge to the natural world. Exhibits such as weather forecasting, animal identification, a real working beehive, archaeological displays, and zoological collections of live reptiles and amphibians make this a special stop. (See our Kidstuff chapter for more.)

Zebulon Vance Birthplace
Reems Creek Road, off Old U.S. Highways 19/23, Weaverville, NC
(828) 645-6706

This charming mountain homestead was home to one of North Carolina's most prominent political figures. Zeb Vance began his career as a lawyer, assuming public office by the young age of 24. He was elected governor of North Carolina three times, most notably during the Civil War. He served three terms as senator from North Carolina. At his death in 1894, this most capable public servant was admired by colleagues and beloved by his constituency. His life and career are profiled in an exhibit in the adjoining visitors center. But better yet is the opportunity to see a period mountain home replete with old utensils, kitchenry, rope-spring beds, and other objects whose uses are explained in the informative and free guided tours.

The two-story cabin and outbuildings are reconstructions, built from hewn, yellow pine logs around the original chimney with its two massive fireplaces. The furnishings and household items depict the period from 1790 to 1840 and include a few pieces original to the Vance family.

Pioneer Living Days are celebrated here each spring and fall. Costumed staff members demonstrate skills and occupations of earlier days. Military encampments and battle reenactments are frequently part of the events. The home-stead is open Monday through Saturday 9:00 A.M. to 5:00 P.M., Sunday 1:00 to 5:00 P.M., and admission is free.

Henderson County

Information about some of Henderson County's attractions, including the Carl Sandburg Home, the Historic Hendersonville Depot and Model Railroad, the Historic Johnson Farm, and the Western North Carolina Air Museum, can be found in the Arts and Culture chapter.

St. John in the Wilderness
U.S. Highway 25 S., Flat Rock, NC
(828) 693-9783
This charming chapel has an interesting background. In 1837 English-born Charles Baring, in search of a healthier summer climate, brought his beloved wife Susan, the former widow of a wealthy Charleston rice planter, to an area between the Watauga settlements in what is now Watauga County and Greenville, South Carolina, known simply as "the Wilderness." Thus began a migration of wealthy families from the coast that turned Flat Rock into "the little Charleston of the mountains." Baring bought hundreds of acres in the area and built a grand home called Mountain Lodge, developed on the order of an English country estate, complete with a gatekeeper's cottage, a billiard house, and a deer park. The hilltop private residence, hidden by tall pines on Rutledge Drive, is one of many grand old homes from this period still in the area.

Most of these homes are private dwellings, not open to the public. However the Barings also built a private chapel that they donated to the Episcopal Diocese of North Carolina in 1836. Here many of the cream of Southern gentry worshipped together with their slaves and were buried together in the same cemetery. The chapel, partially built of now-yellowed bricks thought to have been made by

Barings' slaves, was doubled in size in 1852. The beautiful structure is 2.25 miles south of Hendersonville on the west side of U.S. 25. The site has a marker and can be easily seen from the road. Both the graveyard and the church are open to visitors daily from 9:00 A.M. to 4:00 P.M.

Charles Baring's decision to move his family to this gentle mountain climate each summer must have been the right one, because Susan lived to be 83, and he died at age 92. They are buried in a vault inside the church under the spot where their pew used to sit.

Wolfe's Angel
Oakdale Cemetery, U.S. Highway 64 W., Hendersonville, NC
Just a short distance from downtown Hendersonville on U.S. 64 W., the cemetery plot of a local family, the Johnsons, is marked by an angel. She holds a stone lily in her left hand and extends her right hand upward. This statue, imported from Italy and sold to the Johnson family by novelist Thomas Wolfe's father, W. O. Wolfe, is prominently featured in the author's first novel, Look Homeward, Angel. Today an iron fence protects the famous angel, and a historical marker on the highway next to the cemetery notes its importance. You can enter the cemetery for a close-up look.

Polk County

Foothills Equestrian Nature Center
500 Hunting Country Road, Tryon, NC
(828) 859-9021
Foothills Equestrian Nature Center—FENCE, as it is commonly called—is a 300-acre nature sanctuary dedicated to education, recreation, and preservation. The state-of-the-art equestrian facility hosts more than 18 events each season, including two steeplechases, hunter/jumper and dressage shows, and driving rallies. The facility is home to the Carolina Carriage Club (see our Recreation chapter). It also has bridle trails.

Even if you aren't a horse person, FENCE has great hiking trails that are open to the public free of charge from dawn until dusk all year long. It also offers on- and off-site programs for school classes as well as adult classes in wild-flowers and other nature subjects. Its Bird Center activities are outstanding. In addi-tion to lectures and slide shows, there are frequent bird-watching outings. These include regular Thursday morning bird walks at FENCE or at nearby good birding sites in the spring and fall, as well as local, regional, and international birding "ven-tures" throughout the year.

Rutherford County

Chimney Rock Park
U.S. Highways 64/74-A in Chimney Rock
(828) 625–9611, (800) 277–9611

Chimney Rock Park, in Hickory Nut Gorge, has been a favorite in the Southeast. Its unusual rock formations, spectacular Hick-ory Nut Falls dropping 404 feet to the gorge below, winding mountainside trails, and delicate wildflowers draw a steady stream of visitors annually. From the park-ing area, take a 26-story elevator ride to the Sky Lounge, the park's snack and gift shop area. From the deck just outside, you have a wonderful view of the park's land-mark and namesake, Chimney Rock. Or try the steps to the Chimney—the rock formations and spectacular views along the way are well worth it.

This prominent rocky pedestal gives visitors a spectacular 180-degree view of the Hickory Nut Gorge area and beautiful Lake Lure. Make your way down a stair-way from the chimney and choose one of several beautiful trails threading through the rocky outcrops, cliffs, and mountain-side. The Skyline Trail winds upward through the woods, leveling out after about a quarter-mile and proceeding along a flat path to the top of beautiful Hickory Nut Falls. A new children's trail has playful wildlife sculptures.

Look out! Heading southeast on U.S. 74 just as you come into Chimney Rock is a view so beautiful that you might miss a curve on this windy mountain road. Just take it slow and look to your right at the mountains above with shimmer-ing rock faces and the Rocky Broad River with its swift current tumbling and cascading below.

The park is full of fascinating rocks, ledges, and natural wildlife. You can squeeze through the crevice known as the Needle's Eye; visit the Grotto, the Rock Pile, the Moon-Shiner's Cave (with a replica of an old moonshine still); and journey up to the magnificent heights of Inspiration Point. If you get a little weak in the knees at the thought of high places, don't worry. Chimney Rock Park's Forest Stroll Trail, leading from the parking area, is a leisurely 0.75-mile walk to the base of Hickory Nut Falls. There is a viewing deck with a few picnic tables for your convenience.

The Morse family continues the tradi-tion of private ownership since 1902, as the park evolves as an ecological reserve. One of the most popular of the special events offered throughout the year is the traditional Easter sunrise service. The park is open year-round and offers a number of annual and ongoing activities. A resident botanist and ornithologist offer several workshops and nature walks throughout the year. There are now five hiking trails.

The Sky Lounge snack and gift shop offers light lunch sandwiches and features a costume exhibit from *The Last of the Mohicans* film as well as theme-related gift items. A nature center on the meadows about halfway up the drive to the top of the park is a pleasant stop. Picnic areas, grills, rest rooms, and play areas are nearby.

An annual pass to Chimney Rock Park is a tremendous savings at less than the cost of two visits. Children under four are admitted free. Special group rates are available for groups of 20 or more. The ticket office of Chimney Rock Park is open from 8:30 A.M. to 5:30 P.M. (daylight savings time) and 8:30 A.M. to 4:30 P.M. (eastern standard time). The Park closes at 7:00 P.M. in the summer and one hour and a half after the ticket office closes in the winter.

Lake Lure Tours
Lake Lure Marina
U.S. Highways 64/74-A in Lake Lure
(828) 625-0077

Tour the lake *National Geographic* called "one of the 10 most spectacular man-made lakes in the world." A fleet of modern boats offers deluxe seats, full-length canopies, and clear enclosures to keep you comfortable whatever the weather. Tours take 60 minutes, departing every hour from the Town Marina. Be sure to arrive early enough to enjoy the surroundings. Before hopping on board, stroll the wooden boardwalk along the lake or the mile-long walking trail to the gazebo and picnic area with swings for the kids. Even parking your car is a delight here—the rocky-faced mountains are exquisite (especially when the dogwoods are in blossom in the spring). Tickets cost around $5.00 for children 6 to 15 and $9.00 for adults. Tours operate March through November from 10:00 A.M. to 8:00 P.M. For a special treat take the Sunset Dinner Cruise that includes a stop at Sunset Cove for wine and hors d'oeuvres (BYOB) and dinner at one of three lakeside restaurants. After dessert, climb back aboard for a romantic trip back to port under the summer moonlight. Tickets are approximately $15 plus dinner. Private charters are also available for all occasions.

Transylvania County

Brevard Music Center
1000 Probart Street, Brevard, NC
(828) 884-2011, (888) 384-8682

The hills are alive with the sound of music for seven weeks each summer at this internationally famous music center.

(For more information see our Arts and Culture chapter.)

Cradle of Forestry
U. S. Highway 276, Pisgah National Forest
(828) 877-3130

The Forest Discovery Center and its trails and activities at the Cradle of Forestry are a "don't miss" attraction. (For more information see our Forests and Parks, Art and Culture, and Kidstuff chapters.)

English Chapel
U.S. Highway 276
Pisgah National Forest

This Methodist church just a few miles from the entrance to Pisgah Forest is a simple structure. It is worth a historical exploration and the setting by the Davidson River is lovely. The Rev. A. F. English bought the land for $5.00 and founded the church in 1860. It was built by local folks and continues to serve the community and forest visitors. It is usually locked except for Sunday 9:30 A.M. services. An exercise trail that borders the river's rushing, clear waters leads from the church to the Davidson River Campground. Unlike many trails in the forest, this one is wide and level, making for a relaxed stroll.

Pisgah Center for Wildlife Education
FR 475, Pisgah National Forest
(828) 877-4423

Situated adjacent to the Pisgah Forest Fish Hatchery (see the following entry), this educational facility, operated by the North Carolina Wildlife Resources Commission, has exhibits and programs that explain how human activities affect and are affected by wildlife and the natural environment. The center includes a paved walkway to outdoor exhibits focusing on wildlife and fish management, law enforcement, and conservation education. Indoor exhibits feature aquariums containing coastal, Piedmont, and mountain aquatic species and an auditorium. Wildlife educational programs are offered at the center throughout the year.

The center is open daily from 8:00 A.M. until 5:00 P.M. except Thanksgiving Day, Christmas Day, and New Year's Day. Admission to both the center and its courses is free.

Pisgah Forest Fish Hatchery
FR 475, Pisgah National Forest
(828) 877-3121

First it was a logging camp, then a camp for the Civilian Conservation Corps during the Great Depression. Today the Pisgah Forest Fish Hatchery, just off U.S. 276 and at the base of John Rock, is operated by the North Carolina Wildlife Resources Commission. It raises thousands of trout that are released in area streams. Children really like this place. They particularly delight in the wild frenzies when the fish, which come in all sizes, are fed. Even more, they like to feed the fish themselves.

To get to the hatchery, drive several miles up U.S. 276 from the Brevard entrance to Pisgah Forest and turn off on FR 475, which is well marked and paved. The hatchery is less than a mile down this road. There are also a number of nice hiking trails in the area.

SOUTHERN MOUNTAINS

Cherokee County

The Episcopal Church of the Messiah
Peachtree Street, Murphy, NC
(828) 837-2021

Murphy's "little church around the corner" was organized in 1855, when there were only two Episcopal families in the town. Much of the money to build the church was raised, in 25 cent contributions, by the mother of Lucy Morgan, who is herself renowned for her work at Penland School (see our chapter on Mountain Crafts). The cornerstone of the church dates back to 1896. It is across the street from the blue-marble county courthouse. Its stained-glass windows executed by Tiffany's of New York, its handmade altar, and the herringbone pattern of its heart-pine paneling make this church, which is open to the public, a small work of art.

Field of the Woods
U.S. Highway 294, Murphy, NC
(828) 494-7855

Field of the Woods is unique in the world. Stretched over 200 acres, this Christian theme park is made up of symbols and words taken from the Bible, often presented in a majestic form. One of the most spectacular displays is a 300-foot-wide marker listing the Old Testament's Ten Commandments in letters 5 feet high and 4 feet wide. Another is the representation of a huge open Bible that takes its text from Matthew 22:37–40, with the words painted in bold, black lettering that can be read from a great distance.

A 150-foot cross lies atop All Nations Mountain, surrounded by the flags of all the countries where the Church of God of Prophecy, the park's owners, are active. There is a tomb, constructed in the likeness of the one in Jerusalem where many believe that Jesus' body was taken after his crucifixion. You'll also find a cafe, gift shop, and Christian bookstore. The cafe is closed on Mondays.

The park is open year-round from sunrise to sunset. Admission is free.

Cherokee Indian Reservation

The Qualla Boundary, home to the 13,000 members of the Eastern Band of the Cherokee, is one of America's most-visited tourist destinations. (For more information see our Kidstuff chapter and our chapter on the Cherokee Indian Reservation.)

Cherokee Fun Park
U.S. Highway 441 N., Cherokee, NC
(828) 497-5877

This is a great place to drop off teenagers for a couple of hours while you pursue your own pleasures. The four-acre park

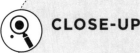

The Bride and Groom of Pisgah

Many years ago 17-year-old Jim Stratton fell in love with Mary Robinson, the 15-year-old daughter of "Old Man" Robinson. Mary lived with her father at Frying Pan Gap, while Jim Stratton lived across the ridge at Bald Mountain.

Old Man Robinson told Jim to leave his daughter alone and to not come around Frying Pan Gap. Jim, however, didn't pay much attention to the warning, because he and Mary were in love. Just about everyone had a still in the mountains in those days, and Old Man Robinson knew that one sure way to get Jim Stratton's attention was to do something grandiose to let Jim know that he meant business.

One late fall day Jim Stratton was stirring the mash at his still, which was hidden high above a clearing of an old trail on the face of Bald Mountain. Suddenly all the animals and insects of the forest fell silent. Jim took up his long rifle and hid amongst the trees as he watched his mash boiling and bubbling. Soon he saw a fellow appear, cautiously at first, then stepping confidently over to the mash bucket. He was a "federal man," one of many, and Jim knew right away that Old Man Robinson had told them where to find his still.

More than a half-dozen federal officers stepped into the clearing. They proceeded to smash the catching bucket and spill all the good "squeezins" onto the ground. With large axes they crushed the mash vat. It was only when the first federal agent held the still's copper worm in the air like some trophy that Jim was seized by anger and lost all control. With a squeeze of the trigger, the bullet entered the left eye of the federal officer, exiting the back of his skull. The other officers ran back into the woods and down the mountain.

Jim leaped into the clearing and scooped up the brass worm and took off up the mountain. He knew that he had a great deal to do before the Feds came looking for him for what he had just done. He headed to Frying Pan Gap, planning to even the score with Old Man Robinson. Crossing the Pisgahs he stopped off at the Widow Peggy Higgins's cabin. He had helped her when she lost her husband. He told her he did wrong, and he had to go higher in the mountains. But there were two things he had yet to do: The first was to even the score, and the second was to get Mary to go away with him. The widow said she'd fetch Preacher Ball and that Jim should return with Mary so they could be properly joined.

Jim got to Frying Pan Gap, and he looked for Old Man Robinson. He was actually relieved when Mary said that her daddy left for town that morning and would be gone into the late evening. Mary said that she'd go anywhere with Jim and that she'd be with him forever.

When the two of them got back to the Widow Higgins's cabin, Preacher Ball was there and ready to perform the wedding ceremony. However, the bride didn't have a proper wedding gown, and they didn't have a wedding ring. Peggy Higgins resolved that right away. She pulled an old trunk from the foot of the bed, and digging down deep, she pulled out a dusty bridal veil, yellowed from age. It was the one she had worn more than 40 years ago. She shook out the dust and smoothed out the wrinkles. Next Peggy Higgins worked the old wedding band off her hand and offered it to the new bride.

When all the right things had been said, the "I Dos" and the "I Promise," Preacher Ball called down a blessing on them—and it was then they could hear, off in the distance, the braying of the bloodhounds.

The couple went out the back of the cabin and followed the trails that led high up in the Pisgahs. They could hear the hounds coming closer. They climbed higher and ran faster. Soon they could hear the shouts and calling of the men.

Now it's not unusual to see snowfall in the higher elevations in late fall. The snow melts by day and refreezes by night forming Rhine Ice. And that very night a soft snow did begin to fall. As their feet carried them higher and higher, the snow fell faster and faster. The little flakes turned into big flakes. Soon their footprints began to be covered by more snow, and the dogs couldn't follow their scent any longer. The snow got up to their ankles. As they went higher and deeper into the woods the snow reached up to their knees, and when they broke into the clearing on the east face of Pisgah, they were waist deep in the snow.

It was then that winter really set in to the mountains, and it wasn't until the next spring that the federal officers resumed their search. The couple was never found. What was found was a rusted out old long rifle and an old copper worm from a still.

Some say that they got away on that snowy night, over many ridges and through many mountain ranges until they found a place where no one knew them, and where no one ever questioned strangers.

Others know that they are still up on the east face of Pisgah. In fact whenever there is a very hard snowfall, and when it melts and refreezes, you can see Mary standing with her bridal veil down her back, Jim Stratton kneeling beside her with his head bowed. Just stand in Asheville on such a day facing Pisgah, and you'll see them, too.

contains, among other things, minigolf courses, go-cart track, bumper boats, a large arcade, and rides designed for young children. (See our Kidstuff chapter for more information.)

Harrah's Cherokee Casino
777 Casino Drive, Cherokee, NC
(828) 497-7777, (800) HARRAHS
The casino, three football fields in size, is open 24 hours a day. Here you'll find 2,300 video gaming machines, including video blackjack, video poker, and video craps, plus many other games. When you've gambled up an appetite, you can satisfy it at three restaurants: the 125-seat Range Steakhouse, open nightly and specializing in steaks, seafood, and chicken dishes; the 400-seat Fresh Market Square Buffet, open daily, featuring a wide array of cuisine and fresh bakery items; and the 60-seat Winning Streaks Grill, open daily, a quick and easy stop for sandwiches, appetizers, and such. Tribal Bingo, run by the Eastern Band of Cherokee Indians, takes place at Harrah's also.

Harrah's also contains a gift shop and a 1,500-seat multipurpose entertainment center that offers big-time shows with big-name stars. And while you shoot for that new pair of shoes, a large, professional, culturally themed child care center will keep your young ones entertained.

Santa's Land Fun Park and Zoo
U.S. Highway 19, Cherokee, NC
(828) 497-9191
Christmas comes alive in the summertime in this theme park with its Rudi-Coaster ride, Santa's Overland Express train and, of course, Santa himself. (See our Kidstuff chapter for more information.)

Unto These Hills
U.S. Highway 441 N., Cherokee, NC
(828) 497-2111
From mid-June to late August, a cast of 130 brings to life the long-forgotten history of the Cherokee. Presented in a beautiful outdoor theater, this pageant captures the legends, rituals, and dances of the tribe.

(See our Cherokee Indian Reservation chapter for more information.)

Graham County

Chief Junaluska's Grave
off Main Street, Robbinsville, NC
In 1814 a Cherokee leader joined the U.S. Army in a fight against the Creek Indians, vowing that he would kill all the Creeks. During the Battle of Horseshoe Bend, he saved General Andrew Jackson's life but had to admit he left some of the enemy alive. It was then that he was given the nickname of Junaluska, which means "he tried repeatedly but failed." Despite his service to Jackson, who became a U.S. president, he also failed to stop the forced removal of his fellow Cherokee and himself to Oklahoma on the infamous Trail of Tears. The chieftain reportedly remarked at the time that had he known what the future would bring, he would have killed Jackson himself at Horseshoe Bend. Later Junaluska walked from Oklahoma all the way back to the North Carolina, where he continued to struggle to keep the remaining Cherokee in their mountain home.

On January 2, 1847, the state legislature made him a North Carolina citizen and gave him a tract of land. When he died on November 8, 1858, he was more than 100 years old. His grave and that of Nicie, his wife, are on a hilltop outside Robbinsville. To reach it, drive past the courthouse on Main Street and turn right toward the Stanley Furniture plant. The gravesite is on the left, marked by a sign. A trail leads up to the two boulders that mark the graves, which are surrounded by an iron fence. It's said that it took eight yoke of oxen a half-day to pull Junaluska's gravestone up the hill. Plans are underway to open a museum near the site devoted to Junaluska.

Fontana Dam
N.C. Highway 28, Fontana Dam
You can drive across this 480-foot-high dam, the highest east of the Rockies, but

don't be satisfied with that. Stop at the visitor's center for a breathtaking view and make use of the picnic tables there. Inside the center you can take in a short video and other exhibits to learn about the dam's construction and history. After that spend a dollar for a ride in the stainless-steel tram to the dam's base for a look inside the plant itself, where you'll get a lesson on hydroelectric power. This 2,365-foot-wide structure began providing power in 1942 to produce goods during World War II, and it closed in 1944. Today it impounds the 10,600 acres of water that form 29-mile-long Fontana Lake. Historic Fontana Village, now a resort community, was built to house the workers who constructed the dam. The visitor center is open from 9:00 A.M. until 8:00 P.M. and is staffed by volunteers who are former TVA employees.

Haywood County

Carolina Nights Music Comedy Show
Soco Road, U.S. Highway 19, Maggie Valley, NC
(828) 926-8822, (888) 622-7469
A cast of locals and entertainers from elsewhere offer dinner theater with a twist. You can stomp your feet to mountain music and shed a tear with the "Grand Old Flag" and patriotic songs. The grand finale pulls out all stops with a good dose of patriotism and nostalgia in song and dance, complete with a backdrop of the Statue of Liberty, Old Glory, and symbols of "old-time religion." It's hokey, but fun family entertainment. Bus groups are welcome with advance arrangements.

Soco Gardens Zoo
3578 Soco Road, U.S. Highway 19, Maggie Valley, NC
(828) 926-1746
Wild animals, an animal petting section, guided tours, and two snake shows make this a great stop for families. (See our Kid-stuff chapter for more.)

Stompin' Ground
Soco Road, U.S. Highway 19, Maggie Valley, NC
(828) 926-1288
The folks in Maggie claim that this is the "Clogging Capital of the World." It features some of the area's best mountain clogging teams from May to October on Friday and Saturday from early evening to late. (The opening event for Folkmoot USA is always held at the Stompin' Grounds. It takes place the last week in July. See our Annual Festivals and Events chapter.)

Jackson County

Great Smoky Mountains Railroad
119 Front Street, Dillsboro, NC
(828) 586-8811, (800) 872-4681
There are few attractions more popular in Western North Carolina than this railway, and there's no better way to watch some of our area's great scenery glide by than from one of its passenger cars. When you catch a ride on the Great Smoky Mountains Railway, you have your choice of diesel, electric or steam locomotives, with seating in heated and air-conditioned coaches and open-sided cars. Some seating options at a small additional charge are the Club Car (for adults only) and the Crown Coach. Several different excursion options are offered: the Tuckaseigee River Excursion, the Nantahala Gorge Excursion, the Red Marble Gap Excursion, Raft 'n' Rail Excursion, and the Twilight Dinner Train.

- **The Tuckaseigee River Excursion:** This is a 34-mile-long, three-hour Dillsboro-Bryson City round-trip that follows the Tuckaseigee River past the spot where the train wreck in *The Fugitive* was filmed. It also takes you through the 836-foot-long Cowee Tunnel and over many trestles before reaching Bryson

City, where you'll have a 45-minute layover for shopping, browsing, and eating.

- **The Nantahala Gorge Excursion:** From Bryson City you can take a 44-mile, four-hour round-trip tour that brings you through the Nantahala Gorge, created by a river that's become one of North Carolina's prime spots for canoeing, kayaking, and white-water rafting. En route you'll cross a portion of Fontana Lake on a trestle that is 791 feet long, on piers that are 180 feet tall. There's an hour layover in the gorge for eating and viewing the white-water activity.
- **The Red Marble Gap Excursion:** This 38-mile, four-hour trip departs from Andrews and climbs east toward Red Marble Mountain. It passes through the hand-dug Will Sandlin Tunnel, crosses the 400-foot-long Hawksnest Trestle, and descends a 4-plus percent grade from Topton down to Nantahala. Here, too, you have an hour for white-water viewing and lunch. The mountain scenery on this excursion is particularly spectacular. There are no steam trains from Andrews.
- **Raft 'n' Rail Excursion:** This seven-hour trip offers a 22-mile train ride, an 8-mile guided raft trip, a picnic lunch, and a return by bus.
- **Twilight Dinner Train:** The most recently added excursion is the Twilight Dinner Train. It departs from the Dillsboro Depot for a luxurious, leisurely two-hour round-trip that follows the Tuckaseigee River through the historic Cowee Tunnel to Whittier and back. A gourmet four-course dinner, elegant ambience—candlelight, china, and white linen—and old-fashioned attentive service are presented in the beautifully restored dining cars. You can select from four seasonal entrees at the time you make your reservations; cocktails and a selection of premium wines are available from the bar. The Dinner Train operates every Saturday evening from April through

December and selected Friday evenings from July through October.

Judaculla Rock
off N.C. Highway 107

Judaculla (a name corrupted from the Indian *tsulkalu,* meaning "slant eyes") was a fearful giant of Cherokee lore whose farm was on Tanasee Bald at a point where Jackson, Haywood, and Transylvania Counties converge. One day, it's said, he jumped from his mountaintop home to a valley near what is now Caney Fork Creek, leaving the marks of his landing on a large, exposed piece of soapstone. These marks—pictographic writing on the rock—long predate the Cherokee. There are many theories as to their meanings. Is the rock a boundary marker? A battle commemoration? A peace treaty among unknown tribes? Or is it just ancient graffiti?

Judaculla Rock, well marked by signs, is off N.C. 107 between Cashiers and Cullowhee on Caney Fork Road (SR 1737). A lovely 3-mile drive through a bucolic valley of scattered two-story, white frame farmhouses will bring you to the rock, which sits under an open-sided shed next to a cow pasture.

Macon County

Bascom-Louise Gallery
554 Main Street, Highlands, NC
(828) 526–4949

This gallery shares space with the Hudson Library. It was established in 1982 as a nonprofit art center. The original funding came from the estate of New York theater designer Watson Barratt to honor his deceased wife, Louise Bascom Barratt. Mrs. Barratt was a writer and descendant of the Bascoms, early settlers of Highlands who in 1883 built an inn known as The Bascom-Louise. Hours of operation are from 10:00 A.M. to 4:00 P.M. Tuesday through Saturday. During the months of

December through March, it is open only for special events.

Highlands Nature Center and Botanical Gardens
Horse Cove Road, U.S. Highway 28 S., Highlands, NC
(828) 526-2623

Drive a short distance out of Highlands on East Main Street, and you'll come to this interesting place. The Highlands Biological Station, one of the oldest research facilities in the country, operates both the center and the gardens. The center is a showcase for the animals and plants found on the Highlands Plateau, a unique ecosystem that attracts top researchers from around the world. Here you'll find user-friendly exhibits, American Indian artifacts, mineral and rock specimens, snakes, salamanders, and mounted specimens of area mammals and birds. In the Botanical Gardens, the trails, with their excellently identified plants and trees, will take you around Lake Ravenel, along a creek, and up to a small waterfall.

The center is open from 10:00 A.M. to 5:00 P.M. Monday through Saturday from Memorial Day to Labor Day. Admission is free. The gardens are there for you to enjoy anytime. Even in winter thick growths of rhododendron, galax, and doghobble make it a deep-green little paradise.

Museum of American Cut and Engraved Glass
472 Chestnut Street, Highlands, NC
(828) 526-3415, (828) 526-3427

This is a rare museum in many ways. Its collection is one of the most eclectic anywhere in the world of American cut glass. It was opened as a not-for-profit corporation, exclusively for charitable and educational purposes. The exquisite contents are basically the collection of Bonnie and George Siek. They continue to operate the museum without charge and support it philanthropically with 100 percent dona-

tions and income from the sale of cut and engraved glass.

There are more than 400 pieces of glass on display. Another 250 pieces are in storage, affording a rotational display. Throughout the exhibition refracted light sparkles off each individual cut with diamond clarity. You'll find other objects in shades of green, cranberry, blue, gold, and turquoise. Names of grandeur and tradition abound, such as Royal, Trellis, North Star, Wedgemere, and Arbaresque. *Pueblo* and *Nautilus* by Hawkes are examples of the world-class objects here.

This museum is worth a stop and can open a new world of beauty. Don't be surprised by the log cabin structure that houses this priceless collection. The final rarity is that George Siek insists that you call him on his home phone, listed above, if the museum is closed. He'll make every effort to host you personally.

Perry's Water Garden
136 Givson Aquatic Farm Road, Franklin, NC
(828) 524-3264

Even if you never intend to have a water garden, this 12-acre aquatic plant nursery—with its hundreds of lotuses, water lilies, blue-flag irises, and other old and new water- and bog-loving plants—might change your mind. Claiming to be the largest such nursery in the country, it offers a tropical greenhouse, exotic koi and goldfish, old-fashioned antique rose beds, picnic tables, and walking trails. Perry's is open from 9:00 A.M. to noon and 1:00 to 5:00 P.M. Monday through Saturday and 1:00 until 5:00 P.M. on Sunday from March through September.

John Wasilik Memorial Poplar
Nantahala National Forest, near Rainbow Springs

To see the United States' second-largest yellow poplar, named for a former Wayah district ranger, drive west out of Franklin on U.S. 64 and turn on FR 67 toward the Standing Indian Campground. Park a little more than a mile down the road at the

Rock Gap sign before reaching the campground. It's a 1.5-mile, easy-to-moderate, round-trip hike on the Wasilik Poplar Trail, which is lined with second-growth trees up to 8 feet in diameter. The giant memorial tree is 25 feet in circumference, and until a storm blew off its top, it was 125 feet tall.

The Ritter Lumber Company took the rest of the virgin timber out of this area in the early 1930s. They even cut down another yellow poplar of the same size. However the oxen had such a hard time hauling it away that the lumbermen decided not to bother with this now-famous tree.

KIDSTUFF 👫

North Carolina's mountains are even more fun with kids in hand. Try to view the world the way they do. They can see Daniel Boone behind every log cabin and wood nymphs playing in the shelter of rhododendron thickets. See Santa Claus in the summertime (although there's a logical explanation for that one . . . read on).

Hiking is popular with families. Take the kids hiking on many of the numerous trails appropriate for younger ages and abilities. Stop for a picnic along a mountain stream and watch your kids turn rocks and water into adventures only their uninhibited imaginations can know. Or teach them to ski before adult-size fear paralyzes their sense of adventure.

Organizations throughout the region offer exciting programs for little people. Libraries are always a rich source of activities, storytelling, and, of course, books and tapes. Area arts councils provide opportunities for kids to explore their nascent creativity, setting it free with paints and clay, paper and yarn. Art exhibitions of their work are scheduled throughout the year.

Parks and attractions in the mountains welcome pint-size visitors. Trains, Ferris wheels, swimming pools, natural wonders, clowns, and festivals all beckon, as do seasonal activities, such as Easter egg hunts, jack-o'-lantern carvings, and Christmas decoration classes. (Our Summer Camps and Rockhounding chapters have additional resources for kid entertainment. Both offer kids a lifetime of memories. See also our Annual Festivals and Events chapter.)

Many of our chapters offer lots of fun things to do with kids, but in this chapter we gathered some of our favorites.

NORTHERN MOUNTAINS

Watauga County

Magic Mountain Mini Golf & Gem Mine
1675 N.C. Highway 105, Boone, NC
(828) 265–GEMS, (828) 265–GOLF
The kids simply won't get bored here. Open Monday, Tuesday, and Wednesday 10:00 A.M. to 6:00 P.M.; Thursday, Friday, and Saturday 9:00 A.M. to 9:00 P.M., spring through fall, Magic Mountain is a kiddie paradise. Adults probably won't mind sifting through the enriched ore either, because there's a chance of finding a ruby, citrine, garnet, amethyst, aquamarine, sapphire, emerald, or other such rocks.

A sandwich and ice-cream parlor provide indoor or patio dining, and a video game room provides entertainment for those members of the family who just don't want to get their hands dirty. The minigolf course is set on a mountainside amidst foliage and waterfalls.

Mystery Hill
129 Mystery Hill Lane, between Boone and Blowing Rock
(828) 264-2792
www.mysteryhill.com
This is the place to go for interactive fun with your family or group of friends. Celebrating more than 50 years in business, Mystery Hill explores the relationships of science, optical illusion, and natural phenomena in a hands-on entertainment center. Defy gravity in the Mystery House, where the ball rolls up hill or leave your shadow on the wall. (Just try getting the kids out of this one.) The Appalachian Heritage Museum and the Native Ameri-

can Artifacts Museum are included in the tour for one low price.

Open seven days a week, year-round, Mystery Hill is open 8:00 A.M. to 8:00 P.M. June through August, and 9:00 A.M. to 5:00 P.M. September through May. Admission is $7.00 for adults, $5.00 for children, $6.00 for seniors, and free for kids under 5. Group rates are available.

Tweetsie Railroad
U.S. Highway 321, between Boone and Blowing Rock
(828) 264-9061, (800) 526-5740
www.tweetsie.com
Long before there was a Carowinds or Six Flags, there was Tweetsie Railroad. A charming theme park, now more than 30 years old, Tweetsie brings out the little kid in all of us. Not as overwhelming as those other parks, this one gives families a chance to go a little slower and savor the sight of their little pardner all decked out in cowboy hat and six-shooters, waiting for the bad guys on the train to be vanquished by the good-guy sheriff and his deputies.

Remember when things seemed this simple? The innocence and measured pace of this park are its true charm, as is the 1914 Tweetsie locomotive, which still runs. Simple rides, a petting farm with deer, Mouse Mine No. 9, homemade fudge, caramel apples, a Ferris wheel, and those souvenir shops where you have to spend a dollar or bust make Tweetsie a special, unhurried attraction that's hard to find these days. The amusement park also holds special events for certain holidays, such as Halloween, July 4, and others.

Tweetsie Railroad is open daily from 9:00 A.M. to 6:00 P.M. from May through August. Late August through October weekend hours (Friday through Sunday) are 9:00 A.M. to 6:00 P.M. Tweetsie Railroad is also open some evenings in October for the Ghost Train Halloween Festival. Admission runs around $24 for adults, $18 for children and senior citizens; children 2 and younger are admitted free. If you enter after 3:00 P.M., the next day is free. Group rates and discounts are available, and check out the Golden Rail Season Pass.

CENTRAL MOUNTAINS
Buncombe County

Odyssey Center for the Ceramic Arts
236 Clingman Avenue, Asheville, NC
(828) 285-0210
www.highwaterclays.com
This recreational craft center offers some very special programs for children. Odyssey's kids' classes have been filling up quickly with eager faces and curious hands. Nine-week classes are offered for after-school kids and home-schoolers. Kids of all ages learn basic skills in wheel throwing and hand building, making anything from animals and castles to cups and bowls. Call for a detailed course schedule. (For more information on general classes, see our Mountain Crafts chapter.)

Pack Place Education Arts and Science Center
2 South Pack Square, Asheville, NC
(828) 257-4500
www.packplace.org
Four museums and a performing arts theater make this a must-see with kids, especially if the weather isn't cooperating. The Asheville Art Museum, Health Adventure, Colburn Gem & Mineral Museum, YMI Cultural Center, and Diana Wortham Theatre all offer special programs for children.

Health Adventure (meant to be enjoyed by the whole family), especially, is a blast for kids. Learn how the body works, with a life-sized torso—you put in the organs like solving a puzzle! Learn how the ear works. Learn about nutrition while "shopping." Learn mechanics and engineering with fun and games you can try. Check your eyesight; look at a bug, a hair, and other objects through a microscope. The ultraviolet light room will make your whites glow and your teeth green! Two floors of tactile fun can keep kids busy and entertained for hours. (See our Arts and Culture chapter for more information.)

Western North Carolina Nature Center
75 Gashes Creek Road, Asheville, NC
(828) 298–5600
www.wildwnc.org

The Western North Carolina Nature Center offers a remarkable blend of services to the area. Officially it's "an environmental educational resource, exhibiting and inter-preting plants and animals native to the Southern Appalachian Mountains." But it is much more than that. From the moment you step through the door and a three-dimensional, full-size diorama of woodland creatures greets you, you know you are crossing that bridge to the natural world.

Well-planned exhibits in the educa-tional facility offer a hands-on approach to everything from weather forecasting and animal identification to a real working beehive! In the next building are archaeo-logical displays and zoological exhibits of live reptiles and amphibians. In another area a special darkened room allows visi-tors to observe owls, bats, and other noc-turnal creatures.

Outside there's more: bobcats, rac-coons, cougars, otters, foxes, bears, hawks, eagles, sheep, goats, chickens, peacocks, and even wolves. The center has made spectacular use of limited acreage to create a special experience for the whole family. Make sure you walk along the boardwalk in the treetops; it takes you back to those days of childhood tree houses.

The Nature Center is open 10:00 A.M. to 5:00 P.M. seven days a week. Admission is $4.00 for adults, $2.00 for children ages 3 through 14, and $3.00 for senior citizens.

Henderson County

Carl Sandburg Home
1928 Little River Road, Flat Rock, NC
(828) 693–4178

Be sure to let your kids pet the kids (and goats) at Connemara, the home of Carl Sandburg that is now a National Historic Site. (See our Arts and Culture chapter for more information.)

Disposable cameras are small, light-weight, and within their limitations take pretty good snapshots. Consider taking one along to capture the moment at a moment's notice.

The Historic Johnson Farm
3346 Haywood Road, N.C. Highway 191,
Hendersonville, NC
(828) 891–6585
www.johnsonfarm.com

This well-preserved, 15-acre farm, its his-toric house, many outbuildings, and nature trails will take children back to a lifestyle once common earlier in this cen-tury. (See our Arts and Culture chapter for more information.)

Rutherford County

Chimney Rock Park
Entrance on Main Street, Highways
64/74A, Chimney Rock, NC
(828) 625–9611, (800) 277–9611
www.chimneyrockpark.com

Families can picnic in the meadows and elsewhere throughout the park. Self-guided trails are available for explorations or schedule a time with the naturalists for more exciting adventures. Ride the eleva-tor within the mountain itself, going up 30 stories to the Sky Lounge. More adventure lies ahead in exploring the upper trails. Contact Chimney Rock Park for their fam-ily adventures that include a visit by Santa and rock-climbing demonstrations. Their events calendar features their traditional Easter sunrise service and other events occurring monthly throughout the year.

Lake Lure Fun Center
Highways 64/74A, the Beach at Lake
Lure, Lake Lure, NC
(828) FUN-4-ALL, (828) 625–0077

All ages can enjoy trampoline games, minigolf, foosball, Ping Pong, bungee jumping, scooters, the children's inflatable play area, motorized Jeeps, and more at the Lake Lure Fun Center. Swimming is another obvious attraction with ever-watchful certified lifeguards. Boat tours of the lake are offered at the marina, and self-propelled boats can be rented as well.

Transylvania County

Cradle of Forestry
U.S. Highway 276, Pisgah National Forest
(828) 877-3130
www.cradleofforestry.com
Children of all ages love the Forest Discovery Center at the Cradle of Forestry. They can see a short movie about the first forestry school in America, which was situated here—and that's only the beginning. There are 15 educational exhibits on the workings of the forest ecosystem and what it takes to manage an ecosystem. For example, there is a replicated hillside, complete with a forest summit. Below, a 30-foot tunnel lets one crawl underground through "The Great Tree and Burrow" exhibit, complete with all the animals that live there. Another exhibit explains the dynamics of a watershed, all the way to the household faucet. Adventure seekers can experience the "Fire-Fighting Helicopter Simulator" that flies into the depths of a wildfire to drop retardant to quench the flames, complete with visuals, sound, movement, and smells.

Outside the building there are two beautiful, mile-long paved trails, each with guided tours that will tell you of the Cradle's history and teach you a lot about the plants and trees along the way. The Forest Festival Trail has many forest demonstration projects, an old sawmill, the first little fish hatchery in Pisgah, and an old Climax logging train. Children love to climb into the cab and ring the bell. The Biltmore Campus Trail winds through the school's old campus of original and reconstructed buildings.

On Saturday and Sunday afternoons craftspeople in period dress demonstrate crafts such as weaving, spinning, quilting, basketry, and toy making, and life at the turn of the century. There are also a number of special events happening throughout the year, such as Fiber Arts Week and the huge Forest Festival Day held in October.

The Cradle, open seven days a week from 9:00 A.M. to 5:00 P.M., is located on U.S. 276, 11 miles from the intersection of U.S. 64, 276, and 280 at Pisgah Forest, or 4 miles south of the Blue Ridge Parkway at milepost 412. The use fee is $5.00 for adults, $2.50 for students 4 to 17, and free for children 3 years and under. (See our Cradle Keeps Rocking Close-up in the Forests and Parks chapter.)

Pisgah Center for Wildlife Education
FR 475, Pisgah Forest
(828) 877-4423
This center focuses on natural habitats and how to preserve them. It offers exhibits and free programs on raising trout, trees, birds, streams and water quality, backcountry wisdom, and more. (See the listing in our Attractions chapter.) Admission to the center is free.

Pisgah Forest Fish Hatchery
FR 475, Pisgah National Forest
(828) 877-3121
The Pisgah Forest Fish Hatchery raises the thousands of trout that are released into area streams. There are fish-food vending machines, and your kids'll love watching the wild feeding frenzies when the fish, which come in all sizes, are fed.

To get to the hatchery, drive several miles up U.S. 276 from the Brevard entrance to Pisgah Forest and turn off onto FR 475, which is well marked and paved. The hatchery is less than a mile down this road. (For more information see our Attractions chapter.)

Sliding Rock
U.S. Highway 276, Pisgah National Forest
Sliding Rock is just 7.6 miles from the junction of U.S. Highways 276 and 64 outside Brevard. Here you're invited to "take the plunge" down a 60-foot slippery cascade into the 55 to 60-degree, 6-foot-deep pool

below. If you don't care to make the slide, it's fun to watch the action from paved viewing areas at the top or bottom of this natural, exhilarating ride that's fueled by 11,000 gallons of water a minute.

There's a large parking lot adjacent to Sliding Rock (the parking fee is $3.00) as well as a bathhouse. Lifeguards are on duty from 10:00 A.M. to 6:00 P.M. from Memorial Day through Labor Day. The rock, while slick, can take the bottom out of an ordinary bathing suit, so old jeans or cutoffs are best for this fast ride. Also, be careful while getting in and out of the water. The surface of the rock, even where the water isn't flowing, can be slick and accounts for some hard tumbles.

SOUTHERN MOUNTAINS
Cherokee County

John C. Campbell Folk School
1 Folk School Road, Brasstown, NC
(828) 837-2775, (800) FOLK-SCH
www.folkschool.org
This fine, 70-year-old craft school offers Little/Middle Folk School each June for one week for youngsters ages 7 to 17. The week is full of crafts, games, and lots of fun. Classes fill quickly so early registration is essential.

Contact the Folk School to be included in a separate mailing for this program. (See our Mountain Crafts chapter for more information on the school's other offerings.)

Haywood County

Soco Gardens Zoo
3578 Soco Road, U.S. Highway 19,
Maggie Valley, NC
(828) 926-1746
www.animalpark.org/socozoo
In addition to many of the usual wild animals, this zoo allows touching and feeding in its petting section. There are guided

tours, two snake shows (one venomous and the other nonpoisonous; in the latter visitors can touch or hold the performers), and a gift shop made for animal lovers.

Hours change with the season: 10:00 A.M. to 5:00 P.M. in May, September, and October; 9:00 A.M. to dark in June, July, and August. It is closed in the winter. Admission is $7.00 for adults, $6.00 for seniors, and $4.00 for children ages 4 to 12. There is no charge for children 3 and younger as long as they are with the family and not a part of a children's group.

Cherokee Indian Reservation

For more information on the reservation and other attractions here, see our chapters on Attractions and the Cherokee Indian Reservation.

Cherokee Bear Zoo & Plaza
Main Street, Cherokee, NC
(828) 497-4525
www.cherokeezoo.com
When seeing a bear in the wild, it's always best to keep your distance (see our Outdoor Safety and Forests and Parks chapters), but here's a chance for children to get a close-up look at all kinds of bears, big and small—and even feed them! This petting zoo also has monkeys, big cats, deer, and other animals.

It opens at 10:00 A.M. during the week. Closing hours can be as late as 11:00 P.M. according to the season. The entrance fee is $3.00, with children 3 and younger admitted free.

Cherokee Fun Park
U.S. Highway 441 N., Cherokee, NC
(828) 497-5877
www.cherokeefunpark.com
This is a great place to drop off teenagers for a couple of hours while you pursue your own pleasures. The four-acre park contains, among other things, two challenging miniature golf courses, a go-cart

track, bumper boats, a large arcade, and rides designed for young children.

It opens daily at 11:00 A.M. on weekdays and 10:00 A.M. on weekends from May through October. Closing time is around 11:00 P.M. in midsummer and 8:30 or 9:00 P.M. in the spring and fall. Admission is free, but there is a charge of $5.00 for boats and go-carts and $5.00 for golf (play all day). After 6:00 P.M. it costs $5.00 for each golf game. Kiddie rides are $2.00 each.

Santa's Land Fun Park and Zoo
U.S. Highway 19, Cherokee, NC
(828) 497-9191
www.santaslandnc.com

Christmas comes alive in the summertime in this theme park. We expect that young children will refuse to miss its Rudi-Coaster ride, Santa's Overland Express train and, of course, Santa. The family can also paddle boats around Monkey Islands in the lake, view Cherokee from the top of a Ferris wheel, and visit a wealth of shops.

In the zoo kids will enjoy petting baby bears and feeding deer and trout. A visit to the gristmill will show them how corn-meal is made, and they can watch pork rinds being cooked. You'll also find a picnic and playground area in the park. It's open from early May until the first weekend in November.

Admission is around $17. Children younger than 2 get in free. Prices are, however, subject to change.

Macon County

Highlands Chamber of Commerce
396 Oak Street, Highlands, NC
(828) 526-2112
www.highlandschamber.org

Located in one of the main botanical centers in North Carolina, young folks can hike the numerous trails of the Nantahala National Forest. Breathtaking views are available throughout this entire area. Early morning hikes provide spectacular views of the mist rising off of Mirror Lake and Lake Sequoyah. An energetic mountain trek can be followed by a welcomed dip in the lake. Canoes and boats are available for rent as well. Not to be missed are the bountiful waterfalls cascading throughout the mountains. Bridal Veil Falls can be viewed from the car, while Dry Falls are an easy walk from U.S. 64, where both these falls can be found. Glen Falls is located 3 miles south of Highlands off N.C. 106.

The Kelsey & Hutchinson Lodge is a "welcome center" for adults who want solitude and comfort, as well as for families traveling with pets. An entire area of the lodge provides a separate, disconnected section to accommodate these lodgers.

The Adventure Depot provides llama trekking and camping experiences.

November and December are months especially geared to kids and the family. During the week of Thanksgiving, the Tree Lighting Ceremony is held at the Gazebo on Pine Street. The Olde Mountain Christmas Parade is held on the first Saturday in December at 11:00 A.M. It goes down Main Street and the town is dressed for the holidays.

The Highlands Ranger District has a visitor center in downtown Highlands just off Main Street, directly beside the restaurant Wolfgang's on Main. Trail maps and other information for outdoor activities are available at the center.

BILTMORE ESTATE AND WINERY

Amid the central North Carolina mountains, just outside of Asheville, you will see what appears to be a castle rising out of a mountainside. Biltmore Estate, the largest private residence in the United States, was home to George Vanderbilt, grandson of Cornelius Vanderbilt, founder of one of America's foremost shipping and railroading dynasties. George Vanderbilt first traveled to Asheville with his mother in 1888. Enchanted by the majesty of the mountains, he returned home to enlist the greatest designers and architects for the country estate he envisioned. Richard Morris Hunt, one of the foremost architects of the 19th century, patterned the magnificent 250-room mansion after 16th-century chateaux in the Loire Valley of France. Preeminent landscape architect Frederick Law Olmsted, noted for his design of Central Park in New York City, shaped the original 125,000 acres of the vast working estate. Vanderbilt's extensive personal collection of 70,000 objects from all parts of the world filled his country home, which was completed in 1895.

In 1914, after Mr. Vanderbilt's death, nearly 87,000 acres of the estate were sold to the U.S. government to form the nucleus of Pisgah National Forest, America's first national forest east of the Mississippi. The 8,000 remaining carefully and colorfully landscaped acres maintain much of the original estate's grandeur. The 250 acres of gardens are internationally renowned for annual and perennial displays of tulips, daffodils, roses, dogwoods, and azaleas, among other plants. Each April, the Annual Festival of Flowers heralds spring with a Victorian celebration.

Continuing the tradition of superlatives begun a century ago, William A. V. Cecil, grandson of George Vanderbilt and owner of Biltmore Estate, established the Biltmore Estate Wine Company in 1983. The first vineyards on the estate, planted in 1971, contained French-American hybrids and were planted in an area just below Biltmore House and behind the greenhouses, with vinifera plantings following a few years later. After years of experimentation and research, the winery opened in 1985 with state-of-the-art production technology. It is considered to be the most visited winery in the world, with over 500,000 visitors annually. It continues the tradition of Biltmore Estate as a self-sufficient working estate. (A French winemaker oversees the winemaking operations.)

The new generation continues family ownership and operation of Biltmore Estate. The company is headed by William A. V. Cecil Jr. Other family members serve in the operation as well.

The turn-of-the-century mansion covers an incredible four acres of floor space. It took 50 servants to see to the needs of the Vanderbilts and their many frequent guests. These guests included famed writers Edith Wharton and Henry James, and presidents William McKinley and Woodrow Wilson.

More than 850,000 guests from all over the world visit this legendary home each year. Over one-third of the 250 rooms on four floors, lavishly furnished, often as the Vanderbilts left them, are open to the public. Describing rooms such as the Winter Garden, Banquet Hall, Music Room, Billiard Room, Tapestry Gallery, Louis XVI Room, Sheraton Room, Chippendale Room, Bowling Alley, Swimming Pool, Gymnasium, guest rooms, and even the kitchens calls for a good thesaurus to

CLOSE-UP

Stone Roberts and the Family Portrait

At age 5, Stone Roberts discovered his interest in painting when he pulled art books from his parents' bookshelves in Asheville, North Carolina. He attended the private Gibbons Hall for Boys in Asheville with classmate Donald Sultan, later a venerable New York artist. After receiving a degree from Yale, Roberts returned to Asheville and studied art with Tucker Cooke of UNCA. Roberts's first major piece, *Janet,* evocative of Vermeer, is now in the permanent collection of the Metropolitan Museum of Art. Stone Roberts is now a New York resident artist at the top of his profession.

In 1990, William Cecil, owner of Biltmore House, commissioned Roberts to paint a group portrait of the Cecil family for the centennial of the Estate. Titled *The William A. V. Cecil Family,* the oil on canvas work hangs in the second floor Living Hall of the Biltmore House. In the background, Roberts has depicted a painting by the 19th-century American artist Seymour Guy of the last formal portrait of the Vanderbilts, executed in 1873. The position of the Guy painting is depicted as it was for many years until replaced with the current work. The 1873 family portrait is mounted at the opposite end of the Sitting Room.

avoid using words like *opulent* and *majestic* over and over.

The Winter Garden, a sunken room with marble floors and glass ceiling, is the first stop on the self-guided tour. The Banquet Hall, which hosted formal gatherings around a table large enough for 64 people, was designed specifically to house five handwoven, 16th-century Flemish tapestries depicting mythical characters. The 70-foot-high, barrel-vaulted ceiling is worth a look. In fact all the ceilings are notable, so don't forget to look up.

The Vanderbilts' daughter, Cornelia, and her husband, John Cecil, took over the Halloween Room in 1924 for a party during their wedding festivities. Some of their unusual decorations remain on the walls.

With so many spectacular rooms and gardens to choose from, the movie industry is drawn to the estate. A number of films have been shot here, including *The Swan* with Grace Kelly, *Being There* with Peter Sellers, portions of *Mr. Destiny* with Michael Caine and Jim Belushi, *The Last of the Mohicans* with Daniel Day-Lewis, *Richie Rich* with Macaulay Culkin, *My Fellow Americans* with James Garner, Jack Lemmon, and Dan Aykroyd, and most recently *Hannibal* with Sir Anthony Hopkins.

For an extra fee a special tour called Behind the Scenes takes you into the depths of the mansion. In the subbasement, for example, stand Mr. Vanderbilt's powerful boilers and power generators, which assured the estate's self-sufficiency. The tour includes the Butler's Pantry, which was the central command location for the servant infrastructure. Other tours are continuously being added. Weather permitting, Rooftop Tours and Garden Treasure Walks are just two of them. There is an extra fee for these tours, and reservations are required.

After touring the main house, you can visit Victorian gift shops chock full of decorative accessories, books, toys, and confections. Several dining opportunities await you at Deerpark Restaurant, the Stable Café, and the Bistro, Biltmore's newest restaurant at the Winery.

Take a stroll in the many landscaped gardens just as Vanderbilt's guests did—strolling through the Azalea Garden and Spring Garden, sheltered by a grove of white pines and hemlocks. The Walled Garden of four acres includes the Rose Garden with over 2,300 rose bushes in more than 350 varieties. Closer to the house, the Shrub Garden provides a "ramble" through flowering bushes on a small path. The Italian Garden is marked by three symmetrical pools, graveled paths, and a manicured lawn reminiscent of Italian Renaissance landscape design. Benches and a classical statuary make this a peaceful and relaxing garden. Farther along the estate's gladed road, notice the Bass Pond and Lagoon.

General admission to Biltmore Estate varies based on seasonal offerings. Adult admission begins at age 17. Children age 5 and younger are admitted free with a paid adult admission; youth ages 6 to 16 are offered a reduced price. The estate is open from 9:00 A.M. to 5:00 P.M. daily, except Thanksgiving and Christmas. The estate is open on New Year's Day. Hours and admission prices change on a seasonal basis, so call ahead for the most up-to-date information. Allow four to six hours to fully enjoy your visit. If you arrive after 3:00 P.M., your ticket will also be honored the following day. During the Christmas season take advantage of the Candlelight Evening Tours of Biltmore Estate. But call early—these popular, reservation-only tours book up quickly, and space is limited. Other special annual events include the Annual Easter Egg Hunt, Festival of Flowers, and Festival of Flowers Evenings (also reservations-only evening tours) in the spring and Summer Evenings Concerts in the summer. Michaelmas: An English Harvest Fair is a fall festival at Biltmore. Call (800) 289-1895 for reservations. Audiotapes are available for rent at the entrance desk. They add a lively narrative to your tour along with gurgling water as you pass fountains, servants' footsteps, and even Coco the Parrot squawking her greeting. Other acoustics add reality to your visit.

Biltmore Estate is on U.S. 25 at the junction of Hendersonville Road and McDowell Street in Asheville. From I-40, Biltmore Estate is located just north of exit 50 or 50B on U.S. 25. For more information on the estate, gardens, or winery, call (828) 225-1333 or (800) 543-2961. These numbers will connect with all facilities at Biltmore. Also try the Web site, www.biltmore.com.

BILTMORE ESTATE WINERY

To assure the success of the enterprise, a sixth-generation French winemaster, Philippe Jourdain of Provence, was chosen in 1977 as winemaster for the Biltmore Estate Winery. Mr. Jourdain was not only experienced in the operation of a family vineyard but was also a respected teacher of viticulture and oenology, the sciences of grape growing and wine making. The winery flourished, and the first wine was sold in 1979. When he retired in 1995, Jourdain was replaced by Bernard Delille, a fellow Frenchman who has been winemaker at the estate since 1986. The Biltmore Estate wine-making operation has evolved into a premier vineyard, producing 120,000 cases of wine each year and garnering more than 160 medals at wine competitions nationwide. Since its inception as North Carolina's third licensed winery, Biltmore has provided leadership in this agricultural industry. Just as George Vanderbilt's dairy trucks were a familiar early-morning sight as they collected milk from farmers throughout Western North Carolina from 1897 to the 1970s, the Winery has provided the impetus for the North Carolina Grape Council's report that there are now more than 250 vineyards with a total acreage of 1,100 under vine

CLOSE-UP

Fruit of the Tarheel Vine

Prior to passage of Prohibition, North Carolina was legendary for its vineyards and wine production. When America went "dry," only a limited amount of wine could be produced, and for medicinal and religious purposes.

In the case of the Waldensian Winery in Valdese, the huge redwood tankards were sunk—empty—into the mountain lakes. It wasn't until the 1980s that they were retrieved and the Waldensian Vineyards was reactivated.

In 1972 the Fussen family of Rose Hill, North Carolina, in concert with North Carolina State University, explored the idea of making North Carolina a wine-producing state. Using the Muscadine and Scuppernong grapes of eastern North Carolina, they opened the Duplin Winery. Their wine was as sweet as the fresh pressed grapes, and the industry reemerged. Their first fermentation tanks were bought from a dairy; thus milk was turned into wine . . . in a sense.

Other experimental wineries opened, and in the 1970s Biltmore Estate planted its first grapes. By 1982, third-generation wine maker Philippe Jourdain of Carcasson, France, had arrived in North Carolina and applied his techniques in developing the Biltmore Estate Winery. In 1985 the owner of Biltmore Estate, William Amhurst Vanderbilt Cecil, renovated the dairy barn of 1890s vintage, reopening it as the home of Biltmore Estate Winery.

Other wineries followed and are continuing to open, particularly in the northern mountains, where the soil is rich and the climate just right. Of the 26 wineries currently operating in North Carolina, nine are found in the western mountains. The remainder stretch out across the state all the way to Knotts Island, accessible only by ferry. As you tour the Tar Heel state, you have many options to "taste the wine where the grape was grown."

and 25 new wineries now in the state. The economic impact is estimated at $79 million, providing 855 jobs. As the cash crop, tobacco, diminishes, farmers' fields of North Carolina are ripe with rows of vines for this evolving industry.

The vineyard itself is located in the Long Valley, where George Vanderbilt's dairy herd once grazed, across the French Broad River from Biltmore House. A 35-acre lake constructed near the vineyards provides irrigation and frost control. During the spring budding cold spells often sweep

through the mountains. Buds are sprayed with lake water that turns into an icy sheath that incubates the buds and protects them from freezing internally. (Ongoing research and development at Biltmore Estate Winery are as essential as the grapes in producing fine-quality wines.)

With more than 500,000 guests visiting the winery annually, the Biltmore Estate Winery has the distinction of being the most-visited winery in the United States. Officially opened for tours in 1985, the 90,000-square-foot facility is housed in the expanded original dairy barn and includes offices and the winery production works. The handsome pebble-dash building is crowned by a distinctive European-style clock tower from the estate. The expanded and renovated buildings feature a Welcome Center, the Bistro, Tasting Room, and Gift Shop.

The winery tour begins in the Welcome Center, an open area with hand-stenciled walls and Portuguese tiling that lend it a distinctly European flavor. Sample some of Biltmore's special seasonal wines or take advantage of the innovative menu at the newest restaurant on the estate, the Bistro.

An exhibit in the Welcome Center acquaints visitors with the ancient history of the grape and the more recent history of the building. A stylishly produced film runs daily at various times in a small theater just off the inner courtyard, beyond the main welcome area. From the theater visitors can move to the wine-making operation and view fermenting, aging, and bottling rooms; cool cellars; gleaming machinery; and row upon row of barrels and bottles.

Your next stop is the Tasting Room, a relaxed, open room with several tasting bars. Wine stewards are eager to accommodate your taste buds with whatever sample you desire from an expansive wine list that includes white wines made from sauvignon blanc, chardonnay, and Riesling grapes and red wines from pinot noir, cabernet sauvignon, cabernet Franc, and merlot. Zinfandel and cabernet sauvignon rosé wines are also available. For the children a tasty Biltmore blend of grape juice is on hand.

Complete your visit to the Biltmore Estate Winery with a visit to the gift shop. Biltmore Estate wine is available for purchase in a multitude of package options. Wine accessories, gourmet foods, upscale kitchen and dining accessories, and other gifts with a Victorian flavor are attractively displayed. Biltmore Estate wines can also be found in fine wine shops and restaurants throughout North Carolina, South Carolina,

Georgia, Tennessee, Virginia, and Florida.

The winery is open January through March from 11:00 A.M. to 6:00 P.M. Monday through Saturday and noon to 6:00 P.M. Sunday. April through December, the hours are 11:00 A.M. to 7:00 P.M. Monday through Saturday and noon to 7:00 P.M. Sunday. Hours change from season to season and year to year, so be sure to call before you visit. For general information on Biltmore Estate and Winery, call (828) 225-1333 or (800) 543-2961. The winery's self-guided tour is included in the price of admission.

Biltmore Estate is worth an entire day. You're welcome to drive along the meandering estate roads, walk the estate trails, stop off in the many gardens and meadows, have a rest by the lagoons and fishponds ... take full advantage.

STAYING AT THE ESTATE

**The Inn on Biltmore Estate $$$$
(828) 225-1333, (800) 922-0084
www.biltmore.com**
The new Inn on Biltmore Estate with 213 rooms and suites, offers guests the unique opportunity to stay on George Vanderbilt's grand estate. It is located on a hill above Biltmore Estate Winery. With unparalleled mountain views, the inn also offers special amenities, such as afternoon tea in a delightful library, an elegant lobby bar, and dinners in the Dining Room. Relax in the outdoor pool and hot tub surrounded by more views. Fine furnishings and decor inspired by English and French manor houses decorate the interior. Choose from Deluxe rooms, Grand King, Terrace rooms, or Balcony rooms. You'll also appreciate the nightly turn-down service with chocolates.

Plush chairs decorate the library. Sink

For a total Christmas-at-Biltmore experience, book dinner reservations at the restaurant.

into one during your stay for traditional afternoon tea, served daily between 3:30 and 4:40 P.M., and enjoy hot tea, freshly baked pastries, and tea sandwiches. The 165,000-square-foot facility includes banquet rooms, board and meeting rooms, and a variety of guest rooms, including suites. It also incorporates a full-service, 150-seat restaurant, a library, a lobby bar, an exterior swimming pool, and a fitness center. Shuttles take guests to Biltmore House, the winery and to other parts of the estate.

BILTMORE OUTDOOR CENTER

Biltmore Estate offers float trips on the French Broad River as it passes through the Estate. Biking and guided Saddle Rides from Biltmore Stables are other fun activities. Carriage rides provide a tour of Biltmore as they did in 1895, and other outdoor activities can be scheduled at the Outdoor Center located just above the Winery.

Try one—or more—of the restaurants after your stroll through the Biltmore House. These are not your standard bland and generic tourist stops. Deerpark chefs have won awards, and the restaurant is often host to lavish wedding receptions. The Bistro is exceptional in flavor and freshness of the food. The atmosphere is comfortable and intimate. Don't forget to visit the eclectic shops as well.

DINING AT THE ESTATE
PRICE CODE

Our price code is based on a two-person dinner, excluding drinks, dessert, and tip. Please note that prices vary in all restaurants depending on the season and the time of day, i.e., lunch or dinner. All the restaurants mentioned accept credit cards. (For more dining facilities in the area, see our Restaurants chapter.)

$	Less than $20
$$	$20 to $35
$$$	$36 to $50
$$$$	More than $50

You will certainly want to include dining as part of your Biltmore Estate experience. Deerpark Restaurant, the Stable Cafe, and the Bistro offer creative menus that take advantage of the freshest and finest ingredients. Dining at all of the estate's restaurants is presently open to touring guests only.

The Bistro $$-$$$
(828) 225-6231
The Bistro offers wild mushroom appetizers, seasonal entrees, wood-fired pizzas, fresh pasta creations, and creamy desserts, which are enhanced by a wide selection of estate wines by the glass. A patio provides an exceptionally attractive setting for alfresco dining, weather permitting.

Deerpark Restaurant $$-$$$
(828) 225-6260
Deerpark Restaurant is in an expanded and renovated old calving barn with a central courtyard framed by dining space. The menu changes each season, and the chefs use fresh produce from gardens on the estate. The Deerpark is open for lunch daily, serving a lavish buffet that includes beef from the Biltmore cattle, mountain trout from Biltmore's lake, pasta, a soup bar, a dessert bar, and an expansive salad bar as well. A candlelight dinner buffet is

offered here during special holidays, but due to its popularity, reservations are required and should be made as soon as your plans are set.

The Stable Cafe   **$-$$$**
(828) 225-6370
The Stable Cafe in the courtyard adjacent to the mansion underwent renovation and expansion for the 1995 centennial celebration. Rotisserie chicken, soup, salads, hamburgers, and desserts are served in the quaint surroundings of the former carriage house and stable, just steps from the mansion itself. The Stable Cafe is open for lunch daily and in the evenings during Festival of Flowers and Christmas.

THE ICE CREAM PARLOR

Although the Biltmore dairy herd left the estate in 1981, and Biltmore Dairy closed its doors, the original Biltmore Ice

Cream formula is still produced exclusively for Biltmore Estate and the Biltmore Dairy Bar at the Biltmore Double Tree Hotel. The latter is owned by the family of George Vanderbilt's older grandson, George H. V. Cecil. The Double Tree is located just outside Biltmore Estate at the entrance to Biltmore Forest on Hendersonville Road and Vanderbilt Road. Long lines of guests at the Ice Cream Parlor on the Estate indicate that the tradition of the Biltmore Dairy is as strong as when GWV's advertising for his ice cream stated, "It's so pure; watch it melt."

THE BAKERY

Located across the courtyard is the Bakery. Find delectable pastry treats here with aromas that snake out the door. A strong cappuccino pick-me-up, or latte, can be taken out to tables in the courtyard.

CHEROKEE INDIAN RESERVATION

Idyllically tucked into the valley where the Great Smoky Mountains National Park connects with the Blue Ridge Parkway is the Nation of the Eastern Band of the Cherokee Indians. Also known as the Qualla Boundary, this "land of enchantment" encompasses nearly 60,000 acres. The people comprising this nation are numbered as 13,000 registered Cherokees.

The continuing influence of this tribe on the life of today's western North Carolinians is more prevalent than most of us realize. Cherokee words form the basis for many names given to our towns, rivers, mountains, resorts, real estate developments, and businesses. Old folk remedies derived from Cherokee medicine still have their place in the homes of many longtime residents. Cherokee legends endure in the mountains, valleys, and coves where we live and play. Their food—squash, beans, corn, potatoes, and more—deliciously graces our tables. The natural dyes they discovered and their craft techniques color and shape our handmade heritage. Their newest enterprise, Harrah's Casino and Hotel, continues to bring tourists to the area. Importantly, employment opportunities for the Cherokee cover all aspects of operating the casino and hotel, including key management positions.

All registered Cherokee of the Eastern Band of the Cherokee Nation receive a bi-annual stipend from the casino's profits. These funds are put in interest-bearing escrow accounts for those under 18. Upon high school graduation the funds can be withdrawn. Accordingly, the funds are not available until age 25 if the student drops out of school. The value of this plan is multifaceted. Total scholarships to any institute in the world are offered to all qualifying students. Likewise, at age 18, a youngster born today would be a millionaire.

These funds have also been allocated to the tribe and have been used for upgrading social services, hospitals, and schools on the Qualla Boundary. Currently the nation is seeking a land swap with the U.S. government to build new and updated schools on land adjacent to the Boundary that is located within the Great Smoky Mountains National Park.

Instead of being the downtrodden, this sovereign nation is not only working toward improving the quality of life among their own, they have extended charitable offerings where needs exist across the state of North Carolina and throughout the United States.

ANCIENT MOUNTAIN CULTURES

For more than 10,000 years, primitive ancestors of Native American Indians have roamed the Western North Carolina mountains. Artifacts of these prehistoric tribes—classified under names such as Upper Valley People, Middle Valley People, Hiawassee People, and Dallas People—have been unearthed at their campsites, villages, battlefields, and tribal mounds. At times some groups coexisted in the same area but in separate villages. Yet, sooner or later, one would drive the others out and take control of the rich hunting grounds. The Cherokee had broken away from the Iroquois perhaps around the time the group crossed the Mississippi River looking for permanent homes in the eastern United States. Linguistic analysis suggests this division happened at least 3,000 years ago. Despite similar languages and identical arrow types, the two groups were separate nations and bitter enemies by the time the Iroquois took over the territory north of the Great Lakes and moved into central New York.

WAR WITH THE IROQUOIS

Ancient legends of the Cherokee and other tribes indicate that the Cherokee once claimed a vast region that stretched from the Great Lakes to the Ohio River. But when they tried to move into New York from the south, a bitter war with the Iroquois and their allies, the Delawares, ensued; eventually the Cherokee were defeated. Thus, it is said, they began their slow retreat down the Ohio River and into West Virginia, fighting opposing tribes all the way. Eventually they moved south and west into the mountains of North Carolina and Tennessee. Here they found a beautiful land with a favorable climate, rich in plants and game. Once conquered, the mountainous terrain was easy for this tribe to defend.

By the time the Europeans arrived in the mid-1500s, the Cherokee had been here for 1,000 years and were second only to the Iroquois federation in strength and population. Numbering around 25,000, they controlled some 135,000 square miles of territory, and they fought victoriously against the surrounding Catawbas, Sara, Cheraw, Tuscaroras, Creeks, Chickasaw, and Shawnees to retain it.

This great Cherokee nation stretched from the Ohio River in the north all the way down into Georgia and Alabama, taking in parts of eight states, including all of Western North Carolina, the eastern section of Tennessee, and parts of South Carolina and West Virginia. They claimed all of Kentucky as hunting grounds. Much of the area was used as a game preserve, while permanent settlements were built along rivers and streams in Western North Carolina, eastern Tennessee, northern Georgia, and northwestern South Carolina.

These settlements were made up of as many as 100 small, rectangular log homes, and each town had a large council house and extensive communal agricultural fields. Even the smaller towns would have at least 200 acres planted in corn, potatoes, beans, squash, and peach orchards.

THREE CHEROKEE REGIONS

The Cherokee nation itself was divided into three regions, each with its own dialect and principal town that also served as a religious center. The Over Hill Towns, in Georgia and along the Little Tennessee and Tellico Rivers, contained the major capital of the whole tribe. It was called Echota (Chota) and was regarded as a sacred city of refuge. The Middle Towns were found along the Tuckasegee River, the headwaters of the Little Tennessee River, and along the Hiawassee and Valley Rivers. Their principal town and religious center, a kind of subcapital, was Nikwasi, built on the site of what is now Franklin, North Carolina. It has been said that the Cherokee regarded Kituwah, a large settlement in southeastern Swain County, as the "Mother Town." The Lower Towns, in South Carolina and farther east in Georgia, had a principal town on the Tugalo River called Keowee.

When visiting the Cherokee Indian Reservation, your first stop should be at the Cherokee Visitor Center across U.S. 441, facing the Museum of the Cherokee Indian (828-497-9195 or 800-438-1601). Here you'll find brochures and information on all Cherokee and area attractions, local restaurants, and sightseeing. It's open daily from 8:00 A.M. to 9:00 P.M. from mid-June through late August, 8:00 A.M. to 6:00 P.M. from late August through October, and 8:00 A.M. to 4:30 P.M. from November through mid-June.

Cherokee Lands

Historically the land of the Cherokees encompassed parts of the following states: Kentucky, Tennessee, Alabama, Georgia, South Carolina, North Carolina, Virginia, and West Virginia. Today the nation of the Eastern Band of the Cherokee encompasses less than 60,000 acres in Western North Carolina.

The 1838 removal of the Cherokee has become known as "The Trail of Tears" for the thousands who died en route to the Oklahoma Territory. Each Cherokee was allotted 110 acres in the Northeast corner at Thalequah, Oklahoma. Unscrupulous "land grabbers" were able to reduce acreage significantly.

The Cherokee, unlike the Iroquois, had no strong central government. Until they had to make treaties with the English colonies, no single leader headed their nation, though there were wise men and women who wielded great influence over the entire tribe. Instead town councils made up of male citizens elected their own town chiefs: one who presided over tribal affairs and one who was in charge of military matters. Each Cherokee was also a member of one of seven matriarchal clans. Children belonged to the clan of the mother, and one could not marry into his or her own clan. Divorce was fairly easy, and once a couple divorced, the children stayed with the wife's clan, and the husband returned to his own clan.

A single town or clan could declare war, particularly acts of revenge, or it might be undertaken by the entire Cherokee nation. It was the women, however, who had the vote on war or peace. The women chosen to announce such decisions were known as War Women or Pretty Women. Punishment of captives—including torture, death, or pardons, as well as adoptions—also were decided by women.

EUROPEANS ARRIVE

The first contact with Europeans occurred in May 1540 when Hernando de Soto arrived in Cherokee country in search of the gold and silver he had been told existed in the region. He, along with 300 horsemen, 300 footmen, and a herd of 200 hogs, entered the area just east of Rabun Gap in Georgia, passed through what is now Highlands, North Carolina, and came to the town of Nikwasi (Franklin). From there, he went over the mountains to present-day Hayesville and on to Gauaxula, close to where the town of Murphy now stands. De Soto's scribe called the people he met here Chalaque, a designation given to them by an eastern tribe. One hundred years later, a Frenchman wrote the name Cheraqui, which the English later transformed into Cherokee. The Cherokee, however, had always called themselves simply the Principle People.

Finding only copper mines, de Soto's expedition continued west toward the Mississippi River.

Twenty-seven years later, another Spaniard, Juan Pardo, led a more violent—

and financially lucrative—gold-hunting expedition, coming into the mountains through present-day Toxaway. It is said that Pardo "left death, destruction, and terror in his wake." For the next 125 years, Spaniards prospected quietly in the area, while life for the Cherokee went on much the same as it always had.

It wasn't until the late 1600s, when the English began to settle and explore the Carolinas, that everything changed. Between 1716 and 1743 trade between the Cherokee and the English flourished: More than 200,000 furs were exchanged for guns, blankets, broadcloth, calico, mirrors, teakettles, and other goods. In 1767 Josiah Wedgwood imported "Cherokee Clay" from Franklin, North Carolina, and used it as the basis for the world-renowned English jasperware. But by the middle of that century, game was already growing scarce from years of overhunting to supply the demand for furs, and many Cherokee were in debt to unscrupulous traders.

Adding to the degeneration of what had been fairly decent relations between whites and natives, the English, French, and Spanish drew the Cherokee, along with many of their longtime enemy tribes, into their own conflicts for territory, including the French and Indian War. During that conflict the Cherokees' sympathies tended toward the French, but they were coerced into raising a force to fight for the British. As time went on misunderstandings and mistreatments of American Indians increased, and the Cherokee were frequently at war with the European settlers they found constantly encroaching upon their lands. In 1760 Col. Archibald Montgomery and 1,650 soldiers destroyed the Lower Towns along Georgia's Savannah River, forcing survivors to flee into the mountains. Montgomery and his men then advanced on the Middle Towns but were driven back. The following spring, however, another British force burned 15 of these settlements and destroyed 1,500 acres of crops, causing a widespread famine and the subsequent death of nearly half the Cherokee population.

Treaties were made and just as quickly broken, and intruding white settlers saw the Cherokees' sense of justice, which was like the old Hebrew concept of an eye for an eye, as savage. During the Revolutionary War, Britain provided the Cherokee with guns and offered bounties on the scalps of the rebellious American settlers on the east and west sides of the Blue Ridge. Discovering this, the rebels, under Gen. Griffith Rutherfordton, marched through the Swannanoa Gap through present-day Waynesville and carried out raids throughout the Middle Towns, leveling 66 of them and burning crops and food supplies, while the terrified Cherokee population fled into hiding. This scorched-earth policy forced the Lower Towns into a treaty that ceded almost all their land in South Carolina to the federal government. It was only one of many exchanges of land for temporary peace, for by this time the Cherokee had little left to bargain with.

Trout season opens the last Saturday of March and ends the last day of February the following year. Fishing is permitted from one-half hour before sunrise to one-half hour after sunset. The daily creel limit is 10 per permit holder. For more information contact Fish & Game management of the Eastern Band of the Cherokee Indians at (829) 497–5201.

SUCCESS AND TRAGEDY

Though the size of their territory shrank drastically by the early 1800s, many Cherokee managed to prosper. One of their own, Sequoyah (George Gist), an illiterate, non-English-speaking child of a Cherokee mother and an absent white father, invented an alphabet so that the Cherokee could read and write in their own language, the first Native Americans to do so. A few years later, in 1828, the first Cherokee-language newspaper,

Do you have Cherokee ancestors? If so, and if you have some knowledge of your family tree, you may be able to expand on it by doing your own research in the library at the Qualla Civic Center on Acquoni Road. You can also check out Cherokee Roots' companion publications listing the rolls of the Eastern and Western Bands of the Cherokee. To purchase the publications, write to Cherokee Roots, P.O. Box 525, Cherokee NC 28719, or call (828) 497-9709. The books are also for sale in some area shops, such as the gift shop of the Museum of the Cherokee Indian.

Cherokee Phoenix, came into being. Some Cherokee, educated in mission schools, went on to get their degrees in higher education from American universities. Many owned large farms and slaves.

This success, however, only provoked resentment and covetousness in the surrounding white settlers. Then gold was discovered on Cherokee land in Georgia. Georgia refused to recognize the existence of the Cherokee nation and therefore disallowed them from owning land. They were given until June 1, 1830, to leave Georgia, and the state offered white settlers "gold lots" of Cherokee land by lottery. Though the Cherokee under Chief Junaluska had helped Gen. Andrew Jackson's forces in their successful fight against the British in the War of 1812, President Jackson, as he had now become, failed to support the Cherokee against the state of Georgia. Instead the federal government offered the Cherokee $4.5 million for their eastern territory and told them to move to Oklahoma. When they overwhelmingly rejected these terms, the Cherokee were forcibly removed from their tribal lands in the tragedy we now call the Trail of Tears.

Chief Tsali, known to whites as Old Charley, was rounded up with his wife and family. Tsali and his sons and son-in-law overpowered the soldiers. In the skirmish

a soldier was killed, and Tsali and his family fled into the mountains to take refuge with others hiding there. The government soon realized there was no way to flush or starve out Tsali and other knowledgeable survivors from remote hiding places in their old hunting grounds. Gen. Winfield Scott offered terms to Tsali and his sons for their surrender. His clan could stay in North Carolina. Tsali and his sons, hearing this, turned themselves in. His own people were forced to execute the old man, his oldest son, and son-in-law by firing squad, but his youngest son, because of his tender age, was allowed to live. A marker stands at the courthouse in Bryson city describing this event.

THE FORMATION OF THE QUALLA BOUNDARY

After the federal troops withdrew from the mountains, the ragtag remnant of the once-great Cherokee Nation turned to William Holland Thomas, who was born on a farm near what is now Waynesville. At the age of 12, Thomas had become manager of an Indian trading post at Qualla; by the age of 14, he owned it. He bought it from Felix Walker, a farmer, trader, land speculator, and representative to Congress. Thomas spoke and wrote Cherokee and studied American law on his own. Trusted and loved by the Cherokee, he was adopted by their old chief, Yonaguska. When Yonaguska died, Thomas, a white man, was elected chief of the eastern band of Cherokee, and he immediately went to Washington to obtain their share of the money that had been offered to the Cherokee for their land. After years of struggle, he was appointed federal agent to this eastern band of Cherokee, and the money was put in his trust. With it, he purchased 57,000 acres around the present village of Cherokee, plus a smaller tract known as the Snowbird Reservation near Robbinsville. Today, to those who come here by the thousands, this land is known as the Cherokee Indian Reservation, but to the people living on this acreage, it is the Qualla Boundary. *Qualla* is Cherokee for the name *Pauline*, a Cherokee matriarch.

THE PRESENT-DAY QUALLA BOUNDARY

It is the nearly 13,000 residents of this region and their ancestors (who were, for many years, more isolated than the Western Band of Cherokee forced into Oklahoma) who have been largely responsible for keeping alive so much that is authentic about the Cherokee culture. This may not be apparent immediately to the first-time visitor to the reservation, with its string of stores, motels, shops, and tourist attractions that serve hordes of visitors each year. The tourist who simply comes for a relaxing vacation can enjoy hiking, swimming, trout fishing, river trips, shopping, and other attractions, such as Tribal Bingo, Harrah's Cherokee Casino, Santa's Land Theme Park and Zoo, and Cherokee Fun Park (some of these are listed in our Attractions and Kidstuff chapters).

You'll also find 44 motels and 84 cabins and 28 campgrounds with more than 2,200 sites at in-town locations as well as along the Oconaluftee River and tucked away on the mountain slopes. Several of these facilities are associated with national chains. (Not all are open in the winter.) A visitors guide and directory that lists facilities, amenities, and phone numbers can be picked up at the Cherokee Visitors Center located across U.S. 441 facing the Museum of the Cherokee Indian. Or call (800) 438-1601 to get a copy by mail or visit www.cherokee-nc.com. But even the casual visitor can learn a great deal about the history and the culture of the Cherokee People by including the following sites and events in your plans.

Cherokee Heritage Museum & Gallery
Saunooke Village, U.S. Highway 441 N.,
Cherokee, NC
(828) 497-3211

This museum and gallery will be a particularly nice stop for those who appreciate the very best in contemporary Cherokee art. The theme here is discovering the past through the present. It offers displays of art and cultural items such as masks, crystals, the uketena, and more. The gallery presents a new exhibit each month. Cherokee Heritage also features educational taped tours, books, and craft demonstrations. It is open daily from April through November. Admission is $2.50 for those 11 years and older; $1.50 for children ages 6 to 10; under 6 free.

The Museum of the Cherokee Indian
U.S. Highway 441, at Drama Road,
Cherokee, NC
(828) 497-3481, (888) 665-7249
Plan to spend at least two hours at this museum, which has been called "a cutting-edge" example of "how all museums should be." Outside the building is a 20-foot wooden sculpture of Sequoya (the Cherokee genius who is—as far as we know—the only human to create a written form of language all alone), and inside you can literally walk through Cherokee history. Interactive displays and multisensory exhibits allow you to experience the past. You can listen to storytellers, play the ancient butter bean game, travel the infamous Trail of Tears, and much more.

The fine gift shop is loaded with a large selection of books, crafts, artwork, and other Cherokee or Native American items. The museum is open year-round except on Thanksgiving, Christmas, and New Year's Day. Hours are 9:00 A.M. to 5:00 P.M. September through May and 9:00 A.M. to 8:00 P.M. June through August. Admission is $8.00 for adults, $5.00 for children ages 6 to 12. There are group rates, AAA, AARP, and other discounts available.

Oconaluftee Indian Village
Drama Road off U.S. Highway 441 N.,
Cherokee, NC
(828) 497-2315, (828) 497-2111
www.oconalufteevillage.com

CLOSE-UP

The Invisible Warriors

The town of Franklin was built where the Cherokee settlement of Nikwasi once stood. Nikwasi was one of the oldest Cherokee towns and an important ceremonial center. In the old days Indians built their town lodges on large manmade mounds, and Nikwasi's was one of the few that possessed the "everlasting fire," or spiritual connection, hence the lodge was used in religious ceremonies.

Once, long ago, a powerful, unknown tribe invaded the land, destroying the villages and killing the people. One morning at dawn the intruders were seen approaching Nikwasi. The villagers rushed to defend their town but were eventually forced to retreat.

Suddenly a stranger appeared. He spoke and dressed like a chief from the Overhills settlements. The villagers thought he had come to their aid with reinforcements. He shouted to the Nikwasi chief to call off his men—he would defeat the enemy. As the Nikwasi villagers fell back toward the lodge, they saw hundreds of warriors, armed and painted for battle, streaming out of an open doorway in the side of the mound where no doorway had existed before. It was then the villagers recognized the warriors as *nunnehi*—"Immortals," or the "people who live anywhere."

Theirs was a race of spirit people, fond of music and dancing, who lived in the highlands and had a great many town lodges, especially on mountain balds. As soon as the nunnehi got a short distance from the mound, they became invisible. The invaders could see the weapons but could not see who wielded them; frightened, they began to flee. They tried to hide behind large rocks as they retreated, but the nunnehi's arrows flew around the boulders and killed them. When only six or so of the invaders were left alive, they were so upset they just sat down and cried. Since that day the Cherokee have called that spot at the head of the Tuckasegee River *dayulsunyi*, "where they cried."

It was Indian custom to spare a few warriors to return home and tell of their defeat. Thus the invaders went home to the north and the nunnehi returned to the mound.

There are countless Cherokee stories involving this spirit race who, when they chose to show themselves, looked like ordinary people. They also appeared to whites during the Civil War. It's said that a large troop of Union soldiers came to Franklin to surprise a small number of Confederates posted there but, upon seeing so many soldiers guarding the town, they turned away.

Get ready to step back more than two centuries in time when you visit this recreated 1750s Cherokee village. Indian guides in native costumes will take you through the village, while others demonstrate such life skills as weaving, pottery, beadwork, food preparation, canoe construction, and arrow-making and hunting techniques. You will see Cherokee homes, a sweat lodge, and the important seven-sided council house. Cherokee history, culture, and social customs will be explained, and you'll have ample opportunity to ask questions. Afterward go back to the areas that interested you and spend as much time as you like exploring further. The village is open from 9:00 A.M. to 5:30 P.M. daily May 15 through October 25. Admission is $12.00 for adults and $5.00 for children 6 through 13 years old. A combined ticket for the Museum and the Village is $17.00 for adults and $9.00 for children.

Qualla Arts and Crafts Mutual, Inc.
U.S. Highway 441 and Drama Road, Cherokee, NC
(828) 497-3103

Just across the street from the Museum of the Cherokee Indian, you'll find a cooperative that displays the works of 300 Cherokee craftspeople and a section of American Indian crafts from other areas of the country. The store also has a large section of historical baskets, masks, pottery, finger weaving, wood carving, and the like. It's open 8:00 A.M. to 8:00 P.M. June through August, 8:00 A.M. to 6:00 P.M. September through October, and 9:00 A.M. to 4:30 P.M. November through May. Admission is free.

Unto These Hills Outdoor Drama
Drama Road and U.S. Highway 441 N., Cherokee, NC
(828) 497-2111, (800) 554-4557
www.untothesehills.com

Every summer from mid-June through late August, one of the world's longest-running outdoor dramas takes the stage in the 2,800-seat Mountainside Theater just outside the town of Cherokee. In the half-century since the play opened in 1950, millions of visitors have watched the rich pageant of Cherokee legends, rituals, dances, and history unfold before them. Even if you've seen this outdoor drama in years past, a recomposed musical score makes a return trip a new experience.

June and July performances, which run two hours and 15 minutes, start at 8:45 P.M., with preshow musical entertainment beginning at 8:10 P.M. In August shows begin at 8:30 P.M. and preshow entertainment at 7:50 P.M. Reserved seating in the front half of the theater is $18.00 for all ages; general admission is $16.00 per adult and $8.00 per child through age 12. Group rates are available for 20 or more people. Tickets may be purchased at the box office at the intersection of U.S. 441 and Drama Road from 9:00 A.M. to 6:30 P.M. Monday through Saturday. After 6:30 P.M. you can buy them at the Mountainside Theater for that evening's performance. You can also order reserve tickets by calling (828) 497-2111 or (800) 554-4557. Both the theater and the box office are closed on Sunday.

WATERFALLS

Whether it's the roar of a great cataract forming rainbows in its drenching spray or a slender, misty stream of water musically splashing in a shallow pool, there are few places where the call of the falls can be so fulfilled as in Western North Carolina. There are literally hundreds of waterfalls in these mountains, more than 250 in Transylvania County alone.

Nature and time have provided waterfalls throughout the mountains. Some are on private property, and others can only be reached by long and strenuous hikes though rugged country. Most of the ones we've chosen are just a short jaunt from a roadway, and some of these falls can be viewed simply by parking your car and taking a look. We have listed several worth the extra effort required to reach them, even though it sometimes means traveling on a narrow, curvy, graveled secondary road (SR) or Forest Service road (FR).

A few words of caution are in order: Water-drenched rocks are extremely treacherous, and a number of serious accidents and deaths occur each year to people who slip and fall from the tops of these falls or from the spray- and moss-slick rocks, steps, and trails nearby. (Even when fording mountain streams, extreme care is needed.) Use common sense and caution. Keep a sharp eye on children. Stay well away from the tops of falls and never try to climb or walk across them. Avoid tragedies.

Care for the forest. Stick to the trails and don't scramble around the stream and riverbanks, destroying vegetation and loosening the soil. Such impact from humans and our carelessness with fishing lines, cigarettes, bottles, cans, and other litter endangers fish, wildlife, and rare plants and plays a large role in destroying many of these ancient and lovely places.

In order to support highly visited areas, a small admittance fee has been levied. The money collected is returned directly to each site to make improvements and pay employees. Areas where nominal fees are collected include Sliding Rock, Dry Falls, and Whitewater Falls. A season pass costs $15. However one pass is needed for Sliding Rock and another is required for and provides access to Dry Falls and Whitewater Falls, as well as nearby Whiteside Mountain. Both Golden Age and Golden Access Passports are honored.

NORTHERN MOUNTAINS
Avery County

Elk Falls
off U.S. Highway 19 E.
Sixty-five-foot Elk Falls, just inside the Tennessee-North Carolina border, is one of the most beautiful waterfalls in the mountains. Its lovely pool, one of the largest and deepest around, makes this a super-popular swimming hole, but beware of the fast water here.

Elk Falls is easily accessible; just go north on U.S. 19 E. to the town of Elk Park. A short distance up Main Street (SR 1303), turn right on Elk River Road (SR 1305), a residential street. Travel just over 4 miles to a parking area beside the Elk River. Here a short trail leads to the top and on down to the base of the falls.

Burke County

Linville Falls
Mile 316.5, Blue Ridge Parkway
Well-known Linville Falls, at the head of Linville Gorge, pours downward in several

stages into one of the deepest gorges in the eastern United States. Its upper and lower cascades, we're told, used to be about the same height. But a heavy flood around the turn of the century broke off part of the ledge on the upper falls and deposited it at the top of the lower falls, decreasing the height of the former but increasing the height of the latter. You can reach the falls by hiking from the Linville Falls Visitors Center at milepost 316.5 on the Blue Ridge Parkway. For specific directions check the maps posted at the center. The trails to various overlooks of the falls range from easy to difficult.

Upper Creek Falls
off N.C. Highway 181
The main part of this cascade tumbles some 100 feet into a pool of thrashing water. This and the fact that it's moderately easy to get to make Upper Creek Falls a popular swimming and sunbathing area. To reach it take N.C. 181 south from the Blue Ridge Parkway for just more than 5.5 miles to a parking area on the left. A nearly mile-long, steep switchback trail descends through the woods to the falls.

Yancey County

Crabtree Falls
Mile 339.5, Blue Ridge Parkway
This 70-foot waterfall, considered to be one of the most photogenic in the state, is in the Crabtree Meadows Recreation Area (elevation 3,700 feet) on the Blue Ridge Parkway, 8.4 miles south of the junction of N.C. 226 at milepost 339.5. The steep, rocky trail makes for a moderately difficult hike from the parking lot in the Crabtree Meadows camping area (you can pick up a trail guide at the campground's entrance during the summer months). In winter, when the campgrounds are closed, you'll have to park outside the gate and walk in. A loop trail, lined with birch and hemlock and, in spring and summer, a great variety

Famous Linville Gorge and Linville Falls were named for William Linville and his son, John, who were killed by Indians in 1766. The Cherokee called the river "eeseeoh" or "river of many cliffs."

of wildflowers, leads to this beautiful 70-foot falls. To get to the falls by the shortest route, nearly a mile, descend the trail to the right. You can come back the same way for a trip of slightly less than 2 miles or continue on the 2.5-mile loop. If you do the latter, bear to the left to avoid trails leading into the campground.

Setrock Creek and Roaring Fork Falls
3 miles off of N.C. Highway 80 N.
From the Blue Ridge Parkway, exit onto N.C. 80 N. (at milepost 344) and go approximately 2 miles north to Forest Service Road 472. Make a left onto FR 472 and drive 4.7 miles to the Black Mountain Campground. Inside the campground you'll see a sign leading to the Briar Bottom group camp. Drive the short distance to a sign on the right that marks the way to this 75-foot cascade. When the trail forks, bear right. This is a round-trip excursion of a little more than a 0.5 mile.

When you return to your car, continue your journey another 3.9 miles down FR 472 (when the road changes from gravel to pavement, it becomes SR 1205). At the BUSICK WORK CENTER sign, turn right and park at the gate. The trail, an old logging road to the right of the gate, will take you to Roaring Fork River. Turn right on a path at the river. You'll find the falls, which drop in beautiful 5-foot cascades, about a mile away.

The mossy rocks and leaves form alcoves worthy of the Garden of Eden! A trail running up the forested right side of the falls let you into a small pool at the top. Be very careful and use only the trail to get to the top.

Waterfall on Big Creek
off U.S. Highway 19 W.
This gushing waterfall, which can be viewed from the road, is reached by taking U.S. 19 E. west out of Burnsville and then turning right on U.S. 19 W. toward the Tennessee border. Drive 17.5 miles to a marked pull-off on the left for a view of the 25-foot falls.

CENTRAL MOUNTAINS
Buncombe County

Douglas (or Carter Creek) and Walker Falls
5 miles south of N.C. Highway 197
A journey into Pisgah's Craggy Mountain Scenic Area to view Douglas Falls offers an added attraction: The falls are surrounded by a stand of rare virgin hemlock. To reach the area take U.S. 19/23 north out of Asheville for 13.5 miles and then go east on N.C. Highway 197 to Barnardsville. Turn south on Dillingham Road (SR 2173) about a half-block past the post office. About 4 miles down this winding road, veer to the left and continue until it becomes graveled FR 74; stop for a view of two-tier, 50-foot Walker Falls on the left.

Continue on another 5 miles or so until you dead-end at the Craggy Mountain Scenic Area parking area. Take the trail on the south end (right side) of the parking lot. It's a little more than 0.5 mile to a viewing area at the base of 70-foot Douglas Falls, named in honor of Supreme Court Justice William O. Douglas. Unless you are an experienced hiker armed with a good topographical map and compass, return the way you came. Most trail maps of this area are outdated and confusing. For the best viewing, visit both these falls after heavy rains.

Glassmine Falls
Mile 361.1, Blue Ridge Parkway
This waterfall is on private land, and its water flow can be thin when rain is scarce. (It's been known to dry up completely.)

However after heavy rains, Glassmine Falls, with its immense slide downward, can be impressive. You can view the falls from Glassmine Falls Overlook at milepost 361.1 on the Blue Ridge Parkway. This overlook is about 200 feet from the parking area, which is 5.7 miles south of N.C. 128, the road that leads to Mount Mitchell's summit. It will be on the left when driving south from Mount Mitchell and on the right when driving north. Look east to locate the fall's steep rock face (estimated at 800 feet), framed by stark skeletons of red spruce that have died from air pollution.

Polk County

Pearson Falls
off Pearson Falls Road (SR 1102)
There is a $1.50 fee for adults and 50 cents for children 6 to 12 (children younger than 6 are admitted free) to Pearson Falls Park, which is owned and maintained by the Tryon Garden Club, and it's well worth the price. Take U.S. 176 south out of Saluda or north out of Tryon. Watch for a small sign on the Pacolet River side of the road that marks Pearson Falls Road (SR 1102). The entrance to the 250-acre park is slightly less than a mile down this road. This biologically rich glen with its profusion of wildflowers was purchased in 1931 and is now a North Carolina Natural Heritage Area. It's a great place for hiking, bird-watching, and picnicking. The park is open from 10:00 A.M. to 6:00 P.M. daily in the summer. From November 1 to March 1, it's closed on Monday and Tuesday and is only open from 10:00 A.M. to 5:00 P.M. the rest of the week.

Shunkawauken Falls
White Oak Mountain Road, SR 1136
This cascade begins its tumbles practically from the summit of 3,102-foot White Oak Mountain, with the main portion measuring around 150 feet high. Though it's on private land, it can be viewed right from

the roadside. From I-26 drive east on N.C. 108 for just less than a half-mile and turn left on Houston Road (SR 1137). After another half-mile, take the fork to the left onto White Oak Mountain Road (SR 1136). You'll come to the waterfall in another 2 miles. There is a pull-off on the left just beyond it. If you continue on down the road for just a little more than 0.5 mile, you'll reach an overlook with a great view of Columbus and the surrounding area.

Rutherford County

Hickory Nut Falls
Inside the park off U.S. Highway 64 E.
This waterfall spilling 404 feet over a granite face is just over the Henderson County line at Lake Lure and can be seen from quite a distance. Hickory Nut Falls are located in the privately owned Chimney Rock Park (see our Attractions chapter). Admission ($9.50 for adults and $5.00 for children 6 to 15; children under 6 are free) includes a 26-story elevator ride up through solid rock and access to nature trails offering unparalleled views of the falls (the best is from Inspiration Point). It also offers a smashing view of Lake Lure, craggy-faced Rumbling Bald Mountain, and the surrounding countryside. For a preview of the falls, you may want to rent the 1992 movie *Last of the Mohicans,* which featured the majestic falls prominently. To reach the park take U.S. 64 E. off I-26 and drive approximately 15 miles through Bat Cave to the park.

Transylvania County

Courthouse Falls
off N.C. Highway 215
You'll have to walk a short distance to reach this waterfall, but it's one of our favorites and one of the most beautiful in the mountains. Take N.C. 215 for 10.4 miles into Pisgah Forest from its junction with U.S. 64 near Rosman. Turn right on FR 140

National Forest Service visitor centers often carry maps to waterfalls in the area.

and drive approximately 3 miles to a small bridge that crosses a creek; you can park on the far side, on the right. Take the trail on the right for a few hundred yards to a narrow trail that bears left. This 300-foot, short, steep trail leads to the beautiful pool at the base of the falls.

Daniel Ridge Falls
FR 475
Two other fine cascades—Cove Creek and Shuck Ridge Creek Falls—are in this general area, but Daniel Ridge, also known as Toms Spring Falls, is the largest and easiest to find. Drive 5.2 miles up U.S. 276 to FR 475 and go 3.9 miles to a parking area on the right. From there follow the logging road for less than a mile. You'll see the 150-foot falls on the left.

The Horsepasture River Falls
off N.C. Highway 281 S.
The series of waterfalls here are some of the most awe inspiring in the region. To reach the falls from the intersection of U.S. 64 and N.C. 281 in Sapphire, turn south on N.C. 281 and drive 1.8 miles to the Horsepasture River, 4.2 miles of which have been designated as part of the National Wild and Scenic River System. Find a parking spot along the guardrails near the bridge. Drift Falls, known to locals as "Bust Your Butt Falls," can be seen just downriver. Recently it came under private ownership and is not open to the public. The falls can still be viewed from the parking area. There's a pull-off on the right for about three or four cars next to the trailhead, marked by a small green sign on the guardrail. (Make sure your vehicle is completely off the road, or you may get ticketed.) From the trailhead descend the trail for 100 yards until it joins the trail paralleling the river. Privately owned Drift Falls will be to your right. Drop Off/Turtleback Falls, named for its

domelike rock, is a few hundred feet farther on your left. Though it looks like a
great place for some slide-and-swim fun,
don't attempt it; the currents in this pool
have caused a number of drownings, and
it's dangerously close to the top of Rainbow Falls. A few years ago a girl was
swept by the current over Rainbow and
killed. Her two companions narrowly
escaped the same fate.

Viewing the other beautiful falls along
this wide, deep gorge will require a 1.5-mile
steep descent on a sometimes-strenuous
trail with precipitous ledges. It is not suitable for young children or those less than
physically fit. Even if you're in shape, care
is needed.

Continue down the gorge to the top
of roaring, 200-foot Rainbow Falls, where
you can often see rainbows in the thun-
derous spray. Again, *stay away from the
brink of this waterfall!* Instead take the trail
to an upper overlook or descend to the
lower overlook (if you don't mind a
drenching) for a picnic or swim. Avoid
these falls in winter; the spray freezes and
it makes walking dangerous.

It's another fairly difficult half-mile trek
to the base of Stairstep Falls, where the
river tumbles down seven 10-foot-tall,
river-wide steps. If you're wise, you'll turn
around and make the hike back to Turtle-
back Falls at this point; only the most
experienced and intrepid should continue
down the strenuous and dangerous 1.3-
mile trail to Windy Falls. That series of
nine violent cascades plunges 700 feet so
mightily that they create their own wind
through the narrowing gorge. We definitely advise not attempting this one.
There isn't even a viewing place to see all

---

*Due to the glare of sunshine on water,
waterfall photos usually come out best
if shot in the early morning, late
evening, or on a cloudy day. If you
can keep your camera lens dry, try
shooting during light rain or fog for
wonderful effects.*

---

of Windy Falls. A final word of caution:
When visiting this wild river gorge, one of
the most beautiful and spectacular in the
mountains, remember that accidents in
the area have kept the local rescue squad
busy through the years, and deaths have
been a common occurrence.

Looking Glass Falls
U.S. Highway 276
You barely have to get out of your vehicle
to enjoy the most visited of Transylvania
County's many waterfalls. This rushing 30-
foot-wide, 60-foot-high cascade is set
alongside U.S. 276, 5.5 miles into Pisgah
Forest from its junction with U.S. 64. A
short flight of stone steps leads down to
the base of the falls from a paved pull-off
area right beside Looking Glass Creek.

Moore's Cove Falls
0.7 miles off U.S. Highway 276
One mile north of Looking Glass Falls on
U.S. 276, keep a sharp eye out for the first
bridge ahead and pull off in the wide,
unpaved area just before reaching the
bridge. (When driving south, it's 1.6 miles
from Sliding Rock.) A wooden pedestrian
bridge will take you across Looking Glass
Creek to the lovely, easy 0.7-mile-long
Moore's Cove Trail, which is steep only for
the first few hundred yards. At its end a
small stream tumbles over a deeply
recessed ledge that allows you to walk
behind the free-falling, 50-foot falls. Avoid
the steep path to the top of the ledge; it
can be dangerous.

Slick Rock Falls
FR 475B
To reach this watery attraction just a
short distance up the road from Looking
Glass Falls, follow the sign to the Pisgah
Fish Hatchery (FR 475) on the left. Drive
1.6 miles and turn right on FR 475B. After
1.1 miles you'll come to a sharp bend in
the road. Park at the small pull-off on the
right, where a trailhead leads up to the
summit of Looking Glass Rock. The small
but pretty 30-foot-tall Slick Rock Falls,
some 50 yards away, spills over a rocky

CLOSE-UP

Macon County: Slick Rock

Slick Rock is a granite rock outcrop on an eastward facing slope, the summit of which offers an impressive view of far-off mountains. From Highlands take Horse Cove Road to the end of the pavement, then take the right fork onto Bull Pen Road and drive about 1.5 miles. When you reach a sharp left curve, look for a pull-off and a steep, unmarked path on the right (if you pass a road that intersects Bull Pen on the right at a 45-degree angle, you've gone too far; turn around and go back). This timber sale road runs right beneath Slick Rock. The hike to the top is less than a quarter-mile, and it's a great place to watch a sunrise.

---

ledge of this rugged mountain. This waterfall well deserves its name "slick," so please don't try to climb it or any other falls.

Sliding Rock
U.S. Highway 276

Just 1.6 miles farther up U.S. 276 (or 7.6 miles from its junction with U.S. 64) is Sliding Rock, one place where you're invited to "take the plunge" down a 60-foot slippery cascade into the 50 degree to 60 degree, 6-foot-deep pool below. If you don't care to make the slide, it's fun to simply watch the action from paved viewing areas at the top or bottom of this natural, exhilarating ride that's fueled by 11,000 gallons of water a minute. There's now a $3.00 per vehicle parking fee that helps pay for lifeguards, who are on duty from 10:00 A.M. to 6:00 P.M. from Memorial Day through Labor Day; the parking fee includes the use of a bathhouse.

The rock, while slick, can take the bottom out of an ordinary bathing suit, so old jeans or cutoffs are best for this fast ride. Also be careful while getting in and out of the water. The surface of the rock, even where the water isn't flowing, can be slick and accounts for some hard tumbles.

Toxaway Falls
off U.S. Highway 64

In 1916 the first Lake Toxaway dam burst after a flooding downpour. The water from the lake washed away huge amounts of vegetation and soil and exposed a huge granite dome. Now, as you drive over this dome on a bridge, you get a bird's-eye view of the great quantities of water, sometimes more than 300 feet wide, that pour 250 feet over this ledge into the valley below. In 1997, busy, twisting U.S. 64 was widened and an easier pull-off was created for the many people who wished to look down on and/or get a photo of the falls. (The bottom of the falls is on private land.) For a more leisurely view, you might want to stop for a meal at October's End, a nice Italian restaurant with a terrace overlooking the falls. (See our Restaurants chapter.)

Twin Falls on Henry Branch
2.2 miles off FR 477

Since we sometimes are able to take this lovely hike to Twin Falls without meeting anyone else along the trail, we almost hesitate to risk jeopardizing such solitude by writing about it. Note that at 4.4 miles for the round trip, this is the longest trek in this list. While it's not a particularly difficult trail, it does involve negotiating a number of log bridges, so we always equip ourselves with a long, sturdy walking stick to help keep our balance, a good idea almost anytime you're walking forest trails that often have slippery and eroded sections.

To reach these two 100-foot waterfalls, drive 2.2 miles north on U.S. 276 from its junction with U.S. 64. Turn right on FR 477 and travel just more than 2.5 miles to a small parking area on the right side at the sign to Avery Creek Trail. Take this yellow-and-blue-blazed path for slightly more than a mile, until Avery Creek Trail crosses orange-blazed Buckhorn Gap Trail, which you should take to the right. In a little more than a half-mile, you'll come to a Trail Falls Loop sign. It's just a short distance in either direction of the loop to Twin Falls (the left loop is usually less overgrown), which are formed by two separate streams. There is no trail to the very base of the falls. Don't try to make one. You'll only disturb the wonderful plants that live here.

Never ever climb around the tops or sides of a waterfall. Always view the falls from below. Every year a curious visitor tragically falls to his or her death.

Whitewater Falls and Laurel Falls
off N.C. Highway 281
At 411 feet, Whitewater Falls lays claim to being the highest unbroken falls in the Southeast. To reach it take U.S. 64 to N.C. 281 and travel south for approximately 9.5 miles. Turn left at the Whitewater Falls Scenic Area for the short drive to the parking area, where there is a $2.00 per vehicle fee. From there a 0.2-mile trail leads to the upper overlook. Be extremely careful when negotiating the steep trip down to a lower overlook for an even better view. An old roadbed leads to the top of the falls, but we don't recommend any

close-up viewing, as a number of deaths occur in the area almost every year.

If you're in excellent shape, you can turn right on the trail that brings you to the middle overlook, and it will take you on a very strenuous hike of just less than a mile down to Laurel Falls, also known as Corbin Creek Falls. When the trees have shed their leaves, you can view this waterfall from Whitewater. It's made up of a series of broken cascades that tumble about the same distance as Whitewater, but only the lowest one, which drops approximately 75 feet, can be easily seen. It's much too dangerous to try to get a close-up view of the others.

SOUTHERN MOUNTAINS
Clay County

Leatherwood Falls
FR 340
Compared with some falls, 25-foot Leatherwood is not particularly grand, but Fires Creek, which rushes past the falls' base, is great for swimming and fishing. To find it go west out of Hayesville on U.S. 64 for just short of 5 miles and turn right on SR 1302. After 3.7 miles turn left on SR 1344, which will become FR 340 as it enters the Nantahala National Forest. Drive 1.9 miles to the Leatherwood Falls parking and picnic area. You can view the falls from here or wade into the creek (it can be rushing and dangerous after heavy rains), or you can cross the bridge upstream and work your way back to the foot of the falls. Don't, however, be tempted to climb the cascade. It may not look dangerous, but it is. From the picnic area, paved trails provide access for fly-fishing from wheelchairs.

Haywood County

The Graveyard Fields Falls
Mile 418.8, Blue Ridge Parkway
Three waterfalls, Upper Falls, Second Falls, and Yellowstone Falls (the largest of the

three), are in Graveyard Fields, a vast area left nearly treeless by a devastating forest fire in 1925. Second Falls can be seen from the parking area at milepost 418.8 on the Blue Ridge Parkway, but most people prefer a closer look and walk to the Graveyard Fields Loop Trail. The parking area is very crowded on weekends. Some parts of the trail are badly eroded, as are many side trails. Do Graveyard Fields a favor and stick to the main routes, avoiding the area altogether during wet weather. Check the information board at the parking area for the most direct routes to the falls and be careful at the overlook at Yellowstone Falls, which can be treacherous (see our chapter on the Blue Ridge Parkway). As with all falls, stay out of the water at the top of the falls and stay on the trails.

Midnight Hole and Mouse Creek Falls
1.5 and 2 miles off Waterville Road

Seeing these falls requires a 4-mile round-trip hike, but it's an easy walk on a graded road that runs along beautiful Big Creek. To reach Big Creek drive west on Interstate 40 to the Waterville exit (just before you reach the Tennessee border). Turn left on Waterville Road, which will enter the Great Smoky Mountains National Park. After approximately 3 miles, 0.8 mile past the ranger station, the road will end at a parking area of the Big Creek Campground. (In winter the gate is closed at the ranger station, so you'll have to walk from there, adding 1.6 miles round-trip.) Take the road (Big Creek Trail) just a few feet back from the parking area. A little less than 1.5 miles along this easy route, an obvious path will lead to Midnight Hole, where small (7-foot) but gorgeous twin falls flow into a fantastic 80-foot-wide, 15-foot-deep swimming hole. Back on the road/trail, continue on slightly over another half-mile, and you'll see Mouse Creek Falls, which drop a total of 50 feet, rushing into the creek.

For those with the energy, there is another series of waterfalls called Gunter Fork Cascades. The longest one drops 100 feet, making it one of the tallest waterfalls

Mountain water is cold! Icy cold. Be sure to have dry clothing to change into after swimming in these pools. Believe it or not, hypothermia could become a threat even in warm weather.

in the park. They're 8.2 difficult miles from the parking area and are reached by a wonderful route that runs mostly along this beautiful creek then just over 2 miles up Gunter Fork Trail. That, however, is a hard 16.4-mile round-trip, and you'll have to make a number of wet-stream crossings. You should get a trail map and specific directions if you want to see these falls.

Jackson County

Hurricane Falls and Glassy Creek Falls
N.C. Highway 107 and Norton
Road (SR 1145)

Hurricane and Glassy Creek Falls are both on private property, but they can be viewed from the roadside on the same trip. To reach Hurricane Falls drive north out of Cashiers on N.C. 107 for 1.8 miles and turn left on Norton Road (SR 1145). It's just more than 0.5 mile to a pull-off where you can see the waterfall, which has an average height of 40 feet that varies according to the height of Lake Thorpe, into which it flows.

For Glassy Creek Falls return to N.C. 107 and continue north for 8.6 miles to a pull-off on the left (because of the sharp curve at this location, pass the pull-off, turn around farther up the road, and come back to park). The 100-foot curling falls is formed by the Little River Creek. The river in front of the falls is the West Fork of the Tuckasegee.

Silver Run Falls
N.C. Highway 107

Would you like a waterfall-fed pool to cool off in on a hot day? Then, from Cashiers drive south on N.C. 107 for just more than 4 miles and park at a graveled pull-off on the

A self-guided, 1.5-mile loop trail will take you over the highest mountain in the Great Balsam Mountains, 6,410-foot Richland Balsam, and through a remnant of a spruce fir forest. Drive to the Haywood-Jackson County Overlook at milepost 431, just north of the highest point on the Blue Ridge Parkway. The trail begins at the upper end of the parking lot and is paved at its start.

left with a utility pole at its corner. Follow the short path over a fallen log that bridges the creek or wade the water to this picturesque 20-foot waterfall. Its lovely, sandy beach and pretty pool make it a relatively safe and popular swimming area.

Macon County

Big Laurel Falls and Mooney Falls
FR 67

Big Laurel Falls is a small but beautiful waterfall that plunges 30 feet in two stages into a tempting pool deep in the Southern Nantahala Wilderness Area. To get there take U.S. 64 W. out of Franklin for about 12 miles and turn left onto Old U.S. Highway 64. In slightly less than 2 miles, turn right on FR 67, which is only partly paved, and drive for just short of 7 miles to a marked parking area. Take the easy trail (it's less than a half-mile) to the falls, bearing to the right each time the trail forks. Mooney Falls, actually a series of falls, is just more than a half-mile farther up the road on FR 67. Park at the Mooney Falls sign and take the short trail for several different views of the falls. None of the cascades is more than 15 feet high, but the overall effect is exceedingly breathtaking.

Bridal Veil Falls
off U.S. Highway 64

Only a few dozen feet from U.S. 64, 2.5 miles west of Highlands, you can see this 120-foot, ethereal cascade right from your car. U.S. 64 used to run right behind the falls, but there was a problem with ice on the highway in winter, so the highway was moved. You can still use an old piece of the original highway to detour behind the falls. For a more leisurely view or to take a photograph, there's a pull-off just beyond the falls.

Cullasaja Falls
U.S. Highway 64

The 250-foot Cullasaja Falls is one of the more majestic of the many cascades in the Cullasaja River Gorge, so it's unfortunate that U.S. 64 is so busy, narrow, and dangerous at this point 8.8 miles west of Highlands, making more than a drive-by glimpse difficult. To get a good look, find a parking place in one of the narrow, frequently crowded, unmarked pull-offs on the highway's precipitous shoulder, keeping a careful eye on traffic when getting in and out of the car. Then be satisfied with a view and photo from the road. The primitive paths down to the base of the falls are much too dangerous to attempt.

Dry Falls
U.S. Highway 64

Less than a mile from Bridal Veil Falls, Dry Falls drops 80 feet; 40 feet of that distance is free fall. The neat thing about this falls is that an easy, paved path leads down from the parking lot, taking you inside the recessed ledge behind the roaring and sometimes-drenching waters for a view from the other side. There is a $2.00 per vehicle fee.

Glen Falls
SR 1618

There are several beautiful falls and accompanying cascades here that drop 640 feet in only a half-mile. So, though the well-maintained trail to the 70-, 60-, and 15-foot waterfalls in the Glen Falls Scenic Area is less than a mile long, it is steep and tough to hike back up. But it's worth it! In addition there are marvelous views of the Blue Valley as well as great picnic spots along the route. To reach the area take N.C. 106 just south of Highlands for less than 2 miles until you see the Glen Falls Scenic Area sign on the left and take SR 1618 immediately on the right. From there it's a mile to the trail that leads from a parking area.

Upper and Lower Satulah Falls
off N.C. Highway 28

Upper Satulah Falls, which looks like a steep waterslide, is on private property, but you can see it easily from the road. From Highlands drive south on N.C. 28 for 2.3 miles and look to your left at the foot of the vast rock face of 4,543-foot Satulah Mountain. Park at the overlook a short distance farther on the right side of the road. Continue on N.C. 28 for just more than a mile to view the high, narrow Lower Satulah Falls (also known as Clear Creek Falls). It's across the valley from a wide pull-off that also overlooks the Piedmont, including the Blue Valley, Rabun Bald, and Scaly Mountain. This 100-foot, lower waterfall is best seen in the winter when the foliage is off the trees.

Swain County

Juneywhank Falls, Toms Branch Falls,
and Indian Creek Falls
off Deep Creek Road

All three of these popular falls in the Great Smoky Mountains National Park can be found by going out Deep Creek Road just outside Bryson City. However you'll have to jog around several different streets as you pass through town to find this road, so the simplest thing is to go to Bryson City and ask directions to Deep Creek Road. You'll travel 2.2 miles up this road before you enter the actual park. From that boundary it's a little more than a half-mile to the parking area at the end of the road. The quarter-mile trail to 80-foot Juneywhank Falls begins about 100 yards from the picnic area.

To get to another 80-foot-drop cascade, Toms Branch Falls, go past the gate and take the gravel road (part of the

Some of the waterfalls listed here are deep in the area's forests, so be sure to take food and drink along with you and always wear comfortable shoes with nonskid soles. Packing a towel, a bathing suit, and a change of clothing also isn't a bad idea, but be warned: The water in any mountain pool will be chilly, to say the least. Make sure, too, that the pool you choose to swim in is absolutely safe. Currents near waterfalls can be treacherous. And as we've noted numerous times, never, ever wade above a waterfall, where a slip can be fatal.

park's popular Deep Creek Trail) a quarter-mile to the falls on the right. A half-mile upstream is the well-used tubing launch site, so expect to see hordes of tubers floating by in the summer. Actually you can see the falls much better in the winter when the surrounding trees and bushes have lost their foliage.

Continuing on the Deep Creek Trail for less than a mile will bring you to Indian Creek Trail. The wide 25-foot waterfall known as Indian Creek Falls is just a few hundred yards down this path, where a side trail will take you to the base of the falls.

Mingo Falls
off Big Cove Road

Mingo, on the Cherokee Indian Reservation, is one of the most fabulous falls in the whole Smoky Mountains area, though the landscape around it has been somewhat marred in the past few years by storm damage. To reach it take U.S. 441 out of Cherokee, where it becomes Newfound Gap Road once it enters the Great Smoky Mountains National Park. Just short of a mile after the junction with the Blue Ridge Parkway, turn right at the Jobs Corps Center sign. The road will end after a half-mile at Big Cove Road. Turn left and drive 3.3 miles to the Mingo Cove Campground and park. The trail is only a quarter-mile long, but the first part of it is very steep.

BLUE RIDGE PARKWAY

It was fewer than 70 years ago that the first mules and workmen began carving a ribbon of road that would span from Virginia, through North Carolina, and complete its journey in the Great Smoky Mountains in Tennessee. The Blue Ridge Parkway is such a natural part of the landscape that it seems to have always wound through these mountaintops. This scenic highway was born in the 1930s out of a need to provide work for people forced from their jobs by the Great Depression. The parkway was conceived as a link between the Shenandoah National Park in Virginia and the Great Smoky Mountains National Park in North Carolina and Tennessee. After the political wranglings ended and financing was ironed out, the project employed thousands of workers and engineers. The inspiration of a particularly gifted young landscape architect, Stanley Abbott, and northern Italian stonemasons contributed to the parkway's beauty and grace.

The designers' goals were as lofty as the parkway itself: to create for the traveler a sense of connection to the land and its history and to inspire future generations to preserve this connection. They succeeded. As you travel along the 250 miles of the parkway in North Carolina, you pass sights that fill your soul and summon you to be part of this beautiful place. Scores of overlooks, designed for their grand vistas, invite you to pull over and stop. More often than not, a hiking trail will tempt you up the hill where wildflowers with colorful names such as pink lady's slipper, skunk cabbage, and joe-pye weed grow in abundance from April through October. Several endangered species live on parkway lands, including wildflowers such as Gray's lily, Heller's blazing star, and small-whorled Pogonia,

and animal species such as bog turtles, flying squirrels, salamanders, and bats. More than 100 bird species can be seen during the spring migration season. Picnic tables scattered along the parkway make the slightest stopover a special occasion. Visitor centers and roadside historical markers bring to life the story of the mountains and regions, their people, and natural beauty.

When the parkway flows into North Carolina from Virginia at milepost 216.9, you find yourself in the rolling pasture land of Alleghany and Ashe Counties. Those cows grazing in the northern meadows, the pioneer cabins just off the road, and the lichen-covered split-rail fences are part of the parkway by design. These farms in the northern stretches of the parkway were welcomed, their owners encouraged to stay and work in harmony with the National Park Service to preserve the look of a simpler time. It's as if you turned down a country road with no particular destination in mind and found yourself in a tranquil yesteryear.

As you get closer to Watauga, Avery, and Mitchell Counties, the mountains grow taller, the mountaintops stretch higher, and the horizon spreads farther. (Elevations on the parkway range from 649 to 6,047 feet.) The section of the parkway known as the Linn Cove Viaduct, near Grandfather Mountain at milepost 304, is the newest link and an engineering marvel. This section swings 1,243 feet around the curve of the rugged mountain. Borrowing construction techniques developed in Switzerland, the viaduct was designed and built "from the top down" to create the least impact on delicate Grandfather Mountain. The structure was built of 153 precast concrete sections, no two exactly alike, and was completed in the 1980s.

Milepost 355.4 marks the entrance to Mount Mitchell State Park, where the highest peak in the eastern United States rises up to 6,684 feet. The mountainside becomes more rugged, the terrain more imposing, and views even more panoramic. Misty blue mountains in the distance cradle the small towns in the valleys below. In recent years the mountains and valleys have been victims of traveling pollution blown in on the transcontinental jet stream. The result is reduced long-distance visibility. The vistas are still remarkable, although compared with less-polluted times, the difference is sadly evident.

The parkway changes again as it approaches Asheville and Buncombe County from the north. Many overlooks provide the opportunity to scan the communities down below. Asheville, the largest metropolitan area in the mountains, is a thriving small city with a unique mix of cosmopolitan and mountain flavors. Crossing over the French Broad River at milepost 393.6, look to the left for a glimpse of the Biltmore House in the distance, rising out of the trees and looking like a fairy tale castle.

Just prior to reaching this milepost note the signs to the North Carolina Arboretum. It is a "must" stop.

Heading south, panoramas widen into vistas that surely must extend to the edge of the world. Many of the parkway's 27 tunnels are in this section. Above Pisgah National Forest near Transylvania County stands the prominent peak of Mount Pisgah, milepost 408.6, at an elevation of 5,721 feet, taking its name from the Biblical mountain from which Moses first viewed the Promised Land.

Past Pisgah the road winds around more incredible peaks and spectacular sights, such as Looking Glass Rock, elevation 4,493 feet. This massive sculpted mountain of rock sits majestically in the valley near the Pink Beds (pink with flowers in May) of Pisgah National Forest below. As the parkway leads south, the names of the land take on a wilder, more mythical flavor: Graveyard Fields, Devil's

Courthouse, Shining Rock, Big Witch. Many were derived from Indian legend and pioneer folklore. The road climbs to its highest point at Richland Balsam, elevation 6,047 feet, milepost 431, before beginning its descent to the terminus at milepost 469.1, near the entrance to the reservation of the Eastern Band of the Cherokee Nation and the gateway to Great Smoky Mountains National Park.

There are so many places to stop, by whim or design, it's no wonder that the parkway, with 25 million visitors annually, is the most visited of all the 367 territories in the National Park System. Visitor centers are equipped with amenities to make your trip easier, and you'll find accommodations, rustic inns, and restaurants off many parkway exits. Most are within easy driving distance from the parkway. (Two outstanding choices right on the parkway are Bluffs Lodge, 910-372-4499, at milepost 241, and the Pisgah Inn, 910-235-8228, at milepost 408.6. Both are highlighted in our Other Accommodations chapter. Just across the parkway from Bluffs Lodge is the Bluffs Lodge Coffee Shop (910-372-4744), where you can sip coffee and soak in the incredibly breathtaking vistas. (See our Restaurants chapter for more eateries in the area.)

Plan on taking some extra time if you're traveling the parkway—this is far removed from interstate driving. The speed limit on the parkway is always 45 mph, though between the sharp mountain twists and turns and the plodding recreational vehicles, you'll often find yourself driving much slower than that. Just relax

If you love the Parkway and would like to spend more time there than just a drive, consider volunteering with the Friends of the Blue Ridge Parkway's Volunteer in Parks Program (see www.blueridgefriends.com). You may find yourself clearing one of the beautiful trails or doing other beautifying, healthy work in your spare time.

and enjoy the scenery of one of the most beautiful drives in the country. As a courtesy of the road use the pull-off areas along the drive so that you can enjoy driving at your own pace without holding up others. You'll be glad you did.

FRIENDS OF THE BLUE RIDGE PARKWAY

For over 60 years the Blue Ridge Parkway has propelled countless thousands to inspirational heights. But in recent years the federal government has drastically reduced crucial financial support for this national treasure. Now maintaining the parkway in all its irreplaceable splendor has become an important challenge. Taking up the gauntlet is a vigorous group, the Friends of the Blue Ridge Parkway, a nonprofit organization started in 1989. The grassroots support that characterizes the Friends has helped the organization flourish. The group's mission is to preserve and protect this national treasure through a series of initiatives focusing on the historical heritage of the parkway and the region and by developing a wider environmental awareness and public education on the issues. The organization works to preserve historic sites and structures along the parkway and lobbies Congress for the protection of scenic vistas and natural habitats.

The Friends of the Blue Ridge Parkway has varying levels of membership and financial support. You can become a "Friend" for a contribution as small as $15 or as high as your pocketbook will allow. Corporate and group donations are welcome. Children can join Grover Groundhog's Nature, which offers special learning and fun events. All members receive the newsletter *High Vistas* and a subscription to *Parkway Milepost,* the official Blue Ridge Parkway news magazine. Programs and conferences are scheduled throughout the year. Memberships of $50 or more receive special benefits. Financial gifts to the Friends of the Blue Ridge Parkway are tax deductible. Your time as a volunteer is also appreciated. Headquarters for this organization have recently moved to Roanoke, Virginia. You can call them at (540) 776–PARK or write to P.O. Box 20986, Roanoke, VA 24018. In North Carolina contact the satellite office by calling (828) 687–8722 or (800) 228–7275, accessing www.blueridgefriends.org, or writing Friends of the Blue Ridge Parkway, 2301 Hendersonville Road, Arden, NC 28776.

STOPS ALONG THE WAY

In the pages that follow, we've described some of our favorite stops along the Blue Ridge Parkway in North Carolina, beginning at the state line at milepost 216.9 in Alleghany County and traveling south to the parkway's southern terminus at milepost 469.1 at the Oconoluftee Visitors Center. Mileposts are markers that stretch the length of the parkway, each posted a mile apart. Overlooks and other sites of merit are also noted by milepost numbers. This list is by no means exhaustive—there are literally hundreds of overlooks and other stops along the parkway, and all have merit. But these are some of our favorites.

Cumberland Knob
Mile 217.5
Cumberland Knob, elevation 2,885 feet, was the first recreational area completed on the Blue Ridge Parkway back in 1937. The Civilian Conservation Corps, a government-authorized jobs program during the Great Depression, built the structures at this site and many like it along the parkway and in surrounding areas. On the 1,000 acres at Cumberland Knob, you can picnic, hike, listen to lectures by rangers, or simply marvel at the view. A pleasant 20-minute loop trail starts at the visitors center and passes by Cumberland Knob. For the hardier hiker try the two-hour loop trail from the center of the knob into Gulley Creek Gorge. Drinking water, rest rooms, a book shop, and a public telephone are also available.

Jackson County: Wet Camp Gap

This 3-mile, round-trip hike to a lovely mile-high meadow with superb views of the Pisgah National Forest is not difficult. For part of the walk, you will be on sections of the Mountains-to-the-Sea Trail. Be sure to take a sharp left at the trail junction about 15 minutes from the start of your walk. To reach the trail drive to the Bear Pen Gap parking overlook at milepost 427.6 on the Blue Ridge Parkway in Jackson County. The trail begins at the lower end of the parking lot.

Little Glade Mill Pond
Mile 230.1
This scenic stop overlooks a delightful pond near an old turbine-type mill. The water is smooth as glass, and a picnic area makes this a restful stop.

Air Bellows Gap
Mile 237.1
Air Bellows Gap, elevation 3,729 feet, is designated as the Crest of the Blue Ridge. The spectacular vista includes a 180-degree view into the valley below, which is chock-full of Christmas trees. The rich green of the tree farms stands out in a patchwork of patterns. Hawks soar on the updrafts of this windy gap, and rich autumn colors turn this into a leaf looker's paradise!

Doughton Park
Miles 234.8 to 238.6
This 6,000-acre park has picnic areas (milepost 241), a campground (milepost 239), trailer sites, comfort stations, and drinking water. The park has 30 miles of trails over bluegrass bluffs (see our Autumn in the Mountains Close-up).

Brinegar Cabin
Mile 238.5
The Brinegar Cabin, an authentic mountain homestead covered in hand-hewn shake shingles, stands as testament to the harsh, isolated, self-sufficient life of mountaineers that lasted even into the 20th century. This tiny cabin was home to Martin (1856–1925) and Caroline (1863–1943) Brinegar. The toll that mountain life takes can be seen in a simple photo portrait of Caroline at her mother's loom inside the cabin. The springhouse is still down a steep rocky path, and the garden patch that once yielded the necessities of life is now overgrown and barely discernible. The couple is buried nearby. (Admission to the cabin is free.)

The Cedar Ridge Trail (4.3 miles) and the Bluff Mountain Trail (7.5 miles) take off from points that begin at the end of the parking area.

Wildcat Rocks
Mile 241.1
This is the Caudill family homestead, where visitors can get a glimpse into the rugged mountain life.

Northwest Trading Post
Mile 259
(336) 982-2543
Near Glendale Springs, this delightfully rustic craft shop of knotty pine with a genuine rock fireplace sells all kinds of items made by North Carolina residents in 11 neighboring counties. Home-baked goodies, handmade baskets, bowls, old-time wooden toys, quilts, and jewelry

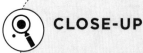

Autumn in the Mountains

Sometimes gradually, sometimes overnight the verdant peaks and valleys do a slow burlesque, teasing with a hint of color here, a little more there, each stage more exciting until the grandest week of all when the mix of red and gold, green and yellow present their breathtaking finale.* Somehow Mother Nature can wear colors you'd never put together—chartreuse and red, orange and green—and still look stunning. And even when the inevitable happens and the autumn color leaves us, usually no later than mid-November, something special is left behind. Like colorful wrapping paper torn away, the fallen foliage exposes a precious gift—the mountains themselves. Breathtaking vistas, obscured much of the year by the lush vegetation that flourishes in our diverse ecosystem, are revealed until spring works its way north again.

The kaleidoscope of colored trees is more than a treat to the eye. It gives those of us who have forgotten our high school botany a break. We can easily identify hickories and poplars glowing their bright yellow against a Carolina-blue sky, or mountain favorites such as dogwood, sourwood, blackgum, and maple turning deep red, sassafras a vivid orange. The various oaks turn russet and maroon, while some trees can't decide which color to turn, offering a rainbow mix on the same tree.

It seems no one wants to stay indoors this time of year. In celebration of the fine weather and natural beauty, festivals and craft fairs abound. Harvest dances, apple cider pressings, mountain music and dances, special tours, steam-driven trains forging through the red and gold are scheduled throughout the season.

A special breed of wildflowers bloom late in the year. Joe-pye weed nods its foot-wide head high above the rest. Purple-blooming blazing star and ironweed, golden sneezeweed, and lilac aster bloom throughout the fall.

As you travel down the highways and byways, you'll pass fanciful Mr. and Mrs. Scarecrows, dressed in flannel shirts and jeans, hay for their body and jack-o'-lanterns for their heads. They sit in welcome at roadside stands selling pumpkins, gourds, honey, sorghum, and cider. Take home colorful gourds and doll-size Indian corn for Thanksgiving table decorations. Many stands sell jams and relishes, dried apples and apple butter, pumpkin bread, and pies in anticipation of the coming holidays.

Every year thousands upon thousands of nature's admirers return to North Carolina's mountains to drink in the beauty. Touring the Blue Ridge Parkway is the most favored way of taking in this long sweep of fall color. From Boone and Blowing Rock to Asheville and Cherokee, each turn of the road offers a new horizon, a new definition of beautiful. The ever-popular Mount Mitchell State Park area, just off the Blue Ridge Parkway, as well as the communities of Spruce Pine, Linville Falls, and Little Switzerland, and the North Carolina Minerals Museum, are other popular leaf-looking sites along the parkway.

The fall foliage season generally reaches its peak in mid-October, but the degrees and intensity of color and peak for each area are determined by elevation. At 6,684 feet, Mount Mitchell, the highest peak in the eastern United States, enjoys the distinction of having the early jump on fall leaf color. The peaks of the High Country of the Boone area are next, about mid-October. And the Asheville area and southern stretches near Cherokee along the parkway peak around the third and fourth weeks in October. But if you choose the Blue Ridge Parkway as your vantage point for viewing fall color, you can pick any time in October. From parkway overlooks high above, you can scan the valleys below to see autumn's transformation at many different elevations.

During that intense tourist trek in October, parkway rangers suggest that you can get maximum enjoyment and avoid the crowds by making your trip here Monday through Friday, when traffic is less heavy. The weekends in October can quickly become a bumper-to-bumper snail's pace of leaf lookers, especially on Sunday afternoons.

If the you find the parkway busier than you prefer during this time of year, get off the beaten track. Take one of the side roads that branch off the parkway. These dirt and gravel roadways, maintained by the U.S. Forest Service, wind down the mountain to the valleys below. One word of caution: Check with the rangers at the visitors centers along the parkway for information on these roads, their end points, and current driving conditions. Four-wheel-drive vehicles will have a better go of it on these twisting mountain roads, but front-wheel drive is adequate. Just make sure your vehicle is in good working order, and you have plenty of gas. There are no tow trucks or gas stations just around the bend back here in the mountain wilderness!

Other alternative routes include the major connecting highways to the parkway or maybe a less-traveled two-laner just outside the major towns and cities. The state of North Carolina published a 90-page guide, *North Carolina Scenic Byways,* featuring 11 mountain roads (31 statewide) that give visitors and residents a chance to experience the diverse beauty and culture of the Tar Heel State. Routes are clearly marked with signs stating NC SCENIC BYWAY surrounded by green-mountain and blue-sea motifs. For more information contact the North Carolina Department of Transportation, P.O. Box 25201, Raleigh, NC 27611; (919) 733-2520.

U.S. Highway 194 is a good example of a scenic byway. This winding back road passes near Valle Crucis on its way to Boone, then on to picturesque hilltop ridges near Todd in rural Ashe County. Another gorgeous option is U.S. 321 from Boone to the rocky hills of west Watauga County and the charming country cross-road communities of Sugar Grove and Vilas on the way to the Tennessee state line. Schulls Mill Road off N.C. 105 at Foscoe, outside Boone, is a locally used short-cut to Blowing Rock along a beautiful but very winding two-lane road. Cruising along U.S. 221 from Boone through Linville and the Christmas tree country of Linville Falls before heading down the mountain to the beautiful fields of the North Cove Valley area near Marion is a lovely way to spend an October afternoon.

Farther south take the Barnardsville exit off U.S. 19/23 N. in Asheville for another quiet backroad lined with rural farms and old homesteads, or you could take N.C. 151 up to the parkway from the pleasant little farm community of Hominy Valley, west of Asheville. U.S. 276 from the parkway down to Brevard is a very popular road in leaf season. It winds down past tumbling creeks and waterways, waterfalls and picnic areas, and the well-known Cradle of Forestry area. The scenic winding roads around Highlands and Cashiers have always been noted for their breathtaking fall beauty. And the exquisite forests and country roads around Fontana Lake and Robbinsville are just being discovered by visitors to the North Carolina mountains.

A good many of those 1.5 million visitors to the Blue Ridge Parkway area during leaf season often decide to stay for a night or an extended family vacation. You can understand why local officials and innkeepers suggest booking your visit in advance for maximum satisfaction. Some veteran leaf lookers book as much as a year in advance for their favorite bed-and-breakfast inns or family hotels. If you're a spontaneous traveler and miss out on those hoped-for accommodations, check with local chambers of commerce for possible alternative accommodations that spring up during this busy tourism month. (The numbers for local chambers are listed in our Area Overviews chapter.)

Whether you travel the Blue Ridge Parkway or the road less traveled, remember to guard and respect the fragile beauty of nature so that it remains a sight of miracle and majesty for generations to come.

*The scientific explanation of leaf changes: The intensity of the color season is determined by a number of weather variables that change from year to year. It is generally accepted, however, that more vivid leaf color is preceded by a weather year marked by long dry spells in summer and cool, moist days in fall. When this happens, and the sunlight diminishes, the trees are "tricked" into quicker cessation of the process of photosynthesis. No sugar is produced to keep the lush green of the chlorophyll, so the underlying pigments emerge.

made from antique buttons are just some of the wares offered by this nonprofit group that donates all profits to local charities. The trading post is open from April 15 to October 31, 9:00 A.M. to 5:30 P.M. Rest rooms (wheelchair accessible) are also available.

Boone's Trace
Mile 285.1

Daniel Boone passed by this site on his trek westward. An information marker provides details about his blaze to the West.

Moses H. Cone Memorial and Visitors Center
Mile 293
(828) 295-3782

Near the town of Blowing Rock, this former 3,600-acre estate of textile giant Moses Cone was donated to the National Park Service in the 1950s. Today the rambling white manor house is home to a craft shop that displays the work of the Southern Highland Handicraft Guild. The mansion faces a picturesque lake, and the grounds are threaded with miles

of hiking trails and include two trout ponds (check at the center for fishing information).

Julian Price Memorial Park
Mile 295
(828) 963-5911

This popular park of 4,344 acres includes a lake, campground, hiking trails, picnic area, and limited boating. There's an easy 2.5-mile loop trail around the lakeside.

Linn Cove Viaduct
Mile 304

Built around environmentally fragile Grandfather Mountain, this incredible bridge is a marvel of engineering and gives you the sense of flying over the valley below—breathtaking! There's a visitor center and trails underneath the viaduct. Walking is not allowed on the bridge.

Linville Falls and Gorge
Mile 316.5

An easy-to-moderate lower trail leads to the falls. A spectacular example of nature's power, these waterfalls were carved from massive quartzite rock millions of years ago. An upper trail with a steeper incline gives you quite a different view (see our Waterfalls chapter).

Chestoa View
Mile 320.7

Chestoa is derived from the Cherokee word for rabbit. From this spot you can enjoy a scenic view of granite-faced Table Rock.

Museum of North Carolina Minerals
Mile 331
(828) 765-9483

Informative geology exhibits, rock and mineral displays, parkway information, a book shop, gifts, and rest rooms make the museum a pleasant diversion for children and rock hounds of all ages (see our chapter on Rockhounding).

Crabtree Meadows Coffee Shop
Mile 339.5
(828) 675-4236

You can get a good lunch here, as well as parkway guidebooks, maps, and the *Asheville Citizen-Times* newspaper. Facilities also include rest rooms, a service station, and a craft shop near Little Switzerland, a community on the edge of the mountain, that are open May 1 through November 1. The coffee shop is open from 10:00 A.M. to 6:00 P.M.; the craft shop until 7:30 P.M.

Crabtree Meadows Recreation Center
Miles 339.5 to 340.3 (ranger kiosk)
(828) 675-5444

This 250-acre site includes a picnic area, numerous hiking trails, and a campground. Primitive camping is available for tent and RV campers for approximately $10.00 per night for two adults; add about $2.00 for each additional adult. Children 18 and younger stay free. Comfort stations are also located here. The 40-minute trek to Crabtree Falls rewards you with a beautiful 125-foot waterfalls (see our Waterfalls chapter). Look for wildflowers in spring.

Although the Blue Ridge Parkway was designed for motor travel, bicyclists can enjoy the drive as well. Have reflectors and wear high visibility clothing and helmets, and avoid the Parkway during fog and periods of low visibility. Also, bring plenty of water and energy bars for those stringent uphill climbs.

Mount Mitchell State Park
Mile 355.4
(828) 675-4611

Take N.C. 128 to the summit of Mount Mitchell, the highest peak in the eastern United States. Hiking trails, a memorial to Elisha Mitchell (for whom the peak is named), a small natural history museum, comfort stations, a snack shop, and a picnic area make this a pleasant stop. In June 2001 a new museum opened at Mitchell State Park. This is an amazing facility that is user-friendly. A life-size wood carving of Big Tom Wilson, the mountaineer whose legend is connected with the mountain, stands on his front porch—a facade within the museum—and greets the visitor with a touch of a button. His great-great-great grandson, David Boone, world-class carver, was commissioned for this sculpture. Pictorials and stuffed animals of the mountains are showcased. The highest peaks in the Appalachia chain are rendered in a stair-step manner for easy comparison. Interactive displays permit the viewer to cause a miniature movement of the earth to form a mountain. The entire museum is of interest to children and adults.

Unfortunately you can see the dramatic evidence of acid rain on Mitchell's slopes from several vantage points. On a brighter note keep your eyes peeled for the deer that dart through these woods. Bring a jacket because the weather is windy and cool up here, even in summer.

The massive stone-and-frame restaurant in the park is about two-thirds of the way up N.C. 128 leading to the summit, which makes it the highest restaurant in the eastern United States. Open from May 1 through October 31, the restaurant serves lunch and dinner daily and breakfast on weekends and holidays. It closes one hour prior to park closing, which varies seasonally. Call (828) 675-9545 for more information on the restaurant.

Craggy Gardens Visitors Center
Mile 364.4
This popular stop offers nature exhibits, comfort stations, and parkway and national forest information. The center is open from May through October. At the rear of the visitor center, a narrative directs your view to the village of Dilling-

ham, which is at the foot of Craggy. It states that the flora from that village at 2,000 feet, up to the mountain top of Craggy, contains all the varieties found from Georgia to Maine. (See our Autumn in the Mountains Close-up.)

Bull Creek Valley Overlook
Mile 373.8
This scenic stop-off point overlooks what was once the home of the great bull buffalo.

Folk Art Center
Mile 382
(828) 298-7928
Home of the renowned Southern Highland Handicraft Guild, this 30,000-square-foot contemporary structure of rock, timber, and glass is an attractive complement to the natural woodland surroundings.

Visit Allanstand Craft Shop, America's oldest craft shop, on the main level for exquisitely crafted handblown glassware, functional pottery, handmade toys, handcrafted jewelry, and handwoven coverlets and rugs. The Blue Ridge Parkway also maintains a bookstore and staffs an information center here. Up the sweeping ramp, the second-floor gallery houses the guild's permanent collection as well as changing exhibits by some of its 700-plus members. A library of handcraft and its history is also on the upper level. Craft demonstrations, interpretive talks, and special events keep the Folk Art Center a vital and continuously interesting place for area visitors.

The center is open daily 9:00 A.M. to 6:00 P.M. April through December and 9:00 A.M. to 5:00 P.M. January through March. It's closed for Thanksgiving, Christmas, and New Year's Day. The bustling city of Asheville is just off the next exit (see our Mountain Crafts, Attractions, and Annual Festivals and Events chapters).

French Broad River Overlook
Mile 393.8
One of the few north-flowing rivers in the United States, the French Broad River figures prominently in the history and development of the Asheville/Buncombe

County area and all of Western North Carolina. This overlook at milepost 393.8 is an especially good place to get a view of the river. It is from here that you can exit just a few feet to the North Carolina Arboretum. More than a thousand world-class botanists gathered here for their first international conference in the year 2000.

Hominy Valley Overlook
Mile 404.2
This pull-off from the parkway is a scenic view of the pastoral mountain valley farm community west of Asheville.

Mount Pisgah
Mile 407.4
At 5,721 feet Mount Pisgah is visible for miles around, holding court over the vast land once owned by George Vanderbilt that is now part of Pisgah National Forest. The summit can be reached by a moderate-to-strenuous winding trail from the parking area below. The junction of U.S. 276 and the Blue Ridge Parkway is just south of Mount Pisgah. Traveling down this winding and scenic road to Brevard in Transylvania County, you'll pass the Cradle of Forestry, the site of the first forestry school in America, once a part of the Biltmore Estate. Following U.S. 276 toward Waynesville, you'll come to Cold Mountain, the site and title of Charles Frazier's award-winning book. The parking area just past this road intersection is Wagon Road Gap. It is here that the monarch butterfly passes in September as they migrate to South America. They return in the spring. (See the Close-up Finding Cold Mountain.)

Looking Glass Rock
Mile 417
This spectacularly sculpted monolith in the valley below is one of the largest masses of granite in the eastern United States. Its name comes from the shimmering effects of sunlight on its surface when wet. Elevation is 4,493 feet. Though you can't get to Looking Glass from this stop, the view is fantastic. (A trail that leads to the top is off the road to the Pisgah Fish Hatchery, off U.S. 276, just past Looking Glass Rock.)

Graveyard Fields
Mile 418.8
These flats were once overgrown with mounds of moss that inspired the name Graveyard Fields, but a fire destroyed the moss mounds in 1925. (See our Autumn in the Mountains Close-up.)

In summer views from the parkway can be obscured by haze—partly natural and partly pollution. At those times it's often best to visit the parkway in the morning, before the day heats up and when the air is cleaner. This time of day provides the added beauty of ground fog curling up out of the valleys.

Devil's Courthouse
Mile 422.4
The top of this rocky, rugged cliff can be reached by a steeply ascending, well-worn trail from a parking area below. Legend has it there is a cave inside the mountain where the devil still holds court. Due to the nesting of the peregrine falcon, the rock face is closed to climbers.

Haywood/Jackson Overlook
Mile 431.0
This self-guided loop trail climbs with moderate difficulty 1.5 miles to the summit of Richland Balsam.

Waterrock Knob
Mile 451
Adjoining this parking area is a short trail that leads to an incredible four-state view (North Carolina, Tennessee, South Carolina, and Georgia) with a panorama of the Great Smoky Mountains just ahead. Information and a comfort station are available here.

Plott's Balsam Range Overlook
Mile 457.9
Yet another beautiful overlook, here you'll see the mountain range that's named for

CLOSE-UP

Finding Cold Mountain

Ever since Charles Frazier's *Cold Mountain,* a novel about a Civil War soldier's walk home to his beloved Ada, became a best-seller, people have been wanting to know how to find this 6,030-foot peak, located in Haywood County. There is a trail to the top, but only very experienced hikers should take it. It's steep, poorly marked, and according to how you go, 14 to 16 miles round-trip.

Those not so footworthy can take U.S. 276 from the Blue Ridge Parkway toward Waynesville. This roughly follows along

Wagon Road Gap along the east side of the mountain. Near Cruso turn onto U.S. Highway 215, which will run along the western side of the peak. This 50-mile circle will take you past many of the coves, creeks, and churches mentioned in the book and bring you back to the Blue Ridge Parkway not very far south of where you left it.

If you haven't time for this wonderful tour, just stop at the parkway's milepost 420. The massive peak in the distance is Cold Mountain.

the German immigrant who settled here in the early 1800s. The Plott Hound, a legendary dog used for bear hunting, and the state dog of North Carolina, was brought from Hannover, Germany, by these settlers.

Big Witch Overlook
Mile 461.6
The interesting name honors one of the last of the great Cherokee medicine men. An exhibit tells of the early Cherokee eagle killers.

Oconoluftee Visitors Center
Mile 469.1
(828) 497–1900
This milepost marks the terminus of the Blue Ridge Parkway, or its starting point, if you are traveling north. The popular visitor center, a half-mile north on U.S. 441, hosts several events during summer, including Women's Day and the Mountain Life Festival, which celebrate the heritage of these mountains (see our Annual Festivals and Events chapter). Park information and rest rooms are available. The center is open

daily year-round (except major holidays). Hours vary with the season.

Do be sure to visit Mountain Farm Museum, an open-air museum featuring historic farm buildings brought here from the surrounding area. The old cabin belonged to the John Davis family and was built in 1901. It is a good place for children to see how things used to be. Watch out for the chickens, ducks, and other farm animals strutting around the barns filled with antique farm implements. It feels as though the Davises have just gone down the road for a bit and asked you to set a spell and make yourself at home 'til they return.

Just ahead lies the Cherokee Indian Reservation and the Great Smoky Mountains National Park. For park information call (423) 436–1200.

CAMPING

Camping is allowed along the Blue Ridge Parkway from May 1 through October 31.

Designated camping sites require a daily fee of approximately $10.00 (subject to change) for adults, $5.00 for Golden Age Passport holders, free for youths younger than 18. Golden Age Passports (62 or older) and Golden Access Passports (visually handicapped or permanently disabled) can be obtained at any visitor center or campground along the parkway. Each of these campgrounds has only primitive facilities, including a fireplace and table. Other amenities may include access to public telephones, water, picnic sites, gasoline, camping supplies, and sanitary dumping stations. There are no electrical hookups. If you are a hardy soul, you can camp in winter, weather permitting. One of the campgrounds is open year-round, at the park's discretion. (The open campground rotates from year to year, so call to find out which one will be open this year.) No fee is required in the winter, but facilities are limited, so you'll need to call in advance. For general parkway and campground information, call (828) 298-0398.

Campground regulations are posted at campsites; additional copies are available at parkway visitors centers. In case of emergencies, call (800) PARKWATCH.

(See our Recreation chapter for additional campground listings.)

CAMPGROUNDS

None of the campgrounds along the Blue Ridge take reservations. All are filled on a first-come, first-served basis. Again, the cost is approximately $10.00 per adult, $5.00 for Golden Age Passport holders, youths younger than 18 free.

Doughton Park
Mile 239.0
One hundred and ten tent sites, including tent pads, picnic tables, grills, and lantern posts, are scattered in wooded areas and around a grassy hillside. A smaller area with 25 RV sites lies across the road, though none of the sites have hookups.

The Weather Channel (www.weather.com) provides an extensive "Fall Foliage Forecast," helpful in planning your trip on the Parkway.

Rest rooms and water spigots are available at this park but no showers. This is camping as it was meant to be! The park itself covers approximately 6,000 acres in Alleghany and Wilkes Counties, and is the largest park on the parkway. It was named after Robert Lee Doughton, a U.S. representative who served from 1911 to 1953 and who was an advocate for the construction of the parkway.

Julian Price
Mile 297.0
(828) 963-5911
This campground sprawls across both sides of the parkway near Price Lake. One hundred and twenty-nine tent sites lie fairly close together, divided by blossoming rhododendron bushes. Sixty-eight RV sites are also available, though with no plug-ins. Tent-pads, picnic tables, grills, and spigots provide adequate comforts. There are rest rooms but no showers, and firewood may be purchased nearby. The park is marked by mild terrain, covered by a dense hardwood forest. Poplars, chestnut trees, and maples make a pleasant canopy for hikers and campers. Canoes may be rented at the lake, and hiking trails nearby lead to two smaller lakes and creeks.

Linville Falls
Mile 316.3
(828) 765-7818
Fifty-five tent sites and 20 RV sites are available in the campground of this 440-acre wooded park. Tent site 15 is the most secluded. The surrounding forest seems almost primordial with moss-covered trees and waterfalls plunging through the granite walls of Linville Gorge. Fishing in the nearby Linville River is allowed, and a

visitor center and bookstore provide campers with plenty of area information.

Crabtree Meadows
Mile 339.5
(828) 675-5444

The 71 tent sites and 22 RV sites of Crabtree Meadows lie close to large grassy clearings. The lawn of wildflowers runs up to the forest edge, with mountains visible in the distance. The campground is rarely full and offers the requisite picnic tables, grills, and tent pads but no showers. Water fountains and hand water pumps are centrally located. It is a quiet, peaceful area, awash with rhododendrons and hardwood trees. This is a good base camp for hiking in the Pisgah National Forest; trails lead to scenic falls on Crabtree Creek. Crabtree Falls Trail, a strenuous 2.5-mile loop, begins near the campground entrance. A camp store, gas station, and restaurant/gift shop are also nearby.

Mount Pisgah
Mile 408.6
(828) 235-9109

The entrance to Mount Pisgah Campground with its 70 tent sites and 70 RV sites lies directly across from Pisgah Inn on the parkway. The small sites, close together, are arranged in three landscaped loops. A dense forest adds privacy. There are no showers, but central hand water pumps and individual picnic tables, grills, and lantern posts are provided. Maps of the area, including hiking trails, are avail-

able at the camp. A picnic area lies in a meadow bordered by rhododendron.

HIKING

Towering trees, awe-inspiring vistas, gurgling mountain streams, colorful birds on the wing, flaming and delicate wildflowers, and the comfort of a well-trod path mark hiking trails on the parkway. This is all free for the taking when you leave the car behind and take advantage of the thousands of miles of trails winding in and around the parkway. Hiking is an easy, inexpensive way to enjoy the outdoors: You don't need much gear, and the rewards are priceless. Just follow basic hiking rules to keep it safe and fun (see our chapter on Outdoor Safety; for additional hiking possibilities see our Recreation chapter).

Northern Mountains

CUMBERLAND KNOB

The relatively easy trails of Cumberland Knob (mi. 217.5) allow you to walk where the Blue Ridge Parkway began back in 1935. Cumberland Knob Trail, an easy, paved 0.5-mile walk, starts at the visitor center, swings through a picnic area, and continues up to the Cumberland Knob overlook shelter. This is a good leg-stretching trail, especially if you've been riding the parkway for a while without a stop. It's a good one for kids, too. Gully Creek Trail here is a more strenuous two-hour hike along a mountain stream. Bring your wildflower field guides—these mountain springs give life to some amazing plants.

TANAWA TRAIL

This 13.5-mile course, which runs more or less parallel to the Blue Ridge Parkway and Grandfather Mountain from Beacon Heights (mi. 305.5) to Julian Price Park (mi. 297.1), deserves special mention. The trail offers a great deal of variety and plenty of access points along the parkway as it winds along the ridge. One particularly popular section, noted for its breathtaking views, is the access just below the Linn Cove Viaduct (mi. 304.4). The Linn Cove information station and access spot are south of the viaduct. The trail passes directly under this bridgelike span and rises steeply up stone steps, then past a massive wall of rock. Next the trail levels and leads into a shady stand of birch and beech trees, then traverses Wilson Creek to a clearing scattered with so many flat rocks that the trail seems more like a flagstone path. The sharp rise to Rough Ridge is followed by the surprise of a 200-foot-long boardwalk. From this point the view of the Piedmont below, which encompasses Linn Cove Viaduct, Table Mountain, and Hawks Bill, is breathtaking.

CRAGGY DOME TRAIL

The parking area just through the tunnel to the north of the visitor center (mi. 364.4) is the beginning of the trail leading to Craggy Dome. This well-marked path winds through beautiful rhododendron thickets and ascends to the breathtaking summit of Craggy Dome, a 360-degree sight to behold. The trail isn't strenuous,

but it does have a continuously rising grade, so allow yourself plenty of time. Besides, seeing the unique wildflowers, velvety mosses, and gnarled, lichen-covered trunks of the rhododendron is worth the extra time. Look for the color-less white stalks of the Indian pipes under cover of the rhododendron.

Central and Southern Mountains

GRAVEYARD FIELDS

Take the hiking trails to Upper and Lower Falls (see our Waterfalls chapter), just off the parking area at milepost 418.8. This is a popular area for backpack camping and blueberry picking (which accounts for some of the many side trails) and includes Shining Rock Wilderness, just over the ridge to the southeast.

PISGAH NATIONAL FOREST

Pisgah National Forest is a hiker's delight with its varying terrain: the steep slopes of Mount Pisgah, granite monoliths such as Looking Glass Rock, and the level flats of the Pink Beds. There are also a number of relatively easy roadside jaunts along U.S. 276 to Brevard from the parkway junction south of Mount Pisgah. This highway cuts a twisting path down the mountain along a creek bed leading to Looking Glass Falls. Many smaller trail spurs shoot off from the overlooks, and parking turnouts are always worth a look for different views and angles of the falls.

Many deli-style shops in our mountain towns will create a splendid picnic basket for taking on the Parkway.

ROCKHOUNDING

We've all heard of fantasy cities with streets paved with gold and the Emerald City of Oz, but what about real highways paved with rubies? That's occasionally the case in Western North Carolina, where, if you look closely enough, you can see ruby-flecked gravel along the roadsides. That should give some idea of the copious amounts of gemstones in many sections of these mountains.

Important gems you might find are beryl (aquamarine, blue, golden, and green); corundum (bronze sapphire, pink, ruby, and sapphire); feldspar (moonstone); garnet (general, almandite, and rhodolite); olivine; opal; quartz (agate, amethyst, chrysoprase, jasper, and others); spinel; tourmaline; turquoise; and zircon. Rock hounds collect at least 37 other minerals, some of which can occasionally be classified as gem quality. In the late 1800s even a few diamonds supposedly turned up, but we know of none that have been found for more than 100 years.

It's rather ironic that in 1540 Hernando de Soto visited the Cherokee village of Nikwasi (now known as Franklin, the county seat of Macon County) in search of gold, never realizing he was passing through an area awash in precious and semiprecious stones. Admittedly most of the gems and semiprecious stones found in the mountains have no great commercial value, but many are attractive enough to be custom set and taken home as special souvenirs of an exciting and rewarding afternoon of sluicing through buckets of rock and dirt.

Of course there are the true tales of turning up a really big one! In 1989 a longtime Cherokee County rock hound found a 10.5-pound (18,000-carat) sapphire 2 feet underground in an undisclosed location that was cut and polished to a grapefruit-size 9,719.5-carat star sapphire worth several million dollars. In 1991 a 1,497-carat sapphire was found by a teenager in a Macon County mine, and in 1992 a Haywood County mine produced a 12.5-pound sapphire. Likewise, rubies of several thousand carats and a number of large emeralds have been found here over the years. Grandiose gems are surely there to be discovered by the lucky or inspired rock hound.

But even if these large and valuable stones are few and far between, it's not uncommon for even the most casual amateur to luck out on a gem worth a few hundred dollars while grubbing in a sluice box of mud and rocks. Gem mining, even when not richly profitable, is good fun, especially for children, whose eyes widen with amazement when they unearth a nice rock. It can be educational, too, as school groups on field trips have discovered.

Gem mining can be wet and messy, so make sure you approach this exciting search in old clothes. Because you'll be standing at the flumes for a considerable length of time, a comfortable pair of shoes is a must. So is sunscreen. Although many mines offer some shade in the form of shelters, tents, or big, beach-type umbrellas, the sun reflecting off the water can give you an unexpected burn. Besides this can be such a fascinating pastime that you may not realize how much time is passing. Certainly, if you find a fine gem in your first load or two of ore, you're likely to come down with rock-hound fever—you'll be hooked.

Some Western North Carolina colleges and universities have regular and continuing education classes that will help you identify and prospect for gems and other minerals. Often these classes include field trips.

You don't necessarily have to go to a commercial gem mine to find precious and semiprecious stones—that is, if you know what to look for. A wide array of land, both public and private, contains igneous, sedimentary, and metamorphic rock types, along with the individual minerals associated with such rocks. On private land, of course, you will have to get the permission of owners for any rockhounding activities. On national forest lands (though not in national parks or wilderness areas), there is no objection, as a rule, to taking a handful of rock, mineral, or petrified wood specimens from the surface of the ground.

There is no fee, special permission, or permit required as long as such collecting doesn't conflict with existing mineral permits, leases, or sales—and even if it does, you can seek the permission of the minerals' owners to do some collecting. These areas can be identified from maps in the ranger district offices. Any collected specimens must also be for personal and noncommercial use, and they cannot be of archaeological value (artifacts, including projectile points, chips, and flakes, may not be collected).

Certain areas are designated as archaeological sites or geologic interest areas, and ground disturbance of any sort is prohibited in these and any unrecorded archaeological sites. You must also be sure that your rockhounding doesn't cause any significant surface disturbance to the land, air, or water. Obviously no explosives or mechanical equipment may be used.

The NFS district ranger offices are the best sources for current rules, maps, and information on local access and road conditions within the forests. (See our Forests and Parks chapter for a listing of these offices and phone numbers.) Although they don't normally keep information concerning minerals or collecting localities, they may have some knowledge about these subjects. For this information it's best to contact the state's geological survey office (919-571-4000), university geology departments and libraries, mineralogical societies, and rock-hounding and lapidary clubs.

GEM MINES

Although the heaviest concentration of gem mines by far is in the jewel-rich Cowee Valley of Macon County, there are other places scattered throughout the mountains where you can try your luck at finding a jewel or two.

The following list includes several gem-mining operations that are open to the public.

Northern Mountains

MITCHELL COUNTY

Blue Ridge Gemstone Mine & Campground
626 McKinny Mine Road, Little Switzerland, NC
(828) 765-5264
Established in 1984, this family-owned and -operated mine maintains a 320-foot flume line. It is enclosed and heated in the spring and fall, so you can comfortably sift through buckets of dirt any time, May through December. It is open seven days a week. Inspect the rock and gift shop and bring a lunch for the picnic area, overlooking the mountains. Or, if you would like to camp, full hookups, water, and electricity are provided. For a small fee the Blue Ridge Gemstone will cut, grind, and polish the stones you find. You can also have them set into handcrafted jewelry.

To get to the Blue Ridge Mine, exit the parkway at Little Switzerland. Take your first right before the stop sign. Turn right onto Chestnut Grove Church Road. Go under the parkway and continue for 1 mile and then turn left onto McKinney Mine Road. The mine is 2 miles farther, on the left.

Emerald Village
McKinney Mine and Crabtree Creek Roads
Little Switzerland, NC
(828) 765-6463
www.emeraldvillage.com

This mining attraction just 2.5 miles off the Blue Ridge Parkway in Mitchell County not only provides a guaranteed gem find at the Gemstone Mine but also has a mining museum underground in a genuine mine. The unusual antique displays are worth a look. A gift shop is filled with lapidary supplies and souvenirs, and attendants in the shop will answer your gemstone questions. Emerald Village is open from 9:00 A.M. to 5:00 P.M. April to Memorial Day, Memorial Day to Labor Day 9:00 A.M. to 6:00 P.M. The cost of ore buckets ranges from $4.00 to $500.00, depending on the size.

Gem Mountain
137 N.C. Highway 226 S., Spruce Pine, NC
(828) 765-6130
www.gemmountain.com
Open seven days a week from 9:00 A.M. to 5:00 P.M. March through December, and 9:00 A.M. to 7:00 P.M. June through August, this gemstone mine maintains modern gem-washing facilities and covered flumes. A picnic area by a nearby stream completes the outdoor hounding experience, or you can rest easy and dine in the Gem Mountain restaurant. There are ice-cream cones for the kids, and a gift and jewelry shop—fun for the adults in the group. Gem Mountain will cater birthday parties or special events celebrations and offers discounts on mining and lunches for these catered affairs. Call for details.

The cost is approximately $10 per bucket. Gem Mountain is located on N.C. 226, between Spruce Pine (U.S. 19E) and the Blue Ridge Parkway.

Rio Doce Gem Mine
14622 N.C. Highway 226, Little Switzerland, NC
(828) 765-2099
www.riodoce.com
Open mid-April (or May 1, depending on the weather) to Halloween from 9:00 A.M. to 5:00 P.M., seven days a week, the Rio Doce mine is owned by the Jerry Call family. Jerry Call, a gemologist who worked in Brazil's Vale Rio Doce (Sweet River Valley) for over 20 years, is currently involved in large-scale mining in the Brazilian valley. Some of the fine gem exports from the Brazilian valley end up in Spruce Pine's Rio Doce flumes. Rock hounds may be unearthing Mitchell County gems or Brazilian stones! Jerry Call and his family are master gem cutters and offer a complete gemological laboratory and appraisal services. The adjacent gem and gift shop offers 14k gold, sterling silver, and mineral specimens and provides

gem cutting, and rough and cut gems. There is also a picnic area. Rio Doce offers group rates. The mine is located a half-mile north of the Blue Ridge Parkway and the North Carolina Mineral Museum.

WATAUGA COUNTY

Magic Mountain Mini Golf & Gem Mine
1675 N.C. Highway 105, Boone, NC
(828) 265-GEMS, (828) 265-GOLF
The kids simply won't get bored here. Open seven days a week, 9:00 A.M. to 11:00 P.M., Magic Mountain is kiddie paradise. Adults won't mind sifting through the enriched ore either, because there's a chance of finding a ruby, citrine, garnet, amethyst, aquamarine, sapphire, emerald, or other such rocks. The minigolf course is set on a mountainside amidst foliage and waterfalls. (See our Kidstuff chapter for more on this Magic Mountain.)

Central Mountains

HAYWOOD COUNTY

Old Pressley Sapphire Mines
286 Pressley Mine Road, Canton, NC
(828) 648-6320
Some of the world's largest sapphires, including the 1,445-carat "Star of the Carolinas," have been found in this Haywood County mine. In addition to the opportunity to flume for sapphires and other gems, Old Pressley has picnic tables and a rock shop. Better yet, it's open all year, weather permitting, seven days a week from 9:00 A.M. to 6:00 P.M. The flume is shut down during freezing weather, but people still can come here to prospect. There is a $5.00 entrance fee and a charge of $1.00 for each 10-quart bucket of ore. Premade buckets range from $10 to $45. To get here take exit 33 off I-40 onto Newfound Road, then onto North Hominy Road, and left onto Willis Cove Road, and finally left to the mines' address.

Southern Mountains

MACON COUNTY

This is the heart of gem mining in Western North Carolina. In Macon County's famous Cowee Valley, you can go to more than a dozen gem mines where the entrance fee is usually $4.00 to $5.00 for adults and $1.00 to $3.00 for children ages 3 to 12. There is an additional charge of $1.00 to $5.00 for buckets or bags of gem-bearing gravel that you can sluice in search of that "find of the century." However prices vary with the size of the buckets from mine to mine. Some in Macon County, as well as those in other counties, offer ore "enriched" or "seeded" with minerals not native to this locale; others offer strictly North Carolina stones.

Most gem mines, especially during the busy midsummer season, are open seven days a week from April 1 until October 31, and many are open from 8:00 A.M. until sunset, but times can vary. It's always a good idea to call before heading out to the mines; some closing times may vary according to the numbers of visitors and the weather during the season that you visit. Contact the Franklin Area Chamber of Commerce, 180 Porter Street, Franklin, NC 28734; (828) 524-3161 for a listing of the county's many gem mines.

SWAIN COUNTY

Nantahala Gorge Ruby Mine
11900 U.S. Highway 19 W., Bryson City, NC
(828) 488-3854
This Swain County mine, which uses enriched and native ore, has been known to produce rubies of good color and clarity. It's open from mid-March or mid-April through the end of October or on into November, depending on the weather. Ten- to twelve-pound bags of ruby ore run $3.00 a bag or two bags for $5.00; sapphire ore is $4.00 or two for $7.00; emerald ore is $5.00 or two bags for $9.00. More heavily enriched bags of ore

The annual Original North Carolina Mineral and Gem Festival at Spruce Pine takes place during the first weekend in August. Demonstrations, loose stone and mineral fossil displays, and the sale of lapidary supplies make this an entertaining event for everyone. Call the Mitchell Area Chamber of Commerce for more information at (800) 227-3912.

(called "super-ruby," "super-emerald," and "super-sapphire" bags) cost a bit more. There is no entrance fee.

Smoky Mountain Gold and Ruby Mine
U.S. Highway 441 N., Cherokee, NC
(828) 497-6574

In addition to all the other attractions on the Cherokee Indian Reservation, you can come here to search for such gems as amethysts, garnets, sapphires, rubies, citrine, topaz, and smoky quartz. Gem ore is $4.00 per bag or two for $7.00. Smoky Mountain also offers ruby and sapphire specialty buckets for $10.00 and a colored "fun bucket" for $5.00. Gold Ore is $5.00 per bag, $10.00 per bag for a bag with more ore, and $25.00 for a one-gallon bucket. Fifty dollars will get a mixed gem bucket with a cut gem somewhere in the mix. Next to the shaded and covered water flumes is a gem shop that will also cut and mount your finds. The mine opens at 9:00 A.M. seven days a week from early spring through November.

For over three decades one of the biggest gem shows in the area, called Gemboree, is held at the Macon County Community Building (US 441 S.) in Franklin each July and October. Call the Franklin County Chamber of Commerce at (800) 336-7829 for more information.

GEM MUSEUMS

Aside from small museums associated with some gem mines, there are some outstanding gem museums in the region. At these you can get the scoop on the history of rockhounding in North Carolina and a general education on gems and geology.

Northern Mountains

Museum of North Carolina Minerals
off Blue Ridge Parkway at Mile 331
(828) 765-2761

This museum is a great side trip off the parkway. It displays a fascinating collection of minerals in various forms, from raw materials to the cut and polished items we know best. Spruce Pine, just down the road, and Little Switzerland, nearby, are both well known as sources of one of the highest and most varied concentrations of minerals in the United States. A gift shop offers a good variety of rock collections for any young rock hounds and enough material to keep them occupied quite a few miles down the road. The museum is open seven days a week in the summer season. Admission is free. The Mitchell County Chamber of Commerce (828-765-9483) is in the same building.

Central Mountains

The Colburn Gem and Mineral Museum
2 South Pack Square, Asheville, NC
(828) 254-7162, (828) 257-4500

This gem and mineral museum in the Pack Place Education Arts and Science Center dazzles the eyes. The museum was founded in 1960 and highlights gems and minerals of all shapes and sizes from around the world. North Carolina-specific garnets, rubies, emeralds, and gold deposits also feature heavily. Admission is

$4.00 for adults; children ages 4 to 15 and senior citizens receive a discount.

Southern Mountains

Franklin Gem and Mineral Museum
25 Phillips Street, Franklin, NC
(828) 369-7831

The museum building, with its barred windows, is interesting in itself. It's the old county jail, located between Palmer and Main Streets, which was built in the 1850s and used as a jail until 1972. Now converted to displays, the North Carolina Room contains a huge sapphire, a 49-pound corundum crystal, and a baseball-size ruby crystal, all found at Corundum Hill Mine in Macon County, along with a rock collection, cut and faceted gems, an exhibit of mica types, and so on.

The Fluorescent Room, a one-time solitary confinement cell, displays the phenomenon of fluorescence and phosphorescence—what the narrative tape calls "nature's hidden rainbows."

The States Room contains specimens from each of the 50 states, including large specimens of fluorite that you can touch. There is also an Indian Artifacts Room with articles, many of which are centuries old, on loan from members and friends of the Gem and Mineral Society of Franklin.

A former high-security lockup known as the Slammer holds a display on rocks used in the manufacture of glass. The museum also has a nice collection of fossils and corals as well as beautiful minerals from more than 30 nations.

In addition to all this, there is a fine library full of gems and mineral books and a special Writings in Stone exhibit. The small gift shop helps support the museum. Admission is free.

Ruby City Gems and Minerals
130 East Main Street, Franklin, NC
(828) 524-3967

There are several "rock shops" in and around the Franklin area, but this establishment also has a great museum section, the result of more than 40 years of collecting specimens, artifacts, ivory carvings, and rare gems. Here you'll find a 385-pound sapphire and a 162-carat gem-quality ruby. The shop carries jewelry, lapidary equipment, and many rough stones. Other treasures found here include arrowheads and old tools, plus pre-Columbian Aztec and Inca vases and statues.

Franklin's gem mines are too numerous to detail in this chapter. Do make a stop at the Franklin County Chamber of Commerce at 425 Porter Street or call (866) 372-5546 to get maps and brochures of the many mines in this area. The Web site www.franklin-chamber.com also has a page about gem mining.

ANNUAL FESTIVALS AND EVENTS

Our North Carolina Mountains are a celebration in and of themselves, and just living here seems to give rise to all manner of joyous, lively, enlightening, wondrous festivals. Here's a month-to-month sampling, broken down under the geographic regions of the Northern, Central, and Southern Mountains. The events are free unless we've noted an entry fee. Please note: While we update these events with each new edition, it's still best to check with the chambers of commerce in each county to make sure events planned far ahead of time are still scheduled.

Get set to find a bit of everything: woolly worms, dogwood blossoms, gospel music, Scottish clans, Grandma's finest quilt, and even "whimmy-diddles" (Appalachian wooden toys) and washtub race cars. Have fun!

JANUARY

Northern Mountains

Winterfest
Beech Mountain Ski Resort, Beech Mountain, NC
(828) 387-2011
This town festival on Beech Mountain in the first week of January features an ice show, beauty contest, and tube and box races. Nominal entrance fees are charged for the various events.

Old Christmas Hickory Ridge Homestead
591 Horn in the West Drive, Boone, NC
(828) 264-2120
A traditional Christmas celebration held annually on January 6, this community event is free and welcomes everyone to take part. A roaring bonfire (it's cold up here this time of year!) is built from the holiday trees and branches brought by the community as a good luck gesture for the new year. And the good luck begins when delicious food and beverages are provided at the event.

Central Mountains

Annual All That Jazz Weekend at the Grove Park Inn
290 Macon Avenue, Asheville, NC
(828) 252-2711, (800) 438-5800
Hot jazz warms up a cold January weekend. This annual event features two evening concerts, Saturday afternoon jazz, and legendary talents on Saturday night. Admission is charged for concerts.

Martin Luther King Jr. Annual Birthday Celebration
Various locations, Asheville, NC
(828) 259-5800, (828) 253-3714
A variety of events in a five-day celebration at various locations around town honor the birth and contributions of the famed civil rights leader. It all begins the third Monday of the month. Events include a peace march through town, singing, poetry readings, lectures, and music. The event is cosponsored by the city of Asheville.

FEBRUARY

Central Mountains

Arts and Crafts Conference at the Grove Park Inn
290 Macon Avenue, Asheville, NC
(828) 252-2711, (800) 438-5800

This annual professional conference in praise of the Arts and Crafts Movement of Gustav Stickley and his contemporaries working in furniture, pottery, and metalware could have no better surroundings than the Grove Park Inn, a veritable shrine to the movement. The richness of the red-shingled stone resort and its fine collection of arts and crafts pieces exemplify the natural elements and clean lines of this radical design movement, which set the Victorians on their ears at the turn of the last century. The conference is usually held the third week in February.

Big Band Dance Weekend at the Grove Park Inn
290 Macon Avenue, Asheville, NC
(828) 252-2711, (800) 438-5800
It's swing time at the famed Grove Park Inn. This annual event, on the first weekend in February, draws lovers of the Big Band sound of the 1940s and dancers from all over the country. The professional instruction and exhibitions—dancers sweeping across the ballroom in amazingly synchronized steps—are a special treat.

Winterfest Arts and Crafts Show
3 South Tunnel Road, Asheville, NC
(828) 252-3880
This annual regional crafts display fills the corridors of the Asheville Mall and offers a pleasant diversion from winter's chill for three days in early February. This show is sponsored by the High Country Craft Guild and features traditional mountain crafts, such as quilts, ceramics, dolls, and other items.

Black Mountain to Mount Mitchell Marathon Challenge, Black Mountain, NC
(828) 669-2300
This is a 26-mile and a 40-mile foot race on the extreme sports level as it changes elevations drastically and takes place in the middle of winter.

Club Day at the Blue Ridge Mall
1800 Seasons Boulevard, Hendersonville, NC
(828) 697-1745
During the last week in February, local clubs and organizations set up booths to show the community what's offered within the groups.

Chili Cook-off
Kelsey and Hutchinson Lodge, Highlands, NC
(828) 526-2112, (888) 245-9058
One great way to shake off the chills of winter is to warm up by the fireplaces at this upscale and inviting lodge. Another way is to participate in the Chili Cook-off. This fiery potion will stir the gentlest of souls and turn boys into men. Forget winter and welcome spring. The event is cosponsored by the Highlands Chamber of Commerce.

MARCH
Central Mountains

Comedy Classic
290 Macon Avenue, Grove Park Inn, Asheville, NC
(828) 252-2711, (800) 438-5800
Always a sellout, this popular weekend features an exciting lineup of top professional talent. It is always scheduled for the first weekend in March.

Saint Patrick's Day Celebration
Various locations, Asheville, NC
Asheville's cobblestoned Market Street is the starting point for this lively celebration of the wearing of the green. Crafts, entertainment, food, and an energetic parade complete the festivities for those with a bit of Irish in their soul.

*Don't underestimate the popularity
of the festivals and events in these
mountains. Most attract hundreds, if not
thousands, of visitors. Therefore calling
ahead to inquire about the best place
to find parking is a wise idea. It can
save time that'll be better spent enjoying a festival.*

Western Carolina Home Show
**87 Haywood Street, Asheville, NC
(828) 259-5544**
Always popular, this annual event fills the
Asheville Civic Center with streams of visitors, merchants, and an eye-popping array
of the hottest items for the modern
homeowner. It's fun to go, even if your
dream house is still a dream. Parking is
available in the municipal parking garage
next door, just behind the public library.
There's a small charge for admission.

Horse Shows
**Western North Carolina Agricultural
Center, N.C. Highway 280, Fletcher, NC
(828) 687-1414**
Throughout the month, WNC Agricultural
Center hosts the Western North Carolina
Quarter Horse Show, the Roping Horse
Show, and the Carolina Mountain Arabian
Horse Show. Call for exact dates.

Other horses such as palominos, sad-
dlebreds, and racking and walking horses
are on parade throughout the year from
March to November. (See our Recreation
chapter for more information.)

Spring Craft Show
**1800 Four Seasons Boulevard,
Hendersonville, NC
(828) 697-1745**
The Henderson County Crafters Association brings handicrafts to the Blue Ridge
Mall on Four Seasons Boulevard toward
the middle of this month. Dolls, jewelry,
pottery, homemade greeting cards, and
brooms are only part of what you'll see.

Super Saturday
**Various locations, Tryon, NC
(828) 894-3051**
Downtown is transformed into a children's
festival with puppet shows, theater performances, jugglers, magicians, and arts
and craft activities. The city of Tryon
sponsors the event.

APRIL
Central Mountains

Biltmore Estate's Festival of Flowers
**1 Approach Road, Asheville, NC
(828) 225-1333, (800) 624-1575**
Not only is Mr. Vanderbilt's 250-room mansion a magnificent sight, but the grounds
and gardens, designed by noted landscape
architect Frederick Law Olmsted, are just
as breathtaking. This month-long festival
celebrates the exquisite beauty of the
estate's wildflowers, formal plantings, and
exotic blooms of the gardens. The mansion
itself is arrayed in Victorian floral design,
while live music serenades you in the
house and gardens. The house is also open
for Festival of Flower Evenings by reservations on Fridays and Saturdays during the
event. The festival lasts from mid-April to
mid-May, and the price is admission to Biltmore Estate. (See our Biltmore Estate and
Winery chapter.)

Old Depot Association Art & Crafts Show
**Old Depot, Black Mountain, NC
(828) 669-2300**
This is a juried art show held at the his-
toric train station in downtown Black
Mountain.

Earth Day Celebration
**Chimney Rock Park, U.S. Highways
64/74-A, Chimney Rock, NC
(828) 625-9611, (800) 277-9611**
Join environmental speakers and guided
nature walks in celebration of Mother
Nature. Programs, demonstrations, and

hands-on displays including animals, dulcimer music, and magic shows compose this celebration.

Annual Easter Sunrise Service
Chimney Rock Park, U.S. Highways 64/74-A, Chimney Rock, NC
(828) 625-9611, (800) 277-9611

Deep valleys and craggy ridges are an inspiring backdrop for this service conducted by a guest minister, a free, ongoing tradition for more than 40 years.

Easter Egg Hunt
Jackson Park, Hendersonville, NC

Just before Easter you can bring the young and young-at-heart for an old-fashioned egg hunt in the area's largest park. This free springtime event, when more than 11,000 eggs are hidden in the park for children to find, starts at 11:00 A.M.

Historic Johnson Farm Festival
3346 Haywood Road, N.C. Highway 191, Hendersonville, NC
(828) 891-6585

At the end of April, there are tours, an auction, demonstrations, arts and crafts, and food at this old tobacco farm, a heritage education center and farm museum now owned by the Henderson County Public Schools. It's 4 miles north of Hendersonville on N.C. 191. The festival runs from 10:00 A.M. until 4:00 P.M.

Olde Tyme Music Festival
Downtown, Hendersonville, NC

On the second Saturday in April, acoustic musicians will entertain you from 10:00 A.M. until 5:00 P.M. on Appalachian and hammered dulcimers, fiddles, guitars, Autoharps, and banjos.

Hickory Nut Gorge Dogwood Festival
Lake Lure, NC
(828) 625-0204

Lake Lure shimmers, and a cascade of white petals dots the mountains of the gorge, providing inspiration for this festival in honor of the return of spring. Food, entertainment, tournaments, and crafts abound. Saturday includes a parade and a 5K run. The festival, usually held the third weekend in April, runs from 10:00 A.M. to 7:00 P.M., with entertainment going well into the evening.

Appalachian Spring Celebration
Cradle of Forestry, Pisgah National Forest, U.S. Highway 276, Pisgah Forest, NC
(828) 877-3130

Starting the last week in April and running for a full month, the Cradle of Forestry celebrates our mountains' diversity of birds, wildflowers, and waterfalls with a variety of programs for children and adults, including guided bird and wildflower walks and a wildflower photography contest. There is an entrance fee of $4.00 for adults and $2.00 for students.

The Block House Steeplechase
500 Hunting Country Road, Tryon, NC
(828) 859-6109, (800) 438-3681

This free mid-month event, one of the region's most famous and well attended, marks over 55 years of running the horses. It takes place at the Foothills Equestrian Nature Center (FENCE). Gates open at 10:00 A.M.

Revolutionary War Encampment at FENCE
500 Hunting Country Road, Foothills Equestrian Nature Center, Tryon, NC
(828) 859-9021

Experience revolutionary times with South Carolina's Second Regiment at the Foothills Equestrian Nature Center (FENCE). See demonstrations of period crafts, cooking, musket shooting, and an authentic campsite. This free event is held near the end of April.

Pioneer Living Day
911 Reems Creek Road, Zebulon B. Vance Birthplace, Weaverville, NC
(828) 645-6706

Walk into the North Carolina mountains of yesteryear at the Zebulon B. Vance Birthplace. Pioneer Living Day at this state historic site is a fascinating event for the whole family, who can all become involved in demonstrations of the day-to-day life of early mountaineers at this country homestead, surrounded by meadows and mountains. Cooking, candle making, and spinning are just a few of the delights. This event occurs the third Sunday in April.

Southern Mountains

Ramp Festival
Various locations, Robbinsville, NC
(828) 479-3790
On the last Sunday in April, the whole town celebrates the pungent ramp. This wild cousin of the onion is the star of this occasion sponsored by the local rescue squad. The day's activities feature a duck race, dinner with ramp-flavored dishes, and a craft fair.

Razzle Dazzle Saturday
Various locations, Waynesville, NC
(828) 452-0593, (800) 334-9036
Even the name sounds like fun. On the second Saturday in April, children of all ages enjoy a downtown, daylong celebration of arts and entertainment. There are live performances and hands-on art, food, face painting, and fun.

MAY
Northern Mountains

Spring Arts Festival
Town Square, Burnsville, NC
(828) 682-7413, (800) 948-1632
This young festival on the second May weekend is only three years old. Saturday from 10:00 A.M. to 4:00 P.M., the town square is home to artists and their works. Browse the booths for some creative gifts and fine art, while the children paint and draw to their hearts' content on the Expression Wall. Sponsored by the Toe River Arts Council and the Business Owners Association, this event is free.

Spring Studio and Garden Tour
Various locations, Spruce Pine, NC
(828) 765-9483, (800) 227-3912
The first Friday and Saturday in May, the artists and garden businesses of Yancey and Mitchell Counties open their studios and garden spots for informal viewing just before Mother's Day. Fine handcrafted works and garden accoutrements make for a delightful shopping mixture. The tour runs from 10:00 A.M. to 5:00 P.M. and is sponsored by the Toe River Arts Council. Pick up a map of studios on the tour at the Mitchell County Chamber of Commerce at the North Carolina Museum of Minerals or at the Mitchell News Journal in downtown Spruce Pine.

Central Mountains

Folk Art Center Fiber Day
Mile 382, Asheville, NC
(828) 298-7928
The Folk Art Center, east of the city on the Blue Ridge Parkway, hosts a special day in the middle of the month to celebrate the fiber arts. The professional demonstrations attract large crowds, who get to watch how these folks spin thread and weave cloth out of the wool from sheep. This demonstration usually includes all the stages, from watching the sheep being shorn to the weaving on the loom.

Spring Herb Festival
Western North Carolina Farmer's Market
off I-26, Brevard exit, Asheville, NC
(828) 689-5974
This event on the first weekend in May offers educational gardening programs as well as an opportunity to speak to herbalists and master gardeners. This festival is free, so you can save your money to buy herbs, books, and herbal products.

Lake Eden Arts Festival
Camp Rockmont, 377 Lake Eden Road,
Black Mountain, NC
(828) 686-8742

Lake Eden Arts Festival is a new event celebrating the world of folk arts. On the sprawling grounds of a boy's summer camp, this fest features dancing and music, drumming and handicrafts, poetry and storytelling over the three-day Memorial Day weekend in May, then again in October. There are also spiritual and healing workshops, a farmers market, ethnic food booths, massage and aromatherapy, and a vast and funky mixture of world music, folk, and country sounds, all running concurrently on four different stages. This is one very hip festival—call for a brochure with pricing.

Camping during the festival is available.

Carl Sandburg Folk and Poetry Festival
1928 Little River Road, Connemara, Flat Rock, NC
(828) 693-4178
One of the mountains' favorite people is the namesake and inspiration for this free entertainment. Carl Sandburg loved to sing, and music still graces Connemara, his farm, now a National Historic Site just outside Hendersonville. The last weekend in May, professional musicians and actors perform songs and poems from Sandburg's works from 10:00 A.M. until 5:00 P.M.

Flat Rock Playhouse
2661 Greenville Highway, Flat Rock, NC
(828) 693-0731
From late May through early September, North Carolina's official state theater presents comedy, American classics, whodunits, musicals, and farces. (See our write-up in the Arts and Culture chapter for more information.)

Annual Main Street Antique Show
Main Street, Hendersonville, NC
(828) 692-9057
Seventy-five antique dealers show their wares on Main Street from 9:00 A.M. until 5:00 P.M.

Garden Jubilee
Visitors Information Center, 201 South Main Street, Hendersonville, NC
(828) 693-9708, (800) 828-4244
The last week in May brings arts and crafts, a plant sale, garden talks, food, and more to the Visitors Information Center. The event is sponsored by downtown merchants, who hold sidewalk sales and treasure hunts, and a free flower drawing and bring in live music that day.

Sunday Melodies in the Park
Jackson Park Amphitheater, Hendersonville, NC
(828) 697-1745, (800) 828-4344
A free summer concert series begins the second Sunday of the month. Call for more information.

Montreat Kirkin' o' the Tartans
Montreat Scottish Society, Montreat, NC
(828) 669-8011
Memorial Day Sunday is when the 100 clans of the Scots at Montreat gather. At 10:30 A.M. the Montreat Pipe Band brings the tunes of Scotland to the mountains of Appalachia in front of the great stone building of Anderson Auditorium on the grounds of the Montreat Conference Center and Montreat College. At 11 on the hour, the pipers lead the standard bearers, 100 strong, into Anderson Auditorium for the traditional worship service and blessing of the tartans. Among the illustrious preachers has been Montreats own resident, the Rev. Dr. Billy Graham.

The idea of Kirkin' in the United States began with the Scottish preacher, Peter Marshall. He was pastor of the Pennsylvania Avenue Presbyterian Church in Washington, D.C, and chaplain of the U.S. Senate. It was during World War II that he initiated the practice, which included gift bearing of goods to send overseas during those times of scarcity in war torn countries.

Southern Mountains

Taste of Highlands
Highlands Plaza, Highlands, NC
(828) 526-2112
The plaza is bedecked by a festive tent with chefs of the area, wineries and breweries from everywhere, and a lively band exuding sound and excitement. The event begins in the early evening on the first Thursday in May. Admission is charged.

Great Smoky Mountain Trout Festival
Waynesville, NC
(828) 456-3021, (800) 334-9036
This Memorial Day event held in Recreation Park honors the greatest catch in the mountains with exhibitions, contests, crafts, food, and entertainment. The Haywood County Chamber of Commerce sponsors this free event.

Ramp Convention
Various locations, Waynesville, NC
(828) 456-3021, (800) 334-9036
Early May brings a genuine mountain hoedown to again honor the ramp—a rare, wild onionlike plant—in downtown Waynesville. It adds zest to all the day's dishes. There'll be country and bluegrass music, square dancing, and clogging, too. But beware—it's been known to inspire a politician or two to make a speech.

JUNE
Northern Mountains

North Carolina Rhododendron Festival
along Mitchell Avenue, Bakersville, NC
(828) 765-9483, (800) 227-3912
For a half-century this festival has coincided with the blooming of the 600-acre Rhododendron Gardens atop Roan Mountain. A 10K road race, golf tournament, two pageants, historic tours, a car show, and a street dance round out the three-day weekend in the third week of June. These events are free.

Yancey County Clogging-Art & Craft Show
Town Square, Burnsville, NC
(828) 682-7413, (800) 948-1632
This dance festival runs for two days in mid-June. Burnsville's town square hosts a pig-pickin' the first night of the fest, serving succulent barbecue, while cloggers dance the traditional mountain jigs handed down through the generations. The first evening culminates in a street dance. Saturday includes more clogging and arts and crafts booths.

Singing on the Mountain at Grandfather Mountain
off N.C. Highway 221 (entrance of Grandfather Mountain), McRae Meadows Linville, NC
(828) 733-4337
This traditional Southern gospel sing at magnificent McRae Meadows has been going strong since 1924. Drawing crowds in the tens of thousands, this event hearkens back to old-time preachin', when the message was delivered outdoors under the heavens and voices were lifted up to the skies. Lively gospel singing, entertainers, picnic lunches, preaching by well-known speakers, and wide-open vistas create a joyful good time for the entire family. This event, which takes place on the fourth Sunday in June, is free.

Blue Ridge Mountain Fair Craft Festival
Crouse Park, Sparta, NC
(910) 372-5473, (800) 372-5473
Crouse Park in Sparta is the setting for an old-time mountain fair of food, fun, crafts, and music held the last Saturday of the month.

Central Mountains

Brevard Music Center
Probant Street, Brevard, NC
(828) 884-2011, (888) 384-8682
The renowned music center opens for its summer run of more than 70 concerts.

Ice-Cream Social/Spring Kickoff
Silvermont Mansion, Main Street, Brevard, NC
(828) 884-5255
This early June benefit for the Brevard Little Theater, held at the Silvermont Mansion on Main Street, gives participants a preview of the community theater's coming season. Admission is free.

French Broad River Month
Various locations in Buncombe, Henderson, Madison, and Transylvania Counties
(828) 252-8474
June is French Broad River Month. This menagerie of events along the riverfront of the French Broad is sponsored by River-Link, a nonprofit group devoted to improving the river and its banks. Boat races, a Bridge Party and Triathalon, white-water raft trips, biking, and rock climbing are all a part of this outdoors celebration. Activity charges vary, so call ahead.

Annual Tryon Horse Show
500 Hunting Country Road, Foothills Equestrian Nature Center, Tryon, NC
(828) 859-9021, (800) 4-EVENT-1
Sponsored by the Tryon Riding and Hunt Club at the Foothills Equestrian Nature Center (FENCE) early in June, this is a free can't-miss event for horse lovers. Events include dressage, cross-country, and jumping.

The Blue Ridge Barbecue Festival and N.C. State Barbecue Championship
Harmon Field, Tryon, NC
(828) 859-6236
On a weekend in mid-June, the North Carolina state championship barbecue cook-off is held at Harmon Field, attracting even out-of-state barbecue specialists. There's nonstop bluegrass, Piedmont blues, rock and country music, crafts, and children's activities. There is an admission fee.

Summer Nights at Fence Schooling Show
Foothills Equestrian Nature Center
500 Hunting Country Road, Tryon, NC
(828) 859-9021, (800) 4-EVENT-1

From late June through the middle of August, a series of horse shows designed for family fun and friendly competition are held at the Foothills Equestrian Nature Center.

Southern Mountains

Bluegrass Festival
Happy Holiday Campground, U.S. Highway 19 N., Cherokee, NC
(828) 864-7203, (800) 438-1601
You can join in the foot-stompin' that goes on during this three-day, late-June event at the Happy Holiday Campground.

Dillsboro Heritage Festival
Various downtown locations, Dillsboro, NC
(828) 586-3943
On the second Saturday in June, Dillsboro, one of the mountains' most craft-filled towns, closes off its main shopping street for a festival full of food, arts, crafts, and demonstrations.

Taste of Scotland
Square and grounds of Burrell Building Franklin, NC
(828) 524-7472
For the past five years the town of Franklin looks a great deal like "yon, bon bonnie banks of Scotland" on the Saturday before Father's Day. This celebration of Scottish heritage is a joint venture of the Scottish Tartan Museum and the Franklin Chamber of Commerce. The day begins with a parade of bagpipe bands, followed by dancing, children's games and activities, a display of crafts, and food to please an eclectic taste—if it is Scottish.

Innkeepers Tour
Throughout the area, Highlands, NC
(828) 526-2112
The innkeepers of Highlands open their doors and hospitality the second Tuesday and Wednesday in June. Chat with the innkeepers, peek behind the scenes, and select the room of your choice for your overnight stay, either then or later. Nibble

a cookie here, a cup of tea there, or even a refreshing glass of lemonade. The inns' adornments range from antique-filled rooms to extraordinary gardens. Many have wraparound porches, while others offer decks. When you spend a night or two, the innkeepers will be certain to guide you to some of the finest restaurants in the mountains. Three of the restaurants have the *Wine Spectator*'s Award of Excellence. The Highlands Chamber of Commerce has a map of the inns so you won't have any trouble finding your way around.

JULY

Northern Mountains

Old-Fashioned July 4th Celebration on the Square
Town Square, Burnsville, NC
(828) 682–7413, (800) 948–1632

The picturesque Town Square is the scene of a Fourth of July like our grandparents enjoyed. Don't miss the wagon train parade, crafts, food, and mountain music. When twilight falls, you would swear it's still 1900.

Grandfather Mountain
Highland Games and Gathering of the Scottish Clans, McRae Meadows, Linville, NC
(828) 733–1333

Expansive McRae Meadows on Grandfather Mountain is the gorgeous venue for a sea of kilts and tartans during the second full weekend in July. For more than 40 years, this gathering has brought Scottish hearts together for ancient games, traditional food, and bagpipes galore. Because there is no on-site parking, shuttle buses are provided from the entrance to the top of Grandfather Mountain for around $1.00 each way, per person.

Don't miss the spectacular Torchlight Opening Ceremony on Thursday evening, invoking the "spirit of the clans" upon the games. This stirring parade of torchbearers and traditional highland bagpipes and drums makes the centuries seem to fall away. A 5-mile foot race from the town of Linville to the top of Grandfather Mountain is also part of the opening night festivities. Evening activities continue throughout the weekend. Charges vary, so call for an informational brochure.

Christmas in July Festival
West Jefferson, NC
(336) 246–9550

This festival, which is held in mid-July, is heralded as a celebration of Ashe County's thriving Christmas tree industry. What better fun than to pretend it's Christmas in the heat of midsummer! Christmas crafts, from roping and wreaths to decorated trees, are on display along with traditional mountain crafts. Music to suit just about everyone's tastes, including bluegrass, gospel, and classic rock, fills the air. Helicopter rides, children's activities, and all kinds of mouthwatering food round out the fun. (The exact date of the festival varies from year to year, so call ahead of time.)

Central Mountains

The Asheville Poetry Alive Festival
UNCA, Asheville, NC
(828) 298–4927

This event is a treat. Poetry workshops and events, many featuring Pulitzer Prize winners, are held in Asheville the second weekend in July. Readings, lectures, and seminars devoted to the written word are open to amateurs, professionals, and the general public. Come watch a "slam," write your own poems, listen to the masters . . . experiment. Admission is charged and varies for the whole event, workshops, or individual days. There is a charge for the weekend pass. Call for event, workshop, or day rates.

**Old-Fashioned Grove Park Inn Family
4th of July
290 Macon Avenue, Asheville, NC
(828) 252–2711, (800) 438–5800**
Strolling music and sing-alongs, musical
fireworks, a bingo scavenger hunt, and
tennis and golf clinics at this historic inn
help celebrate our national birthday.

**Bele Chere
Various downtown locations, Asheville, NC
(828) 253–1009**
This tremendously popular annual street
festival has grown over almost two
decades to become one of the premier
events in the Southeast, attracting upward
of 350,000 people over its three-day span.
This is Western North Carolina's largest
outdoor festival, featuring more than a
hundred national and regional entertainment acts. At least five different stages
grace various key parts of downtown, and
canopied booths line the main streets.

Multicultural crafts and food set the
tone—the Greek Orthodox Church always
sponsors a booth or two with excellent
Mediterranean fare, and the fajitas, gyros,
Indian samosas, Thai noodles, and many
other mouthwatering selections keep festival goers fairly content. Funnel cakes
and shaved ice are sold every few steps.
Local restaurants join in, often hosting
booths in the central Pack Square.

The musical entertainment, as well as
poetry and dance, is excellent, ranging
from Andean pan flute music, to throw-
down gospel, to reggae, rock and roll,
Brazilian samba, zydeco, bluegrass, swing,
and much, much more. Street dances continue throughout the day and evening.

Vendors offer colorful batiks, jewelry,
leather, pottery, and sundry handcrafted
items. Special events like face painting,
puppet shows, kiddie concerts, and
numerous other activities are geared
toward children, making this a terrific family outing. Bele Chere is always held the
last Friday, Saturday, and Sunday of the
month. Many sophisticated shopping
booths mingle with the more carnival-fare
type, presenting hand-wrought furniture,

clothing, handmade jewelry, and the popular Indian henna temporary tattoo art
mhendi. Best of all, it's free!

**4th of July Gala
Various downtown locations, Asheville, NC**
A spectacular shower of fireworks illuminates the skyline of historic City/County
Plaza in downtown Asheville. Get there
early for the food, music, and fun. A variety of food booths, including Greek, Italian, German, Scottish, and all the usual fair
fare, line the plaza. Funky tunes from
zydeco to rockabilly to country set the
stage for inspirational street dancing.

**Guild Fair
Asheville Civic Center, 87 Haywood
Street, Asheville, NC
(828) 298–7928**
One of the most popular of the annual
mountain crafts fairs, Guild Fair is sponsored by the Southern Highland Handicraft
Guild. A juried craft exhibition, professional
demonstrations, and fine traditional mountain music set this fair apart from the rest.
Artisans from nine different states in the
Appalachians descend on the downtown
civic center on the third weekends in July
and October, offering every kind of craft
from wood furniture to glassware to calico
dolls and sofa cushions. Here you can get
a taste of both the traditional, simple craft
and high-end, one-of-a-kind pieces. It's not
just a place to observe: The Guild Fair also
makes for excellent gift shopping for a
special piece of craft heritage. Admission
is usually $5.00.

**Shindig-on-the-Green
City/County Plaza, Asheville, NC**
Every Saturday night in summer, starting
the first weekend in July, old-fashioned
mountain music thrives in the modern
world on Asheville's central City/County
Plaza. The Shindig-on-the-Green, now in
its 29th year, is the best free entertainment in the region, drawn from the area's
many talented musicians, singers, and
dancers. The program, cosponsored by
the City of Asheville Parks and Recreation

Department and the Asheville Area Chamber of Commerce, began with the simple desire of a few dedicated area musicians to preserve our region's musical heritage. The first stage was set up on the steps of City Hall.

The traditional method of passing down mountain music is by playing it— here, banjo pickers, buck dancers, ballad singers, cloggers, and fans fill the audience and the stage for this celebration of musical heritage. The City/County Plaza swells with a sea of mountain music lovers and spontaneous dancers who begin gathering at 6:00 P.M. The fun usually goes on until 10:00 P.M., or until the last banjo picker or guitar player goes home. A house band usually starts the action, followed by an invited team of cloggers or "smooth dance" square dancers. Musicians come from all over the area to be a part of the evening's entertainment. What began modestly almost three decades ago as a simple desire to keep the ancient strains of mountain music alive has become a living, breathing perpetuation of a unique cultural heritage.

Carnival!
South Broad Park, South Broad Street, Brevard, NC
(828) 877–4777
For four days in mid-July, carnival rides, pony rides, clowns, jugglers, food, prizes, a white elephant sale, dance lessons, and free health screenings are offered, all to benefit the Transylvania Community Hospital. Admission is free, but there is a charge for the rides and some of the games.

Summertime Saturday
Various downtown locations, Brevard, NC
On Saturday afternoons throughout July, Brevard's musicians and others from the area perform in the downtown shopping district.

Harambee
Historic Depot and Seventh Avenue district, Hendersonville, NC
(828) 884–3278

This multicultural festival takes place on the first Saturday in July. Here you'll find arts and crafts, entertainment, food, and more.

Coon Dog Day
Various locations, Saluda, NC
This downtown celebration of the coon dog on the Fourth of July weekend is one of the more popular festivals in the region. It a great day for both dogs and their people, with contests and judging for the dogs and crafts, live music, and a street dance for the people.

Swannanoa Chamber Festival
701 Warren Wilson Road, Warren Wilson College, Swannanoa, NC
This annual festival of chamber music is a rarity and a delight. From the campus of Warren Wilson College, a visiting contingent of classically trained professional musicians produces a series of five marvelous concerts. Traveling workshops and concert series for the Hendersonville and Waynesville communities are also part of this five-week-long musical celebration. The festival also combines lectures, demonstrations, and a benefit recital with the regularly scheduled program.

Fabulous Fourth Metric
Century Bicycle Tour, Tryon, NC
(828) 859–6042, (800) 440–7848
As many as 300 participants and many visitors come from throughout the South to enjoy this 63-mile Independence Day tour that begins in Harmon Field in Tryon. The challenging course has ascents to almost 5,500 feet. After cheering the bicyclists on, visitors can go "next door" to Columbus and enjoy that town's Fourth of July festival, an all-day affair that offers food, crafts, a street dance, and evening fireworks.

Southern Mountains

Andrews Wagon Train
Andrews to Franklin
(828) 837–6492

Since the 1960s this wagon train has wound its way through the mountains, leaving Andrews in late June and arriving in Franklin by the July 4th weekend.

Christian Harmony Singing
John C. Campbell Folk School, 1 Folk School Road, Brasstown, NC
(828) 837-2775, (800) FOLK-SCH
This annual gathering around the second weekend in July draws nearly 80 singers from much of the Southeast. The four-part, unaccompanied shaped-note singing takes place from 10:30 A.M. until 3:00 P.M., broken only by a covered dish dinner from 12:30 to 1:30 P.M.

Fourth of July Freedom Fest
Town Square, Bryson City, NC
(828) 488-3681, (800) 867-9246
Independence Day in Swain County is celebrated with a bevy of live entertainment, food, crafts, and fireworks, of course.

Art Fest
Downtown, Cashiers, NC
(828) 743-5050
On the second weekend of the month, several thousand people come to view and buy the best in local arts and crafts. Box lunches of tasty barbecue are for sale.

Mountain Heritage Day
N.C. Highway 107, Cullowhee, NC
(828) 227-7272
This most "mountainy" day of the year attracts some 50,000 people. You can watch chain saw demonstrations, ax-throwing contests, and cat and dog shows. There are also mountain arts and crafts and food. Favorites on the day's program are gospel, bluegrass, and country music with lots of clogging, square dancing, and line dancing.

Annual Gemboree
Macon County Community Center, U.S. Highway 441 S., Franklin, NC
(828) 524-3161, (800) 336-7829
The "Gem Capital of the World" will show off its rough and cut gems, minerals, fine

jewelry, and equipment in late July. You can also shop for gem-related books and supplies, attend lectures, and maybe win a door prize. Admission is free.

Mountain Artisans Summer Arts and Craft Show
Macon County Community Building, U.S. Highway 441 S., Franklin, NC
(828) 524-3405
More than 70 exhibitors from six states show off their country and traditional crafts and fine arts at this show in late July.

Kirkin' o' the Tartans in July
First Presbyterian Church of Highlands
471 Main Street, Highlands, NC
(828) 526-3175
The pipes and drums bring a measure of nostalgia, dignity, and majesty to these mountain communities, which were founded by the Scots. Historic First Presbyterian Church of Highlands is only one of many that honors the tradition of Kirkin'. This is the time when the kilts, tartan banners, and the pipes and drums lead the procession into the church in thankfulness and for the traditional blessings. The Ravenel family played an important role in the Highlands community in financing this church in its founding days. At one time a good portion of Whiteside Mountain was part of their holdings as they summered in Highlands.

Mountaineer Antique Auto Show
U.S. Highway 276, Maggie Valley, NC
(828) 926-1686, (800) 334-9036
This is one of the largest gatherings of spiffed-up vintage cars you're likely to see. It takes place over the Fourth of July weekend. There have been more than 500 participants in the past.

Annual Snowbird Mountain Gospel Singing
Jacob Cornsilk Community Center, Robbinsville, NC
(828) 479-8984, (828) 479-3926
This three-day event, which attracts singers from the entire Southeast, is held in the middle of July in the Jacob Cornsilk

Community Center. The singing starts around 7:00 P.M. on Friday and Saturday and at 2:00 P.M. on Sunday.

July 4th Heritage Festival
Various downtown locations,
Robbinsville, NC
(828) 499-3790
Join the downtown parade featuring local bands. The festival features lots of food and crafts, too.

Folkmoot USA
Waynesville and other locations
(800) 334-9036
From late July through early August, beginning with a parade through downtown Waynesville, the mountains become the world's stage, as musicians and dancers from different countries gather in a celebration of music, dance, and culture. (See the Folkmoot USA Close-up.)

AUGUST
Northern Mountains

Banner Elk Art Festival
Hickory Nut Gap Road, Old Cannon
Hospital, Banner Elk, NC
(828) 898-5605, (800) 972-2183
This juried fine art exhibit and sale is held the fourth weekend in August. It's sponsored by the Avery-Banner Elk Chamber of Commerce.

Mount Mitchell Crafts Fair
Town Square, Burnsville, NC
(828) 682-7413, (800) 227-3912
Here's a spectacular slice of Americana on the grassy Town Square in the quaint village of Burnsville. A splendid array of traditional mountain crafts, food, and music make for an enjoyable day in mid-August.

Mineral and Gem Festival
97 Pine Bridge Avenue, Pine Bridge
Coliseum, Spruce Pine, NC
(828) 765-9483, (800) 227-3912

A rock hound's dream come true, this weeklong event draws crowds to its displays and sales booths. More than 50 dealers descend during the first week in August.

Central Mountains

Goombay Festival
Eagle Street and South Market Street,
Asheville, NC
(828) 252-4614
This spirited weekend festival celebrates African-American culture in exciting African and Caribbean style. *Goombay* is a West African term meaning rhythm, and this festival is based on a centuries-old celebration filled with music, dance, and the joy of life.

For more than a decade, Goombay has personified joyous multiculturalism at the corner of Eagle and South Market Streets in Asheville. Steel drums; jazz and reggae music; traditional African clothing, jewelry, and decorations; and an incredible assortment of delectable food are all part of the fun. More than 50,000 visitors a year from all over the country step to the Goombay beat, many returning year after year. The festival takes place in late August.

Mountain Dance and Folk Festival
Downtown, Asheville, NC
(828) 259-6107
This granddaddy of all U.S. folk music festivals started informally back in 1927 as just "a little pickin' and a-grinnin' and a-steppin" at the home of Bascom Lamar Lunsford in Turkey Creek in Buncombe County. Today it has evolved into one of the most revered folk music festivals of its kind in the country.

Lunsford, the festival's founder, devoted his life to the perpetuation of our mountain music heritage. He died in 1973, but his festival still retains the naturalness and spontaneity that gave it life 70 years ago on that porch on Turkey Creek. This toe-tapping, knee-slapping event, cospon-

Folkmoot USA

Dancers in traditional Kazakh headgear and flowing gowns, Turkish sword dancers with fezes, French stilt dancers in lambskin vests, New Zealand Maori in grass skirts, Bavarian oompah bands, and sombrero-wearing Mexican ensembles are only a few of the multicultural treasures you might encounter at Waynesville's Folkmoot USA festival.

For 10 days every July, this small mountain town transforms itself into a miniature United Nations, melding folk music, dance, and culture from around the world in an event much like one you would have to travel abroad to see. Each year 10 premier folk groups representing different parts of the world demonstrate their cultural heritages through colorful authentic and original reproduction costumes, lively dance, and music played on unique instruments that are often hand-crafted. Through the years more than 70 countries have sent more than 130 groups to take part.

It's amazing to look back at the humble beginnings of this festival in 1984. America was in the midst of the Cold War, apartheid ruled South Africa, and yet in one mountain village we could speak to our Russian guests one-on-one or have them visit in our houses. Poles, Kazakhs, Turks, Germans, Lithuanians, Kenyans, and so many others joined together in song and dance, music being the common language. Even today the profound sense of "global family" that this festival evokes is hard to mistake.

Folkmoot is patterned after classic European festivals. More than 300 musicians and dancers from around the globe descend on Waynesville and make their home base in a converted old schoolhouse, now known as the Folkmoot Center. From there, they travel to perform in city, college, and school auditoriums around Western North Carolina. During intermission the foyers turn into eastern bazaars, with the foreign visitors offering traditional souvenirs from their homelands.

International Festival Day is another opportunity to find a mélange of international crafts and to watch some inspired street performances. This street fair was added to Folkmoot USA's lineup in 1986 and attracts 20,000 visitors who mingle among the one hundred canopied handicraft and ethnic food booths, along with the costumed performers who might just break into an informal sidewalk song and dance. Local artisans and vendors also join in.

The annual Folkmoot festival closes with a poignant all-group candlelight performance at the Lake Junaluska auditorium. Lights flicker on the water, crickets sing, and a light dew descends on the cool night air as foreign friends bid us good-bye.

For more information on Folkmoot, including a performance schedule and admission costs, call (828) 452-2997. You can also write to Folkmoot USA, P.O. Box 658, Waynesville, NC 28786.

sored by the city of Asheville, begins in early August each year at various downtown locations.

Village Art & Craft Fair
Throughout Historic Biltmore Village
Asheville, NC
(828) 274-2831
What a fabulous setting! Historic Biltmore Village and the grounds of the Cathedral of All Souls in south Asheville, opposite the entrance to Biltmore Estate, come alive the first full weekend in August for this annual arts festival. The historic shopping district, once the village of Best, was purchased by George Vanderbilt in the 1890s to accommodate the army of crafters, artisans, and laborers necessary to complete the five-year construction of Biltmore House (see our chapter on Shopping Destinations). More than 150 artists offer beautiful jewelry and fiber, pottery, and metalworks. Food and beverage sales benefit community charities.

Sourwood Festival
Various locations, Black Mountain, NC
(828) 669-2300, (800) 669-2301
More than 150 art, craft, and food vendors set up in this picturesque town, a 15-minute ride east of Asheville. A music tent, battle of the bands, and carnival for children are just some of the fun in store Tuesday through Sunday on the third week in August. Stroll the old-fashioned main street and peek into the numerous galleries and antique stores. Many of them have special sales in conjunction with the festival. It features a lot of good old Americana—bring out the corndogs, watermelon, and, of course, the sourwood honey.

Annual Jazz in Brevard
Brevard, NC
(828) 884-2787
The Transylvania Arts Council sponsors a day of world-class jazz. This mid-August event takes place in various locations.

Summer Social
Tryon Fine Arts Center, Downtown,
Tryon, NC
(828) 859-8322
The Fine Arts Council holds an all-day, outdoor arts and entertainment festival on the second Saturday of the month at the Tryon Fine Arts Center. It includes local and regional art, food, fun, dances, live music, and magic.

Southern Mountains

J. C. Campbell Annual
August Auction, 1 Folk School Road,
Brasstown, NC
(828) 837-2775, (800) FOLK-SCH
Spend the first Saturday of the month bidding on outstanding craft items. It's a great way to support this unique craft school.

Annual Antique Show
Blue Ridge School, N.C. Highway 107,
Cashiers, NC
(828) 743-5191
Held the first weekend in August, this juried show at the Blue Ridge School draws dealers from all over the Southeast. Come early: The place fills quickly, and people do come to buy!

SEPTEMBER
Northern Mountains

Olde Boone Streetfest
Various locations, Boone, NC
This country fair on the streets of Boone has the added appeal of the early fall leaf colors as a backdrop for fun. You can munch all day on traditional mountain foods or go for more modern tastes. The arts and crafts are excellent, and music sets a lively mood. The festival is held in late September.

Music in the Mountains Festival
Toe River Campground Park, N.C.
Highway 80, Burnsville, NC
(828) 682-7413, (828) 682-7215,
(800) 948-1632
Mountain folk music and food at the Toe
River Campground Park are a magical
combination, especially with Mother
Nature's beautiful backdrop. Various bluegrass and mountain music bands play at
this all-day jamboree in late September,
often jamming into the night with visitors
who happen to bring along instruments.
The small fee is usually under $5.00.

Overmountain Victory Trail Celebration
Mile 331, Spruce Pine, NC
(828) 765-9483, (800) 227-3912
Relive the lives of the "overmountain
boys," who walked a trail toward history
defending our rights and freedoms.
Scheduled events are complemented by
demonstrations of frontier cooking,
leatherwork, beadwork, spinning, and
other Revolutionary-era lifestyle skills. The
celebration is held on the third weekend
of the month at the North Carolina
Museum of Minerals.

Central Mountains

Celebrate Folk Art Day
Folk Art Center, Blue Ridge Parkway,
Asheville, NC
(828) 298-7928
Head for the Folk Art Center, east of the
city on the Blue Ridge Parkway, for a day
dedicated to those who carry on our
Appalachian craft heritage. The early crafts
of the mountains were made by combining
local materials with skills brought over
from England and Europe. Chairs, dolls,
musical instruments, knives, quilts, weavings, and carvings are all part of the show,
plus musicians and storytellers.

Greek Festival
City/County Plaza, Asheville, NC
(828) 253-3754

Asheville's Greek community has contributed richly to the multicultural fabric
of the city for more than 100 years. This
annual festival is a special treat for young
and old alike. Ethnic music and crafts line
the City/County Plaza downtown near
Pack Square. And the food! Spanakopita,
pastitchio, gyros, baklava—try one of
everything! A cafe tent features Greek
sweets and rich strong demitasses of
finely ground Greek coffee; just don't
swallow the dregs.

Kituwah
Asheville Civic Center, 87 Haywood
Street, Asheville, NC
(828) 254-0072
This young festival celebrates the art and
culture of the American Indian through
dance, storytelling and arts and crafts. Call
for more detailed information, and for a
schedule of performers and events. It is held
for two days the last week of the month.

Oktoberfest
Grove Park Inn, 290 Macon Avenue,
Asheville, NC
(828) 252-2711, (800) 438-5800
This annual Oktoberfest happens during
the last week of September at Grove Park
Inn. Hearty German food, music, and (of
course) beer help to celebrate the time of
harvest. Though it's not as raucous as the
one in Munich, it can still quench your
thirst for the real brew and taste for herb-
infused sausages.

Annual Apple Festival
Hendersonville, NC
(828) 692-1413, (800) 282-4244
For almost a half-century this has been
Henderson County's biggest event. It
takes place from September's first Friday
through Monday and includes a huge
street fair, food, crafts, entertainment, and
sporting contests. There are 41 individual
events and 25 kinds of entertainment taking place all over town, including the
Mountain Music Jamboree, Sunday in the
Park, a bike tour, a 10K run, Apple Jack

Local newspapers print special supplements for larger events. Take these with you. They are excellent sources for information, schedules, and event locations.

and Apple Jill golf tournaments, and the King Apple Parade.

Fall Pioneer Living Days and Military Encampment
Zebulon Vance Birthplace, 911 Reems Creek Road, Weaverville, NC
(828) 645-6706

The 1800s come alive at the Zebulon Vance Birthplace, a state historic site. Here mountain crafts and traditional cooking are demonstrated, and a 19th-century military encampment is reenacted on the grounds.

Southern Mountains

Fireman's Day Festival
Town Square, Bryson City, NC
(828) 488-9416

Held on Town Square on the first Saturday of the month, this is a day and evening of festivities in the mountain tradition with music, entertainment, and crafts.

Haywood County Fair
Haywood County Fair Ground,
Lake Junaluska, NC
(828) 452-0152, (800) 334-9036

There are barbecues, cotton candy, gospel singings under the tent, old-fashioned horse and tractor pulls, a man's biscuit-making contest, a petting zoo, food and craft exhibits, and more! The event takes place at the Haywood County Fair Ground in Lake Junaluska.

Smoky Mountain Folk Festival
Stuart Auditorium, Lake Junaluska, NC
(800) 334-9036

A freewheeling Labor Day celebration of the finest traditional and old-timey music and dance, this mountain festival is held in the cool, open-air Stuart Auditorium and on the surrounding grounds. There's even a separate show where kids can kick up their heels!

Homecoming Parade
Downtown, Robbinsville, NC
(828) 479-3330

Remember the good ol' days? This is an old-fashioned homecoming the last Saturday of the month, complete with a football game at the high school and the crowning of a homecoming queen.

OCTOBER
Northern Mountains

Woolly Worm Festival
Banner Elk, NC
(828) 898-5605, (800) 972-2183

A fuzzy weather prognosticator? Tradition says it's so. The woolly worm has earned this distinction here in the mountains, and people gather high up in Banner Elk to celebrate the fact every year during the third weekend in October, just before the winds blow chill. Stripes on the woolly worm are traditionally inspected by town elders. Depending on the color, the elders can predict what kind of winter it will be. Along with the honored woolly worm, more than 120 craft artists, races, entertainment, and food make the festival a hit for the whole family.

Apple Festival
591 Horn in the West Drive, Boone, NC
(828) 264-2225, (800) 852-9506

High in the Northern Mountains come apples, apples, and more apples late in October. This annual festival celebrates the esteemed fruit with a traditional harvest-time good time. Crafts, entertainment, and food, particularly the apples, "round" out the festival.

Madison County Heritage Festival
Various locations, Mars Hill, NC
(828) 689-9351, (828) 689-1424

The first Saturday in October is set aside for this celebration of the community and family life of the people of "the Mountains of Madison." Traditional mountain crafts such as rug braiding, basketmaking, spinning and weaving, and musical instrument making are among the exhibitions. This delightful, small college town opens up all of Main Street, serving a wonderful assortment of pies, cakes, breads, and home cooking. Forty craft booths, local musicians, clog dancers, storytellers, and shape-note singers add to the festivities.

Mountain Heritage Festival
Various locations, Sparta, NC
(336) 372-5473, (800) 372-5473

Enjoy an old-time celebration of early mountain life in the "unspoiled province" of Alleghany County, tucked up against the Virginia border. This is harvest time as it used to be. Sparta (population 1,957) serves up an energetic good time with all the ingredients that these events are noted for: food, fun, crafts, and crowds.

Fall Celebration of the Arts
Spruce Pine, NC
(828) 765-9483, (800) 227-3912

This annual juried and invitational exhibition that takes place on the third weekend in October features traditional and contemporary glass, fiber, ceramics, metal, wood, sculpture, and jewelry by some of the region's finest artists. It's a good place to start a little early Christmas shopping.

New River Festival
Various locations, Todd, NC
(336) 877-1128, (336) 877-1067

Todd, a historic village in Ashe County, is the scene of a new festival on the ancient New River in early October. Once a bustling train town, Todd is now a quiet hamlet frequented by the traveler who wants a different, more leisurely getaway.

This festival offers an old-fashioned gospel sing, checkers playoff, horseshoe toss, arts displays, storytelling, a fishing tournament, and much more. And don't miss the town's main attraction, the Todd General Store. And you thought community socials were a thing of the past. Admission: one smile.

Valle Country Fair
Apple Barn, N.C. Highway 194, Valle Crucis, NC
(828) 264-1299, (800) 852-9506

When the colors of the autumn leaves set the mountains afire and the air carries a slight nip, you know it's time for the Valle Country Fair. This delightful mountain festival is the premier arts, crafts, and mountain music event in the High Country, drawing upwards of 15,000 visitors annually for an entire weekend in mid-October.

Set on the grounds of the old Apple Barn near the Valle Crucis Conference Center in picturesque Valle Crucis, the event takes you back to simpler times when country fairs were the prime social events in the mountains. Every year more than 150 artisans unveil their handcrafted treasures.

The atmosphere is highlighted by the strains of mountain music, and you might even catch of a glimpse of old, buckskin-clad Dan'l Boone himself. It's actually actor Glenn Causey, who, since 1955, has played the venerable frontiersman in Horn in the West, the popular outdoor drama staged in nearby Boone (see our Attractions chapter). All proceeds from the fair benefit local High Country charitable organizations. Don't miss this one! Come early and stake out a parking spot.

To find the Apple Barn, take N.C. 194 S. past the Mast General Store. You'll find the Apple Barn in just under 2 miles.

Central Mountains

Guild Fair
Asheville Civic Center, Asheville, NC
(828) 298-7928

One of the most popular of the annual mountain crafts fairs, Guild Fair is sponsored by the Southern Highland Handicraft Guild and features a juried craft exhibition, professional demonstrations, and fine traditional mountain music. It's held in the downtown civic center on the third weekends in July and October.

Thomas Wolfe Festival
Various locations, Asheville, NC
(828) 253-8304
The Thomas Wolfe Memorial Welcome Center and downtown Asheville host two days of events on the first weekend of October saluting Asheville's most famous writer. Included are readings, discussions, walking tours, a birthday party, music, and theater events. Most events are free.

Urban Trail Arts Festival
Park Square, Asheville, NC
(828) 258-0710
This new arts festival highlights fine arts and crafts from around the region, by celebrating the Asheville Urban Trail, a series of sculptures and plaques, with tours and lectures.

Lake Eden Arts Festival
Camp Rockmont, Black Mountain, NC
(828) 686-8742
The Lake Eden Arts Festival is a fun new event filled with dancing and music, drumming and handcrafts, poetry and storytelling. There are also spiritual and healing workshops and a farmers market during the three-day weekend in late October and again in May.

Annual Forest Festival Day
Cradle of Forestry, Pisgah National
Forest, Brevard, NC
(828) 877-3130
The Cradle of Forestry, a National Historic Site, celebrates our past and future forest resources with old-time demonstrations of carding, spinning, natural dyeing, weaving, whittling, basket making, crosscut sawing, fence rail splitting, and trail building. This popular event takes place the first week in October. Admission charged. Over 50

craftspeople, exhibitors, and entertainers take part.

Halloween Fest in
Transylvania County, Various locations,
Brevard, NC
(828) 883-3700
What better place for a fun and scary Halloween than in Transylvania. From 10:00 A.M. until 6:00 P.M., there are food vendors, crafters, a musical competition, a bicycle rodeo, and a mask-making workshop. In the afternoon participants can sacrifice their blood, not to a vampire, but to the Bloodmobile; join or watch a costume parade; trick or treat in the downtown area; compete in a pumpkin-carving contest; enjoy a kids' carnival; and much more.

Pioneer Day at the Deaver House
Deaver House, U.S. Highway 280,
Brevard, NC
(828) 884-5137
The Blue Ridge Mountains' oldest frame house, on U.S. Highway 280, is open for tours, food, and entertainment. Admission is $6.00 for adults and $3.00 for children and includes dinner, served between 11:30 A.M. and 2:00 P.M. Funds raised are used to preserve and restore the house.

Transylvania Art Guild Annual
Fall Show and Sale, Courthouse Lawn,
Brevard, NC
(828) 884-4366
Original art in all media including wood carving and batik is for sale on the courthouse lawn on the second weekend in October.

Southeastern Animal Fiber Fair
WNC Agricultural Center, Airport Road,
Fletcher, NC
(828) 891-2810
The end of October brings a fair that features hundreds of fiber animals, including llamas, Angora goats, rabbits, and many breeds of sheep. Demonstrations teach how to harvest and use such fiber "crops."

Fall Quilt Show
National Guard Armory, Hendersonville, NC
(828) 891-5027

In mid-October cozy covers transformed into works of art are on display at the National Guard Armory. The brilliant colors rival Mother Nature's fall display! Admission charged.

Farm City Day
Jackson Park, Hendersonville, NC
(828) 697-4884

The free, daylong event, held in Jackson Park, includes tractor pulls, sheep herding, and shearing demonstrations. Here you'll find antique and modern farm equipment, square dancing, clogging, arts and crafts, and food booths. The festivities end with a Civil War reenactment. A special children's section features activities such as a greased pig contest.

Annual Any and All Dog Show
Harmon Field, Tryon, NC
(828) 859-6109, (800) 4-EVENT-1

Calling all dogs! Bring your people and join in the fun the second weekend in October at 1:30 P.M. Categories include master and dog look-alike, most unusual tail, best trick, and more.

Southern Mountains

Annual Andrews Antique Car Show
Andrews, NC
(828) 321-4411

For nearly two decades 100 to 200 cars and trucks from as far away as Knoxville, Chattanooga, and Atlanta have been put on display at this huge show held the first Saturday of the month. There is an entry fee for vehicles; spectators get in free. It's a lively event with all-day 1950s music, car-related booths, and lots of food. In years past entries have included the world's fastest '57 Chevy.

J. C. Campbell Fall Festival
1 School House Road, Brasstown, NC
(828) 837-2775, (800) FOLK-SCH

This is a two-day fair of food, crafts, children's activities, music, dance, and good company held the first weekend of the month.

Bryson City Chili Cookoff
Railroad Station, Everett Street, Bryson City, NC
(828) 488-3681

Teams of chili cookers compete for trophies, accompanied by live music, on the last Saturday of the month.

Maroon Devil Classic Band Contest
Graham County High School, Lakeview Drive, Bryson City, NC
(828) 488-2152

On the third Saturday of the month, country and western bands from North Carolina, Tennessee, and Georgia converge on this town, along with appreciative crowds.

Pumpkin Fest
Various locations, Franklin, NC
(828) 524-3161, (800) 336-3704

On the last Saturday of the month, school children show off their decorated pumpkins and gourds during this town-wide celebration, which also features costume contests, crafts, and food vendors.

Church Street Art and Craft Show
Main Street, Waynesville, NC
(828) 456-3021, (800) 334-9036

On the second Saturday of the month, Main Street is transformed into an arts and crafts marketplace that showcases the region's finest artisans. There are food booths and traditional mountain music. Only original works of art are accepted in this juried show.

NOVEMBER
Northern Mountains

Old Fashioned Christmas
Various locations, Blowing Rock, NC

The town of Blowing Rock launches a series of seasonal festivities that continues through the end of December. It begins after Thanksgiving and includes a Christmas parade, "Christmas in the Park" with caroling in the town's Memorial Park, Christmas decorations throughout the town, and various day and evening activities in conjunction with the season. Call the Blowing Rock Chamber of Commerce (828-295-7851) for a complete listing of Yuletide activities.

Central Mountains

The Asheville Film Festival
Asheville Parks and Recreation, Asheville, NC
(828) 259-5800
A start-up festival for films from around the world, the AFF takes place in venues around Asheville.

Christmas at Biltmore Estate
1 Approach Road, Asheville, NC
(828) 274-6333, (800) 289-1895
This magnificent re-creation of a Victorian Christmas of a century ago begins just before Thanksgiving and continues through December. Daytime visits to George Vanderbilt's mansion are wonderful, but make a point to include on your agenda this nighttime delight—the Biltmore House bathed in the glow of candlelight and blazing hearth fires. It's exquisite, but it's by reservation only, so book early. The cost is admission to the estate.

Christmas Parade
Patton Avenue, Asheville, NC
This is a vibrant, rousing, rollicking beginning to the fun of the Christmas season. Always held before Thanksgiving, Asheville's Christmas parade is alive with colorful floats, whirling Shriners, energetic marching bands, high-stepping steeds, tiny twirlers, raucous clowns, and ol' St. Nick himself showering the throngs with candy canes and peppermints. This parade is always well attended by young and old and swells downtown to bursting. Get there early to stake out your spot.

A Grove Park Inn Christmas
Grove Park Inn, 290 Macon Avenue, Asheville, NC
(828) 252-2711, (800) 438-5800
Here is a special place to fill your family with the Christmas spirit. In addition to beautifully decorated trees, there are gingerbread houses made by area artists, storytelling, caroling, and craft demonstrations. The famed Grove Park Inn Staff Chorus performs daily in the Great Hall, with special appearances by the inn's ambassador, Major Bear. Holiday activities continue from late November through New Year's Day.

Home for the Holidays
Various locations, Hendersonville and Flat Rock
(828) 693-9708, (800) 828-4244
Concerts, exhibits, tours, and special holiday events are scheduled beginning the day after Thanksgiving through Christmas. It starts with the mayoral downtown holiday lighting ceremony and includes tours of historic bed-and-breakfast establishments, Christmas carols, open house at the Curb Market, the Kris Kringle Kids Karnival, and much more.

Southern Mountains

J. C. Campbell Annual
Blacksmith Auction, 1 School House Road, Brasstown, NC
(828) 837-2775, (800) FOLK-SCH
Taking place on the second Saturday of the month, this auction offers pieces by some the nation's greatest masters. Proceeds help keep the craft school's smithy one of the best.

Annual Hard-Candy Arts and Crafts Show
Macon County Community Building, Franklin, NC
(828) 524-9801, (800) 336-7829
In the old days, when times were hard, kids might receive only a few hard candies and perhaps a handmade gift for the holidays. This became known as a Hard-

Candy Christmas. You get a free stick of peppermint at this popular show, held just after Thanksgiving. The exhibitors are first class: There are apple crafts, a children's section full of dolls and doll houses, a host of angels, and other crafts reflecting the holiday spirit. Bring your Christmas list!

Town Lighting
Highlands Town Hall and Main Street,
Highlands, NC
(828) 526-2112
Once again the population of Highlands swells with the guests joining the year-round folks for the lighting. It occurs on the Saturday following Thanksgiving. This traditional event ushers in the excitement of the holiday season. The shops are adorned with seasonal decorations, subtle, yet beckoning. It's time to experience the holidays in a tasteful manner.

DECEMBER
Northern Mountains

Choose and Cut Weekend
Ashe County (336) 246-9550
Sparta/Alleghany County (800) 372-5473
Watauga County (800) 852-9506
The Northern Mountains region is the land of Christmas trees, and fragrant "groves" of evergreens spread over remote hillsides begin to bustle with activity as Christmas nears. Choose and Cut Weekend provides the ideal opportunity to select the family Christmas tree. All locations offer tree-cutting festivities, including caroling and cider and cookie sampling in early December. After you tie the fir to the car roof, go have a mug of hot chocolate and join in the holiday events and festival fun. Christmas card memories!

North Pole at Beech
Various locations, Beech Mountain
(828) 387-9283, (800) 468-5506
A lively old-fashioned holiday celebration starts at Fred's General Mercantile in this

cozy ski village. You can ride on a caroling hayride and bring the little ones to see Santa in a real horse-drawn carriage. Christmas snow in the Northern Mountains comes more often than not.

Boone Christmas Parade
Downtown, Boone, NC
(828) 264-2225, (800) 852-9506
The first Saturday in December is set aside to herald the holiday season in this picturesque college town. Choose a Fraser fir from the mountains and watch the magic of the holiday season begin at this old-fashioned parade.

Central Mountains

Christmas with the Guild
Folk Art Center, Blue Ridge Parkway,
Asheville, NC
(828) 298-7928
The Southern Highland Handicraft Guild displays Christmas decorations and holiday craft exhibits at the grand showcase venue of the Folk Art Center at the Blue Ridge Parkway entrance just east of the city. Free holiday concerts are featured on weekends throughout December.

First Night Asheville
Various downtown locations, Asheville, NC
Take to the streets and bring in the new year Asheville style. First Night Asheville is an alcohol-free, community cultural arts celebration that is oriented toward families. Festivals are held throughout the town and are sure to please all ages.

Before or after an event at Asheville's Civic Center or Thomas Wolfe Auditorium, we like to stop by the Gold Hill Espresso and Fine Teas at 64 Haywood Street, just across the way. The walls display local art, and the rack of magazines may just make you miss your show if you're not careful.

Music, entertainers, food, and brilliant fireworks displays welcome the new year. Many galleries stay open late for a nighttime stroll, and if you are craving bubbly to toast at midnight, numerous taverns, cafes, and restaurants in the downtown area are practically flowing with rivers of the liquid gold.

Kwanzaa
YMI Cultural Center, 39 South Market Street, Asheville, NC
(828) 252-4614

The historic YMI Cultural Center (corner of Market and Eagle Streets) in downtown Asheville is the setting for this African-American celebration of the holiday season. *Kwanzaa* is a Swahili word meaning "first" and signifies the first fruits of the harvest—a time when people come together to celebrate and give thanks for their good fortune. In 1966 these basic principles were adopted in America to create this celebration that includes lighting of the ceremonial Kinara candelabrum, traditional music, readings, and a bounty of ethnic foods. The celebration takes place from December 26 to January 1.

Black Mountain Christmas Parade and Community Candle Lighting
Downtown, Black Mountain, NC
(828) 669-2300, (800) 669-2301

The unique village of Black Mountain just east of Asheville is the setting for a traditional parade down a picturesque Main Street to Lake Tomahawk, just a few blocks north of downtown. The event begins in late afternoon the first Saturday in December and is capped by the lighting of candles and carol singing around the rim of luminaria-lit Lake Tomahawk (where Santa has been known to make an appearance).

Festival of Trees
Silvermont Mansion, East Main Street, Brevard, NC
(828) 883-3692

You can buy or just enjoy looking at the exquisitely decorated trees, Christmas cakes, candies, cookies, and gifts prepared for this four-day event in early December that benefits the Children's Center. A raffle is also held.

Twilight Tour and Dickens on Main
Various locations, Brevard, NC
(828) 884-3278

During this evening event the first Saturday in December, horse-drawn carriages transport revelers through the twinkling lights and luminaria-lit streets of downtown, past carolers, musicians, and food vendors. Most stores are open and serve free hot cider and cookies. This event, regardless of the weather, is extremely popular with local residents.

Santa and More
Chimney Rock Park, Chimney Rock, NC
(828) 625-9611, (800) 277-9611

Enjoy winter scenes of Hickory Nut Gorge, sounds of the season, and visits with Santa throughout the month of December.

Christmas at Connemara
Connemara, 1928 Little River Road, Flat Rock, NC
(828) 693-4178

Follow the luminaria-lined path up the hillside to the Carl Sandburg Home and savor a simple time of Christmas past just as the Sandburg family celebrated it. The one-day event, usually held the third week in December, costs $3.00 for adults. Children younger than 16 are admitted free.

Christmas Parade and Kris Kringle Karnival
Downtown, Hendersonville, NC
(828) 692-1413, (800) 828-4244

In early December, after a traditional Christmas parade down Main Street, enjoy the Kris Kringle Karnival, which features Santa Claus, crafts, carnival games, entertainment, and food.

Festival of Lights
Jackson Park, Hendersonville, NC
(828) 697-4884

Held on Friday and Saturday nights, from 5:30 until 9:30 P.M. on the second weekend of the month, this festival includes the lighting of the Hospice Tree, Santa, hayrides, and refreshments. On Saturday evening 2,000 luminarias light up the park.

Southern Mountains

J. C. Campbell Fireside Sale
1 Folk School Road, Brasstown, NC
(828) 837–2775, (800) FOLK–SCH
This craft sale extravaganza on the first Sunday in December is just one of many community events happening around the hearth and the big Christmas tree at the John C. Campbell Folk School.

Luminaria in Dillsboro
Various locations, Dillsboro, NC
(828) 586–3943
The first two weekends in December, all shops hold open houses with thousands of luminaria lighting up the streets and Christmas caroling filling the night. Complimentary refreshments are served.

Highlands Christmas Parade
Main Street, Highlands, NC
(828) 526–2112

Jolly Old St. Nick has the key to the city gates and occupies the mayor's chair during this festive time. The parade winds its way through this mountain town on the first Saturday in December. B&Bs and the restaurants open their doors to guests, offering hospitality and Christmas theme meals. The surrounding mountains offer the enchantment of the season and sleigh bells can be heard, especially if one listens carefully. Chestnuts are roasting on an open fire, and hot chocolate couldn't taste better. Highlands at the holidays is always special.

Christmas at the Lake
Lambuth Inn, Lake Junaluska, NC
(828) 452–2881, (800) 222–4930
From December 1 to Christmas Eve, enjoy this three-week celebration that includes self-guided tours of the Lambuth Inn's beautiful Christmas trees, gingerbread houses, and nativity scenes.

Holiday Tour of Historic Homes
Various locations, Maggie Valley, NC
(828) 926–1686, (800) 334–9036
This is a feast for the senses in old-fashioned homes decked out in their Christmas best. It takes place the first week in December and is free of charge.

ARTS AND CULTURE

Alone tobacco barn with a red tin roof perches on a bald hillside. Horses whip their tails lazily about in a wildflower-dappled meadow. Mountain ridges mist over blue in the evening, while the sun's setting rays cast splashes of angry pinks, oranges, and golds across the puff-clouded skies. A town square comes alive with warm lights, as the silhouettes of dining patrons bob in silent conversations through picture windows.

No doubt these scenes of life in the mountains, not to mention the powerful stimulus of the primordial visions of nature surrounding us, unleash a certain creativity within. The pure beauty of the natural canvas inspires. And the provocative mix of people who reside within these mountains enlivens the arts and creates refreshing debate.

The visual arts spring to life here in the traditional crafts of the area like pottery, glass, jewelry, fiber, and wood that are so keenly attuned to the highland heritage. Artists' studios can be found in every hollow and each back road, side street, and suburban neighborhood in Western North Carolina. Contemporary crafts with novel material or new techniques have made their mark on the area, propelling this part of the state to the top of "arts destination" lists nationwide. Professional painters and sculptors have infused new energy into the contemporary art scene in the mountains. Community art leagues and artists' guilds nurture the growth of emerging artists in nearly every county and town. Even the proliferation of coffee shops and poetry slams and the changing face of this Southern region can be attributed to this new population's focus on creative endeavor.

Theater arts are threaded through the fabric of our everyday life, giving breath to the personal dramas that drive us all and illuminating the joy of being human.

In the mountains we find our humanity represented by scores of creative sources: neighborhood little theater, public school productions, university theater departments, readers' theater, experimental groups, semiprofessional little theater companies, and Actor's Equity players. More than 40 theater troupes are listed with the Asheville Area Arts council alone.

Music, too, echoes a mountain heritage, derived in part from the historically isolated life of our early settlers. These mountaineers culled their music from the soul of the hills and from the melodies carried on the wind. Born of the first front-porch sing-alongs, with "banjo pickin' and guitar playin' " at sundown and the bittersweet ballads rising out of the mountain coves, the musical legacy found in North Carolina's mountains continues to thrive. More interesting is that it flourishes alongside the strains of a classical symphony, delicate chamber music, inspirational choral music, fervent black gospel, lively barbershop harmony, jazz, swing, and contemporary folk music.

Dance is so effortless here in the mountains. We have a thousand images of inspiration right outside our doors: trees swaying in the wind, leaves whirling across the hill, water tumbling over a rocky creek bed. The mountains have numerous groups for ballet, contemporary dance theater, traditional mountain clogging, international folk dance and Old World contra dance, even country-and-western line dancing.

Museums document the history of these mountains. Some are more academic museums devoted to departmental disciplines and regional displays of traditional mountain life, while others are restored farmhouses, grand old homes, and vast estates that stand as tributes to the virtues and careers of pioneering citizens. Best of all, these museums are not of the stodgy, cement-building stock. These home museums transport you into the past with the scent of aged wood, slightly musty attics, and wildflower-filled surroundings. They welcome you to step onto the back porch and drink in the deep valley views just as the mountain settlers of yore did.

This chapter gives you a glimpse into the melting pot of artistic interests that mirrors the quality of life here—and helps define it. The abundance of arts and crafts in this region and their many similarities often make it hard to characterize what is an "art" and what is a "craft." Here we have tried to differentiate between arts and craft galleries or artisans' studios (these studios are described in the Mountain Crafts chapter). Consult both chapters closely, as you may well find part of what you are looking for in both.

Some of the following organizations are operated out of private homes. If that is the case, we don't furnish the address. Do call the number that's provided to get more information.

ORGANIZATIONS

Northern Mountains

ALLEGHANY COUNTY

Alleghany County Arts Council
Grayson and Cherry Streets, Sparta, NC
(336) 372-2578
The Alleghany County Arts Council, housed in a charming historic house in Crouse Park in downtown Sparta, is a young organization that sponsors local artists in yearly exhibits held in the local public library. The council also puts on the annual Blue Ridge Mountain Craft Fair on the last Saturday in June at the Justin Higgins Agricultural Center and Fairgrounds on U.S. 21 in Sparta. (See our Annual Festivals and Events chapter for information about county fairs.)

ASHE COUNTY

Ashe County Arts Council
West Sixth Street off East Main Street, West Jefferson, NC
(336) 246-2787
www.ashecountyarts.org
This organization is headquartered in a lovely old stone building known as the Ashe Arts Center. This structure, constructed as a community center during the Great Depression, was a Works Progress Administration project. The Ashe County Arts Council is an active organization that sponsors 32 in-school arts programs, numerous arts residencies in the school system, and eight community concerts. The group also sponsors continuously changing exhibits of the work of local artists in its Ashe Arts Center gallery.

AVERY COUNTY

Avery County Arts Council
P.O. Box 2505, Banner Elk, NC
(828) 898-8755
The Avery Arts Council coordinates myriad cultural activities for county residents. The group sponsors numerous arts festivals during the year, such as a Christmas Craft Show and the Very Special Arts Festival in the spring. It also creates opportunities for arts through education and programming.

WATAUGA COUNTY

Watauga County Arts Council
604 West King Street, Boone, NC
(828) 264-1789
www.wataugaart.org
This county arts council is housed in the Jones Community Center in downtown Boone, a building that's also home to two art exhibition galleries. The council is a vital part of the community, sponsoring a number of events during the year and promoting education in the arts with fund raising for the support of art scholarships. The council office is open Wednesday through Saturday.

YANCEY COUNTY

Toe River Arts Council
Town Square, Burnsville, NC
(828) 682-7215

This incredibly busy arts council serves two counties (Yancey and neighboring Mitchell) with an inordinate number of artists and craftspeople—in part due to the presence of the revered Penland School of Crafts in Mitchell County (see our Mountain Crafts chapter).

Services provided by the Toe River Arts Council include a winter arts program and a symphony program. After-school art classes are available to school children. The group also sponsors art and music festivals each summer, along with summer art workshops. The group has developed a map outlining the location of the numerous studios of Yancey County artists and craftspeople and a free directory listing all the cultural offerings in the two-county area served by the council.

Central Mountains

BUNCOMBE COUNTY

Asheville Area Arts Council
11 Biltmore Avenue, Asheville, NC
(828) 258-0710
www.ashevillearts.com

This nonprofit organization has been dedicated to the support and perpetuation of the cultural arts in the Asheville/Buncombe County area for more than 40 years. The group provides technical support, management assistance, and allocation of grants and other funding to emerging artists and area cultural activities and organizations. The Arts in Education program brings art into the schools. The arts council works closely with the community in an effort to identify these needs. Regular exhibitions are displayed in the gallery space, and an annual ball raises funds for the arts.

HandMade in America
67 North Market Street, Asheville, NC
(828) 252-0121
www.handmadeinamerica.org

This evolving community organization is hard at work to make Western North Carolina a nationally recognized center for the fine handcrafts indigenous to our area. (See HandMade in America Close-up for more information.)

HENDERSON COUNTY

The Arts Center of Henderson County, Inc.
538 North Main Street, Hendersonville, NC
(828) 693-8504
www.theartscenterofnc.com

This center offers openings of art collections and juried competitions. One such opening featured a gala evening with a jazz band in support of The Outside/Folk Art Exhibition—The Blackwell Collection. A silent auction was held in conjunction. Another event was the juried competition entitled "The Human Figure." An educational program is offered as well.

Camera Club of Hendersonville
Hendersonville, NC

For over 25 years this club has brought together photographers who enjoy sharing and learning from one another. The inexperienced can learn from the experienced, and the latter can compare ideas, techniques, equipment, materials, and results. The club meets the fourth Tuesday of each month at the Opportunity House (see the subsequent listing in the "Visual Arts" section) for talks and demonstrations by professional photographers and members. Classes, workshops and field trips are also offered, along with a quarterly club competition night, with each photograph judged on its own merits by outside judges. Special events have included exhibitions of members' prints at the Four Seasons Arts Council Gallery on Main Street and showings at the Hendersonville Library.

Henderson County Arts Council, Inc.
401 North Main Street, Hendersonville, NC
(828) 697-9278
www.hendersonarts.org
Henderson County Arts Council, a super-active organization, sponsors special art events throughout the year, including the spring Jubilee Arts Festival and a performance of Folkmoot, the International Dance Festival. In cooperation with the North Carolina Museum of Art, the council promotes art education through its Art Appreciation School Slide Program in Henderson County schools. It's also responsible for the Mountain Arts Program, the Regional Arts Project Grant Program, and the distribution of public and grant monies for the arts in the county. Open Tuesday through Friday, 10:00 A.M. to 5:00 P.M.

The Henderson County Art League
Opportunity House, 1411 Asheville Highway, Hendersonville, NC
(828) 692-0575
The Art League was established in 1958 and is a tax-exempt, not-for-profit corporation. Its purpose is the promotion, development, and the enjoyment of the visual arts. Currently over 220 members represent all levels of artistic achievement from professional to beginners. The league meets at the Opportunity House on the third Wednesday of each month at 1:45 P.M. Each month it offers a new exhibit of its members' work and a demonstration of techniques or methods by qualified artists. On the first Sunday of each month, the league holds a reception and exhibit for a guest artist. All of these events are open to the public. The Sidewalk Art Show has been held on Main Street in downtown Hendersonville for over 40 years. This two-day event features over 100 artists from many locations. In a recent show artists reported over $80,000 in sales. During the summer many members gather at interesting local sites for outdoor paint-outs. The league also has a program called Education Progress that benefits art students in the local high

schools. An All Member juried show with cash prizes is held in November. For additional information call (828) 692-0575 Monday through Friday.

Western North Carolina Quilters Guild
P.O. Box 3121, Hendersonville, NC 28739
No phone
This guild was founded in 1982 to promote the art of quilting and provide an opportunity for area quilters to get together—a modern-day version of the old "quilting bee." Meetings are held on the third Thursday of each month at the First Congregational Church, 1735 Fifth Avenue W. at White Pine Drive. The guild features lectures, workshops, and quilt shows. An extensive lending library filled with current books, patterns, magazines, and videos is available to all members, who also receive an informative newsletter called *Grainlines*.

POLK COUNTY
Carolina Camera Club
Tryon Fine Arts Center, 34 Melrose Avenue, Tryon, NC
(828) 859-8322
Photography buffs in this group get to share their mutual interests and improve their skills at monthly meetings and through other programs. The club is affiliated with the Photographic Society of America and is one of more than 30 camera clubs in six states that form the Southeastern Council of Camera Clubs. A monthly newsletter is available, and there is an annual contest for members' photographs. Award-winning images are exhibited in the Tryon Fine Arts Center lobby in January and February. Anyone interested in photography may become a member, and visitors are always welcome.

Tryon Crafts
Tryon Fine Arts Center, 34 Melrose Avenue, Tryon, NC
(828) 859-8322
www.tryontfac.org
A nonprofit organization, Tryon Crafts sponsors classes that include weaving,

CLOSE-UP

HandMade in America

Long before the first tourists came to Western North Carolina, quilts and baskets, tools and furniture were being crafted as necessities of life. Although they were rarely seen by anyone but family members, these handcrafts were created with an integrity that speaks volumes about the people who made them. Today thousands come each year to see the woodworking, pottery, blacksmithing, and weaving that are now considered treasured keepsakes. They come, too, to reconnect with that part of themselves that longs to create.

HandMade in America is hard at work garnering national and international recognition for this creative heritage. The formal development of HandMade began with a three-year grant received from the Pew Partnership for Civic Change in December 1993. More than 360 people participated in a six-month regional planning process that shaped and defined its mission.

Working with three tourism-related organizations (Blue Ridge Hosts, High Country Hosts, and Smoky Mountain Hosts), HandMade is guiding the development of a craft "heritage corridor" across 22 Western North Carolina counties. The Blue Ridge Parkway serves as the main link by which visitors can access a series of loop trails that take them to historic craft locations, scenic byways, and other attractions. A 120-page guide book, *The Craft Heritage Trails of Western North Carolina,* takes you on seven exciting trails carefully designed to traverse 400 of the region's most fascinating and historical shops, inns, restaurants, galleries, and historical sites. Many were not open to the public before, but HandMade's careful planning and negotiations have created new opportunities. And training

silversmithing, enameling on copper, rug hooking, crewel and needlepoint, macramé, wood carving, knitting, chair caning, stained glass, lampshade making, and oshibana. New classes are opened if enough interested students and qualified teachers are found. Tryon Crafts also has a weaving cottage on Tryon Fine Arts Center, property called the Cate-Hall Weaving Center. Member shows are held each year at Christmas and in spring, and a newly remodeled shop is open next to the Tryon Crafts office on the lower level of the TFAC building. The organization also sponsors out-of-town trips to various craft centers, such as Penland School in Penland and the John C. Campbell Folk School in Brasstown. Hours are 9:00 A.M. to noon, Monday through Friday.

The arts center for the town is 100 percent privately funded. Built in 1969, the center contains a 345-seat theater with a hearing-impaired system, an exhibition room called Gallery I, a Mural Room for meetings and receptions, art studios, a crafts room for classes, and an outdoor garden. In addition to all the activities of its affiliates—the Tryon Concert Association, Tryon Crafts, Tryon Little Theater, Tryon Painters and Sculptors, Foothills Savoyard, Tryon Youth Center, Carolina Camera Club, and the Thermal Belt Model

sessions for all participating sites mean that you are greeted by people knowledgeable not just about their specialty but all the stops along the way.

Consider the names of the trails: High Country Ramble, Circle of the Mountain Trail, Farm to Market Trail, Mountain Cities Trail, Cascades Trail, Shadow of the Smokies Trail, and Lake Country Trail, and you learn of the diversity of the region, the scope of the project, and the theme each has to offer. All destinations have been carefully researched, their authenticity as truly American and/or handmade scrupulously verified. Many of the sites in our book are included on HandMade's self-guided trails.

HandMade is also involved in programs to provide craftspeople with some of the advantages that employees of large corporations enjoy. There are, after all, 739 full-time and 3,369 part-time craftspeople in the region. Their total economic contribution to the state by the mid-1990s exceeded $122 million. To support this burgeoning industry, HandMade is establishing an investment bank that provides low-interest loans to craftspeople and crafts-related businesses, job training programs, a crafts registry, a teacher certification program, and an Institute of Creativity, Research, and Design. They are also working with Andrews, Bakersville, Chimney Rock, and Mars Hill on a Mainstreet Program that pairs these small towns with similar towns already involved in and benefiting from revitalization.

Contact HandMade in America at 67 North Market Street, P.O. Box 2089, Asheville, NC 28802, call (828) 252-0121, or access www.handmadeinamerica.org to purchase a copy of *The Craft Heritage Trails of Western North Carolina.*

Rail Road Club—TFAC offers musical performances by local and professional artists, recounting of personal travel experiences, benefits, lectures, slide shows, Christmas song fests, summer socials, North Carolina Shakespeare Festival performances, jazz bands, contemporary subject seminars, and more.

Tryon Youth Center
N.C. Highway 176, Tryon, NC
(828) 859-3192
This organization provides social, artistic, recreational, educational, and cultural experiences for the young people of the area. Each year the center puts on a Youth Center Summer Musical in the Tryon Fine Arts Center auditorium, but most of its activities are centered in a 5,300-square-foot building on N.C. Highway 176 that's also available for rent by other community organizations and individuals.

TRANSYLVANIA COUNTY

Brevard Camera Club
Brevard, NC
(828) 862-5622
This club, affiliated with the Photographic Society of America, meets on the second Tuesday of the month in Brevard's Parks and Recreation building on South Main

Street. Meetings are usually instructional or entertaining. Dues are $8.00 per year. A similar organization, the Connestee Camera Club, is made up mostly of photographers from the Connestee Falls residential community. They support the Amateur Photo Exhibition by the Transylvania County Arts Council (TCarts) in July and have an exhibition during May and June at the Connestee Club House. This organization can be contacted at (828) 884-4646.

The Connestee Art League
Connestee Falls, Brevard, NC
(828) 885-2001

This art group has over 50 members, made up of talented inhabitants of the large residential development of Connestee Falls. They meet at 9:30 A.M. on Monday mornings at the Art Room in the Connestee Falls Overlook Lounge. Live models and art demonstrations are a part of these gatherings.

Paul Porter Center for Performing Arts
400 North Broad Street, Brevard, NC
(828) 884-8330

An elegant and stately structure, the center features the Concert Hall with superb acoustics, the Morrison Theater, and the Institute for Sacred Music. Events range from orchestral, chamber, and folk concerts to theatrical productions, art exhibitions, and seminars. The activities are planned to match this distinctive milieu tastefully and to reflect the rich cultural diversity found in Western North Carolina. Tickets and information regarding upcoming events may be obtained by contacting the box office at (828) 884-8330.

Transylvania Art Guild
P.O. Box 655, Brevard, NC
(828) 884-8727
www.tcarts.org

The guild's 65 or so professional and amateur members meet the first Thursday of each month at the Lutheran Church of the Good Shepherd, 808 North Broad Street, for an art demonstration or lecture. Members of the group conduct classes in vari-

ous painting media. Paintings by members of the art guild are exhibited in the Chamber of Commerce Gallery, at the Transylvania County Library, and at the Transylvania County Arts Co-op, as well as various commercial establishments in Brevard. There are three shows each year—in June, August, and October—held on the lawn of the county courthouse.

Transylvania County Arts Council
324 South Caldwell Street, Brevard, NC
(828) 884-2787

"TCarts" is now headquartered at 321 South Caldwell Street in Brevard. In 1998 the arts council purchased an old church and renovated it completely. This new Community Arts Center houses the arts council, an exhibition/performance hall (where exhibits change monthly), and an educational wing where classes are held throughout the year.

Operating as a program of the arts council, #7 Arts, an Artists Cooperative, now occupies the council's former location at 7 East Main Street in downtown Brevard. This gallery offers shoppers a chance to view and purchase fine arts and crafts at reasonable prices.

In its effort to provide inspiration and support to local artists, art groups, and school children, TCarts oversees 30 art programs and services, including Grassroots Arts and Regional Artist Project grant programs. The Arts in the Schools and Take Art to Heart programs foster creativity by giving students the best possible experience through in-school performances, artists in residence, and monthly visits from volunteers who use the visual arts to teach critical thinking skills to students.

TCarts also joins Brevard College in presenting the Performing Arts Series for the community.

The council holds a fall and a spring gala fund-raising event each year. The annual Holiday Tour of Homes and Studios is held the second Saturday in December.

This organization sponsors a summer Festival of the Arts, a weeklong celebration of the visual and performing arts, usually held the second week in July. TCarts also sponsors a juried show of regional artists from six Western North Carolina counties at the Transylvania Fine Arts and Crafts Exhibition, held at Brevard College's Spiers Gallery in July.

Transylvania County Handcrafters Guild
P.O. Box 7, Brevard, NC
(828) 862-8554

This friendly, active group of some 90 members welcomes newcomers with open arms. Meetings are held the second Tuesday of the month at 7:00 P.M. in the social hall of the Sacred Heart Catholic Church (4 Fortune Cove) in Brevard. A business meeting is followed by brief craft demonstrations. The guild also has shows in the summer and fall as well as a couple of Christmas shows, but you don't have to show to be a member. Nearly every type of craft is represented, including weaving, stained glass, basketry, batik, fabric painting, and woodworking.

There are other guilds in the Brevard area, including the French Broad Weavers, the Western North Carolina Quilters Guild, the Mini-Quilters, and the Laurel Chapter of the Embroiders Guild. For more information on these organizations, call the Transylvania County Arts Council at (828) 884-2787.

Southern Mountains

HAYWOOD COUNTY

Haywood County Arts Council
37 Church Street, Waynesville, NC
(828) 452-0593
www.haywoodarts.com

HCAC, in cooperation with the Friends of the Library, sponsors free concerts the fourth Sunday of each month at the Waynesville Library. These can include chamber music, bluegrass, or jazz. Since 1995 it also has sponsored a series of five concerts called the Swannanoa Chamber Festival Concert Season.

Another group HCAC supports is Spotlight, a children's theater that stages monthly or bimonthly plays at Haywood Community College's new auditorium. Past plays have included *The Glass Slipper* and *The Beauty of the Dreaming Wood*. In addition to producing Razzle Dazzle, an annual street festival for children in April, HCAC sponsors an International Festival— a day of dance, music, food, and a juried crafts show—each July in association with Folkmoot, the International Dance Festival. HCAC also is involved in Haywood's own production of *The Nutcracker* and the annual Holiday Tour of Homes.

The council brings the Atlanta Ballet to Waynesville for its two-week annual residency in late summer—one of the most popular arts events of the year. In addition to open rehearsals, the ballet holds workshops for area youth. One year they worked with local football players; another time they entertained eighth graders from across the county and the Cherokee Indian Reservation. The ballet group also offers at least two performances at the Haywood Community College auditorium.

The council also sponsors the Autumn Showcase of fine handcrafts of Haywood County and the Smoky Mountain Folk Festival held each Labor Day at Lake Junaluska, where more than 250 performers play old-time music on the stage of the Stuart Auditorium and on the auditorium's grounds.

JACKSON COUNTY

Jackson County Arts Council
Sylva, NC
(828) 293-5458

Whether it's dance, literature, drama, or the visual arts, this council lends its support to dozens of activities and performances each year, including lectures, concerts, and exhibitions. Here are some examples that demonstrate the types of cultural events to enjoy in the county.

• For students: The council sponsors summer art classes for children, a storyteller program in the schools, and two Jackson County Youth Solo Scholarships. It also brings many performers to the schools, including the North Carolina Symphony, theatrical groups, and puppet shows.

- Music: The council sponsors the Valley Chamber Festival, the Western Carolina University Jazz Festival, the North Carolina Percussion Society Convention, and two performances each by the Western North Carolina Community Chorus and the Western North Carolina Civic Orchestra.
- Art: The council sponsors the Jackson County Visual Art Association, Dillsboro Sidewalk Art Show, North Carolina Teachers-Only Art Show, and the Best in Jackson County Art Show.

The council, which puts out a quarterly newsletter, is also responsible for distributing Grassroots grants and other monies.

Jackson County Visual Arts Association
Main Street, Sylva, NC
(828) 293-3407

The approximately 60 member-artists of this group meet monthly and sponsor monthly exhibits (featuring mostly local artists) at Gallery One in Sylva. The association provides art classes for adults and especially for youth and children. A special Membership Show is held each November, and the association sponsors Art from the Jackson County Schools and Art in the Park Shows. It also participates in other local and regional shows and events, such as Mountain Heritage Day at Cullowhee in September. The group takes several field trips each year to such places as the Campbell Folk School, Bob Jones University, and the Greenville Art Museum.

The gallery, run entirely by volunteers, is closed in the winter except during special events, but from May through October, it's open on a regular schedule.

Western Carolina University
N.C. Highway 107, Cullowhee, NC
(828) 227-7211

Western Carolina University provides a year-round showcase for artistic performances, featuring WCU students and faculty and entertainers of national renown.

Its 8,000-seat Liston B. Ramsey Regional Activity Center regularly stages national-caliber sports and entertainment events. The university's Lectures, Concerts, and Exhibitions Series brings music, dance, and theatrical productions to campus each year, and the department of communications and theater arts stages its own high-quality plays. Western's galleries regularly play host to art exhibitions.

Last Minute Productions, WCU's student-run programming organization, maintains a regular schedule of events that brings music groups, comedians, and other acts to campus. The talents of Western's student body and faculty are highlighted in recitals held throughout the year, and the artist-in-residence programs of the Art and Music Departments bring nationally recognized artists to WCU to share their expertise in classroom lectures and their talents through concert and exhibitions. The English Department's Visiting Writers Series bring new voices and legendary names to WCU to share the written word with the WCU community and visitors.

Western's Mountain Heritage Center, located on the ground floor of the H. F. Robinson Administration Building, depicts the natural and cultural heritage of the southern Appalachian region through exhibitions, publications, educational programs, and demonstrations. Mountain Heritage Day, WCU's annual celebration of the mountain spirit, draws more than 30,000 visitors to the campus on the last Saturday of each September.

MACON COUNTY

Arts Council of Macon County
3 East Main Street, Franklin, NC
(828) 524-7683

Macon County's Arts Council, which is dedicated to getting people actively involved in the arts, describes itself as "extremely volunteer driven." Here you'll find ongoing, year-round programs and performances, including concerts, lectures, and other presentations. Regular monthly programs are given, and they often concentrate on a particular subject. A recent program, for example, included a slide show on women's art. During the summer there might be two or three such presentations a month.

Two performances of Folkmoot, the International Dance Festival, are also under the council's auspices. In addition it sponsors one-day craft classes and has an extension program that brings art into the schools.

The Arts League of Highlands
Highlands, NC
(706) 746-2556

The Arts League of Highlands, founded in 1980, is a nonprofit association of artists and supporters of visual arts and serves the Western Carolina/North Georgia mountain areas. The league, with over 100 members, sponsors several shows a year, supports and helps publicize visual arts in the area, and takes field trips to galleries, art shows, and other places of interest. Monthly meetings are held on the last Monday of the month at the Bascom-Louise Gallery in Highlands from May through September. Off-season, members host informal luncheon meetings. For further information, please write to the Arts League of Highlands, P.O. Box 2133, Highlands, NC 28741, or call the above number.

Macon County Art Association
30 East Main Street, Franklin, NC
(828) 349-4607

One of the oldest art associations in Franklin (1962) continues to grow and

If old cemeteries fascinate you, check out the large one at Old Mother Church on Fort Hill, overlooking the town of Robbinsville in Graham County. Its exact founding date is unknown, but it probably dates back to the 1840s. The present building at the site, constructed around 1875, has served as a one-room school, a court of justice, and a place of worship.

flourish. Members are artists of oil, pastel, watercolor, acrylics, mixed media, and sculpture. These members run the Uptown Gallery for displaying and selling their artwork. Many of these originals depict the surrounding Appalachian Mountains, in addition to genres of all subjects.

Membership is by board approval. The association emphasizes participation in activities enhancing and encouraging a better understanding of the inclusion of the fine arts in society. This also includes support for the Macon County Art Association scholarship fund for students attending Western Carolina University. Through help from the arts council in Franklin, programs for children such as summer camps in art are encouraged.

Monthly meetings are held on the second Monday at the gallery, offering programs for members and the general public. Workshops in all media are scheduled during the year for all who wish to attend. Summer outdoor shows are on the first Saturdays of July, August, and September at Our Lady of the Mountains Catholic Church in Highlands. Hours are from 10:00 A.M. to 4:00 P.M.

The Uptown Gallery is open all year. Summer hours are 10:00 A.M. to 4:00 P.M., Monday through Saturday. Winter hours are from 11:00 A.M. to 3:00 P.M. Wednesday through Friday.

SWAIN COUNTY

Swain County Center for the Arts
Bryson City, NC
(828) 488-7843

Because only a small group of people makes up this council, it concentrates its efforts as a funds and grants distributing agency for supporting existing groups instead of sponsoring any special events itself. One exception is its cosponsorship of some of the town's festivals, and it works with the local recreation department on a number of activities. One of the council's main areas of support is a countywide program that brings special teachers of arts, crafts, and music into the schools.

VISUAL ARTS
Northern Mountains

ASHE COUNTY

Ashe County Studio Hop
Various locations, Ashe County, NC
(336) 246-ARTS
Rural Ashe County is full of wonderful artists working in all media, from pottery to glass, woodworking, and painting. The easiest, and certainly one of the most enjoyable, way to experience the artistry of this area is to participate in the Ashe County Studio Hop. This event is held during one weekend in early fall every year.

DePree Studio & Gallery
109 North Jefferson Avenue,
West Jefferson, NC
(336) 246-7399, (877) 639-5808
The spacious gallery specializes in mountain themes, as well as original artwork, prints, giclees, and boxed note cards. The owners, Lenure and Gordon DePree, have lived around the world and created some interesting work inspired by 1400s Persian art.

River Rock Gallery
101 North Jefferson Avenue,
West Jefferson, NC
(336) 219-0089
Fine art and handcrafted works from over a dozen cooperative members mark this new gallery's repertoire. The gallery's long-term objective is to provide and promote art education and appreciation in

Ashe County. A number of projects are in the works to assist artists, aspiring artists, and the community at large. With over 1,000 square feet and high ceilings, track lighting, and wood floors, this gallery leads the way in West Jefferson's growing arts community. The gallery features paintings, drawings, sculpture, pottery, woodturnings, woodworking, jewelry, stained glass, pressed flowers, woodblock prints, music, weaving, and more.

Silver Designs by Lou E and Art Gallery
off N.C. Highway 16, Glendale Springs, NC
(336) 982-4102
Just a few steps down from Holy Trinity Church (one of the Churches of the Frescoes; see our Close-up in this chapter) lies this interesting little gallery/shop. Silversmith Lou Eremita, a member of the Southern Highland Handicraft Guild, made his way to the mountains about 18 years ago from New York City. Finding the solitude of rural Ashe County to his liking, he has been inspired to create wonderful hand-wrought silver jewelry of all descriptions. You can watch him work in this open studio and also take in the interesting gallery of stained glass, crafts, and paintings (primarily watercolors) by Ashe County artists on display.

AVERY COUNTY

The Art Cellar
N.C. Highway 184, 920 Shawneshaw
Avenue, Banner Elk, NC
(828) 898-5175
Along with a wonderful selection of fine art representing the work of local artists, The Art Cellar in Banner Elk features animation art and the latest wrinkle in the art world, "outsider art." It's folk art created by those outside the art world's mainstream.

James P. Kerr Gallery & Studio
N.C. Highway 184, next to Louisiana
Purchase, Banner Elk, NC
(828) 898-8696
The owner of this gallery is a master of painting the landscapes and seascapes of the American continent and the islands

of the Caribbean. His paintings of the entertainment world of New Orleans are especially favored by those who collect his works. Kerr's paintings are exhibited in many prominent galleries throughout the country and are in hundreds of private and corporate collections throughout the United States, Canada, Europe, and the West Indies. Hours vary, so call for an appointment.

MITCHELL COUNTY

Ken Sedberry Clay Studio
Mine Creek Road off U.S. Highway 226, Bakersville, NC
(828) 688-3386
Trained at the Rhode Island School of Design, Ken Sedberry works in clay, drawing from his artistic intuition and a wealth of experience as an instructor in Helena, Montana, at the Archie Bray Foundation, and the Catholic University in Washington, D.C. Today he fills his studio, near Loafer's Glory, with marvelously imaginative decorative pottery as well as wood-fired, functional tableware, all illuminated with a brilliant palette of color.

Penland School of Crafts
Visitors Center, Penland Road, off U.S. Highway 19 E., Penland, NC
(828) 765-6211
We discuss this wonderfully unique, historic school in greater detail in our Mountain Crafts chapter, but it bears repeating that this facility and staff play a crucial role in preserving North Carolina's mountain heritage of arts and handcrafts. You can visit the school's gallery, which has a collection of the works of students and former students. Blown glass, handcrafted jewelry, wood sculpture, weaving, watercolors, and works in oil are all artfully displayed and available for purchase.

Twisted Laurel Gallery
333 Locust Street (Lower Street), Spruce Pine, NC
(828) 765-1532

This charming gallery represents more than 140 artists in all media from the tri-county area: Mitchell, Yancey, and Avery Counties. You'll find exquisite handblown glass as well as colorful stained-glass work. Wood sculpture of all types, some featuring those fanciful, carved faces of wood sprites, is well-represented. Functional and decorative pottery, fiber art, handmade jewelry, watercolor, and oil and acrylic pieces are also available at the Twisted Laurel Gallery.

WATAUGA COUNTY

Art in the Park
Town Park, Main Street
Blowing Rock
For over 25 years Art in the Park has been a central focus of the Blowing Rock tourist season. These monthly events are staged from May to November in Blowing Rock's Town Park off Main Street and offer an ongoing festival of arts and crafts, featuring work of artisans from all over the Southeast. You can browse any number of booths exhibiting wood works, sculpture, fine art, handmade silver and gold jewelry, photography, and leather crafts.

Bolick Pottery
Blackberry Road off U.S. Highway 321, Blowing Rock, NC
(828) 295-3862
You'll want to make the special trip to Bolick Pottery on Blackberry Road, just minutes south of Blowing Rock. Here you'll find a family tradition at work. The Bolick family pottery was begun in 1973 by Lula Owens Bolick and her husband, Glenn. Before locating near Boone, the Bolicks worked with Lula's potter father, M. L. Owens, near Seagrove, North Carolina, a place steeped in the pottery tradition.

These fifth-generation potters continue to fashion traditional pieces, candleholders, mugs, bowls, pitchers, and miniature tea sets in the old-time colors of oatmeal, gray, and cobalt blue. All pieces produced by the Bolicks are microwave and dishwasher safe.

CLOSE-UP

The Frescoes of Ashe County

Remote Ashe County, in the far northwest corner of North Carolina's mountains, seems an unlikely place for a collection of religious frescoes.

Noted American artist Ben Long, born in Statesville, has found his niche as an artist who keeps alive the ancient art of the fresco. Fresco painting is a tenuous art based as it is on the immediate application of pigment to wet plaster. So quickly does the bonding of the two take place that great skill and meticulous planning must be maintained in order to achieve beautiful results.

In two picturesque Episcopal churches, St. Mary's in West Jefferson, on N.C. 194, off U.S. 221, and Holy Trinity, just off N.C. Highway 16 at Glendale Springs, are housed a collection of wonderful religious frescoes created by Long and his students, spanning a period of years from the mid-1970s to the mid-1980s. The marvelous beauty of the work and the powerful subjects have drawn thousands of visitors from all over the country to witness firsthand the evocative frescoes that decorate the walls of these tiny churches.

Both churches date to early in the 20th century, and each seats a congregation no larger than 100. The white frame buildings, trimmed in scrollwork, are described as Carpenter Gothic in style. Neatly trimmed lawns and carefully tended gardens surround these tiny islands of worship. Both are open day and night for prayer and meditation and accept only donations for the privilege of seeing these splendid works of art.

At St. Mary's in West Jefferson, the smaller of the two churches, you can listen to an eloquently recorded description of the works that grace the altar and line the rich, chestnut sanctuary walls. At the altar you have the opportunity to see the exquisite portrayal of *Mary, Great with Child*. This luminous fresco, modeled by Long's wife and bearing the face of a local mountain girl, was completed in 1974. On

---

Doe Ridge Pottery
149 West King Street, Boone, NC
(828) 264-1127
Doe Ridge is an appealing pottery gallery in downtown Boone. You can find both functional stoneware and decorative works here. Handmade Christmas ornaments are an unusual feature of Doe Ridge. Commissions are also accepted.

Gallery 9
10244 Highway 105 S, Foscoe, NC
(828) 963-6068
www.gallery9.com

This gallery features contemporary and traditional painting, indoor and outdoor sculpture, wearable art jewelry, photography, vibrant glassworks, clay, wood turnings, raku, and original pastels by nationally and internationally known artists.

Hands Gallery
543 West King Street, Boone, NC
(828) 262-1970
This gallery has been a part of the Boone arts scene for more than 25 years. A consistently fine selection of wearable fiber

the opposite side of the altar, John the Baptist, completed in 1975, is pictured standing on the banks of the Jordan River; the face of this subject speaks volumes. In the center is the powerful fresco *The Mystery of Faith,* completed in 1977. This fresco, rising the full height of the altar, depicts the crucifixion of Christ and the celebration of the Eucharist. Works by Long's students line the walls of this tiny church. *The Laughing Christ,* completed in 1975 by then-19-year-old artist Bo Bartlett, is an unusual rendition of the face so familiar to the modern world.

Down the road about 10 minutes away is Holy Trinity Church at Glendale Springs. Sitting on a commanding hill, framed by the North Carolina sky, the little Gothic-style frame building is as much a work of art as the magnificent fresco of *The Last Supper,* which fills its altar wall. When you enter Holy Trinity, you are struck by the immediacy of this fresco. So strong are the personalities of the life-size figures, so

vibrant is the texture, it's as if you have come upon that private meeting of Christ and His disciples quite by accident. You can almost hear them speak. The luminous quality of the fresco is achieved by the sealant, which is a centuries-old mixture of white wine and fresh egg white.

Long came to Holy Trinity in 1980, completing this work that summer. He successfully enlisted the aid of area residents, who served as his models, along with his wife, two children, and an errant dog, who found a home at Holy Trinity for the duration and is included in the foreground of the piece. The white cloth at the apex of the fresco, fluttering heavenward, is described by Ben Long as the mystery of that inexplicable quality of life's force that is within all of us.

If you visit the city of Charlotte, you can see more examples of the spectacular fresco art of Ben Long, as well as in Black Mountain at Montreat, where the chapel houses *The Prodigal* by Long.

art, wood sculpture, and imaginative, functional and decorative pottery is featured here.

Main Street
Main Street, Blowing Rock, NC
(828) 295-7839
This lovely gallery features a variety of glass pieces, prints, photography, stained glass, functional and decorative pottery, woven pieces, leather work, and wearable art. Special exhibits are on display each season.

Parkway Craft Center
Mile 294, Blue Ridge Parkway, Blowing Rock, NC
(828) 295-7938
In the splendid Victorian-era home known as Flat Top Manor, this distinctive craft center offers room after room of traditional and contemporary crafts of the finest quality. Since 1951 the center has come alive every May through October with demonstrations and displays by members of the prestigious Southern Highland Handicraft Guild of works in clay,

fiber, wood, fabric, metal, and materials native to the mountains. Be sure to save some time to sit on a rocking chair on the expansive front porch and take in one of the most inspiring views in the mountains.

Tumbleston Studio of Art
525 Harrison Road, Boone, NC
(828) 264-7147
Richard Tumbleston is one of the best-known artists in the High Country of North Carolina. He continues to produce exceptional work and take on new challenges, working in new media. His egg tempera still lifes are luminous. You may visit his personal studio/gallery by appointment.

YANCEY COUNTY

The Design Gallery
7 South Main Street, Burnsville, NC
(828) 678-9869
www.the-design-gallery.com
A mother/daughter team has amassed the work of more than 100 local artisans. The selection includes original paintings, etchings, art glass, pottery, woodwork, furniture, textiles, sculpture, metals, book art, and jewelry. A new feature is Mayland Court Furniture, which is a full line of furniture, handcrafted and handpainted to the buyers' specifications.

The Pot Hole
390 Seven Mile Ridge, 7 miles south of Micaville
(828) 675-5217
The Pot Hole features the functional pottery of Danielle LeHardy. Each handmade stoneware piece is freehand-painted in a range of colorful geometric designs. You can find this tucked away studio/gallery by driving 7 miles south of Micaville, turning left onto Seven Mile Ridge Road, and following the signs.

Toe River Crafts
4590 U.S. Highway 80 S., Burnsville, NC
Six miles south of tiny Micaville, on U.S. Highway 80 S., is Toe River Crafts. This rustic crafts cooperative gallery repre-

sents the work of several nationally known Yancey County artists and craftspeople, many whose work has been shown across the country. You will find finely crafted, one-of-a-kind works at Toe River Crafts, from prints to metals, fiber arts, paper, wood works, photography, pottery, and watercolor.

Central Mountains

Asheville Gallery of Art
16 College Street, Asheville, NC
(828) 251-5796
This downtown gallery represents a fine assortment of leading area artists, such as popular local watercolor artist Ann Vasilik, whose interesting impressionistic interpretations of Asheville are quite striking. The gallery is a co-op, where the artists run the gallery themselves. A fine variety is represented here, including oils, acrylics, lithographs, etchings, and sculpture.

Bellagio
5 Biltmore Place, Biltmore Village, Asheville, NC
(828) 277-8100
www.bellagioarttowear.com
Gallery entrepreneur John Cram continues his representation of fine art in the Asheville area with Bellagio. This shop in Biltmore Village is a venue for "wearable art." Exquisite handwoven, high-fashion clothing and handcrafted jewelry and accessories fill this wonderful corner gallery/shop.

Blue Spiral 1
38 Biltmore Avenue, Asheville, NC
(828) 251-0202
www.bluespiral1.com
The elegant and airy gallery space of Blue Spiral 1 in downtown Asheville is a masterfully planned multilevel showcase for fine painting, sculpture, and fine crafts. Changing exhibits cover the expansive 15,000-square-foot space. A new wing, added in 1997, includes pull-out display "walls" on

wheels for more exhibition space. This is a true state-of-the-art gallery.

The Blue Spiral 1 is also home to the largest collection of paintings by Will Henry Stevens (1881–1949). Stevens was a renowned regionalist and modernist who worked in oils, watercolor, pastels, and mixed media.

Craven Handbuilt Porcelain
11 Roberts Street, Asheville, NC
(828) 232-1401
www.cravenstudio.com
This gallery and working studio for internationally known artists Ian and Jo Lydia Craven features elegant dinnerware, orchid pots, bowls, and sculptures. This couple spent years in Spain and France perfecting their art of creating magnificent porcelain works with the imprints of heirloom lace.

Fine Arts League of Asheville
25 Rankin Avenue, Asheville, NC
(828) 252-5050
www.fineartsleague.org
This nonprofit art instruction studio is dedicated to the development of the Realist Artist. The League offers seminars and workshops with visiting artists, art historians, and related experts in the field of fine art. Intensive classes cover anatomy, craftsmanship, color theory, perspective, composition, etc. A gallery in the League's space features guest artists as well as student works.

Gallery of the Mountains
The Grove Park Inn, 290 Macon Avenue, Asheville, NC
(828) 254-2068
Treasure hunting—that's what a visit to this gallery is all about. Here, amidst the grand setting of the historic Grove Park Inn (see our Resorts chapter), you can find a treasure at every turn, including charming handcrafted wearables, jewelry, pottery, Arts and Craft movement lamps and accessories.

Grovewood Gallery
111 Grovewood Road, Asheville, NC
(828) 253-7651
www.grovewood.com
This fine gallery is in the 79-year-old former home of the Biltmore Industries woolen homespun operation. The interior of this interesting English-style cottage adjacent to the Grove Park Inn has been wonderfully renovated as gallery and shop space without sacrificing the integrity of its origin. The Grovewood Studios, in the next cottage, houses eleven artists, specializing in wood work, blown glass, stone carving, jewelry and furniture. Their work, along with the work of other area craftspeople, is represented by the Grovewood Gallery. The furniture gallery upstairs has expanded and features fabulous designs from the Southeast.

Jewelry Design—Jewels that Dance
63 Haywood Street, Asheville, NC
(828) 254-5088
The imaginatively conceived jewelry pieces of Jewelry Design gallery are works of art wrought in gold and silver. Rings, pins, and necklaces sport unusual features that will catch your fancy. The gallery is next door to Asheville's Pack Library, downtown.

New Morning Gallery
7 Boston Way, Biltmore Village, Asheville, NC
(828) 274-2831
www.newmorninggallerync.com
Started in 1972 as a modest crafts gallery, the New Morning Gallery is one of the best showcases of fine handcrafts in the region. Owner John Cram describes New Morning Gallery as "art for living." You can enjoy browsing the newly expanded shop filled with lovely sculptural pottery, handmade jewelry, fine art glass, and unusual furniture.

Seven Sisters Gallery
117 Cherry Street, Black Mountain, NC
(828) 669-5107
www.sevensistersgallery.com
The wonderfully rustic brick interior, original pressed-tin ceiling, hardwood floors,

and antique furniture—all serving as display space for gallery work—set the mood for this relaxed gallery that has been an integral part of Black Mountain for more than 16 years. Seven Sisters Gallery is an anchor for the Cherry Street Historic District in this quaint old resort town. Artists from all over the region and Western North Carolina in particular are represented in wood, pottery, beadwork, handcrafted jewelry, fiber arts, and other lovely crafts. Thought-provoking, themed exhibitions (one recent exhibit was titled "The Human Form—In Dance and Repose") draw tourists and residents alike to this popular gallery of fine art and craft work.

Southern Highland Handicraft Guild
Mile 382, Blue Ridge Parkway off U.S. 70 E., Asheville, NC
(828) 298–7928
www.southernhighlandguild.com
The Southern Highland Handicraft Guild was founded in 1930 as an educational, nonprofit organization to provide economic support for the many talented craftspeople in the Southern Appalachian region. Today the guild is composed of more than 700 members in a nine-state Southeast region. Members submit applications and are selected by a board, based on the merit of their work. The Allanstand Craft Shop in the Folk Art Center (milepost 382), east of Asheville, and the gift gallery of the Moses Cone Memorial and Visitors Center (828–295–7938; milepost 293) near Blowing Rock in Watauga County, serve as retail outlets for members' works.

(See our Blue Ridge Parkway and Attractions chapters for more about the Folk Arts Center and the Moses Cone Memorial.)

Swannanoa Valley Art League
1132 Old U.S. Highway 70,
Black Mountain, NC
(828) 669–7224
This community arts group is the oldest in Western North Carolina, serving amateur artists in the Swannanoa Valley area surrounding Black Mountain, east of Asheville. Members meet monthly at the Black Mountain Library. Classes in oil painting, calligraphy, print making, piano, drawing, and watercolor are available at the studio on Old U.S. Highway 70. Yearly exhibits at the library showcase members' work.

Vadim Bora Gallery & Studio
30½ Battery Park Avenue, Asheville, NC
(828) 254–7959
www.vadimborastudio.com
Vadim Bora Gallery & Studio allows you to enter the artist's "kitchen." Visit with the artist, originally from the republic of Ossetia in the Caucases Mountains of Russia, while he creates his sculptures, paintings, and sketches. Vadim Bora is a multimedia artist, specializing in sculpture, painting, and jewelry design. The bright upstairs studio is located conveniently on a major shopping street. Oil paintings and sketches adorning the gallery walls are for sale, but you can also request your own commissioned portrait, sculpture, or jewelry. Bora teaches sculpture classes in this studio-gallery. Gallery hours are 11:00 A.M. to 6:00 P.M., by appointment, or "if the gate is open."

Vitrum Gallerie
Biltmore Village, 10 Lodge Street, Asheville, NC
(828) 274–9900
Glass and more glass is the object of this gallery in historic Biltmore Village. From reverse-glass painting to cast and blown glass, Vitrum features the works of fine contemporary glass artisans Peiser, Beecham, Sikorsky Todd, Littleton-Vogel, and others.

HENDERSON COUNTY

The Arts Center
538 North Main Street, Hendersonville, NC
(828) 693–8504
This is, indeed, the center for art information and a good starting place for getting involved in the arts in Henderson County. The center, founded by the Four Seasons Arts Council (FSAC) in 1992 (see previous

listing under Organizations), houses the council's offices, as well as those of the Hendersonville Symphony Orchestra. Here also is the D. Samuel Neill Gallery, with shows by local, regional, and national professional artists that change approximately every six weeks. The Hall Gallery (actually a long hallway) offers the works of local artists, students, and art organizations. There are also two artist studios for rent and a classroom for lectures, children's art classes, and other events.

Calico Gallery
317 North Main Street, Hendersonville, NC
(828) 697-2551
Hendersonville has attracted any number of fine artists and craftspeople, and here's a place where you can buy their paintings and handmade crafts. The shop also stocks antique dolls, furniture, jewelry, and other items.

Opportunity House
1411 Asheville Highway, Hendersonville, NC
(828) 692-0575
The Opportunity House was established as an Arts, Crafts, and Cultural Center in 1958. Exhibits of artwork done by members of The Art League of Henderson County and guest artists are presented monthly. The Art Gallery is open to the public for viewing and purchases Monday through Friday from 9:00 A.M. until 5:00 P.M. The Opportunity House Gift Shop offers a wide selection of handcrafted items made by its members. In addition many talented artists and craftspeople teach classes year-round in basic drawing, acrylics, oils, sketching, watercolor, stained glass, lapidary, weaving, wood carving, pottery, and sculpture.

Touchstone Gallery
318 North Main Street, Hendersonville, NC
(828) 692-2191
Touchstone has long been one of the more lighthearted contemporary galleries in town. In 1998 *Niche* magazine recognized Touchstone as one of the top 100 craft galleries in the country. When it opened a number of years ago, it concentrated on exhibiting mostly local artists. Now it has expanded its reach to the whole region and occasionally throws in an out-of-region artist to spice things up. Most shows last from 60 to 90 days.

With the wealth of talent available, even the more popular artists usually wait for more than a year for a repeat show, so there's an ever-changing array of new items to enjoy here. You'll find exceptional art and craft works in a variety of mediums: pottery, fused and blown glass, wood, metal, ceramics, marble, acrylics, oils, watercolors and collages, to name a few. This is also one of the few shops in the area that carries UNICEF cards and calendars.

Many arts councils in various towns hold "gallery hops" or "gallery crawls" every few months. During these events galleries and studios throw their doors open wide to the public, sometimes offering light hors d'oeuvres and wine, while visitors stroll from gallery to gallery for some art appreciation and a bit of socializing. Often the artists are on hand to discuss their works. Check local newspaper listings or consult individual art councils.

Wickwire
423 North Main Street, Hendersonville, NC
(828) 692-6222
Wickwire, a fine art/folk art gallery, "seeks the bread that sustains the heart." It goes out of its way to display the visions of emerging local artists. At the same time the gallery also represents some very well established names, including three Smithsonian artisans and two "North Carolina Living Treasures."

POLK COUNTY

Heartwood Contemporary Crafts Gallery
Main Street, Saluda, NC
(828) 749-9365
With a focus on a more contemporary collection, this gallery is the perfect place

for anyone who not only enjoys fine crafts, but also likes to bask in the small town atmosphere that makes Saluda special. Regional and national craftspeople of the highest caliber display their wares in a well-lit, comfortable shop that highlights the qualities of the work. You'll find delicate porcelain sculpture, pottery (one of the finest collections in the region), jewelry in all its forms, wood items, garden sculpture, wind chimes, stylish birdhouses and feeders, and original prints and painting by the area's finest artists. And this is just a short list of the numerous arts and crafts on display.

Saluda Mountain Crafts Gallery
I-26 and exit 28, Saluda, NC
(828) 749-4341
Despite its proximity to a busy interstate highway, this gallery has a country feel. It's housed in a two-story home built in the 1920s, complete with a wraparound porch. Inside you'll find pottery, jewelry, furniture, weavings, quilts, prints, some original paintings, and a vast array of other items, 99 percent of which were made right here in the mountains by some 200 different artists, many of them from the Saluda area. The gallery is open all year.

When visiting Saluda Mountain Crafts in Saluda, take the time to visit the old-fashioned ice-cream parlor right next door. Fudge Mountain Ice Cream makes its own ice cream and fudge and serves it up in an authentic atmosphere, created with antique items from old ice-cream parlors, old RKO movie theater marquees, and cabinets made from the lockers of the Virginia Senate Building.

Tryon Painters and Sculptors
208 Melrose Avenue, Tryon Fine Arts Center, Tryon, NC
(828) 859-9755
Composed of 160 amateur and professional artists, some of whom are nationally

known, this organization presents 10 art show openings a year, including artists from all over the United States. The group's shows are held both at the Tryon Fine Arts Center and at the Arts Palette in the Farwell Annex next door. The Arts Palette holds an open house the second Saturday of the month. Workshops and regular art and sculpture classes are held in the studio, which also contains a retail store featuring members' creations.

The Upstairs Gallery
409 North Trade Street, Tryon, NC
(828) 859-2828
www.upstairsgallery.com
The Upstairs Gallery got its name from former upstairs locations. Now, 21 years later, though definitely in a downstairs space, the name has stuck. The Upstairs is a well-known contemporary art gallery that features fine arts and crafts, children's art, literary readings, musical performances (including a monthly Pickin' Parlor), art education, Southern Writers Summer Series, and an annual Christmas Craft Festival. The gallery is run entirely by volunteers and is closed in July, August, and January. Exhibitions open on Fridays with a public reception and run for four weeks. Family Day, with a gallery tour, is held the first Sunday after an opening.

TRANSYLVANIA COUNTY

Brevard College Visual Arts
400 North Broad Street, Brevard, NC
(828) 883-8292
Exhibitions of visual art at the college can be found in two locations: the Mezzazine Gallery in the Paul Porter Center for Performing Arts (see Organizations) and the Spiers Gallery in Sims Art Center. In addition to displays of art produced by the faculty and students, visitors may enjoy the talents of regionally and nationally known artists. Exhibitions include work that spans the spectrum of the visual arts, including ceramics, painting, sculpture, photography, and installations. Recent exhibitions have featured work by Canadian sculptress Jocelyn Salem, as well as

such nationally recognized artists as Joe Molinaro, Michael Mallard, Michael Voors, Olga Alexander, and Darryl Halbrooks. Gallery hours are Monday through Friday from 10:00 A.M. until 5:30 P.M.

Not only does this gallery provide exposure to some fine artists, it also serves as a teaching tool for the college's art department. (Visiting artists often spend a few days on campus interacting with the students.) The shows, which include both two- and three-dimensional art, change approximately every five weeks. The exhibitions are representative of both regional and national artists, traditional and nontraditional. The public is invited to opening receptions, which often include musical presentations and poetry readings.

The works of area artists can also be seen in the Transylvania County Library at 105 South Broad Street, the Brevard Chamber of Commerce, and the Transylvania County Courthouse; the latter two are on Main Street.

The Frame-Up
4 West Main Street, Brevard, NC
(828) 883-2385

In addition to fantastic archival framing, The Frame-Up also carries one-of-a-kind jewelry, woodturnings, handmade furniture, and beautiful (framed, of course) prints, as well as blown glass, porcelain, and pottery.

Gallery on Main
53 East Main Street, Brevard, NC
(828) 885-7299

You'll find originals and limited editions prints here as well as a lovely selection of collectibles.

Transylvania County Arts Co-Op
7 East Main Street, Brevard, NC
(828) 883-2294

Occupying the former gallery and offices of the Transylvania County Arts Council and associated with that council (see Organizations), this gallery gives shoppers a chance to purchase beautiful, locally made arts and crafts at wonderful prices.

Southern Mountains

HAYWOOD COUNTY

Blue Owl Studio and Gallery, Inc.
11 North Main Street, Waynesville, NC
(828) 456-5050

If you wonder how the cities and landscapes of the mountains appeared in yesteryear, you can relive some of those days in this gallery. Filled with antique graphics of the past, the artists at Blue Owl bring them to life in brilliant hand-painted colors. Better yet, the prices for these works of art are surprisingly affordable.

Earthwork's Environmental Gallery
21 North Main Street, Waynesville, NC
(828) 452-9500

Earthwork's is one of our Waynesville favorites. Its goal is to "celebrate the beauty of the earth through the eyes of the artists." This large gallery covers Southwestern arts and crafts and Native American wildlife themes. You'll find rugs, pillows, and runners from the Zapotec Indians of Mexico; woodturnings by local artists; gourd art; stone carvings from Africa; and captivating paintings and prints by Native American artists. There are also jewelry, books, music, and many other items of superb taste at reasonable prices. The Earthwork's Frame Gallery (828-456-3666) is at 152 South Main Street.

T. Pennington Art Gallery
15 North Main Street, Waynesville, NC
(828) 452-4582

Waynesville's Mast General Store (63 North Main Street) makes interesting browsing anytime (see our Shopping chapter). Now its Mast Store Crafter Series demonstrations make it the home of a real learning experience. Several times a month, talented craftspeople show off their skills in such things as doll making, jewelry design, raku masks, and stenciling. Call (828) 452-2101 for more information about the series.

You'll be amazed by the excellent colored-pencil drawings of Western North Carolina created by Teresa Pennington. In addition to original works, the gallery also carries limited-edition prints of local mountain scenes.

JACKSON COUNTY

Belk Art Gallery and Chelsa Gallery
Western Carolina University,
N.C. Highway 107, Cullowhee, NC
(828) 227-7327
Both of these galleries on the university's campus offer art exhibits by local, regional, and national artists on a year-round basis.

City Lights Bookstore & Cafe
3 East Jackson Street, Sylva, NC
(828) 586-9499
In addition to offering new and used books, good food, and live entertainment, City Lights has an interesting gallery of rotating exhibitions.

Dogwood Crafters
90 Webster Street, Dillsboro, NC
(828) 586-2248
Housed in a large, renovated log building around the corner from Front Street, this is one of Dillsboro's most charming stores. We are particularly taken with the lovely, artistic cornhusk dolls here, but there also are hundreds of contemporary and traditional handicrafts on display, including pottery, pillows, art, and toys.

Gallery One
Main Street, Sylva, NC
(828) 293-3407
Operated by the Jackson County Visual Arts Associations, the gallery sponsors monthly exhibits, mostly by local artists, and has an artist in residence. (See Organizations.)

Gallery Z
Front Street, Dillsboro, NC
(828) 586-3383
The mountains are becoming world famous for studio glass, and at Gallery Z you can see some samples of it in the form of candleholders, lamps, vases, and perfume bottles.

Mountain Pottery
Front Street, Dillsboro, NC
(828) 586-9183
At Mountain Pottery you can see pottery being made in an open studio. It's also got the town's largest selection of handmade porcelain, stoneware, and raku pottery. The pottery is supplied by more than 50 craftspeople from the region.

Riverwood Pewter Shop
N.C. Highway 411, Dillsboro, NC
(828) 586-6996, (800) 530-2547
The Riverwood Shops developed around a hand-hammered pewter business established in 1930. The Riverwood Pewter Shop is still here making hand-hammered pewter on the premises.

Riverwood's Oaks Gallery
N.C. Highway 441, Dillsboro
(828) 586-6996, (800) 580-2547
Right next door to the Riverwood Pewter Shop, this cooperative of more than 80 Appalachian craftspeople showcases weaving, jewelry, glass, wood, wearables, and pottery.

Village Studio
Front Street, Dillsboro, NC
(828) 586-4060
The talents that flower in these mountains are beautifully expressed in this gallery. Area artists fill it with paintings and prints, handmade dulcimers, gifts and cards. The gallery-style shop also displays decorative accessories for home and office. Professional framing is available.

MACON COUNTY

The Bascom-Louise Gallery and the
Highlands Center for the Visual Arts
554 East Main Street, Highlands, NC
(828) 526-4949
The Bascom-Louise Gallery stages impressive showings of works by regional and

national artists. Exhibitions change every three weeks from May through November and are accompanied by public receptions for the artists. Lectures are also held here. A new permanent collection gallery houses artwork by some of the finest regional artists along with a sales gallery of original fine arts and crafts. The new workroom in back of the Bascom-Louise Gallery is bright, spacious, and well equipped. It contains audiovisual, painting, and drawing areas, plus a darkroom and raku kiln.

Workshops, taught by some of the finest artists in the Southeast, are open to beginning artists and professionals at the Highlands Center for the Visual Arts. They include classes in painting, drawing, sculpture, photography, crafts, and more. Class sizes are kept small for close interaction with instructors. The cost of these intensive workshops ranges from $85 to $200. Sometimes there's a small additional fee for materials or the use of equipment. The center and gallery both are closed during the winter.

Bryant Art Glass Studio
260 Franklin Road, Highway 64, Highlands, NC
(828) 526-4095

Dwight Bryant has rediscovered the secrets of the pharaohs. Dipping into antiquity for the process of handmade fused-glass plates, bowls, and platters, as perfected by the ancient Egyptians, Bryant has brought this to life with colorful designs of pink dogwood, purple iris, pansies, and orange and yellow sunflowers. He has also infused numerous other designs, including birds and other fauna and flora.

His commissions have included crafting the commemorative cobalt and clear glass plates designed by artist Richard Jolley for the Charlotte Mint Museum of Craft and Design. Another was for the 24th annual Decorators' Show House, benefiting the Alabama Symphony Orchestra Endowment Fund. Among those who have acquired his works are Secretary of State and Mrs. Colin Powell,

the Ted Kennedy family, and the Bush family. Bryant is in residence April through Christmas Eve. Open Monday through Saturday from 10:00 A.M. to 4:00 P.M.

Maco Crafts Inc.
652 Georgia Highway, Franklin, NC
(828) 524-7878

This huge craft cooperative and fabric shop has thrived for more than a quarter century. It assures high-quality work from more than 200 local craftspeople through a jurying process, yet it is still able to maintain an average inventory of more than 10,000 items. It is particularly famous for its quality quilts and also offers all the supplies a quilter could ever need.

In addition to its craft work, which includes jewelry, wood, pottery, paintings, stained-glass art, dolls, and toys, there is a Christmas room that's open year-round. Maco also has the area's largest selection of fine cotton fabrics and the latest patterns and books. The co-op's craftspeople will create custom work in both traditional and contemporary designs. You can also enroll in one of the many craft classes offered. Maco Crafts is 2 miles south of Franklin on U.S. 441.

Museum of American Cut and Engraved Glass
472 Chestnut Street, Highlands, NC
(828) 526-3415

The brilliance of cut glass illuminates the interior of the log house in which it is exhibited. Curator and collectors George and Bonnie Siek share their love of this medium. The American Brilliant Period, acknowledged to have started with the 1876 Centennial Exhibition in Philadelphia, ended in 1916 with the onset of the First World War. This museum opens up a dazzling new world to many; it is as overwhelming as the myriad of patterns of frost on a windowpane or a waterfall glistening in the sun. Not only is the collection spectacular, but the owners are as well. Should you find the museum closed, just call George at home, and he'll arrange a private showing. There is no admission charge as there are a number of pieces from the Brilliant Period for sale at reasonable prices. These sales go toward paying the bills.

Summerhouse Gallery
N.C. Highway 106 S., Highlands, NC
(828) 526–5577
Tiger Mountain Summerhouse Gallery is the showroom for woodworks. This shop sells handcrafted furnishings, including custom lodge furniture and country reproductions including beds, tables, dressers and other items for the entire house.

The Uptown Gallery
30 East Main Street, Franklin, NC
(828) 349–6708
Members of the Macon County Art Association (see Organizations) display their oils, pastels, watercolors, acrylics, mixed media, and sculpture here on a year-round basis.

THEATER

Northern Mountains

ASHE COUNTY

Ashe County Little Theater
Various venues, West Jefferson, NC
(336) 246–ARTS
Ashe County is well represented by this amateur theatrical group, which features local actors of all ages in an energetic annual program of popular Broadway productions. Past productions have included *Oliver!, The King and I,* and *The Sound of Music.*

AVERY COUNTY

Lees-McRae College
Main Street, N.C. Highway 194, Banner Elk, NC
(828) 898–5241
Mile-high Banner Elk is the lovely location for this dynamic little college (see our Education chapter). The college is innovative both academically and culturally and promotes a yearlong calendar of cultural arts events that is amazingly

diverse for a school its size. The Lees-McRae College Summer Theater, established as a semiprofessional theater in 1984, is one of the foremost theatrical attractions in the High Country.

Past productions have included *Fiddler on the Roof, Man of La Mancha,* and *Guys and Dolls.* The Performing Arts Series, sponsored by the college's Performing Arts Department, offers consistently interesting dramatic productions, one-act plays, traditional mountain dance performances (clogging), and other concerts throughout the academic year. All are open to the public.

WATAUGA COUNTY

Appalachian State University
Boone, NC
(800) 841–ARTS
Boone's community-minded university offers a series of cultural events throughout the year. The Department of Theater and Dance at ASU presents a wide array of one-act plays, full dramatic productions, and dance performances, all of which are open to the public. The ASU Forum Series is the university's formal lecture series that has featured national speakers addressing topics of national and international importance.

During the summer the community is treated to An Appalachian Summer Festival, offering the best in music, dance, theater, visual arts, and symposia. The Performing Arts Series also brings national and international performers to the campus. These events are also open to the public. (See the "Music" section in this chapter for information on recitals and concerts.)

Blowing Rock Stage Company
Blowing Rock Arts Center,
Sunset Drive, Blowing Rock, NC
(828) 295–9627
The Blowing Rock Stage Company is the High Country's resident professional theater, drawing the services of professional Actor's Equity players every summer. The

artistic home of the theater company is the Blowing Rock Arts Center, adjacent to Blowing Rock Elementary School. Local and summer residents of the High Country, as well as scores of tourists, fill every performance of this fine theatrical company mid-June through mid-August.

Blue Ridge Community Theater
Various venues, Boone, NC
(828) 297-3155
For over 25 years Blue Ridge Community Theater (BRCT) has brought the best in amateur theatrical production to the High Country. The 200 local actors who regularly participate in BRCT stage two yearly productions: a fall drama and a spring musical.

YANCEY COUNTY

Burnsville Little Theater
Various venues, Burnsville, NC
This is Yancey County's resident amateur theater group. Drawing talent from the surrounding area, the Burnsville Little Theater stages two or three productions a year. Check local listings for venues because this is an amateur theater with no home stage.

Parkway Playhouse
202 Green Mountain Drive, Burnsville, NC
(828) 682-4285
The Parkway Playhouse opened its doors in 1947 as the "Burnsville Playhouse." Eventually it was housed in a former school gymnasium, which was moved up the South Toe River to its present location. As the oldest continuously producing summer stock theater in North Carolina, it is now looking to the future for year-round performances, with a winterizing feasibility study under way. The most recent season has been expanded to 10 weeks. It includes a Youth Theater Institute. Collaborative relationships have been established with Mayland Community College, the Toe River Arts Council, and the Southern Appalachian Repertory Theatre.

Central Mountains

BUNCOMBE COUNTY

Asheville Community Theatre
35 Walnut Street, Asheville, NC
(828) 254-1320
This award-winning theater is ranked one of the best in the Southeast, consistently providing the Asheville area with the best in live theater since its inception in 1946. This long tradition of excellence has a colorful heritage that includes an association with famed motion picture actor Charlton Heston. Heston was codirector of ACT in the 1947 season, making it his springboard to stardom the following year when he returned to New York.

The Asheville Community Theatre produces a six-show season that includes the best of Broadway musicals, comedies, and classics. The Heston Auditorium has continental-style seating in its air-conditioned space, is wheelchair accessible, and is equipped with an enhancement system for the hearing impaired. Local restaurants offer dinner and show packages. New director Peter Carver, plucked from the Big Easy to run the ACT is breathing new life into each upcoming season. Tickets for the five-show season cost around $60. During intermission visitors can enjoy rotating exhibitions in the lobby gallery space.

Montford Park Players
Montford Park Recreational Facility,
Montford Avenue and Pearson Drive,
Asheville, NC
(828) 254-5146
This legendary Asheville theater company grew out of one woman's fascination with the English Bard. Founder Hazel Robinson created the Montford Park Players on a financial shoestring back in 1973, bringing the works of Shakespeare to the public. The plays in those days were performed in the natural, grassy amphitheater of old Montford Park, with costumes and props scavenged by Ms. Robinson and her loyal

thespian followers. As the Great Man said, "The play's the thing." And so it was.

The performances of the Montford Park Players gained in popularity and attracted attention from city leaders, who provided a space in Asheville's Montford Park Recreational Facility nearby and enough free lumber to build a real stage. That was 1983. Every summer since this vigorous and dedicated amateur company, with steadfast Hazel Robinson at the helm as artistic director, continues to be a favorite Asheville entertainment.

Two separate works by Shakespeare, usually one comedy and one tragedy, are performed each summer season. You can bring a blanket and a picnic and stake out your space on the hillside. There's nothing like Shakespeare under the night sky to set the mood. The performances are free, but in the true tradition of early Shakespearean troupes, a hat is passed at intermission. You can find the Montford Park Players at the outdoor amphitheater of Montford Recreation Center, 1 block off Montford Avenue at the intersection of Montford Avenue and Pearson Drive.

A highlight of the Christmas season is the Montford Park Players' production of *A Christmas Carol*. This energetic production has been performed at the auditorium of Asheville High School and also at Diana Wortham Theatre at Pack Place.

HENDERSON COUNTY

The Belfry Players
**131 Fourth Avenue W., Suite 215, Hendersonville, NC
(828) 698–8288**
Sherry Raker is the artistic director of this theatrical group, which began in 1988 with just a few participants using a small performance space at St. James Episcopal Church in Hendersonville. It now draws on a large paid membership and produces three plays a year in the Sumner Pingree Theatre at Christ School, 500 Christ School Road, Arden. Although its base remains in Hendersonville, the group now draws both its membership and audience from Asheville, Tryon, and Brevard. The Belfry Players productions cover a broad range of material from *Spoon River Anthology* to *Sylvia* to short opera. Single show tickets are $9.00; season tickets to all three productions are $24.00.

The players also maintain an outreach program called "Bits & Pieces," which presents programs to retirement centers and various organizations. These may include music as well as drama and readings.

Flat Rock Playhouse
The State Theatre of North Carolina
**2661 Greenville Highway, Flat Rock, NC
(828) 693–0731**
Flat Rock Playhouse, the State Theatre of North Carolina, is a professional theater operating under a contract with the Actors' Equity Association, the national union of professional actors and stage managers. Founded in 1937 the playhouse entertains more than 65,000 guests each season. Eight productions are offered between late May and mid-October annually. A variety of comedies, musicals, and dramas, which range from world premieres to the latest from Broadway and London to the classics, compose the summer/fall series.

Flat Rock Playhouse endeavors to produce plays that have a wide range of appeal and are appropriate for the entire family. For example, included in the 2001 playlist were *Bye-Bye Birdie, I Do, I Do, Stand by Your Man, Romance in D*, and *Dial M for Murder*.

The performance schedule is Wednesday through Saturday at 8:15 P.M. and Wednesday, Thursday, Saturday, and Sunday at 2:15 P.M. The box office opens in late April, and reservations can be made by calling the above number. Musical productions cost $25 and nonmusicals cost $22. Discounts are offered for students, seniors, and groups of 13 or more.

Flat Rock Playhouse is located 3 miles south of Hendersonville on U.S. 25; from I-26 take exit 22 and follow the signs.

The Vagabond School of the Drama operates Flat Rock Playhouse and has two main educational divisions: the summer Apprentice/Intern Program and the fall through spring Theatre for Young People. Between these two divisions, classes are offered to students from the first grade through college graduates and pre-professional students. The summer programs are accredited through the University of North Carolina in Asheville.

Hendersonville Little Theatre
The Barn on State Street, Hendersonville, NC
(828) 692-1082

This all-volunteer group of players has entertained the town since 1966, putting on four shows in a refurbished barn from September to May. These shows usually include a couple of comedies, a mystery, and sometimes a serious drama. There are more than 400 members in this organization, and a large number of them actively work on each production. Tickets are $8.00, but there are various memberships available that range from $25.00 for a season ticket for three plays to $500.00 for a life membership that entitles you to see the plays free for life.

POLK COUNTY

Tryon Little Theater
Tryon Fine Arts Center, 208 Melrose Avenue, Tryon, NC
(828) 859-8322, (828) 859-3545 (info. line)

Since 1969 this organization has produced more than 100 plays and musicals. The nearly 800 members create six productions a year at the Tryon Fine Arts Center, including at least one musical each season. There are more than 150 individuals participating in some facet of every production. Recent works presented have been as disparate as *My Fair Lady* and *The Glass Menagerie*. It is not unheard of for such shows to be sold out and for popular demand to require additional performances. Tryon Little Theater also holds acting workshops and play-reading groups. It has sponsored various theatrical events, premiered original pro-

ductions, and won a North Carolina Theater Award. Tickets range from $10 to $15, depending on the show.

TRANSYLVANIA COUNTY

Brevard Little Theater
P.O. Box 544, Brevard, NC
(828) 884-2587

This theatrical group, which celebrated its 50th season in the year 2000, is the official theater company of the city and county. It's also the Resident Community Theater Company at Brevard College. The Barn Theater, overlooking scenic King's Creek on the Brevard College campus, was renovated and refurbished for the 1999 season.

The group produces four plays for a season that runs from October through August. It also puts on children's plays, including the very popular *The Nutcracker* in December. In addition there's a very active "BLT to Go" group that provides benefit performances for community and charitable organizations.

Reservations are advised due to the limited seating in the Barn Theatre. Certain productions are also staged at the larger Dunham Auditorium on the college campus.

Southern Mountains

CHEROKEE COUNTY

The Valleytown Arts Center
Third and Chestnut Streets, Andrews, NC
(828) 321-3453

This center, originally the First Baptist Church, has been renovated with the purpose of providing a facility for the community to stage performing and visual arts. It houses both the Community Youth Players, an ensemble of young local talent that has been active since 1986 and that performs a Christmas play in early December and presents another performance in the spring, and the Andrews Community Theater, which offers plays throughout the year. Concerts and other events are also staged here. Call for information.

CLAY COUNTY

Licklog Players
Peacock Playhouse, Hayesville, NC
(828) 389-8632

This volunteer organization was started as a small community theater in 1977 by Diane Teague, Jimmy Hicks, and Susan King. In searching for a name that reflected this area, they thought of the Davis family, early settlers who felled trees and cut notches in the logs to hold salt for their cattle. This area became known as Licklog, and so the name was adopted.

Today, Licklog Players has grown into a regional theatrical group with talent drawn from several surrounding states. It's housed in the 250-seat, air-conditioned Peacock Playhouse with state-of-the-art facilities. Last year for the first time the players offered productions year-round, including comedies, farces, mysteries, dramas, musicals, and children's performances. Recent productions included *Cabaret, Annie, The Sound of Music, A Delicate Balance, The King and I, Trip to Bountiful, A Tuna Christmas,* and *Rumors.*

Members of the board of directors, a theater manager, paid directors, choreographers, and music directors produce the wonderful works seen here. Some 300 volunteers perform all the other jobs. Tickets for plays are $10.00 for adults and $6.00 for students and children; musicals cost $12.00 for adults and $7.00 for students and children. Each year Licklog offers a summer theater workshop for youth, which includes instruction in acting, dance, music, and other areas of theater arts.

HAYWOOD COUNTY

Haywood Arts Repertory Theater
250 Pigeon Street, U.S. Highway 276 S.,
Waynesville, NC
(828) 456-6322

HART is the region's most active theater company, producing seven main stage productions each year and up to six "studio" shows, including major musicals, classics, and new plays. In recent years the theater has hosted a production direct from Off-Broadway, sent a production to New York, and staged a new play in its studio that won honors at the John F. Kennedy Center. The group moved into its new home, the Performing Arts Center at the Shelton House, in 1997. The center, a summer stock barn-style facility, sits in the middle of an eight-acre National Historic Site shared with the Museum of North Carolina Handicrafts. It includes a 250-seat auditorium, a visual arts gallery, and a 75-seat studio theater. The center is located just 2 blocks from Waynesville's pretty Main Street. In addition to an acoustically fine, all-wood interior, there are earphones for the hearing impaired, and the facility is wheelchair accessible.

The group has more than 700 season ticket holders and involves hundreds of volunteers, with an annual budget of more than $130,000. Tickets for plays are around $10 for adults.

JACKSON COUNTY

Kudzu Players
P.O. Box 834, Sylva, NC
(828) 586-8133

The Kudzu Players, a community theater group of around 50 people, offers popular plays on a regular basis in the former courtroom of the historic Old Jackson County Courthouse. Call for information and ticket prices.

Niggli Theatre and Studio Theatre
Western Carolina University,
N.C. Highway 107, Cullowhee, NC
(828) 227-7491

The university's Department of Speech and Drama produces dramas, comedies, and musicals throughout the year. Call the above number for information and ticket prices.

MACON COUNTY

Highlands Playhouse
Oak Street, Highlands, NC
(828) 526-2695 (tickets)
(828) 526-9443 (information)

This community theater has been active for 60 years and is still going strong. It has been housed in the same building for more than 50 years, and work is under way to place it on the National Register of Historic Places. The playhouse stages four productions in a season that runs from June into August. It combines professional talent with outside equity guest stars. Showtimes are Tuesday through Saturday at 8:00 P.M. and Sunday at 2:00 P.M. Tickets are $20.00 for adults and $7.00 for students. Group rates for 10 or more are available.

SWAIN COUNTY

Smoky Mountain Community Theater
Main Street, Bryson City, NC
The Smoky Mountain Community Theater presents four plays a year in an old movie theater on Main Street. The group itself refurbished the more-than-50-year-old structure, installing a sophisticated lighting system, building dressing rooms, and more than doubling the size of the stage. Members are undaunted by large-scale productions. In the past they've presented *Oklahoma, Fiddler on the Roof, The Music Man, South Pacific, The Sound of Music, The Wizard of Oz,* and *Into the Woods.* A summer children's theater that offers a workshop and production has been established. Check local listings for workshop programs.

MUSIC

Northern Mountains

ASHE COUNTY

Ashe County Choral Society
First Baptist Church, West Jefferson, NC
(336) 246-ARTS
This group of community singers works each year to stage both a holiday and a spring concert. The holiday concert in December features religious and secular music, while the spring concert consists of a blend of contemporary pops and religious music.

WATAUGA COUNTY

Music in the Mountains with Joe Shannon
Various venues, Boone, NC
(828) 264-8118
This lively concert series is also a weekly television show taped every Friday evening at 8:00 P.M. in Boone. Remarkably entertaining, it's part traditional mountain shindig, part Appalachian cultural history lesson.

Every week a musical guest takes the stage, setting the tone for the evening's entertainment. Guests have provided gospel, bluegrass, banjo, fiddle, old-time string band music, and even songs of the Civil War, accompanied by traditional instruments. The program is highlighted by a one-on-one interview with one of the "old masters" of our Appalachian musical and cultural heritage. The shows are taped and aired on local Boone radio.

In the summer the concert series takes place at various venues. During the fall all shows take place at the Blowing Rock Arts Center on Sunset Drive.

School of Music
Faculty Recital Series
Appalachian State University, Boone, NC
(828) 262-4046, (800) 841-ARTS
The Appalachian State University School of Music Faculty Recital Series is an eagerly anticipated series of concert events in the High Country. These performances are scheduled monthly during the academic year and are also open to the public.

Central Mountains

BUNCOMBE COUNTY

Asheville Bravo Concerts
(828) 252-6777
This venerable cultural arts membership organization, now in its 66th season, is responsible for bringing the finest in national and international ballet, jazz, choral groups, and classical orchestral music to Asheville. The Thomas Wolfe Auditorium of the Asheville Civic Center is

the location for all performances. Individual tickets are available, and a season membership for the entire series of five concerts is approximately $85.

Asheville Chamber Music Series
(828) 253-2579

This 46-year-old organization sponsors five concerts a year featuring nationally renowned artists of chamber music. The concerts are presented in the Unitarian Universalist Church, 1 Edwin Place, off Charlotte Street in north Asheville. Season or individual tickets are available. Students are admitted free.

Asheville Choral Society
(828) 669-8695

Founded in 1977, the Asheville Choral Society has a membership of about 60 to 85 amateur and professional singers. The society's choral director, Robert P. Keener, is also the retired chairman of the Music Department of nearby Warren Wilson College in Swannanoa. The group performs concerts that include classical and contemporary masterpieces of choral literature. The Asheville Choral Society has appeared with both the Asheville Symphony and the North Carolina Symphony Orchestras.

A season ticket is roughly $24.00 for three concerts, $18.00 for seniors; tickets at the door are $10.00 and $8.00, respectively. Students with valid identification are admitted free.

Asheville Lyric Opera
Pack Place, Asheville, NC
(828) 236-0670

David Craig Starkey brought his talents from the New York and the Metropolitan Opera Company to Asheville, as founder and general and artistic director of the Asheville Lyric Opera. World-class artists, brought from the fine opera houses of New York, Vienna, and from across the United States, grace the Asheville stage. Together with local talent, they've brought the stage of the Diana Wortham Theater at Pack Place alive with the fun of Gilbert

and Sullivan's *The Pirates of Penzance,* the tragedy of *I Pagliacci* and *Madama Butterfly,* and the poignancy of *La Bohème* and *Amahl and the Night Visitors.*

The opera company also serves the schools of the area with educational outreach. Traveling troupes perform in schools, or lectures and demonstrations are made available for in-class production. School groups then travel to the theater to experience the real thing.

The Asheville Symphony Orchestra
Asheville Civic Center, Asheville, NC
(828) 254-7046

The distinguished Asheville Symphony Orchestra, led by maestro Robert Hart Baker, is celebrating its 43rd season. This community orchestra consistently provides exceptional concerts and continues to set new challenges for itself each season. The popular Masterworks Series, composed of six concerts, features distinguished, internationally known guest artists. In addition the orchestra performs its annual Children's Concert in October, a holiday pops concert in December and a spring pops concert in May.

Mid-Day Musicals
Park Square Pack Place, Asheville, NC

This lively musical series, cosponsored by the city of Asheville, is highlighted by a feeling of spontaneity. For the past seven years, a changing cast of some of the area's most talented singers has been performing these free lunchtime minimusicals Thursdays at 12:30, starting the last weekend in August through the first weekend of October outside Pack Place on historic Pack Square. Each performance features a different theme. A variety of pieces, such as the music of famed Broadway composer Stephen Sondheim, light opera by Gilbert and Sullivan, the classic standards of sophisticated Noel Coward and legendary Broadway composers Rogers and Hammerstein, are performed by these energetic and talented performers. Lunchtime has never been so entertaining!

HENDERSON COUNTY

Blue Ridge Community College Concerts
Blue Ridge College, College Drive,
Flat Rock, NC
(828) 692-3572, ext. 306

On Monday nights in a season stretching from September to April, the college's Division of Community Services sponsors eight classical music concerts in the 150-seat auditorium of the Patton Building. Many of the performers have national reputations, and about half the concerts feature outstanding students from the North Carolina School of the Arts in Winston-Salem. One concert is reserved to display the talents of a local professional. In addition around three times a year, special benefit performances are given to help support the college's music department. Tickets to the Monday night series are $6.00; season tickets are $45.00.

The Hendersonville Chorale
(828) 692-3211

This group was founded in 1974 and was incorporated as a nonprofit organization in 1979. Ever since, it has enriched the lives of the residents here, both singers and listeners, by presenting two concerts a year of quality chorale literature of all historical periods. Eighty-five to 100 voices strong, these volunteers (it's a nonaudition group; no one is turned away) perform in December and May at the acoustically fine First Baptist Church. There is a membership charge of $5.00 per concert to join the chorale. Tickets to the performances are $6.00 for adults and $3.00 for students.

Hendersonville Symphony Orchestra
538 North Main Street, Hendersonville, NC
(828) 697-5884

Talented guest artists from around the nation are delighted to perform with this jewel of an orchestra. Totally community supported, it's made up of 60 to 70 music professionals, talented retirees, and students and is conducted by Dr.

Thomas Joiner. This results in six vibrant concerts a year of a quality normally found in large cities. The group also gives pops and children's concerts and an occasional special benefit. Since 1978 it has been the mentor to a string of educational programs in the Henderson County Public Schools. The symphony supports a coaching program for youth ensembles, adult ensembles, a full youth orchestra, a young artist competition, and a one-week summer string camp. Tickets to the concerts, which are held in the Hendersonville High School auditorium (the Christmas concert is at the First Baptist Church), are $12.00 for adults and $5.00 for students.

North Carolina is ranked among the top three states in national film production. Blue Ridge Motion Pictures opened its studios in Asheville in 2001. The 1921 film Conquest of Canaan *was the first to be produced in Asheville and the surrounding area. Since then, some 44 movies have been filmed or partially filmed in North Carolina's mountains.*

POLK COUNTY

Tryon Community Chorus
no phone

The Tryon Community Chorus is an all-volunteer group of people from the foothills. Two concerts are given each year: one during the Christmas season and another in the spring. Participation is open to all singers. Rehearsals are held on Mondays at Tryon Congregational Church, beginning approximately 10 weeks prior to performances. These are presented in the Polk County High School auditorium on a Friday night and Sunday afternoon. Proceeds from the concerts go toward scholarships sponsored by the Tryon Rotary Club. For further information write to Chorus, P.O. Box 54, Tryon, NC 28782.

Tryon Concert Association
Tryon Fine Arts Center, 208 Melrose
Avenue, Tryon, NC
(828) 859-8322, (828) 859-9050
This association sponsors a series of quality musical programs featuring artists of
note from October through May at the
Tryon Fine Arts Center. Membership is by
subscription and open to anyone who
enjoys a wide variety of musical presentations. Volunteers manage all aspects of
the concerts.

TRANSYLVANIA COUNTY

Brevard Chamber Orchestra
P. O. Box 1547, Brevard, NC
(828) 884-2823
Established in 1978, this 55-piece orchestra
of paid professionals from the Carolinas
and Georgia has been conducted since
1980 by Virginia Tillotson, head of the
Music Department at Brevard College. The
five-concert season has performances
scheduled in September, November,
December, February, and April. Two programs feature the full orchestra, while two
showcase smaller, more intimate ensembles. Each concert highlights critically
acclaimed guest artists. The fifth concert is
a festive Christmas program featuring the
orchestra and the choirs of Brevard. A benefit concert, always something special in
the way of guest artists and themes, is held
once a year, usually in March. The BCO is
Orchestra in Residence at the Paul Porter
Center for Performing Arts at Brevard College. Season tickets are available. Individual
tickets for specific concerts are available in
advance only at the Porter Center box
office. That number is (828) 884-8330.

Brevard College
400 North Broad Street, Brevard, NC
(828) 883-8292
Long known for its outstanding music curriculum, the college schedules a number of
cultural events throughout the school year.
These have been greatly enhanced by the
new Paul Porter Center for Performing
Arts. The public is invited to enjoy recitals,
musicals, choral groups, and instrumental
ensembles as well as dance and drama
that involve students and teachers.

Through its Life and Culture Program,
Brevard also sponsors lectures, concerts,
and writers and poetry series and has
sponsored musical performances by such
renowned groups as the Russian Folk
Ensemble, the Audubon String Quartet,
the Dutch vocal ensemble Quince, The
National Opera, and the Preservation Hall
Jazz Band. Performances by the likes of
Sukay and the Nai-Ni Chen Dance Company are joint productions with the Transylvania County Arts Council. The college
also brings in famous theatrical companies and lecturers. Many of the performances are free of charge.

Brevard Music Center
1000 Probart Street, Brevard, NC
(828) 884-2011, (888) 384-8682
Held on 140 beautiful acres just on the outskirts of town, the Brevard Music Festival
had its beginning in 1936. Today it presents
more than 70 different concert events from
mid-June through mid-August in the center's 1,800-seat, open-sided auditorium.
Lawn tickets are available after all house
seats have been sold. Performances include
symphony orchestra, opera, jazz, Broadway
musicals, pops, and those of internationally
acclaimed guest artists. Included in the
past seasons' appearances were com-
poser/entertainer Marvin Hamlisch, harpist
Deborah Henson-Conant, pianist Garrick
Ohlsson, Rhythm & Brass, the U.S. Army
Orchestra, and staged productions of
Gilbert and Sullivan's *The Mikado,* Puccini's
La Bohème, Massenet's Manon, and Her-
bert's *Naughty Marietta.* During the most
recent season, Kathleen Battle of the Met
performed for two sold-out houses. She
was originally scheduled for only one date.
In addition an intimate chamber music
series is scheduled on weeknights, along
with various student performances.

Integral to its impressive concert
series, the center provides a unique training experience for 400-plus gifted students from across the nation. They, along

with teaching professionals from leading college/conservatories and performing organizations, perform beside internationally known guest artists, working together to present seven weeks of fabulous music.

More than half of the events are free to the public. Among these have been *Peter and the Wolf* and *Beauty and the Beast,* special young persons' concerts, free for kids on Saturdays. Bach's Lunch and BYOP (bring your own picnic) are lunchtime favorites. Have lunch with the students as they perform delightful music.

Single tickets can range from free to $25 for adults and from free to $13 for children. Special events concerts are fundraisers and are priced accordingly. For ticket information or to request a schedule of events, call the above phone numbers or visit the center's Web site at www.brevardmusic.org, where tickets may be purchased on-line.

Calico Chorus and Men's Chorus
Brevard, NC
(828) 883-2297

For more than 27 years, the Calico Chorus, founded and directed by Ruth Hunter, has presented spring and Christmas concerts. In addition this group of nine women entertains nursing home residents and community and civic organizations all over Western North Carolina with its delightful repertoire of mostly American popular music. About 11 years ago, eight male singers, called the Men's Chorus, were added for some of the performances, both to sing with the women and to do their own numbers.

The major concerts are usually held at the Brevard Presbyterian Church, 300 East Main Street, or at the First Methodist Church, 500 North Broad Street. The group has also proven very popular when participating in the town's Festival of the Arts and has performed in the Great Hall of the Grove Park Inn at Christmas.

Transylvania Choral Society
Brevard, NC
(828) 884-2645

This is a nonauditioned group of about 45 singers. Formed by Ruth Hunter about 20 years ago to offer church choir members in the community a forum for singing major sacred works, it's now open to anyone who loves to sing. It meets at Brevard-Davidson River Presbyterian Church weekly except during the summer. Concerts of classical choral music are offered twice a year, in the spring and at Christmas. The concerts are usually at the Presbyterian Church.

Southern Mountains

CHEROKEE/CLAY COUNTIES

The Brasstown Concert Association
P. O. Box 105, Brasstown, NC 28902
(828) 837-8822

Since 1927 this association has brought artists from the outside world to what, until a few decades ago, was a beautiful but remote area of the mountains. Today it presents six concerts, three in the spring and three in the fall, that vary from flute to harp to string quartets to brass quintets to fabulous performers of ethnic music from around the world. These concerts, which takes place at 3:00 P.M. on Sunday afternoons, can be enjoyed at the John C. Campbell Folk School. (See our chapter on Mountain Crafts.) Season tickets are $40.00 for all six concerts; $20.00 for a series of three concerts. Tickets are usually $8.00 for a single concert, and discounts are available to students.

The association also occasionally sponsors dance and performance arts programs, and schedules music workshops in the local schools.

John C. Campbell Folk School Concerts
1 Folk School Road, Brasstown, NC
(828) 837-2775, (800) FOLK-SCH

Free Folk School Concerts are held most Fridays at 7:30 P.M. at the school's historic Keith House Community Room on Brasstown Road. During late spring and summer, weather permitting, the event moves to the Festival Barn. (Bring a lawn chair and follow the signs from the Keith House parking area.) These concerts range from traditional gospel and bluegrass to music for handbells to western song and cowboy poetry.

MACON COUNTY

Highlands Chamber Music Festival
P.O. Box 1702, Highlands, NC 28741
No phone

Since 1981 the Highlands Chamber Music Festival has presented a stunning monthlong series of chamber music. The July-August season features about 15 concerts held at the Episcopal Church of the Incarnation and the Highlands United Methodist Church. Write to the above address for current information on performers and ticket prices.

DANCE

Central Mountains

BUNCOMBE COUNTY

Asheville Contemporary Dance Theatre and The New Studio of Dance
20 Commerce Street, Asheville, NC
(828) 254-2621

This fascinating, experimental dance/theater company presents lavishly produced original works adapted from ancient legends of different world cultures—particularly the richly imaginative Aztec and Mayan legends, such as the story of the feathered serpent Quetzalcoatl. Meticulous research, typically taking as long as eight months, incorporates experimental movement, puppets, sword play, mime, traditional music, and interpretive costuming (including some interesting ones of sculpted foam) for each production. The 6- to 15-member company has performed across the Southeast and in France and offers artistic exchanges with international dance theater companies.

Fletcher School of Dance/Land of the Sky Civic Ballet
177 Patton Avenue, Asheville, NC
(828) 252-4761

This distinguished school of dance, started more than 50 years ago by the late Beale Fletcher, is an institution in Asheville. The school's performing arm, the Land of the Sky Civic Ballet, annually produces a polished, well-received version of *The Nutcracker* for holiday audiences.

POLK COUNTY

Tryon Dance Guild
Columbus, NC

Twice a year, in the spring and fall, this guild, under the auspices of the Polk County Community Schools, presents performances by renowned national dance groups. Shows are held in the 700-seat Polk County High School Auditorium. Call (828) 894-3051 for ticket information. Free performances are presented to students throughout the county.

LITERARY ARTS

Many bookstores in all the mountain areas offer a fine schedule of literary readings. Poets and authors from all parts enjoy a turn in the mountains and read from their best-sellers, offering a question-and-answer session afterward. Check local listings in the *Mountain Xpress,* daily papers, and free weekly entertainment papers.

Northern Mountains

ASHE COUNTY

Blue Ridge Writers Group
Ashe County Library, 148 Library Drive, West Jefferson, NC
(828) 246-9087

This group supports the creative efforts of area writers of fiction, nonfiction, and poetry. The Blue Ridge Writers Group sponsors literary contests, offers a critiquing service and provides tips on getting work published.

Central Mountains

BUNCOMBE COUNTY

Poetry Alive!
20 Battery Park Avenue, Asheville, NC
(828) 255-7636, (800) 476-8172
www.poetryalive.com
Interaction is the life's blood of this arts organization, which was formed back in 1984 with the express purpose of popularizing poetry and making it more accessible to the general public, children in particular. The prime focus of Poetry Alive! is making poetry, education, and fun synonymous, a feat accomplished over and over again by this innovative organization.

From five to nine teams of poets/performers travel the nation, bringing the richly illustrative world of poetry to all who will listen and watch. Transfixed audiences from kindergartners to college students watch as the words leap off the page, and all manner of poetry—epic poems, sonnets, classics from world culture, doggerel, and humor—come to life before their eyes.

Team members are college graduates in fine arts or education. They also work with teachers to incorporate these materials into the classroom by providing workshops, scripted material, and tapes. And fortunately for the rest of us, Poetry Alive! offers performances for adults as well.

The Writers' Workshop
387 Beaucatcher Road, Asheville, NC
(828) 254-8111
This busy organization is geared to writers—amateurs, professionals and youthful budding scribes—of all ages. For the last 17 years, this membership group has been dedicated to the promotion of all things literary.

The Writers' Workshop offers support, evaluation, competition, and valuable workshops designed to enhance the spark of inspiration and help it grow. A quarterly newsletter and regular literary competitions are yearly highlights. Nationally known professional writers are judges for these contests and participate in an annual professional writers' forum in Asheville, sponsored by the Writers' Workshop. This special series is open to the public. Past participants have included such literary greats as Eudora Welty, Alex Haley, John Le Carre, E. L. Doctorow, Kurt Vonnegut, and Peter Matthiessen.

TRANSYLVANIA COUNTY

Transylvania Writers' Alliance
c/o Michael DeNike, 92 Thunder Road,
Brevard, NC
(828) 883-8688
Both professional and amateur writers meet to share and critique their works and hear tips from successful authors. In addition to monthly meetings, there are weekly critique sessions. These sessions, for both poetry and prose, are held on separate days. There are also occasional workshops with professional leaders. For more information on the Alliance, call Mr. DeNike.

MUSEUMS

Northern Mountains

WATAUGA COUNTY

Appalachian Cultural Museum
University Hall Drive, Boone, NC
(828) 262-3117
You must visit this fine museum of Appalachian cultural heritage. Located in University Hall in Boone just off the campus of Appalachian State University, it has a fascinating collection of artifacts spanning eons—from prehistoric times to the present. You can view special exhibits depicting highlights of life in our mountain region. Groups can take advantage of the specially guided tours led by museum staff (call for a reservation). These personalized illuminations of history focus on all

aspects of living in the mountains, now and in the past. University Hall also houses the Appalachian Collection, a wonderfully varied assortment of music, books, and documents pertinent to the region. The offices of the Appalachian Consortium and the Center for Appalachian Studies are also here.

Hickory Ridge Homestead
591 Horn in the West Drive, Boone, NC
(828) 264–2120
This living history museum, sponsored by the Southern Appalachian Historical Association, is composed of a series of log structures, a main log cabin, a weaving room, and a smokehouse, all depicting the period of the late-18th century in the Appalachian mountains. The homestead reflects the same period covered by the outdoor drama *Horn in the West,* also on the site. The Olde Christmas Celebration and the Hickory Ridge Homestead Apple Festival in October are two special events celebrated here.

Central Mountains

BUNCOMBE COUNTY

Biltmore Estate
N.C. Highway 25, Asheville, NC
(828) 255–1700, (800) 543–2961
Don't miss the spectacular private working estate established in 1895 by railroad heir George Vanderbilt. Vanderbilt chose his original 125,000 acres well and created a lavish 250-room mansion styled after his favorite chateau in France's Loire River Valley, and it's filled with antiques and artifacts (for much more information, see our chapter on the Biltmore Estate and Winery).

Biltmore Homespun Museum
111 Grovewood Road, Asheville, NC
(828) 253–7651
Built in 1917, the English-style pebble-dash cottage housing the museum was one of the original Biltmore Homespun Shop

buildings. Photos and artifacts preserve the old weaving operation begun almost a century ago under the auspices of Edith Stuyvesant Vanderbilt, wife of railroad heir George Vanderbilt of Biltmore Estate. Artifacts such as bolts of cloth, antique handmade looms, and an original, old-time clock bring back the flavor of the Biltmore Industries and Biltmore Homespun Shops of days gone by. During the week there are weaving demonstrations throughout the day. There's no entrance fee.

Biltmore Village Historic Museum
7 Biltmore Plaza, Biltmore Village,
Asheville, NC
(828) 274–9707
The 100-year history of Biltmore Village and its integral connection to George Vanderbilt and his magnificent Biltmore Estate is displayed in an exhibit of period photographs and Victorian artifacts in this free museum in Biltmore Village (see our chapter on the Biltmore Estate and Winery for more information).

Estes-Winn Antique
Automobile Museum, 111 Grovewood
Road, Asheville, NC
(828) 253–7651
Next door to Grovewood Gallery, in the massive original weaving shed that once housed 40 looms for the old Biltmore Industries, is the Estes-Winn Antique Automobile Museum. This delightful collection is a veritable history of how America took to the highway, from the first Model T to shiny post–World War II roadsters. You can fantasize about grand old autos such as a 1926 Cadillac and a 1927 La Salle convertible. There's even a 1922 La France fire engine on display that once was used by the Asheville Fire Department. They just don't make 'em like they used to!

Pack Place Education Arts and Science Center
2 South Pack Square, Asheville, NC
(828) 257–4500
This spectacular, 92,000-square-foot complex is a monument to the determination

CLOSE-UP

A Hillside in Highland Park

A bright star among the Montgomery, Alabama, Southern Belles, Zelda Fitzgerald left a path of broken hearts behind her. An accomplished painter, she also wrote. The dark shadows of her mind eventually brought her to Highland Psychiatric Hospital in Asheville, founded in 1904 by Dr. Robert Carroll. In 1939 Dr. Carroll gave 100 percent interest in the hospital to Duke University. Zelda, who earlier had been diagnosed in Europe with schizophrenia, frequented the sanitarium from the 1930s until her death in an all-consuming hospital fire in 1948. Meanwhile, her husband, author F. Scott, resided at the Grove Park Inn during his visits with her.

The former hospital grounds are now known as Highland Park. Amid this landscape Zelda once painted; you will find a plaque dedicated to her.

of such leading Asheville citizens as the late Roger McGuire, whose vision was to realize the potential of downtown Asheville. The success of Pack Place has finally become reality, and visitors and citizens alike are discovering the delights of this diverse cultural center. Pack Place is the union, adaptation, and renovation of several historic structures and is home to the Asheville Art Museum, the Colburn Gem and Mineral Museum, the Health Adventure, Diana Wortham Theatre, and the YMI Cultural Center.

The Asheville Art Museum, founded in 1948, is contained on three floors of the old Pack Memorial Library, now a part of Pack Place. This first-rate museum maintains a fine permanent collection of 20th-century American art, including the work of such renowned artists as Romare Bearden, Jacob Lawrence, and George Inness; the sculpture of Louise Nevelson; and contemporary abstracts of Asheville natives Kenneth Noland and Donald Sultan. Tours are available for group visits.

The Colburn Gem and Mineral Museum is an exploration of the geological world around us. The museum, founded in 1960,

highlights gems and minerals of all shapes and sizes from around the world, as well as those specific garnets, rubies, emeralds and gold deposits that make North Carolina a rock hound's delight (see our chapter on Rockhounding).

The Health Adventure, founded in 1968, is a marvelous hands-on learning center, providing children and adults special insights into the human physical condition and related applied sciences. Two theaters accommodate school groups for educator-led programs. Thoughtfully planned, hands-on exhibits such as Brain Storm, Body Works, Miracle of Life, and the Creative Play Space (for children younger than 8) invite young curiosity.

The Diana Wortham Theatre is a gem of a performance space for audiences, performers, and technicians. The 500-seat theater is an intimate, sophisticated setting with a full-size stage, exquisitely detailed woodwork, impeccable acoustics, and accessibility for people with disabilities. Diana Wortham Theatre presents, produces, and hosts performing arts events that range from Shakespeare to Mamet, classical ballet to modern dance, lectures to performance poetry, symphonies to Brubeck, and world-renowned storytellers to local school pageants.

The YMI Cultural Center, also a part of the Pack Place complex, is on the corner of Market and Eagle Streets, southeast of Pack Square, in an architecturally rich, century-old structure commissioned by George Vanderbilt. This museum is the home of changing exhibits and a permanent collection of artifacts that focus on the local, national, and international African-American heritage.

The Adventure Place is an imaginatively stocked gift shop designed to complement the various museums found at Pack Place. A fascinating lobby exhibit entitled "Here is the Square. . . " traces three centuries of Asheville history and the evolution of Pack Square itself.

Tickets are required for admission to each of the museums. A single adult ticket for each museum is $3.50, with a discount for senior citizens and students (with ID) and for children ages 4 to 15. Your best bet is a one-day pass covering admission to all museums at $6.50, $5.50, and $4.50, respectively. Children younger than 3 are admitted free. Hours are Tuesday through Saturday from 10:00 A.M. to 5:00 P.M. From June through October, Pack Place is also open on Sundays from 1:00 to 5:00 P.M. The Art Museum is open Friday night until 8:00 P.M.

Smith-McDowell House
283 Victoria Road, Asheville, NC
(828) 253-9231

This fine old Asheville residence is on the campus of Asheville-Buncombe Technical Community College. The stately, early Victorian-era home, built around 1840, is Asheville's oldest brick residence, furnished with period antiques. You'll enjoy the marvelous architectural details and appointments of this palatial beauty. Personalized tours are available. Admission is $5.00 for adults and $2.00 for children. Regular hours are Tuesday through Saturday from 10:00 A.M. to 4:00 P.M. and Sunday from 1:00 to 4:00 P.M. Hours during

January, February, and March are Tuesday through Friday from 10:00 A.M. to 4:00 P.M.

Swannanoa Valley Museum
225 West State Street, Black Mountain, NC
(828) 669-9566

The Swannanoa Valley Museum, open seasonally from April through October, is the guardian of a remarkable collection of artifacts of everyday life in Western North Carolina, from pioneer times to recent years. Local residents donated many of the items here. This unique museum is also home to an exhibit honoring Rafael Guastavino, architect and designer of the century-old Basilica of St. Lawrence in Asheville; displays spotlighting Billy Graham's crusades; the U.S. Navy artifacts of Rear Adm. G. C. Crawford; and an extensive collection of wildflower photography. The museum is open Tuesday through Saturday 10:00 A.M. to 5:00 P.M. and Sunday 2:00 to 5:00 P.M.

Thomas Wolfe Memorial
48 Spruce Street, Asheville, NC
(828) 253-8304

Asheville's native son, noted author of the classic coming-of-age novel, *Look Homeward, Angel,* spent his boyhood here in his mother's rambling old boardinghouse on Spruce Street, just off legendary Pack Square. This old house figured prominently in Wolfe's work and is important for its ability to convey the forces that helped shape this remarkable American writer. Tragically the house was badly burned in a fire in late 1998 but is presently undergoing renovations. The Thomas Wolfe Welcome Center adjacent to the house is still open and offers information about the house and the author.

Zebulon Vance Birthplace
Reems Creek Road off Old U.S. Highways
19/23, Weaverville, NC
(828) 645-6706

This charming mountain homestead was home to one of North Carolina's most prominent political figures. Zeb Vance began his career as a lawyer, assuming

Gift of the Magi

William Sidney Porter claimed to his final day that it was only a coincidence that both he and a large sum of money were missing from the Texas bank where he was a teller in 1894. Eventually Porter found his way to Asheville and as both a widower and as the noted author, O. Henry, married a local girl, Sara Lindsey Coleman. He obviously became familiar with many of the mountain folks as he used mountain names and the circumstances of folks from this region in "The Gift of the Magi." To commemorate this tale, the Urban Trail of Asheville displays a plaque with items from the story (cast in bronze) surrounding it. It is located on Patton Avenue close to Pack Square. Meanwhile, in death, O. Henry remains in our area noted by a simple grave marker in Riverside Cemetery, William Sidney Porter.

public office by the young age of 24. He was elected governor of North Carolina three times, most notably during the Civil War. He also served three terms as a U.S. senator. At his death in 1894, this most capable public servant was admired by colleagues and beloved by his constituency. His life and career are profiled in an exhibit in the adjoining visitor center.

The two-story cabin and outbuildings are reconstructions, built from hewn, yellow pine logs around the original chimney with its two massive fireplaces. The furnishings and household items depict the period from 1790 to 1840 and include a few pieces original to the Vance family.

Pioneer Living Days are celebrated here each spring and fall. Costumed staff members demonstrate skills and occupations of earlier days. Military encampments and battle reenactments are frequently part of the events (see our Annual Festivals and Events chapter). Admission to the homestead is free.

HENDERSON COUNTY

Carl Sandburg Home
1928 Little River Road, Flat Rock, NC
(828) 693-4178

Carl Sandburg—poet, author, lecturer, musician, onetime political activist, social thinker, and winner of two Pulitzer Prizes for his four-volume *Abraham Lincoln: The War Years* and his *Complete Poems*— spent the last 22 years of his life at Connemara, a 240-acre farm 3 miles south of Hendersonville. The main house was built in 1838 as a summer home for Charleston's Christopher Gustave Memminger, who served as secretary of the treasury for the Confederacy from 1861 to 1864. Like many mountain residents today, Memminger wanted to escape the heat and humidity of the coast, while Sandburg sought relief from cold northern winters.

Sandburg moved here in 1945 with his wife, three daughters, grandchildren, and his wife's prize-winning Chikaming goats— a herd that grew as large as 200; the milk was turned into a successful dairy operation. The Sandburgs spent happy and productive years in a lovely setting of rolling pastures, ponds, lakes, and wooded mountains. Sandburg died in 1967, and Connemara became a National Historic Site the following year. It's open daily except on December 25.

To reach the site drive south on U.S. 25 and turn onto Little River Road at the Flat Rock Playhouse. Park at the Visitors Information Center and, after viewing the exhibits there, take the lovely walk past a small lake up to the main house for a guided tour. (Access assistance for the handicapped is provided.) Later, stroll about the farm and pet the goats and other farm animals if you don't mind risking an occasional bite, peck, or kick. Hike the 2.6-mile round-trip trail up to Glassy Mountain, one of Sandburg's favorite walks, for a mountain ridge and valley view.

In midsummer there are free dramatic renditions of some of Sandburg's writings offered by the Apprentice Company of the Flat Rock Playhouse in the outdoor theater (call for performance times). Connemara is particularly festive during the Christmas season, which is celebrated in "Sandburg style" on Saturday evenings from Thanksgiving until Christmas. The park is closed only on December 25.

The Historic Hendersonville Depot and Model Railroad
Seventh Avenue and Maple Street, Hendersonville, NC
(828) 693-0605

Hendersonville got its first train depot in 1879, which was replaced in 1902 by the present structure. Now the quaint building is under an ongoing restoration program. Dressed up in its original colors, it houses an operating, 420-square-foot model railroad in its old baggage room. The model features the Hendersonville, Asheville, Brevard, and Saluda Stations, including the Saluda Grade (the steepest grade in the country), plus mountains, waterfalls, lakes, towns, and industries. The train runs over 500 feet of track and has more than 100 switches. It's open to the public free of charge year-round (donations are appreciated) from noon to 3:00 P.M. on Wednesday and 9:00 A.M. until noon on Saturday.

The Historic Johnson Farm
3346 Haywood Road, N.C. Highway 191, Hendersonville, NC
(828) 891-6585

Located 4 miles north of Hendersonville on N.C. 191, this late-19th-century, 15-acre tobacco farm became a popular summer tourist retreat in the 1920s. Today, owned by the Henderson County Public Schools, an 1870s brick farmhouse, 1920 boarding house, barn-loft museum, 10 historic buildings, and two nature trails are operated as a heritage education center and farm museum. Guided tours are available at 10:30 A.M. and 1:30 P.M. Tuesday through Saturday from May through October, and Wednesday through Saturday from November through April. A small admission is charged for guided tours.

Western North Carolina Air Museum
1340 Gilbert Street, Hendersonville, NC
(828) 693-9708, (800) 828-4244

It's appropriate that this air museum, in the state where flight was born, is located at the Hendersonville Airport. That also enables it to feature spring and fall air shows. Award-winning, beautifully restored airplanes as well as restored replica antique and vintage planes are on display here. They range from a 1917 Nieuport 11 (Bebe) replica to a 1950s Ercoup, and a Corbin Ace. You can even view a 1510 ornithopter designed by Leonardo da Vinci. The museum is open each Wednesday, Saturday, and Sunday from noon until 6:00 P.M. Admission is free, but donations are welcomed. Gifts and souvenirs are available. Museum memberships and lifetime memberships are also available.

POLK COUNTY

Polk County Historical Association & Museum
1 Depot Street, Tryon, NC
(828) 859-2287

Housed in the old but charmingly renovated Tryon railroad depot, the association exhibits household, agricultural, and historical artifacts used by the early settlers and Indians in this area. There is also a collection of folklore, old maps, records, and pictures, including important items in American history such as "the cannonball that started the Civil War," said to have been picked up at Fort Sumter by a young Union officer, Abner Doubleday. Monthly historical meetings are held, and the public is invited. The museum is open on Tuesday and Thursday from 10:00 A.M. until noon and by appointment. Admission is free, but donations are appreciated.

TRANSYLVANIA COUNTY

Allison-Deaver Historical House
N.C. Highway 280, Pisgah Forest, NC
(828) 884-5137

Just two days before it was scheduled to be demolished, Western North Carolina's oldest frame house west of the Blue Ridge Mountains was saved by the Transylvania County Historical Society. Built in Quaker or Federal architectural style in the early 1800s by Benjamin Allison, it housed his family of 11 children. In 1830 he sold the house and its 420 acres to William Deaver, who, in the early 1840s, remodeled the six-room, 1,100-square-foot structure into a Greek Revival house and expanded it. Then in the 1860s, the roof was raised to make room for second- and third-floor Charleston-, or Low County-style porches. This "house-restoration museum" is open for tours from April through October from 10:00 A.M. to 4:00 P.M. on Friday and Saturday and on Sunday from 1:00 to 4:00 P.M. There is no admission charge, but donations for this ongoing project are appreciated.

The Allison-Deaver House is located on N.C. 280 just north of its intersection with U.S. 64 in Pisgah Forest. It is adjacent to the Forest Gate Shopping Center and Taco Bell restaurant.

Cradle of Forestry
U.S. Highway 276, Pisgah National Forest
(828) 877-3130

There is an old story, though probably not true, that claims someone told George Vanderbilt that if he was going to build a baronial estate (Biltmore House and Gardens certainly qualifies), he should have a baronial forest—and that's how scientific forestry got started in America. True or

not, in the late 1800s George Vanderbilt hired Gifford Pinchot to restore and manage the forest on the 8,000 acres surrounding his famous estate. His holdings were later expanded to 125,000 acres that, after his death, became part of Pisgah National Forest.

In 1895 Dr. Carl Schenck, a brilliant German forester, succeeded Pinchot and was a magnet for young men wishing to learn the new sustainable forest methods. As a result, in 1898 Schenck started the Biltmore Forest School, the first forestry school in America. For his campus he utilized an old schoolhouse and abandoned farm buildings in a 3,200-foot-high valley that was named the Pink Beds, after its lush bloom of flowers. In 1964, 6,500 acres in this area were established as a National Historic Site and became known as the Cradle of Forestry.

Special interpretive programs and guided tours are offered here, and you can view an excellent 18-minute movie depicting the relationship between Vanderbilt, Pinchot, Schenck, and the Forest School students. The Forest Discovery Center has a Biltmore Forest School exhibit with a collection of artifacts as well as "Schenck's Office," where you'll find period furniture and artifacts and can look through the windows and listen to a conversation between Dr. Schenck and a student. (See the Cradle of Forestry Close-up in our Forests and Parks chapter.)

There are two beautiful, mile-long paved trails, each with guided tours that will tell you of the Cradle's history and teach you a lot about the plants and trees along the way. The Forest Festival Trail has many forest demonstration projects, an old sawmill, the first little fish hatchery in Pisgah, and a old Climax logging train on display—children love to climb on it and ring the bell. The Biltmore Campus Trail winds through the school's old campus of original and reconstructed buildings. In addition to the schoolhouse, there's a general store, a two-story frame house built in 1884, another farmhouse that was used as student quarters, a blacksmith shop, an old barn that Schenck converted to an office, two former ranger houses designed by Schenck (known as the Black Forest Lodge and the Cantrell Creek Lodge), an old-time vegetable garden, and more.

On Friday, Saturday, and Sunday afternoons, craftspeople in period dress demonstrate crafts like weaving, spinning, quilting, basketry, and toy making and give you a glimpse of life at the turn of the twentieth century. There are a number of special events throughout the year, such as Fiber Arts Week and the huge Forest Festival Day, held in October. The Cradle, open seven days a week from 9:00 A.M. to 5:00 P.M., is on U.S. 276, 14 miles northwest of Brevard and 4 miles south of the Blue Ridge Parkway at milepost 412. The use fee is $4.00 for adults and $2.00 for children ages 6 to 17. Children 5 and younger are admitted free.

Jim Bob Tinsley Museum and Research Center
20 West Jordan Street, Brevard, NC
(828) 884–2347

Transylvania County may seem an unlikely place to find a cowboy museum, but this is a great one. It houses the extensive collection of art, memorabilia, and research records of Jim Bob Tinsley, a Brevard native and famous author, educator, and musicologist. He performed with Gene Autry in the late 1940s and has received many awards for his work, including one from the National Cowboy Hall of Fame for his book (one of 10) *He Was Singing This Song*, a compilation of traditional American cowboy songs.

Here you'll find original art, lithographs, photographs, and bronze statues by famous sculptors of the caliber of Frederick Remington. There is also, as you might expect, a lot about country-and-western music, including a large collection of records, tapes, and CDs. There are reels and TV tapes of western movies and old television programs that are played during office hours. And there are all those other things connected to cowboys: saddles,

spurs, branding irons from famous ranches, Florida Cracker cowboy whips, and an original Zane Grey 30-foot riata, to name a few items.

But Tinsley's interests go far beyond cowboys. The museum contains his historic Transylvania County memorabilia, including one of only six known Gillespie rifles. The gun dates from the early 1880s and was manufactured at the Gillespie rifle factory in nearby South Mills River. You'll also find art and literature concerning two of his other passions: pumas and sailfish. And then there are Tinsley's waterfall photos, many of which appeared in his popular book *The Land of Waterfalls: Transylvania, North Carolina*.

The museum's summer hours are Tuesday through Saturday from 10:00 A.M. to 4:00 P.M.; in winter hours are Tuesday through Saturday from 1:00 to 4:00 P.M. Admission is free.

Silvermont Mansion
East Main Street, Brevard, NC
No phone

John Silversteen and his wife, Elizabeth, moved to Transylvania County in 1902. He opened the Toxaway Tanning Company, around which the town of Rosman grew, and later established the Gloucester Lumber Company. His enterprises, the largest in the county, provided work for several hundred people until the 1950s. He was active in and generous to the community, building the first brick elementary school in Rosman and donating the land for that town's high school.

But he's most remembered for Silvermont, the 1917, 33-room, Colonial Revival house that still stands on its spacious grounds on East Main Street. Here the Silversteens raised their three daughters—two went into business with their father; one became a noted singer who performed with the likes of Arturo Toscanini and Leopold Stokowski under the name of Adelaide van Wey.

Silvermont was willed to the county when the last daughter died in 1972. It was placed on the National Register of Historic

Places in 1981. Full of interesting furniture and Silversteen memorabilia, its first floor is used for community club meetings, by private groups, and as a senior meal and recreation center. The eight-acre grounds have tennis and shuffleboard courts, a basketball court, a playground, and a picnic area. On summer evenings square dancing takes place on Tuesday, ballroom dancing on Wednesday, and mountain music "on the porch" on Thursday. Christmas at Silvermont features decorations by the Transylvania Council of Garden Clubs, usually involving musical performances.

The mansion is available for weddings, receptions, family reunions, class reunions, and other special events, but is closed when not in use. For more information call Herman Rahn at (828) 877-3939 or Harley Raines at (828) 883-9223. For information about the park, call (828) 884-3156.

Southern Mountains

CLAY COUNTY

Historical Arts Museum
U.S. Highway 64 Business, Hayesville, NC
(828) 389-6814
The museum, housed in the town's old jail, is devoted to local history and is sponsored by the Clay County Historical and Art Council. Here you'll see a cross-section of memorabilia—the first telephone switchboard and a kitchen from the 19th century—from earlier time. Receptions and showings of local artists are also held here. It is open from June through September.

CHEROKEE COUNTY

Cherokee County Historical Museum
205 Peachtree Street, Murphy, NC
(828) 837-6792
This museum is housed in the former Carnegie Library building, right next to the even grander county courthouse. Its largest collection is devoted to the life of the Cherokee during their many centuries

in the mountains and their removal to Oklahoma. Murphy itself was established near the site of the ancient Cherokee village of Guasili (pronounced "gau-ax-u-le"), visited by de Soto in 1540, and was also the site of Fort Butler, the largest of the forts built in the area for the Cherokees' removal via "The Trail of Tears."

In the museum are leftover weapons from Spanish explorers and another large collection of tools, housewares, and other items from the early pioneer days in the region. Some of the most interesting things among the mineral and rock collections are "fairy crosses" (see our Close-up, Little People and Fairy Crosses). These naturally occurring little stone crosses, called staurlite (pronounced "starlight") crystals, are supposed to bring the finder good luck. Some can be as large as 3 inches across. They still turn up around Hyatt Creek southeast of Marble and around Fishermare Branch, Almond Creek, between Parsons Branch and Burnt Branch, and around the Brasstown area.

The museum also houses a collection of more than 700 priceless dolls donated by Louise S. Kilgore. They include, among other things, representations of famous personalities (including Elvis and Princess Diana) and unique older dolls made in prefactory days. The collection takes up about one-fourth of the space on the museum's top floor. The museum is open Monday through Friday from 9:00 A.M. until 5:00 P.M. Admission is free.

HAYWOOD COUNTY

Canton Area Historical Museum
36 Park Street, Canton, NC
(828) 646-3412
With its library of old family histories and historical documents, this city-run museum, housed in the town's old library building, is an excellent place to research local history. Displays include artifacts, records, heritage handicrafts, and pictures from the past, all of which combine to tell the story of the settling of Canton and the Pigeon River area, Haywood County, and Western North

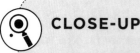

Little People and Fairy Crosses

Those of us steeped in Western culture know all about the Old World's fairies, elves, gnomes, trolls, and the like, but few of us are acquainted with the Little People who reside in these mountains, though some folks of European descent have encountered them over the years. James Mooney, in his classic work, *History, Myths, and Sacred Formulas of the Cherokees,* first published in 1900 by the Bureau of American Ethnology, identifies a whole pantheon of spirit folk, some of whom are mentioned in other legends in our book.

The Cherokee's name for Little People is *yunwi tsunsdi.* They usually live in rock caves on mountainsides, though one group, called *yunwi amaiyinehi,* lives in water (they are the ones fishing enthusiasts should try to please). When full grown, *yunwi tsunsdi* are only as tall as a man's knee, but they are well formed and handsome, with long hair down to their heels. They love music and spend a lot of time singing and dancing.

They are also powerful workers of wonders. Generally speaking, they are kind and helpful (particularly to children or people lost in the woods) but not always. If you hear their drumming in the distance, don't follow the sound: If disturbed in their homes, Little People will cast a spell that will make you lose your way. Even if you are found, you may spend the rest of your life in a daze. If you find an object, such as a knife or other item in the woods, you must say,

"Little People, I want to take this," because if you don't and it belongs to them, they will throw stones at you on your way home.

Like the busy elves in Western lore, they will sometimes come near a human house at night and, before morning, finish a great task like clearing a field that would require the efforts of a huge workforce. However, if you hear them at work, don't go out to see them, or you'll die.

Many little footprints were seen, and a number of encounters with these little folk were described in accounts by both Indians and whites (mainly hunters) at the end of the 19th century. Some of these took place near or at the head of the Oconaluftee River, which flows through the present-day Cherokee Indian Reservation. There is also a certain spot in what is now the Great Smoky Mountains National Park where yunsi tsunsdi came to the Cherokee during summer solstices to tell them, among other things, tales of the Cherokee nation's history.

One day, the Little People were near Brasstown, doing their favorite things—singing and dancing—when a foreign "messenger" arrived and told them the sad tale of Christ's death on a cross. They were so moved, they cried. As their tears fell, they turned into little stone crosses that can still be found today. A wonderful collection of these Fairy Crosses can be seen in Murphy's Cherokee County Historical Museum (which is described in this chapter).

Carolina (in that order of importance). The artifacts include everything from Indian arrowheads and tools to butter molds, quilts, glassware, and pottery.

Special shows, such as an exhibit of old medical equipment and an exhibit of local primitive painters, are frequently held. You can also explore a Champion display room, which features a video on the role of Champion paper in the area. The museum also participates in educational programs at local schools and civic clubs. It's open Monday through Friday from 10:00 A.M. until noon and from 1:00 P.M. until 4:00 P.M. and on Sunday from 2:00 to 4:00 P.M.

The Museum of North Carolina Handicrafts
307 Shelton Street, Waynesville, NC
(828) 452-1551

The Shelton House, built in 1875 and listed on the National Register of Historic Places, is the setting for these comprehensive exhibits of 19th-century crafts. It also has an interesting exhibit of handicrafts made by artisans who have participated in the educational demonstration of heritage crafts in the North Carolina State Fair's Village of Yesteryear since 1951 (see our Mountain Crafts chapter for more information). New exhibits include a working Pioneer Village and a collection of railroad memorabilia. The museum is open from 10:00 A.M. to 4:00 P.M. Tuesday through Friday, May through October. There is an admission charge of $4.00 for adults; for groups of 15 or more, it's $2.00 per adult.

JACKSON COUNTY

Mountain Heritage Center
Western Carolina University, Administration Building, U.S. Highway 107, Cullowhee, NC
(828) 227-7211

If you're of Scotch-Irish ancestry, this museum is a must! Even if you're not, it's a very special place for learning about the land, culture, and people of the Appalachian region. A large permanent exhibit, "Migration of the Scotch-Irish People," relates the saga of this group's

departure from their native Scotland to settle in Northern Ireland, and in a later generation, its journey from Ulster to the New World. It also highlights the homes and culture that developed here in the coves and hollows of Western North Carolina. Murals and a life-size, 18th-century Irish cottage make the story come alive. Other exhibits illustrate the mountains' natural history and society, both past and present.

This section also preserves objects of historical significance, including the heirlooms of hundreds of families who lived here. There are exhibits on cornshuck handcrafts and the traditions of milling, tilling, and stilling corn. A good place to start your tour is in the museum movie theater, where nine-projector, multiimage shows complement the thematic exhibits. The center also publishes books and other materials on mountain culture. All these— the exhibits, the shows, and the literature—are based on thorough and extensive research.

The Mountain Heritage Center is also the focus for Mountain Heritage Day, held in September, which attracts more than 35,000 visitors (see our Annual Festivals and Events chapter). During this event the center puts together a folk festival featuring musicians and craftspeople who maintain authentic mountain traditions. The center also sponsors a variety of special mountain heritage events in the schools and communities throughout the region. It is open year-round, Monday through Friday from 8:00 A.M. to 5:00 P.M. and from 1:00 to 4:00 P.M. on Sunday. There is no admission charge.

MACON COUNTY

Macon County Historical Society Museum
36 West Main Street, Franklin, NC
(828) 524-9758

This museum, supported by the Macon County Historical Society, preserves the area's heritage through displays of artifacts, documents, and photographs that illustrate the social, cultural, and historical

CLOSE-UP

Macon County: Jones Knob and Whiterock Mountain

A fairly easy, round-trip hike of about 5.2 miles will reveal some special vistas of the Nantahala Mountains to the west. First, from the corner of Fourth and Main Streets in Highlands, take U.S. 64/28 toward Franklin for 4.2 miles. Turn left on Turtle Pond Road (SR 1620) and drive for 1.1 miles to SR 1678. Turn right and drive 1.4 miles to the top of a hill. Turn left on Jones Gap Road (FR 4522) and drive 2 miles to the parking area.

The trail leaves the parking area on the right, goes on an access road, and crosses a wildlife management field. At the end of the field, the trail spur marked in blue leads 0.3 mile to Jones Knob and views to the left and down from the flat rock area at the top. The right fork (yellow blazes) is the Bartram Trail. Take it 1.3 miles to Whiterock Gap for views to the west. Continue for almost 0.75 mile to the blue-blazed spur trail to the left. This trail ascends less than 0.5 mile to a spectacular rock outcropping and view. Keep in mind, however, that seasonal closing of the road may occur.

The place where the ancient Cherokee village of Guasili (near Murphy in Cherokee County) probably stood was at what is now known as the Peachtree Mound, where Peachtree Creek joins the Hiwassee River. Hardly a mound any more, this ceremonial center was flattened by excavations in both 1885 and 1933. More than a quarter-million artifacts were removed from the site and are housed in the Smithsonian and the Valentine Museum in Richmond, Virginia. Peachtree Mound was occupied during the Archaic period (8000 to 1000 B.C.), right up until historic times. Hernando de Soto visited it briefly in 1540. To reach it drive 5.5 miles out of Murphy on U.S. 64 E. A historical marker provides information on the area.

background of the county. The museum is open Monday through Friday from 10:00 A.M. to 4:00 P.M.

Scottish Tartans Museum and Heritage Center
95 East Main Street, Franklin, NC
(828) 524-7472

If you can't get to Scotland this year, this museum, recognized and authorized by the Scottish Tartans Society (the official registry of all publicly known tartans), is the next best thing. Opened in 1994, the 3,200-square-foot facility includes exhibits of tartan and Highland dress from 1700 to the present and shows the evolution of the kilt and the weaving of tartan. It also traces the influence of the Scots and other settlers on Appalachian and Cherokee culture and the history of North Carolina. Those of Scottish ancestry can investigate the tartan research library and find their family's tartan in the Tartan Room. There is also a great gift shop full of Celtic and Scottish treasures. All tartan items are imported from Scotland and come in 100 percent new wool. You'll also find scarves, shawls, sashes, tams, men's ties, caps, and children's items. Immediate delivery can be had on books, music, clan videos, jewelry, Highland dress items, dirks, skean dubbs, and Scottish weaponry. The museum is open year-round from 10:00 A.M. to 5:00 P.M. Monday through Saturday and 1:00 to 5:00 P.M. on Sunday. Admission is a $1.00 donation for adults, and children 10 and younger with an adult are admitted free.

OTHER CULTURAL EVENTS, ORGANIZATIONS, AND INFORMATION

Northern Mountains

MADISON COUNTY

Mars Hill College
off U.S. Highways 19/23 N., Mars Hill, NC
(828) 689-1217
Mars Hill College is a fundamental source for a variety of cultural activities in the Madison County area. The celebrated theater, art, history, and music departments continually provide excellence in each of those disciplines.

The Southern Appalachian Repertory Theater (SART) at Mars Hill College grew out of the exceptional talent of the college drama department and has, for 22 summers, perpetuated the best in classic and popular theater. SART has also served as the premiere stage for a number of emerging playwrights. The college's Department of Art maintains gallery space and features the exceptional talent of both students and faculty members.

The Department of Music at Mars Hill is well known for the talent that continues to emerge from its academic program. Concerts and recitals by students and faculty are open to the general public. This department, in cooperation with the Student Activities Department, has been instrumental in bringing the finest in musi-

cal concerts and dance performance (such as the Joffrey Ballet, among others) to the campus.

Mountain heritage is a vital focus of this college. To that end Mars Hill's Rural Life Museum is devoted to the presentation and preservation of the history of the unique lifestyle of our pioneer forebears. The museum is also home to the William A. Barnhill Collection, a personal photographic legacy illustrating mountain life in Western North Carolina in 1914, seen through the eye of the young roving photographer. The college also features a series of public service forums and a variety of speakers during the year, addressing current national and international issues.

WATAUGA COUNTY

An Appalachian Summer Festival
229 Rivers Street, Boone, NC
(828) 262-6084, (800) 841-ARTS
For one glorious month each summer, Boone comes alive with an intense, exciting celebration of the arts. This July explosion of theater, music, dance, and art is Appalachian State University's annual arts blowout, drawing visitors from across the Southeast. Now in its 18th season, An Appalachian Summer Festival is an interactive arts festival, with workshops, art competitions, concerts, and exhibits designed to please the entire family.

Children can participate in their own special art and creative writing workshops. All tastes are satisfied during Appalachian Summer. Music ranges from the classic strains of the North Carolina Symphony to New Orleans jazz, traditional bluegrass, and from well-known singer-storytellers to the country/folk stylings of musical artists. The Atlanta Ballet, the Parsons Dance Company, international folk dancers, and mountain cloggers and buck dancers all perform during that one month in Boone. The excitement is contagious.

You can purchase individual tickets for different events, but your best bet is the subscription package that covers the whole shebang. A full season package costs approximately $230. You can purchase a series of six or more adult tickets at a variety of discounts, or pay $16 each for individual events. Student admission costs about $9.00, and children ages 12 and younger are admitted for $2.00.

Central Mountains

BUNCOMBE COUNTY

Fine Arts Theater
36 Biltmore Avenue, Asheville, NC
(828) 232–1536

This newly restored movie theater (a triple-X cinema in the 1970s) screens award-winning independent and foreign films. The main theater is an ode to the finer days of cinema, with dimmed brass sconces, plush seats, a high ceiling, and finely draped stage. The smaller upstairs cinema is as cozy as the main hall is elegant. More than just your regular Milk Duds and Goobers, the snacks at the Fine Arts range from beer to biscotti. Catch the excellent first-run films shown here, because it's the only place in town you can!

University of North Carolina at Asheville
1 University Heights, off Weaver
Boulevard, Asheville, NC
(828) 251–6600

This exceptional liberal arts university (see our Education chapter) provides the city of Asheville and surrounding area with a diverse and continuously entertaining array of cultural arts offerings. The departments of music, drama, and art and the UNCA Cultural and Special Events Committee coordinate everything from international and experimental music/theater to folk music and dance, Broadway touring companies, and Shakespeare with the renowned North Carolina Shakespeare Festival company.

The in-house cultural arts departments of music, drama, and art offer an equally impressive schedule of events: first-rate

theater productions, Tanglewood Children's Theater, university gallery shows for both students and faculty, and community-based organizations such as the UNCA Community Chorus, the UNCA Community Concert Band, and the UNCA Community Jazz Band. These are open by audition to any musically trained or inclined citizens of any age in the Asheville area. The groups present various public concerts during the year.

One of the best-received UNCA cultural events is the summer Concerts on the Quad Series. These free performances on the grassy stage of the university quad in the center of the campus happen every Monday from 7:00 to 8:30 P.M. during June and July and are always well attended by area residents as well as UNCA students. Get there early and be ready for incredible entertainment. Summer performances have included avant-garde poetry slam artists who fill the air with alphabetical arias, the talent of international folk dance teams from the acclaimed Folkmoot international dance festival (headquartered in Waynesville), big band jazz, and African-American ethnic dancing.

WCQS-FM
73 Broadway Street, Asheville, NC
(828) 253–6875

This is the Asheville area's exceptional public radio station. The community-based FM station began back in the 1970s on the campus of the University of North Carolina at Asheville and moved to its present location in 1984. Programming features classical, jazz, folk, and traditional music; in-depth local news and information; and National Public Radio. It's available on several frequencies in the Western North Carolina area: 88.1 FM in Asheville and Hendersonville; 89.7 FM in Waynesville, Clyde, Cullowhee, and Webster; 91.3 FM in Franklin and North Georgia; 90.7 FM in Brevard; 95.3 FM in the Cherokee and Waynesville area; and 104.5 on the Asheville InterMedia Cable FM.

HENDERSON COUNTY

The Blue Ridge Radio Players
P.O. Box 993, Hendersonville, NC 28793
(828) 692-0621

These talented volunteers dramatize literary classics on audio cassettes for broadcast and distribution free of charge to the visually impaired all over the United States, including Hawaii. A number of public radio stations air these tapes, and many libraries specializing in tapes for the visually impaired make them available.

Each year, the Radio Players put on An Evening with the Blue Ridge Radio Players, consisting of a comedy and a mystery at the Blue Ridge Community College auditorium. This gives the public a behind-the-scenes look at radio production and helps to let the community know what the group is up to. If you would like to contribute your talents to this fine group, or you wish to learn how to gain access to the cassettes, write to the above address.

TRANSYLVANIA COUNTY

RiverRun International Film Festival
Brevard College, 400 North Broad
Street, Brevard, NC
(828) 884-8209

The first annual RiverRun International Film Festival held at Brevard College in the fall of 1998 and cosponsored by the Belle Visione Film Society adds a new dimension for the college and the region. Independent filmmakers have a venue for screening feature films, documentaries, and shorts. Internationally known actors, filmmakers, directors, producers, and cinematographers conduct professional labs/workshops. Each week during the festival, Brevard College and Cinema Paradiso screen independent films in Durham Auditorium. The public is welcome. Call for information at the above number.

MOUNTAIN CRAFTS

All areas of the United States have their talented craftspeople, but few places have the fabulous hand-wrought heritage found in the southern Appalachians. Tucked away in our coves or working in downtown studios, there are cadres of citizens to whom "handmade" is a large part of both life and livelihood.

Many of these crafts flourished in the isolation caused by the lack of good transportation to and from the remote mountain regions. With the advent of good roads in the middle of the 20th century, the crafts of "makin' do" were transformed into beautiful art forms. The Cherokee Indians who occupied the area for countless generations influenced handcrafts, as did the Old World settlers, passing down skills that eventually evolved into the region's style. And there's no doubt that many crafts were inspired by the wealth of natural resources. There were honeysuckle, river cane, and white oak for baskets; willows for furniture; silver bell and rhododendron for making canes; and the country's largest variety of wood for carving bowls, spoons, and statues.

Natural dyes were derived from wild pokeberries, blueberries, black walnuts, yellow root, and any number of other plants. Skilled hands transformed pinecones and weeds of the fields and roadsides into wreaths and stunning dried-flower arrangements. Corn shucks became dolls, flowers, and fans. Handmade toys that amused our great-grandparents still delight our children today. Clay for pottery was there for the digging, and some of this malleable earth was of such high quality that it ended up as table settings for royalty.

The land surrounding Franklin in Macon County is most famous for producing rubies and other gemstones, but it also contains a more humble treasure: kaolin. In 1767 an English tableware manufacturer, Josiah Wedgewood, sent a South Carolina planter, Thomas Griffith, to make an arrangement with the Cherokee to export the high-quality clay. Huge amounts of kaolin were shipped to Wedgewood and transformed into the famous Queensware. A Wedgewood dinner service of Macon County clay graced the table of Catherine the Great.

Gemstones, too, can be found in abundance in our fields, mines, and rivers (see our chapter on Rockhounding). These, in turn, inspired generations of jewelry makers. To fend off cold mountain winters, craftswomen turned scraps of old clothing into quilts; many of these works of art can be found in national museums. While spinners and weavers kept old skills alive out of necessity, today's fabric artists delight in introducing new and beautiful creations for the sheer joy of it.

The abundance of hardwoods and the need to create entertainment spawned some of the finest instrument makers around. Their delicate fiddles and sturdy dulcimers have inspired a wealth of accomplished musicians, unique songs, and joyous dances, a tradition that also continues.

Handmade is, in fact, such an integral part of our lives in Western North Carolina that we probably take it for granted. A visitor to this area will find this rich heritage everywhere: in our homes, museums, shops, and galleries, as well as at roadside stands and at our craft fairs and festivals (see our Annual Festivals and Events and Arts and Culture chapters). That this fine legacy will continue is guaranteed by the hundreds of craft classes conducted by a variety of educational institutions, senior citizens centers, summer camps, and parks and recreation departments, to name a few.

Three of the country's best craft schools are found in the region, attracting hundreds of craftspeople to settle in places such as Brasstown, Asheville, and Penland. In addition to large and highly influential guilds, such as The Southern Highland Craft Guild, there are also numerous small local guilds for weavers, spinners, quilters, and other crafters that meet in members' homes. And, thanks to the efforts of HandMade in America, many artists' studios are open to visitors for the first time (see our HandMade in America Close-up in the Arts and Culture chapter).

Here we describe schools and our favorite crafts studios in the mountains. We also include crafts such as glassblowing and ceramics in this chapter. Though they're not intrinsically "mountain crafts," they are indeed practiced to near perfection in the Western North Carolina mountains.

NORTHERN MOUNTAINS

Bea Hensley & Son Blacksmiths
Rt. 1, off Mile 331, Spruce Pine, NC
No phone
There aren't many working blacksmiths around, especially in this country. That's what makes this three-generation black-smithing studio so special. Bea Hensley, winner of the National Endowment of the Arts Heritage Award in 1995, maintains this successful forge with his son Mike. Grandson Luke is still in school but spends his vacations observing and learning bits of the trade. Schooled in the apprentice-ship style, which has not changed much from the 1600s, Mike Hensley does major smithing in wrought iron, fashioning elab-orate made-to-order gates and other home ornamentation in this shop.

The sheer power and stamina of these men is staggering. Beefy forearms, cal-lused hands, and thick back musculature are the results of years of working at the anvil. When the blacksmiths make the anvil "sing" while forging a particular piece of iron, smithing is especially transfixing. The "teacher" moves his smaller hammer over the anvil and hot iron, beating out a rhythm and directions that the "appren-tice" must follow with the powerful blows

of a heavy mallet. Though both Bea and Mike Hensley are past the apprenticing stage, they still make the anvil sing for vis-itors at times or while working on a par-ticularly intricate project that needs the both of them. This trade is fascinating and rare in this modern world.

Don't miss this, you can't help but be mesmerized by the song of the anvil.

Many mountain crafters who don't have other outlets for their wares sell them exclusively at the numerous annual street fairs and celebrations held throughout the year. (See our Annual Festivals and Events chapter for detailed descriptions.)

Carlton Gallery at Creekside
Aldridge Road, N.C. Highway 105, Foscoe, NC
(828) 963-4288
This adobelike building features the Carlton Gallery of fine woven works, and contempo-rary art. (See our Arts and Culture chapter.)

J & S Beaumont Pottery
N.C. Highway 194, Valle Crucis, NC
(828) 963-6399
Located in the Red School House behind the Mast General Store, this pottery studio and gallery makes for wonderful browsing and picking up those little hand-crafted gifts to take back home.

Visitors can view turning, glazing, and decorating processes from a special area just a few feet away from the work area. We spent a good two hours mesmerized by the spin of the potter's wheel and the scent of fresh clay being manipulated.

Adjacent to the airy manufacturing hall is the retail store. Here you'll find handmade and handpainted dinnerware and other functional pieces for the home. The rich patterns are influenced by Euro-pean and American art pottery styles. We found the soap dish and water cup com-bos especially charming. The colors and patterns on display could match just about any bathroom decor. Wonderful urns, pitchers, and salad bowls also tickled our fancy. A special shelf for "seconds" offers some perfectly gorgeous pieces with only slight flaws at reduced prices.

The Penland School of Crafts
Penland, NC
(828) 765-2359
www.penland.org

Resting on the crest of a remote mountaintop in Mitchell County, The Penland School is one of the country's finest institutions devoted entirely to the study of crafts. It was founded by Miss Lucy Morgan in 1929 after an inspirational sojourn to the craft haven of Berea, Kentucky, where she spent a summer learning to weave. On her return Miss Lucy set forth with a twofold purpose: to revive the mountain tradition of weaving here at home and to help the economically distressed women add to their livelihood. Word spread; students wanted to learn to weave. Soon new crafts were added, and suddenly Miss Lucy found her project becoming a school.

Today the school has a 450-acre campus and boasts a broad curriculum that includes book arts, glass, photography, printmaking, wood, surface design, metals, iron, drawing, clay, and fibers. The Penland community includes staff, resident artists, and students, who are composed of a mix of college students and graduates, professionals looking for a different career, and retirees who seek the arts as an avocation. This diversity of life experience only adds to the flow of creativity and the quality of Penland.

The purity of Miss Lucy's original idea is woven into the fabric of Penland School. The beauty of the art, the love of the work, and the preservation of the heritage are ingrained in every student who makes the trek up the mountain to Penland. A shared spirit for creativity permeates the log walls of the old dormitory, the chinks in the studio sheds, the light-filled drawing spaces, the ordered looms, the steady forge, and solid kiln.

This is a place where inspiration lives, high on the mountaintop close to the sky. Many of the light-filled classrooms overlook a grass-covered bald and ridge upon ridge in the gloaming. Guest teachers, like master Venetian glassblowers, fiber artists from Australia, and many others, conduct two-week workshops. A cozy dining room serves buffet-style meals—the menu changes each day to include wholesome preservative-free organic meals.

To receive information on classes, tuition, or any other aspect of the school, write to the Penland School of Crafts, Penland, NC 28765, or call (828) 765-2359.

The Weaving Room/Crossnore School
205 Johnson Lane, N.C. Highway 221, Crossnore, NC
(828) 733-4660, (800) 374-4660
www.crossnoreschool.org

The Weaving Room is a self-help project of Crossnore School. All proceeds benefit the boys and girls of Crossnore School, children from the Carolina mountains and foothills. These children from families in crisis find a stable environment on the school's 72-acre campus.

At the Crossnore School watch weavers at their looms, creating traditional patterns and contemporary wares. Since 1920 the school has kept alive the almost forgotten art of producing handwoven clothing and home furnishings in patterns used by the early settlers of the Appalachians. In the Weaving Room, you will find throw rugs in the Lee's Surrender pattern, capes and stoles in a Honeysuckle pattern, and table runners and baby blankets in the Bronson Lace pattern. The weavers use all natural cotton, wool, and linen, as well as some easy-care materials like rayon, orlon, and synthetics.

Woody's Chair Shop
110 Dale Road, Spruce Pine, NC
(828) 765-9277

All-in-the-family trade has spanned three generations at Woody's Chair Shop. Rocking chairs, made by hand and by special machinery constructed and designed solely by Woody are the specialty here. The front shop sells fabulous wooden doodads, from smoothly fashioned business card holders to gravity-defying wine bottle holders, old mountain children's games and adult chess sets, humidors, and grand mirrors.

Woody's chairs are his pride, though, and are sought the world over. Special deliveries are sent to Europe yearly. Ask Woody or his wife for a quick peek into the workshop and he might just oblige. Expect lots of sawdust, some fascinating machinery, and workers in deep concentration. Ask the master chairmaker to show you the machine that evens up irregular chair legs. Also cast a glance at the workshop floor; under the sawdust there's an intricately placed wood floor.

CENTRAL MOUNTAINS

Ariel Gallery
46 Haywood Street, Asheville, NC
(828) 236-2660
This cooperative arts and craft gallery features the crème-de-la-crème of local artisans. With everything from modern textiles to pottery, jewelry, furniture in wood, glass and metal, numerous decorative items, and wearable art, this is a treasure trove of the region's handcrafted works. The artists themselves man the store, so you may be striking up a conversation with the person who created your find.

Black Mountain Gallery
112 Cherry Street, Black Mountain, NC
(828) 669-2450
This downtown gallery is the only one in the area primarily dedicated to lathing turned wooden bowls, both artistic and functional. In a workshop adjacent to the gallery, father and son artists Eddie and Marshall Hollifield, transform Mother Nature's abnormalities—the knots of a tree or dome-shaped growths in tree trunks, known as "burls"—into works of art. Feel free to watch this fascinating process. The

gallery also features the works of other local artists.

The Folk Art Center
Mile 382, Blue Ridge Parkway, Asheville, NC
(828) 298-7928
www.southernhighlandguild.org
The Folk Art Center is the grand showcase for the work of the more than 700 members of the Southern Highland Craft Guild. The guild was founded in 1930 as an educational, nonprofit organization to provide economic support to the many fine craftspeople of the southern Appalachian region. Guild members come from a nine-state region and produce some of the finest traditional mountain crafts as well as outstanding contemporary craft work being done today.

The Folk Art Center, Asheville's gateway to the Blue Ridge Parkway off U.S. 70, welcomes 350,000 visitors annually from all over the country and the world. They come to see the fine traditional mountain heritage on display in the permanent collection and the traditional and contemporary crafts in the ever-changing exhibitions. Allanstand Craft Shop, America's oldest craft shop, is a feast for the eyes with its displays of glassware, blankets, dishware, wooden toys, exquisitely crafted jewelry, prints, brooms, and baskets.

The main level houses a 250-seat auditorium that serves the guild's educational purposes and is also used by the NPS. Here, as well as in the foyer, demonstrations are produced throughout April through December. Special events, such as Clay Day and Fiber Day, involve the public with hands-on participation projects and provide fun for the entire family. (Call to find out about the special events.)

Pick up a copy of Rapid River Entertainment Digest, *a free monthly newspaper with literary reviews, artists' showcases, and art gallery listings in the Asheville area. You'll find stacks of the* Digest *in any gallery or cafe.*

CLOSE-UP

Artisans in Residence at Asheville's River District Studios

The mountains of North Carolina are well-known for artisans' studios dotting their countryside. We, the viewers, are no longer just satisfied with the finished product; instead, we crave and are given the opportunity to experience the sweat and the inspiration behind American craftspeople's creations. Asheville, in particular, has amassed a group of studios concentrated in one area of the city, now considered an established arts and crafts community. The River District Studios, located along the French Broad River in Asheville's old industrial area close to downtown, is home to no less than 35 working studios. Some include galleries, and all welcome visitors, provided a phone call precedes the visit. Ceramics, printmaking, painting, woodworking,

sculpting, garden art, photography, welding, candle making, and many other crafts can be found here. Twice a year the River District Studios host a "sunset stroll" through studios and courtyards. Feel free to wander and watch and make a purchase or two. You'll be sure to run into a bevy of local supporters. Strolls take place in the fall and summer. The Cotton Mill Studios offer tours of certain studios year-round. For more information call (828) 252-9122.

Be sure to call and see if the artisans are in before you venture out (828–285–9700). The River District Studios are concentrated on Riverside Drive, Clingman Avenue, and Roberts Street. Check local listings for the dates and times of the Studio Strolls.

The essence of the guild and the Folk Art Center is described by a lifetime member, wood-carver and dulcimer maker Edsel Martin of Old Fort, who in 1970 wrote: "The Southern Highland Handicraft Guild is not just a business...it is people. People who are proud, who live close to the earth, and who live with an independence and dignity that money can't buy. The Guild is not people who stand behind or in front of each other; it is people standing side by side."

The Folk Art Center is open April through December from 9:00 A.M. to 6:00 P.M. daily except Thanksgiving, Christmas, and New Year's; 9:00 A.M. to 5:00 P.M. January through March. Admission is free.

Great Southern Glassworks
9 Riverside Drive, Asheville, NC
(828) 255-0187
This is a working glassblowing studio. Come witness the inspired "performance" of the "craft rogues" molding liquid glass into gorgeous and useful forms and then buy something to take home.

Odyssey Center for the Ceramic Arts
236 Clingman Avenue, Asheville, NC
(828) 285-0210
www.highwaterclays.com
This is another new studio that has found a home in Asheville's Historic River District. Close to the train tracks and the banks of the French Broad River, this large

pottery center offers courses in clay crafts for beginners and advanced students. Nine-week classes are offered in pottery, hand building, and figurative sculpture, as well as kids' classes for after school and home schoolers. (Read more about these in our Kidstuff chapter.)

Weekend and weeklong workshops, along with frequent lectures, feature nationally and internationally known ceramic artists. An independent study program gives returning students the opportunity to use the facility during open studio hours and work independently. The Odyssey Gallery markets and exhibits ceramic works from local and national artists and serves as an educational tool for students as well as the public. Call for a detailed course brochure and workshop schedule.

SOUTHERN MOUNTAINS

Haywood Community College Craft Production Program, 1 Freelander Drive, Clyde, NC
(828) 627-4670

This two-year program in jewelry, pottery, weaving, and woodworking is considered one of the finest in the nation. In addition to teaching technique and design, the school is noted for its marketing courses that help turn aspiration into economic reality for the craft artists. Students design their own graduation show at the completion of their chosen program. (See our chapter on Education for more information about Haywood Community College.)

John C. Campbell Folk School
1 Folk School Road, Brasstown, NC
(828) 837-2775, (800) FOLK-SCH
www.folkschool.org

The John C. Campbell Folk School has been a mountain institution for 75 years, and there's really no other place like it. Though Brasstown is only two hours from Atlanta, Chattanooga, and Asheville, the school—set in a mountain-rimmed farming valley—seems to be from another century.

If you are planning to attend one of John C. Campbell's regular concerts, why not enjoy a meal at the school's table beforehand? Make reservations at least one day in advance by calling (800) FOLK-SCH or (828) 837-2775. Then prepare yourself for a tasty repast!

Actually it began in the twentieth, when Indiana-born educator John C. Campbell took his new bride, Olive Dame, on a fact-finding survey throughout the Appalachian Mountains. While he investigated the agricultural practices, she studied the music and handicrafts.

After John's death in 1919, Olive Campbell and friend Marguerite Butler went to Scandinavia to study hands-on schools without credits, degrees, grades, or competition. They returned to the mountains to see if such a school would be welcomed in the region. More than 200 enthusiastic people showed up at an organizational meeting at a Brasstown church. Fred O. Scroggs, the local storekeeper, donated 75 acres of land, and the people pledged labor, building materials, and most importantly, their heartfelt support.

Today the 372-acre campus contains 27 buildings, some designed by Belgian architect Leon Deschamps in a romantic European style, while others are more typical of Appalachian farm houses. It has fully equipped craft studios, a sawmill, meeting rooms, a covered outdoor dance pavilion, a nature trail, a craft shop, a vegetable garden, rustic lodgings, and the Community Room, which has one of the best dance floors in America. The National Register of Historic Places has declared the campus a Historical District.

Over the years the school's role in the community has changed as many of the needs it served (such as health care and job training) have been taken over by public programs. It continues, however, to enrich and serve the local community. Its craft shop, for example, sells the work of more than 200 mountain craftspeople,

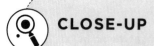

The Swannanoa Gathering

Making music in the mountains is a natural occurrence. Birds sing year-round, their rich summer choruses dwindling to delicate solos come winter. The wind plays a medley of tunes, at times whistling through the leaves, at times roaring through the coves. Crickets, katydids, and grasshoppers start their washboard bands when the weather gets warm, and, of course, the people make music too. From cabin porches to concert halls, we have a reputation for being home to some of the finest folk, bluegrass, and country music—sounds influenced by the early Scotch-Irish settlers and distilled into a distinct style all its own.

In the heart of the summer, about the time the katydids crank up, folks from all over the country converge upon the Asheville area for the Swannanoa Gathering at Warren Wilson College (see our Education chapter). These four weeks of music workshops run through July and into early August. The schedule is full of special weeks that focus on specific styles and disciplines, including Celtic Week, Performance Lab, Dulcimer Week, Dance Week, Old-Time Music & Dance Week, Contemporary Folk Week, and Guitar Week. Some years include Blues Week as well. With an advisory board that reads like a Who's Who in Folk Music—David Holt, John McCutcheon, Fiona Ritchie, Billy Edd Wheeler, and Asheville's own David Wilcox—it's no wonder the programming and attendance improves every year.

The workshops convene at various sites around the Warren Wilson campus. Classes are open to everyone, and many are structured for beginners. Students are free to create their own curriculum for each week (with the exception of some restrictions by individual teachers), although concentration on one or two classes is recommended.

Programs are offered during certain weeks for children ages 6 to 12. Classes in crafts, field trips to local attractions such as Pack Place and the Nature Center, and swimming activities are scheduled during the daytime class sessions.

A typical week begins with supper, an orientation session, and socializing on the Sunday before the courses begin in earnest. Most classes meet for morning or afternoon sessions Monday through Friday. Some may meet in the evenings for performance critiques, rehearsals, or jam sessions. Other evening activities include concerts by staff instructors, dances, song swaps, and impromptu happenings, such as picking sessions and slow jams (tune-learning sessions). Especially popular are the "sippin' & pickin'" activities under one of the heavy-duty tents overlooking the college's rich farmland and postcard-perfect mountains.

For sports and recreation, the college's facilities include a gymnasium, weight room, aquatic center, and tennis courts, as well as a pond, nature trails, a working farm, and a kayak run on the nearby Swannanoa River.

The musical traditions of Scotland and Ireland, possessing separate and distinctive personalities, nonetheless share a common heritage. Celtic Week acknowledges this dual heritage with a program featuring the best from each tradition. Irish flute, Irish step dancing, uilleann pipes, Celtic harp, tin whistle, Scottish fiddle, hammered dulcimer, bodhran (traditional Irish frame drum), Celtic guitar, and bouzouki (like a large, long-necked mandolin) are just some of the courses offered.

Performance Lab Week is designed for those who have a serious interest in moving to a higher level in their performing activities. The first three class days are spent on the campus, working on performance skills in a lab setting. Then it's put-your-music-where-your-mouth-is time as the acts hit the road to perform three concerts in the region. They are presented as a revue, with each act doing a short set as a part of each show. Set in well-known acoustic music venues, they offer a tremendous opportunity to work in optimal situations before an appreciative audience.

Old-Time Music & Dance Week explores the rich music, dance, singing, and storytelling traditions of the southern Appalachian region. Last year's programming included 23 courses plus visits from local master musicians, ballad singers, and buck dancers. Old-time fiddle is a popular course, as are old-time banjo, old-time guitar, and autoharp. Shaped-note singing, a fascinating musical tradition stretching back to the 16th century, is also offered. Combining the sacred music of the earliest New England colonists, Southern white spirituals, and the gospel hymns of the great nineteenth-century camp meetings, shaped-note singing creates a remarkably democratic four-part harmony with each part a separate and engaging melody. The music is notated using differently shaped notes—squares, triangles, circles, and diamonds—which make it easier and more fun for untutored folks to participate in a venerable old Southern tradition.

Dulcimer Week includes instruction in both the mountain dulcimer and one of the most appealing and accessible of folk instruments, the hammered dulcimer. Students have an opportunity to learn either or both instruments from the country's finest teachers and players. Four skill levels are offered in each instrument.

Contemporary Folk Week is a unique program of workshops for anyone who has ever had the desire to play music for other people. If you're a closet songwriter who likes to go to "open mike night" at your local folk club, if you've been performing for a while and are ready to make the commitment to a career, or if you'd just like to feel more confident when you pull that guitar out at parties, this week is for you. Programs are divided into broad subject areas covering a variety of related topics: songwriting, performance, sound reinforcement and recording, and vocal coaching.

New since 1996 is Guitar Week. Contemporary fingerstyle guitar, flatpicking (taught by a three-time national champ!), blues, and guitar accompaniment are featured.

Whether you are a musician or not, there's a magic in the air at the Swannanoa Gathering. A series of concerts showcasing workshop staff is scheduled at the end of each week and is open to the public.

The Swannanoa Gathering has earned a well-deserved reputation for its quality programming and careful attention to details.

For more information contact the Swannanoa Gathering at (828) 298-3434 or www.swangathering.com.

including the famous Brasstown Carvers, whose delicately carved animals are all-time favorites.

Lifestyles and relationships to tradition have changed since 1925. Most of today's 3,000 annual Folk School students come from all over the United States for a week or two to learn a craft, pick up an instrument, or learn to dance. But the individual expression and social interaction that have been encouraged by crafts, music, and dance are still needed today—perhaps more than ever.

Regularly scheduled concerts of traditional music, along with dances are open to the public. For those who want to learn a new skill or improve an old one, there are literally hundreds of weekend and one- or two-week-long courses offered year-round in basketry, beadwork, blacksmithing, book arts, broom making, calligraphy, chair seats, clay, crochet, dance, dolls, drawing, dyeing, embroidery, enameling, felting, food, genealogy, glass, jewelry, kaleidoscopes, knitting, lace, leather, marbling, metalwork, music, nature studies, painting, paper art, photography, printmaking, quilting, recreation, rugs, spinning, stone carving, storytelling, thread art, tinsmithing, weaving, wood carving, wood turning, woodworking and writing. Phew!

Tuition ranges from $168 for weekends to $294 for the average week, plus the actual costs of materials (such as the student's clay in a pottery course). There are discounts for students from a number of surrounding Georgia and North Carolina counties as well as for members of Elderhostel on most, but not all, courses. Three family-style meals are served each day. Lodging (meals included) is provided in a number of on-campus buildings. Costs vary.

There are 12 campsites with full hookups and modest bathroom facilities on campus. Campsites are available for a cost.

To receive a catalog call one of the numbers above or write to the John C. Campbell Folk School, 1 Folk School Road, Brasstown, NC 28902.

The Museum of North Carolina Handicrafts
49 Shelton Street, Waynesville, NC
(828) 452-1551

If you're looking for crafting inspiration, or if you'd simply like to see some of the skills demonstrated by past and present North Carolinians, this museum offers you both. The white-framed Shelton House, built in 1875 and listed on the National Register of Historic Places, is as interesting as the museum and offers a perfect setting for the comprehensive exhibits of 19th-century crafts.

Just a short walk from Waynesville's charming Main Street, the museum contains examples of furniture from the 19th century, a Victorian bed and shaving stand, a dining table, handcrafted cupboard, toys (including a handmade miniature farmstead), and a working pioneer village.

It also features an exhibit of handicrafts made by artisans who have participated in the educational demonstration of heritage crafts in the North Carolina State Fair's Village of Yesteryear since 1951. You'll see such once-necessary tools as Saxony spinning wheels and walking spinning wheels. There is also a fine collection of Cherokee Indian artifacts—dolls, baskets, pottery, and woodcarvings—as well as the Will Shelton collection of Navajo rugs, pottery, jewelry, and baskets.

A small gift shop carries pottery, braided rugs, hand-carved birds, and other handcrafted items and a selection of regional craft books.

Allow yourself at least an hour to enjoy this step back into the past. The museum is open from 10:00 A.M. to 4:00 P.M. Tuesday through Friday, May through October. There is an admission charge.

Woodcraft "On the Hill"
Main Street, Highlands, NC
(828) 526-2400

Sylvia Sammons is so versatile that when she performs century-old ballads of Scotland in a coffeehouse setting or in a 7,000 seat auditorium, she accompanies herself

CLOSE-UP

Potters of the Roan

"Potters of the Roan" is a guild of professional potters living and working in the Bakersville area of the mountains of Western North Carolina in Mitchell County. Roan Mountain dominates the views of the area with extensive balds and huge natural rhododendron gardens. "Potters of the Roan" can be rec-ognized throughout Mitchell County by red signs with white interior ovals. Inside the ovals are the individual names of their studios. (For information contact Fork Mountain Pottery, 1782 Fork Mountain Road, Bakersville, NC; 828–688–9297; www.forkmountain pottery.com.)

on guitar, harmonica, soprano and alto recorder, French horn, piano, autoharp, and lute. Her music wafts out over the Main Street in Highlands during the summer months when she is in residence. Her shop is filled with originally designed wooden articles ranging from candlesticks to end tables. According to Sylvia, "Although blindness may have made me more cautious in the use of power tools and certainly more deliberate in my work, I feel that it has enhanced my appreciation for the art of woodcraft." Another treat is that Sylvia performs balcony concerts in Highlands every Friday night from 8:00 to 9:00 P.M. from June through October.

SUMMER CAMPS

For generations children and young people have delighted in the many summer camps that thrive in the Western North Carolina mountains. They often attend the same camps that their grandparents enjoyed.

There are 24 camps in Henderson County alone and another 17 in neighboring Transylvania County, plus a number of others in surrounding counties. Some camps are coed, others single sex. Some are privately owned, while others have religious affiliations or are sponsored by scout organizations or civic clubs. A number of camps have focused activities, such as music, drama, rock climbing, white-water skills, and horseback riding. So, with such a wide range of camping options available, how do you go about choosing the right one for your child? At the very least, you should ask the following questions:

- Is the camp accredited by the American Camping Association, and if so, when was it accredited?
- How many years has it been in operation?
- How long has the director been there, and what are his or her qualifications? Does he or she own the facility?
- What is the camp's philosophy?
- What are the staff members' qualifications? How thoroughly is staff interviewed and investigated? What percentage of the staff returns each year?
- What percentage of campers return each year?
- What is the camper-counselor ratio?
- Does the camp supply references from past campers' families?
- Does the camp maintain a safe environment concerning such things as fire prevention, emergency drills, first aid, medical procedures, and regular evaluations and inspections of the food and facilities?
- What kind of vehicles are used to transport children? Are they owned or leased? Are drivers trained in ongoing safety-awareness programs?
- Does the camp carry liability insurance?
- Does it belong to any organizations that can help it maintain and improve its professionalism?

Although summer camps can vary in size, price, duration, and age ranges of the campers, most include such activities as hiking, camping, canoeing, swimming, archery, mountain biking, horseback riding, tennis, golf, team sports, and nature studies—thanks in part to the vast recreational opportunities offered by the nearby public lands (see our Forests and Parks chapter). As the late Frank "Chief" Bell Sr., founder of Mondamin Camp, put it, "The wilderness can be a magnificent playground and a great university." The cultural heritage of the area's arts and crafts, such as drama, blacksmithing, and pottery, play a big role in summer activities.

Although most camps draw the majority of their participants from the Southeast, many come from as far away as Alaska, Hawaii, and South America for this mountain experience. Campers have been known to spend every summer for 5 to 15 years at the same camp. Many have come back as camp counselors, and some have even become camp owners. A number of the camps have been in continuous operation for more than seventy years. We've included just a few of the long-established facilities. For complete camp listings, contact local chambers of commerce.

CENTRAL MOUNTAINS

Camp Arrowhead for Boys
(828) 692-1123
Camp Glen Arden for Girls
off Green River Road, Tuxedo, NC
(828) 692-8362

Arrowhead is a Christian camp for boys 7 to 15 years old. Set along sparkling Rock Creek, a tributary of the Green River, it has more than 1,000 acres of woodland, streams, meadows, and trails that offer endless opportunities for playing, exploring, camping, and riding. J. O. Bell Jr. started the camp in 1937, and it's been owned and directed by the Bell family for more than 50 years. In 1951 its sister camp, Camp Glen Arden for Girls joined it. The vast grounds contain two lakes, a swimming pool, archery fields, tennis courts, a gym, stables, a woodworking shop, a blacksmith shop, and a great variety of other facilities and cabins. Just inside the Glen Arden gate, a towering 300-foot waterfall greets campers. Both camps offer almost all the activities found at the other camps mentioned in this chapter. The camps believe in providing moderate structure, but with enough free time to "watch a hawk circling above against fluffy clouds."

These two affiliated camps have a 4 to 1 camper-counselor ratio, although in the youngest camper cabins the ratio is two to one. Camp Arrowhead holds two four-week sessions, and two two-week sessions.

Camp Carolina for Boys
Lamb's Creek Road, Brevard, NC
(828) 884-2414, (800) 551-9136

Though Camp Carolina is only 2.5 miles from Brevard, its 22 acres feel far from town life. It's bordered by mountain ridges and on two sides by the Pisgah National Forest, and it's only a half-mile from the forest's entrance. The camp, established in 1924, has three streams and a four-acre lake for swimming, canoeing, kayaking, and fishing for mountain trout. Both group and individual tennis instruction is provided on six tennis courts. Other activities include riflery, archery, soccer, table tennis, basketball, football, baseball, lacrosse, hang gliding, mountain biking, skateboarding, weightlifting, and arts and crafts. Horseback riding in Western and English saddles, forward seat, and jumping are taught, and campers take day and overnight rides in Pisgah Forest. Wilderness classes are also beginning.

Younger campers who have proven their skills on the camp's lake take river trips on Mills River and the upper French Broad. More advanced campers tackle the Green and Tuckasegee Rivers, and the skilled have the opportunity to challenge the Nantahala, Pigeon, and Chattooga Rivers. All ages have the opportunity to experience white-water rafting. In addition to Pisgah Forest camping, more challenging hiking and camping trips go deep into the Nantahala National Forest, Linville Gorge Wilderness Area, and Mount Mitchell State Park. All campers may participate in rock climbing and rappelling, starting on the camp's wall.

Carolina's nature program involves collecting and identifying area plants and animals; pioneering projects include using hand tools to build tree houses, forts, dams, bridges, and cabins.

The camp, which is open to boys ages 7 to 17, has a capacity of 200. It provides an average of one counselor for every four campers. For younger groups there is one counselor for every three boys in a cabin. There is a lodge for each age group where meetings, evening programs, and rainy-day activities take place. The camp's infirmary is staffed by two registered nurses, and a doctor is on call. There is a three-week session in June, a four-week session in July, and a two-week session in August.

Camp Gwynn Valley
1080 Island Ford Road, Brevard, NC
(828) 885-2900

Camp Gwynn Valley is somewhat newer than some of the other camps listed in this chapter and is also different than the others in that it provides a special, sheltered environment for younger children, ages 5 to 12. Mary Gwynn established the camp in 1935, and it has been in continuous operation ever since, attaining an international reputation for dealing with the needs and interests of the younger child. Camp Gwynn Valley, altitude 2,240 feet, sits in a secluded cove that opens

To prevent bugs in cabins, most summer camps now have policies that ask friends and families not to send care packages containing food. You might instead order a "Camp Pack" from Main Street Ltd., 22 East Main Street, Brevard; (828) 884-4974, (800) 248-CAMP. It'll custom-make a gift pack and deliver it locally or ship it nationally. (See our Shopping chapter for more information on Main Street Ltd.)

onto a sunlit valley with a view of the Pisgah Range.

The camp's 300 acres are comprised of 250 acres of woods and a 50-acre working farm, where children can take turns feeding the animals, weeding and hoeing the garden, and milking the cow and goats. Cabin cookouts often begin with a trip to the farm to gather fresh eggs and pick vegetables in season. Baby animals—lambs, rabbits, calves, piglets, and kittens—are favorite members of the camp's "family."

Swimmers gain confidence in the pool before graduating to the camp's lake. Most boating and canoeing also take place on the lake, although older children who meet the requirements take short trips on the nearby French Broad River. They can also fish for bream and bass in the lake and for trout in the millpond, where a historic mill has been renovated and is once more grinding corn and wheat, providing electricity, and performing other functions, such as churning ice cream. Children get to participate in the entire food-producing process—from field to table—picking, shelling, sifting, bagging, baking, and eating the cornbread.

Horseback-riding instruction concentrates on the basic skills of English saddle seat; advanced riders do some open field and trail riding on the property. Campers also learn something of the care of tack and horses, including Loeb, the draft horse that pulls the wagon for after-supper hayrides. Cookouts and sleep-outs are conducted mostly on camp property. The younger children use closed-in, fixed tent sites, while older ones backpack to more remote areas.

Crafts include ceramics, weaving, copper enameling, tie-dyeing, macramé, puppetry, mosaics, and broom- and candle making. There is no formal arts program, but in the relaxed time after supper, children can choose to learn Braille, plan a play with their cabin mates, or learn mountain and international dances in the lodge. Sketching, painting, and collage are also taught. Campers participate in campfire readings of poetry and children's classics, and the children are encouraged to write about their camp activities.

Children are placed in cabin groups according to grade completed in school, with 6 to 10 children in a cabin, depending on their ages (the younger ones are in smaller groups). The camper-staff ratio is three to one. Younger children have inside bathrooms in their cabins. The older children heat water with wood and have battery-powered lights in their cabins— lessons in energy conservation and resource management. Home-cooked meals are served in an open-air, screened dining room. A physician and nurses are in residence.

Camp Hollymont for Girls
475 Lake Eden Road, Black Mountain, NC
(828) 686-5343 (winter)
(828) 252-2123 (summer)
Founded by George W. Pickering, who has served in this Christian camp's ministry since 1946, Camp Hollymont's tradition is continued by the McKibbens family. Located on the 300-acre campus of the private Asheville School, Camp Hollymont provides for a fun-filled summer for girls from age 6 to 15, in refined living conditions. Acres of rolling hills and lush green forests provide the perfect summer setting for sports, fun and games, and learning crafts and skills. Girls live in the lodges, in clusters divided by age and

grade. A cluster consists of four rooms, with one of the four for the counselor. There are 120 campers per session.

Rocking chairs sit on the wide open-air front porches for better viewing of the panoramic Blue Ridge Mountains. An air-conditioned dining hall, stone chapel, professional stage and theater, athletic center with a gymnasium, and indoor pool facilitate an excellent camp atmosphere. Seven athletic fields, seven tennis courts, an archery range, a track, cross-country trails, horse stables with training ring, and miles of riding trails through the woods offer the perfect backdrop for the recreation-filled weeks that campers will spend at Hollymont. Several registered nurses staff the well-equipped infirmary 24 hours a day, and an Asheville physician is available for campers. Creative and nutritionally sound meals are served family style in the dining hall; campers can also visit the canteen for snacks. The food service sees that all dietary needs are honored.

Because it is a Christian camp, Hollymont closes each day with evening devotions—quiet, sharing moments, inspirational stories, and prayer. Most memorable to campers, however, will be the action-packed weeks of exploration, games, and recreation overseen by the youthful and energetic staff. Qualified instructors teach girls horseback riding, tennis, archery, gymnastics, ceramics, cheerleading, climbing, singing, photography, sign language, music, camping, and a number of other recreational skills and hobbies. Campers select five instructional skills per two-week session.

Buncombe County lends itself well to the pursuit of nature, and one of the special offerings of the camp is the Hollymont Ranger Program, emphasizing safety, leadership skills, teamwork, camping, hiking, and high-adventure trips. The camper rangers hike and explore the Blue Ridge Parkway, the Great Smokies, and Pisgah National Forest. The ranger program is limited to 12 girls per session, ages 13 to 16. These campers will experience white-water rafting, rock climbing, high ropes course, rappelling, water skiing, mountain biking, and caving, and spend weekends at the camp, joining in the camp's regular activities. Whatever programs Hollymont campers choose, they will be nurtured and taught by well-educated counselors, who make an effort to extend the camp's motto to all children attending: "Living and Learning with Love and Laughter." In this atmosphere, the campers develop self-confidence, build lasting friendships, and grow spiritually, all while having a whole lot of fun.

Camp Illahee
Illahee Road, Brevard, NC
(828) 883-2181

Illahee means "heavenly world" in the Cherokee language, and this camp for girls ages 6 to 16, which was established in 1921, abounds with natural beauty and high spirits. The grounds are beautifully landscaped. They contain 30 cabins, a dining hall, a new recreation lodge that includes a stage and gymnastics area, an infirmary, a crafts shop, a barn, a canoe lake, tennis courts, an open-air woodland chapel, riding rings, rifle range, two climbing walls, and many other facilities.

Each camper sets her own schedule, which can include such activities as riflery, team sports, archery, dance, drama, gymnastics, aerobics, painting, drawing, weaving, stitchery, ceramics, printing, woodworking, synchronized swimming and diving, tennis, horseback riding, hiking, white-water canoeing, rappelling, backpacking, and kayaking.

Camp Joy
Bonclarken Conference Center, Flat Rock, NC
(828) 692-2223

This is a special camp for exceptional children. An opportunity is provided for youngsters who are mentally and physically challenged to experience an exceptional life adventure.

Camp Merri-Mac for Girls
1229 Montreat Road, Black Mountain, NC
(828) 669–8766

Set in the lush Black Mountain area, Camp Merri-Mac offers two four-week sessions for girls aged 6 to 16. Since 1978 Spencer and Dorothy Boyd, parents of six children themselves, have operated Camp Merri-Mac. They have some 40 years of professional camp experience. The camp is located on a 150-acre tract of land in the Blue Ridge Mountains, at an elevation of 2,800 feet. Campers are divided by age groups into Junior, Intermediate, and Senior Camps and are housed in 13 screened and shuttered cabins with adjoining baths. The front porches make for great gatherings at dusk. The dining hall, infirmary, laundry, and camp offices are located in the Big House, a former private home. Between mealtimes, campers may purchase a limited amount of snacks and drinks. The Mike, or the gym, is a central place for recreation, including indoor volleyball, basketball, as well as musical and drama productions. Three tennis courts, volleyball courts, and sports fields assure physical fitness is a large part of the program.

A member of the National Riflery Association and the Camp Archery Association, Camp Merri-Mac teaches range and field safety in target sports. Merri-Mac teaches camp craft skills, with emphasis placed on woods safety, proper equipment, and a real appreciation for the outdoors. Operating on a tribal system, life at Merri-Mac takes on a distinctly Native American air. Girls are assigned one of three tribes—Choctaw, Iroquois, or Seminole—during the first session and remain a member of the respective tribe during their future years at the camp. These tribes compete in various activities throughout the session and choose leaders, who plan and organize many tribal events with staff advisors. These groupings foster healthy competition and leadership qualities in young girls attending the camp.

A 15-minute chapel service is held each morning before girls begin their busy days. Not only sports are on the schedule; fine arts classes taught by college art majors; drama programs, comedy, and modern jazz dancing as well as traditional clogging are also offered. Girls have the opportunity to enjoy water sports: canoeing, diving, and just fun splashing around. Merri-Mac's riding program has drawn a good bit of praise. The Boyd family's experience with horses in national shows, circuit, and foxhunting has given them an outstanding group of school horses. The camper-staff ratio of 3.5 to 1 enables each girl to feel the individual attention of a college-level counselor who may have been a camper here once herself.

Camp Mondamin for Boys
Lake Summit, Tuxedo, NC
(828) 693–7446, (800) 688–5789 (information)
Camp Green Cove for Girls
Lake Summit, Tuxedo, NC
(828) 692–6355, (800) 688–5789 (information)

In 1922 Camp Mondamin, for boys ages 7 to 17, was established by the late Frank "Chief" Bell Sr. on the then-new 350-acre Lake Summit. It has been owned and operated by the Bell family ever since. The lake and surrounding 800 acres of private woodlands make sailing and nature studies a large part of the curriculum. The camp also includes five tennis courts, a crafts shop, an indoor rifle range, a gymnasium, a barn, and three riding rings.

Camp Green Cove, for girls ages 8 to 17, was founded by the Bells in 1945 at Rockbrook Camp in Brevard (see the Rockbrook Camp entry). In 1949 the Bells moved the camp to the upper end of Lake Summit. The buildings surround a beautiful cove where a dammed-off stream forms a smaller, private lake for swimming and canoeing. The main building houses the dining room, lounges, offices, and craft shops where such subjects as weaving, pottery, macramé, copper enameling, silk-screen printing, and drawing are taught. This building and the camp cabins are on one side of the lake. On the other side are four tennis courts, an archery field, a ball field, a barn, and five riding rings, including a jumping course.

Each of these adjoining camps has its own infirmary with two nurses on staff; one physician in residence serves both camps. Sailing, horseback riding, and woods skills are emphasized, and both offer swimming, canoeing, backpacking, rock climbing, a ropes course, wilderness camping, mountain biking, tennis, crafts, and nature studies. Minor activities include archery, riflery, photography, volleyball, and at Mondamin, an amateur radio program. Mondamin has a gymnasium; Green Cove offers gymnastics and dramatics.

These camps are unique in that they maintain a long, unbroken camp session of six weeks and don't accept campers for shorter times during that session. (They do have separate three- and one-week sessions.) These long-term camps accommodate a strong wilderness trip that gives participants the time to build skills and use them in the woods and on the water. The white-water canoeing program—headed by Gordon Grant, technical editor for Canoe magazine and former head of instruction at the Nantahala Outdoor Center and a Mondamin camper in the 1960s and '70s—has been recognized as one of the best of its kind.

The Bells' philosophy that it is not necessary to inflict a defeat in order to win a victory guides the camps' noncompetitive programs—an advantage for participants who aren't the best athletes. Programs are structured but unregimented to encourage self-direction and initiative.

Each camp has a combined capacity of 180. The camper-counselor ratio is 4 to 1.

Camp Rockmont for Boys
375 Lake Eden Road, Black Mountain, NC
(828) 686-3885

Driving up a tree-shaded lane, you approach Camp Rockmont at the same time you cast your first glance over Lake Eden and the Black Mountains in the distance. The lake's central position on the

600 acres of the camp's secluded property is a telling symbol of days by the water to come. Only 15 miles east of Asheville, near the town of Black Mountain, Camp Rockmont welcomes boys ages 6 to 17.

Under Christian leadership, the camp carries a prestigious reputation with it, serving more than 1,200 boys in the Blue Ridge Mountains each summer. Ranging from 13-day to 20-day sessions, the camp is divided into Junior Camp, Intermediate, and Senior Camp; campers range in age from 7 to 16. Within each camp the boys are further divided into two tribes according to age and grade. Junior campers live in large lodges with private baths and stone fireplaces in the cavernous lobbies, while Intermediate and Senior campers stay in spacious cabins tucked into wooded slopes and use newly constructed bathhouses. Each camper chooses six instructional activities every two weeks. The recreational activities are sporty in nature—Red Cross swimming, riflery, archery, tennis, weight training, canoeing, sailing, climbing, horseback riding, kayaking, and team sports. More reflective activities include pioneering, crafts, and Bible study.

Rockmont places a spiritual emphasis on the whole camp experience. Counselors enjoy devotional times with their cabins, and a Morning Watch and Sunday services are times set aside for worship through singing, learning, and sharing. Every Sunday evening each camp gathers at a Council Ring site on the mountainside to reflect on the prior week. Boys are recognized according to personal performance as it applies to attitude, enthusiasm, and cooperation.

Also unique to this boys' camp is the ranger program, not unlike the program at Rockmont's sister camp Hollymont for Girls. A Rockmont ranger keeps a daily journal of his outdoor experiences, learning to live in the wilderness, identify flora and fauna, maneuver rope courses, whitewater raft, hike, and camp. Each ranger receives a patch of completion at the closing ceremony. Rangers must be at least 14 years old.

The counselors-in-training program is aimed at young men 16 and older, who would like to assert their leadership as future Rockmont counselors. Choosing from 13-, 20-, or 27-day sessions, trainees act as assistants to the counselors in cabin life, in skills-class instruction, and in everyday camp life. They also attend leadership training classes where they learn special skills and leadership techniques that will last a lifetime.

Provide your children with a variety of fun stationery for letter writing. Should they get homesick, they may feel better writing you or friends on stationery that you picked out together expressly for this purpose.

Camp Timberlake for Boys
**1229 Montreat Road, Black Mountain, NC
(828) 669–8766**

Due to the popularity of Camp Merri-Mac for Girls, the Boyd family founded Camp Timberlake for Boys in 1983. Providing a challenging adventure for boys ages 6 through 16, Timberlake operates on the same campground as Merri-Mac but has a separate program run by its own staff of skilled young men. The two four-week sessions and a smaller two-week session allow boys to familiarize themselves with the outdoors, and with a variety of sports they may not have access to in school.

The backpacking program, geared toward learning safe independence in the wilderness, provides instruction on how to plan a trip, what to bring, and how to set up camp. Experienced instructors lead overnight trips into the Pisgah National Forest. Swimming, diving, wrestling, tennis, horseback riding, archery, and riflery are taught by qualified instructors, as are canoeing, climbing, and fencing, a unique

sport for a summer camp. Fencing, which the Timberlake describes as "physical chess," enables each boy to use his own distinct skill—be it athletic ability and quickness or a strategic approach to the activity. Climbing is practiced on one of the three climbing walls before moving out to the fine granite of the Southeast. The camp also offers instructions in mountain biking and guitar. Lodging and board costs are similar to Merri-Mac's. The infirmary, also like Merri-Mac's, is staffed 24 hours a day by a registered nurse and assistant.

All activity and recreational equipment is checked before each day's use, and instructors are highly skilled at the activities they teach as well as in first aid. Services in a chapel by the lake begin each day with rousing singing and reflective Bible study. Two hours of free time a day give each boy the chance to make his own decisions about pursuing an extra activity, resting, reading, or playing.

Eagle's Nest Camp
**43 Hart Road, Pisgah Forest, NC
(828) 877–4349**

The staff of Eagle's Nest Camp believes that the big missing ingredient for American children is membership in a tribe, a village, and a nature-based homeland. This sense of "belonging" is one of the missing links that they strive to create for their campers. One way they achieve the goal is through the joy children gain in knowing that they are, according to the camp's brochure, "responsible and viable parts of a greater idealized whole."

This journey to wholeness takes place in a "village" setting surrounded by the natural beauty of a serene, mountain-enclosed valley. Its quadrangle is bordered on one end by an open-air dining room, where whole and natural foods have been served family style for the past 20 years, and at the other by the 60-year-old lodge with a stone fireplace and stage. Many of the rest of the camp's buildings have been rebuilt in the last 15 years, and the kitchen, infirmary, laundry, and offices are brand new.

Activities—including swimming, lake and white-water canoeing, fishing, rock climbing, backpacking, dance, Native American ceremonies, dramatics, musical instrument instruction, ceramics, weaving, woodworking, photography, sewing, crafts, sketching, sculpture, and nature skills—meet in large open-air buildings, in the meadows, by the lake, at the horse-riding ring and stable, on the athletic or archery fields, on the tennis court, in the theaters, at the canoe dock, in the garden, and in the apple orchard. The camp's three hilltops provide plenty of breathing room, and the surrounding forests, trails, river, streams, and mountains offer opportunities for adventure and development of wilderness skills. An Indian Village brings children to the heart of the mythic story and ceremony each week. Full-stage musical productions can involve one-third of the camp. Campers and counselors alike share in the chores of keeping Eagle's Nest running smoothly.

This coed camp, now in business for 72 years, is designed for children age 6 through high school and offers three three-week sessions. It has a camper-counselor ratio of 4 to 1.

Eagle's Nest also offers expanded wilderness adventures to teenagers, such as 100-mile hikes on the Appalachian Trail.

Falling Creek Camp
off Falling Creek Road, Tuxedo, NC
(828) 692-0262

Though conveniently close to I-26 and the Asheville airport, Falling Creek's home in a hidden cove deep in the mountains seems incredibly remote. Its campus spreads over 1,000 acres. The main section surrounds two lakes with many miles of trails and outpost cabins between its mountain-top and the river pastures in the Green River Valley.

This camp for boys offers many competitive activities while realizing it's more important for a boy to work and cooperate with others than to consistently try to outrank his peers. The facility's 220 partic-

ipants are divided into three age groups—Cherokee, Catawba, and Iroquois—with about 12 cabins in each division. Each boy lives with seven cabin mates and one or two counselors. Care has been taken in the construction of all Falling Creek's building to preserve the natural beauty of the surroundings.

Each boy selects six different activities in which to participate on a daily basis. These include archery-riflery, sailing, water-skiing, swimming, canoeing, horseback riding, track and field, land sports, lacrosse, soccer, mountain biking, hiking, rock climbing, nature programs, photography, crafts, woodcrafts, tennis, basketball, Indian lore, weightlifting, and radio (the camp has its own radio station: WFCC-640 AM). The camp also has its own camp doctor and dietitian and is the brother camp to Camp Greystone for Girls, about 7 miles away on Lake Summit.

Rockbrook Camp for Girls
N.C. Highway 276, Brevard, NC
(828) 884-6151

Rockbrook Camp, which serves girls ages 6 to 16, has been in existence since 1921. The 200-acre site, 4 miles from Brevard on the French Broad River, is replete with beautiful forests and waterfalls, all of which are accessible by numerous hiking trails. It is also just minutes away from Pisgah National Forest, which is used for day hikes, overnight backpacking trips, and rock-climbing trips. Rockbrook has excellent in-camp rock-climbing facilities as well. These include a 70-foot climbing tower, an indoor climbing wall, and rock faces.

Campers chose weekly from many fun-filled activities in a noncompetitive environment. Emphasis is placed on canoeing, rafting, and kayaking. (Rockbrook is a licensed outfitter on the Nantahala River and has an outpost at this location near the Great Smoky Mountains.) Other sports include tennis, swimming, soccer, and horseback riding, with all levels of hunter-jumper instruction. Creative outlets include drama and pottery (the camp has a year-round commercial pottery operation that's devoted entirely to campers during the summer).

Campers live eight to a screened cabin with two counselors per cabin. The main buildings are composed of a dining hall, gym, three stone lodges, a barn, two log cabins, and the pottery studio. There are five tennis courts, a rifle range, an archery range, and a lake. The camper-counselor ratio is approximately 4 to 1. A full-time registered nurse is on duty in the health lodge, and a licensed physician is on call. All staff members are trained in CPR and first aid.

The camp can accommodate 190 campers per session; the girls are organized into three age groups.

SOUTHERN MOUNTAINS

Camp Merrie-Woode
100 Merrie-Woode Road, Sapphire, NC
(828) 743–3300

Camp Merrie-Woode has completed 83 seasons. It was founded in 1919 by Mrs. Jonathan C. "Dammie" Day, born of English parents, who founded the camp on "English traditions and Christian principles" as a place where girls could come for adventure and discover the strength in themselves. Since 1978, when former campers bought the operation, Merrie-Woode has been run as a nonprofit foundation.

Though only a mile off U.S. 64, the camp, nestled at the foot of Old Bald Mountain and overlooking the headwaters of Lake Fairfield, sits secluded at 3,300 feet among rhododendron, hemlock, and hardwood forests. Instruction is offered in archery, arts and crafts, canoeing, ceramics, dance, dramatics, horseback riding, jewelry, kayaking, hiking, climbing, land sports, music, nature, photography, sailing, swimming, tennis, tumbling, and weaving. Special emphasis is given to hiking, backpacking, wilderness camping, trail riding, rock climbing, white-water canoeing, and kayaking. Emphasis is placed on the process by which a girl attains skills or grows in self-confidence, rather than on competition or the final product.

Many camp traditions have developed over the years, not the least of which is the camp uniform. The gray "middy" and green ties and shorts are the same as uniforms used in the past that link present campers to generations before them. All except the oldest campers live four to a cabin plus a counselor.

Merrie-Woods offers three sessions: a three-week session for ages 7 to 16; a five-week session for ages 8 to 17; and a two-week session for ages 6 to 14.

RELOCATION

The great stretch of the Appalachian Mountains spreads from Canada to Alabama. The highest peaks in the eastern United States swoop down through North Carolina, across the Asheville plateau swelling up into the Great Smokies. Rich soils deposited here from the receding glaciers of the Ice Age provided these mountains with the seeds of flora ranging from Georgia to Canada. It is in this verdant land of forested mountains, richly silted bottoms, rushing streams, and brilliant waterfalls that villages, towns, and cities have developed.

The largest city in Western North Carolina is Asheville. With a population of over 68,000, it swells with an additional 150,000 visitors per week arriving off the Blue Ridge Parkway, via the Asheville Airport, or motoring in on I-40 and I-26. These visitors attend seminars at Grove Park Inn, Inn on Biltmore, the YMCA's Blue Ridge Assembly, Billy Graham's Conference Center, the Cove, and in the multitude of other conference centers and camps tucked among these mountains.

There's plenty of elbow room for more folks to settle into Western North Carolina, though they are coming rapidly. Western North Carolina reaches from the northern mountains of North Carolina to the borders of neighboring Virginia, West Virginia, Tennessee, Georgia, and South Carolina. You can always be certain of access to interstates, major U.S. highways, and the Blue Ridge Parkway, while maintaining a sense of quiet Southern relaxation.

Even in the towns and cities, one can spot a black bear now and then. One senses the wilderness is never too far away. Deer are abundant as well, while mountain otter splash in the streams and an elk herd has been reintroduced. There are those who swear to having seen a mountain lion, often called a "Painter."

Hospitality continues to be one of the leading industries in these mountains. But recreation and sports, particularly mountain biking and kayaking, have overtaken almost even hunting and fishing as favorite pastimes. Golf courses lead from flat land to the high mountains. Artisans gather, wooed by Penland School of Crafts in the northern mountains and John C. Campbell Folk School in the southern mountains.

Agriculture and aquaculture provide world leadership in the Christmas tree industry, forestry, viniculture, and farm produce. Caviar and trout from Dick Jennings Trout farm in the western mountains can even be found in the restaurants of New York. Industry and technology abound in the mountains, with various national and international firms embedded in the infrastructure. Some of these firms are Sonopress of Germany, BASF of Germany, Volvo of Sweden, and Blue Ridge Paper Mill in Canton.

The University of North Carolina at Asheville blazed the trail with its College for Seniors. Community colleges throughout the mountains now provide opportunities for seniors to enter new hobbies.

At the mayors' conference in Denver, Colorado, in 2003, Asheville was noted as an outstanding city. It has been listed as an ideal place to live in magazines such

There's a lot to be said for a house sitting high on a plateau or mountainside with a spectacular mountain view. But while these higher elevation homes are cooler in summer, they are also much colder in winter. Hilltops, too, are often subject to high winds, while homes snuggled in a protected valley or cove may experience little or no wind at all.

as *Modern Maturity, Southern Living, Money Magazine,* and *Places Rated Almanac.* With such national attention, locals and those who now consider themselves locals (after five years or so) are keen on not stretching the resources of these mountains too thin. Move here . . . and you, too, may eventually find yourselves defending the beauty of the land from overdevelopment by "outsiders"— and wisely so.

People moving to our mountains from crime-ridden cities often pay premium prices to be in gated, security-conscious communities. Although rules in such places do protect property values from unwanted developments in the neighborhood, longtime residents have to smile at what they consider unnecessary paranoia.

REAL ESTATE

With so many professional real estate companies in all 18 counties of North Carolina's mountains, we first provide you with a registry of real estate publications. Also, every town paper in the mountains runs a Sunday real estate section.

Apartment Finder
(800) 222-3651
www.livingchoices.com
This complimentary booklet covers Asheville and Hendersonville and provides contacts for rental and for-purchase apartments.

Century 21 Mountain Lifestyles Home Guide
(866) 812-2100
www.c21mountainlifestyles.com
This free monthly publication showcases 500-plus homes, commercial properties, and land. Find it available at many freestanding displays in restaurants, airports, and on the street.

Homes & Land of Asheville
(800) 277-7800
www.homesandland.com
Look for this free monthly publication throughout Buncombe and Madison Counties. It serves both counties.

Mature Living Choices
(Senior Selections Carolina Mountains & Upstate)
(800) 222-5771
www.maturelivingchoices.com
This complimentary booklet assists seniors in finding enjoyable housing. A questionnaire at the front of the book can be of assistance. A call to the toll-free number will get an issue mailed to you for your relocation consideration.

Real Estate Weekly
Published by Asheville Board of Realtors
209 East Chestnut Street, Asheville, NC
(828) 255-8505
Published weekly, this tabloid is available at newsstands throughout the area and provides color photographs and good descriptions of area homes.

Northern Mountains

ALLEGHANY COUNTY

Alleghany County still is a treasure waiting to be discovered. This largely undeveloped county owes its pristine state to the geographical isolation imposed on it by the limited road system here. It is the northernmost county in North Carolina's mountains and is bordered by Virginia to the north and the Blue Ridge Parkway to the east. Access into the county from any direction is by twisting two-lane roads. However this isn't necessarily a drawback. If you like the feel of wide-open, rolling land without urban clutter, then Alleghany County is for you.

Real estate is still reasonably priced in this county of 11,550 residents, and a surprising variety of properties are available, but as the general populace discovers the pastoral beauty of this area, the prices go up. The land outside the town is sparsely populated; homes perch on mountaintops surrounded by views of farmland valleys that spread toward the Virginia border.

Here and there in the more remote areas of the county little communities are clustered around a typical crossroads and a convenience store.

Alleghany County, for all its rural charm, also has the allure of old money. Southeast in the county is Roaring Gap, a spectacular ridge with an unbelievable 180-degree view of metropolitan Winston-Salem, about 75 miles away in the valley below. This area was settled in the 1930s as a summer retreat by prominent Winston families such as the Bowmans, Hanes, and Grays. The grand homes here, many with the chestnut-bark siding characteristic of the era, are nestled along the ridge with the confidence of established tradition. Adding to the landscape of this venerable region are the occasional private club, placid mountain lake, or old stone church. When homes in Roaring Gap do become available, they tend to change hands quietly, without ever reaching the open market. Inquire about these areas with a local Realtor.

ASHE COUNTY

Ashe is a rural county on the move. Like its neighbor, Alleghany County, Ashe has been isolated in the past by an undeveloped road system. Roads have improved, and city leaders are seeing more interest from outside business. Businesses aren't the only ones attracted to this area, though; the rolling countryside is becoming more and more intriguing to individuals and families, retirees and couples. This could make a real estate investment now in Ashe County a glowing prospect.

Riding north from Boone along U.S. 221, you'll see the hills of Ashe County rise out of the valleys. Instead of the haphazard residential growth you might see elsewhere in the region, you see geometric plantings of Christmas trees—a big business here—and unmarked pasture land dotted with cows and horses. Fairly large expanses of acreage are still available. You can even be a gentleman farmer if you can find one of the county's many marvelous old two-story farmhouses down a gravel road or restored mills on a waterway.

Most of Ashe County's population is gathered around the towns of West Jefferson and Jefferson. Some apartment complexes and condominium units are also scattered over the two towns.

The virgin land out in the county has also attracted luxury golfing communities. Both Mountain Aire Golf Club and Jefferson Landing are upscale recreation-centered developments with condominiums, town houses, and single-family residences.

At Mountain Aire Golf Club, just off Old U.S. 221, Fairway Ridge offers year-round residence or a seasonal retreat alongside a new golf course. Large homesites, cleared or naturally wooded, offer breathtaking mountain views; most of the sites overlook the fairways. Paved roads and underground utilities are additional features.

AVERY COUNTY

From the Christmas tree farms sprawling over the hillsides like vineyards in the southern part of the county to the seasonal activity of the ski areas and the multimillion dollar exclusivity of the Linville area, Avery County offers a diverse real estate market.

Closer to Boone, bordering N.C. 105, is Linville, a resort area that has attracted seasonal visitors and moneyed jet-setters for about 100 years. Today's seasonal guests from all over the country make their second nest in several exclusive developments such as Linville Ridge and

The local chamber of commerce will always have a stash of real estate newsletters and newspapers. Pick one up to familiarize yourself with the offerings of particular companies.

Grandfather Golf and Country Club. These gated communities all have spectacular views (some 360 degrees!).

Banner Elk, northeast of Linville, is home to Lees-McRae College; Sugar Mountain, a ski resort; and Elk River Country Club, a gated community. The prime real estate focus here is seasonal rentals. Modern condos, mountain chalets, and rustic one-bedroom bungalows are among the places rented in season, winter or summer. Time-sharing is also a popular concept here.

Contact the chambers of commerce or tourism and visitor bureaus of the areas you are interested in; they will send you relocation packets with up-to-date local information about city services, real estate, and more.

For retirees in Avery County, resident-controlled communities such as Linville Land Harbor are appealing. A sense of community and cohesion is evident in this development 20 miles from Boone, where RVs, executive homes, and vacation bungalows stand side by side. Recreational facilities that include an 18-hole golf course, a boating lake, tennis courts, a heated pool, and shuffleboard courts are also available to members who pay a one-time fee. Most residents of Linville Land Harbor are seasonal, but a number of permanent families have also made this development their home, perhaps drawn by its unhurried pace, recreation options, security, and sense of community.

The county line runs through the center of Beech Mountain, a ski community, making it a part of both Avery and Watauga Counties. (See Watauga County for information on Beech Mountain.)

MADISON COUNTY

The allure of mountain hollows, coves, winding country roads, and rushing water makes Madison County, only 35 minutes

from Asheville, a great retreat for all ages. This county remains largely rural and features some of the most remote, undeveloped mountain areas available in Western North Carolina.

There is still a considerable amount of acreage to be had in Madison County, some of it rather steep and densely wooded, such as Shelton Laurel and Walnut, communities near the Tennessee line.

Largely undisturbed, the principal towns of Marshall and Hot Springs are basically much as they were in their heyday at the turn of the century. Hot Springs was once a fashionable resort, famous for its curative springs. As a result many of the area's grand old homes are waiting to be rediscovered. Hot Springs is also home to seasonal residents and a vital resting point off the Appalachian Trail.

Mars Hill, home to Mars Hill College, is a quaint Main Street hamlet with only a few traffic lights, but the expansion of the campus has impacted the town, bringing in more diverse groups and a growth in businesses along the road that links the town with U.S. 19/23. The completion of a massive interstate corridor link over the mountains with Tennessee is expected and should significantly open up this area for development.

Modern residential housing is in a state of transition in Madison County. The average basic three-bedroom home sells for about $100,000, and rentals are few and far between. There are a few planned subdivisions in Madison County, but not many.

MITCHELL COUNTY

If you want your own special place in the woods or at the top of a mountain, and you enjoy simple outdoor pleasures, Mitchell County will delight you. Tucked back in these high woods and atop spectacular mountain peaks are some of the more reasonably priced getaway properties you'll find in the mountains.

The influence of Little Switzerland, a community with a decidedly Swiss architectural flavor that was settled in the early 1900s, is evident in the many nearby gingerbread-trimmed chalets and cabins. And even properties with a view are surprisingly reasonable here. The mountaintop views are not the only appealing land parcels in Mitchell County. Down winding mountain back roads, you can find acreage with your own personal waterfall or trout stream, minifarms with barns, outbuildings, and quaint old homesteads.

The hamlets of Spruce Pine and Bakersville are reminiscent of a bygone era. Here marvelous old homes can be purchased at low prices. More modern homes are also moderately priced. Upscale homes, such as a three-bedroom, two-story cedar with vaulted ceiling and stone fireplace, are also tucked away in the mountains of Mitchell County.

If you prefer even more seclusion, a few properties with some acreage are still available near the border of the Pisgah National Forest and the Blue Ridge Parkway.

People who settle in Mitchell County seem to prefer the rustic seclusion, but when the urge for city comforts arises, they take solace in the easy driving distance to Asheville and Boone.

WATAUGA COUNTY

Tourism, a university, and geography play equal parts in the development of property in Watauga County. The mountain communities of Boone, Blowing Rock, Beech Mountain, and Valle Crucis have grown up around the tourist trade. This is ski country, and the character of home design—much of it log—and property prices reflect the influx of seasonal money.

Many of the exclusive gated communities in the area are populated by seasonal residents who build homes costing from $200,000 to several million. Here homes built with natural materials—stone, timber, and a wealth of glass—perch on the mountaintops with views that seem to go on forever. The upscale Mayview section

of picturesque Blowing Rock, 15 minutes southeast of Boone, commands a breathtaking view and equally breathtaking home prices.

A basic three-bedroom, two-bath bungalow on about two acres, which was available 10 years ago in Watauga County for about $60,000, today sells for $85,000. This makes it tough for first-time home buyers, whose problems are worsened by a scarcity of year-round rentals. When you add to the mix the 13,000 students at Appalachian State University, who are only guaranteed one year of campus housing, coupled with the reality that seasonal tourism doubles the population, the scarcity is understandable.

Acreage in Watauga is at a premium. The tourism industry has created a lack of prime farmland, and large tracts held through the generations are particularly difficult to locate on the market. The best possibilities for this type of real estate are generally found a good 20 minutes north and west of Boone.

Tourist rentals and time-share options are popular in the resort sections of the county. Beech Mountain, the mile-high ski community that evolved from the tourist trade, straddles both Avery and Watauga Counties, but the major portion of its active real estate lies on the Watauga side. In this tiny community with a year-round population of only 300 or so, there are three subdivisions and about 600 seasonal rental units. Rentals are available either as condominiums or individual chalets and cottages.

YANCEY COUNTY

Variety is the draw for newcomers to Yancey County. This lushly wooded county has high peaks—Mount Mitchell is here—as well as the wide sweep of valleys. Individual lots varying in size and price are spread throughout the county.

The area has numerous seasonal residents and a growing retiree population. The pace is slower here, and Burnsville, the county seat established in 1833, with its picturesque town square, recalls a simpler era.

An exclusive new development, Mountain Air Country Club, is now in its first phase of development on a 500-acre mountaintop site 35 minutes northeast of Asheville and 4 miles west of Burnsville. This private equity country club community features an 18-hole, par 71 golf course designed by Pete Dye associate Scott Pool (see our Golf chapter); a private paved airstrip located 4,400 feet above sea level; and homesites for approximately 264 single-family dwellings. There will also be about 336 cluster homes, town homes, and luxurious condominiums. For more information on living at Mountain Air, call (800) 247-7791.

Central Mountains

BUNCOMBE COUNTY

This is the site of the largest private real estate sale in America: George Vanderbilt purchased 125,000 prime acres 100 years ago and created the incomparable Biltmore Estate. You can't buy anything of that magnitude here today, but Buncombe County does have an amazing array of property. The unique character of the county is visible in its real estate landscape: classic turn-of-the-century country farmhouses, the Queen Anne "ladies" of old Asheville, French Country cottages from the 1920s, lavish homes of Biltmore Forest, stately Georgian-columned domiciles and pastel Victorian dream houses in historic Montford, and contemporary timber and glass aeries hugging the mountainsides.

The influx of newcomers from all over the country has boosted the market price of building lots and residential properties. The spectrum is broad. Acreage, found more easily in the western and northern sections of the county, sells at a premium. You have to be cautious about your selection of a hilltop in Buncombe County—especially if you plan to enjoy that view in the future, since zoning is variable.

Homes run the gamut from a fixer-upper for $70,000 to the grandeur of multimillion-dollar palaces in the exclusive Biltmore Forest. There are many upscale subdivisions planned for all points of the county, and some have already been completed. Still, the average three-bedroom, two-bath home in Buncombe County sells for about $160,000, and there's much variety on both sides of that figure, usually the higher end.

Each end of the county reflects a distinct character, and builders and developers are quick to accommodate these varying tastes. The northern part of the county is more rustic with log homes and refurbished farmhouses. Cedar homes are popular throughout the county. The western end of Buncombe is punctuated by quaint bungalow homes of the 1940s and an array of modern rustic-style homes. In the east are Black Mountain and Montreat, tourist spots since the early 1900s. Classic homes here reflect the 1920s and '30s rustic camp look as well as the classic white frame of the 1940s.

But it's the south end of the county that seems to be experiencing the most rapid growth. The terrain here is more level and the mountains more open, making the land more conducive to development. Stretching toward the Asheville Regional Airport off I-26 are numerous new upscale subdivisions geared to the young urban professional. These modern, mostly cedar or traditional brick homes range from $180,000 for a three-bedroom, two-bath home on three-quarters of an acre to the $400,000-plus executive home with all the expected amenities. Also in south Buncombe several country-estate subdivisions offer acreage or run along the crest of a mountain, commanding much higher prices: from $450,000 to $1 million. A new posh subdivision, Biltmore Park, on the edge of the Biltmore Estate, sells building sites for $50,000 and higher.

HENDERSON COUNTY

Back in the early 1830s, wealthy planters from Charleston, South Carolina, were already building majestic summer homes in this cool, mountain-ringed county. Because it sits on a high plateau, much of Henderson County is made up of lovely, rolling hills—as opposed to the steep, mountainous terrain found in many other areas—so there's ample opportunity for residential developments, horse farms, grand estates, and golfing communities. And while retirees find perfect spots throughout Western North Carolina to live out their golden years, Henderson County has long been the retirement mecca of the region.

This has driven up prices, relatively speaking, but the county is still affordable, with real estate in all price ranges. The median price of a single-family home, for example, is around $115,400, but you can still find small, older, one- or two-bedroom homes in town or out in the country for $65,000. If you'd like, you can also pay $1 million-plus for a grand old estate or one of the modern ones on several acres.

Among developments, Champion Hills, a relatively new golfing community, is the most expensive. Kenmure, another golfing community near fashionable Flat Rock, is slightly less expensive, as are nearby residential developments. The Mills River area, between Asheville and Hendersonville and handy to the Asheville Airport and I-26, was mostly devoted to farming two decades ago. It still manages to maintain a rural atmosphere, although it's become upscale and pricey.

Some of the best buys—and some beautiful country to boot—are to the east of Hendersonville. Like it or not, this prime

apple-growing region probably is destined to go as suburban as much of the rest of the county has done in the last 20 years as its popularity continues to grow.

POLK COUNTY

The area around Saluda, Tryon, and Columbus on the edge of the Blue Ridge is full of great scenery and laid-back charm. This area boasts two additional attractions: the thermal belt—a warm microclimate—and horses, for Polk County is true horse country. This horse country land, an area filled with old and established horse farms, is going to be expensive, even on its perimeter.

TRANSYLVANIA COUNTY

Few places have been chosen so many times as the best place to retire or live as Brevard, the small county seat of this pretty, tree-covered, river-filled county known for its 250-plus waterfalls. Brevard forms a triad with Hendersonville and Asheville. Now a five-lane connector to I-26 and the Asheville Airport has brought the three towns even closer together. It's also increasing development and land prices, which have jumped dramatically in the last few years.

Prices around Lake Toxaway (reached by a steep, sharply curved section of U.S. 64 W.) match or surpass those in the Highlands-Cashiers area. (See our information on Jackson and Macon Counties in this chapter.) While there are houses tucked along back roads and coves that are still affordable, homes that sell for $500,000 and up are common here. A lakefront lot on Lake Toxaway, if you can find one, begins at $895,000.

Southern Mountains

CHEROKEE COUNTY

One of the most desirable areas around Murphy, the county seat, is within 10 to 15 miles of town. Many delightful homes are priced under $100,000. For undeveloped land near Murphy, the average one-acre, wooded lot with views and underground utilities runs about $14,500. Five acres will cost between $3,000 and $5,000 an acre.

There is less property for sale around the historic old railroad town of Andrews, but you can still find some good buys. This is a beautiful valley of farmland and rolling hills with quiet, but growing communities.

CLAY COUNTY

You won't find smokestacks in this mostly rural county, but you will find a wide price range in real estate. You can pay a small price for a one-bedroom cottage on a half-acre in the country or as much as $250,000 to $500,000 for a four-bedroom, four-and-a-half-bath home on 10 to 12 acres. Property on Lake Chatuge is probably the most expensive. On the other hand large tracts of 25 acres and more elsewhere in the county can be as low as $4,000 an acre.

ℹ️ *Meet new people in the area by contacting local hiking, biking, wine-tasting, or other special interest clubs. Asheville even has a newcomer's club. Find up-to-date contact numbers in the "Organizations" section of the local free weekly newspaper.*

GRAHAM COUNTY

Though national forest land covers nearly 60 percent of Graham County, and Lake Fontana and Lake Santeetlah cover a lot more, good buys abound in this beautiful lake and mountain region. Real estate prices here are still fairly low compared to other areas in the mountains, but developers are coming here, too, ready to offer pristine land for a price.

There are, as in other counties, what locals think of as high-priced properties. Both a seven-bedroom and a two-bedroom on one acre on deep water on Lake Santeetlah were selling for $395,000, and the asking price of a nearby three-bedroom on one acre on a creek was $315,000. These prices are headed skyward.

HAYWOOD COUNTY

This beautiful mountain county with its easy access to Asheville and the Great Smoky Mountains has long been popular—and is becoming more so—with retirees moving in from out of state. Many people own summer homes here, and older developments still demand a high dollar as new ones do. In the upper range, a four-bedroom, three-bath home near the Waynesville Country Club or the Laurel Ridge Country Club will cost around $375,000.

Some of the best buys in the county are in Canton. An I-40 interchange on the eastern side of Canton has made access to Asheville and other parts of the region easy.

There are some darling older homes in Canton at extremely reasonable prices. On the whole homes are 10 to 14 percent less expensive than in the western part of the county—if you take the time to look, you might come up with a superbargain.

JACKSON COUNTY

In this mountainous county relatively flat land is at a premium and is priced accordingly. Sylva is an interesting community with a neat little downtown. Dillsboro

Macon County: Wayah Bald

On a clear day from the 5,200-foot Wayah Bald in Macon County, you can see north to the Great Smoky Mountains in Tennessee and south into the rolling hills of Georgia. You can also climb an old fire tower, built in the days of the Civilian Conservation Corps. To reach Wayah Bald, take SR 1310 out of Franklin. Turn on to FR 69 (a steep, gravel road) to the bald. This is also where the Appalachian Trail and the Bartram Trail join and briefly merge. Visitors are also welcome at the 1916 Wilson Lick Ranger Station, situated along FR 69, where you can view the history of the first ranger station in the Nantahala National Forest.

maintains the feel of a bygone era with small cabins and houses to be found on the outskirts. The Cashiers-Highlands area is a whole different—and more expensive—story. Many homes run into the millions in the charming and exclusive community of Cashiers-Highlands area.

The main real estate market, however, is in the club resorts in areas such as Sapphire Lakes, Fairfield-Sapphire Valley, High Hampton, Highland Falls, Highland Country Club, and Wildcat Cliffs that offer sought-after amenities, restrictions, and a secured gate. Cashiers is still a "bargain" compared with prices in Lake Toxaway to its east or Highlands to its west, but property values here have sometimes doubled in the last two years.

MACON COUNTY

Here you'll find everything from open valleys to steep, rugged terrain and elevations from 1,900 feet to 5,500 feet. Two major towns are Franklin and Highlands.

Just down the road from Franklin, and past three glorious waterfalls, sits the town of Highlands, at 4,118 feet, one of the highest incorporated towns east of the Mississippi. Property prices around the historic resort village of Highlands are much higher. Large resort developments have driven costs up in this spectacularly scenic region—Heavenly Highlands, it's called. Prices soar heavenward, too, being even higher than those around Cashiers, which was discussed in the Jackson County section. Homes costing more than $3 million are not uncommon here. However there is still breathing space for those with middle-income budgets. Unique to Highlands is that it is conservation oriented with their "Land Stewards of the Highlands Plateau" program. Private enterprise has teamed with government services, community garden clubs, local merchants, innkeepers, restaurants, and the community as a whole to assist in designing homes and gardens to preserve the beauty of the mountains.

SWAIN COUNTY

People who like the outdoors will like Swain County. Surrounded by the Cherokee and Nantahala National Forests and the Great Smoky Mountains National Park, residents have access to some of the largest expanses of wilderness in the eastern United States while still living an easy drive from Asheville, Knoxville, and Atlanta.

ℹ️ *Jackson County has a number of historic homes, churches, and commercial buildings. If you'd like to check some of them out, call the Jackson County Travel and Tourism Authority at (800) 962-1911 and ask them to send you a free tour brochure and map. This self-guiding driving tour will take you to 29 sites, 10 of which are listed on the National Register of Historic Places.*

WORSHIP IN THE MOUNTAINS

Long known as the Bible Belt of America, the South continues its tradition of spiritual offerings. This nomenclature can be attributed to the early settlers who pushed into a wilderness to scratch out a living. They needed to call upon all the help they could get. One such helper came over the mountains as a circuit rider. One of the earliest was Bishop Asbury, who firmly established the Methodist church in these mountains. Many Methodist churches carry his name. Major world religions have representations in North Carolina's mountains. Also, independent religious and philosophical faiths have found root here.

Churches and Related Conference Centers

NORTHERN MOUNTAINS

Valle Crucis Conference Center
P.O. Box 654, Valle Crucis, NC 28691
(828) 963-4453
www.highsouth.com/vallecrucis
This conference center is host to the Labyrinth of the ministry of the Episcopal diocese of Western North Carolina. It is patterned after the ancient labyrinth at Chartre Cathedral in France. This ancient spiritual tool provides a winding, circuitous walk symbolizing a pilgrim's walk with God. The center is open to all who wish to make a reservation.

Wildacres Retreat
Wildacres Road, Little Switzerland, NC
(828) 756-4573
www.wildacres.org
Wildacres is a conference center offering its facilities to nonprofit groups that conduct educational or cultural programs and seminars. In 1946, it was dedicated by I. D. and Madolyn Blumenthal to the betterment of human relations and interfaith dialogue. It is situated on 1,600 acres at an elevation of 3,300 feet atop a mountain called Pompey's Knob, near the Blue Ridge Parkway in Little Switzerland, North Carolina. It is about halfway between Asheville and Blowing Rock. Among the many groups using the facilities are music and art master classes; religious and interfaith groups; mineral and lapidary societies; and medical, social science, natural sciences, academic, environmental, and senior citizen groups. All groups must be nonprofit and have planned educational programs.

CENTRAL MOUNTAINS

Basilica of St. Lawrence
97 Haywood Street, Asheville, NC
(828) 252-6042
The 34th Minor Basilica in the United States of the Roman Catholic Church is the Basilica of St. Lawrence in Asheville. This downtown church was built by Spanish architect Rafael Guastavino. A remarkable feature of this church is that the architect is buried in an alcove in the Chapel of Mary. In that same chapel is the restored Stanzionni painting *The Visitation,* which was discovered to be the missing painting from the set of four he painted for the Vatican.

The Basilica has a sister church of the same design in Wilmington, North Carolina. In Asheville, services are in both English and Spanish to serve its diverse parish. In celebrating its 10th year as a Minor Basilica, a litany written for the opening of the church in 1908 by architect Guastavino was discovered and was used for the first time.

Cathedral of All Souls
9 Swann Street, Biltmore Village, NC
(828) 274-2681
This Episcopal church was built as part of George W. Vanderbilt's Biltmore Village. It served as an anchor for the many buildings in the village that now house boutique shops, restaurants, and other functioning businesses. The stained glass windows are especially noteworthy as they were created by LaFarge. The church, as are other original buildings in the village, was designed in a style similar to that of the Yorkshire Moors in England.

The Cove/Billy Graham Training Center
1 Porters Cove Road, Swannanoa, NC
(828) 298-2092, (800) 950-2092
www.thecove.org
The Billy Graham Training Center at the Cove is situated on a secluded 1,500 acres of solitude with a bubbling stream and winding trails. The four-story Chatlos Memorial Chapel, with its 87-foot steeple and 8-foot cross, is open to visitors. An eight-minute video is offered that depicts the various events at the Cove. A walk around the next level of the chapel presents a photo exhibit of Billy Graham's worldwide crusades. A bookstore is also on that level. The next two levels offer the chapel and a prayer room.

The Cove property is an idyllic setting, with mountain streams, hiking trails, and open fields. The cove camp is open for ages 9 to 15. In addition, other camps and retreat sites are provided for junior and senior high school students. The Cove Camp includes full-facility cabins, a dining hall, and recreational sites. Weekend conferences, summer retreats, and other ongoing seminars are offered in Christian leadership training. The 80,000-square-foot training facility can accommodate groups of up to 450 and offers rooms especially designed for teaching, studying, and worship.

First Baptist Church
5 Oak Street, Asheville, NC
(828) 252-4781
America's leader in the Art Deco movement, Douglas Ellington, lived on Chunns Cove Road. After studying architectural design in Europe, he relocated to Asheville from his birthplace in eastern North Carolina. A group of Baptists in Asheville commissioned him to build them as beautiful a church as he could. He recalled being enthralled with the great architectural style of the Duomo in Florence, Italy. Thus he inculcated the concept of that great Roman Catholic edifice into the design of First Baptist Church of Asheville. One result is that many mistakenly believe this to be Asheville's Minor Basilica of St. Lawrence. The Basilica is located across from the Civic Center. Since 1927 both the building and the ministry of First Baptist church have become a widespread ministry that includes a child development center and a family ministries center.

Kanuga Conferences
Hendersonville, NC
(828) 692-9136
www.kanuga.org
This Episcopal center hosts conferences and retreats for Episcopal groups. Other church groups, nonprofits, and corporate meetings for educational training are welcome when retreats are not taking place. The center accommodates 450 overnight guests. Ropes courses and team building are available.

Lake Junaluska Conference Center and Retreat
Lake Junaluska, NC
(800) 222-4930, ext. 2
www.lakejunaluska.com
This conference center is the headquarters of the Southeastern Jurisdiction of the United Methodist Church. It is located in Haywood County south of I-40, exit 27, off U.S. 23/74. The center is tucked in among 18 of the peaks that are over 6,000 feet. The 200-acre lake is surrounded by 1,200 acres of rolling hills and valleys.

Communion of Saints Fresco at St. Eugene's Parish in Asheville

This 9-by-12-foot fresco is the first in Asheville. It depicts Christ ascendant over St. Francis, St. Paul, Mary Magdalen, and a pair of anonymous followers. The traditional technique of fresco involves mixing water with lime and plaster, then painting directly onto the plaster. This was the method used by Michelangelo in the Sistine Chapel paintings and Leonardo da Vinci's *The Last Supper.* For more than six years artist James Daniel studied with fresco-master Ben Long of Asheville. He has assisted Long with painting the domes of the TransAmerica Building in Charlotte, the Charlotte Law Enforcement Center, the Chapel of the Prodical in Montreat, and the Statesville Civic Center. The wall in the new day chapel at St. Eugene's was built to the artist's specifications. It is set into a 15-foot freestanding stone wall. St. Eugene's Parish is 1 block north of Merrimon Avenue just off Beaverdam Road. Open daily 7:30 A.M. to 7:30 P.M. For information call (828) 254–5193.

The center hosts church-related programs, youth conferences, educational seminars, spiritual retreats, vacations, and family reunions. Lodging and conference facilities can accommodate up to 2,000 people. Lodging is in private cottages, the majestic Terrace Hotel, and the Lambuth Inn, which jointly have 231 rooms.

Closing ceremonies for Folkmoot USA have been held each summer for the past 20 years at Stuart Auditorium. (See Close-up about Folkmoot USA in our Annual Festivals and Events chapter.)

The center takes its name from the Cherokee Chief Junaluska, who led his warriors in victory with Gen. Andrew Jackson and his federal troops against the British at Horseshoe Bend in the War of 1812.

Montreat Conference Center
101 Assembly Drive, Montreat, NC
(828) 669–2911
www.montreat.org
The Scots brought with them the banner of Calvinism and the Presbyterian church

as they explored these mountains. Schools and churches were established. An outgrowth has been a conference retreat center known originally as Mountain Retreat, now known as the town of Montreat. The Presbyterian Scots established a grammar school for boys, which has grown into Warren Wilson College, and their school for girls is now Montreat College. One prominent resident at Montreat is the world-renowned evangelist—a boy who came off a dairy farm in Charlotte, North Carolina—Rev. Dr. Billy Graham.

The books and movie about the chaplain of the U.S. Senate and pastor of the New York Avenue Presbyterian church in Washington, D.C., Peter Marshall, were penned by his wife Catherine, a resident of Montreat. She later wrote about her mother, who was an educational missionary in these mountains. Her book, *Kristy,* became a television series as well. Within this small mountain enclave reside around 300 registered voters. The population swells as summer homes are filled, the

Montreat Conference Center conducts business, and Montreat College operates two campuses between Montreat and Black Mountain, with advanced degree programs offered across the state in various centers. With the erection of the Chapel of the Prodigal on the college campus in 1998, the Ben Long fresco *Return of the Prodigal* has been visited by more than 20 million people.

Ridgecrest Conference Center
Ridgecrest, NC
(828) 669-8022
www.ridgecrestconferences.com

This conference site is owned by the Southern Baptist Convention. Established in 1907, it is situated on 1,300 acres with spectacular views of the mountains and seasonal changes. It offers conferences for Baptist groups and is also available to non-Baptist groups. It operates year-round. The center is 17 miles east of Asheville off I-40.

St. Matthias Episcopal Church
1 Dundee Street, Asheville, NC
(828) 285-0033

Located on Catholic Hill in Asheville is this integrated church that once served the Afro-American Episcopal population of Asheville. It has specific links to the Vanderbilts. In the 1880s segregation was the key word in the South. Freed men were not permitted to worship at All Souls. Vanderbilt donated materials and craftsmen from his estate to build St. Matthias in 1895. Much of the interior is similar to that of Biltmore House. The building is on the National Register of Historic Buildings. The contracting builder was James Victor Miller. Across the street from the Young Men's Institute (YMI) on South Market Street in Asheville is a station of the Urban Trail honoring James Miller. Today the ministry of the church includes Sunday afternoon concerts, unusually beginning at 3:00 P.M. There is no admission charge.

YMCA Blue Ridge Assembly Inc.
84 Blue Ridge Circle, Black Mountain, NC
(828) 669-8422
www.blueridgeassembly.org

In 1906 Willis Duke Weatherford Sr. climbed a tree to see whether this site provided an inspirational view. It certainly did, as this is where thousands have come since then to enjoy all aspects of inspiration. It hosts international conferences as well as serving as a day camp in the summer. It is a full-service, year-round conference center and is available to groups and organizations, particularly not-for-profit, religious, educational, government, and social services groups and family reunions. The Assembly can accommodate 950 overnight guests. Rope courses and team building programs are offered. Cameras captured this site with Sandra Bullock in the film *28 Days*.

Synagogues

Beth Ha-Tephila Congregation
43 North Liberty Street
Asheville, NC
(828) 253-4911

Congregation Beth-ha-Tephila was founded in 1891. At that time the Conservative congregation met at the Lyceum Hall on Biltmore Avenue. Property for a Jewish cemetery was purchased in 1902 at Riverside. In the same year, a building was purchased at Spruce and Woodfin Streets.

Beth Israel Synagogue
229 Murdock Avenue, Asheville, NC
(818) 252-8431

Not only are there Jewish temples and synagogues in the mountains, but Riverside Cemetery in Asheville has incorporated within it a special Jewish cemetery with all stones engraved in Hebrew. A hemlock hedge outlines the area.

RETIREMENT

North Carolina's mountain towns and cities have been at the top of leading publications' lists of "top places to retire" for some time now. But many retirees discovered this area years ago, long before the lists were a twinkle in publishers' eyes. Some of us locals were once visitors or summer vacationers who were so delighted with the beauty, the climate, the amenities, the price of properties, and the services offered that we ended up moving here permanently. Another important factor that makes this area attractive for retirement is the low crime rate and active lifestyle.

This large and vital segment of the mountains' population is growing by leaps and bounds. By the year 2010 Henderson County, one of the fastest growing retirement regions here, will have a population of which 40 percent is older than 65. This county, along with others in the region, is responding by making long-term plans to assure that essentials such as health care, housing, transportation, and social support services are adequate to meet this growth. Although the majority of older adults in the area have ample income (Henderson County's poverty rate is one of the state's lowest), the costs of such services are more than offset by the talent, wisdom, life skills, and energy senior citizens bring to our area.

But what draws people here for retirement anyway? When moving to the North Carolina mountains, you won't feel like you are retiring, but rather beginning a second career of healthy recreation, travel, cultural enrichment, culinary arts, entertainment, and the discovery of nature. Whether settling down in the placid seasonal community of Blowing Rock, where fine and unique restaurants line the main street along with quality antique stores, bakeries, and sweet shops, or the rolling green countryside of Valle Crucis, where

your visitors will adore the many bed-and-breakfasts they will encounter in this rural valley, you will not go wrong in choosing to continue your lives here. With all the cultural treats of the area—universities and music schools, museums and galleries, mountain craft schools and studios, unique shops and arrays of excellent restaurants, botanical gardens and nearby forests and waterfalls—you would be hard pressed to find time to while away the hours sitting in a rocking chair!

A number of counties around North Carolina hold Senior Games competitions, which were founded in 1983 to create a year-round health promotion and educational program for North Carolinians 55 and older. Today over 36,000 seniors participate in 52 local games that serve all 100 counties across the state. For example, in Transylvania County, these qualifying games are sponsored each spring. To participate you must be 55 or older and reside in the county for at least three months out of the year. Competitions include the running and standing long jump, a 1,500-meter race walk, men's and women's tennis (both singles and doubles), men's and women's horseshoes, bowling, billiards, a basketball shoot, table tennis, a football and softball throw, spin casting, golf, swimming events, cycling, racquetball, and badminton. Gold, silver, and bronze medals are awarded in each age category in each event. All winners are eligible to participate in the North Carolina State Senior Games in Raleigh during the autumn. For more information call North Carolina Senior Games (919–851–5456).

At the same time Transylvania and other counties also sponsor the Silver Arts Competition. Entries must be the original work of the artist, must be work created after the age of 55, and must have been completed within two years of the local games' qualifying date. First-place winners in each visual and heritage arts subcategory are entered in the state finals.

If help is needed, it's available. In counties that have long dealt with seniors' needs—such as Buncombe and Henderson—such services are broad and highly organized. In some of the more rural counties, what may be lacking in highly organized structures is more than made up for in small-town and community caring. (See our Health Care chapter for information on the health services in the area.) Here—aside from the usual government agencies, such as health departments, departments of social services, the public libraries, parks and recreation departments (which coordinate annual Senior Games), and commercial in-home health services that can be located in the Yellow Pages—is just a partial list of places you may call on for support systems, socializing, and just plain fun.

REGIONAL SERVICES
Northern Mountains

Area Agency on Aging Council of Governments
155 Furman Road, Boone, NC
(828) 265-5434
www.regiond.org
This agency serves senior citizens in the seven northwestern counties of North Carolina. The agency directs a Long-Term Care Ombudsman Program for the region and serves as a funding and information resource for agencies involved in senior care, education, and public awareness in Alleghany, Ashe, Avery, Mitchell, Watauga, and Yancey Counties to the north. Senior centers in each of these locations offer a variety of programs that include group meals at the centers as well as home-delivered meals, In-Home Aide, recreational programs, legal services, health screening, and nutrition guidance. Transportation and adult day care are also pro-

vided through some locations. They also publish a helpful directory, listing agencies and telephone numbers.

Legal Services of the Blue Ridge
171 Grand Boulevard, Boone, NC
(828) 264-5640, (800) 849-5666
Senior citizens can get advice for problems with Social Security, Medicaid and Medicare, food stamps, housing, institutional care, and consumer issues.

ALLEGHANY COUNTY

Alleghany Council on Aging Inc.
Senior Center, Greyson and Whitehead Streets, Sparta, NC
(336) 372-4640
This organization oversees In-Home Aide, group meals, home-delivered meals, health promotion, Senior Games, AARP, recreation, and educational classes.

American Association of Retired Persons (AARP)
Greyson and Whitehead Streets, Sparta, NC
(336) 372-4640
This branch of the national organization meets the fourth Tuesday of each month at 6:00 P.M. at the Alleghany Senior Center for discussion, support, counseling, and social time.

Blue Ridge Opportunity Commission
1747 U.S. Highway 21 N., Sparta, NC
(336) 372-7284
The BROC provides information and referral, housing weatherization, and repair.

Cooperative Extension Service
90 South Main Street, Sparta, NC
(336) 372-5597
This office provides advice on energy resources conservation, homemaking, and personal financial management counseling for Alleghany County senior citizens.

Department of Social Services
182 Doctors Street, Sparta, NC
(336) 372-2411, (336) 372-2414 (food stamps)

The Department of Social Services can help you arrange for health support services, Medicaid, protective services, senior citizens transportation, emergency assistance programs, and nursing home placement. Food stamps are also available through this office.

When visiting or living in a mountain county that lacks a daily newspaper, buy or subscribe to the county weekly. These are great, up-to-date sources for our cultural events, educational opportunities, and other activities.

ASHE COUNTY

American Association of Retired Persons (AARP)

This group meets the first Wednesday of each month from noon to 4:00 P.M. at the public library in Jefferson to discuss issues concerning seniors in the area and to provide mutual support.

Ashe Services for Aging Inc.
180 Chatty Rob Lane, West Jefferson, NC
(336) 246-2461
www.asheaging.org

This agency oversees programs for transportation, In-Home Aide II, group and home-delivered meals, and educational classes. Senior Tar Heel discount cards, the Health Insurance Information Program, adult day care, and daily activity programs are some of the benefits available here for Ashe County's older residents.

Blue Ridge Opportunity Commission
169 Warrensville School Road,
Warrensville, NC
(336) 384-4543

The group offers assistance with weatherization and repair, housing and community action, and crisis intervention regarding fuel and electricity.

Department of Social Services
303 East Main Street, Jefferson, NC
(336) 246-1900

This public agency offers senior citizens resources, information, aid for medical expenses, adult protective services, food stamps, and (home-heating) fuel assistance.

Health Department,
Senior Companion Program
707 Ray Taylor Road, West Jefferson, NC
(336) 246-4898

Companionship is key to the success of this in-home service that involves active senior citizens working with disabled or less-active senior citizens in the community and provides assistance with light housekeeping, meal preparation, laundry, bookkeeping, bill-paying, and transportation.

USDA Rural Development
525 East Main Street, Jefferson, NC
(336) 246-8818

Low- and moderate-income grants for senior citizens for housing and home repair are available through this agency.

AVERY COUNTY

Avery County Veterans Office
205 Administrative Building, Newland, NC
(828) 733-8211

This local office assists veterans with claims to the Veterans Administration for such things as education, medical care, insurance, and loans.

Avery Senior Services Senior Center
165 Shultz Circle, Newland, NC
(828) 733-8220

Transportation, In-Home Aide I, group and home-delivered meals, and health promotion are a few of the many services Avery provides.

W.A.M.Y. Community Action
260 Eastotoa Avenue, Newland, NC
(828) 733-0156

This group provides community center crafts, weatherization and home repair, job training, a garden program, and transportation assistance. (W.A.M.Y. stands for Watauga, Avery, Mitchell, and Yancey Counties.)

MADISON COUNTY

Department of Social Services
Main Street, Marshall, NC
(828) 649-2711
Food stamps and assistance with Medicaid and fuel bills are provided though this office.

Madison County Department of Community Services Senior Center
462 Long Branch Road, Marshall, NC
(828) 649-2722
This site is the central location for a network of centers that offers activities, health screening, chore services, nutrition information, and home-delivered meals as well as congregate meals on site and information on other vital services of interest to Madison County senior citizens.

Mars Hill College Programs for Senior Citizens
Mars Hill, NC
(828) 689-1167
Mars Hill College participates with Elderhostel, a worldwide continuing education enrichment series for senior citizens. Programs from history and music to science and art are part of this learning opportunity offered 22 weeks each year. The college provides a regular continuing education program linked with the Mars Hill curriculum. The Summer Alternative Vacation Program and the Learning Institute for Elders (LIFE) have learning tours on a variety of subjects.

MITCHELL COUNTY

Cooperative Extension Service
County Building, Annex E., 10 South Mitchell Avenue, Bakersville, NC
(828) 688-4811

This county extension service provides senior citizens with advice on energy resources conservation, financial management, and homemaking.

Department of Social Services
271 Crimson Laurel Way, Bakersville, NC
(828) 688-2175
Senior citizens around Bakersville can find resource information, In-Home Aide services, food stamps, energy assistance, health support services, transportation, and home improvement assistance through this agency.

Mitchell Senior Center
152 Ledger School Road, Bakersville, NC
(828) 688-3019
Transportation, In-Home Aide I, group and home-delivered meals, and health and nutrition assistance are some of the services provided by this center.

Veterans Service Office
130 Forest Service Drive, Suite C, Bakersville, NC
(828) 688-2200
This local office assists veterans with claims to the Veterans Administration for such things as education, medical care, insurance, and loans.

W.A.M.Y. Community Action Inc.
213 Oak Avenue, Spruce Pine, NC
(828) 766-9150, (828) 765-9151
Transportation, weatherization and home repair, elderly nutrition, and gardening programs are some of the services provided by this office.

WATAUGA COUNTY

American Association of Retired Persons (AARP)
Boone, NC
This group for Boone-area retired folk meets the third Monday of each month at 11:30 A.M. for a Dutch treat lunch at a local Shoney's. This AARP chapter is active in legislative lobbying and in local and regional issues.

AppalCART Transportation
274 Winklers Creek Road, Boone, NC
(828) 264-2280, (828) 264-2278
AppalCART provides county and town transportation service to seniors and the general public. Call for schedules and arrangements.

Cooperative Extension Service
971 West King Street, Boone, NC
(828) 264-3061
Homemaking and housing information as well as energy resources conservation and financial management counseling are provided through the county extension service.

It's said "to learn, teach" and "to receive, give." Both sayings are particularly applicable to the thousands who volunteer their time and energy to enrich the lives, nature, and culture here in the mountains. Opportunities in every field abound. Contact local chambers of commerce for agencies that coordinate volunteers. Give it a try!

Department of Social Services
132 Popular Grove Connector, Suite C,
Boone, NC
(828) 265-8100
Health support services are among the many types of aid available through this department.

Veterans Service Office
Courthouse Annex, Room 100, Boone, NC
(828) 265-8065
This local office assists veterans with claims to the Veterans Administration for such things as education, medical care, insurance, and loans.

W.A.M.Y. Community Action Program
Main Office
152 Southgate Drive, Suite 2, Boone, NC
(828) 264-2421

Watauga County senior citizens benefit from the active participation of this office in the areas of weatherization and home repair, transportation for elderly, and job and gardening programs.

Watauga County Project on Aging
132 Poplar Grove Connector, Suite A,
Boone, NC
(828) 265-8090
www.wataugacounty.org/aging
Transportation, In-Home Aide I and II, group and home-delivered meals, and health screenings are provided to Watauga County senior citizens.

YANCEY COUNTY

Cooperative Extension Service
10 Orchard Street, Burnsville, NC
(828) 682-6186
Financial management counseling, housing information, homemaking services, and information on energy resources conservation, agriculture, and home horticulture are offered by the county extension service.

Department of Social Services
222 Lincoln Park, Burnsville, NC
(828) 682-6148, (828) 682-2470
Health support services, transportation, and aid for medical expenses and family and veteran support services are some of the services of this department.

W.A.M.Y. Community Action Program
22 E. Bypass, Burnsville, NC
(828) 682-2610
Above Pollard's Drug Store, the W.A.M.Y. program offers limited home repair assistance as well as elderly transportation.

Yancey County Committee on Aging
Senior Center, 10 Swiss Avenue,
Burnsville, NC
(828) 682-6011
This lively place offers In-Home Aide I, group and home-delivered meals, transportation, and health promotion like blood pressure and cholesterol checks. Senior Tar Heel Discount cards and the Senior's Health Insurance Information Program

(SHIIP) are also part of the services offered here.

Yancey Transportation Authority
Courthouse, 15 East Boulevard, Burnsville, NC
(828) 682-6144
Yancey offers senior transportation assistance through a contract with the senior center.

Central Mountains

BUNCOMBE COUNTY

Buncombe County Council on Aging
Community Services Center, 50 South French Broad Avenue, Suite 141, Asheville, NC
(828) 258-8027, (828) 258-8028
This private, nonprofit corporation, a United Way agency, is composed of senior citizens groups and organizations providing services to Buncombe County senior citizens. Outreach services include friendly visitation, senior companionship, home repair, weatherization, and fan distribution. The agency coordinates various county-wide programs that offer nutrition assistance, congregate meals at 17 locations, the Senior Tar Heel discount program, and volunteer opportunities for older citizens and other people.

Buncombe County Mountain Mobility
185 Coxe Avenue, Asheville, NC
(828) 258-0186
This service provides door-to-door transportation services for the elderly, disabled, and transportation disadvantaged.

Buncombe County Sheriff's Department
Reassurance Program
Sheriff's Department, 202 Haywood Street, Asheville, NC
(828) 250-4492
This helpful program, staffed by citizen volunteers, provides daily telephone check-in service for a number of Buncombe County's elderly. This program also works in connection with Visiting Health Professionals, Department of Social Services, and the Meals on Wheels program. The Buncombe County Sheriff's Department makes home visits when needed.

Center for Creative Retirement
College for Seniors, University of North Carolina Asheville, 1 University Heights Asheville, NC
(828) 251-6140, (828) 251-6384
www.unca.edu
The University of North Carolina Asheville was one of the first to establish a college for seniors. Through the generosity of the Janirve Foundation the college found a home as the Center for Creative Retirement. This newest building on campus, known as the Reuter Center, is named for the founder of the foundation.

This innovative university program, begun in 1988, offers learning, leadership, and community-service opportunities for older adults. Among these are the College for Seniors, a peer learning and teaching program; Schools and Campus Volunteer Programs, a variety of student/mentor learning experiences; Leadership Asheville Seniors, a series of daylong sessions geared toward community service; and a continuing program of research into issues concerning older adult education.

Land of the Sky Regional Council
25 Heritage Drive, Asheville, NC
(828) 251-6622
www.landofsky.org
The following counties comprise Land of the Sky Regional Council: Madison, Buncombe, Henderson, and Transylvania. Its purpose is to provide total services for seniors in all these counties. Two of the Council's guide books that contain contacts for all services from health services to activity clubs and beyond are *Senior Adult Directory for Buncombe County* and *Madison County Senior Services Directory.*

HENDERSON COUNTY

American Association of Retired Persons (AARP)
314 Oklawaha Circle, Hendersonville, NC
(828) 697-0187
This organization offers a 55 Alive/Safe Driving Course for senior citizens and tax aid services. A member of the organization coordinates the Senior's Health Insurance Information Program (SHIIP). It informs and educates seniors regarding relevant issues through speakers and literature and is one of the sponsors of the Widowed Persons Services (see later). It is an advocate for seniors' issues at the state and national level.

Blue Ridge Community College
College Drive, Flat Rock, NC
(828) 694-1700
BRCC offers a variety of courses, day adventures, and cultural events. Most important for retirees, it operates the Center for Lifelong Learning, which provides adults older than 50 the opportunity to buy a lifetime membership.

Council on Aging
304 Chadwick Avenue, Hendersonville, NC
(828) 692-4203
The council provides a variety of services that help older adults cope with physical, social, or other aging problems. Specific programs include Meals on Wheels, Service Advocates for the Elderly (SAFE), Elder Neighbors, minor home repairs, installation and repair of smoke alarms (Fire Alert), and an Information and Referral Helpline (828-697-4357). Other services include lending out heaters and fans, a hearing-aid bank, a thrift shop (213 South Church Street, 828-693-7756), and living wills. The council also offers congregate meals at the Sammy Williams Senior Center located at Third Avenue W. and Justice Street (828-692-3320), for those persons wishing to travel to the center.

FISH Volunteer Medical Transportation
P.O. Box 2411, Hendersonville, NC 28731
(828) 693-5100
FISH provides round-trip transportation within the county and, when medical services are not available, to Asheville for health-related appointments. Although the organization does not provide emergency medical transportation, it will take patients home from the hospital after outpatient surgery.

Lifeline Personal Emergency Response System
Pardee Hospital/Lifeline, 2029A Asheville Highway, Hendersonville, NC
(828) 692-9061
This program offers round-the-clock, professional monitoring of every emergency call for help direct to Pardee Hospital.

Opportunity House
1411 Asheville Highway, Hendersonville, NC
(828) 692-0575
This arts, crafts, and cultural center is a nonprofit organization that opened its doors in 1958. Now, as then, it continues to offer fellowship and learning opportunities to individuals of all ages and faiths. Activities include bridge, crafts, dance, golf, ladies club, seminars, and smoke-free bingo. The gift shop on the premises features many handcrafted items and is open to the public. Opportunity House is open Monday through Friday from 9:00 A.M. to 5:00 P.M., and visitors are always welcome. The annual membership fee is $25 for singles and $45 for couples; a lifetime membership fee is $200 for singles and $380 for couples. (See our Arts and Culture chapter for more information.)

Pardee Pavilion (Adult Day Care)
104 College Drive, Flat Rock
(828) 696-7070
This adult day-care facility has planned activities to meet an individual's specific needs. It provides educational, recreational, social, diversional, and volunteer programs. They moved to their new facility in mid-2000.

Seniors Health Insurance
Hendersonville, NC
(828) 692-4600

Personal insurance counseling provided by the Senior Health Insurance Information Program (SHIIP) is available at Pardee Hospital's Health Education Center in the Blue Ridge Mall. The trained SHIIP volunteers provide free counseling to older adults on long-term care insurance, Medicare, and Medicaid Supplement insurance. Contact the Pardee Health Education Center, 1800 Four Seasons Boulevard, Hendersonville; (828) 692-4600, for more information.

Western Carolina Community Action
526 Seventh Avenue E., Hendersonville, NC
(828) 693-1771

This organization develops and administers programs of interest to older adults that include weatherization, a heating appliance replacement and repair program (HARRP), FISH medical transportation answering and dispatch, a variety of transportation services, emergency assistance, emergency fuel, plastic for windows, a garden program, a food closet, job placement with supportive services, liquid nutrient supplement (Ensure), and Section 8 Housing Assistance, to name a few.

YMCA
810 Sixth Avenue W., Hendersonville, NC
(828) 692-5774

Adult programs include fitness classes, health enhancement programming, swimming classes, volleyball, basketball, special events, and workshops. Specifically for older adults, the "Y" offers a Water Exercise program, an Arthritis Water exercise program, a Senior Pep Exercise program, and a Deep Water Aerobic program.

POLK COUNTY

The Meeting Place
Jervey-Palmer Building, 330 Carolina Drive, Tryon, NC
(828) 859-9707

This center serves both congregate and in-home lunches Monday through Friday. It also offers classes in exercise, quilting, and sewing, but one of its biggest draws is its ceramics workshop.

The Meeting Place also has a pool room, a television lounge, and frequent games of cards, bingo, and checkers. It has its own library and is visited regularly by a bookmobile. There is also a regular Wednesday music session. Other services include regularly scheduled transportation for shopping and medical appointments, and special holiday trips are offered. Seniors may also take advantage of nutrition education programs, legal services, and tax services. There are satellite centers with many of the same services in both Saluda and Green Creek.

Polk County Transportation Authority
Columbus, NC
(828) 894-8203

The authority provides transportation to senior centers and elsewhere by appointment.

TRANSYLVANIA COUNTY

American Association of Retired Persons (AARP)
P. O. Box 1336, Brevard, NC 28902
(828) 883-8486

AARP meets at 10:00 A.M. on the fourth Tuesday of each month in the Fellowship Hall of the First United Methodist Church in Brevard to hear speakers and participate in other programs of interest to the retirement community.

Brevard College Community Education
400 North Broad Street, Brevard, NC
(828) 884-8256

Reaching beyond the college-aged population, Brevard has a wide variety of continuing education programs for adults. The Office of Community Education currently offers more than 200 courses annually, with an enrollment for nearly 2,000 participants that include intellectual and academic subjects, cultural experiences, local orientation, hobbies and self-improvement, and health and physical fitness classes. Classes are noncredit. However CEUs are offered for specific programs. In addition musical performances, dramatic presentations, art gallery exhibits, and lecture series are presented throughout the year and are open to the public.

Computer courses are offered as well as a program that is lauded by the Transylvania newspaper as being one of the finest: the "Inside Transylvania" program. This course is designed for newcomers, but open to all. Participants meet face to face with leaders in Transylvania County. It offers 3.0 CEUs.

The Brevard College library is also an integral part of the intellectual life here. It has over 45,000 books, 200 periodical subscriptions, valuable electronic resources available on CD-ROM, Web access, and access to nearby colleges through the Mountain College Library Network.

College for Seniors and Elderhostel programs are offered through the University of North Carolina at Asheville. Contact the university for more information and turn your vacation into a journey of knowledge.

Koala Adult Day Care
19 Carolina Avenue, Brevard, NC
(828) 884-2980

Caregivers can leave loved ones here while they work or just take time for themselves. It offers its clients crafts, remotivation, reminiscing, fun and games, medication, and a hot lunch. The fee is $26 a day, and grants are available to those unable to pay the full amount.

Lifeline: Emergency Response
Transylvania Community Hospital,
Home Care Hospital Drive, Brevard, NC
(828) 883-5254

Lifeline provides 24-hour access to emergency help when a person is at home alone or with a caregiver who may be unable to provide necessary assistance in an emergency. It links, via telephone and specialized electronic equipment, with continuous emergency assistance at Tran-

sylvania Community Hospital.

Meals on Wheels of Brevard
Transylvania Community Hospital,
Hospital Drive, Brevard, NC
(828) 884-5298

Like so many other of these helpful programs, MOW provides hot, well-balanced noontime meals, weekdays, to shut-ins without age or income restrictions. Volunteers deliver the meals, and the cost-based on the client's ability to pay.

Telephone Reassurance Program
Brevard Police Department, City Hall,
Brevard, NC
(828) 883-2212

This 24-hour service is for people who live alone. They can leave their name, age, address, doctor's name, and who to call in an emergency. Every morning these people call or are called by the police department to make sure everything is okay. If there is no response or if help is needed, a police officer is sent to the address and proper steps are taken.

Transylvania County Med-Drive
Transportation
(828) 884-3203

Med-Drive volunteers provide transportation to medical appointments for any person over 60 within Transylvania County. Limited out-of-county transportation is available for chemotherapy, radiation, and renal dialysis. Med-Drive doesn't accommodate emergency medical transportation.

Western Carolina Community Action
203 East Morgan, Brevard, NC
(828) 884-3219

A branch of the WCCA in Henderson County, Transylvania's office serves congregate lunches Monday through Friday at both Silvermont in Brevard and in Quebec on U.S. 64 W. and provides transportation to both sites as well as out-of-county medical transportation. It joins with the AARP in providing trained tax preparers to assist with tax returns and oversees the Senior Health Insurance

Information Program (SHIIP), job-training for those older than 55, a weatherization program for both renters and homeowners with limited incomes, emergency assistance, liquid nutrient supplement (Ensure) program, plastic for windows, spring and fall garden supplies, a heating appliance repair and replacement program, and rental assistance. Program eligibility is based on income.

Southern Mountains

CHEROKEE COUNTY

Cherokee County Senior Services
69 Alpine Street, Murphy, NC
(828) 837-2467
Many activities take place at the Penland Senior Citizens Center, including craft classes and exercise programs conducted by the health department. A Friendly Visitor Program visits homebound seniors for "cheers and chores," and there's a congregate meal program at the center Monday through Friday, as well as a home-delivered meals program. It also offers information and referrals to various community services.

The organization's red vans offer regularly scheduled runs into each section of the county. Out-of-county trips are also scheduled for shopping, recreation and medical appointments. SHIIP (the Senior Health Insurance Information Program) is active here with trained counselors helping senior citizens with health insurance information. It also supports annual Senior Games and holds an annual picnic. In the Andrews branch (The Sunshine Club, 19 Business, Andrews; 828-321-4505), there is also a nutrition program, an exercise program, and classes.

CLAY COUNTY

American Association of Retired Persons (AARP)
Ritter Road, Hayesville, NC
(828) 389-9271

This group meets at the Clay County Senior Center (see the following entry) on the second Monday of the month for refreshments and to hear speakers talk about a variety of topics.

Clay County Senior Center
Ritter Road, Hayesville, NC
(828) 389-9271
The center provides a congregate "Meals with Friends" and Meals on Wheels, Monday through Friday. It also holds classes in painting, wood carving, crocheting, and exercise, and has popular Thursday Morning Music Sessions.

GRAHAM COUNTY

Senior Citizens Center
Moose Branch Road, Robbinsville, NC
(828) 479-7977
A congregate lunch is served at the center five days a week with home-driven meals to homebound seniors. There are also art and carving classes and bingo.

HAYWOOD COUNTY

Canton Senior Center
Old Canton Armory, 1 Pigeon Street, Canton, NC
(828) 648-8412
The center promotes wellness in older adults through group socialization, special activities, crafts, speaking, educational opportunities, and organized trips. A meal is offered at 11:45 A.M., Monday through Friday. They also serve as a conduit for Meals on Wheels for the Department of Social Services.

Council on Aging
1271 East Street, Waynesville, NC
(828) 452-2370
The council provides information and referral, resource directory, advocacy, coordination of services, special programs, and the Senior Games. The council is also the lead agency for CAP/DA, which serves elderly adults needing care in an in-home setting. A more recent

program is Faith in Action. It provides aid to the handicapped in installing railings and ramps and other devices necessary for well-being.

Haywood Community College
185 Freelander Drive, Clyde, NC
(828) 627-4500

Tuition is free to persons over 65, except for an activity fee and the cost of materials in arts and crafts classes. (See the HCC listing in our Education chapter.)

Intentional Growth Center
959 North Lakeshore Drive,
Lake Junaluska, NC
(828) 452-2881, ext. 721,
(800) 482-1442

The center, an agency of the United Methodist Church, is a nationally accredited provider of continuing education courses and programs of clergy and laity. It also serves as a popular center for the national Elderhostel program and for church-related older adult events, such as Fall Flings and Christmas at Lambuth Inn.

Meals on Wheels
Department of Social Services, 486 East
Marshall Street, Waynesville, NC
(828) 452-6620, ext. 377

Meals are provided five days a week based on need. Fees are based on income.

Mountain Projects Inc.
2251 Old Balsam Road, Waynesville, NC
(828) 452-1447

This organization is a community action agency serving Haywood and Jackson Counties. It operates numerous programs for low-income and disadvantaged persons. These currently include housing rehabilitation, Head Start, a congregate nutrition program, foster grandparents, a retired senior volunteer program, Section 8 rental assistance, Haywood Public Transit, employment and training programs, and in-home chore services for the elderly. The eligibility for program participation is determined by the particular grant funding the program.

Waynesville Old Armory Recreation Center
44 Boundary Street, Waynesville, NC
(828) 456-9207

Senior citizens meet here for lunch Monday through Friday. The center, which serves the entire community, also offers special activities, crafts, bridge, lectures, and organized trips.

JACKSON COUNTY

American Association of Retired Persons (AARP)
Sylva, NC
(828) 631-0193 (president)

This active chapter holds a monthly meeting. Additionally they support the functions at the Golden Age Club and programs that present topics of interest to senior citizens. On an as-needed basis, they offer a seven-week course teaching personal financial management to women and a 55 Alive driver refreshing course.

Cashiers Senior C.A.F.E.
Cashiers Community Building, off U.S.
Highway 64 W., Cashiers, NC
(828) 743-9215

This center provides congregate meals, home delivered meals, and social activities for senior citizens in the Cashiers area. Seniors can also use and receive instruction on the center's public access computer with Internet access.

Golden Age Club
1 Central Avenue, Sylva, NC
(828) 586-4944

This is one of the more active senior citizen centers in the mountains. Its 300 members enjoy classes in exercise, beginner and advanced line dancing, square dancing, tai chi exercise, wood carving, basic computer instruction, tennis, hiking, and creative writing. There are coffee klatsches for men and women, organized card games, and co-ed softball games. A philosophy group uses the center for its discussions. Another group is devoted to bowling. There is also a singing group and a line-dancing group that give performances around the area. Other activities include income tax preparation, a walking program, Senior Games, shuffleboard, horseshoes, billiards, fund-raisers, and intergenerational programs. A covered-dish supper is held once a month with dancing afterward. The fourth Saturday of every month, the center serves an "All You Can Eat" country breakfast for $3.00. The public is invited. Membership fees for those 50 and over are $5.00 a year, and seniors get a lot for their money!

Jackson County Department on Aging
30 Central Street, Sylva, NC
(828) 586-8562

This active agency provides programs and resources for county seniors. In addition to coordinating services with other agencies and councils, it provides information and referral services on a variety of subjects and health issues, initiates new services, and is a senior advocacy group. It also publishes a monthly newsletter, Jacksonian, with information about local senior events and happenings.

Jackson County Transportation
(828) 586-3133

This organization fills a need that many residents in rural counties encounter. It provides on-call transportation for medical visits to nutrition sites. One day a week it follows established routes in outlying areas to take people shopping, to banks, and to doctors. It also visits the county's rehabilitation center and offers low-cost, zoned transportation to the general public.

Mountain Projects, Inc.
23 Schulman Street, Sylva, NC
(828) 586-2345

For information on this agency's services, see our Mountain Projects, Inc. entry in this chapter under Haywood County.

Southwestern Community College
Highway 107, Sylva, NC
(828) 586-4091

SCC's Continuing Education program—serving Jackson, Macon, Swain, and the Qualla Boundary—offers classes in every-thing from computers to crafts. You can reach the center nearest you by calling the Sylva campus number above, the Cherokee Center (828-497-7233), the Macon County Center (828-369-7331), or the Swain County Center (828-488-6413).

Sylva Senior C. A. F. E.
Community Services Building, 538 Scots Creek, Sylva, NC
(828) 586-6710

A congregate lunch is served here Monday through Friday, and the Home-Delivered Meals Program delivers hot, nutritious meals daily to Jackson County's homebound elderly seven days a week. This center has a public access computer with Internet connection for seniors in the Sylva area, and instruction is available. It also offers occasional programs, including exercises, bingo, and adventurous outings, but simply socializing is one of the biggest attractions.

Western Carolina University
N.C. Highway 107, Cullowhee, NC
(828) 227-7397

In addition to all the arts and culture found at a large university, this institution offers an outstanding continuing education program. (See the WCU entry in our Education chapter for more information.)

MACON COUNTY

Center for Life Enrichment
Peggy Cross Center, Corner of Fifth and South Streets, P.O. Box 2046, Highlands, NC 28741
(828) 526-9381

The center is aligned with four regional institutions of higher education: Western Carolina University, Southwestern Community College, Piedmont College, and Brevard College. Programs are offered for personal enrichment. One such offering is "Cooking with Culinary Herbs," taught by Stewart House B&B owner, Barbara Werder. She is an avid gardener who raises spectacular herbs and flowers. Another course entitled "Wine Trends" is taught by restaurateur, Steve Pignatiello, at his colleagues' restaurant, "Wolfgang's On Main." Mindy and Wolfgang Green now list over 280 wines on their menu. Other programs present computer knowledge, art and music, and much more, including resources for everyday living.

Macon County Department of Aging
125 Hyatt Road, Franklin, NC
(828) 349-2058
The department is the only full-service agency to serve anyone older than 60 west of Hickory. A sampling of the services provided: congregate meals, home-delivered meals, chores, respite care services, in home services, an Alzheimer's support group, an Alzheimer's day-care center, overnight respite, case management, information and referral, SHIIP, a lending library on dementia, and medical equipment for loan.

Many local restaurants, museums, and movie theaters offer senior discounts—inquire and bring proof of age!

SWAIN COUNTY

State of Franklin Services to Senior Citizens
Courthouse-on-the-Square, Bryson City, NC
(828) 488-3047
The Swain County Senior Center provides an Elderly Nutrition Program for people older than 60 at noon Monday through Friday as well as transportation to the center. Transportation is also provided for medical appointments and shopping. On certain days of the month, there are regularly scheduled trips for out-of-town medical appointments.

Through the National Council of Senior Citizens, a Senior AIDES Program provides an employment service for people older than 55 for 20-hour-week jobs with non-profit organizations and governmental positions. Other activities include line dancing and classes through Southwestern Community College. Bingo is played on Wednesdays and Fridays, and there's a health screening at the center twice a month.

RETIREMENT COMMUNITIES

Because Western North Carolina is so popular with retirees, it naturally follows that many retirement communities have sprung up here. Although most are concentrated in the Asheville-Hendersonville area, others are sprouting in surrounding areas. They offer everything from an independent living style to total life care. They also offer a wide range of options to fit various retirement needs and budgets: manufactured homes, cluster or attached homes, town houses, condominiums, apartments, and luxurious life-care facilities.

Some offer basic services, such as lawn care, at the option of individual residents. Others take care of all maintenance. Some include a variety of recreational amenities. A number provide meals, housekeeping, social activities, transportation, and nursing care.

Most counties have low-cost retirement apartments through their departments of social services that are priced according to income levels, though there is often a waiting list for these. Here are a few examples of what is available. For more information contact local chambers of commerce.

Northern Mountains

Appalachian/Brian Estates
163 Shadowline Drive, Boone, NC
(828) 264-1006, (800) 333-3432
This 91-residence community for older adults is unique in that it offers both annual and seasonal apartments. Appalachian/Brian Estates is strictly a rental retirement community developed as a cooperative venture between Appalachian State University Foundation and Don Beaver of Beaver Sports Properties. Because residents are not required to

liquidate their assets and no endowments or purchase plans are required, the rental option is a big drawing card.

Modern facilities, including a variety of thoughtfully designed floor plans for studio, one- and two-bedroom residences, a community dining room, and several recreational areas cater to the carefree retirement lifestyle. Lounges, a club room for parties, exercise facilities, a professional hair salon, library, and sundry store are all on site. A guest suite is provided for visiting family members. Services are well planned and involve community outreach. At nearby Appalachian State, the "A/BE" residents enjoy university programs geared toward retirees. The university library is also open to the residents.

Community security includes a 24-hour emergency call system and smoke detectors and sprinkler systems in every residence. Staff members are available around the clock. Prices start at $1,200 per month for an unfurnished studio apartment and vary depending on the six different floor plans, annual or seasonal.

Central Mountains

College Walk
Neely Road, Brevard, NC
(828) 884-5800, (800) 280-9600

At College Walk you'll find a stimulating community planned exclusively for your pleasure and customized to your lifestyle. Whether you relish long, solitary walks in picturesque woods, love learning and broadening your horizons, or simply prefer a busy schedule of activities, there's something that will satisfy you here.

College Walk borders Brevard College and is convenient to the Brevard Music Center, shopping, and Pisgah National Forest.

This community offers two- and three-bedroom cluster homes; studio, one-, and two-bedroom apartments; and a state-licensed assisted-living facility. Apartments, which can range in size from 430 to 1,300 square feet, have no entry fee. Monthly fees range from $1,275 to $2,545

and include one meal daily, housekeeping, maintenance, transportation, linen service, utilities, a 24-hour emergency call system, security, and a large number of activities.

The two- and three-bedroom cluster homes all have screened porches and garages and range from 1,250 to 1,650 square feet. The fee includes one meal daily, land lease, outside maintenance, security patrol, and use of the clubhouse, library, game room, auditorium, workshop, and other common areas.

Crescent View
2533 Hendersonville Road, Asheville, NC
(828) 687-0068

This Lutheran-sponsored planned community in Buncombe County has a variety of studio, one-, and two-bedroom apartment homes for retired seniors. Fine dining, housekeeping, and linen services are available here, as well as 24-hour security and transportation. Crescent View also offers assisted-living residences. On the south end of Asheville, it is close to major supermarkets, movie theaters, shopping, and easy access to the Blue Ridge Parkway.

Deerfield
1617 Hendersonville Road, Asheville, NC
(828) 274-1531, (800) 284-1531

This pleasant Episcopal retirement community on Asheville's south end offers apartments and cottages for seniors. The attractively landscaped estate maintains a health center, a central formal dining room with wait service, and a community center with a host of amenities. Deerfield maintains Life Care assisted living and will be expanding over the next few years. Just off a main thoroughfare on Asheville's south side, Deerfield is close to shopping, restaurants, cinemas, and access to the Blue Ridge Parkway.

Givens Estate United Methodist Retirement Community, 2360 Sweeten Creek Road, Asheville, NC
(828) 274-4800

This United Methodist retirement community is spread over 160 wooded acres in south Asheville. The retirement village has residential options that include apartments, duplexes, and individual houses scattered across the campus. Asbury Hall, in the community's center, offers congregate living with dining and recreational facilities. Also within this facility is Sales Health Care Center, designed to provide domiciliary or skilled nursing care to residents who can no longer live alone. A campus nurse and 24-hour emergency call system and housekeeping are additional services. The purchase price of houses, duplexes, villas, and congregate-living apartments range from $47,500 and up. Apartment rental under the federal government's HUD program is based on income.

Highland Farms Retirement Community
200 Tabernacle Road, Black Mountain, NC
(828) 669-6473

Highland Farms was one of the first retirement communities in Western North Carolina. This beautiful spot, nestled in the mountains in Buncombe County near the village of Black Mountain, has drawn retirees since the 1970s. Cluster homes, condominiums, apartments, individual homes, a residential lodge, a health care center, and a rest home are spread over a lovely campus with the mountains in view.

Residents enjoy a number of services and activities. A library, music area, art and craft studio, and even a vegetable garden keep those at Highland Farms active. Seminars and on-campus workshops foster a close relationship with the surrounding communities of Asheville and Black Mountain.

Lake Pointe Landing
333 Thompson Street, Hendersonville, NC
(828) 693-7800, (800) 693-7801

The 32-acre complex has easy access to I-26 and is less than a mile from Hendersonville's restaurants, shopping, banks, and medical offices. The lush landscaping and one-plus-acre lake make it seem more a "country place."

Lake Pointe is made up of patio homes known as the Villas, where retirees can enjoy 100 percent equity ownership. There are two- and three-bedroom units, each with a second-floor loft to use as a study or for extra storage. Both units come with two baths; a living room; a fully equipped, all-electric kitchen; a fireplace; a screened-in back porch; and an enclosed garage. For more space there are special homes with a lakeside view, retirement center proximity, or seclusion and privacy.

Homes range in price from $170,000 and up. The monthly service fee is $450 and includes the use of the Club House, which has an arts and crafts room, an auditorium, a library, a general store, an exercise room/spa, a swimming pool, a beauty and barber shop, a billiards room, a bridge room, a woodworking shop, and garden plots. Dining service for one dinner meal a day is $240 a month. Lake Pointe Landing homeowners are give priority places into the Health Center and independent/assisted living apartments.

Rental apartments, called The Harbor, are also available. Residents here have biweekly maid service and evening meals in a full-service dining room. All utilities except personal telephone service are included in the rental fee, along with maintenance and a full calendar of activities, with scheduled transportation and use of the Club House. Special guest suites are available for family and friends when they come to visit.

In addition there are assisted living apartments at the Inn at Lake Pointe Landing with a choice of alcove and one-bedroom apartments. A licensed staff provides help in monitoring medications, grooming, housekeeping, and access to transportation and other assistance.

Lake Pointe Landing also offers an on-site, long-term-care facility, Life Care Center of Hendersonville. It provides rehabilitation, skilled, and long-term care services.

Pine Park Retirement Inn
2601 Highway 64 E., Hendersonville, NC
(828) 692-1911

Pine Park is a month-to-month rental retirement center with no "buy in" or long-term lease. There is, however, a processing fee, payable in advance, (refundable until the day of occupancy).

The center has 110 units: 63 independent-living units and 47 assisted-living units. Prices for apartments include three meals a day; a social activities program; once-a-week housekeeping, including linens; all utilities and cable television; two-way intercom service; 24-hour attendant services; and transportation to medical services, shopping, and other outside activities.

Additional services associated with the activities of daily life—such as bathing, supervision of medications, and personal laundry service—are available in assisted-living units. There is a charge for using the on-site beauty/barber shop. Pets are allowed for a monthly pet charge.

Riverwind Adult Community
100 Riverwind Drive, Hendersonville, NC
(828) 891-2010, (800) 452-3058

This community of manufactured homes, created by the Oakwood Homes Corporation, is just off U.S. 64 W. in Etowah, between Brevard and Hendersonville. It's also just a mile from two championship golf courses (Etowah Valley Country Club and the Cummings Cove Golf Course; see our Golf chapter for more info) and is convenient to medical facilities and shopping (including groceries). Riverwind offers Freedom, Oakwood, and Virginia homes in two- and three-bedroom, two-bath models with brick/block foundations that contain approximately 1,950 to 3,940 square feet. The prices include the property that the home is on. Its cable, city water, electricity, natural gas, and telephone lines are all underground. Home-owners Association dues are accessed monthly and include sewer service, street, and entrance lights; common area maintenance; garbage collection; and use of the recently built clubhouse, swimming pool, and whirlpool spa.

Tryon Estates
617 Laurell Lake Drive, Columbus, NC
(828) 894-3000, (800) 633-2718

Tryon Estates—owned and operated by ACTS, Inc., a not-for-profit corporation—lies on a 215-acre wooded site in Polk County's Thermal Belt. It offers both one-, two-, and three-bedroom apartments and two- and three-bedroom villas with all buildings connected by covered walkways. Chef-prepared gourmet meals are served each day in an elegant central dining room. There are also private dining rooms. It has a regular activity schedule and a full-time activity director. Other amenities include a theater-style auditorium, library, woodworking shop, billiard room, an activity-craft room, a card room, a beauty/barber shop, a pharmacy, banking and postal services, a gift shop, and an indoor, heated swimming pool. Outside you'll find garden plots, walking and biking paths, a stocked fishing pond, croquet, and shuffleboard. Maid service is available.

Residents are also offered portable emergency-call buttons, home health care, and a state-licensed, Medicare-approved health care center with a medical staff on duty 24 hours a day. This community includes 44 personal-care units (assisted living) and 52 skilled-nursing units. There is a dining room/activity area in the healthcare center with three meals served daily. Health care costs are covered under the monthly fee. The cost also covers daily breakfasts and dinners, all utilities except telephone, weekly bed linen laundry, maintenance, transportation, landscaping, activities, and security. The entrance fees to this life-care community—which provides a lifetime apartment lease, guaranteed access to all medical care, and use of all community facilities—currently range from $115,900 to $179,900 (a second person's entrance fee is $10,000). Overnight guests/children are welcomed, and pets are allowed.

HEALTH CARE (H)

E ven before the turn of the century, when these mountains became a haven for sufferers of tuberculosis, health care held a prominent position in Western North Carolina. Carriage upon carriage of visitors arrived to "take the air" and enjoy the healthful climate at local spas. Many of these visitors remained as permanent residents. Today the legacy of these early mountain sanitariums forms a strong foundation for the rapidly expanding modern medical facilities found in each county of the region.

Increased national focus on health care and technological advancements is one important reason that the latest medical services are available to residents of even the most remote mountain counties. Innovative pooling of related or crossover medical services is also a growing trend here. Buncombe County's Memorial Mission Hospital and St. Joseph's Hospital, for example, have merged. Asheville and Buncombe County, especially, boast a thriving and continually growing medical community.

The level of medical care available is equal to that of a major university research center, with some important differences. Savvy consumers like the fact that hospitals in Western North Carolina are still nonprofit and focused on quality. State-of-the-art medical care is delivered with individual concern and friendliness. The patient, not the stockholder, comes first.

Throughout the region services ranging from large, centrally located full-service hospitals, 24-hour emergency treatment centers, urgent-care and outpatient centers to community hospitals, community medical centers, and special private clinics directed to the needs of the underinsured can be found. Special medical concerns, such as cancer treatment, heart care, women's services, orthopedics, pediatric medicine, psychiatric services, rehabilitative therapy, and veterans' services are a major focus at many of the region's medical facilities. The latest diagnostics services, including ultrasound, mammography, CT scan, and MRI (magnetic resonance imaging) are available at all the region's larger medical facilities. With the increasing accessibility of technology, even some of the smaller community hospitals in the region can offer this level of medical service.

In this chapter we offer you an overview of the region's larger medical facilities, the community hospitals, a number of the community clinics, and their basic and specialized services. To find out more about the many services that each of the health care outlets offer, call the information numbers that we've provided.

If you unfortunately encounter a medical emergency in Western North Carolina, all our counties offer 911 emergency telephone service. For nonemergencies, check the front of the local phone book for other important phone numbers.

NORTHERN MOUNTAINS

Alleghany County

Alleghany Memorial Hospital
233 Doctor's Street N.C. Highway 18, Sparta, NC
(336) 372–5511
Just off the intersection of North Carolina Highways 21 and 18 N., in the heart of Sparta, Alleghany Memorial Hospital has served this rural, northern county since 1951. Personalized service and quality care are the mission of the 150-member staff at Alleghany Memorial. Comprehensive services are provided 24 hours a day. These include a well-staffed emergency room; radiology services such as CT scanning, mammography, ultrasound, MRI, and fluoroscopic services; rehabilitation services;

obstetrics; and restorative, respite, and terminal care. An additional primary care clinic handles specialty services like urology, orthopedics, cataract surgery, and everyday health problems. An In-Home Aide program, home-care program, and Lifeline provide outreach services to the community.

Ashe County

Ashe Memorial Hospital
200 Hospital Avenue, Jefferson, NC
(336) 246-7101

About 40 minutes from Boone, this small rural hospital maintains a sophisticated level of care for a county population of just 23,000. The hospital, established in 1939, is licensed for 76 beds and has a staff that includes two general surgeons, nine family practitioners, one radiologist, two ophthalmologists, one pediatrician, and one internist. A full-service hospital, Ashe Memorial offers general, laparascopic, and orthopedic surgery; complete eye care, including cataract treatment and laser surgery; diagnostic imaging; pediatric medicine; cardiopulmonary therapy and testing; nutritional counseling; Lifeline emergency response program; and a 24-hour emergency unit. The hospital also runs the Mountain Hearts Cardiac Rehabilitation Center and Segraves Care Center, a 60-bed skilled nursing home.

Avery County

Charles A. Cannon, Jr., Memorial Hospital
434 Hospital Drive, Linville, NC
(828) 737-7000

The Sloop Memorial and Charles A. Cannon Hospitals have merged and operate under the umbrella of the Avery Health Care System, 1955 Newland Highway; (828) 733-4410. Both are full-service facilities serving small rural communities.

Cannon, with a 79-bed capacity, was founded in 1908 and is in Banner Elk, just 17 miles from Boone. Sloop, with 38 beds and a staff of 15 doctors, was founded in 1929 and is in Crossnore, 25 miles from Boone. Both offer a wide range of modern services, including critical-care units, obstetric services, and radiology departments, featuring CT scanning, nuclear medicine, and MRI services. A 24-hour emergency service is available in both hospitals. Cannon also houses an inpatient psychiatric unit.

Two community clinics—Foscoe Family Health Center, N.C. 105, Sugar Grove, (828) 963-7161; and Newland Family Medical Center, 358 Beech Street, Newland, (828) 733-9276—serve as outreach affiliates of the hospitals.

Madison County

Mars Hill Medical Center
119 Mountain View Road, Mars Hill, NC
(828) 689-3507

Mars Hill Medical Center is in the small college town of Mars Hill, roughly 20 minutes north of Asheville. This private medical group, founded in 1971, serves the primary health care needs of the remote rural communities of Mars Hill, Marshall, Hot Springs, and Laurel in Madison County.

The Mars Hill location is the coordinating site for the various community services encompassed by the Hot Springs Health Program, and caregivers spend a great deal of hands-on time in the community. The 150 health care professionals and support staff of the Hot Springs Health Program all work with a high degree of mobility, providing primary medical care, pharmacy and dental services, home health and hospice care, occupational and physical therapy, and social services.

This group is professionally affiliated with the schools of medicine of the University of North Carolina at Chapel Hill, Duke University, the Mountain Area Health Edu-

Alternative Health Care in the Mountains

Ever had an ache or unhealthy condition that you'd like to get rid of without scads of medication? Or have you exhausted all medical avenues and don't seem to be getting better? Do the fluorescent lights of hospital corridors and the rubbing alcohol smell of austere clinics make you cringe? And how do you feel about a waiting room full of weary, sour faces and tattered magazines? We're not saying our hospitals and clinics are like that—but folks sometimes perceive things that way. Many Americans are venturing down another path to wellness these days. Healing of the whole body—rather than an ache or just one body part—is increasingly becoming an alternative or addition to established medical treatments. "Alternative medicine," practiced in a soothing aesthetic atmosphere, is becoming more and more widely accepted, even by the media.

"Alternative Medicine: Not So Alternative Anymore" was the headline of a lead-

ing news magazine article. More than one-third of Americans now use alternative therapies such as chiropractic, acupuncture, and massage. For a number of years the Asheville area has been drawing alternative healing practitioners to these mountains. The population has been receptive enough to create an abundance of newsletters, several weekly and monthly newspapers, magazines, and Web pages devoted to the subject, just in this area alone.

The mountains have drawn alternative healers and educators for many reasons—the air, the climate, the calming landscape, the natural beauty, community interest, and even a spiritual calling. *Holistic medicine,* another term that describes the art and science of healing through natural means, includes a wide range of methods for treating various ailments or for simply making the body function better. Various forms of massage, Rolfing,

cation Center of Asheville, and Bowman-Gray in Winston-Salem, acting as a teaching site for each. The experience in this rural community offers young medical students a perspective different from the usual city hospital internship.

The Marshall/Walnut Medical Center (828-649-3500) is at 8625 U.S. 25/70. The Hot Springs Medical and Dental Center (828-622-3245) is on U.S. 25/70 close to the BP gas station. The Laurel Medical Center is at 400 Cook Farm Road off N.C. Highway 208, which leads to Greeneville, Tennessee.

Mitchell County

Bakersville Community Medical Clinic
86 North Mitchell Avenue, Bakersville, NC
(828) 688-2104
The tiny, rural community of Bakersville is served by this private clinic of five family physicians, one chiropractor, and one nurse practitioner. The clinic offers a wide range of primary care services, including obstetrics and gynecology, flexible sigmoidoscopy, orthopedic medicine, drug screening, pediatrics, sports and industrial medicine, geriatrics, and nutrition counsel-

acupuncture, chelation therapy, herbology, reflexology, aromatherapy, biofeedback, acupressure, hypnotherapy, ear coning, and homeopathy are only a few of the therapies that make up the lingo of holistic medicine.

Many of the treatments are ancient in their histories, involving the use of plants and herbs to successfully combat ailments; others are newer derivations of old folk remedies. Rolfing, for example, is a relatively new discipline. It's the popular name for Structural Integration, developed by Dr. Ida Rolf in this century, based on the idea that human function is improved when segments of the body are properly aligned. Acupuncture, on the other hand, originated in China more than 5,000 years ago. The World Health Organization recognizes the use of acupuncture in the treatment of a wide range of medical problems, including digestive disorders, respiratory disorders, neurological

and muscular disorders, urinary and muscular problems, and PMS.

If you are interested in using alternative therapies but put off or confused by the holistic health jargon, consult the bible on the subject: *Alternative Medicine—The Definitive Guide.* It will familiarize you with various forms of holistic therapies. In your search for local practitioners and centers, pick up free locally published newspapers and newsletters in bookstores and cafes in Asheville for current articles and listings. Some of the most well known are *The Re:Source, Spirit in the Smokies,* and the Web magazines *NC Natural* and *Asheville Holistic Alternatives.* AHA offers a complete listing of alternative health care centers and individual practitioners, as well as events and shopping opportunities for those interested in natural health. If you are an alternative practitioner, you can be listed for free.

ing. The clinic is affiliated with the Spruce Pine Community Hospital.

Spruce Pine Community Hospital
125 Hospital Drive, Spruce Pine, NC
(828) 765-4201
Founded in 1955, this 80-bed community hospital is within the town of Spruce Pine, in the mountains north of Burnsville. The hospital serves Mitchell, Avery and Yancey Counties. Spruce Pine Hospital is also a member of the Mission St. Joseph's Health System. The full-service Spruce Pine facility staffs a 24-hour emergency room.

Social workers assist the hospital in arranging nursing home care.

Watauga County

Blowing Rock Hospital
416 Chestnut Drive, Blowing Rock, NC
(828) 295-3136
This 100-bed, full-service community hospital is located in the village of Blowing Rock, north of Boone. It is a private, nonprofit hospital, with an adjacent medical office complex. Facilities include

acute and long-term care; surgery, X-ray, and lab facilities; on-call physicians; and an emergency room. The hospital and long-term care unit are fully accredited by the Joint Commission of Accreditation of Hospitals.

Watauga Medical Center
336 Deerfield Road, Boone, NC
(828) 262-4391

Watauga Medical Center started in 1936 as a humble medical clinic on the campus of Appalachian State Teacher's College in Boone. The clinic quickly developed into a regular 50-bed hospital and by 1967 had expanded to an 83-bed facility at its present Deerfield Road site. Watauga almost doubled its capacity by 1979 and by 1985 began an expansion project to house an enlarged imaging department. In the early 1990s the Medical Center also completed an outpatient facility. Today the hospital is licensed as a 147-bed complex. To reflect the expanding services, the hospital changed its name in 1993 to Watauga Medical Center.

Some of the services at Watauga Medical Center include a critical care center; a complete surgical suite covering general and specialized surgery; an imaging unit offering CT scanning, MRI, X ray, mammography, and ultrasound; a birthing suite featuring relaxed birthing rooms, Cesarean section rooms, two well-baby nurseries, a level II neonatal intensive-care nursery, and an isolation nursery; and a well-equipped, well-staffed pathology department for routine and special procedures, including forensic pathology. A special kidney dialysis unit and a regional cancer center are also part of Watauga Medical Center's comprehensive medical complex. The center has a 24-hour physician-staffed emergency room and has air access via helicopter to Sanger Clinic in Charlotte for heart patients and Baptist Hospital in Winston-Salem for head trauma patients.

Yancey County

Yancey Community Medical Center
320 Pensacola Road, Burnsville, NC
(828) 682-6136

Serving the Burnsville area, this primary care clinic is open Monday through Friday, 8:00 A.M. to 5:00 P.M. with evening hours on Thursday until 8:00 P.M. X-ray facilities are available, and there's a lab operated by Spruce Pine Community Hospital on the premises. The clinic is affiliated with Mission St. Joseph's Health System. This medical center will see walk-ins with emergencies. After hours, it's best to go to the Spruce Pine Community Hospital (828-765-4201), 125 Hospital Drive.

CENTRAL MOUNTAINS
Buncombe County

The Asheville Veterans Affairs Medical Center
1100 Tunnel Road, Asheville, NC
(828) 298-7911

The Asheville VA Medical Center is in the Oteen area, in east Asheville, just minutes from an entrance to the Blue Ridge Parkway. The facility has a 76-year history of service to veterans in the mountains of Western North Carolina, beginning in March 1918 when it became U.S. Army General Hospital No. 19, a cantonlike collection of 104 frame buildings accommodating 1,200 beds. The first patient was admitted in September of the same year. Treatment of tuberculosis was the primary focus.

In 1920 administration of the hospital was transferred to the U.S. Public Health Service. It was during this period that the Cherokee Indian term *oteen,* meaning "chief aim," was proposed for use with the hospital as an encouragement to every patient to adopt as his chief aim "to get well."

The mission of the USPHS hospital continued to be the treatment of tuberculosis. More permanent buildings were constructed on site from 1924 to 1936 to help provide better treatment facilities for this disease. Modernization of these structures was completed and capacity expanded during World War II. The 40-year mission as a tuberculosis treatment center was enhanced and the scope of treatment broadened when the hospital was officially designated as a General Medical and Surgical Hospital in 1961.

Asheville's VA Medical Center is recognized as a major general medical and surgical hospital. The center is known for its strong programs in vascular, thoracic, and cardiac surgery. Its successful cardiac surgery program is the longest-running, continuously cost-effective program of its kind in the VA system and serves veterans from Virginia, West Virginia, upstate South Carolina, east Tennessee, and Western North Carolina.

The VA Medical Center provides a number of special programs, including cardiac catheterization, nuclear medicine, respiratory care, audiology and speech pathology, geriatric evaluation and management, mental health programs, a 25-bed substance-abuse program, a residential rehabilitation treatment program, a community nursing program, and a hospital-based primary care program. The VA Center also has a mutual-use sharing agreement with the region's major hospitals in certain specialized medical areas.

A nonprofit research corporation administers an ongoing research program here. It currently consists of nine projects, most of which are clinical trials.

Mission Hospital in Asheville: St. Joseph and Memorial Campuses
509 Biltmore Avenue, Asheville, NC
(828) 213-1111

This private not-for-profit medical facility began in 1885 as the Asheville Mission Hospital. Today this nearly 500-bed hospital and the staff of 390 physicians and 2,000-member support staff provide medical expertise and high-quality care.

Most specialties are represented at Mission, which has expanded in the last 20 years to cover virtually an entire hilltop in downtown Asheville. It offers a level of sophistication of medical care found at large university medical centers.

Mission St. Joseph's was formed by combining Asheville's two private acute care hospitals: Memorial Mission and St. Joseph's. As a system, Mission St. Joseph's has 5,000 employees, 800 beds, and more than 500 physicians. The health system is private, not for profit, and governed by a board of volunteer leaders. Costs compare favorably with similar health systems. The system operates under continuing governance from the state, which monitors changes, excellence of care, and commitment to service and community outreach. Virtually every medical specialty is available at Mission St. Joseph's. Programs emphasize prevention, cost control, logistical and financial access, and excellent care.

The partnership was the first of its type in North Carolina and one of the first in the nation. Combined, the two large hospitals cover more than 2 million square feet. The 500 physicians—primary care doctors, specialists, and subspecialists—care for patients in the hospitals as well as in the new critical care, heart, genetics, and women's and children's centers. Medical services are organized according to clinical specialty: the Owen Health Center provides for cardiology and heart surgery and a cardiac rehabilitation program. It's also a national leader in minimally invasive and valve replacement surgery. The Ruth and Billy Graham Children's Health Center is an inpatient hospital, pediatric intensive care unit, and neonatal ICU for newborns. Orthopedic care ranks among the top 35 hospitals in the country in the number of joint replacement surgeries done. The Women's Health Center educates and supports women of all ages, including high-risk obstetrics patients. The Fullerton Genetics Center diagnoses and provides laboratory testing and counseling for individuals and families who may be affected by inherited health problems. Services include the Copestone behavioral medicine unit, with geriatric, adolescent, psychiatric, and substance abuse programs.

Surgical services include one-day and laser-assisted surgery and a soon-to-be-dedicated vascular center. Neurosciences, adult medicine, and oncology are, of course, included in the comprehensive hospital program. Emergency trauma services are staffed 24 hours a day and include hospital-operated air and ground transportation services.

Thoms Rehabilitation Hospital
68 Sweeten Creek Road, Asheville, NC
(828) 274-2400

Established as the Asheville Orthopedic Home in 1938 by the Rotary Club and the Junior League of Asheville, Thoms Rehabilitation Hospital was originally a facility for handicapped children from the remote areas of the mountains of Western North Carolina. Thoms is now a nonprofit regional referral center offering acute care, day treatment, and transitional outpatient rehabilitation services to those with physical, cognitive, and developmental impairments. Traditional and specialized rehabilitation programs are offered for all ages.

The hospital works with brain trauma cases, spinal cord injuries, stroke and developmental disabilities, pain and industrial injuries, and conditions of amputation and neuromuscular disorders.

The staff is composed of physicians, psychologists, nurses, and physical and occupational therapists and speech/language pathologists, among other professionals. Thoms is a founding member of Community CarePartners, a postacute continuum of care.

Henderson County

Blue Ridge Dental Practice
1801 Asheville Highway, Hendersonville, NC
(828) 696-0512

Blue Ridge Health Center
U.S. Highway 64 E. and Howard Gap
Road, Hendersonville, NC
(828) 692-4289
Druid Hills Family Practice
1801 Asheville Highway, Hendersonville, NC
(828) 696-0545
George Bond Memorial Health Center
U.S. Highway 74, Bat Cave, NC
(828) 625-9141
Kate B. Reynolds Women's and
Children's Center
U.S. Highway 64 E. and Howard Gap
Road, Hendersonville, NC
(828) 692-7057

Blue Ridge Community Health Service is a private, not-for-profit community health center with five locations in Henderson County. A staff of board-certified family practice physicians, internists, and pediatricians, along with physician assistants, family nurse practitioners, and certified nurse-midwives, work as a team to provide personalized comprehensive health care for the entire family, from newborns to the elderly. Doctors are on 24-hour call and enjoy staff privileges at Margaret R. Pardee Hospital in Hendersonville.

Maternal Outreach and Child Service Coordination Programs support the obstetrics and gynecology services. A nutritionist provides dietetic education and counseling, and home-health nursing services are available for homebound patients.

Board-certified dentists, along with hygienists, provide restorative and preventive dental care to children and pregnant women and emergency care for established Blue Ridge patients. The new dental facility will be a teaching site for dental students from the University of North Carolina School of Dentistry.

Blue Ridge Community Health Services leads the way in providing access to health care and dental care—a major concern for many people throughout Western North Carolina. The doors are open to "everyone" without regard to financial status. Their focus is providing quality health care at affordable rates with an emphasis on the medically underserved. Most insurance plans are accepted, including Medicare and Medicaid. A sliding fee schedule is available for those who qualify, and payment plans can be arranged.

All locations can be reached after hours by calling (828) 692–4289.

Margaret R. Pardee Memorial Hospital
715 Fleming Street, Hendersonville, NC
(828) 696–1000

Founded in 1953 with the help of a $100,000 donation from Ivor Pardee in memory of his aunt, Margaret R. Pardee, this 100-bed facility has grown through the years to its present 222 licensed acute-care beds, which include 21 psychiatric beds. In addition there are 40 skilled nursing beds.

The recently completed hospital surgical facilities house six large operating rooms, 22 day-surgery rooms, and a 13-bay recovery room. Pardee's advanced diagnostic equipment and treatment facilities include a sleep disorder lab, MRI, CT scan, echocardiograms, advanced angiogram equipment, nuclear medicine, endoscopy, mammography, ultrasound, kidney stone lithotripsy, and bone densitometer.

Pardee Hospital dedicated the Kayden Radiation Oncology Center in 1993. The center was built to meet the needs of cancer patients who require radiation therapy five days a week for six weeks or more. The addition of radiation therapy means that all three major treatment modes are available at Pardee: surgery, chemotherapy, and radiation therapy. The American College of Surgeons certified Pardee as a cancer center in February 1997. The certification process takes three years and involves a cancer registry, which records and reports cancers and treatments to the N.C. Central Cancer Registry. This information becomes part of the national database on cancer care. Local cancer conferences, held twice a month, are attended by physicians, nurses, social workers, the chaplain, pharmacists, and others who treat or work with cancer patients. These conferences review cases and share treatment and support possibilities for each patient.

Family-centered, one-room birthing in the Family Way unit allows families to fully appreciate the childbirth experience. Pardee's day-surgery unit, freestanding outpatient radiology department, and large emergency department make treatment more convenient. Express Care (same address as the hospital) is open evenings, weekends, and holidays for care of minor emergencies and illnesses without the waiting time that is sometimes seen in the emergency room.

Pardee's Home Care includes OB and pediatric nursing, psychiatric nursing, and personal care services. Other services include cardiac and pulmonary rehabilitation, respite care of dependent adults, geriatric evaluations, and adult day care. In the summer of 1996, Pardee launched the Hendersonville Family Practice Residency Program in conjunction with the Mountain Area Health Education Center (MAHEC) in Asheville and the University of North Carolina in Chapel Hill. Designed to train family physicians who wish to practice in a rural area, the three-year program trains two residents annually. The program is community based, conceived and initiated by community physicians who want to share their medical expertise and knowledge with doctors in training and to bring excellent family practitioners to our area. The Hendersonville Family Health Center is one immediate benefit of the residency program. As part of the program, the clinic is always accepting new patients.

Pardee provides health education to the community through a variety of means. The Pardee Health Education Center at the Blue Ridge Mall on Four Seasons Boulevard has served the community in health promotions and wellness since 1989. Free or low-cost screenings, seminars by doctors and health care professionals, support groups, and a wealth of literature and videos on health topics are available at the center. The Henderson County Breast Cancer Initiative, sponsored by Pardee, provides education on breast cancer, bringing services such as mobile mammography, breast self-examination education, and a breast cancer awareness speakers bureau to neighborhoods, community organizations, and businesses.

Pardee Care Center is a 130-bed nursing home on land adjacent to Blue Ridge Community College. It shares space with both the college and Four Seasons Hospice. Locating the nursing home and 12-bed home for hospice patients adjacent to the campus provides additional clinical spaces for students in the college's allied health programs, fosters skill upgrading and certification of health care professionals, and facilitates cross-training of staff through the expansion of conferences and seminars to serve all partner organizations.

Park Ridge Hospital
Naples Road, Fletcher, NC
(828) 684-8501

First opened in 1910, the Mountain Sanitarium eventually evolved into Fletcher Hospital. Then in 1986 its new 103-bed facility was opened, and this not-for-profit facility, operated by the Seventh-day Adventists, became the Park Ridge Hospital. The facility is a full-service general, acute-care hospital that has a 24-hour emergency department, OB/GYN, and psychiatric services. With 150 physicians and more than 450 employees, it averages about 23,000 patient visits per year, with a focus on "the well-being of the whole person" that includes a vegetarian option for all hospital meals.

Park Ridge offers the latest in health care technology, including a CT scanner, a mobile MRI unit, and nuclear medicine. Specialized spine and orthopedic surgery capabilities are available at Park Ridge. Comprehensive ophthalmology services also are provided. Approximately 750 cataract surgeries are performed every year. Park Ridge also provides a variety of educational and rehabilitative programs that include child and adolescent psychiatry, occupational health, cardiac and pulmonary rehabilitation, wellness, smoking

cessation, classes for expectant parents, and HOPE, a woman's program that treats eating and psychological disorders.

The emergency department operates 24 hours a day. The Home Health Agency provides skilled nursing care and rehabilitation at home. The hospital also has birthing rooms and a large physical therapy department that's part of its cardiac rehabilitation and occupational health program for area industry. Blending faith and technology, Park Ridge Hospital provides the highest quality health care.

Polk County

St. Luke's Hospital
101 Hospital Drive, Columbus, NC
(828) 894-3311

St. Luke's, founded in 1929, is a private, nonprofit facility serving 34,000 patients annually from Polk, Spartanburg, and Greenville Counties. It offers primary, emergency, and outpatient services, including a geriatric psychiatric unit, a Center of Behavioral Medicine for psychiatric outpatients, a restorative care unit, and ICU and a 24-hour, physician-staffed emergency department. St. Luke's also offers state-of-the-art diagnostics, including a new CT scanner, new GE mammography equipment, a new heart-monitoring system for both the ER and ICU, nuclear medicine, and a new bone densitometer. It also offers physical, occupational, respiratory, and speech therapies.

St. Luke's staff specialties include general, orthopedic, and pain-management surgery, as well as ophthalmology, family practice, gerontology, internal medicine, pathology, psychiatry, urology, and radiology.

Transylvania County

Transylvania Community Hospital
Hospital Drive, Brevard, NC
(828) 884-9111

Transylvania Community Hospital is a 94-bed, not-for-profit community facility. The hospital, formed in 1933, is fully accredited and offers a wide range of services including preventative care, wellness programs, inpatient and outpatient medical/surgical services, a complete physical/occupational/speech therapy department, cardiac and pulmonary disease rehabilitation, and follow-up care. Services include Bridgeway, an inpatient and outpatient alcohol and substance abuse unit; Work Well, an occupational health program that helps injured workers get back to work; and the Living Well with Diabetes program, a comprehensive diabetes management and education service. The Wound Care, Ostomy, and Continence Department offers special care for patients with non-healing wounds or infections, temporary or permanent ostomies, or incontinence.

The medical staff at TCH includes specialists in emergency medicine, ENT, internal medicine, family practice, pediatrics, sports medicine, ophthalmology, oncology, orthopedics, radiology, and urology, among others.

SOUTHERN MOUNTAINS

Cherokee County

District Memorial Hospital
415 Whitaker Lane, Andrews, NC
(828) 321-1200
Nationally accredited by the Joint Commission on Accreditation of Healthcare Organizations, DMH is a state-licensed, 60-bed, acute-care facility located in the beautiful valley town of Andrews. Its growing medical staff of more than twenty physicians includes specialists in cardiology, critical care, emergency medicine, family practice, gastroenterology, general surgery, internal medicine, ophthalmology, orthopedics, pathology, pulmonology, radiology, and urology.

District Memorial's 24-hour emergency department is complemented by its 24-hour laboratory, respiratory, and X-ray serv-

ices. It has a fully equipped intensive care unit and a growing surgical unit for both inpatient and outpatient procedures. DMH also has a Convalescent Unit and offers occupational physical and speech therapy.

Murphy Medical Center
4130 Highway 64 E., Murphy, NC
(828) 837-8161
Located 5 miles from Murphy on the Hiwassee River, the Murphy Medical Center opened in 1979 and is one of the more modern facilities in the region. A full-service hospital with 50 beds and a 120-bed nursing home, MMC serves the residents of Cherokee, Clay, and Graham Counties and adjoining counties in Georgia and Tennessee with a 24-hour emergency room and can respond to most medical needs.

It provides services in the fields of family practice, general surgery, internal medicine, orthopedics, pediatrics, radiology, ophthalmology, urology, obstetrics, gynecology, and oncology. The hospital also provides a personal-response emergency system.

Haywood County

Haywood Regional Medical Center
262 Leroy George Drive, Clyde, NC
(828) 456-7311, (800) 834-1729
Established in 1927, this is the largest hospital west of Asheville serving the westernmost counties as the provider of primary, acute hospital care, and numerous medical specialty services.

The facility's expanding medical staff includes more than 65 physicians and medical professionals representing almost every medical specialty.

The modern 200-bed facility, built in 1979, is a full-service regional hospital utilizing the most advanced technology, equipment, and staff to provide high-quality patient services. Available services include lithotripsy, cardiac care, a cancer center, reference laboratory, rehabilitation services, an osteoporosis center, a diabetes education center, occupational health services, and a home-health/home-service center.

Recent additions involved the opening of a 20-bed restorative care center to provide transitional care to patients who require continued hospital care before returning home; a $3.00 million radiology renovation project, which included the highest level technology available in Western North Carolina for CT scans, nuclear medicine, and ultrasound; a Women's Care Center; a modern OB/GYN and wellness resource for families and women of all ages; and a new building housing the growing home-health services staff and expansion of the hospital's rehabilitation programs and services.

Key preventive programs and services include occupational medicine, mammography, an osteoporosis center, cardiac rehabilitation, a diabetes treatment center, and numerous ongoing support groups.

Home Health Care of Haywood Regional Medical Center
262 Leroy George Drive, Clyde, NC
(828) 452-8292, (888) 456-0011
Now serving all the counties included in this book, Haywood County's Home Care Services' certified nursing assistants provide home care under the supervision of a registered nurse. CNAs perform personal care tasks such as bathing, essential housekeeping, and home management, while a team of RNs and pharmacists provide infusion therapy, skilled nursing, rehabilitation services, and medical social work.

Home Care Services also provides hospice services. Haywood Regional Medical Center also has designated beds for hospice respite care and inpatient use. In addition the organization offers many specialized services, including maternal/infant, psychiatric, respiratory, bereavement, and Lifeline programs.

Jackson County

WestCare Health System
Harris Regional Hospital, 68 Hospital Road, Sylva, NC
(828) 586-7000
Swain County Hospital
45 Plateau Street, Bryson City, NC
(828) 488-2155
WestCare Health System was established in 1994 by Harris Regional Hospital to meet the expanding health needs of a growing Western North Carolina population and to enhance the delivery of health care in the region. Swain County Hospital and its affiliated services joined the system in 1997. WestCare Health System—through Harris Regional Hospital, Swain County Hospital, and affiliated medical resources—offers clinical services, acute-care inpatient services, outpatient services, cardiopulmonary services, emergency departments, an Urgent Care Center, emergency medical services, Home Health and Hospice, imaging services, laboratory services, a medical resource center, nutrition services, wellness services, occupational health management, rehabilitation services, surgical services, and women's and children's services. WestCare Health System and its affiliated hospitals and services and its associated medical staff are widely recognized as a provider of choice in the health care field.

Macon County

Angel Medical Center
Riverview Street, Franklin
(828) 524-8411
The 25 doctors at this modern, multipurpose 59-bed facility specialize in allergies, orthopedics, family practice, internal medicine, pathology, emergency medicine, urology, ophthalmology, OB/GYN and pediatrics. Angel provides 24-hour emer-

gency service and outpatient surgeries. The Home Health Agency is fully accredited, and the American College of Radiology certifies its mammography unit.

ACH also offers, among other services, physical therapy, diet/nutrition classes, MRI, CT scanning, nuclear medicine, speech therapy, pathology, chemotherapy, cardiopulmonary services, family services, and an occupational health program for business and industry.

Two additional services are the Urgent Care Center (828-369-4427), at the intersection of U.S. 23 and 441, that treats nonemergency medical problems, and the 24-hour Angel Medical Answer Line (828-369-4455), which is staffed by nurses.

Highlands-Cashiers Hospital
190 Hospital Drive and U.S. Highway 64 E., Highlands, NC
(828) 526-1200

A private, nonprofit health care provider, Highlands-Cashiers Hospital has served the medical needs of the people of southern Macon and Jackson Counties and western Transylvania County for nearly half a century. A new hospital and nursing facility opened its doors in 1993. It offers a wide range of diagnostic services, state-of-the-art medical technology, and a board-certified medical staff of nearly 30 physicians, including specialists in cardiology, gastroenterology, general surgery, plastic and reconstructive surgery, urol-

ogy, rheumatology, orthopedic surgery, ophthalmology, podiatry, and pulmonary medicine. The hospital has a 24-hour emergency room and offers Saturday morning Urgent Care. It's affiliated with both Mission St. Joseph's Health System in Asheville and Emory Healthcare System in Atlanta, Georgia.

The Fidelia Eckerd Nursing Center, a part of the hospital, offers long-term nursing care, respite care, and assisted living.

Macon County Public Health Center
1830 Lakeside Drive, Franklin, NC
(828) 349-2081

Opened in 1980 this health center offers a wide range of public health services, including family planning, prenatal, child and adult health screenings, orthopedic, and hypertension services. The health center's laboratory offers support for the public health programs and may file forms for Medicare, Medicaid, and some insurance companies. Routine vaccinations are given free; other services are also free or provided at low cost. While no appointments are necessary, Monday and Thursday are generally considered the center's walk-in days. The Macon County Public Health Center also holds clinics in Highlands and Nantahala on a regular schedule.

The center also provides environmental health services, such as water testing, issuing septic system permits, and food and lodging inspections.

EDUCATION

F ormal education came to the mountains in 1793, only 10 years after the first settlers moved west of the Blue Ridge. Scotch-Irish Presbyterians established the first school here, an academy called Union Hill in what is now the city of Asheville. Only two years later the University of North Carolina, the oldest state university in the nation, opened its doors in Chapel Hill.

Father of the geodesic design, forerunner of today's domed stadiums, was Buckminster Fuller, one of the leaders of the formation of Black Mountain College. Now defunct, the college was home to creative minds like John Cage and Robert Rauschenberg.

Today the University of North Carolina, as well as a number of other colleges and prep schools, offer a wide range of educational and cultural options. They provide a wealth of affordable continuing education courses that draw on the skills of the area's large number of talented retirees.

In addition the mountains are home to renowned craft and music schools. Penland School of Crafts is the oldest and largest school for high-quality mixed-media arts and crafts in North America. For some 70 years the John C. Campbell Folk School has offered outstanding courses in traditional crafts, music, and dance (see our Mountain Crafts chapter). At the Brevard Music Center, approximately 300 gifted students from across the nation have the opportunity to join teaching professionals and famous guests in the performance of 50 summer concerts (see our Arts and Culture chapter).

In-state tuition at most of the state institutions is considered reasonable, but costs are subject to increases as specified by state legislation.

As in other chapters, we have divided our discussion of education into three geographic regions. At the end of the chapter, we give a brief overview of public school systems in the North Carolina mountains.

NORTHERN MOUNTAINS

Universities

Appalachian State University
River Street, Boone, NC
(828) 262-2000

From its beginnings as a teachers academy, Appalachian State University has grown into one of the top comprehensive universities in the South. Today students major in a variety of fields, including graphic arts, business, exercise science, criminal justice, and teacher education. University programs, such as Freshman Seminar, have received national recognition. Innovative partnerships with public schools, community colleges, business and industry, retirement centers, and others provide students opportunities to translate classroom learning into real-world experience. Off-campus properties in Washington, D.C., and New York City provide opportunities for special learning experiences.

Appalachian offers approximately 100 undergraduate majors, more than 75 graduate majors, and a doctorate in educational leadership. The university consistently has ranked among the top 15 comprehensive regional universities in the South since *U.S. News & World Report* began ranking colleges and universities in 1986.

Appalachian's enrollment is approximately 12,300 students. Beautifully set in the rugged Watauga County mountains, Appalachian attracts students from the state's larger cities as well as its hometown of Boone.

Appalachian prides itself on creating the right climate for undergraduate learning, bringing together the most advanced resources, a dedicated faculty, and a comfortable living environment.

Four-Year Colleges

Lees-McRae College
375 College Drive, Banner Elk, NC
(828) 898-8780, (828) 898-5241

Lees-McRae College is a coeducational liberal arts institution that, at 4,000 feet above sea level, boasts the highest elevation of any college east of the Mississippi River.

This private college is affiliated with the Presbyterian Church (U.S.A.). Its beginnings go back to 1900 and the Rev. Edgar Tufts, who founded what was then a high school as an outgrowth of his ministry in the Appalachian Mountains. Elizabeth A. McRae was the teacher for the first class of 14 girls. In the ensuing years the school grew, thanks in great measure to the generosity of the school's benefactor Mrs. S. P. Lees. The efforts of these two women were not forgotten when the school was chartered in 1907 as the Lees-McRae Institute. It was renamed Lees-McRae College in 1931 when it gained accreditation as a coeducational junior college.

The college attained senior college status in 1990. The attractive campus has 30 buildings, many built of native stone. There are 13 residence halls, 2 classroom buildings, an 89,000-volume library, an auditorium, a student center, and a physical education center. The 32-member faculty reflects a variety of religious, ethnic, and national origins. Enrollment is 470, and the student-faculty ratio is 15 to 1. More than 90 percent of the students received financial aid in 1998. Scholarships are also available in academics, athletics, and performing arts.

Lees-McRae offers both bachelor of arts and bachelor of science degrees as well as course work in a number of preprofessional areas. The school also maintains study-abroad and community service programs as well as an honors curriculum.

Mars Hill College
124 Cascade Street, Mars Hill, NC
(828) 689-1201, (800) 543-1514

Mars Hill College is tucked away on a ridge in rural Madison County, just over the mountain from Tennessee. This four-year, private coeducational college has the distinction of being the oldest educational institution in Western North Carolina. It was founded in 1856 as the French Broad Baptist Academy by a group of citizens descended from the original settlers of the area. The school was chartered officially as Mars Hill College in 1859 by the North Carolina General Assembly.

The Civil War brought hard times to the South, and Mars Hill College felt its share. Struggling with the deprivations of war, the college was able to stay in operation for the first two years of the war but was forced to close from 1863 to 1865. For much of its history, the school operated as an academy or boarding school, one that provided some college-level courses. In 1921 Mars Hill was reorganized as a junior college and became a pioneer in that field of education. This Baptist-affiliated college subsequently became a four-year institution, awarding the first baccalaureate degrees in May 1964.

The campus lies on 194 acres of rolling hills with a panoramic view of Mount Pisgah, Clingman's Peak, and the Craggies. It's hard to tell where the campus ends and the town of Mars Hill begins, so closely are they linked in every way. The pace is a little slower here, more conducive to inspiration. And when the need for city life arises, Asheville is just 18 miles south.

For all its bucolic charm, Mars Hill College is recognized today as educationally progressive in the fields of innovative curriculum development, continuing education, regional cultural studies, the arts, and international education. The campus houses the Rural Life Museum, which facilitates the collection, preservation, exhibition, and interpretation of rural life artifacts in the southern Appalachian region.

With an enrollment of nearly 1,300 students, Mars Hill College offers a 13-to-1 student-teacher ratio. The college offers 31 majors in its curriculum but also provides students the opportunity to pursue specially designed courses of study, available through three interdisciplinary programs: communications, international studies, and regional studies. The student-to-computer ratio is 6 to 1, which far exceeds the national average at colleges of 13 to 1. Approximately 50 international students come to the campus each year, and out-of-state students comprise 40 percent of the student body. Mars Hill's athletic program includes 13 NCAA Division II sports.

Two-Year Colleges

Mayland Community College
200 Mayland Drive, Spruce Pine
(828) 765–7351, (800) 4-MAYLAND
This small community college offers a unique family atmosphere in a natural mountain setting in the Blue Ridge Mountains on 41 acres just east of the town of Spruce Pine. Nearby is Mount Mitchell, the highest mountain east of the Mississippi. A little to the north is world-famous Grandfather Mountain. The Blue Ridge Parkway also winds its way through this scenic area.

The college, established in 1971, takes its name from the initials of the Tri-County area it serves: Mitchell, Avery, and Yancey. With an enrollment of around 800, this coeducational institution can provide personal student-instructor interaction. Mayland is accredited by the Commission on Colleges of the Southern Association of Colleges and Schools to award the associate in arts degree, diplomas, and certificates.

In addition to curriculum programs, Mayland also provides a wide variety of classes under the umbrella of continuing education. Included in this division are classes in occupational extension, community service, Small Business Center, and Human Resources Development.

The Basic Skills Program offers adults opportunities to develop basic and computational skills necessary to function in employment in the community. Two outreach facilities, the Avery Learning Center in Newland and the Yancey Learning Center in Burnsville, complete the campus of Mayland Community College.

Watauga Campus of Caldwell Community College and Technical Institute
Community College Drive, Boone, NC
(828) 297-2185

This satellite college of nearby Caldwell Community College and Technical Institute provides quality continuing education opportunities for residents of Watauga County. Both two-year degrees and one-year diploma programs are available. Occupational programs offer one or two years of training in vocational and technical subjects. College parallel programs provide freshman and sophomore courses for students who may wish to transfer to four-year institutions.

Established in 1973, the CCC&TI offers instruction leading to completion of certificates, diplomas, and degrees, as well as continuing education courses. A permanent Watauga campus was established in 1998 with the addition of a 23,000-square-foot instructional facility. In addition to this 39-acre site, classes are also taught at four other locations in the county.

CENTRAL MOUNTAINS

Universities

The University of North Carolina at Asheville
1 University Heights, Asheville, NC
(828) 251-6600

The University of North Carolina Asheville is the designated public liberal arts university of the 16-campus University of North Carolina system. The university sits on a wooded 265-acre site a mile north of downtown Asheville. UNCA opened in 1927 as Buncombe County Junior College, and through an ongoing community commitment, has evolved into a small, distinguished public liberal arts university.

Recently named a "best buy" by the *Fiske Guide to Colleges,* UNCA offers

Check in with the local colleges and universities where you are vacationing. They vary in offering summer accommodations in empty dorms and meals throughout the year, all at a great savings.

four-year undergraduate degree programs in the arts and humanities, the natural and social sciences, and selected pre-professional and professional programs. UNCA also offers an undergraduate "2-plus-2" program in engineering with North Carolina State University in Raleigh. Undergraduates spend two years at UNCA and two years at NCSU. The Asheville Graduate Center offers graduate degree programs from NC State, UNC-Chapel Hill, UNC-Greensboro, and Western Carolina University, as well as UNCA's Master of Liberal Arts program.

UNCA is the home of the North Carolina Center for Creative Retirement, including its College for Seniors, an additional avenue for continuing education.

The newly renovated D. Hiden Ramsay Library is the cultural and architectural heart of the campus. It houses nearly 318,000 volumes on open shelves, approximately 50,000 government documents, and several hundred audio- and videotapes. A computerized, one-day library network with sister universities extends the collection to more than a million volumes.

The arts figure prominently in UNCA campus life. The proximity of cosmopolitan Asheville is a definite influence, and the two frequently intertwine. Access to the university is of prime benefit to the citizens of Asheville. The university's theater programs, concerts, dance performances, arts exhibits, and lecture series enrich the community.

Ongoing construction at UNCA provides for the growth of this increasingly popular campus. UNCA has about 3,500 students and an average class size of 21.

Four-Year Colleges

Brevard College
400 North Broad Street, Brevard, NC
(828) 884-8300, (800) 527-9090

Brevard College offers an innovative, inter-disciplinary course of study culminating in a four-year degree. Located on a beautiful mountain campus, the college has a faculty to student ratio of 8 to 1. Environmental studies, wilderness leadership and experiential education, ecology, music, art, theater, and organizational studies (business) are just some of the majors offered here. A strong affiliation with the United Methodist Church dates back to 1853 when the college was established as the first institution of higher learning in Western North Carolina. A small liberal arts residential college, Brevard has approximately 670 students representing 30 states and 15 foreign countries.

Long recognized for its outstanding tradition in music, the college now features the Paul Porter Center for Performing Arts with the acoustically impressive concert hall, Blackbox Theater, and Institute of Sacred Music. Opened in the fall of 1998, the Porter Center provides excellent venues for nationally known performers as well as BC's own student ensembles, choirs, and thespians.

With numerous national championships from competition in the NJCAA, the college's male and female athletes now compete in the NAIA in such sports as soccer, baseball, softball, volleyball, cross-country, track and field, and more. Intramural sports are available and adventure-based sports such as kayaking, climbing, rappelling, and mountain biking are offered through the college's wilderness leadership program. The college runs a variety of "immersion" educational experiences for academic credit, including the 1997 Voice of the Rivers Expedition—a 2,000-mile kayaking experience on the French Broad, Tennessee, Ohio, and Mississippi Rivers to the Gulf of Mexico, where participants have taught some 6,000 students along the way about environmental issues.

The philosophy of Brevard College is that service be a vital part of the classroom experience, so the Center for Service Learning coordinates service activities in the surrounding community.

Montreat College
310 Gaither Circle, Montreat, NC
(828) 669-8011

Seeming to emerge from the woods, Montreat College is a unique, four-year liberal arts college affiliated with the Presbyterian Church (U.S.A.). This lovely, small college has a heritage of quality education founded on Christian beliefs.

In 1916 the Montreat Normal School for women was founded. In 1934, during Dr. Robert C. Anderson's tenure as president, Montreat Normal School was renamed simply Montreat College. The college grew as its academic program expanded. It began a four-year degree program in 1945. After 14 years as a four-year women's college, the college was restructured in 1959 as a coeducational junior college and was given a new name, Montreat-Anderson College. In 1985 the college board of trustees realized the demands and changing circumstances in higher education and made the decision to again become a baccalaureate institution, re-creating the dream of Dr. Anderson. The recent name change back to Montreat College returns the school to its original vision and identity.

Students benefit from Montreat's small classes, and they grow through one-on-one interaction with professors and classmates. Studies challenge them to integrate faith and learning while considering subjects in ways never thought possible. Hands-on experiences in the majors (internships, field studies, mission programs, community service, and independent research) enable students to gain practical career and life preparation.

Montreat College is tucked within the wooded paradise of the community of

Montreat, near Black Mountain, 15 miles east of Asheville. The campus follows a tree-lined valley, woven through with numerous streams. This beautiful campus features buildings constructed of native stone whose interiors are uniquely highlighted by wide use of flint, colorful mica, granite, sandstone, and marble. The facilities of the Mountain Retreat Association and the Presbyterian Department of History are also in Montreat.

Montreat College offers majors in American studies, Bible and religion, business administration, English, environmental studies, history, human services, liberal arts, mathematics, and outdoor education. A teaching certification program is available on the secondary school level. The college's School of Professional and Adults Studies offers associate's, bachelor's, and master's degrees for working adults with campus facilities in Charlotte and Asheville.

A significant aspect of Montreat College is the fact that the college provides extensive financial aid to enable any qualified student to get a college education. More than 80 percent of the student body receives some form of financial aid through a variety of federal and state grants.

Warren Wilson College
701 Warren Wilson College Road, Swannanoa, NC
(828) 298-3325
Warren Wilson College has always combined academic rewards with a strong work effort and service to the community. In 1894 the national Presbyterian Board of Missions started the Asheville Farm School to provide education for boys of the Appalachian mountain area. In the early 1940s the college merged with the Dorland-Bell School for Girls in Hot Springs in Madison County. At that time it became Warren Wilson High School, named in honor of a young sociologist who worked with the school through the auspices of the Presbyterian Church. The year 1942 saw the addition of a junior college division, and in 1966 Warren Wilson finally became a four-year, liberal arts college.

Of the school's 700 students, 25 percent come from North Carolina, 5 percent from outside the United States, and the remainder from 40 other states. The college is known for its unusual curriculum that combines in equal measure strong academics, work for the school, and service to the community. Each student works 15 hours per week on one of 105 essential work crews. These crews range from plumbing and landscaping to farm labor and administrative support. Students also must perform a minimum of 100 hours of community service while they are enrolled. Students generate service projects to fill any needs they see. Projects are also offered through the campus center for service learning.

The 1,100-acre campus sits in the Blue Ridge Mountains just east of Asheville. The campus features a 300-acre working farm, an archaeological site, and 600 acres of forest. Dormitories built of native stone dot the intimate main campus, and 25 miles of hiking trails are available to students right on campus, along with a campus white-water paddling location.

Ties to the land are evident in the fact that the most popular major at Warren Wilson is environmental studies. A highly touted, low-residency program awarding an M.F.A. in creative writing as well as a widely respected program in traditional Appalachian folk music are two additional facets of this creative school.

Two-Year Colleges

Asheville-Buncombe Technical Community College
340 Victoria Drive, Asheville, NC
(828) 254-1921
A member of the North Carolina Community College System, A-B Tech offers associate degrees, diplomas, or certificates in 48 curriculum programs through four academic divisions: Allied Health and Public

Service Education, Arts and Sciences, Business and Hospitality Education, and Engineering and Applied Technology. A fifth division, Continuing Education, offers opportunities for specific job training and retraining, basic skills education, and vocational courses for individual enrichment.

A-B Tech celebrated its 40th anniversary in 1999. Established September 1, 1959, the college was originally funded by a bond election and called the Asheville Industrial Education Center. Over the years community support has helped A-B Tech grow and expand its services so that it currently enrolls approximately 20,000 curriculum and continuing education students annually.

The campus has undergone a metamorphosis over the years, acquiring land from surrounding parcels as they became available.

The main campus is made up of 144 acres off Victoria Road, and 22 buildings house academic programs and campus services. Included are three historic homes: Sunnicrest, one of George Vanderbilt's villas renovated to house the college's Business and Industry Services; the Smith-McDowell Museum, the oldest brick house in Buncombe County, which is leased to the Western North Carolina Historical Association; and Fernihurst, a circa-1875 mansion A-B Tech plans to renovate for its nationally recognized culinary program. The college operates a campus in Madison County that offers adult education and college credit courses. A campus is now located at the Industrial Complex in western Buncombe County, in coordination with the BASF Company.

Blue Ridge Community College, Brevard Campus
1030 Asheville Highway and Osburn Road, Brevard, NC
(828) 883-2520

In the fall of 1997, BRCC in Transylvania County moved to its new, conveniently located campus on the north side of Brevard. The building, which once housed an elementary school, was renovated to

become the college's Transylvania Center and include a student center, a science lab, and computer labs. The space also houses an adult high school program, an industrial maintenance program, and classrooms for curricula programs and continuing education classes. Information Systems replaces the Computer Operations program with not only a new title but also with Internet, networking, and system-management courses. Carpentry has added a planning and estimating course and an OSHA safety certification course. Also, a six-month paramedic continuing education class is offered in cooperation with Transylvania Emergency Service. Other continuing education courses are the popular nursing assistant course and law enforcement training updates.

Regular curricula programs include business administration, health unit coordinator, horticulture, office systems technology and college transfer. In addition the college offers all prerequisites for any BRCC program, including the Associate Degree Nursing program.

Blue Ridge Community College, Flat Rock Campus
College Drive, Flat Rock, NC
(828) 692-3572

BRCC was established in 1969 with campuses in both Henderson and Transylvania counties. The college offers academic credit programs leading to associate degrees, vocational diplomas, and vocational certificates as well as a college transfer program. It enrolls approximately 1,600 curriculum students and serves around 12,000 with both job-related and continuing education courses. In 1997 BRCC opened its Allied Health and Human Services Building. This 66,000-square-foot building houses the Associated Degree Nursing, Surgical Technology, Health Unit Coordinator, Certified Nursing Assistant, Emergency Medical Technician, Cosmetology, and Early Childhood Development Center. The Office for Student Services anchors the building.

The college works closely with area businesses to develop special programs needed by new industries, and its Small Business Center holds workshops, seminars, and classes to aid new and existing businesses and professions.

The college also provides the community with various cultural programs. One of the most popular is the Blue Ridge Concert Series, which brings outstanding artists to the college at affordable prices. (For more information on these events, see our Arts and Culture chapter.)

Isothermal Community College
1255 West Mills Street, Columbus, NC
(828) 894-3092

This two-year institution, chartered in 1964 to serve the people of Polk and Rutherford Counties, offers associate of arts and associate of science degrees in 22 areas of study transferable to four-year colleges and universities. It also serves its communities with technical, vocational, and continuing educational programs, and its libraries are open to the public.

The main 132-acre campus, which serves almost 58,000 students, is at Spindale in Rutherford County. The radio station, WNCW, operates out of the main campus. It is outside the geographic scope of this book, but our coverage does include the 11-acre Polk County satellite campus, located on property adjacent to St. Luke's Hospital in Columbus, which serves some 1,500 students. It offers curriculum classes in business administration, administrative office technology, computers, and liberal arts. There is also a wide range of continuing education classes, which include training for nurse aides, emergency medical technicians, and fire and rescue personnel. Lifelong learning enrichment courses include art, piano, jazz, languages, genealogy, Appalachian/North Carolina history and folklore, other history-related subjects, investing, fitness, classic films, and English as a second language classes. The college also sponsors periodic special events for the community.

Shaw University
31 College Place, Asheville, NC
(828) 252-7635
www.shawuniversity.edu

Shaw University is the oldest historically black university in the South. Its main campus is located in the state capital of Raleigh. The university was founded in 1865. The Asheville campus is located in the former Allen Center, which originally was established as a finishing school for African-American women.

Two colleges, one school, and 10 departments constitute a variety of academic offerings that are geared toward today's employment market. Evening classes are offered to the nontraditional student.

The Center for Alternative Programs of Education (CAPE) allows adult students in nine cities across North Carolina the opportunity to pursue an academic degree through flexible course scheduling and credit for prior learning experiences. Approximately 2,700 students from the United States, the Caribbean, African countries, and the Middle East attend Shaw University.

South College
1567 Patton Avenue, Asheville, NC
(828) 252-2486

Until moving to an eight-acre site west of the city in 1977, South College, formerly known as Cecils College, had been a landmark in downtown Asheville. Founded in 1905 by Robert Talmadge Cecil, the college was well known as a business school, primarily providing secretarial training. Mr. Cecil owned the college until his death in 1956. Through the years Cecils College was owned by a succession of out-of-state corporations operating similar small business colleges elsewhere. In 1972 Cecils College finally returned to ownership by a North Carolina-based, family-owned corporation, Executive Schools Inc. On November 1, 1998, the college was acquired by a family member who formed a new ownership corporation, South College of North Carolina.

The college is accredited as a junior college by the Accrediting Council for Independent Colleges and Schools and is licensed by the Board of Governors of the University System of North Carolina to confer the degree of applied science. The associate of applied science degree is awarded to South graduates in the areas of business administration, computer information systems, medical assisting, office administration, accounting, and paralegal studies.

SOUTHERN MOUNTAINS
Universities

Western Carolina University
215 U.S. Highway 107, Cullowhee, NC
(828) 227-7211, (800) 928-2369
Founded by Professor Robert Lee Madison in 1889 as a semipublic community school to train teachers, Western Carolina University has grown and evolved over the years to become one of the most technologically advanced campuses in the country. The approximately 6,700 students that make up Western's student body hail from North Carolina's mountains and from other regions of the state, the country, and the world.

Undergraduate students may choose from more than 80 majors in one of the four colleges: Applied Sciences, Arts and Sciences, Business, and Education and Allied Professions. Students interested in careers in engineering, law, medicine, dentistry, optometry, veterinary medicine, and pharmacy may enroll in pre-professional programs. The graduate school offers more than 50 programs leading to a master's degree, educational specialist degree, and the doctor of education degree.

A faculty of 330 leads WCU's rigorous academic program. Classes are small enough that individual effort can be recognized and encouraged. The residential Honors College offers a rare learning environment for gifted students.

Numerous service and research centers at WCU serve Western North Carolina, including the Mountain Resource Center, Highlands Biological Station, and the Mountain Aquaculture Research Center. Western's centers in Asheville and Cherokee extend graduate and undergraduate programs to the region.

In the fall of 1998, Western Carolina became one of just 12 public universities nationwide and the first in The University of North Carolina system to require freshmen to come to campus with personal computers. Two computer ports in each residence hall room make it possible for students to connect to the Internet and university computer network from the comfort of their rooms. The use of nine multimedia electronic classrooms puts WCU at the national forefront in the use of educational technology, leading Cullowhee to be called the "most wired" small town in North Carolina.

Western's 230-acre main campus in Cullowhee sits in a beautiful valley between the Blue Ridge and Smoky Mountains, with world-class outdoor recreation opportunities just minutes away. The 8,000-seat Liston B. Ramsey Regional Activity Center regularly hosts national-caliber sports and entertainment events. The university's Lectures, Concerts and Exhibitions Series brings music, dance, and theatrical productions to campus each year. WCU's own department of communication and theater arts stages its own high-quality plays, and Western's galleries maintain a regular schedule of art exhibitions.

Western's Mountain Heritage Center depicts the natural and cultural heritage of the southern Appalachian region through exhibitions, publications, educational programs, and demonstrations. Mountain Heritage Day, WCU's annual celebration of the mountain spirit, draws more than 30,000 visitors to the campus on the last Saturday of each September. (See our Annual Festivals and Events chapter for more information.)

Two-Year Colleges

Haywood Community College
185 Freelander Drive, Clyde, NC
(828) 627-4500, (828) 627-2821

Haywood's facilities are impressive. The 83-acre campus features a student center with a 1,100-seat auditorium and the Regional High Technology Center—one of only two in the state. The Learning Resource Center houses more than 25,000 books, 167 serial subscriptions, and 38,000 microfiche, and offers video- and audiotaping services. Computerized searches of indexes and abstracts are available, as well as an online interlibrary loan service. The beautiful campus also includes a horticulture complex with greenhouses, a dwarf conifer garden, a millhouse with a fishpond, a rhododendron garden, an extensive arboretum, a commercial sawmill and dry kiln, and a 320-acre teaching forest.

Programs take from one semester to two years to complete and lead to a certificate, diploma, or an associate degree in such fields as business administration, engineering technologies, natural resources, human services, and professional crafts. (See our Mountain Crafts chapter for more on the crafts program.) Students also learn skilled trades like welding, plumbing, and electrical installation.

Continuing education programs include GED certification, business and industry training courses, crafts, and emergency medical training. The college also offers small business and occupational training courses.

Southwestern Community College
477 College Drive, Sylva, NC
(828) 586-4091

Established in 1964 to serve Swain, Jackson, and Macon Counties and the Cherokee Indian Reservation, SCC combines a strong vocational-technical program with general education. Its student body of 1,700 attends classes both on its main 57-acre campus between Webster and Sylva on N.C. Highway 116 and at centers in Bryson City, Cashiers, Cherokee, and Franklin.

The centers in Franklin are listed as the Macon Center and the Business Assistance Center. The third center in Macon County is the Public Safety Training Center. It is located between Franklin and Otto at the Macon County Industrial Park.

The programs, courses, and activities, offered in day, evening, and weekend classes, prepare students for the workforce by helping them qualify for jobs in new or existing industries and by providing specific skills training. There are also courses leading to the college's degree programs and transfer courses as well as GED and continuing education classes in such subjects such as basic investment, weaving, computers, CPR certification, law enforcement, fire-and-rescue training, and a National Park Service program. In 1999 SCC added programs in speech and language, literacy, pathology assistant, and environmental science technology.

Tri-County Community College
4600 U.S. Highway 64 E., Murphy, NC
(828) 837-6810 (Peachtree Campus)
(828) 479-9256 (Robbinsville Campus)
(828) 321-2300 (Andrews Site)

This Murphy-based college was originally an extension of the Asheville-Buncombe Technical College, but in 1967 it became an individual unit called the Tri-County Industrial Educational Center. When the state approved its college-transfer program in 1978, its status was upgraded to the Tri-County Community College.

The college serves students primarily from Cherokee, Clay, and Graham Counties at its two campuses in the Peachtree community of Cherokee County and in Robbinsville and offers classes at a site in Andrews. It offers college-transfer and technical and vocational programs, including certificates in real-estate appraisal and horticulture, diplomas in cosmetology and welding, and associate degrees in applied science, accounting, general business, health, nursing, and emergency medical services. The continuing education department offers basic skills programs, occupational extension courses, firefighter training, and community service classes, including cooking classes, craft, and painting courses. A small-business center has opened at the college to help increase the success rate and number of small businesses in the area. Many services and seminars are offered here at little or no cost.

The child care center at the TCCC's Peachtree campus offers model day-care program care for 45 children. It has been rated five stars, the highest rating possible, by the North Carolina Day Care regulatory commission.

PREPARATORY SCHOOLS

The Asheville School
360 Asheville School Road, Asheville, NC
(828) 254-6345

Set on a commanding hill sheltered by woods, the Asheville School is the personification of tradition. This venerable preparatory school was founded in 1900 on the western edge of Asheville. The campus is dotted with majestic trees and graced with architecture from another era, each building having a distinct history. Stately, rambling structures, known in the early days simply as the "House" and the "School," were the heart of the campus, providing basic student housing and classroom instruction. Anthony Lord, an Asheville native and noted architect, designed three of the most beautiful structures on the campus: the Crawford Music House and the Howard Bement House in 1937 and Memorial Hall in 1947. The newest additions to Asheville School architecture in the 1980s and '90s maintain the artistic integrity of existing structures. The school was named to the National Register of Historic Places in 1996.

The rich heritage of this traditionally male boarding school has seen a number of additions brought on by a changing society. The Asheville School is now coeducational, with an average of 200 students, 60 percent male and 40 percent female. Around 17 states and 13 foreign countries are represented.

One thing that has never changed through the years is the commitment to a rigorous academic program designed to foster excellence. The overall student-faculty ratio is 4 to 1, and the average class has 11 students. Study is closely supervised, each day's schedule strictly guided. A full range of advanced-placement courses are offered for college credit. Graduating seniors of the Asheville School are routinely accepted into outstanding colleges and universities, both in this country and abroad, including Brown, Columbia, Duke, Harvard, Oxford, and Stanford.

Extracurricular activities are encouraged and include clubs, publications, philanthropic organizations, chamber choir, and dramatic society. The mountaineering program is a special feature of the Asheville School. Designed to build teamwork and group communication skills, a new Alpine tower and ropes course on campus enable students to learn the fundamentals of climbing, belaying, and rappelling before heading to the mountains surrounding the school. A strong Equestrian Program has also recently been included.

Carolina Day School
1345 Hendersonville Road, Asheville, NC
(828) 274-0757

Carolina Day School, on 28 acres just 15 minutes south of Asheville, is a nonsectarian, coeducational, independent school with approximately 500 students, ranging from prekindergarten to grade 12. The present school, formed by the merger in 1987 of Asheville Country Day School (founded in 1936) and St. Genevieve/Gibbons Hall (founded in 1905) carries on traditions of both schools.

A rigorous academic discipline is carried throughout all grades and subject areas at Carolina Day. The prekindergarten and kindergarten groups are exposed early to literature, number concepts, hands-on science, and computers as well as vital social skills. Grades one through five build on this foundation, with emphasis on reading, writing, and mathematics. Social studies, science, Spanish, and the arts enrich the lower school experience and prepare students for the middle grades. In the middle school (grades 6 to 8), students are encouraged to become both autonomous learners and contributing members of a group. Academic expectations increase and students take part in sports, modern languages, the arts, and projects using multimedia technology. The upper school offers advanced-placement college-level courses, access to information technology, and additional options for fine and performing arts. Carolina Day School graduates are accepted in many of the country's most competitive colleges and universities.

Christ School
500 Christ School Road, Arden, NC
(828) 684-6232

This Episcopal prep school for boys in grades 8 through 12 is 9 miles south of Asheville, 12 miles north of Hendersonville, and 20 miles northeast of Brevard. There are 160 boarding students from 15 states and eight foreign countries. With 18 of the 30 faculty members living on campus, Christ School offers a true sense of community.

The school prides itself in the statement that "teachers at Christ School are instructors, advisors, coaches, mentors, and friends." The core campus and faculty homes make up a small part of the beautifully landscaped, 500-acre wooded campus. Chapel bells ring out daily, reminders of the school's strong emphasis on spiritual growth. The extensive campus acreage encourages a variety of team sports and outdoor activities, including cross-country, soccer, and football. Weekend trips to the surrounding mountains include Outward Bound–style rock climbing, backpacking, kayaking, rafting, and mountain biking as part of the regular outdoor program.

The school work program involves every student and fosters a sense of contributing to the community. Each student is responsible for maintaining upkeep of his personal dorm room, for performing a daily 20-minute task, and for joining in the regular Friday total campus cleanup.

The academic program at Christ School is designed to prepare boys for rigorous college programs. Advanced placement courses are offered in a comprehensive range of subjects. The learning resource program offers academic support in English, math, and study skills within the context of a rigorous college preparatory curriculum. The newly expanded library is completely automated and connected to the North Carolina Information Network, which also connects the school to DIALOG, with access to major university libraries such as the UNC-Chapel Hill and North Carolina State University. Christ School graduates are accepted by some of the finest colleges and universities in the nation, including Duke, Sewanee, University of North Carolina-Chapel Hill, Dartmouth, and Williams.

PUBLIC SCHOOLS

To register a child for school in North Carolina, a parent or legal guardian must present the child's birth certificate, up-to-date immunization record, and previous report cards, if the child was enrolled in another school system.

Western North Carolina public schooling ranges from larger urban schools to small country schoolhouses. Outside of Buncombe County, however, the schools tend to be smaller, and obviously, more rural. Classes are usually small—20 students being the average. Each system offers advanced placement courses, honors programs, and classes for the academically gifted. County and city schools are fully accredited by the state of North Carolina and the Southern Association of Colleges and Schools.

The Buncombe County school system also operates an alternative program for students in grades 7 through 12 who have been identified as "at risk," keeping them in school and focused on life beyond graduation. The county system operates the Progressive Education Program, which offers special education curricula for students. The Career Education Center is an extension of the high school curriculum, offering classes beyond those offered in the "home" schools, like cosmetology, electronics, graphic communications, masonry, and welding. The city school system operates the Accelerated Learning Center for middle grade students. Here a low pupil-teacher ratio (10 to 1) and emphasis on parent involvement encourage students to reach their maximum academic potential. Most schools offer after-school child care, and all elementary schools in the Asheville City school system offer after-school care.

The schools in the smaller communities, especially, are highly supported by the community. The schools in Blowing Rock, for example, maintain a community-sponsored Web page, newsletter, and programs involving the community in the life of the school and the children.

For more detailed information on the school of your interest, contact the information offices of your school system at the numbers we have provided.

The following are brief descriptions of school systems in the North Carolina mountains, divided regionally. Enrollment figures are based on the 2002–2003 school year.

Northern Mountains

Alleghany County School System
85 Peachtree Street, Sparta, NC
(336) 372-4345
There are approximately 1,500 students enrolled in Alleghany County's one high school and three elementary schools serving kindergarten through eighth grade.

Ashe County Public School System
320 South Street, Jefferson, NC
(336) 246-7175
There are three high schools, four elementary schools, and a career center for remedial and at-risk students, adding up to a school population of 3,347.

Avery County School System
775 Cranberry Street, Newland, NC
(828) 733-6006
The students in Avery County are divided among one high school, two middle schools, and six elementary schools.

Madison County School System
115 Blannahassett Island Road, Marshall, NC
(828) 649-9276

One high school, one middle school, and six elementary schools serve the needs of the 2,453 students in this county. As with most counties in North Carolina, Madison has an exceptional-children's program and other special-needs services. An elementary school is on an island in the French Broad River, along with the school system's administrative offices.

Mitchell County School System
72 Ledger School Road, Bakersville, NC
(828) 688-4432

Mitchell has one high school for grades 9 through 12, two middle schools, and five elementary schools.

Watauga County School System
175 Pioneer Trail, Boone, NC
(828) 264-7190

The student population is spread among the one high school and eight elementary schools.

Yancey County School System
100 School Circle, Burnsville, NC
(828) 682-6101

A high school, two middle schools, and six elementary schools compose the school system in this county.

Central Mountains

Asheville City School System
16 South Biltmore Avenue, Asheville, NC
(828) 255-5304

For its student population of 4,414, the city has a system of 10 schools, including one high school, one middle school, six elementary schools, one preschool, and the Accelerated Learning Center. An innovative dropout prevention program, the Accelerated Learning Center, was established to assist students with their school work and return to the regular classroom if they fall behind due to absences, disciplinary action, or other reasons.

Buncombe County Public Schools
175 Bingham Road, Asheville, NC
(828) 255-5921

Buncombe County has by far the largest concentration of students, roughly 23,350, in the North Carolina mountains. The system supports 6 high schools, 8 middle schools, 21 elementary schools, 2 primary schools, and the Buncombe Community School (for at-risk students). In addition there are special programs in place at Roberson High School, Valley Springs Middle School (which added a wing to serve physically and mentally handicapped students), and Estes Elementary School to meet the needs of the county's 431 handicapped students. The Career Education Center provides students special vocational courses such as cosmetology, graphic arts, and computers, which are not offered at their individual high schools.

Henderson County Public Schools
414 Fourth Avenue W., Hendersonville, NC
(828) 697-4512

The Henderson County Public School System, with a student population of 11,369, is a K-12, 21-school district with 4 high, 4 middle, and 12 elementary schools, plus one alternative school that serves middle and high school students. A new elementary school opened in the fall of 2001.

This school system has an impressive history of academic excellence. Twelve of its schools were recently named Schools of Distinction by the North Carolina Department of Public Instruction for academic growth in 2000; while twelve attained Exemplary Growth status due to achievement in the state testing program. The class of 2000 averaged 1038 on the SAT, 19 points above the national average and 50 points above the state average.

Henderson County Public Schools are strongly supported by the community at large. The business community offers financial support, scholarship opportunities, and JobReady programs. Over 2,000 adult volunteers serve students regularly.

Mountain children keep an eye on the sky in winter. It doesn't take much snow to keep school buses from running on icy mountain roads and for the schools to close down for a "snow day." Of course children pay for too many snow-day holidays with an extended school year.

Polk County School System
202 East Mills Street, Columbus, NC
(828) 894-3051

Polk County's six schools serve 2,480 students and employ 180 teachers; more than half of the teachers hold advanced degrees. The high school, completed in 1992, boasts a 750-seat theater, modern athletic complex, up-to-the-minute science labs, a vocational department, and a high-tech media center. Since 1994 the system has invested more than $1 million in technology: Each school has a computer lab staffed by a technology specialist; all schools are connected to the state computer network; every ninth grade English student gets a laptop computer. Eighty-five percent of the year 2000 graduates are pursuing advanced degrees; 56 percent received more than $1 million in scholarships and awards. Polk County High was rated fifth highest statewide in academic growth since 1998. Since 2001 the Tryon Elementary has continuously made the "Top 25" as a "School of Excellence," with 90 percent of students performing at or above grade level. Saluda is an "A-Plus" school where the arts are integrated throughout the curriculum. Based on end-of-grade/end-of-course test scores, all six Polk County schools were rated "Exemplary" by the State Board of Education. Saluda, Sunny View, and Tryon Middle Schools have all been noted as Schools of Distinction.

Transylvania County School System
400 Rosenwald Lane, Brevard, NC
(828) 884-6173

Transylvania's system is made up of a high school, middle school, and elementary school in Brevard; elementary schools in Pisgah Forest, Rosman, and Lake Toxaway; and another high school and middle school in Rosman. The schools employ around 500 people and serve just under 3,845 students. A $26 million building upgrade and expansion program has been completed. It has also added an alternative school, Davidson River School, for middle and high school students with placement by referral only. The system also offers distance learning with dual enrollment opportunities. An emphasis is placed on the academics and the arts. Computer ratio is 1 to 4.5 students. The Transylvania school system consistently scores among the top systems in the state on all North Carolina tests.

Southern Mountains

Cherokee Central Schools
Acquoni Road, Cherokee, NC
(828) 497-6370

Cherokee Central Schools System is located on the Qualla Boundary of the Eastern Band of Cherokee Indians in Western North Carolina. Since 1990 the tribal council of the EBCI authorized the School Board of Education to operate the schools under PL 100-297 grant from the Bureau of Indian Affairs Office of Indian Education. The schools are accredited by the Southern Association of Colleges and Schools.

Its student population of 1,300 is 96 percent Native American. Cherokee Elementary School serves kindergarten through sixth grade, and Cherokee High School serves grades 7 through 12. A middle school is located within the high school facility.

Cherokee language and culture classes are an important part of the curriculum. Language and culture competency is a graduation requirement. The school system has an extensive health center, special services for exceptional students, creative learning center in grades 7 through 12, and reciprocal agreements in the Tech Prep and College Prep programs with Southwestern Community College via Interactive Television, a community link site for students and community members. They also have a reciprocal educational agreement with Oconaluftee Job Corps Center to assist students in completing a vocational/technical course of study.

Cherokee County School System
911 Andrews Road, Murphy, NC
(828) 837-2722

The Cherokee County system is composed of 12 schools: 3 high schools, 2 independent middle schools, 3 middle schools connected to elementary schools, 6 elementary schools, and 1 alternative school. They serve almost 3,500 students. There are also prekindergarten programs available at all the elementary schools.

Clay County School System
154 Yellow Jacket Drive, Hayesville, NC
(828) 389-8513

Clay County has three schools—one each to serve elementary, middle, and high school students—all on one campus. All have been built in the past few years. Total enrollment is around 1,250, and there are over 150 school employees. The system is one of only four in the state that had all their schools classified as exemplary, with students exceeding state expectations in all areas of achievement and performance. It has also posted the lowest dropout rate in the state. Both elementary and middle schools have consistently been ranked in the top 10 in physical education.

Graham County School System
Main Street, Robbinsville, NC
(828) 479-3413

All three of Graham County's schools are in Robbinsville. Enrollment in the elementary, middle, and high schools totals just more than 1,250 students. There are

The North Carolina Department of Public Instruction can be reached at (919) 715-1246.

approximately 225 employees, of whom 108 are teachers.

Haywood County School System
1230 North Main Street, Waynesville, NC
(828) 456-2400

This system serves more than 7,000 students in 10 elementary schools, 3 middle schools, and 2 high schools. It employs a staff of 1,050, including some 525 teachers and 142 teaching assistants. The students habitually exceed the state and national norms. In addition to traditional core requirements, students are exposed to art, music, physical education, media, computer technology, and a second language beginning in kindergarten.

Jackson County School System
398 Hospital Road, Sylva, NC
(828) 586-2311

The county has four elementary schools, one combined school (kindergarten through 12th grade), and one high school. Total enrollment is approximately 3,540 students. The system has around 450 full-time employees, including 254 teachers. More than 50 percent of the teachers hold graduate certificates. In 1997 Jackson County Schools were third in the state for SAT scores and were one of eight North Carolina systems to score above the national average.

Macon County School System
1202 Old Murphy Road, Franklin, NC
(828) 524-4414, (828) 524-3314

The school system encompasses seven elementary schools, one middle school, and three high schools in the Franklin area and two schools for kindergarten through 12th grade in Nantahala and Highlands. The schools teach a total of 3,953 students.

Swain County School System
280 School Drive, Bryson City, NC
(828) 488-3129
This system consists of two elementary schools, a middle school, and a high school and serves around 1,600 students. The schools employ 247 people, including 143 teachers. Its elementary students are consistently among the leaders in the region and the state on the "end of grade test" scores in reading and math and it has received a "Governor's Award for Excellence in Education" twice in recent years. Seventy-three percent of Swain County's high school students enter two- and four-year colleges, and 31 percent of graduating seniors receive a scholarship. The average class size in the high school is 12.7.

INDEX

ABOUT THE AUTHORS

Constance E. Richards is a freelance writer, journalist, and interpreter based in Asheville, North Carolina. She was born in Landstuhl, Germany, to American parents who were international educators. She attended German schools until moving to the United States, where she completed high school and graduated from Georgetown University.

She witnessed the fall of the Berlin Wall while living in Berlin, an event which influenced her decision to become a journalist. Richards was posted in Russia for nearly seven years as a foreign correspondent, where she reported and wrote for *Time Magazine, LIFE, Time-LIFE Books, People Magazine, Moscow Magazine* and the *Moscow Times*. She has reported for the *London Daily Telegraph, Sports Illustrated, Fortune, British Marie-Claire,* and *Condé Nast Traveler.* Richards also worked with the Moscow Bureau of ABC News during major historical events in Russia and the former Soviet Union.

Since returning to the U.S., she has authored *Making Books and Journals* (Lark Books, 1998) and *Creative Giftwraps* (Lark Books, 2000), *Artful Asheville—Along the Urban Trail* (J. F. Enterprizes, 2002), as well as numerous travel articles, children's articles, and a weekly arts column.

Kenneth L. Richards entered the Big Ivy Community of Buncombe County in Western North Carolina in the early 1960s. It seemed only natural that he would meet a mountain girl from North Carolina in London, England, when he was visiting there. He and the former Irene Dillingham (from Dillingham, North Carolina) married in Switzerland and then settled into their work as overseas educators, authors, publishers, winemasters, conference organizers, and lecturers throughout Europe.

Their first trip back to the states brought them over the Blue Ridge Parkway where his first view of his adopted home was 3000 feet down the mountain from Craggy Gardens. Following the logging road carved out by the Civilian Conservation Corps in the 1930s, they bounced their way down the mountain, arriving in Dillingham on Dillingham Road. Traditionally when one has been "kissed by the winds of the Craggies," or "dipped into the Big Ivy Creek," they will always return. And return they did, settling into nearby Asheville, North Carolina, in 1979.

His work in travel and tourism began during college, leading tours across the United States and Canada for Greyhound Highway Tours, Inc. Later, he taught at the International Institute in Detroit and has been an editor and feature columnist—specializing in food, wine, and opera—for newspapers in Detroit, Germany, and North Carolina. Founding director of the Mountain Area Teacher Education Center and of the Buncombe County Schools Foundation, Richards was also a founding director of the Big Ivy Historical Society and a director of education at the Biltmore Estate. Currently in demand as a lecturer and tour guide, he also occasionally teaches about the history and people of Western North Carolina at various colleges and universities. He is North Carolina State Coordinator for Sister Cities International.

Help Us Keep This Guide Up to Date

Every effort has been made by the authors and editors to make this guide as accurate and useful as possible. However, many things can change after a guide is published—establishments close, phone numbers change, hiking trails are rerouted, facilities come under new management, etc.

We would love to hear from you concerning your experiences with this guide and how you feel it could be made better and be kept up to date. While we may not be able to respond to all comments and suggestions, we'll take them to heart and we'll also make certain to share them with the authors. Please send your comments and suggestions to the following address:

The Globe Pequot Press
Reader Response/Editorial Department
P.O. Box 480
Guilford, CT 06437

Or you may e-mail us at:

editorial@GlobePequot.com

Thanks for your input, and happy travels!